# ADVANCE PRAISE

"As Erik Elgersma wisely points out, strategic analysis is a craft. *The Strategic Analysis Cycle* books will inspire those who already master this craft and guide those who are just starting to learn it. If approached from the beginning to the end, these books will keep the reader intrigued by its insights and practical suggestions. If used to deal with a specific aspect of strategic analysis, like setting up a plan or hiring an analyst, it will be exhaustive and complete, as each chapter stands on its own. The books will show the reader how to make strategic analysis a powerful tool for supporting strategy execution. I would recommend reading it to both strategic analysis professionals and to those who are involved in designing and executing a strategy."

**Dr. Anna Giatti,** Market Intelligence manager, Akzo Nobel Chemicals

"*The Strategic Analysis Cycle* books are the most comprehensive review of CI tools and practices that exist today, to the best of my knowledge. Best practices for CI / MI / Strategic analysts is herein explained in a very methodological and clear structure, in a direct way and 'eye to eye' language, demonstrated through real-life anecdotes and case studies, and all of this is spiced with a huge amount of love for the profession and a great sense of humor. These books can serve as a great way for the beginner analyst to understand the terminology and get familiarized with the basics, nevertheless the CI professional can also profit from expanding the knowledge on a breadth of tools and methods."

**Inbal Dembo**, Global Business & Competitive Intelligence Manager, Adama Corporation

Published by
**LID Publishing Limited**
One Adam Street, London WC2N 6LE

31 West 34th Street, 8th Floor, Suite 8004,
New York, NY 10001, U.S.

info@lidpublishing.com
www.lidpublishing.com

A member of:
BPR
Business Publishers Roundtable

**www.businesspublishersroundtable.com**



Printed in Great Britain by TJ International
ISBN: 978-1-911498-36-0

Cover and page design: Caroline Li

ERIK ELGERSMA

# THE STRATEGIC ANALYSIS CYCLE

HOW ADVANCED DATA COLLECTION AND ANALYSIS UNDERPINS WINNING STRATEGIES

HAND BOOK

LID

LONDON MADRID MEXICO CITY NEW YORK BARCELONA MONTERREY SHANGHAI BOGOTA BUENOS AIRES SAN FRANCISCO

# THE STRATEGIC ANALYSIS CYCLE

## HANDBOOK

HOW ADVANCED DATA COLLECTION AND ANALYSIS UNDERPINS WINNING STRATEGIES

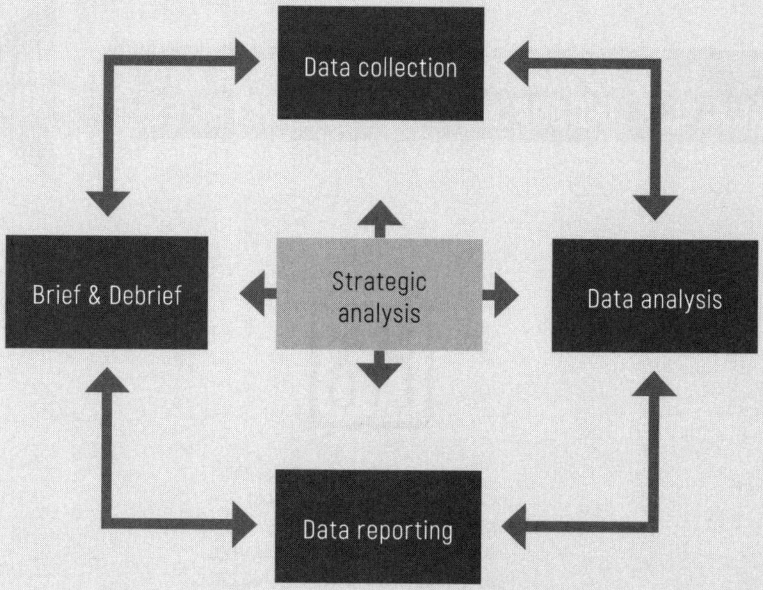

To Louise

# CONTENTS

CHAPTER 1

# INTRODUCTION

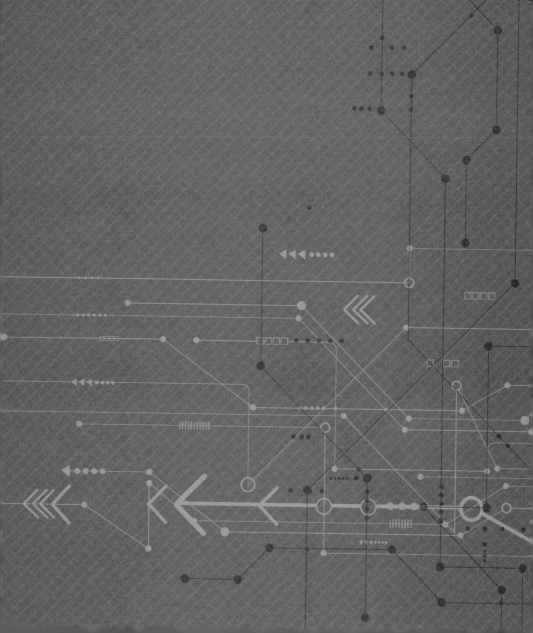

# 1.1 INTRODUCTION

- What is the growth percentage of the car market in Brazil in value?
- What will be the impact of the appointment of the new CEO at Pear Phones?
- What is to be expected from the newly announced bilateral trade agreement between New Zealand and Intellistan on your company's market position in the latter country?
- What will change at packaging supplier QuattroBloc now that it has been acquired by a private equity party?
- What volume of cotton in tons did India export last year to Venezuela and what is expected for this year?

These seemingly random business questions have more in common than is apparent at first sight. Commonalities for all questions include:

- they are future-oriented
- they are open, i.e. not to be answered by a simple yes or no
- they concern the business environment of your company
- they are factual and may require making sense of the data that is requested
- they are generally not answered by the person asking them, with the latter often having a hierarchical relation with the person answering them
- they form relevant input to business decision-making
- they often need to be answered fast

Most of all, these questions are all within the scope of a functional business discipline called strategic analysis of the business environment (sometimes also called market intelligence or competitive intelligence or competitor intelligence). In this book I will refer to this as strategic analysis, taking into account the fact that the business environment is in the scope granted. In this book, strategic analysis exclusively focuses on the external, or business environment, of a firm.

## STRATEGIC ANALYSIS HAS AS ITS SCOPE THE FULL BUSINESS ENVIRONMENT OF A FIRM

Strategic analysis is the umbrella discipline that holistically covers the entire business environment of a firm. It is this broad definition of strategic analysis that will be used throughout this book. Having said this loud and clear, it is fair to say that most examples in this book will originate from and relate to competitors. The analysis methodologies used to assess a competitor's strategy are identical to those suitable for assessing strategies and capabilities of a customer or a supplier. This means that wherever *competitor* has been written, *customer* or *supplier* can be read.

The business environment of a firm is well characterised by the sum of the five forces that shape business strategy, as defined in Michael E. Porter's seminal 1979 *Harvard Business Review* article from which diagram 1.1 has been reproduced (Porter, 1979). The forces include new entrants, suppliers, buyers, substitutes and existing competitors. In addition, the business environment includes stakeholders like governments and non-governmental organizations but also the macro-economy at large.

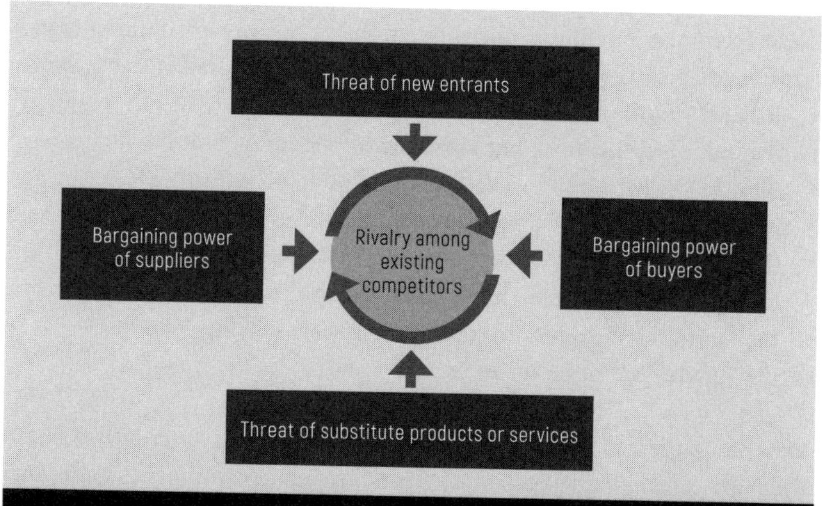


DIAGRAM 1.1 ▸▸▸ THE FIVE FORCES THAT SHAPE INDUSTRY COMPETITION (PORTER, 1979)

It is critical to also define what strategic analysis is not:

- Strategic analysis is not corporate espionage. Espionage is theft; usually by seducing others to betrayal through providing secrets. Strategic analysis only applies to lawful information collection practices. Although, strategic analysis has a lot in common with military intelligence, there are marked differences too. Zero tolerance for espionage is one of these differences.
- Strategic analysis is not market research.
- Strategic analysis does not focus on the inner world of a firm, only on the environment.

## STRATEGIC ANALYSIS IS FULLY ETHICAL AND COMPLIANT BUT SHOULD STILL BE SECRETIVE

As with military intelligence, strategy analysis is a discipline that is and should be in the shadows, even though all procedures are strictly lawful. The reason is that there is no merit in anyone outside knowing what your firm wants to know. As a military intelligence tradecraft one-liner has it: 'Intelligence leaves no traces'. This applies to strategic analysis as well. Leaving no traces is feasible due to a unique characteristic of data. Data is immaterial. Data can be given or taken, without the original holder of the data losing it.

After reading this book I trust you will be a better-informed strategy analyst. In advance I already share a conclusion on the specific discipline of analysis: analysis is a craft of lifelong learning. After some 35,000 flight hours in this field I still thoroughly enjoy finding new insights by applying new analysis methodologies. The discipline of analysis to me feels like a permanent voyage of discovery. This book is the journal of my voyage. I hope your reading this book will also make you enjoy your trips in strategic analysis!

# 1.2 DATA, INFORMATION, KNOWLEDGE AND INTELLIGENCE

For the purposes of this book, strategic analysis of the business environment is defined as:

> *"The systematic and continuous collection, analysis and reporting of changes or trends in the business environment of the firm as input for the firm's future-oriented decision-making."*

The Oxford English dictionary defines 'trend' as 'a general direction in which something is developing or changing' (Hawker, 2006). This definition highlights the relevance of the dimension *time* in trends. In this definition, the business environment as a rule changes over time.

With respect to methodologies, military intelligence is remarkably close to strategic analysis at large. I will draw multiple examples from the world of military intelligence. Fitting a puzzle from seemingly unrelated puzzle pieces is a beloved metaphor for the broader intelligence analysis work process. Fitting puzzles is, a bit snobbishly, referred to as 'puzzle management'. The metaphor is believed to facilitate the understanding of how data are processed to deliver intelligence.

## FROM DATA TO INTELLIGENCE

As we saw in diagram 1.1 the business environment of your firm consists of many dimensions. Think of customers, consumers, etc. Data on the business environment may consist of plain facts, and any of these individual facts constitutes a data point. In a made-up scenario that we will use an example of a data point is: in 2007 Yo-B-Good was a yoghurt producer, operating in the country Yolistan. Data may also be generated by changes in one or more of the business environment dimensions over time. For example: yoghurt sales in Yolistan increased by 3% in the local currency in 2015, versus the sales of 2014.

The previous sentence provided an individual input data point: Yolistani consumers in 2015 spent 3% more on yoghurt than they did in 2014. But a single data point by itself has no meaning. In the jigsaw puzzle, a single data point is like a single puzzle piece; by itself it will not show the rest of the picture.

A second individual input data point – or puzzle piece – is that the volume of sales in the yoghurt market in Yolistan has been stable from 2014 to 2015. A third data point is that the key ingredient in terms of raw material cost for producing yoghurts is raw (i.e., locally produced, fresh) cow's milk. Raw milk generally makes up about 50% of the cost of goods sold for producing yoghurt in Yolistan. In Yolistan the average purchasing price for raw milk for yoghurt producers has increased 6% from 2014 and 2015. Yet another data point is that yoghurt imports into Yolistan have been negligible in both 2014 and 2015. Collectively, these data points are pulled together and make up *information.*

The *deduced information* is that in Yolistan, an average consumer price increase of 3% in yoghurt last year was what, all other things being equal, Yo-B-Good needed to cover the raw material cost price increase of 6% last year in raw milk.

Data points, alone or together as information, are turned into *knowledge* when the puzzle manager, generally known as the analyst, starts processing them with the aim to use the outcome of the analysis to predict future developments. The analyst, for example, may 'know' that higher input (i.e., raw material) costs in this industry, are in this country *generally* fully passed on by producers to retailers and by retailers to consumers. As will be shown below, this data point is of a fundamentally different origin than the data points on price and volume developments of the yoghurt market in 2014 and 2015 in Yolistan. By its nature the data point on the passing-on of price increases resembles the data point that raw milk makes up 50% of the cost-of-goods-sold of yoghurt in Yolistan.

The analysis may now be that in Yolistan in 2015 retail yoghurt prices went up to cover increasing raw material cost of the producer, but did neither change the retailer's nor the producer's margins (again all other things being equal). The mentioned analysis may subsequently be partly validated when another data point comes in that shows that the profitability of the yoghurt producer and market leader Yolofarm in Yolistan, *all other things being equal* (for the sake of the argument) has been stable for the year from 2014 to 2015.

The so-created knowledge is turned into *intelligence*, when as input to a business plan for investing in yoghurt production in Yolistan, the analysis includes that modest cost-of-goods-sold increases (validated for up to 3%/year in retail value) can be passed on via retailers to consumers without volume losses and without affecting producer or retailer margins. Knowledge is turned into market *intelligence* when knowledge is *applied* for future-oriented decision-making. The data-information-knowledge connection has a physiological origin. It is based on human brain processing and not on an artificial or abstract model (Favaro, 2013).[1]

## GENERATING KNOWLEDGE

Combining multiple data points may form information. Individual data points or combinations of data points may lead to the generation of knowledge. The verb *may* in the previous sentence should be emphasized. Knowledge can be generated in distinctive ways. There are four principal ways for generating knowledge (Bruce, 2008b). The four ways are collectively exhaustive but are not fully mutually exclusive:

i. authority
ii. habit of thought
iii. rationalism
iv. empiricism

Each generation process is elucidated in the next section. In strategic analysis, rationalism and empiricism are the most common sources of generating knowledge.

## SUMMARIZING THE DATA-TO-INTELLIGENCE CONNECTION

In table 1.1 the connection from data, via knowledge, to intelligence is summarized. The tradecraft metaphor of fitting together a jigsaw puzzle from seemingly unrelated pieces is elaborated upon. A classic military history example is also given as an additional example. The intelligence work discussed in this example was relevant enough, making the difference between global war and peace. The example is based on the book *One Minute to Midnight* (Dobbs, 2009b).

| HIERARCHY | DESCRIPTION | PUZZLE METAPHOR | CUBA CRISIS 1962 |
|---|---|---|---|
| DATA | single-dimensional fact, often available in time series | single puzzle piece | Oct. 1962: 67-foot-long tubes appear at Cuban military bases routinely pictured by US air force reconnaissance |
| INFORMATION | more-dimensional facts; upon being combined, the value of the sum is more than that of the individual data points that constitute it | multiple puzzle pieces that reveal a (part of a) bigger picture | Soviet May Day parade pictures show nuclear weapon rockets to be 67 feet long; all auxiliary equipment related to and needed for rocket launching now also pictured in Cuba |
| KNOWLEDGE | accumulated insight obtained from multiple sources over time, either by an individual or by a group of individuals that share the same sources | continuous addition of newly connected, formerly loose, puzzle pieces from multiple sources to an analyst's expanding (or possibly new) jigsaw puzzle | given available understanding of Soviet rocket technology, Soviet nuclear weapons could, once ready for deployment, explode over Washington 13 minutes after their launch from Cuba |
| INTELLIGENCE | knowledge analysed to make it understandable and applicable for future-oriented decision-making | conveying the meaning of the emerged jigsaw puzzle image to a decision-maker who is not required to have all the knowledge but needs input before acting | the USSR is setting up a nuclear weapon delivery system base in Cuba, distorting the fragile Cold War power balance by minimizing the US' first-strike attack response time when the USSR strikes first from Cuba |

TABLE 1.1 ▶▶▶ THE CONNECTION OF DATA TO INTELLIGENCE

# 1.3 KNOWLEDGE GENERATION PROCESSES

In the previous section I introduced four ways to generate knowledge that I promised to elaborate on in this section. The four processes are:

i. authority
ii. habit of thought
iii. rationalism
iv. empiricism

## AUTHORITY

A person 'knows' a data point through authority, when the person perceives the source of the data point to be authoritative on the topic. The source may include another individual, such as an individual who just introduced himself by name, but also a source like a newspaper or a TV show. When an individual introduces himself by name the new data point (the name) is normally not questioned by the person who just made a new acquaintance. From that moment on, until other more authoritative data proves otherwise, that individual is *known* by that name. The reliability of the source thus completely determines the accuracy of the (new) knowledge (Bruce, 2008b). The new individual may have misrepresented himself, but there is no way of telling so, without other *reliable* sources. In addition, for authority-gained knowledge it is often hard to assess how the source of authority itself obtained the knowledge and whether that process was affected by unintentional inaccuracies or even whether the source was a victim of an intentional lie or deception.

## HABIT OF THOUGHT

'Habit of thought' most commonly makes its appearance as prejudice in individuals and as conventional wisdom in groups (Bruce, 2008b). The 'habit of thought' of knowledge is to be mistrusted for different reasons:

- Resistance to change: getting people to change their entrenched habits, including habits of thought, is often tough. When things have always been done in a particular way or have always been believed to be so, change may not be comfortable. Copernicus and Galileo both had a hard sell, in spite of their convincing evidence, to change their contemporaries' views on astronomy. 'Habit of thought' can be an analyst's most persistent and dangerous adversary.
- Failure to anticipate discontinuities: 'habit of thought' fails to anticipate innovations. In the following chapters, several biases will be discussed relating to how 'habit of thought' resulted in incorrect intelligence assessments that aimed to predict competitor or market innovations/discontinuities.
- Lacking a specific origin and defying explanation: evidence in support of 'habit of thought' knowledge is often at best anecdotal.

This is not to say that 'habit of thought' – knowledge by definition is knowledge of inferior quality. To the contrary, 'habit of thought' knowledge including industry-specific heuristic rules often makes the difference between guessing and correctly assessing what an adversary will do next in a given situation or how for example a competitor will react to sudden market changes.

The validity of 'habit of thought', however, remains limited to the habit itself remaining unchanged… not in the mind of the source that *knows* the habit but in the mind or the practice of the habit of the competitor or other outside phenomenon that is ultimately intended to be understood in the strategic analysis work at hand. 'Habit of thought' knowledge is thus usually not xenocentric: do not generally expect a 'habit of thought' knowledge source to make the competitor's habits or outside phenomenon central.

## RATIONALISM

Great thinkers like Socrates and Spinoza were proponents of rationalism: the school of thinking that postulates that the mind itself can *create* knowledge (Bruce, 2008b). Rationalism as a word has at its root the word 'ratio' or reason. There are three systems of reasoning:

- Deduction.
- Induction.
- Abduction.

*Deduction* produces conclusions about particulars that follow from general laws or principles:

- All men are mortals.
- Socrates was a man.

▶▶▶ Socrates was a mortal

## DEDUCTION IS OF LIMITED RELEVANCE IN STRATEGIC ANALYSIS

Deduction has been defined quite comprehensively (Gavetti, 2005) as being:

> *"...at its most powerful only in information-rich settings, for instance, mature and stable industries. Deduction works best for modular problems that can be broken down and tackled piece by piece."*

Deduction is of limited relevance to intelligence analysis. In intelligence, general laws do not apply. Consider the following rule related to intelligence which is supported by more empirical evidence than strategic analysts or military intelligence practitioners often like to admit:

> *"An analyst fails to imagine what an adversary will decide to do next and as a result incorrectly informs decision-makers."*

This statement is at best heuristic. If this rule were a law of nature and by *deduction* would thus be universally applicable, all strategic analysis and military intelligence work would be in vain. The latter is not the case. A heuristic rule by definition deals with probabilities. The probability of the above rule to apply declines with improved capabilities (collection, analysis and reporting) of the analyst. In the mathematical sense, the infinite limit of this rule is that it never applies. That would be the case if the analyst were 100% xenocentric. In the infinite limit, which, in mathematics is by definition not achievable the analyst has totally immersed herself in the adversary's or competitor's thinking or so fully understands the outside phenomenon under study, that she produces 100% accurate forecasts on future adversary or competitor moves or phenomenon developments.

Minimizing the validity of the above rule is what developing analysis capabilities aims to deliver. Strategic analysis (and intelligence for that matter) will by definition, however, study human actors that are not obeying laws of physics. This renders deduction a great tool of logic, but more suitable and applicable to disciplines other than to strategic analysis.

## INDUCTION IS LIMITED TO EXTRAPOLATING PAST EXPERIENCES

In contrast to deduction, *induction* searches for general principles or more generalized understandings by reasoning from the particulars to the general (Bruce, 2008b), (Taleb, 2007c):

Swan 1 is white, Swan 2 is white, Swan 3 is white… therefore, all swans are white.

After having empirically only ever seen white swans it may be convenient to postulate that being white is a *generic* attribute of being a swan. The opposite postulate is also possible: swans are not black.

In strategic analysis, by definition data and especially data related to understanding competitors or outside market phenomena are incomplete. The mathematical infinite limit implies that nobody can be 100% xenocentric. As a result, in a strategic analysis deliverable that goes beyond plainly reporting available data points, inductively generated knowledge will commonly be present.

This is a good thing. Knowing that a data set is incomplete, and by using inductive reasoning, multiple premises all believed true or found true most of the time, are combined to obtain a specific conclusion. Inductive reasoning is often used in applications that involve prediction, forecasting, or behaviour. It allows the analyst to make sense of the data available, and generate hypotheses. A hypothesis can be a great instrument to support business decision-making in *uncertainty*. The limitation is that the *gamble* remains upon testing the hypothesis, and indeed proving this to be valid, with the test being the actual *execution* of the decision supported by the hypothesis.

Inductive reasoning is thus concerned with uncertainty and the reduction of uncertainty. Strategic analysis can never claim to remove but only to reduce uncertainty. The degree to which business leaders decide to invest in strategic analysis correlates to the related business tolerance of or appetite for risk (uncertainty). Inductive reasoning and strategic analysis thus focus on assessing the *probability* of business opportunities to emerge or threats to materialize. In summary, inductive knowledge is valid *for now* and *probably for tomorrow*.

## ABDUCTION RESEMBLES THE LOGIC OF SHERLOCK HOLMES

*Abductive* logic is described as the logic of Sherlock Holmes (Bruce, 2008b). Abduction is well summarized as: data points, P, Q, R and S… all imply inference A. Abduction is an implicit technique used by analysts for interpreting ongoing events in the environment. Abduction creates knowledge with a similar uncertainty profile to inductive knowledge – it is inherently heuristic and probabilistic. The difference between abduction and induction is that in abduction the data points and the conclusion are correlated rather than logically prescribed as in induction. An example of abduction is:

- Spending power and size of the middle class in emerging market Yolistan increases sharply year on year on year.
- Urbanization proceeds rapidly with over 50% of the population now already living in Yolistan's five largest cities.
- International retail chains servicing multiple stores from central distribution centres emerge in Yolistan, targeting the aforementioned middle class city dwellers.
- International retail chains operate reliable refrigerated distribution chains.

Abduction-based knowledge now is that a chilled/short shelf life retail yoghurt market is likely to develop. In the absence of data on, for example, severe dislike of Yolistani consumers to yoghurt, the knowledge is no more than a prediction. When no Yolistanian will consume yoghurt, given that they can not stand the taste, the yoghurt market may not develop after all. A strategic analysis report on the business opportunity of launching yoghurt in Yolistan will have to identify such fundamental uncertainties. Decision-makers will decide whether additional research is needed. Doing so entails the risk of all yoghurt market positions having been taken by competitors prior to your company having completed its research. Decision-makers may also tolerate the risks of shooting at a target that doesn't exist, if only to hit the target hard with first-market-mover-advantage when it does.

## EMPIRICISM

Empiricism is knowledge generated by observation of the senses. Different collection methodologies in (market) intelligence resemble the human senses: data are obtained through seeing images and reading (eyes), hearing (ears) etc. (Bruce, 2008b). Empiricism as a process to generate knowledge is neither mutually exclusive from doing so from authority nor from doing so from 'habit of thought'. The observation generates *empirically* derived knowledge through a source, for example a measurement instrument, that is considered *authoritative*. Similarly, habit of thought may have started with empirically reproducible evidence observed by senses.

Bruce provides the narrative of how Americans observed that pre-Second World War Japanese fighter pilots were poorly trained. That knowledge as habit of thought had set in quickly. The knowledge resulted in the US military conveniently underestimating Japanese air force capabilities. In fact, the actual capabilities improved rapidly over time. This soon rendered the empirically acquired knowledge obsolete. When in action against the US as of December 1941, Japanese pilots proved highly capable and, certainly initially, much more capable than anticipated (Bruce, 2008b).

The fundamental premise of all the above knowledge generation processes is that knowledge, however useful, in strategic analysis is only valid *for now*. This is no reason to become apathetic and/or consider all knowledge to be a fraud. Rather it is a signal that in strategic analysis, uncertainty is one of the few certainties. Minimizing uncertainty at the lowest cost and in the shortest period of time is the fundamental challenge of strategic analysis.

In chapter 13, the concept of knowledge that is valid-until-proven-wrong will be discussed in more detail, when both hypothesis definition and testing is covered.

To summarize the above knowledge generation processes, table 1.2 refers to the Yolistan yoghurt example. Each data point is connected to a 'knowledge' type. The data points have been segmented to demonstrate two common features. The first is how often several different types of knowledge underpin strategic analysis conclusions. The second is that often seemingly hard data may actually be surprisingly incomplete. Being aware of those different knowledge-types and the incompleteness of what looks like hard data may assist in preventing an analyst from delivering insufficiently xenocentric deliverables. During processing, yoghurt should turn sour, but your business results should not.

| KNOWLEDGE GENERATION | AVAILABLE DATA POINTS ON YOLISTAN YOGHURT MARKET DEVELOPMENTS | DATA THAT ARE STILL MISSING (LIST NOT EXHAUSTIVE...) |
|---|---|---|
| **AUTHORITY** | The sources of the mentioned empirical data points below | What about the accuracy of these sources? |
| **HABIT OF THOUGHT KNOWLEDGE INTELLIGENCE** | Raw material price increases are passed on via retailers to consumers | What is the strategic intent of Yo-B-Good (YBG for short)? Profit or market share? This may lead to different pricing strategies |
| | YBG is a yoghurt producer | Has YBG changed its name to Yolofarm? |
| | YBG operates in Yolistan | Does YBG still exist? Does it export? |
| | Raw milk makes up 50% of yoghurt cost-of-goods-sold | What are the common yoghurt recipes sold in Yolistan? Does this rule-of-thumb apply? |
| **RATIONALISM** DEDUCTION | Average consumer price increases of 3% are needed to cover 2014 to 2015 raw milk price increase | Logically correct. Does, however, all habit-of-thought knowledge apply in this case? |
| INDUCTION | Yoghurt is generally raw cow milk based, so all yoghurt is based on raw cow milk | Is this the case in Yolistan? What about soy-based yoghurt? Has yoghurt been made from milk powder rather than raw milk? |
| ABDUCTION | Profitability of yoghurt producers and retailers has been stable from 2014 to 2015 | This initially abductive knowledge was later partly validated when the financial data for Yolofarm corroborated this analysis. What about other producers? |
| **EMPIRICISM** | Retail yoghurt sales in 2014 in Yolistan increased 3% in local currency value versus 2015 | What about the local currency exchange rate developments versus the US dollar? |
| | Volume of retail yoghurt sales in 2014 in Yolistan was stable versus 2015 | What about other sales channels? Even for the retail channel this is an aggregate figure. What about different recipes or pack types? |
| | Raw milk purchasing prices have increased 6% from 2014 to 2015 | Do Yolistan-based yoghurt producers only use raw milk, or also milk powder, with the latter being priced in US dollars? If so, what about currency developments? |
| | Yoghurt imports in Yolistan were negligible | What about the reliability of these statistics? How well do customs measure in an emerging market? |

**TABLE 1.2 ▶▶▶ KNOWLEDGE GENERATION PROCESSES ELUCIDATED IN THE YOLISTAN EXAMPLE**

# 1.4 EXPLICIT VERSUS TACIT KNOWLEDGE

In section 1.2, the knowledge generated in the analysis process regarding Cuba was a mix. It consisted of knowledge formed through freshly obtained empirical data and from inductive knowledge that was rationally generated in the analyst brain. Knowledge may also be segmented in another useful split which resembles but does not fully overlap empirically derived knowledge and habit-of-thought knowledge. Ikujiro Nonaka draws a distinction between tacit and explicit knowledge (Nonaka, 1995):

> *"Tacit knowledge is personal, context-specific and therefore hard to formalize and communicate. Explicit or 'codified' knowledge, on the other hand, refers to knowledge that is transmittable in formal, systematic language."*

Nonaka and his co-author Hirotaka Takeuchi have developed a 'knowledge spiral' model. They use the model to relate the connected, sequential generation of tacit and explicit knowledge.

In strategic analysis, the difference between 'tacit' and 'explicit' knowledge is crucial. Separate sources are required for collecting 'tacit' knowledge on topics – i.e., from humans – and 'explicit' knowledge. The latter literally can be solitary desk research. The former, however, is a social rather than a solitary process.

Harvesting tacit knowledge of sales staff can be a source of competitive advantage (Palmquist, 2014). In a business-to-business (B2B) context, sales staff are directly exposed to customer needs. Customers make these needs explicit to sales staff, providing the sales staff with valuable tacit knowledge. Companies should organize both initiatives to build trust between different functional disciplines to create a culture of sharing and *platforms* for tacit knowledge exchange to harvest this knowledge – and act upon it. The latter may include function-led strategy analysis or facilitated monthly or quarterly 'account reviews' with R&D, marketing, operations and sales, to share insights across disciplines to better serve the customer and the company's bottom line alike.

For an analyst, it is important to realize that he is not the only person holding tacit knowledge on a topic. The decision-makers who are the end-users of deliverables already have abundant 'tacit' knowledge, even prior to them receiving a deliverable that discusses a particular topic. This remains true when the decision-makers on the particular topic of the deliverable at hand may have no prior 'explicit' knowledge.

No matter how professionally the deliverable has been created, a decision-maker may still reject the conclusions thereof, when the conclusions lack credibility in light of his already present 'tacit' knowledge.

Chapter 10, on input data quality assurance, covers how *new* input data are received by an *old* analyst – loaded with tacit knowledge. Chapter 16 on analyst decision-maker interaction will cover the similar challenge of how a deliverable with new conclusions is received by an 'old' decision-maker.

# 1.5 PRINCIPLES OF KNOWLEDGE MANAGEMENT

Discussing knowledge management as a discipline, however relevant this discipline is, is out of the scope of this book. I restrict myself to mentioning some 'principles of knowledge management' (Snowden, 2002). The Snowden principles, originally published in 2002 and later extended, have assisted me in optimizing my processes of (intra-company) data collection in support of my strategic analysis work. They may also become your rule of thumb when considering how to collect data, information or knowledge from human sources:

- ***Knowledge can only be volunteered, it cannot be conscripted***
  This is a great principle. The first time I read it, it truly hit me. Simple yet spot-on. The key conclusion of a public domain analysis on the common characteristic of today's best data collectors in military intelligence (popularly framed as spymasters) is that they all exude *friendliness* (Grey, 2016f). What is true for our distant cousins in the military equally holds true for us in business. A human source will only give what she wants to give. What she wants to give is determined by how she relates to you. As an analyst, you will fundamentally never know what else the source knows that may be of value for your analysis. If the source is constructive due to your friendliness and thus offers you enough of what you're seeking, what you get will depend on your questions and your probing.

  This principle is particularly relevant in ensuring group decision-making is based on all available data held by the members of the group. A common problem with group decision-making is that not all relevant data held by individual members of a group are shared. This is usually a result of less-than-optimal group processes. A common version is called 'cascade'. In a group that is about to take some decision, a strong leader speaks first. The leader may not have had all available data, but still favours a clear decision. A second speaker is a common ally of the leader and supports the leader's views, adding no new data. How strong should the personality of a third speaker in that meeting be to offer new data, make a difference to the picture and challenge the wisdom of the decision proposed by the first speaker? Research reveals that there are two cascades: informational and reputational (Sunstein, 2015b):

> *"'n informational cascades, people silence themselves out of the respect for the information conveyed by others. In reputational cascades, people silence themselves to avoid the opprobrium of others."*

Either way, when analysts want sources to share data or knowledge they need to create a climate which is conducive to sharing, both in one-to-one interactions as well as in group meetings.

- ***We only know what we know, when we need to know it***
  When you consider individual data points as puzzle pieces that fit multiple puzzles, it is only then that we decide to make a particular puzzle to discover how many fitting pieces we have and ultimately also what that puzzle looks like. This applies both to yourself as an analyst but also to your source. As an analyst, co-creating puzzles with a source is a great way to unlock knowledge.

- ***In the context of real need few people will withhold their knowledge***
  For strategic analysis, this is an important principle. Obviously, an analyst's real need must be conveyed in such a way that the constructive source starts feeling that same real need. How can you as analyst create a real need for your source? Maybe the source can't deny her newfound friend a helping hand?

- ***Everything is fragmented***
  This principle also resonates with strategic analysis. Almost all data that come in are unstructured. They get structure through metadata addition and/or in the context of an analysis.

- ***Tolerated failure imprints learning better than success***
  This principle emphasizes the inevitable need to make mistakes to learn and build knowledge. In business, strategic analysts making mistakes at times is tolerable. Making the same mistake twice is not. Doing so provides ugly evidence of a lack of learning capability. This is incompatible with the first principle of analysis as I see it: analysis is a profession of lifelong learning. Anyone who has stopped learning, should not consider working in analysis.

- ***The way we know things is not the way we report we know things***
  Later in this book, in the chapters on Reporting and on Analyst–Decision-Maker Interaction, we will dive deeper into this insight.

- ***We always know more than we can say, and we always say more than we can write down***
  Especially when working with highly knowledgeable and constructive human sources, as an analyst one may at times become overwhelmed with all the data (and possibly the links between various data) that a source shares during an interview. It gets even more frustrating when you realize how much more this source knows that you have not heard yet. The best strategic analysis work, however, is not data-driven, but decision-driven. As an analyst you need to prepare your analysis to determine what data are critical to substantiate the management decision. When data are superfluous, rigorously weeding out what is 'nice to know' and only working on what is 'need to know' is a key analyst capability.

# 1.6 BUSINESS ENVIRONMENT MONITORING PROCESSES

All strategic analysis work may fundamentally be segmented into projects and processes. Projects are one-offs. They have a beginning and an end. Processes are continuous. Strategy design projects and continuous strategic planning cycles are both based on the output of strategic analysis work. It should thus not come as a surprise that the mix of continuous and project-based activities resembles that of the tasks to be executed in strategy design and planning (McTaggart, 1994):

> *"There are always significant strategic (and organizational) issues impacting value that need to be resolved (...). These issues do not appear at the beginning of the scheduled (business) planning cycle and conveniently disappear again until next year's cycle starts. Thus, documented plans or forecasts may be produced on a periodic schedule, but the process of strategic planning needs to be continuous to ensure that all important issues are systematically and effectively addressed."*

To serve its principals best, a strategic analysis function will thus generally operate continuous processes next to managing a portfolio of projects. Table 1.3 summarizes some features of projects and processes as they are commonly run by strategic analysis functions. The segmentation of projects and processes is fundamental. Normally, in an annual plan for a strategic analysis function, projects and processes will be planned separately.

| | PROCESS | PROJECT |
|---|---|---|
| EXECUTION | Permanent | One-off |
| SCOPE | Broad: Whole business environment | Narrow: Focused brief |
| ANALYSIS | Shallow if at all: Situation report may suffice | Possibly deep: Depth is subject to justifiable cost of the project versus relevance of the issue |
| CONNECTION BETWEEN PROJECT AND PROCESS | Process generally partly precedes (good) projects by collecting projects' inputs | In the absence of a project portfolio there is limited merit to invest in a continuous business environment monitoring process |

TABLE 1.3 ▶▶▶ FEATURES OF STRATEGIC ANALYSIS PROJECTS AND PROCESSES

## A BUSINESS NEEDS A RADAR SYSTEM SIMILAR TO THAT IN THE MILITARY

A continuous monitoring process in strategic analysis for business metaphorically resembles the operation of observation satellites, sonar and radar in the military. RADAR operates 24/7. It monitors everything in the territory that is believed to be critical to a country's security.[2] Every bleep on the radar screen is recorded and filed. Similarly, in well-run businesses, every relevant move of a major competitor is identified, and where needed, analysed and interpreted. When the instant analysis raises serious concerns, or offers unanticipated opportunity, higher rank is to be informed immediately. Subject to higher rank's request, scenarios for mitigating any possible risks or harvesting any opportunity from the emerging new reality are designed, evaluated and put forward for approval to decision-makers. Let me give two examples of putting the radar to work in business to make my point somewhat less abstract. The first example entails a risk; the second example discusses an opportunity.

First, consider a translated foreign newspaper clipping that your company's strategic analysis data collection process has picked up automatically (see chapter 19 for details). The clipping provides an interview with a competitor's executive who announces that the competitor will build a new local plant in one of your firm's key markets. In cases like this, the earlier the warning is available, the better your business is prepared for the intensified competition that may result from the competitor's planned move. Having the RADAR has paid off for your company.

The second example concerns a sales person who has just heard from a major customer that a key competitor has supply problems due to major hiccup in a key production plant. This very tiny piece of data – when immediately shared among all your firm's sales professionals – could lead to a lot of extra orders and an astonishing amount of extra customer satisfaction. This tiny radar signal needs to find its way to the audience that it needs, and it needs to do so fast. In my experience, a knowledge management system, operated by an in-house strategic analysis function, could be the ideal platform for this (again see chapter 19 for details).

The acceptable time lapse between observation and decision-making in the military may only be minutes. Short response times, for example, apply when military aircraft have to intercept an unknown airspace intruder. Response times may be much longer when a country strives for strategic parity in its defense forces with a potential adversary. Missile gaps do not need to be corrected overnight. Meanwhile, the radar remains online and the satellites continue to collect images to keep higher rank and, where needed, the top brass, informed in real time.

Going back to business terms: every data point on the competitor's moves should in principle be collected. Together all the data points provide insight into the competitor's competencies and possibly also into their intent.

Assuming that in the military the adversary has not developed sufficiently advanced stealth technology or works fully underground, such radar collection initiatives minimize the risk of surprise. For business and for the military, installing a permanent monitoring process itself does not protect against existential threats. It does, however, allow management to be continuously and timely warned of opportunities and threats and to act upon these threats.

## WHAT TO MONITOR IS A BALANCING ACT BETWEEN COMPLETENESS AND BUDGET

The definition of what to collect is critical in the design of a permanent monitoring process (Kahneman, 2010):

> *"(Critical is:) when you decide what information needs to be collected. That's an absolutely critical step. If you're starting with a hypothesis and planning to collect information, make sure that the process is systematic and the information high quality. This should take place fairly early."*

In the military, radar systems monitor the competitor's aircraft or fleet movements. How should what needs to be permanently monitored in business be defined? This depends on the individual business that is being served. Generally speaking, existing or future markets, customers, competitors, categories or channels are key topics to monitor. Trying to monitor everything is as useless as deciding to monitor nothing. Discerning how to attune the radar frequencies to the constantly changing business environment is critical; in other words, what competitors, markets, etc., to monitor with what intensity.

After all, the strategic analysis function has to work with limited resources. No matter how advanced and cost-efficient your companies' monitoring of its business environment, there are budget limits to what can be done. To ensure budgets are spent as to generate the highest returns, choices will have to be made.

There is a catch: it tends to be easier to get management to approve a budget for tangible projects, the deliverables of which management can directly apply in their decision-making, than for an activity perceived to be as hazy as setting up and maintaining a permanent radar on the firm's business environment.

This conclusion is shared by big data expert Thomas Davenport. He stresses that even in today's emerging big data world, even early adapters demand immediate Return on Investment (ROI) when developing new customer propositions based on big data in their big data projects (Davenport, 2014e). Strategic analysts should pre-empt this when defining and defending their budget to their management. The key message to management that I used to use, and to some extent still use, is that the radar-system's collection outputs, connected to a structured filing of the collected snippets, is and will remain a critical enabler to carry out meaningful one-off projects.

## THE 'INTERNET OF THINGS' ALLOWS REAL-TIME ANALYSIS OF THE ENVIRONMENT

Gradually, the real-time dimension of more sophisticated automated data processing changes the picture. The permanent monitoring of the business (transaction) environment already allows the most sophisticated companies to take real-time big data-based decisions, like retailers monitoring the effect of promotions real-time as and when these promotions run (Davenport, 2014f).

Increasingly, online interactions of companies with customers and consumers, 'the internet of things', more sophisticated software tools and previously unimaginable computational power make the military radar metaphor increasingly relevant in the contemporary business reality. Using the above radar example, the entry of an unidentified, potentially hostile airplane into a country's airspace within minutes leads the air force sending its jets into the sky. Similarly, short signal-response times are now facilitated in business and are tested by the early adopters, such as online companies like Google, Amazon and LinkedIn.

In the past, data collection in the more professional companies had developed into a continuous process, but the analysis and management reporting of the data remained a discrete, periodical 'batch' activity. Today and in the future, part of that analysis will be automated and will become so fast that data and analysis will become real-time.

Even so, when the radar is not tuned to the frequency of the management needs, the budget is still wasted. It is thus essential that you as an analyst know the scope of your firm's management agenda. Based on today's, and especially tomorrow's sources of cash, choices should be made on the data regarding which companies (which may include competitors, customers or suppliers), which markets, which channels, which categories, etc., should be collected and filed for immediate or future analysis.

# 1.7 INDIVIDUAL ANALYSIS PROJECTS

Over the years I have never seen thriving strategic analysis teams that exclusively did process work. Data without analysis remain what they are: just data without much meaning. Similarly, strategic analysis work cannot only consist of projects. Projects that lack a sufficient factual database are dangerous, because they can lead to incorrect analytical conclusions and, even worse, incorrect management decisions based on such conclusions.

In allocating a budget for a strategic analysis function, a fine balance between process and project work should thus always be sought for, especially when in the future, some of today's routine analyses will turn from periodical into real-time. Diagram 1.2 connects process and project work in strategic analysis. Where the process is broad and shallow in terms of coverage, a project is normally narrowly defined, but it reaches much more depth.

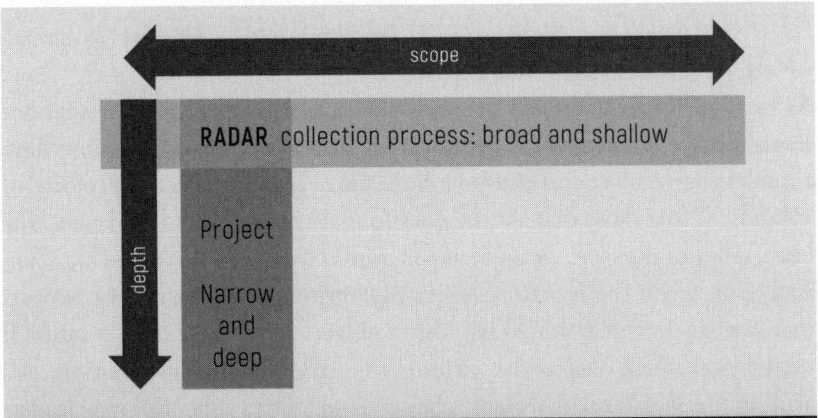


DIAGRAM 1.2 ▶▶▶ CONNECTION BETWEEN STRATEGIC ANALYSIS PROJECTS AND PROCESSES

For any project, the question is not whether it should be detailed and should dive deep. The question is how deep the project should dive. When resources are virtually infinite, such as those available for counter-intelligence during the Second World War in Germany, this question is irrelevant. Hitler's chief of counter-intelligence, Walter Schellenberg, in his memoirs thus made a strong appeal to always ensure details are studied (Schellenberg, 2000):

> *"Questions of detail are most decisive for a secret service (...) Only through scientific and methodological evaluation of the material that comes to one's net, the real basis for policy can be established."*

However, even when details matter in business, often just as much as in countries that are at war, resources in business tend to be finite. It is my experience that the analyst will always have more questions than time and budget allows for.

The analyst and the function at large thus have to set priorities. A good way to do so is to make a back-of-an-envelope assessment of the value of a project to your company. What is the upside or downside potential to a firm's business when this question is answered? What accuracy is needed to do so most cost-efficiently? How do the value calculations for different projects compare? Combined with the strategic priorities set in your firm, such assessments will likely lead to priority settings within your analysis project portfolio.

## A PORTFOLIO OF PROJECTS SHOULD CONSIST OF BOTH SMALL AND LARGE PROJECTS

As we saw, not all questions that land on analysts' desks have a similar potential upside or downside for your firm. Most often, smaller questions have a modest impact but also consume little time. These are 'service projects' or 'errands'. Often those that ask the questions are high-ranking managers. The likely reflex of the strategic analysis function is to answer them quickly. Cynically put, when the function wishes to continue receiving decent budgets that is what the reflex should be. This is all very well, but there is a catch. If there is too much of a service attitude in a strategic analysis function, this leads to numerous small problems being solved. Over time, this may lead to a situation that the English may characterize with 'one hundred small fish don't make a shark'.

I have seen understaffed strategic analysis functions working exclusively on small questions. This causes a widening gap between the strategic issues on the management agenda and the function's agenda. That is dangerous and to be prevented. The function that is ignorant of key management agenda topics will find it difficult to continue delivering directly applicable results to its management. This development may also lead to a lack of focus on and, inevitably, a delay of any large projects that are still in progress, and that does have a high potential up- or downside. In that case, something has gone wrong.

In terms of methodology, research and development (R&D) projects resemble strategic analysis projects well. R&D departments also continuously struggle with how to handle the mix of smaller, often urgent and less important versus larger, important and often not-so-urgent projects. Literature on how to achieve a balanced portfolio of R&D projects discusses this phenomenon in some detail (Roussel, 1991). The approach proposed to prevent this from happening for R&D is highly applicable to strategic analysis.

In this chapter I conclude with the observation that a strategic analysis function, which will generally be working for an individual business unit in a firm, should strive for a balanced portfolio of larger (strategic) and smaller (tactical/operational) projects. An exceptions to this rule may be corporate strategic analysis departments with a predominant focus on longer-term strategic projects.

When resources are tight, as they always will be, work should only be done on those projects that proportional to the efforts have the highest upside potential for the firm.

## SOME QUESTIONS ARE BETTER LEFT UNANSWERED

It may sound weird, but there is a category of questions that land on the desk of the strategic analysis function that I didn't discuss. Believe it or not, answering some questions may have no relevance to your firm at all. This happens when those that ask the question, often willingly, deviate from your firm's strategy. I use strategy here as a another word for allocation choices of corporate resources.

The risk to the function of not working on projects with a corporate relevance increases when the function is not well connected to your firm's (corporate) strategic agenda. In that case the function is not even able to make the call whether a project should be executed or not. Even when the function is sufficiently aware of the corporate strategy and knows what it is supposed to work on, it remains a risk.

The function may be looked upon as a potential ally to help build or further substantiate a business case that had either been rejected earlier by higher management or that is off-strategy but has not yet been officially rejected. Analysts are sometimes coerced by the champions of this type of corporate orphan project to continuously search for results. The hypothesis that the market is there to make their project a big success is by definition true to these project principals. The only thing they want to achieve is for the analyst to find them stronger evidence for their case.

Armed with such evidence they aim to persuade the (in their eyes often old fashioned or short-sighted bunch of) reluctant top executives to (re-) consider (further) funding their project.

Managers, or rather champions, who pursue their own, often highly innovative hobby projects which are not in-line with corporate strategies have a few traits. They are listed here to help a function to recognize these champions early on:

- Champions are driven to get their projects approved and funded; they are prepared to take unconventional steps to achieve their aims.
- Like true believers, they can be passionate and persuasive.
- They will appeal to the function to join them in their pursuit by making the function feel highly important and showing much more appreciation than other customers, for instance by showing how the function contributes to their project's success.
- They more often than not have an R&D or business development background. This will allow them to master the strategic analysis language, making it easier and more fun to work with them compared to other customers.

In short: champions of off-strategy projects may well be the function's favourite customers in terms of work satisfaction. Still, there is a catch. A firm, like an army, needs loyal soldiers to execute strategies that have been chosen, approved and budgeted for. A strategic analysis function that spends big on off-strategy projects, no matter how innovative, risks its own future budget.

## 'NO' IS AN ANSWER

Both in the case of structural work overload, especially with small questions, as well as in the case of requests for off-strategy projects, an imperative for success is a strategic analysis function head who dares to say 'no'. It adds to his credibility when it is clear that business upside potential is the key criterion for his choices. It furthermore helps when the function has the commitment and support to say 'no' from the top executive responsible for the staff cluster which includes the function.

# 1.8 THE ANALYSIS CYCLE

We need to properly define strategic analysis projects. In strategic analysis, virtually all projects happen to have a similar flow, moving from a management brief, through various steps, to a debrief to management. Over time, this common project flow has been captured in a model. This model I call 'the analysis cycle'. Our distant cousins in the military call this model the intelligence cycle. The cycle finds its origin in the world of science; this field of work after all benefits from a variety of research methodologies. The cycle may be applied for any strategic analysis project. It is shown in diagram 1.3

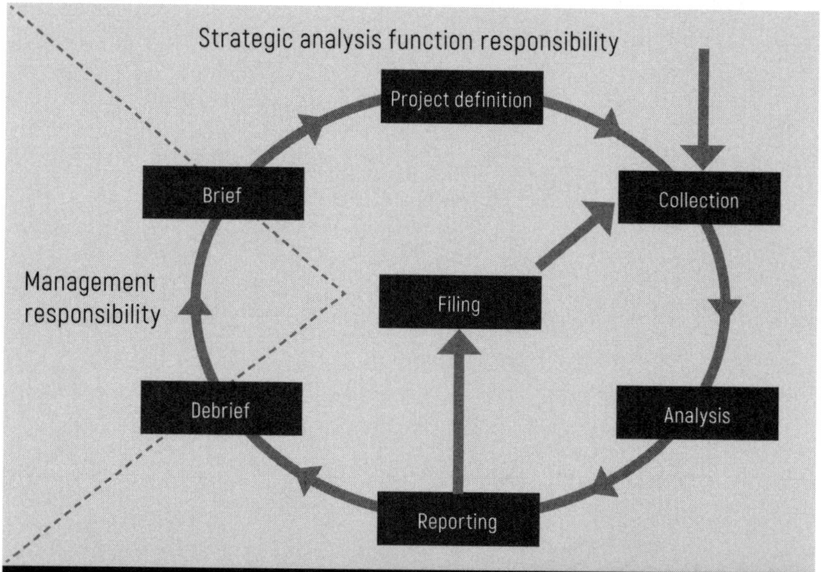


DIAGRAM 1.3 ▶▶ THE ANALYSIS CYCLE

In literature, this cycle has been criticized for being an oversimplification of reality (Meister Johnston, 2005). Meister Johnston postulates that the cycle assumes that the process works the same way for all objectives, regardless of complexity and cognitive demands. He correctly observes that in doing so, the cycle as a project structuring tool fails to recognize the iterative nature of much strategic analysis work. I concur with that view but I consider it a minor shortfall. As a concept, I like the cycle so much that I have used it as the backbone of both multiple strategic analysis projects that I executed over the years and also as a structure in this book.

CHAPTER 2

# BRIEFING AND PROJECT BRIEF

# 2.1 INTRODUCTION

In projects in the field of strategic analysis there is a simple role play, similar to the role play in any other project. For this reason, I will not use many words to discuss generics on project management. I will try to focus on the specifics that deserve attention in relation to running strategic analysis projects.

In such projects, there is normally a principal who assigns the project to a strategic analysis function, and an analyst who executes the project, given certain boundary conditions. These conditions typically include:

- The required timing of the deliverable.
- The resources available to execute the project.
- The requirements set to the quality of the output of the project.
- The project, organization and communication.
- The steps planned to mitigate anticipated risks.

All good projects start with a brief. The principal normally is the source for the 'project brief'. The principal paradoxically rarely is the author of such a brief. Rather the principal usually provides the analyst with some broad questions to be answered. These answers still need to be turned into a project brief. The project brief is the source required to define the actual 'project plan'. In my experience, the principal sketches his analysis request and the analyst patiently listens, aiming to turn what he hears into the project brief. The principal's sketch, for the sake of giving it a differentiating name, I would like to call the 'management brief'. Turning vague questions into a well-defined project plan for a strategic analysis is an art in itself. In running strategic analyses, it is not the only an art that needs to be mastered, when it comes to turning questions (i.e., management briefs) into project plans that result in project deliverables. In addition, an analyst is to in advance properly assess *how* that project deliverables will be used in future decision-making and *by whom*.

All too often the principal is too high up in the organization to be the user of the (detailed) output of the project. Only an aide may be the actual reader of the full report. After a project has been completed, when a principal reads the summary of the project report and acts upon it, that is when the analyst has basically achieved the fundamental aim of a strategic analysis function: generating outputs that are being acted upon. However, it still may be that the action consists of a well-substantiated choice to do nothing. Normally, however, prior to making decisions the principal will tend to check with the aide for their opinion as well. To the analyst, the aide is not a lowly subordinate, but someone who may well prove to be a key stakeholder! This implies that already when making the project brief, the user needs first to be understood and second to be put at centre stage.

This chapter focuses on the processes of first turning possibly ambiguous and broad questions from a principal (the management brief) into a project brief. Secondly, I will discuss how to design the right project brief for creating a deliverable that has a fair chance of being acted upon. Then, I will go on to give a more detailed working process for the management brief phase. In this chapter, we will discuss:

- Why a decision-maker may want to start a strategic analysis project.
- What to define as the scope of such a project.
- When to start the project.

We will conclude first with some final checks that a strategic analysis function be well-advised by its management prior to getting started, and finally with a hopefully useful checklist for the project brief. Based on such a project brief, the analyst can work out a project plan. This step, as mentioned before, is generic and therefore not covered in this book.

# 2.2 THE MANAGEMENT BRIEF

The execution of strategic analysis projects all too often is triggered by the identification of threats, and or opportunities for a business. The trigger may also be called an event. An event in the broadest sense is something happening outside the control of the management team that affects the business. An example of an event is the announcement of a competitor building a new factory. There is also, beyond business, an uneasy relation between decision-makers and events. Once former British Prime Minister Harold MacMillan was asked by a journalist what he feared would most affect the stability of his government. Although the quote has been disputed, he has been said to have uttered:

*'Events, my dear boy, events.'*

To stay in tune with the vocabulary used in this book, we will refer to an event, whether it is an opportunity or a threat, as 'new data'. New data thus often triggers the start of a project. A good start to any new project is to remember the first lines of a short poem (Kipling, 1980).

*"I keep six honest service men*
*They taught me all I knew*
*Their names are what and how and when*
*And where and why and who."*

As I said above, I distinguish between two briefs. The first brief is called the 'management brief'. The management brief should at least consist of the answers to three of Kipling's service men: why, what and when. With the answers to the questions why, what and when the function has what it needs.

After all, Peter Drucker long ago said that:

*"Management is getting things done through other people."*

To a principal, the strategic analysis function tends to be included in the 'other people' bucket. The function is populated with those that are there to get things done. Analysis functions allow management to focus on the *directing* of what things need to be done. After all, focusing on what, when and why actually is a convenience to the principal – it saves time.

# 2.3 WHY WOULD A PRINCIPAL WANT TO START A PROJECT?

The question 'why' is often the most difficult question for the strategic analysis function to find answers for. When asked, some managers may not immediately (or not at all) feel the need to inform the function why they want to know the answers to the what questions they ask the function to work on. Even worse, they may give plausible but incorrect reasons, as they don't want to share the real reasons. Sometimes such secrecy is inevitable. This may be the case for example when the work supports merger and acquisition projects. Absent good reasons for secrecy, the function should better persist in getting to the 'why' before getting started with real work.

My empirical personal experience has taught me that the better the function understands the underlying reasons for the management questions, the more actionable the resulting deliverable of the function will be.

In my opinion it should start with the function being able to truly understand its own firm's strategy. This should not be limited to the headlines. It should also include the way that the strategy is planned to be executed. Understanding the firm's strategy generally is conducive to understanding the 'why' behind the 'what' question.

There is, however, sometimes more to know, beyond the firm's strategy, to identify the drivers behind the 'what' question. For a strategic analysis function, it is essential to be able to look from the customer's perspective. To achieve this the function needs to at times understand the customer as a *person* rather than only as an executive.

No matter how much (most) businesses aim for rational targets to be achieved in a meritocratic culture, managers remain human beings. Humans have functional but also emotional needs that drive their behaviour. Understanding all the factors that drive managers to ask the 'what' question helps strategic analysis functions tailor their work in such a way that it increases the chance of their deliverable being used. Below some questions are provided which may help to indirectly identify the 'why' behind the 'what' questions. The list is not exhaustive but I use it as a checklist in getting a project started.

## WHO IS THE PRINCIPAL?

Consider two possible principals. One is a laboratory analyst, the other is a sales director. Both may approach the function with the same question. However, even though the question sounds the same, each principal may require a different answer. The same question from both of them could for example be: 'What will change when firm ABC upgrades or re-launches its product XYZ?' The laboratory analyst's real information need may well be 'what functional properties will change with the upgrade?' because the analyst uses the current product in some experiments and may, for instance, save time when some product characteristics are improved. The sales director, however, may have another information need: 'what will be the sales price of the upgraded product?' because that is the product she competes with in the marketplace. A question that at first sight may look well-defined actually may not be specific enough once we realize that different users may have different underlying real needs.

Another element of the 'who is the principal' question is the assessment of the competencies of the principal. When the principal is a specialist in a particular area and the question concerns that area, don't worry: the principal will understand every detail.

When, however, the function is more specialized than the principal in a subject matter, always ensure the deliverable is fully comprehensible to the principal. In short: know the principal and his real needs prior to starting a project.

## WHAT BUSINESS TARGETS DOES THE PRINCIPAL OF THE BRIEF HAVE?

The saying is 'Tell me your friends and I will tell you who you are.' In business, I suggest adding a second line to this old wisdom: 'Tell me your (bonus) incentives and I will tell you what you do.' Managers work to further a firm's goals. To stimulate them to achieve success, they get personal targets. These targets, when they are met, directly link to personal rewards. In most companies, such targets are confidential. They will usually not be known by the strategic analysis function.

The budget targets set for an Operating Company, or OpCo, within a larger firm, however, are often known to a large(r) number of staff: those with access to the corporate budget. The personal targets of the management of an OpCo will in any well-managed firm relate to those of the OpCo. When the OpCo targets are known, it means the function knows what management in that OpCo will be incentivized to achieve. If the OpCo targets are to grow the business by acquisitions, quite likely the personal target of the top team will be to realize an acquisition.

Any market data that assists management in realizing an acquisition will be welcome. So, a function that understands the needs and the (bonus) targets of the principal will find it easier to deliver outputs that are being used.

## WHAT EMOTIONAL NEEDS DOES THE PRINCIPAL OF THE BRIEF HAVE?

Training company AchieveGlobal distinguishes six principal emotional needs (AchieveGlobal, 2010):

- Recognition
- Achievement
- Control
- Power
- Affiliation
- Safety

Different managers have different personal needs. The human need for power is for example quite common (Berle, 1969b):

> *"Of the infinite desires of man, the chief are the desires for power and glory."*

There is a danger in generalization. Some managers are self-sufficient in satisfying their need for glory; others thrive on recognition by others. Some want to be firmly in control and thus want to know the smallest details; others prefer to stay at helicopter height. The needs of different project principals have profound implications on what a function needs to do in order to deliver. This indeed already starts in the briefing phase. The better the strategic analyst knows the principal and her emotional needs/character traits, the more effectively and efficiently strategic analysis projects can be executed.

Let me give an example to elucidate this point. A strategic analysis function can work 24/7 all year when the principal customer of the function has a high safety need. The principal will see threats for his business around every corner. He will expect the function to explore each of these threats into sufficient detail.

Why does this impact a brief for an analysis project? The function should in this case aim to provide safety to the principal. Wherever possible, the function, in accepting a brief, should search between lines for the (sometimes hidden) emotional needs of the principal. This is not to say that the personality of the principal changes the facts being explored and the analysis thereof. The latter, of course, remains the core of the work. However, knowing the emotional needs of the principal allows the function to tune the message in the right way to the *person* of the principal. A modest change in tone of voice and tone of delivery, regardless of the content of the message, may make the difference between output being and not being used.

## WHAT DECISION DOES THE PRINCIPAL HAVE TO TAKE?

The better the quality of insight the analyst is given into the items that are on the principal's agenda, the easier it will be to produce immediately actionable deliverables. Analysis departments that are privy to the decisions that top management really need to substantiate will generate the highest return on cost. Before management will share their confidential agenda, trust will have to be built between management and the function. Trust needs to be earned. It will, as always, come on foot, but may, when lost, leave on horseback. In contrast to the answers on the questions 'what' and 'when', the answers to the questions above, as a rule, are not part of the formal written management brief. Yet, the answer(s) to the question 'why' are an essential but unspoken element in the process of coming from new data to a management brief. Time spent on getting behind the formal questions is time well-spent.

## 2.4 WHEN TO START A PROJECT?

The question 'when' is the easiest to answer for management. Management generally wants answers to their questions when they ask their questions. Had they identified the need for the answers yesterday, chances are that they would have asked for them yesterday. Management tends to be focused on today's issues and on this quarter's results. This may sound cynical. Ridiculing management, however, is absolutely not the objective here. The objective is for the strategic analysis function to constantly look from the customer perspective. Management needs to be focused on the day-to-day running of a business. Management that only dreams of remote future cash flows forms a serious risk to immediate business continuity. Management that identifies 'new data' for today generally wants an immediate, or at least a fast, answer from the function on the question(s) these new data trigger.

Timing is of the essence. A competitive move that is pre-empted by adequate and timely countermeasures is the textbook response to high-grade analysis. A nasty surprise that a competitor delivers to us is better framed as a failure to provide a *timely* warning. The critical importance of the timeliness of deliverables is not only valid in the case of threats but also in the case of opportunities. An opportunity loss is just as well a loss indeed.

## NEVER SACRIFICE TIMELINESS FOR COMPLETENESS

In an interview called "Timeliness Trumps Perfection" (Kirkland, 2010), the former CEO of Xerox Corporation, Anne Mulcahy, said the following, and her quote speaks for itself:

> *"If you're creating a category of bad decisions you made, you need to include with it all the decisions you didn't get to make because you missed the window of time that existed to take advantage of an opportunity."*

Vodafone CEO Sir Christopher Gent is not afraid about being too early but admits having been too often, too late, too often (Zook, 2012b):

> *"I'm not sure of a decision that we took too soon. Unfortunately, there is a longer list of decisions that we took too late."*

Clearly, missing the window of time may not only be due to the absence of timely intelligence on the opportunity. It may also be due to slow decision-making upon the intelligence. The opposite made the difference in IBM's turnaround in the 1990s.[1]

What is true in business, is just as true in the military. Admiral John Godfrey, Director of Naval Intelligence of Britain's Royal Navy during the Second World War, emphasizes the need for timeliness just as vividly with another metaphor (Macintyre, 2010i):

> *"Intelligence, like food, soon gets stale, smelly, cold, soggy and indigestible, and when it has gone bad does more harm than good. If it ever gets into one of these revolting conditions, do not try to warm it up. Withdraw the offending morsel and start again".*

In summary, slow decision-making can turn high-grade intelligence sour. When, however, the deliverable is too late, fast decision-making will not be able to make up for it. The strategic analysis function should therefore try to answer (urgent) questions timely. This usually means: as fast as possible, but no faster than that.

# 2.5 WHAT IS THE SCOPE OF A PROJECT?

The question 'what' is focusing on the work to be done itself. I have split this section into two parts. The first part focuses on the content. It covers the objective of the project. The second part covers answers to the 'what' questions, answers that do not relate to the content but are equally relevant for a successful completion of the project.

## OBJECTIVES

The principal of a strategic analysis project should make crystal clear what she sees as the objective of her project. A helpful way to come to an objective of a project that both serves the principal as well as enables efficient project execution is to look for the decision that a principal is planning to take. What particular indicator (fact) would compel a principal to take decision A or decision B?

Consider this example. In many businesses, the quest for growth is the name of the game. When a business executive aims to expand the geo-scope of his business, he may ask the strategic analysis function 'to identify and map attractive future export markets (i.e. countries)'. The function can work on this for ages, finding all imaginable details on the various countries and delivering over 100 slide deliverables by country for over 150 countries – a great way to waste time. For an analyst to get to a much sharper management brief they should ask for three indicators that the principals consider 'must see' to make a first sifting of possibly attractive and possibly unattractive markets. Think of indicators such as the market growth rate of the product category, or the population size, or the applicable import duties of the target market. When import duties are high in a country, exports to the related market will probably be unduly expensive compared to locally produced goods, so the market is probably not attractive. When the population is too small, the market will rarely be attractive either. Finally, when the market growth is negative, why bother to fight for a share in a shrinking market that we are not yet active in? These criteria of course are not universally applicable to any business; the criteria to choose should emerge from understanding your own business. Analysing 100 countries on these three criteria is achievable and based on these the principal may move to step two, asking for in-depth analysis of the top five candidate export markets. The three criteria act as indicators enabling a first rough decision on whether or not to make a deep-dive on a country as candidate export market with priority. More important decisions may be based on the outcome of the in-depth analyses of the priority countries. Principals seldom disagree on these sorts of phased project objectives: phase I enables a rough sifting; phase II dives deeper and decides whether to commit heavy resources to an idea.

The logic of the above example resembles the binary judgment in court: a suspect is guilty or not guilty. For the suspect or his lawyer, one single piece of irrefutable evidence can be enough for an acquittal. This single piece of evidence needs to form a watertight proof that the suspect cannot have committed the act that he is suspected to have committed. The sharper the decision to be taken has been worded, the better the function's search can be focused. Find the evidence – no more but also no less what is needed to base the decision upon. In the age of information overload, defining selectively what really needs to be known can save exceptional amounts of time and effort in executing your projects.

## NON-CONTENT 'WHAT' QUESTIONS CONCERN, FOR EXAMPLE, ACTION STANDARDS

The questions below are 'what' questions that do not concern 'content' but that still need to be answered prior to starting a project. Preferably, the questions are answered by or in consultation with the principal. When the function knows both context of the overall question and the person of the principal well, some questions can be answered by the function because the risk of misunderstandings is deemed small. In case of doubt, however, an analyst should not start regardless. It is indeed recommended that he should bother the principal to get his answers rather than to think in his shoes, make mistakes, waste resources and create an unhappy customer.

## WHAT ACTION STANDARDS?

The most common 'action standard' in analysis is the required accuracy of the result. As a rule of thumb the required accuracy should be proportional to the potential business upside or risk involved.

In military intelligence accuracies are usually expressed as a percentage of the likelihood of some event occurring in a defined future period. On 1 August, 1990, the CIA issued a warning with a 70% probability that Iraq would invade Kuwait. Iraq indeed invaded Kuwait on 2 August, 1990 (Gordon, 1995c). I have not seen such probability percentages being used often in business strategic analysis.

Sometimes it is hard to indicate the required accuracy of the deliverable to be produced. In such cases the analyst should assess the justifiable amount of resources dedicated to an assignment. When I face this issue, on the one hand I mentally consider how much effort is required to check all usual sources in sufficient depth. On the other hand, I consider the potential business impact. High impact, low effort: go. For the opposite scenario, double-check with the principal. Medium impact, medium effort: see whether analyzing a single or a few indicators in phase I of a multi-stage approach may cut resource needs. What this section most of all shows is that strategic analysis management is a pragmatic activity. It is a craft. It is by no means a formal science, where rules of nature determine the game.

## WHAT LEVEL OF DETAIL IS REQUIRED FOR THE DELIVERABLE?

Especially when a lot of information is available or easy to collect, the temptation for a function is to proudly show off to the project principal all the data and analysis that is available. Look, boss, this is how good your function is. This is all that is known. This is understandable and charming, I have seen it happening (here is the new business bible, look at this…) but unfortunately this is wrong. Like in the case of the action standards, the level of detail to be worked out back-office, i.e., in the analysis function, is determined by the potential business upside or risk involved.

Additionally, the chance that the decision-maker will actually use the deliverable increases significantly when the conclusions are unambiguously presented whilst taking a minimum of time to digest. What decisions are based on 200-page reports that do not have a two-page summary? How much more than those two pages do you really need for good decision-making and how much do you need only for your own record? There may be very good reasons to produce 300-page reports. Although, in business there are few instances when the principal needs a report of this level of detail.

## WHAT LANGUAGE TO CHOOSE FOR THE DELIVERABLE?

In any large international firm the answer to this question should be English or Chinese unless otherwise stated. The 'unless' may apply when either for secrecy reasons or because of the language abilities of the principal another language is favoured. Good results have been obtained by offering principals a (short) deliverable in their mother tongue when they are not fluent in English. If it increases the chances of intelligence being used, hiring a translator to translate any non-English language text may be a good investment.

## WHAT FORMAT?

Agreeing in advance with the principal on the format of the deliverable is a key factor in ensuring analysis outputs are being used. This is understood extremely well by the best management consultancy firms, and part of their work essentially boils down to turning data their customer already possesses into graphs or images that radiate a persuasive clarity. This persuasiveness turns management uncertainty into confidence. The result is that the intelligence is being used to support decision-making. This is exactly the aim.

# 2.6 FINAL CHECKS WITH MANAGEMENT

A strategic analysis function that has got appropriate management answers for the questions 'when', 'what' and even, perhaps the unspoken, 'why' will not automatically complete a project. The checks below should be passed before the analyst proceeds from brief to action.

## CHECK ON COMPLETENESS

Sometimes strategic analysis functions do not obtain sufficiently defined answers on the above three questions but a project is started anyway. Often, in these cases, the brief was delivered orally by a member of top management who was in a rush. The high rank of the principal, and/or the persuasive style with which the brief was delivered, intimidated the analyst into submissiveness rather than asking all the right questions needed to get a clear direction for the function's project.

After the project was finished and the deliverable was handed over to management, the management was unhappy. The result did not match their real needs. A frustrated analyst has the reflex to blame management for not giving complete questions. That is understandable but pathetic. The fault really is with the analyst. Rather than being intimidated, the analyst had to ensure he got complete input from management to do useful work in the first place.

## CHECK ON FACTUAL CLARITY

Clarity is not always evident. In the dairy industry the question 'Find me the annual report of Westland company,' is less clear than it looks. In the Netherlands, there is a Westland Kaas company, in Germany, a Westland Milch GmbH exists, whereas in New Zealand there is a Westland Milk Products Cooperative. These companies have no connection whatsoever.

## CHECK ON QUESTION ACCURACY

Questions may not always be accurate. A question like 'Find me the WACC for France' is an example. The abbreviation WACC stands for 'Weighted Average Cost of Capital'. This metric is used in valuation calculations. Unfortunately, there is no such thing as a WACC for a country. A WACC is linked to a stock-listed firm and related to the share price volatility.

Asking for a 'WACC for France' can mean two things: the WACC that *your company* would apply when *you* would invest in France; or the WACC that should be used in calculations for a (stock-listed) French company for their investment in France.

To minimize confusion and maximize results, ensure that you have accurate questions before starting your work.

## CHECK ON AMBIGUITY

Because of either carelessness or a lack of critical thinking – or worse because management is internally divided – questions may not always arrive unambiguously at the strategic analysis function.[2] Ambiguous questions lack clarity. Take for example the question: 'Provide me with some information on the cheese market in the UK'. How would you define 'some'? Does the principal ask for volumes or values of the market? Or the volume and value by sales channel? Or the different cheese types sold by channel (volume/value)? Or which different players are active in the market? Without getting such clarity, starting up the collection phase should be strictly avoided.

Getting clarity is critical. It is the sole responsibility of the strategic analysis function to get a sufficiently defined management brief prior to starting a project. The analyst should keep asking questions for clarification to management up to the point that the 'when', 'what' – and where possible and needed the 'why' of the project – are defined in such a way that misunderstandings between management and the analyst are all but excluded. Once these answers are available, completing the management brief to a project brief is feasible. A checklist for a project brief is the topic of the next section.

# 2.7 CHECKLIST FOR A PROJECT BRIEF

In table 2.1 I provide a simple checklist for a project brief. The three questions what, when and why are covered in table 2.1 and may be answered differently for different strategic analysis projects.

Sometimes there is merit for a strategic analysis function to outsource a project to a third party. In this book, I focus on the 'in-house' strategic analysis function (see chapter 20), so I will ignore the considerations of when and how to outsource intelligence work.

The 'how' question concerns the methodology of the actual project. Methodology is the topic of chapters 3-8 for data collection, chapters 9-14 for data analysis, chapter 15 for reporting and chapter 19 for filing.

Finally, the 'where' question considers the relevance of doing in-field research versus desk research. This topic mainly concerns collection work and is covered in the collection-related chapters.

Now that we have a project brief, we can continue our journey into data collection.

| | |
|---|---|
| WHEN | Timing of the deliverable |
| WHAT | Define objectives and hypotheses to be validated<br><br>Check balance between business' sizing of the price vs, budget (requirements)<br><br>Define non-content attributes:<br>- action standards of accuracy of the result<br>- required level of detail<br>- language<br>- format<br><br>Check 'what' question for:<br>- completeness<br>- accuracy<br>- ambiguity<br>- factual clarity |
| WHY | Define 'real' reason behind the project, taking into account:<br>- upcoming business decisions<br>- current business strategies<br>- current business targets<br><br>Implicitly: consider emotional needs and competencies of the principal |
| WHO | Choose between (partial) internal or (partial) external execution<br>Define organization (principal, project leader, staff, stakeholders)<br><br>When external, consider budget-implications when choosing:<br>- external supplier<br>- between syndicate or tailored work |
| WHERE | Desk research or field work<br>When field work, consider budget implications |
| HOW | Choose collection methods and sources, analysis (tools), reporting media<br>Define clearance level and choose team with full clearance<br>Choose project name<br>Ensure compliance with all applicable law (especially in collection) |

TABLE 2.1 ▶▶▶ FULL PROJECT BRIEF CHECKLIST

CHAPTER 3

# ATTRIBUTES OF SOURCES AND THE COLLECTION PLAN

# 3.1 INTRODUCTION

In chapter 1 I highlighted the fundamental relevance of collection for strategic analysis. This chapter introduces different segmentation dimensions of sources for data collection. The first segmentation dimension is the 'nature' of data sources. Subsequently I will introduce some other useful dimensions to segment data sources.

Then, in subsequent chapters, I will use 'People', 'Papers', 'Pictures' and 'Products' as leading segmentation for the discussion on collection methodologies by data source nature. Prior to that, in this chapter I will discuss other generic segmentation dimensions for data sources, a valuation of source by segment and a methodology to efficiently and effectively execute collection. The latter is commonly known as a 'collection plan'.

# 3.2 SEGMENTATION OF SOURCES

## DEFINING AND SEGMENTING SOURCES

As a first step in this section I aim to define what a source is. A source in this book is:

> *"a book, statement, image, person, object, etc., supplying data for an analysis."*

There are many ways to segment data sources. First, I would like to discuss sources (regardless of their nature), by using some generic segmentation dimensions. The list below, though it is not exhaustive, presents the dimensions that sources are segmented by in this book. But, there may well be other dimensions that are relevant for segmenting such data sources. So be it. The ones below in my experience are relevant in basically all strategic analysis and therefore have made it into this book:

- Open vs. Classified
- Primary vs. Secondary
- Internal vs. External
- Free-of-charge vs. Fee-based
- Small vs. Big
- Good vs. Bad

## OPEN VERSUS CLASSIFIED

In strategic business analysis some sources are confidential. In business analysis confidentiality usually relates to Non-Disclosure Agreements (NDAs) that have been concluded between the different parties and the firm that employs the strategic analyst. Parties involved in NDAs may include suppliers, investment banks, brokers, competitors, other companies and customers. Data obtained from such confidential sources, for instance data to judge the value offered to a firm from a sale in a particular transaction, often is explicitly forbidden to be used for any other purpose.

For example: an auction process is organized to sell a company. In such a case an NDA will first need to be signed by authorized staff in the analyst's firm. Only when the NDA has been countersigned, the seller will be prepared to share detailed, confidential information on the company that is for sale. Such information is contained in what is usually called an Information Memorandum (IM). From a strategic analysis perspective, an IM is a treasure trove. It provides information on a company for sale that will never be available in the public domain. Moreover, IMs have usually been prepared by professional services firms. The latter do not want to end up in litigation when, for whatever reason, the IM contained incorrect information. So, the reliability of the data in an IM is high.

It should, however, be remembered that even when every data point mentioned in the IM is 100% correct and true, the information may still be far from the whole truth (e.g., it may be that essential facts for valuing the company for sale are lacking).

Usually usage clauses of an IM of a company offered for sale limit the IM's value. As a rule, an IM should only be used to judge the value of a potential transaction. The candidate buyer has to guarantee in writing that soft and hard copies of the IM are removed from the computers of the staff involved in the transaction – except for one copy that is usually allowed to be held as a record by the prospective buying firm's legal affairs department. Thus, IMs can only legally be used for a single purpose and afterwards are no longer accessible to the strategic analysis function (or so at least it should be).

Moreover, by implication any analysis will be classified and only available for limited distribution in the context of the purpose for which it has been produced and the use allowed.

In the selling process of a company, even more classified information is made available once a formal due diligence process has started. The due diligence team gets free access to many more and different confidential company facts. What applies to IMs applies even more to due diligence-obtained information: highly useful, but due to confidentiality-related limitations, off-limits for *other* strategic analysis assignments.

Therefore, in general, classified sources are a great and essential asset, but only for the purpose for which they are provided. Therefore, strategic analysis work tends to be based on open sources and the data is collected and available in sources that are 100% in the public domain. There is never, repeat *never* an excuse to break the law (including but not limited to using IMs for purposes other than intended). An analyst who sees no other way to solve his puzzle at hand than through breaking the law is either not competent or lacks integrity. In both cases, such an analyst is not the type of staff any decent firm that embraces fair competition would wish to employ. In summary: open sources are the key source for strategic analysis work.

## PRIMARY VERSUS SECONDARY

Primary sources are defined as sources that themselves possess the data that is looked for. Secondary sources may report data but have generally not created the data themselves.

An example of a primary source is a competitor's annual report, a press release or an investor presentation that is, or at least should be, in the public domain. Primary sources also include humans, who may for instance include the competitor's staff or staff employed by a supplier or a customer.

Secondary sources include all other sources that are not primary sources. The longer the distance between the origin of the data and the source that reports the data, the more significant source reliability issues may become.

Let me provide an example to illustrate this. Secondary sources amongst others include newspaper articles. Newspaper articles, especially those featured in the general press rather than specialized financial newspapers, are notoriously inaccurate when it comes to figures. Turnover or even worse profit is rarely accurately quoted in a newspaper article. A journalist reports that 'profits of company ABC have gone up to US$12 million in Q4'. What profits?

- Gross earnings (i.e., net sales minus variable cost)?
- Earnings Before Interest, Tax, Depreciation and Amortization?
- Earnings Before Interest and Tax?
- Earnings Before Tax?
- Net Earnings?

For each of the four above profit definitions, at least two variations exist: before or after exceptional items.

The good news is that all that is reported is 100% true. There is a caveat. All that is reported, especially by a company on its own performance, is said in such a way as to make the company look great. It is only when reading the fine print that the complete reality and thus the full truth might be revealed.

In the absence of a primary source it is courageous (read 'reckless') for a strategic analysis department to report on a competitor's profit based on a vague secondary source.

A simple rule of strategic analysis work is whenever primary sources are available, secure them. Only use secondary sources when primary sources are not accessible or available. If you have to, in the absence of primary sources, use secondary sources, but do so with sufficient caution regarding the reliability of the data.

## INTERNAL VERSUS EXTERNAL

Internal sources are defined as sources that work in the same firm as the analyst or originate from the same firm that employs the analyst. External sources are not related to the same firm. When working with internal and external sources it is recommended in advance to consider two dimensions:

- Bias
- Accessibility

Internal sources may be deeply biased regarding a topic of strategic analysis. A classic phrase is that it is hard to have a useful meeting with a turkey on Christmas. In other words, don't automatically expect the firm's staff to give a neutral opinion on the situation at a competitor or a customer or a supplier. The firm's staff may feel personally threatened by an issue at hand related to another company. As a result, the source may aim to colour the picture in the way that he perceives to serve his interests best. However, external sources may also not be bias-free. To add to the confusion, the external source bias is probably different from that of the internal source…

Below two generally common biases are discussed to illustrate how analysis can be deceived by missing out on biased sources. The first bias is believing that a human reporting data as a source had the full picture (Friedman, 2010b):

> *"There is value in sources, but they need to be taken with many grains of salt, not because they necessarily lie but because the highest-placed source may simply be wrong (…). If the purpose of intelligence is to predict what will happen, and it is source-based, then that assumes that the sources know what is going on and how it will play out. But they often don't. (…) The purpose of intelligence is obvious: It is to collect as much as*

*information as possible, and surely from the most highly placed sources. But in the end, the most important question to ask is whether the most highly placed source has any clue what is going to happen."*

In this quote, Friedman implicitly suggests that evaluation of the input of the source is ignored. As a result, the source's view on what will happen by definition becomes the strategic analyst's view. That should offend any analyst. A good analyst has the checks and balances in place to evaluate sources, prior to communicating any conclusions to decision-makers about the work that she did. This is not to say that Friedman's warning should not be taken seriously. It apparently is based on experience, unfortunately also my own. Human sources are indeed sometimes indispensable in collecting data. When a human source allows an analyst to turn a mystery into a puzzle, the all-too-human tendency is to overestimate the accuracy of that source's message. The reliability of the source becomes increasingly questionable when more time has passed between the moment of the event reported and the moment of the report. Footnote 1 to chapter 8 encourages keeping a sober view on the limited accuracy of the human memory. These risks are inevitable when working with human sources.

Below I will provide a second example of a human source bias. This bias could well be summarized as the source that happens to have an opinion. Jonathan Powell, the Chief of Staff of the Blair administration in the UK (1998-2007) provides us with an amusing example of this bias (Powell, 2011b):

*"We had two advisers in (Downing Street) Number 10, one madly for the Euro and one madly opposed. I used to think that, if you were a foreign intelligence service and had the first of the two on your payroll, you would be certain Britain was about to join the Euro and be equally sure we were not if you employed the other."*

The advantage of *company-internal* human sources is that they tend to be more easily accessible than external sources. In a firm where cooperation between colleagues is valued, colleagues generally reply positively upon requests for help on data.

Humans are a strange species. On the one hand, humans kill other humans (i.e., animals of the same species.) This is very rare if not absent in the animal world. On the other hand, humans tend to be helpful to other humans, even when knowing there is no reciprocity to be expected (e.g. in charity donations). Intra-company requests to colleagues, even when the purpose of the request, as so often, cannot be fully shared by the strategic analysis department, tend to be answered quickly and correctly. Knowing internally which source knows what therefore is a key asset for a strategic analysis department.

As people tend to work together much easier with people they know than with people they have never met, it also means that the analyst should be known inside his own firm. Those colleagues who benefit from deliverables (e.g., by receiving a regular news and analysis letter), will generally be even more inclined to help. In the best of cases such colleagues will start to send their information proactively to the analyst.

A second benefit of working with internal human sources is that questions can be asked without having to hide the strategic analysis department's intent. The degree of openness that can be used depends on the confidentiality of the topic at hand. With internal sources, at least direct questions are possible.

In contrast, when working with external sources, it is necessary to ensure that no suspicion is created in the mind of the source. Revealing, even unintentionally, what a strategic analysis department wants to know is not a good idea, given the confidentially and/or strategic character of what a strategic analysis department generally works on.

Given the fact that both internal as well as external sources may be biased, with different biases for sure, there is no automatic preference for either of the sources. The big advantage of internal sources is the fact that they, as colleagues, probably collaborate more easily and less suspiciously. Moreover, using internal human sources is usually more time-efficient, not the least because direct questions can be used.

What should be prevented at all times is paying for external sources to discover data that are available within the firm – but only in unknown sources. There are few better options for a strategic analysis department to more quickly and effectively lose its credibility than to pay big-time for data that is already in the possession of the firm.

As a rule, strategic analysis departments should strive to comprehensively explore and approach all internal sources prior to signing off on orders for fee-based external data.

## FREE-OF-CHARGE VERSUS FEE-BASED

The difference between free-of-charge and fee-based sources in strategic analysis work limits itself to public domain or open sources. In any decent firm, the code of ethics rightly prevents the firm from bribing third party human sources. It goes without saying that doing so is unacceptable at all times. Stories about the KGB paying its agents in foreign government jobs are great for history books. For some delightful examples of KGB Christmas bonuses to French agents check out the history of the KGB (Andrew, 2001d). Those type of practices, however, have nothing to do with strategic analysis in business and moreover are generally probably less romantic than spy fiction makes them.

When considering whether to use paid sources the question should not be what amount of cost is involved, but whether the fee paid will be rapidly earned back by the improved quality of the decision-making.

Common paid open sources include databases such as but not limited to Dun & Bradstreet, which provides financial statements on companies in an easy-to-read format. Many structured news providers also charge a price per article or a fixed subscription price. Databases and other free and fee-based sources are covered in chapter 6 and in Appendix 2.

Generally, strategic analysis projects and processes will need a mix of fee-based and free-of-charge open sources. Company statements are of course for free and so are many web-based sources. Few strategic analysis projects, with the exceptions of some small errands, can be executed without using fee-based sources. In budgeting for a strategic analysis department, the subscription cost to various paid sources may be amongst the largest items paid for.

## SMALL VERSUS BIG

In a figurative sense, small sources deliver small amounts of data and big sources deliver big data. Big data as a term has been around since the last quarter of 2010 (Davenport, 2014d).

Big Data may include both internal company data as well external data concerning the business environment of a firm. The criterion that determines whether a data set qualifies to be called big is that the amount of data is truly big: think of petabytes. Big Data forms a rapidly developing field of business information, enabling companies to for example analyse millions and millions of user acts (e.g., user mouse clicks on a website like LinkedIn) per day in search of ever better, more intuitive offers to their customer or visitor base.

Big Data differs from Small Data not only in quantity but also in collection process. Big data tends to come in *continuously* and keep coming in – think of mouse clicks on a 24/7 global website. Small Data comes in 'one-off batches' – think of monthly market share data – a typical recurring external data point, or monthly sales data by country by product – a typical internal data point.

Some Big Data indeed considers the external environment of a firm and thus may qualify for strategic analysis (e.g., *external* visitor interaction with a website) but most focuses on internal data (the firm's *own* performance indicators). Due to their continuous flow and the ever-stronger computer processing power available, Big Data may revolutionize decision-making of organizations. Big Data allows for the response time between an anomaly in a signal and a management response to be minimized – with the latter even possibly being the result of an automated script – so without any human interference. However, direct Big Data applications in strategic analysis are still believed to be in their infancy, even though social media sentiment analysis – for example on the public image of brands, which requires big data technology – starts to take off.

As the discipline of Big Data collection on the business environment is still in its infancy, it is hard to draw conclusions where Big Data will lead strategic analysis to in the future. One thing already seems to be clear: collection isn't and will not likely be the bottleneck in the world of Big Data. Technologies are available to collect the data, whereas making sense of Big Data is proving to be the challenge today. The data analyst profession may be amongst the most promising in the entire computer sector today.

No matter how exciting Big Data and the opportunities Big Data may offer for strategic analysis, it is my experience that often a single data point – so the smallest data set possible – may just make all the difference in an analysis. Though it may be considered to be a bit tongue-in-cheek, here I share a quote I personally quite enjoy, taken from the memoirs of the former head of the East German foreign intelligence service, the extraordinarily capable Markus Wolf. Wolf, I think, highlights just how important it is to find the meaningful small data points, even when big data are available (Wolf, 1998):

> *"Intelligence is essentially a banal trade of sifting through huge amounts of random information in a search for a single enlightening gem or an illuminating link."*

## GOOD VERSUS BAD

The good news is that there are no bad sources. For sure, there are sources that are more and that are less reliable. Knowing the reliability of a source in advance of using it is a great asset when considering the use of sources. The North Korean newspaper *Nodong Sinmun* may, for example, not be the most reliable source on news about South Korea. Meanwhile, it may be one of the few accessible and *reliable* sources on North Korea, which in some instances, but certainly not all, remarkably frankly reports on topics concerning the North (Mercado, 2009b).

Sources are not intrinsically good or bad. A source is an instrument. For accepting or rejecting a hypothesis, one source may simply deliver a key data point more cost effectively than the other. However, when another hypothesis is concerned, another source may be preferable: horses for courses. In the collection plan, which I will discuss later in this chapter, links between hypotheses, key information needs and the (expected) most reliable and efficient source(s) are summarily worked out, for execution during the actual collection.

## SOURCES MAY ALSO BE SEGMENTED BY THEIR NATURE

Where the above segmentation was generic and irrespective of the nature of the source, the nature of the source as such also guides source segmentation. In this book, I present four different natures. To stay close to marketing parlance I will here (again) define the 'four Ps': People, Papers, Pictures and Products.

The four Ps, as they often referred to in marketing, are just a flashy way to present an existing concept, in this case an existing classification – the four Ps link one-to-one to the traditional taxonomy of US intelligence collection (Clark, 2007f):

| | | | |
|---|---|---|---|
| • **people** | or human intelligence | or HUMINT | chapters 4&5 |
| • **papers** | or open source intelligence | or OSINT | chapter 6 |
| • **pictures** | or imagery intelligence | or IMINT | chapter 7 |
| • **products** | or measurement and signature intelligence | or MASINT | chapter 8 |

Other collection methodologies exist in military intelligence, for example ELINT (electronic data interception intelligence) or its sister methodology SIGINT (signal intelligence). ELINT is probably illegal in any business application, so by definition out of scope. SIGINT is a euphemism for eavesdropping. As a rule, all SIGINT for business applications is ethically inappropriate in any company that embraces fair business practices – even when some SIGINT methods may be legal. Therefore, SIGINT like ELINT will not be covered in this book.

HUMINT concerns data collected from and through human sources. OSINT relates to the collection of data from sources that are available in the (written) public domain. IMINT focuses on intelligence collection from images. Finally, MASINT is a collection process to get product samples. The latter are usually processed/analysed to obtain insights by deploying back-engineering or other laboratory analysis techniques. The remainder of this chapter focuses on valuation of sources, subsequently of terminology and on collection as a support process for strategic analysis in general.

# 3.3 VALUATION OF SOURCES

What is true in many management disciplines also holds truth in strategic analysis: garbage in, garbage out. The lower the reliability of the sources, the lower the reliability of the output of the strategic analysis process. The user of the output is unknowingly exposed to serious risks particularly when the output is presented without an indication of the (low) reliability.

There are no firm rules for the reliability of sources. Normally, for example, company annual reports that contain a statement of approval by a certified accountant tend to present reliable figures. After Enron, Parmalat and Ahold, to name a few exciting cases of accounting frauds, real figures may not be what they look. These, of course, were cases of deliberate fraud.

The message is simple: reliability is never to be taken for granted. On the other hand, paranoia over the reliability of sources is also not an approach that is deemed to be effective.

## MASINT TENDS TO BE THE MOST RELIABLE SOURCE

Balancing between naivety and paranoia, diagram 3.1 gives an experience-based review of the reliability of common sources.

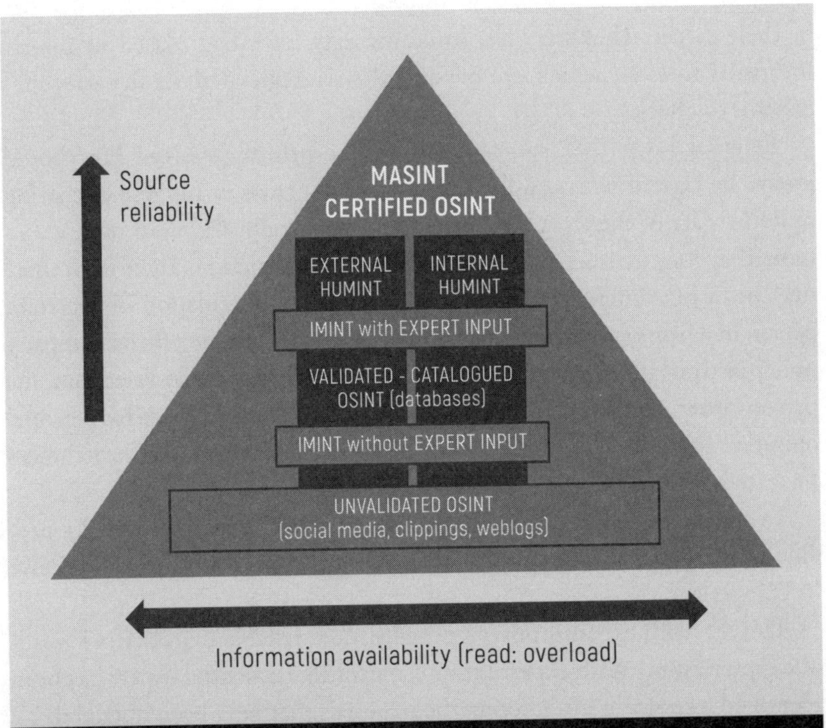


DIAGRAM 3.1 ▶▶▶ OVERVIEW OF THE TYPICAL RELIABILITY OF SOURCES BY THEIR NATURE

MASINT – in other words, the laboratory results of analysis on the competitor's products, for instance – clearly features among the most reliable sources. Provided the analysed sample was representative, there is little room for bias when laboratory best practices have been used.

Certified OSINT delivers, after MASINT, among the most reliable input data or information that is obtainable. When certified it means data or information that prior to their publication have been reviewed by an accountant or a lawyer: for example, a firm's annual report or an Information Memorandum. Both types of documents contain only information that is 100% true. This is true in normal cases, assuming there is no fraud. Information that is 100% true is great, but as has been said before, all that is made available that is 100% true does not necessarily make up the full truth, so having flawless puzzle pieces still doesn't mean that we have a complete puzzle.

External and internal HUMINT sources both rank from highly reliable to not so reliable. Internal HUMINT sources may be biased because, for example, they only want to share part of the story that suits them in their career. They may also unknowingly have had biased or poorly informed sources, which are beyond the strategic analysis department's control to check.

External HUMINT sources may well be primary sources, but should always be treated with caution. They too may have an interest in sharing only the part of the story that suits them personally. Or, even more common, they may themselves simply not have the full picture. There is, or there may be, a big difference between the opinion or speculation of a certain person in a firm on a particular matter in that firm and the official company policy or strategy regarding the matter. As was pointed out by Friedman, the person either may not know the full story or may simply phrase his personal opinion. This source's input may not be allowed to inform the next choices the external firm's management as a whole may make.

In the worst case, a person in a competitor firm may intentionally provide an incorrect story that is illustrated with incorrect facts, just to deceive its competitor.

IMINT with expert input is normally more reliable than IMINT without expert input. With expert input is meant that a neutral expert has been identified to assist in interpreting the materials that have been obtained.

Validated (catalogued) OSINT – information accessible via databases or libraries – tends to be (much) more reliable than information that is just out there (available on a non-validated website. Specifically, information from social media, online blogs and random clippings are among the least reliable sources).

For strategic analysis work, the above general reliability assessment leads to a priority of choosing sources. Remember: sources are an instrument, not a goal. The goal remains to efficiently and effectively solve the strategic analysis project's core problem. Whatever sources are needed to do so should be approached. When, however, choices can be made, the priority that is introduced below may be helpful.

When useful for achieving the objective of a strategic analysis project, MASINT should always be done with priority. Certified OSINT sources should also be used with priority, not the least because they are often accessible 24/7, fast and easy to locate and often cheap. When these sources do not meet all the information needs, think carefully which HUMINT sources could be reliable and (cheaply, rapidly) accessible. Always bear in mind potential biases of the sources to be approached. Think in advance how to avoid getting trapped in a biased story that is great to hear but foolish to believe. Where needed, do take a xenocentric view: it too often matters more who says a thing than what is being said.

When image material is available it should be used. This is especially true when trustworthy experts are around to see what non-experts wouldn't have seen.

Validated/catalogued OSINT sources are normally a good choice: they tend to enable efficient work. These catalogued databases may, however, consist of newspaper articles which may not be as complete and/or correct with quantitative facts as needed.

When all the above sources do not provide all the identified information needs, the inevitable web search is needed. The search may uncover pearls but generally these have to be found among dozens if not millions of shining but worthless glass beads. The Internet in strategic analysis work, however large it may be, is and remains the data provider of last resort. For clarity purposes, catalogued databases that happen to be offered *via* the web are not included in the above reasoning. Non-validated internet sources generally should get the lowest reliability score. They also deserve to get the lowest priority in the collection efforts of a professional strategic analysis department.

# 3.4 SUBJECT TERMINOLOGY

Particular topics may have associated jargon which can only be understood by insiders. Prior to an analyst starting a search, the preferable route is to locate an insider and get initiated into the jargon, regardless of the methodology of searching and/or the sources.

For example, yoghurt drinks, fermented dairy drinks, dairy drinks, sour milk drinks and drinking yoghurts may all mean the same thing, even though dairy drinks may include (flavoured) milk drinks which technically are different. When exploring the market for the entire ready-to-drink yoghurt category (to use another similar term), it is essential to have a grasp of the jargon to avoid missing out on vital data.

Another business discipline that is rich in synonyms is finance. Profits, earnings, results, yields and returns may all be used as synonyms for financial gains (another synonym). The complications get broader when sources in different languages are to be searched.

The recommendation that is made is first to get familiar with the jargon and only afterwards start the search. The preferred source for the jargon is the insider (a trusted human source). In the absence thereof, encyclopedias – either online, like Wikipedia or hard copies – or dictionaries may get you started.

What is true for synonyms is even more relevant for translations of names from different alphabets. Arabic, Chinese or Russian names are easily misspelled in Latin script (and vice versa). Arno Reuser is a great friend of mine. He pointed out that in open sources alone the number of different ways used to spell the name of the former Libyan head of state, Colonel Khadhaffi, in the Latin alphabet went into double digits. When searching for the former Libyan head of state (using a Latin alphabet), checking which spellings are commonly used may assist in not missing out relevant data. In chapter 6 on Open Source Intelligence we cover the challenge of language, spelling and jargon in more detail.

# 3.5 DATA COLLECTION PLAN

Most (larger) strategic analysis assignments are run as projects. Projects usually start with a Project Start Up meeting (PSU meeting). In the PSU-meeting, the objective (or 'what') of the project is defined, next of course to the 'how' which makes up the project plan. The plan also answers questions like 'who' is to be involved, 'when is the deadline' and 'where is the work to be executed.'

In strategic analysis projects, data requirements are usually defined in an early phase of the project, if not at the very start during the PSU meeting. Data requirements are the input to what is normally a sub-task within a strategic analysis assignment: the data collection plan.

Data collection plans are normally organized as source-centred plans. Table 3.1 gives an example of what typically a collection plan's position and content is in a strategic analysis assignment.

| PHASE | Activities |
|---|---|
| PROJECT PLAN | Define data needs |
| COLLECTION PLAN | - Take holistic view on the data needs<br>- Brainstorm on which sources may have relevant data on the topic<br>- List the potential sources:<br><br>**HUMINT**<br>- contact A for not-too-narrow sub-topic P<br>- contact B for sub-topic Q<br>- contact C for sub-topic R<br><br>**OSINT**<br>- check database K for data on need X<br>- check newspaper L for data on need Y<br>- check handbook M for data on need Z<br><br>**IMINT**<br>- have image G evaluated by expert D, etc. |
| COLLECTION EXECUTION | Execute collection by following the so-generated leads, taking into account factors like reliability, cost, time requirement and efficiency |
| ANALYSIS | - Evaluate results of collection: do more collection where needed<br>- Use or reject obtained data points based on actuality, risk of bias,reliability and/or other factors |

**TABLE 3.1 ▶▶▶ SOURCE-CENTRED COLLECTION PLAN**

Table 3.1 hopefully makes clear that compiling a collection plan is not rocket science. The value of formally writing a collection plan is the discipline that it brings to the data collection. By formally brainstorming on what sources to capitalize on for which data need and recording the outcome, the chances of overlooking high-value, low-cost sources of data are substantially reduced. For this reason alone, even after more than two decades of routine in executing strategic analysis assignments I still wouldn't start the smallest errand without making a proper list of data needs and the connected data sources.

CHAPTER 4

# PEOPLE: COLLECTION FROM FRIENDLY OR NEUTRAL SOURCES

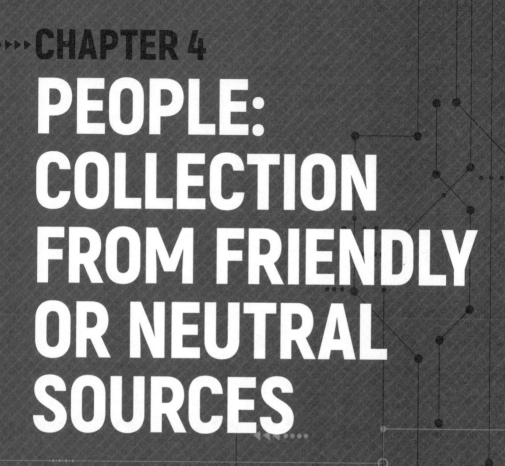

# 4.1 INTRODUCTION

In the previous chapter both the rewards and some of the risks of collecting data from human sources or Human Intelligence (HUMINT) have already been introduced. In this book I define HUMINT as:

> *'the collection method of extracting data, information, knowledge or even intelligence from human sources'*

Section 4.2 will describe the anatomy of HUMINT: why, who, where and when to use it and how to apply it. All humans are equal but some are more equal than others. This explains why different methods are defined in sections 4.3–4.7 for different human-source target groups. The methods discussed in this chapter are limited to those needed for sources that in principle are neutral or friendly (to use military parlance). In business terms, I would characterize these sources as tending to be cooperative. As we will see, even within the group of cooperative sources, we can usefully differentiate methods for data collection. Section 4.8 discusses the protection of sources and section 4.9 looks into HUMINT collection when facing cultural barriers. Chapter 5 also focuses on human intelligence and the obscure art that is sometimes applied to collect data from sources that are not and are not meant to be aware that they have been approached with data collection methodologies.

# 4.2 ANATOMY OF HUMINT

HUMINT is great for collecting data that otherwise may not be available, but it has a dark side. It can at times be ethically dubious. Loading a source with booze to extract a business secret is hardly something to be proud of. In this chapter I wish to focus on HUMINT that is ethically undisputed in terms of methodologies and applications. The next chapter discusses whether and if so how to ethically collect HUMINT from sources that would not spontaneously agree to a formal interview when they would be fully aware that the sole purpose of the conversation would be to collect 'hard-to-get' data.

## WHY TO DO HUMINT?

Key reasons to apply HUMINT include:

**Speed**

HUMINT is often the fastest collection method as the quote below exemplifies. A Special Survey Group in Japan's once deeply-admired MITI (Ministry of International Trade and Industry) in the past has explicitly been set up to report on the US computer industry – an industry known for its rapid changes (Deacon, 1982d):

> *"Japanese agents are aggressively gathering information by both overt and covert means and they eagerly buy samples of new tools and instruments and send them back to Japan. They go for yields, production rates and future plans. What normally might take them a year to discover at home with a tremendous amount of costly research and development can often be obtained in a single conversation in Silicon Valley."*

**Reliability**

Trusted primary HUMINT sources tend to be among the most reliable sources for data. Their value, however, may be overestimated when it comes to making predictions (Friedman, 2010b). Applying checks and balances to all gathered data is the work of the professional analyst. Any journalist knows never to rely on a single human source. The same rule should apply to strategic analysts.

**Uniqueness**

The data that is to be collected through HUMINT may or may not be in the public domain at the moment of collection. In the former case, using the human source channel is simply more convenient; in the latter case, human sources may well be the only sources that can legally provide the required information. There is one caveat to this statement: the statement presupposes that accessible and cooperative sources are available to the collector.

The value of HUMINT from the perspective of military intelligence is highly rated. This former Soviet source also implicitly explains how strongly the former KGB depended on human sources in its data collection (Cherkashin, 2005):

*"Human contributions are by far the most important component of intelligence gathering".*

Part of the typical KGB HUMINT-collection role has by now probably been replaced by digital espionage of non-ethical companies and/or governments. In the 2016 annual report of the Dutch General Intelligence and Security Service (AIVD), one of the three focal points of concern is the unawareness of *digital* espionage in the corporate world (AIVD, 2016). This, however, is not to say that HUMINT as an instrument of data collection is no longer being applied, as HUMINT's speed and uniqueness still makes it a tempting instrument for unethical operators!

A balanced view on HUMINT I believe is provided in the quote below (Grey, 2016h):

*"(HUMINT is) resource-hungry, time-consuming and usually fruitless pursuit at constant risk of backfiring (…) While its impact was usually slight, occasionally, at a very crucial moment, human intelligence could provide the golden arrow, the piece of information that, if it could be corroborated and used correctly, might be decisive, as it was for Stalin with the designs he stole for the atomic bomb."*

## TO WHOM AND WHERE TO APPLY HUMINT

Every analyst needs to understand the basics of HUMINT collection methods and their application. Doing so has a merit first and foremost as a defensive move, as HUMINT may also be applied by competitors (or their mercenaries) against the analyst and the secrets the analyst knows (and that others may be after). Moreover, as ethics and legal risks in HUMINT are as sensitive as in any topic in strategic analysis, full understanding of compliance issues needs to be ensured, prior to (starting to) practicing HUMINT.

HUMINT may be applied on multiple occasions – both in terms of time of the day and activity at that time. It is at the most harmless of occasions, like hanging out in a bar, where the vulnerability of people to unnoticed HUMINT collection efforts is largest – and the collector's success rate is at its highest. Booze and secrets are a poor mix.

HUMINT works best when applied face-to-face, regardless of whether the interests of the source and the collector are aligned or not. Most human communication can be revealed through body language and tone of voice, including sighing etc., Only a limited part of the message is conveyed by the actual text that a source provides to a collector. The body language gets lost in most forms of communication other than face-to-face.

Video conferencing with friendly sources is a good second option after meeting face-to-face. The advantage is the time and cost gained by not having to travel. The disadvantage, however, is that almost by definition the video conference company's room offers a rather formal meeting setting. The latter may in itself impede the source to share 'confidentialities' with the collector, even when the two are on friendly terms, simply due to the intimidating environment of the board room that doubles as video conference facility.

When source and collector have a relationship of mutual trust that has been built over at least some time, a simple call or even an email may be enough to collect HUMINT. It is, however, in the cases when source and collector do not know each other yet – and especially in the case that the two do not have rationally aligned interests – that the HUMINT techniques become relevant, and the ethics and legal compliance may become sensitive. This tricky area I don't want to shy away from; the next chapter covers it.

The question 'who' in this context is operationalized as the question of what attributes a good HUMINT collector has. This question is also answered in the next chapter, as HUMINT collection from sources that may not have an aligned interest with the collector is the most challenging and therefore requires the most sophisticated skills.

Specialized professional service companies offer cold-calling services to collect HUMINT, usually from parties that have no mutual interest or an opposite interest versus the principal of the collector. Given the ethical sensitivities and the difficulty to monitor consistent legal compliance of the operations of such third parties – regardless of what they claim they do – outsourcing HUMINT to third parties is generally to be executed with the greatest of caution.

## WHEN TO APPLY HUMINT

HUMINT is usually applied when either of the three factors mentioned above apply to the collection assignment. Speed, uniqueness and reliability all matter, but the former two generally matter more than the latter.

As described in the previous section, some occasions are more favourable to HUMINT collection than others. More attention to this is given particularly in chapter 5.

## HOW TO APPLY HUMINT

HUMINT is a wide field. HUMINT is therefore segmented in five different methodologies. Each is best applied to particular target groups. Free-flow, interviewing, networking and sampling will each be defined in individual sections below. The special case of elicitation will be covered in chapter 5. Table 4.1 visualizes the five different HUMINT methodologies, applied to eight different target groups.

<table>
<tr><th>SOURCES</th><th>INTERNAL</th><th>EXTERNAL</th></tr>
<tr><td rowspan="2">CLEARANCE[1]<br>EQUAL OR HIGHER<br>FRIENDS<br>CLEARANCE LOWER</td><td colspan="2">Free-Flow</td></tr>
<tr><td colspan="2">Interviewing</td></tr>
<tr><td>NEUTRALS</td><td>Interviewing</td><td>Networking<br>or<br>Sampling<br>or<br>Elicitation</td></tr>
<tr><td>COMPETITOR</td><td colspan="2">Elicitation</td></tr>
</table>

TABLE 4.1 ▶▶▶ HUMINT METHODOLOGIES AND TARGET GROUPS: WHEN TO USE WHICH TYPE

Three different classes of human sources are distinguished, each of which can be internal (i.e., employed by the same firm) or external:

- Friends are parties or persons who (perceive to) have the same interest in the successful outcome of the strategic analysis project as the analyst. Friends are split into those who have the same or an even higher clearance regarding access to (internal) confidential information and those who do not.
- Neutrals are parties or persons who are essentially indifferent to the successful outcome of the strategic analysis project. There's nothing directly in it for them to assist the strategic analysis department.
- Competitors are parties or persons who may negatively be affected by the successful outcome of the strategic analysis project – in the case of internal sources – or may have a negative attitude towards the company the analyst works for in the case of external sources.

Table 4.2 elucidates the concept of table 4.1 by providing characteristic roles of individuals with whom the analyst may interact.

| SOURCES | INTERNAL | EXTERNAL |
|---|---|---|
| CLEARANCE EQUAL OR HIGHER<br>**ALLIES** | colleagues in M&A, strategy, business development who are involved in the larger context of the strategic analysis project, general management, sometimes marketing or sales | staff of involved law firms, investment bankers, advisors – each of these categories has a positive financial interest in the success of the analysis project. |
| CLEARANCE LOWER | colleagues who are active as analysts in other parts of the company and with whom a regular two-way information exchange exists, or colleagues from cooperating departments | staff of data suppliers – e.g., database providers; possibly staff of other suppliers; possibly staff of customers |
| **NEUTRALS** | other colleagues who are not affected by the analysis project | - staff detached from other mothers to common JVs<br>- analysts in other non-competing companies<br>- staff of suppliers<br>- staff of customers<br>- consumers<br>- journalists<br>- NGO staff<br>- trade organization staff<br>- politicians/senior civil servants |
| **COMPETITOR** | colleagues who feel (personally) threatened by either the analysis project or the analyst | staff of competitors and any other source that does not see it as its interest to freely share data with the company the analyst works for |

**TABLE 4.2 ▶▶▶ HUMINT METHODOLOGIES AND TARGET GROUPS: EXAMPLES OF ROLES[2]**

HUMINT is far from an exact science: different methodologies may be applied in different cases and towards different target groups. The objective of this chapter is to offer methodologies that have proven their merits in practice. The objective of strategic analysis work is not to dogmatically apply a particular method to a particular target group in a particular case. Strategic analysis is not prescriptive medicine. Rather, the objective of this chapter is to make the methodologies presented here part of the analyst's data collection toolbox, in order to cost-effectively attain the most accurate, timely and complete strategic analysis deliverable on any management brief. There is one constraint – all that is done needs to be ethical and legal. This is the topic of chapter 18.

# 4.3 FREE-FLOW

Free-flow is the first HUMINT collection methodology that I want to discuss. Free-flow is generally the easiest HUMINT collection method to apply. For an analyst, free-flow basically means to collect the required data directly from sources in open conversations.

For selecting sources, the analyst may just need to know who has clearance. Within the cleared group the analyst needs to know 'who knows what' and to give them airtime or 'mail-time' to get them to respond to requests. Generally, staff clearance levels are proportional to job rank and inversely proportional to unoccupied time in the respective' staff's agendas. Getting their priority to assist the analyst with their inputs may be the only challenge. In free-flow, the analyst tends to leave the lead in the conversation with the source. Like a medical doctor, guiding the source to talk about the topic is often the best way for an analyst to obtain as much data as possible or as required on the selected field of interest.

## GET (EXPERT) SOURCES TO SHARE NARRATIVES

Extensive research is available on how people make decisions (Klein, 1999d). To extract often intuitive decision-making processes from (expert) sources, Klein reports that having the source share their *stories* is a powerful tool to obtain insights (Klein, 1999a). The methodology is directly applicable in data collection for strategic analysis. The following quote elucidates how to operate with expert sources (Klein, 1999a):

*"If you ask experts what makes them so good, they are likely to give general answers that do not reveal much. But if you can get them to tell you about tough cases, non-routine events where their skills made the difference, then you have a pathway into their perspective, into the way they are seeing the world. We call this the critical decision method, because it focuses attention on key judgments and decisions that were made during the incident being described"*

Klein studied how decision-makers operate. In strategic analysis, the holy grail is to define the intent of a competitor. Why did the competitor's decision-makers do what they did? More importantly, what does what they did in the past convey about what the competitor may do next? Would it be possible to extract with any predictive value a pattern from the competitor's past decisions? Free-flow is a HUMINT collection method that allows the analyst to collect data points that together may help to build much more abstract pictures. Along similar lines Klein found abstract rules governing expert decision-making models. The only thing Klein needed was their narratives to go by.

## FREE-FLOW SOURCES MAY ALSO SIT ON A COMPANY'S BOARD

Let me share a narrative. I remember a case about an executive board member of a large company who was once tasked by his own Strategy-M&A project team to be data collector. The strategic analysis was working, offline – desk research only – to assess the attractiveness of an acquisition of a foreign daughter company of a larger conglomerate. The analyst coincidentally learned that his company's board member would meet his counterpart in the larger conglomerate, as the analyst was tasked to prepare a general briefing on the conglomerate for this board member. Following the introduction briefing, an 'analyst-to-collector' collection brief had been prepared to help the board member himself find out whether his counterpart would be open to a transaction regarding this foreign asset, and if so what structure such a transaction could have. The executive board member returned with a positive answer. The top executives on both sides had agreed to an appointment for a designated project leader at the analyst's firm with his counterpart in the conglomerate to further investigate matters. About ten months later, the acquisition was successfully closed.

## FREE-FLOW REQUIRES THE ANALYST TO MAKE FRIENDS BEFORE SHE NEEDS THEM

The above narrative is an example among teamwork of allies: it is about a call on a friend. In the definition of 'allies' it is assumed that the targets and incentives of sources and of us as analysts are aligned, so there should not be typical corporate barriers to a fruitful cooperation. Table 3.3 summarizes the free-flow methodology characteristics.

| | |
|---|---|
| INCENTIVE TO COOPERATE | - Common incentives and targets (e.g., to close a transaction)<br>- Two-way flow of information: the analyst may share facts with sources that are directly relevant to the sources |
| RULES | - Full openness<br>- Mutual exchange of facts and opinions (where useful)<br>- No hidden agendas<br>- No hierarchical barriers; project team culture |
| BENEFITS | - Low-cost<br>- Efficient<br>- Easy to execute<br>- Straightforward methodology<br>- No confidentiality or legal liability risks or exposures |
| RISKS & ISSUES | - Limited number of sources; may not generate complete enough coverage of the topic under study<br>- Sensitive to group-think, especially when in the larger context of the project a dominant principal wishes to steer the analyst<br>- Information reliability risks (a single source may not know or represent the complete picture at the competitor, or may have a personal interest in representing reality in a biased way without saying so) |
| ANALYSIS | - Evaluate results of collection; do more collection where needed<br>- Use or reject obtained data points based on actuality, risk of bias,reliability and/or other factors |

TABLE 4.3 ▶▶ CHARACTERISTICS OF FREE-FLOW

# »»» 4.4 INTERVIEWING

There are two major differences between interviewing and 'free-flow':

- Interviewing is not intended to create a two-way information flow.
- The interviewed staff, also referred to as interviewees or source, should not become aware of the real purpose of the interviewing.

Interviewing centres around questions. Like strategic analysis, asking questions is an art. Three seasoned former CIA officers have written the instructive book *Spy the Lie*, which attempts to discover deception through asking questions. They recommend the following ground rules when asking sources questions that they may not feel comfortable answering in full (Houston, 2012c). The latter may be caused, as in Houston's book's context, because the facts are not the source's best ally, or as in the strategic analysis context, because the source may be reluctant to openly share what he may consider to be valuable information:

- Keep questions short: the longer the question, the more time the interviewee has to make up his mind to avoid answering clearly.
- Keep questions simple: save intellectual grandiosity for your private diary; a well-understood question is likely to be answered clearly as well.
- Keep questions singular in meaning: ambiguity in questions may lead to confusion between interviewee and interviewer and to confused answers.
- Keep questions straightforward: openness may earn the trust of the interviewee. A modest attitude as interviewer may stimulate an interviewee to be more cooperative.
- Keep a catch-all question in reserve: always conclude an interview with the simple question 'what else?' The interviewee may know matters that are of relevance to the topic at hand but that even the most xenocentric

interviewer *could not have imagined* asking. Depending on the trust built during the interview, the interviewee, may be prepared to share those unknown unknowns.

During an interview, it is recommended to generate three categories of follow-up questions, to keep exploring what a source may reveal (Houston, 2012c):

- Evaluation: this type of question is useful to test the accuracy of the source. An example of such question is: How do you know this is true?
- Exploration: this type of question is meant to continue the extraction process. An example is: What more do you know on this business?
- Clarification: this type of question is used to ensure the absence of confusion. An example is: What products did you say were delisted?

Questions may be usefully segmented into two main and several sub-categories (Houston, 2012c). The main categories are recommended and to-be-avoided question segments. The recommended question segments include:

- Open-ended: this question type is used to have the source create a narrative, for example: What can you tell me about the business in Croatia?
- The best questions generally start with Kipling's six honest service men: What, Where, Why, Who, When and How.
- Closed-ended: this question type is useful to establish facts, for example: When did you last visit the production site?
- Presumptive: this question type suggests that the interviewer already knows facts that the interviewee may not yet have shared during the interview. As interviewees in strategic analysis projects are by definition cooperating voluntarily, presumptive questions, unlike, for example, in a law enforcement context, must be used with care not to distort the atmosphere between source and interviewer. An example of a presumptive question could be: What customers did you visit besides Carrefour?
- Bait: this again is a question type that at first sight suits law enforcement better than strategic analysis. In the former context, it may suggest the source withholds information on his actions. This is not useful in a strategic analysis context. This question type establishes a hypothetical situation as a stimulus for triggering a surprise-based response from the source. An example of a bait question in the strategic analysis context could be: Could there be any reason why a competitor may know about our innovative, soon-to-be-launched product?

- Opinion: this is a question type that is neutral and perfectly suitable in strategic analysis as it puts the source on a pedestal by asking them for their opinion. For example: What do you think of the strategy of this competitor? How could they make it work?

Question types to be avoided include:
- Negative: this question type is a recipe for problems as it talks down to the source. As in advertising, questioning negativism is a mortal sin. An example is: 'You don't know the sales of this company, right?'
- Compound: this question type is made up of multiple sub-questions. One of the key risks is that only one of the multiple questions is being answered. An example of a compound question is: 'What do you know about last year's sales, profits and cash flow?'
- Vague: this question type refers to questions that are not specific. Due to the lack of specificity an answer to such question is rarely useful. An example of a vague question in a strategic analysis context is: 'What is going on in the cheese market in Isolattia?'
- Closed: this question type is characterized by the fact that it can be answered by a 'yes' or a 'no', and does not encourage the interviewee to elaborate on their answer. An example is: 'Did you know of the contamination?' A much better question would have been: 'What did you know about the contamination?'

## ASKING GOOD QUESTIONS IS AN ART THAT IS LEARNED BY PERSONAL EXPERIENCE

Defining the right questions is an art, and it is just as important to be able to assess the accuracy and completeness of the answers. The questions above provide hints to discover (intentional) deception by sources who are unwilling to share the full truth.

During the interview the interviewee may know what is being asked, but essentially no more than that. The context should remain hazy (e.g., 'working on some project'). In the case of highly sensitive projects, it is sometimes even advisable, though ethically it's a light shade of grey, to define a cover story and work with it, to avoid curious non-involved colleagues catching a glimpse of what is being worked on.[3] Preparation of a cover story pays off.

Table 4.4 summarizes the characteristics of interviewing.

| | |
|---|---|
| INCENTIVE TO COOPERATE | - In internal functional hierarchy situations, incentive to cooperate is a call to support a project executed by a functional superior.<br>- In internal 'cooperating department' colleague relations, it is plain generosity that is called upon, serving the interest of the company as a whole. Sort of 'please do this for me, next time i will help you.'<br>- In external contacts, it is basically asking a favour as an existing or prospect customer or even as a supplier. |
| RULES | - Only ask questions related to the topic the source is knowledgeable about, so never share a complete picture with the source.<br>- Ask questions in such a way as not to reveal the hidden objective (e.g., ask for a report on topic X that by definition covers topic Y as a sub-topic) but don't refer to topic Y, if topic Y is key to you.<br>- Ask questions that have nothing to do with the objective to hide the objective in the so-created 'protective fog'. |
| BENEFITS | - Low-cost.<br>- Efficient.<br>- Comparatively easy to execute.<br>- Not too complex methodology.<br>- Essentially no confidentiality or legal liability risks or exposures. |
| RISKS & ISSUES | - Don't underestimate the source's ability to deduct the objective behind the questions – there could be an info-security-risk.<br>- There is no such thing as a free lunch: asking a supplier or even worse a customer for a favour (e.g., data) always has a price. |

TABLE 4.4 ▶▶▶ CHARACTERISTICS OF INTERVIEWING

# 4.5 INTERVIEWING COLLEAGUES WHO ARE FORMER COMPETITOR STAFF

Internal sources may know your competitor well. Your colleagues today may in the past have been working at the competitor. A separate section has been dedicated to this topic as this is an area where ethical and legal issues must overrule corporate curiosity at all times.

In some countries, it is not even lawful to ask people about their experiences at their former employer. Asking them to share internal documents of their former employer obtained during their tenure there is obviously off-limits. They shouldn't have these documents in the first place, because usually employee contracts explicitly forbid workers who leave a company to keep such files. Everybody knows that employees do not always comply with this, but it is critical for a company to ensure that no material offered in this way is touched.

In many companies, competitor review sessions are regularly held as part of preparing strategy reviews. Ex-employees of the competitor may participate in such sessions, provided they are not put in potentially embarrassing situations. When their former employer is discussed, based on open source information, it is tempting for them to complement the facts that are shared with loads of non-public facts and insights.

In these cases, when the strategy analyst is facilitating these sessions, it is good practice to first identify each competitor to whom this situation in the group of participants applies. Then, in plenary, the strategy analyst should set out the rules of engagement of the session. Rules of engagement that worked well in my own work experience include:

- Participants who are ex-employees of the to-be-discussed competitor are free not to contribute or should even be asked to leave the room.

- Participants may never be coerced to contribute to such sessions by a peer group of colleagues or even worse by their boss (threatened by losing career opportunities, etc.).

Having formulated these rules in advance, an option is to ask the ex-employee to remain silent during the session and afterwards, and after the analysis has been completed give some nuances, without revealing non-public data. Statements by the ex-employee like, "As you can read in the latest Annual Report, the focus is really on developing this business line," is harmless in terms of competition law and ethics. Yet, it can validate or reject a hypothesis on future competitor plans, provided the ex-employee had access to, or was privy to the plans of the company, in the first place. If not, or if the strategic analyst doubts that was the case, the input by the ex-employee source should be seen as just another minor puzzle piece – a puzzle piece that should be just as rigorously validated as any other puzzle piece.

In discussing competitors in the presence of their ex-employees, the one-liner by Peter Drucker, so often, applies: "The most important thing in communication is to hear what isn't being said." (Drucker, 1990)

# 4.6 SAMPLING

Sampling is a sister-methodology to interviewing. It is normally only applied when working with external, neutral sources. It is or can be powerful, but the power comes at the price of it being rather time consuming.

Sampling is basically asking the same question to say 60 different yet comparable neutral sources. I applied this technique on several occasions when aiming to understand the retail market dynamics in emerging markets, where in the past other sources were few and far between.

In 2003 I chose to visit eight different cities, over eight consecutive days, in this case in Guangdong Province, a southeastern province in the People's Republic of China. Cities were chosen that had different sizes – first tier: Shenzhen, Guangzhou; second tier: Meizhou, Dongguan, etc. When I was driven through each city, I would randomly choose retail outlets that sold products in the category of my interest. From mom-and-pop shops selling 1,000 Yuan per week to hypermarkets with 50 cash machines and everything in-between. I had not announced anything in advance to any retailer. Together with my translator we simply walked in, looked at the shelf, bought a product or two and had a general chat: "Is your business doing well, etc." We introduced ourself as our firm's business development staff and asked whether we could ask a few questions. Apart from one occasion, not one single retailer refused cooperation, even though admittedly some provided more answers than others. The one that didn't want to cooperate was just having lunch. We as team learned two important lessons:

- You may not always get a positive reaction if you try to pepper a small-town Asian shopkeeper with micro-economic analysis questions during meal time.
- It is remarkable how open neutral sources can be when they are treated respectfully.

In eight days, we collected so much high-level, detailed information – with remarkable consistency among the various sources – that we felt comfortable enough to base significant business decisions upon this so-obtained foundation. Looking with hindsight the intelligence collected proved to be high-grade: the predictions made for how this business would develop proved invariably (and honestly, amazingly) correct in the decade since. Table 4.5 gives the characteristics for sampling.

| | |
|---|---|
| INCENTIVE TO COOPERATE | - First, buy some goods in their shops<br>- Second, make a friendly chat (followed by respectfully asking some questions) |
| RULES | - No misrepresentation<br>- Patience<br>- Stick to a topic that is of interest to the source, in this case: their retail margin, what they saw as their best customers and why, etc. |
| BENEFITS | - Information that is hard to get and even harder to get reliably, especially in emerging markets. |
| RISKS & ISSUES | - Time-consuming and thus costly.<br>- It will be a risk to start asking leading questions, that would seem to attribute the responses of the first 40 interviewed sources to interviewee number 41. |

TABLE 4.5 ▶▶▶ SAMPLING CHARACTERISTICS

# 4.7 NETWORKING

Setting up a network is a basic requirement for anyone in strategic analysis. Networks are based on mutual benefits. Network-building will not work when there is nothing relevant to give to other network participants. Get to know people who understand the industry. Give them (harmless) data (e.g., data that is in the public domain or data that concerns another competitor) when that information will assist these potential sources in their work.

Invest time in setting up and maintaining the network. Every industry has its trade association; their meetings are ideal networking occasions. Unfortunately, access to such meetings is usually limited. If the strategic analyst can't be the representative of her firm to the trade organization in some board, do be sure to know who does represent the firm. Our analyst subsequently should ensure this colleague becomes her ally.

Another great venue for networking is business conferences. At such events, employees can look for competing companies' staff, if only to pick up the latest rumours. Strategic analysts, even of competitors, who get acquainted may develop a modus of quid pro quo exchange of (open source) information.

Strategic analysts may also benefit from customer network conferences, organized by larger market research companies. This is where all the market research and possibly strategic analysis buyers from the different peers in an industry segment come together to discuss topics of mutual interest (e.g. the future definition of market segments).

Third parties who are in the know can also be sources in a network. First and foremost, there are investment bankers who work for or regularly connect to several competitors in a single company sector, as all are or may be their customers. Equipment suppliers are of the same breed. Both will, however, always trade information: you give some, you get some – looking as they are for creating their next deal. They will usually want much more than they give. The most professional bankers are also the most useless from this perspective, which in principle speaks in their favour. If they give any data that are not in the public domain, they will only give it hush-hush to what they call 'C-level' – i.e., executive board members. The data they do give freely always tends to originate from sources a good analyst already has (companies like Euromonitor are big suppliers to the financial service companies).

Moreover, investment bankers, like management consultants, will always claim they have Chinese walls: they don't know what goes on at the analyst's competitor. Some bankers and equipment suppliers may nonetheless at times be quite informative, but that is also the moment when the analyst needs to put ethics before getting more data (see chapter 18). Moreover, sources that are too talkative to you about others may be just as talkative about you to others. Watch out for who you work with!

Table 4.6 gives the characteristics of networking.

| | |
|---|---|
| INCENTIVE TO COOPERATE | - Quid pro quo (meaning: we cooperate because we perceive that we will get more than we give). |
| RULES | - No misrepresentation.<br>- Strict adherence to all applicable competition law.<br>- Avoid asking too many questions.<br>- Ensure that what is 'given' is public domain or a view on a topic that is relevant to the source but not concerning your company.<br>- When it is unavoidable to ask questions, limit them to the topic the source is knowledgeable about; never share a complete picture with the source and ensure not to reveal the real objective. |
| BENEFITS | - Access to information that is hard to get through other means.<br>- Often, this provides the earliest warning signal of changes at a competitor. |
| RISKS & ISSUES | - Hard-to-locate the sources and sometimes it may even be harder to trust them.<br>- Time-intensive.<br>- Costly.<br>- Information reliability risks.<br>- Prone to intentional deception.<br>- Prone to underestimating the capabilities of the competitor to benefit from the information provided in the exchange. |

TABLE 4.6 ▶▶▶ SAMPLING CHARACTERISTICS

Take care at all times to never underestimate the capabilities of the competitor. In 1944 master spy Richard Sorge stated in his trial case (Whymant, 2006):

> *"The mercantile class is made up of men of average or less than average intelligence, and the agent who assumes such a cover would be quite safe from detection."*

Sorge, however, met a tragic end. Moreover, the mercantile class may well be composed of more intelligent people than it was in the 1930s and 1940s, when Sorge was highly successful in his work. In short, use HUMINT through networking where useful but ensure always to be on the net receiving side.

Also, avoid at all times the discussion of product prices, market shares and individual customers with anyone outside the company you work for, unless vetted by your company's legal department. It is in these areas that anti-trust laws are applicable, and they are increasingly harshly implemented.

# 4.8 SOURCE PROTECTION

When applying HUMINT, sources should always and at all cost be protected from exposure, especially when the source is not even aware he is a source in the first place.

Source protection in corporate HUMINT collection is very important.[4] I believe protection is just as relevant in corporate data collection as it is in law enforcement, in military intelligence or in journalism for that matter. A source should not be revealed.

The responsibility to ensure source protection lies with the strategic analyst. As a rule, in debriefs of HUMINT collection efforts, no source (nor collector) names, not even code names are ever used. I tend to use meaningless phraseology such as but not limited to 'market rumors have it' or the politically-correct 'team analysis.'

There is a good reason for protecting both the source and the collector. Consider this example: the head of strategic analysis in corporation XYZ brags to his CEO that he has good connections to his counterpart in a competitor company. His counterpart has more than once provided him with useful data that is hard to find in the public domain, simply by carelessness, or in exchange for other open source information, collected by the strategic analysis team of XYZ. Next, the CEOs of the two companies plan to meet. These things happen. The head of strategic analysis in XYZ is tasked to prepare a brief for his CEO. He provides a proud briefing with all the data he has, even the hard-to-find data points.

During the meeting for the two CEOs, the CEO of XYZ brags that he understands the competitor company quite well and in doing so reveals, inadvertently, his knowledge of these hard-to-find data. The competitor's CEO kindly asks how this information found its way XYZ. XYZ's CEO states he has a talented strategic analyst who liaises with his peers. Consider the damage to the relationship with the source … if the source is not fired in the first place. This is a fictional example, but that doesn't mean it cannot happen. When an analyst has such sources for information, they should do their utmost to protect them. Good HUMINT sources are among the most valuable assets a strategic analyst has. Protecting them in their own, and your own, interest is truly imperative.

# 4.9 HUMINT COLLECTION ACROSS CULTURAL BARRIERS

A special case of HUMINT collection is when the collector is originating from another culture than the source. For the sake of the argument, let's say the collector is Western and the source non-Western. This certainly complicates the collector's role. In strategic analysis, ethnocentrism is a common source of flawed data analysis (Johnston, 2005c). The data collector should thus avoid interpreting obtained data in an ethnocentrically flawed way.

For all HUMINT collection methods it is critical to appreciate cultural differences. For an Arab it may be more important to help someone save face than to be truthful (Naffsinger, 1964). This reference may be an old source. Culture may, however, be quite timeless. The versatility of truth in non-Western cultures has also been reported more recently, in this case related to the Turkish culture (Berlinski, 2010):

> *"(…) and you just can't trust a word they say. As one Turkish friend put it (a man who has spent many years in America, and thus grasps the depth of the cultural chasm):*
> *It's not that they're bad; they don't even know they're lying.*
> *My friend is right, and his comment suggests a point about Turkish culture that I doubt many Westerners grasp. People here—and, I would guess, throughout the Middle East and Mediterranean, though Turkey is the only country I know well—see 'truth' as something plastic, connected more to emotions than to facts or logic. If it feels true, it is true. What's more, feelings here tend to change very quickly—and with them, the truth."*

Personally, I have lived for many years in Malaysia and I have on multiple occasions experienced similar behaviour. For a Western cultural origin data collector this may initially not be easy to grasp. There is only one solution. The collector has to find a way to deal with it, as the culture phenomenon will not go away.

T.E. Lawrence, who as British officer during the First World War united the Arabian forces against the Ottomans, said that working towards a xenocentric view of other cultures merely requires taking (much) more time (Lawrence, 2011):

> *"Arab minds moved logically as our own, with nothing radically incomprehensible or difficult, except the premise: there was no excuse or reason, except our laziness and ignorance, whereby we could call them inscrutable or Oriental, or leave them misunderstood."*

So, patience does the job. Take the Japanese, for instance who have a marvelous reputation as data collectors. This may have a cultural background. Even in a Western context they have, especially during their stellar economic rise in the period 1950-1980, been highly effective. They really took the trouble to understand how the West worked, prior to approaching the West on data collection tours. A common model that the Japanese often applied is that they pretended to have no clue about what they are being told. Displaying their feigned ignorance confirmed (or was used to confirm) Western superiority feelings. This was a strong motivator for the Western sources to tell them more in exchange for getting more recognition a hidden belief the Japanese understood well and, even better, capitalized upon. So, Westerners tended to be even happier to tell even more secrets to impress their Japanese guests. This earned them even more 'ahhh' recognition signals and a few more gentle bows. Until, that is the Japanese launched a cheaper *and* better product and it was the Westerners' turn to say 'ahhh' – not expressed out of gratitude but out of cash flow pain.

What was and probably still is true for the Japanese certainly is true for the Chinese. The Chinese in my own experience are also much clearer about and persuasive on what they want to know than on what they want to share.

CHAPTER 5

# PEOPLE: COLLECTION FROM UNSUSPECTING SOURCES

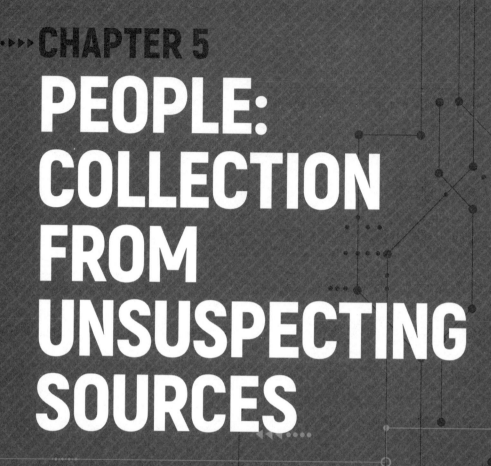

# 5.1 INTRODUCTION

In the previous chapter I discussed ways to collect data from sources that in principle stood neutral or even positive towards the data collector achieving his objectives. The data collector thus could openly share what data was required in pursuit of his strategic analysis. He may not have been able to tell what exactly he was working on at all times in terms of the content of the analysis, but he could communicate with the source that he was after this data. Knowing this would not and did not upset the source. The roles and rules were clear.

However, there may be times that data collectors do not want to share the fact that they are collecting data. They may be just as eagerly looking for data, but they may not want anyone, let alone the source, to know. There may be two reasons for this type of prudence on behalf of the collector:

- The sensitivity of the topic for which data are being collected.
- The collector not wanting the source to realize that he *is* a source and is actually meeting a collector.

The first reason for data collection discretion is that when the source knows *what data* are being collected, the *reason* for the data being collected is inevitably revealed. When a strategic analyst, introducing herself as an analyst, inquires of any potential source (no matter whether that source is friendly, neutral or has no incentive to cooperate) about his interests in the potato business in Paraguay, the inevitable conclusion by any source is that apparently the analyst's firm has some business plan in progress relative to potatoes in Paraguay. Such business plan, however, may involve a deal with another listed company. Any leaking of a potential deal with a listed company is legally highly dubious. Knowledge of such negotiated transactions may even lead to insider trading.

In this case, a source remaining unaware of being one and a collector not explicitly introducing herself as collector may not be ethically questionable. This statement presupposes that the interests of the source are not hurt due to this undercover form of data collection. The source may, for example, be a colleague who is simply not required to know what exactly the analyst works on, but who may have data that should be obtained for the analysis. As long as the source's interests are not hurt, the source may still feel taken by the nose by the collector whenever they find out, but it is unlikely to lead to enmity. The collector played their undercover role for a good reason and that's about it.

## HUMINT COLLECTION FROM UNSUSPECTING SOURCES MAY CAUSE AN ETERNAL LOSS OF TRUST

The second reason for discretion is that a source realizes that the friendly socializer they had a good drink with was actually a shrewdly operating data collector. The source would feel rightly cheated, and perhaps stop being a source.

I would. Even worse, I once did. One day an investment banker played one of the collection tricks on me that I will discuss later as a warning in Appendix 1. It was late at night. I had arrived at Schiphol Airport in Amsterdam after a foreign trip. Upon my arrival I switched my mobile phone back on and received a notification of a missed call from a banker who I knew but was not too close with. I had no clue why he had called me, but I decided to call him back, and this is what happened:

*"Hi John. I saw your missed call, so I decided to call you.*
*Just arrived at Schiphol, that's why I didn't reply any earlier. What's up?"*

*"Hi Erik. Yeah, you must be busy.*
*I saw your company announcing two big deals today!"*

He was right in the sense that we had announced a significant M&A transaction that day. We were working on another major transaction but to my knowledge that transaction was not yet ready for any announcements. I had, however, been abroad so I had not monitored our press releases of the day, and in fact I hadn't heard of any such deals. He clearly confused me, and before I knew it I said:

*"What do you mean two? I know of one.*
*Has another transaction been announced as well?"*

In spite of me being tired, I was very careful to hide what transaction I knew about. However, through my answer I did confirm there was something big going on… which is exactly what he wanted to get confirmed, because that would colour his pitch policy for his next service offer to us. This banker lost my trust forever, and on top I despised him for not being good enough in the job of data collection – even when he scored this hit.

This is as clear of an example of elicitation as it gets. Elicitation is the collection of data from an unsuspecting human source during what the source, initially and possibly until the end, perceived to be an innocent conversation.

The most savvy HUMINT collectors apply elicitation, conveniently ignoring the ethical dimensions involved. They are trained to intentionally distort the memory of their sources. To them, sources should not remember that they shared (sensitive) data, and by intentionally loading their memory with gratifying experiences that are neither relevant to the data given nor the de facto theft thereof, they don't remember this event later. This serves to protect the collector (and his principal) from being unmasked. It is taking the intelligence paradigm of 'not leaving a trace' as far as is possible – and clearly way beyond what is ethically appropriate in fair business practice. Don't think that it will never happen to you. I did, until I switched my mobile phone on that one night at Schiphol.

# 5.2 ELICITATION

Elicitation as described above is a craft which on some occasions is ethically justifiable, but on many it is not. This methodology will be briefly discussed below, because even to an ethical data collector the use of elicitation is in some cases justified. For obvious reasons, literature about elicitation is scarce, just as literature on how to break into houses would be. It is far from my intention to write a manual on how to steal data from innocent, unsuspecting sources who would never have provided the data voluntarily had they known the objectives the collector had. On the other hand, I believe a strategic analyst has to have a minimum awareness of elicitation, because when not knowing how crooks break into houses, how can you effectively protect your house from break-ins?

Elicitation is defined here as the collection of information through *talking* to knowledgeable people, without the people becoming aware that data is being sought from them. The US Army defines elicitation as follows (US Army, 2006a):

> *"Elicitation is the gaining of information through direct interaction with a human source where the source is not aware of the specific purpose for the conversation. Elicitation is a sophisticated technique used when conventional questioning techniques cannot be used effectively."*

The US Federal Bureau of Investigation (FBI) defines elicitation as (FBI, 2014):

*"The strategic use of conversation to extract information from people without giving them the feeling they are being interrogated."*

The elicitation targets are to be seduced through smart verbal manoeuvring by the elicitor into releasing the data the elicitor is after. When operated according to the standards of this duplicitous trade, the target becomes the source. The target is meant to release the data without:

- Ever realizing what the intent of the elicitor is or has ever been.
- The elicitor leaving traces, because the elicitor executes the elicitation operation in a disguised and deniable way.
- Without the source even remembering that he released information that was elicited in the first place.

## PEOPLE CANNOT HOLD SECRETS

Elicitation originates from the military/law enforcement/government intelligence world. It is amongst other methods used to assist law enforcement authorities in lie detection (Javers, 2011b). The underlying assumption that drives elicitation is that somewhere deep in people's souls, people can't hold secrets.

As long as humans are vulnerable to being seduced by psychological rewards, such as personal recognition, elicitation has a chance.

The key in elicitation is that, strange as it may seem, questions will be avoided[1] by the elicitor. Questions are memorable, and in the elicitation tradecraft these are not good as they may leave traces in the target's memory of the conversation. One of the key tenets of intelligence, after all, is not to leave traces. Therefore, elicitation is all about open dialogue (Carpe, 2005):

*"One of the most interesting elements (…) is the ability to keep talkative sources talking for an unpredictably long time. When a source is well engaged and well controlled by the researcher, they can keep the conversation going for as long as humanly possible, provided there are no scheduling conflicts or major interruptions.*
*In countless instances, sources will state that they have only five minutes to speak and in turn wind up (…) for well over an hour; this is the nature of human behaviour."*

When questions are being used by elicitors, they will be non-pertinent. This means the questions may not pertain to the data collection objectives. This is to avoid alerting the target about the real purpose of the conversation. In other words, questions may be used only during rapport-building dialogue, aimed only and exclusively at making the unsuspecting target feel (more) comfortable (Carpe, 2005).

## ELICITATION TENDS TO BE OUTSOURCED

Professional elicitors often have an intelligence agency or related law enforcement training background (Javers, 2011c). Nowadays they work for private firms to extract data from targets under the assignment of large firms that don't want their staff to do the work themselves. This relates to the need for plausible deniability of some large firms.

This is also exactly why this is the place to sound a loud warning signal (Carpe, 2005). Outsourcing of elicitation to specialized agencies is possible. Control over the ethics of such agencies, however, is much less easy.

Whenever outsourcing elicitation (e.g., through cold-calling) is considered, be 100% sure that the agency operates ethically. The reputation or even litigation risk for your firm is unacceptable when non-ethical practices are executed.

## WHETHER WE LIKE IT OR NOT: ELICITATION EXISTS

The reasons for covering the topic are threefold. The first is that elicitation exists in this world. Even when it is not being used for your or my collection efforts in an unethical way, it may still be used unethically against us.

The second reason for covering elicitation is because it is human nature, which is the reason why elicitation works so well. Awareness of the human tendencies that make it work may assist you in protecting yourself against others applying elicitation to you, although just knowing about them, as we saw above, does not protect you against being trapped by them.

The third and final reason is somewhat tongue-in-cheek. To some there may be a little bit of naughty boy or girl charm in it. Those readers who don't see this charm and or will never want to use elicitation – not even in infrequent ethically sound applications – are encouraged to skip reading the remainder of this chapter. For those, however, who would like to see some examples of real-life elicitation in history, the intermezzo at the end of this section has been added as an illustration. In addition, section 5.3 discusses some characteristics of the elicitor – positioned as the villain, but written from the villain's perspective of putting collection above ethics or possibly even legality.

The characteristics of elicitation are given in table 5.1 below.

| | |
|---|---|
| INCENTIVE TO COOPERATE | - Good elicitation triggers sources to speak to an elicitation professional without them later even remembering that in doing so they have revealed information.<br>- The elicitor intuitively maps what emotional needs the source has, plays on them and gets rewarded with data. Often the need for recognition is strong in experts. Rather than keeping (company-confidential) data to themselves, they talk openly to peers, even when the elicitors work at competitors, if only to show how elegantly they solved a complex problem. The instant satisfaction of personal recognition gain may for vain personalities outweigh the long-term cost of loss of data to their employer. People with such profiles are suitable elicitation targets. |
| RULES | - No misrepresentation.<br>- No bribery.<br>- No asking of questions.<br>- No note-taking during the conversation.<br>- No facts about the elicitor's company are shared in return for data (as in networking: quid pro quo); in this case the reward to the source is exclusively psychological/emotional. |
| BENEFITS | - Access to data that may be difficult to collect otherwise. |
| RISKS & ISSUES | - Time-intensive and thus costly.<br>- Data reliability risks (one source may not know or represent the complete picture of the competitor).<br>- Legal compliance and reputation damage are risks when the elicitor 'in the heat of the data battle' breaks ethical and/or legal rules. |

TABLE 5.1 ▶▶▶ ELICITATION CHARACTERISTICS

There is some good news in all this as well. The chances of successful elicitation causing serious damage to a firm can be reduced. Companies are well advised to implement clear counter-intelligence training programmes. Need-to-know staff should participate in them. The best counter-intelligence training to my knowledge was delivered to a company's R&D community and exclusively focused on training these R&D staff elicitation techniques. The trainer never mentioned to the R&D staff that the real objective of the training was not to make them elicitors but to raise awareness of elicitation as a defensive measure – as a way to train them in counter-intelligence. After an hour of sharing all the elicitation tradecraft tricks, suddenly one senior scientist, quite shocked, blurted out:

*"So these techniques can also be applied against us!"*

The objective of the training had been achieved. Being aware of elicitation techniques is recommended. Appendix 1 provides examples of word play that elicitors often use. Using the tricks given in Appendix 1 is for ethical reasons not recommended against adversarial sources, even when applying them may at times be legal on paper.

## INTERMEZZO: ELICITATION – EXAMPLES COLLECTED AS WARNINGS

Government intelligence books and even novels give great examples of elicitation in practice. In the first-ever Russian psychological novel, *A Hero of Our Times*, written in 1840 by Michael J. Lermontov, the lead character gives a brilliant summary of elicitation:

> *"I wanted to make you relate something, for the following reasons: firstly, listening is less fatiguing than talking; secondly, the listener cannot commit himself; thirdly, he can learn another's secret; fourthly, sensible people, such as you, prefer listeners to speakers."*

Another example is provided in the biography of Second World War agent Eddie Chapman (Macintyre, 2007). When describing MI5 officer T.A. Robertson, Macintyre summarizes what it takes to be good at elicitation:

*"T.A. Robertson had the rare knack of being able to talk to anyone, anywhere and about anything. Bishops, admirals, whores, crooks and revolutionaries all found it equally easy to confide in T.A. Robertson. (...) T.A. Robertson was no bookworm. Instead he read people. He excelled in a job that 'involved a great deal of suspect people in pubs... meeting, greeting, charming, chuckling, listening, offering another drink, observing, probing a little, listening some more and ending up with all sorts of confidences the other person would never thought he would utter."*

Journalism is another discipline where characters who are effective in extracting data flourish. A historical example of a smart elicitor is William Russell, reporter for *The Times* during the Crimean War (1854-1856). In Orlando Figes' book on that war, Figes describes Russell as (Figes, 2011):

*"A vulgar low Irishman, an Apostate Catholic... but he has the gift of the gab and uses his pen as well as his tongue, sings a good song, drinks anyone's brandy and water, and smokes as many cigars as foolish young officers will let him, and he is looked upon by most in Camp as a 'Jolly Good Fellow'. He is just the sort of chap to get information, particularly out of youngsters."*

In his analysis of the Cuban Missile Crisis, Dobbs gave a clear-cut example of elicitation (Dobbs, 2009b). Dobbs provides a portrait of Washington-based KGB operative Aleksandr Feliksov and his standard technique of elicitation (a mix of a provocative and a suggestive statement; see Appendix 1)– which indeed yielded him new facts:

*"He (Feliksov) had been meeting the ABC correspondent ( Scali) over coffee and occasional lunch for more than a year. If nothing else, the meetings were a way to improve his English. A voluble Italian-American, Scali was 'an exuberant type' from whom it was relatively easy to extract information. Feliksov's standard technique was simply to raise a topic that interested him and then insist at a certain point, 'No, it can't be.' Eager to display inside knowledge, Scali would reply with a comment like "What do you mean it can't be? The meeting took place last Tuesday at 4 PM and I can even tell you it was on the eleventh floor."*

# 5.3 ELICITATION

How do we recognize a good elicitor as either a helper or an opponent? A good elicitor is an effective elicitor. In other words: a collector who brings home the hard-to-get data she was out to obtain.

The US Army rightly emphasizes the importance of listening and memorizing skills for an elicitor (US Army, 2006b). When using elicitation – no matter whether ethically or not – the best way to scare a source into silence, or worse, is to write down what is being said. That is not the casual conversation a potential source thought he was having and that the elicitor aimed to keep going:

> *"(…) in elicitation, memory is the only viable recording method. However, in general, using the memory exclusively to record information is the most inaccurate methodology."*

Interrogation of, for example, prisoners of war (POWs) resembles elicitation, assuming the nation that has captured the POWs respects the Geneva Convention (Johnson, 2009c). Next to name, rank and serial number, a PoW is entitled to refrain from sharing data, just as an elicitation target does not have the slightest obligation to participate, let alone cooperate in a conversation. A good POW interrogator, however, succeeds in getting data beyond these basics without coercion. The preferred characteristics for an elicitor and a POW interrogator to achieve this are given in table 5.2 (Johnson, 2009c), (Jähne, 2009). A good elicitor radiates a feeling of comfort that allows the free flow of confidentialities between source and elicitor – without a second thought.

## ELICITORS ARE KIND AND ARE IN CONTROL OF THEIR EMOTIONS

For a good elicitor, it is key to have a good understanding of themselves and a full control of their own emotions. The elicitor should take a perfectly neutral stance towards their target, as a good doctor takes opposite a patient. Clearly, the elicitor will act their role. Like a pickpocket, they are only friendly until they have got what they want; that is when their task is accomplished and they will normally vanish from their target's life thereafter. It is not only the theft by sophistry, but it is also this hypocritical duplicity that makes elicitation so ethically shady; pretending to be a friend while in fact only being after data that is hard to pull off.

Scientific research reveals that two factors contribute significantly to elicitors succeeding in extracting more data out of their targets compared to classical interrogation (Oleszkiewicz, 2014).

The first factor proved to be the elicitor's kindness and empathy towards their elicitation target. The second factor was the elicitor's ability to make their elicitation target perceive that the elicitor already knew it all. The elicitor providing multiple facts casually contributed to an atmosphere where the elicitation targets let down their guard and added many facts to the discussion that they, in the experimental context, were supposed to hold as secrets – secrets that were kept in the interrogation context. Kindness and sharing were dangerously effective.

| QUALITIES | APPEARANCE |
|---|---|
| - Determined<br>- Resilient<br>- Sensitive<br>- Discrete<br>- Broad general knowledge<br>- Decent, but not expert, knowledge of the subject at hand<br>- Flexible<br>- Spontaneous; need to communicate<br>- Diplomatic<br>- Working knowledge of psychology<br>- Patient listener<br>- Strong in maintaining eye-contact | - Innocent<br>- Harmless<br>- Friendly<br>- Calm<br>- Empathic<br>- Curious – within tolerable limits |

TABLE 5.2 ▶▶▶ CHARACTERISTICS OF A GOOD ELICITOR

An elicitor may of course face resistance from a target or even downright rejection. That is inevitable and part of the game. There is, however, solid advice to elicitors on how to handle resistance (Borum, 2006):

*"Never try to teach a pig to sing.*
*It wastes your time, and it annoys the pig."*

A final relevant characteristic of a good elicitor, even in the face of some resistance, is to be persuasive. Persuasion has been defined as (Jähne, 2009):

*"The ability to induce beliefs and values in other people by influencing their thoughts and actions through specific strategies."*

Six factors determine 'tried and true' strategies in achieving interpersonal influence (Borum, 2006). These also link to persuasion:
- Likeability
- Authority
- Reciprocity
- Commitment/consistency
- Social validation
- Scarcity

In other words, to be effective an elicitor should (adapted from: Joyner, 2007):
- Determine and control the context, including the place (or at least attempt to). This is why preparation of elicitation is time-consuming, since when possible it should include a reconnaissance visit to the venue selected for the elicitation approach.
- Show empathy with the target. With enough empathy, an elicitor literally turns targets into friends whilst persuading them to meet his data needs.
- Defuse resistance up front. The elicitor should show imperfections in his logic or knowledge. Targets won't go looking for flaws when the elicitor has offered some of these in advance. Doing so contributes to building trust.
- Frame the approach in positive aspirational tones. Any negativism or touching on topics that may lead to negative associations will have to be avoided.

Elicitation, almost like sales, starts with likeability as a key determinant for rapport (Borum, 2006):

*Research – conducted primarily on Westerners – shows that we tend to like others who:*

- *appear physically attractive*
- *appear to like us (directly and indirectly communicated)*
- *behave in a friendly and positive manner*
- *are similar to us*
- *are familiar to us*
- *cooperate with us or generally behave consistently with our own interests*
- *appear to possess positive traits such as:*
    - *intelligence*
    - *kindness*
    - *honesty*

Similar key attributes determine the quality of an elicitor (Canadian Land Forces, 2001c):

- properly attired and groomed
- alert
- confident

In conclusion, we can see that a good elicitor is dangerously friendly and impossibly suave. Elicitation may be needed in law enforcement, but some parties also have been, are and will be applying it in business. As strategic analysts, we need to recognize the elicitor before they hurt our interests. This section has hopefully been instrumental in doing just that. We may also need to organize training in the companies we serve to share how to identify concealed data collection initiatives before they hurt us.

There are rare cases where analysts have to apply elicitation. I would recommend to limit using elicitation to those cases where, if one is found out, nothing is lost – such as in the case of hiding the real purpose of data collection from a colleague who has no knowledge of a confidential dossier. All other applications I tend to see as shady.

To conclude this chapter on a positive note, I wish to share a Japanese proverb I once read. Remembering this proverb may be a great asset in handling hostile elicitation and in protecting your data and secrets from whomever is after them (Benedict, 1954):

> *"Behold the frog who when he opens his mouth displays his whole inside."*

CHAPTER 6

# PAPERS: COLLECTION FROM PUBLIC DOMAIN SOURCES

# 6.1 INTRODUCTION

By far the most important source in strategic analysis is the sources public domain sources. In this chapter, for brevity reasons I wish to use the common military intelligence term for sources of this nature: Open Source Intelligence or 'OSINT'. There is something funny about the term OSINT. The term suggests that data collected from public domain sources by default constitute intelligence, whereas in actual fact data are just data: intelligence is the output of analysis; data is the input. Still, as the term OSINT has been so widely embraced in the world of military intelligence and is so practical in our world of strategic analysis for business that I prefer to stick to it.

OSINT is so wide-ranging a topic that it can easily fill a vast book of its own. Such a book exists. It can be retrieved from the web and it only covers web searching. Thanks to the activities of a certain Mr Snowden a few years ago the US National Security Agency (NSA) is now well-known. The NSA has since 19 April, 2013, declassified a 2007 manual on OSINT that measures 639 pages (NSA, 2007).

It would be superfluous to repeat that neither OSINT nor strategic analysis has anything to do with tapping the German Chancellor Angela Merkel's mobile phone, as the NSA reportedly did around 2010. Still, there are valuable thoughts in the NSA manual, some of which have inspired the chapter that follows.

At this point two disclaimers need to be made. The first disclaimer concerns the degree of detail with which OSINT will be discussed below. This chapter gives no more than an introduction to OSINT as a topic. Readers are encouraged to use this chapter and the related appendices to get familiar with the basics of OSINT. Applying the basics will facilitate executing most OSINT-based collection work for individual strategic analysis projects. For sophisticated OSINT work, consulting specialized sources is recommended.

A second disclaimer relates to the fact that in this chapter the collection of OSINT is implicitly assumed to be carried out for a defined 'strategic analysis project'. OSINT collection, however, may also be executed as a permanent 'radar' monitoring tool for a firm's business environment. For both permanent collection processes and for specific projects, OSINT as a discipline remains the same, but the collection methodology differs. For permanent radar monitoring tools, relatively highly automated OSINT-collection tools have been built which are instruments for permanent corporate strategy monitoring. Such tools may directly and automatically file OSINT data-points, turning unstructured data into searchable, structured filed data. In contrast, OSINT collection for an individual strategic analysis project tends to be operated in batches.

## OSINT IS COLLECTED FROM PUBLIC DOMAIN SOURCES

Prior to diving into the endless sea of OSINT (Mercado, 2009b), I first wish to define OSINT:

> *"OSINT is the data that is available and can be collected from public domain sources."*

OSINT is segmented into internet and non-internet-based sources. The latter have lost some of their past relevance but less than one may think, so they should not be overlooked.

In 2011, McKinsey & Company assessed that the total gross value of internet search across the global economy equaled US$780 billion in 2009 (Bughin, 2011). This equals approximately US$120 per global citizen per year. Focusing in on the countries Brazil, India, France, Germany and the US, McKinsey estimated that knowledge workers experienced search-related productivity gains of up to US$117 billion. Meanwhile, the internet continues to grow fast in relevance around the world. The figures above probably reflect only a fraction of the value internet searches have globally today.

The intermezzo at the end of this section provides nine identified sources of the value of internet searches as pointed out in the McKinsey report. These nine sources do not form an exhaustive list. Each of these sources of value will be covered in more detail later in this chapter.

In a more recent McKinsey study, Chui calculates that US$3 trillion globally (or more) in value could be annually generated from the use of open sources in several sectors, including education, consumer goods and healthcare (Chui, 2014). These large figures show the increasing economic relevance of OSINT in today's internet-based society.

OSINT is probably the most dynamic collection method in strategic analysis work. The possibilities of searching the web alone increase day-by-day. It is impossible to provide an actual review of all searching tricks that are possible in as classic and old-school a medium as a book. By the time the book is published, the text is already obsolete. This is the caveat of the NSA manual mentioned earlier. It has been declassified because it is no longer actual enough to be top of the bill in the latest thinking on internet searches. What is aimed below is to give some timeless truths on OSINT as a collection tool, intended either pretending to be actual or to be fully complete.

Next in this chapter I will cover the anatomy of OSINT, followed by some of its potential pitfalls and finally provide some OSINT applications.

## INTERMEZZO: ON THE VALUE OF APPLYING INTERNET SEARCHES

A McKinsey & Company team identified nine sources of search value (Bughin, 2011). We repeat these verbatim below, indicating, as did the authors, that the list is not exhaustive:

- **Better matching**
  Search helps customers, individuals, and organizations find information that is more relevant to their needs.

- **Time saved**
  Search accelerates the process of finding information, which in turn can streamline processes such as decision-making and purchasing.

- **Raised awareness**
  Search helps all manner of people and organizations raise awareness about themselves and their offerings, in addition to the value of raised awareness from an advertiser's perspective that has been the focus of most studies.

- **Price transparency**
  This is similar to 'better matching' in that it helps users find the information they need, but here the focus is on getting the best price.

- **Long-tail offerings**
  These are niche items that relatively few customers might want. With the help of search, consumers can seek out such offerings, which now have greater profit potential for suppliers.

- **People matching**
  This again entails the matching of information but this time focusing on people, be it for social or work purposes.

- **Problem solving**
  Search tools facilitate all manner of problem solving, be it how to build a chair, idenfity whether the plant your one-year-old (child) has just swallowed is poisonous, or advance scientific research.

- **New business models**
  New companies and business models are springing up to take advantage of search. Without search, many recently developed business models would not exist. Price comparison sites are a case in point.

- **Entertainment**
  Given the quantity of digital music and video available, search creates value by helping to navigate content. For a generation of teenagers who pass on TV to watch videos on YouTube instead, search has also enabled a completely different mode of entertainment.

# 6.2 ANATOMY OF OSINT

Characteristically, for writing this section, I collected most underlying materials I required by indeed using OSINT. The background on OSINT has, like most sources in this book, been obtained from collection steps in public domain literature. Five of Kipling's *six honest service men* will be employed in this section: why, where, who, when and how. The question what OSINT exactly is has, I believe, already been sufficiently answered in the previous section.

## WHY TO APPLY OSINT?

The ultimate driver of strategic analysis is the need for timely, complete and accurate intelligence that is delivered in such a way as to allow for immediate support of management decision-making.

In common strategic analysis practice, OSINT is by far the most intensively used collection method. The same apparently is increasingly true in military intelligence environments (Aldrich, 2011e). In the CIA, 'an OSINT service produces the lion's share of its intelligence' (Mercado, 2009a). In the Cold War, even the East German Intelligence service and the KGB, both known for their highly effective HUMINT operations, depended heavily on OSINT.[1,2,3]

OSINT is remarkably powerful. To substantiate this statement, I treasure three examples from my hobby world of military history and intelligence:

***The unnecessary surprise of the Blitzkrieg***

Surprise as a strategic instrument tends to be effective. Remarkably enough, this is even the case when hints that could have prevented the surprise have already been out on the open OSINT sea. Think of the book *Achtung Panzer*, which in the public domain described the Blitzkrieg doctrine. This book had been published long before the Blitzkrieg had ever been applied (Guderian, 1999). The fact that Poland, Russia and France were surprised by the Blitzkrieg was not because they couldn't have *known* the Blitzkrieg doctrine. Based on OSINT they could have been better prepared to counter it. This is not to suggest that Poland could have withstood the 1939 Wehrmacht assault, but the Polish resistance to it may have been more effective. This may have changed the Second World War in the European theater to some extent.

***The creation of the Chinese atomic bomb***

The biggest secret of the early Cold War was how to make 'the bomb'. The Soviet KGB and GRU were much more successful in rapidly obtaining these secrets than the West had ever expected them to. They relied on HUMINT; think of notorious characters like Klaus Fuchs and Julius Rosenberg. Not so the Chinese. Up until 1982 the Chinese secret service had almost entirely relied on OSINT to collect all the necessary information to build their (operational) atomic bomb (Deacon, 1982e). Admittedly, it took the Chinese longer to build it than the Russians, but they got there anyway.

***The unveiling of the most secret of HM's Government's organizations***

Around 1980, two UK journalists decided to research the most reclusive UK government organization, called Government Communications Headquarters or GCHQ. GCHQ is Britain's intelligence collection agency for radio traffic (or Signals Intelligence – SIGINT in government parlance). The results of their work were of staggering accuracy and thus deeply embarrassing for the UK government, which had to admit having an intelligence service that it had never before admitted it had (Aldrich, 2011f). This research...

> *"...confirmed a fundamental truth: that there are no secrets, only lazy researchers."*

The lesson from these examples for us in business strategic analysis seems to be a simple one, if even before the internet the most secret of organizations could have been unveiled through the use of OSINT methodologies, the Blitzkrieg could have been pre-empted and the atom bomb secrets may have been obtained. OSINT is indeed a powerful source.

So, if OSINT can lead us to the world's best guarded secrets, why should we ever even consider using illegal collection means? The above may well be summarized by strong urges to "*never … neglect overt sources*", even when accuracy risks may play a role when using open sources (Johnson, 2009a).

Other reasons to use OSINT as a collection instrument are summarily discussed below:

**Speed**

OSINT is or at least looks to be fast. What a relief. In MASINT a sample from a competitor product has to be (physically) collected and subsequently painstakingly analysed. In HUMINT the 'talking head' has to be located and successfully approached. In IMINT the image has to be acquired, which may involve travelling and/or planning. In contrast, OSINT can start the same second the strategic analysis project brief is available. Speed is one of the two main drivers of the economic value of internet searches (Bughin, 2011). In 'always-on' multitasking work environments, getting tasks accomplished fast gives instant satisfaction (Dean, 2011). But there are two catches. These relate to accuracy and completeness.

The reflex of many people is 'to look up the answer to the strategic analysis question on Google' or by using a similar (high-quality) search engine on the web. Make no mistake, for many small strategic analysis questions this is an adequate approach. Getting to good results fast, however, more often than not means that the question will require a well-defined search query. Defining such queries is much more of a science than it looks. How to mitigate the risk of catching many millions of useless hits will be covered later in this chapter. Google and its peers are generally known as 'search engines'. However, they are not driven to deliver objectively optimal search results from the collector's view, but by advertisement sales to drive their earnings. The latter doesn't have to be a problem at all, provided the collector realizes the risk of the possible bias in the search outcome.

No matter how fast the results are attained, it remains imperative to check the accuracy of the data collected. This is a step that tends to be overlooked. There is often a trade-off between too fast and wrong on the one hand, and fast and timely enough on the other hand. Moreover, the output of an internet search may be far from complete.

To facilitate achieving speed, completeness and accuracy in OSINT collection, one option is to develop an intranet-based, in-house news and analysis database that offers a permanently actualized business environment repository. This will essentially be a database of business news. Any data point that enters the system can be pre-checked by a data analyst. This data analyst overlooks an automated process that provides the news item with key words on a number of dimensions (country, company, publication date, etc.).

The latter greatly facilitates searching the system, as search queries can be defined to combine free text terms with database dimensions. For most OSINT work, the system as an internally structured and validated database replaces web-based searches completely. The system does not compromise the key attribute of OSINT, which is speed. Yet it allows its users to work with a more complete, refined and accurate database to do their collection work. Setting up such a system takes a significant effort but leads to a tremendous improvement in the quality and quantity of the output of strategic analysis work.

**Cost**

OSINT collection usually starts with using the web or an intranet- or extranet-based database such as the system described above. For the user in a corporate environment these tools are often cheap or even free-of-charge to use.

In many firms, there is an annual internal charge for using extranet-based databases. Next to all news and analysis collected through various internal means, a good intranet OSINT portal also features access to extranet sources. Providers include Planet Retail, Mintel, Merger Market and Euromonitor. The background for the selection of for these sources is given later in this chapter.

Pay-per-view database subscriptions are also commonly used by strategic analysis departments. These databases may contain data that:

- are rarely used
- are costly
- require specialist knowledge to use for which reasons it is not useful to facilitate access to such databases to a broad audience

Some databases simply do not offer a lump sum contract. In Appendix 2, which relates to the 'how to apply OSINT' section below, lump sum subscription and pay-per-view databases are covered in more detail.

In spite of OSINT being perceived as cheap, a large chunk of the entire (corporate) out-of-pocket strategic analysis budget in large firms is often dedicated to securing access to OSINT-databases, either home-made or purchased like Euromonitor. OSINT forms the backbone of strategic analysis-directed collection and tends to take the lion's share of out-of-pocket cost. This is where government intelligence agencies are fundamentally different from business strategic analysis departments. In the former, speaking for the CIA, (Mercado, 2009a):

> *"OSINT's share of the overall intelligence budget has been estimated at roughly 1 per cent."*

**Compliance and ethics**

OSINT is by definition compliant and ethical: it is open source. OSINT does not require walking an ethical or even legal tightrope by collecting information through some sensitive instruments of HUMINT, as discussed in the previous chapters. This is why, almost by definition, in any strategic analysis project collection plan, OSINT should get priority in execution. Non-OSINT collection methods can and have to be used only in those cases where OSINT does not deliver the required information.

**Convenience**

Cost per search, legality, ease of access (24/7, any place that offers WiFi for most OSINT) and speed/time considerations underscore the convenience aspect of executing OSINT.

**Completeness**

As indicated above, it is a common and tested choice to start strategic analysis collection efforts by executing OSINT. Due to OSINT's sheer infinite size, and providing that the right query is used, the internet alone may answer the question at hand rapidly and reliably. The internet may have brought speed, but as we saw before, OSINT has always been a rich source – even when the web didn't exist.

As a result, it is reiterated here that most strategic analysis projects can fully be based on OSINT as the only collection tool. OSINT for many projects offers a sufficiently complete range of data or information to offer a result that is ready for decision-making.

The most effective way of OSINT-collection is permanent monitoring, rather than one-off deep-dives. Permanently monitored OSINT allows us to mitigate business risks by timely identification of threats. Even more important than having a permanent radar in place and tuned to the right competitive frequencies is to have credibility as a strategic analysis department, so that when warnings are given, they are treated seriously by higher management and are adequately acted upon. This brings us to Keegan's Law, which also applies to OSINT collection (Keegan, 2003a):

*"Intelligence is only as good as the use that's made of it."*

Collection tools other than OSINT are thus only needed when OSINT as a source is depleted and questions still remain.

**Matching**

The search part of OSINT allows us to match an information supply with an information demand easily (Bughin, 2011). Depending on the search question, this is the result of the completeness of the supply. Another dimension of matching is people matching. When looking for information, OSINT will provide the tangible or codified information immediately. In doing so, however, it may also reveal the people behind that codified information. These very people may possess tacit knowledge that may be unlocked for strategic analysis work as well.

## WHERE TO APPLY OSINT?

As was pointed out in the previous section, OSINT is a comparatively convenient collection method. When searching many potential sources, it is possible to execute OSINT in any location worldwide that has an internet connection. Since the 2010s these locations even include passenger aircraft that feature WiFi.

Over the last 25 years, access to online data has grown at a phenomenal rate. Through the use of mobile devices, the places where this data can be accessed *instantaneously and 24/7* has completely changed people's lives. Only three decades ago, data or information ranging from last week's newspaper to a database system like Chemical Abstracts could only be accessed in a formal library. Getting access to such data required physically visiting such libraries (or archives) during often all-too-limited opening hours.

The internet has changed all of this. Or hasn't it? It is to be expected that any library collection (books, monographs, databases) will ultimately be fully digitalized and thus be accessible online. I, however, strongly doubt whether this is already the case. Visiting physical archives and databases may, in strategic analysis work, lead to collecting OSINT that would have been impossible to unearth otherwise. Three examples from my own experience are discussed below to illustrate this point.

**Beyond internet filings**

In strategic analysis, financial statements of other companies often are key information inputs. For listed companies, such statements normally are featured in great detail at the respective companies' websites. In the text that follows below information needs are coupled in more detail to potential OSINT sources. For private, cooperatively- or family-owned companies, such filings may be harder to get.[4]

In the Netherlands, financial statement filings are available at the Chamber of Commerce for a particular geo-region. The Chamber offers online filings of all limited companies registered in the Netherlands. The exception is the group of companies that, for whatever reasons, good or bad (usually the latter), refuse to meet the obligation to file their statements and choose to pay the related fine. Visiting an online filing repository of the Chamber of Commerce is as reliable a source as it gets – it is cheap (modest pay-per-view), fast (there is no waiting line at a desk) and it is open 24/7. There is only one OSINT attribute missing here: the online filings are not always complete. Sometimes files are missing because they 'were still to be scanned' or 'were too old' or 'have been overlooked' or were for yet another poor excuse not disclosed online. Getting to a desk during office hours to go browsing through hard copies is time-consuming and inconvenient but has on several occasions proven to deliver valuable, missing puzzle pieces. Depending on the business value of getting the strategic analysis output right, going the extra mile by looking beyond the internet-filed documents may pay off nicely.

**Permission to a permit**

What is true for the Chamber of Commerce's financial statement filings equally holds true for (environmental) permit (application) filings.[5] Such filings relate to existing – or to be built or expanded – fixed assets of a competitor. Such filings, like financial filings, are 100% public domain. The permit (application) filings, however, may only be public domain during a limited timeframe. This timeframe is the legally defined period during which stakeholders can review a permit application prior to deciding to register objections before the relevant legal body that grants the permit.

**No traces left behind**

Chamber of Commerce filings exist in multiple countries. Some are easier to access than others. Online searches do, of course, leave traces behind. The chances, however, of such traces leading to inconvenient exposure of a firm nosing around in their competitors filings, even when these are public domain, are next to nothing. During physical visits to a Chamber of Commerce archive there is usually no need to provide identification to review copy filings. Even when identification is requested and filed, the strategic analysis department staff member providing identification is generally not a publicly known person. Again, the risk of reputation-related exposure is minimal.

In foreign countries (think of emerging countries), an undesirable rumor machine may be triggered more easily – when visiting an online government database, if such a database exists, or when visiting an archive at the registrar of companies in person. In such cases, it is a good practice to involve a trusted, silent third party (e.g., an auditor) to collect financial filings on your firm's behalf. Balancing the risk of exposure versus the known delay and inconvenience of outsourcing is a strategic analysis department task. Assessing that balance needs to be done in advance and on a case-by-case basis.

The above examples serve to substantiate the point that there is more to OSINT than is available anywhere on the internet. It may be more inconvenient and it will for sure be more time-consuming to collect, but the efforts may pay off nicely. This is especially the case as uneducated collectors, hopefully employed at a competitor, simply may never think that OSINT exists over and above the OSINT collected from the web.

## WHO SHOULD APPLY OSINT?

If digitalization has accomplished one single, most peculiar, change it is probably company employee empowerment.

### Empowerment

First and foremost, digitalization tools have been set up to empower any company employee with timely, daily-updated, accurate and complete information on the business environment. Such tools provide employees with access to unclassified market information that has ever been collected by their respective firms, any time and from any location.

### Professionalization

The system, in contrast to common web-based search engines, should provide high-grade intelligence far beyond what is available with an unsorted, incomplete and unreliable mix of high- and low-grade data collection results. The accuracy, completeness and timeliness of the business environment data in the system should form the basis for making any business plan. In facilitating the process of business planning the system should, even more importantly, also drive the quality of the actual plans itself. As senior management gets easy access to the external facts and figures for their strategy development, they have less time to worry about the data quality and the collection itself – this way they can spend more time on turning the data into insights and through doing so turn insights into competitively superior strategies.

This introduction answers the question of who to apply OSINT to. The answer is a firm 'everybody except…'. And there are exceptions.

Advanced collection (and in a later phase, analysis) of data remains a speciality, although with the system everyone can now easily retrieve data. For solving straightforward strategic analysis questions, the whole organization has been empowered. For answering sophisticated questions, however, specialist skills remain relevant.

Gone are the days when companies had librarians who were either the only ones who had passwords to access useful but costly databases online, or were the only ones who knew how to retrieve information from intimidating multi-volume encyclopedic works. While in-house librarians have become almost extinct some of their skills in information collection are still in need inside strategic analysis departments. A strategic analysis department is well advised to employ at least one dedicated data specialist.

**Outsourcing OSINT is easy**

OSINT collection work, given its virtually negligible legal and/or reputation exposure risk, is comparatively easy to outsource to third parties. Doing so to a trusted and proven third party is common practice. The third party focuses on collection. They deliver data in pre-defined detail to facilitate any current or later critical analysis step by the in-house strategic analysts. Only the latter are fully aware of strategies and sensitivities of individual dossiers that are critical to execution of the analysis part. However, the process of turning data into intelligence that is ready for decision-making should be kept as an in-house activity. When regularly working with the same third party OSINT collector and possibly data processor, this third party will inadvertently have learned a lot of your firm's secrets. However, the third parties who are exposed to such secrets would have signed an NDA. In addition to this, the firm and the third party could have an agreement in place which prohibits the third party from undertaking assignments for a (limited) list of the firm's competitors. This ensures that all the heuristic rules of business that the external provider has learned while working with the firm cannot too easily travel to its competitors.

As in all outsourcing, once confidence has been established that the third party collector delivers accurate and complete data, it all boils down to cost and workload. Hiring a third party will be much more expensive per hour than doing the collection in-house by hiring junior staff. The latter's salary, however, is a fixed cost, whereas a third party is a variable cost that will only be incurred when needed. The variable cost of in-sourcing collection efforts is charged to the principal of the project, so it doesn't involve the 'overhead' budget of the strategic analysis department. In doing so the number of fixed full-time strategic analysis staff equivalents is minimized, whilst maintaining quality control of the deliverables to (top) management.

## WHEN TO APPLY OSINT?

As was pointed out above, OSINT is generally the default starting tool in any strategic analysis project, unless in advance it is clear that the information needs will not be served by OSINT.

## HOW TO APPLY OSINT?

A recent strategy book called *The Strategist* by Cynthia Montgomery contains a Frequently Asked Questions section. In this section the question 'How do I go about analysing my industry?' is answered briefly (Montgomery, 2012a). The author refers to a Harvard Business School case study under the title 'Finding Information for Industry Analysis' (Rivkin, 2010). This case study focuses on listing sources. The study deserves credit for pointing out that there are more sources than just those available online.

In the next section, the focus is on providing some of the most common sources that have not yet been mentioned. The second part of this section will focus on internet search techniques.

### Sources are plentiful – a source book may be helpful

This section is one of the most challenging to write. OSINT is an endless sea, with wave after wave after wave of sources crashing down on the data collector. It is not difficult – no, it is literally impossible to attempt to list all sources, even structured sources, that offer information topic-by-topic. By the time the list is ready it is already obsolete as sources may come and go.[6] The sources listed below may not include sources that are or could be highly relevant and useful to a reader. The sources provided in Appendix 2 may offend those offering highly useful (structured) databases that do not find themselves listed in there. I readily admit to not having attempted to provide an exhaustive list. There is simply too much out there.

That is today's reality. There is nothing that can be done about it, except for accepting what you cannot yourself change. It is better to find a way to deal with it. Such a way exists and it is a simple way. Each strategy analyst should build their own 'sources book'. List the sources that are useful to the data requirements that need to be satisfied regularly. Cherish the list: it is your navigation tool on the OSINT sea. As in any voyage of discovery, share the data treasure islands as well as the dangerous spots you discover with fellow analysts – if only to continuously find new sources that may surprise you. Keep the layout of the list simple, as long as it serves your needs. Sometimes it helps to segment sources on your list.

There are multiple ways to segment OSINT sources:

- by reliability of the content (as in diagram 3.1 in chapter 3)
- by cost of use (free or fee-based)
- by ease of accessibility (web-based, or in non-digital physical libraries)
- by the data need that the source satisfies

The latter segmentation is probably the most relevant dimension to a strategic analyst. Cost, reliability and accessibility matter, but for a real strategic analysis, getting the facts matters most. Appendix 2 at the end of this book provides the core sources in OSINT from my own source book, by theme, inspired by Michael Porter's 'five forces model' (Porter, 1979). It covers:

- countries (politics, economics, culture)
- companies (financials, facts, analysis)
- categories & markets
- channel-specific & general news
- best practices

The sources listed in Appendix 2 form a mix of free and fee-based choices. I consider the sources useful, but I may be biased. The sources inevitably relate to my job background in chemicals, minerals and consumer (dairy) foods. Thus, my source book is inevitably skewed to those particular lines of business. The source book is meant to serve as an example to any reader and as source of particular inspiration to readers with a similar business background. The internet offers several source books compiled by dedicated

OSINT professionals. Two examples are mentioned here:

- http://rr.reuser.biz
  This is Arno Reuser's long-list. It is general in nature. It is skewed to serve analysts in security-related topics. It offers multiple Dutch sources.
- http://www.onstrat.com/osint/
  This is another broad long-list of US sources.

Appendix 2 and the lists therein should not be construed as a verdict that the sources mentioned either provide reliable information at all times and concerning all topics that they cover, or that they are superior to other sources. They simply worked for me and provided useful input in the strategic analysis projects I was involved in over the past two decades.

A special class of sources are social media. Social media can offer rich, high-grade intelligence, especially on people. These are data that people personally offer on their social network profiles. These profiles may also contain data on their current or previous employer(s) that is hard to find in other ways. A social media platform like LinkedIn, for example, offers a specific search function that allows searches for individuals that reveal one past company and one present company. This function offers you an easy tool to identify which one of your current colleagues may have worked in another company of interest.

Data from social media may be applied in multiple applications. For example, a social network profile of a particular senior manager contained a detailed description of his previous job at a competitor. It shared the number of staff in his factory, the turnaround he had realized, including some relevant operational efficiency numbers and details on investments he had been responsible for. His previous employer may not have liked this former staff member publishing all of this information, but to a data collector it is public domain information. Provided the usual scepticism is maintained, the data may possibly be used – and it may have been impossibly difficult to get the data in any other legal and ethical way.

Another strategic analysis application of social media is brand tracking. It serves to monitor whatever is said about a firm's brand. Twitter is a great platform for this. This is a highly relevant, defensive approach that formally falls a bit outside the normal scope of outside-in oriented classical strategic analysis. That's not to say that social media has no role with respect to strategic analysis. What can be monitored on the company's own brands can just as easily be monitored for its competitor brands. In cases like installing such monitoring programmes on competitor brands, it is first and foremost critical to ensure that the output of the monitoring leads to decision-making. Not everything that can be done, should be done. Only those initiatives are worth executing by the strategic analysis department that directly or indirectly support current or future management decision-making.

Using sources ultimately remains no more than a means to an end. The end remains the processing of source-provided data into intelligence. The intelligence deliverable should be sufficiently accurate, timely and complete to improve the quality of business decision-making that the strategic analysis department is to serve. Reliable and complete sources certainly contribute to the overall aim. The intelligence output, however, is and remains the sole responsibility of the analyst. It is the latter's duty – for each and every analysis – to value the credibility, accuracy, completeness and actuality of its sources. A poor or non-reliable source should never be blamed for a poor quality strategic analysis!

**Internet search techniques: knowing the tricks saves time and effort**

Searching the internet efficiently is a valued but rare competency in data collection. In this section, we will differentiate between one-off search strategies and permanent internet search 'robot' queries.

When searching for a particular data point in a one-off task, the objective is to find that data point as rapidly as possible and with as little effort as possible. This almost by definition means that the search query should be so well-defined that distracting and irrelevant search results are limited or that they do not appear at all.

The practice of one-off internet searching often forms a mix of pure and elegant mathematical logic (set theory) and the down-to-earth instructions that are specific to a particular internet search engine. The next intermezzo covers the fundamental elements of the set theory applied to the work of strategy analysts. The set theory supports making useful selections in (online) OSINT.

## INTERMEZZO: ELEMENTARY SET THEORY FOR BUSINESS STRATEGY ANALYSTS

To define queries that maximize the number of relevant search results, minimize search time and effort and also minimize retrieving irrelevant search results, applying set theory is recommended. Below an elementary introduction to set theory is provided, focused on its application in defining effective one-off internet search queries.

Consider the following example. There are two transportation means: cars and bicycles. Both cars and bicycles come in four different colours: red, blue, green and yellow. The four colours make up the whole set; in data jargon: they are collectively exhaustive.

The OR-operator (mark the capital font) means just the word **or**. It is called a Boolean operator.

A search for a red car reads:

**car AND red**

The AND-operator (again: mark the capital font) has the meaning of the word **and**. A search for a car that is either red or blue or yellow reads:

**car AND (red OR blue OR yellow)**

The brackets are put around the colours red, blue and yellow to show that a car can either be red or blue or yellow and still meet the search criteria. It is a more efficient way of writing of the line below which means the same:

**(car AND red) OR (car AND blue) OR (car AND yellow)**

A search for a green bicycle may also be written as:

**bicycle AND NOT (red OR blue OR yellow)**

The NOT-operator is another useful operator. This operator excludes options, whereas its opposite operator AND includes options. Whether using AND or NOT is more efficient in a search assignment depends on the problem at hand. When for instance the set of options is large, say one can choose out of 30 colours rather than four, NOT green is more efficient than listing all the ANDs that specify that the 29 other colours would meet the search criterion.

With the three Boolean operators AND, OR and NOT most search assignments can be written. It is emphasized that the objective remains to maximize finding documents that match what is looked for and to minimize finding documents that do not with the least possible effort.

Set theory links to a method called 'successive fractions'. In the latter method, more qualifications are successively added to a search query. In doing so, the number of search hits is gradually brought down to manageable quantities while the number of relevant hits (normally) increases. The next intermezzo covers the successive fraction method in limited detail.

## INTERMEZZO: SUCCESSIVE FRACTIONS

The Boolean operator AND alone is potentially already a powerful selection filter. Repetitively using the AND operator allows to continue adding more qualifications to a search query, to generate ever-more-specific output. This method is called successive fractions. The example below shows how successive fractions turn the endless sea of OSINT into a mapped territory that becomes manageable.

| | |
|---|---|
| "The Netherlands" | 42,600,000 hits |
| "Processed cheese" | 1,380,000 hits |
| "Producer OR producers" | 146,000,000 hits |

The query 'The Netherlands' AND 'Processed cheese' is the first successive fraction. This query yields 146,000 hits.

The quotation marks are used as an adjacency operator, applying the Google format for this operator. The use of this operator in the Google search engine limits result hits to only those outputs where the two terms – in this case The *AND Netherlands* and Processed *AND cheese* – are immediately adjacent. This is a highly useful function which is covered in slightly more detail in Appendix 3. In Google format, the query reads "The Netherlands" "Processed cheese". In Google, the logical operator AND is a simple space. Different search engines use different formats for operators. It is outside the scope of this book to cover the peculiarities of individual search engines in more detail.

**The second successive fraction is the *query***

"*The* Netherlands" AND "processed cheese" AND "Producer OR producers". This query yields 70,500 hits. The results of this query prove to be useful: hits 3 and 8 in the search give the home pages of two important Dutch-based processed cheese producers.

Language matters. The Dutch word for processed cheese is smeltkaas. A query for smeltkaas alone gives 25,800 hits. Running this query alone leads straight away, on the first results page, to the identification of two more Dutch processed cheese producers. It also leads to the home page of the Dutch processed cheese producer association. In its members list, featured one click further, it provides another two names of players. After two minutes, now, six players have been identified.

Adding smeltkaas to the search gives the third successive fraction:
"The Netherlands" AND "processed cheese" AND "Producer OR producers" AND smeltkaas.

This query yields only 19 hits. This query yields no more new results.

Using successive fractions is a powerful way to narrow down search results. Without using successive fractions all but the simplest searches will easily fail due to the sheer endless numbers of results obtained in internet searching.

Internet search engines offer additional tools to facilitate narrowing down search queries in a smart way. Appendix 3 covers a few commonly used and often useful internet search operators. This general book on data collection for strategic analysis does not cover all the operators of internet searching in detail. It gives some hints that are commonly useful for a strategic analyst. OSINT specialists or those who aim to be OSINT specialists should consult specialist literature for more details, for example the NSA guide, even though that is becoming out-dated (NSA, 2007).

# 6.3 APPLICATIONS OF OSINT

This section provides two examples of OSINT applications. OSINT is the recommended start of almost any strategic analysis project that does not have all data ready for analysis, so it is not hard to provide applications of OSINT. The two examples below serve foremost as illustration. They also elucidate some of the possibilities and typical challenges of using OSINT as collection tool.

## THE CEO BRIEFING

CEOs meet a lot of people, including many outside the firm that they are running. They may for example meet their counterparts in competitor companies. Prior to such a visit, the CEO may ask his strategic analysis department to provide him with a briefing on the competitor. The briefing always covers the most recent developments at the competitor, including for example an assessment of their current strategic plans and their success in executing them. When the CEO is to meet a counterpart in the competitor for the first time, he may also ask for a personal profile on the person he is to meet.

This last request, a personal profile, is a specific strategic analysis deliverable. In the US-based OSINT references library multiple sites offer person-specific data (Rivkin,2010). For such profiles, OSINT (especially collected through social media sites) is a common source.

Next to asking for an updated strategy assessment of the competitor and/or a personal profile on the person the CEO is to meet, a CEO may ask for more. From a business development perspective, the CEO may in parallel task her strategic analysis department with identifying useful discussion topics. Such topics may for example include the mapping of options for potential mutual business benefit between the two companies.

The strategic analysis department will use multiple OSINT sources to compile the competitor's company profile. OSINT news sources will be reviewed. Even NGOs may be great sources. When NGOs try to influence the competitor's policies (e.g. in the field of environmental protection) they may report details on the competitor's policies and on their actual performance on the issue at hand. When the competitor is operating in a high-tech environment, even its patent filings or its (future) blockbuster R&D pipeline, as in pharmaceuticals, may need to be reviewed. The strategic analyst, however, should avoid being drowned in data or writing the ultimate review this competitor in six heavy volumes. The clearer the CEO briefs the strategic analysis department, the more selectively the sources can be chosen. The better the brief, the better the briefing and usually also the better the output of the top-top meeting. Let me share a hard-learned rule. A briefing usually has an impact that is inversely proportional to the number of slides that the analyst uses. In my experience, a five slide maximum is best.

Strategic analysis departments can consider themselves blessed when, after a visit, the CEO copies the analyst in on his competitor visit report to the board. Such debrief allows the analyst to sharpen her own view on the competitor and implicitly validates the quality of the analyst's input to the meeting. Complications can (and do) arise when the firm's CEO is given a different perspective on the competitor by a counterpart than was given in the briefing. Briefings by a strategy analyst are, or rather should be, prepared by sceptical analysts. Such analysts value what is being done rather than what has been said by competitors, mercilessly distinguishing cheap talk from big, tangible commitments to choices. To achieve a balanced view, the analyst tries to base her view on as many different sources as possible.

The competitor's CEO may, however, have intentionally tried to deceive the firm's CEO with an upbeat view. The competitor's CEO may also simply have been selling his firm. Any CEO is probably by nature more of an optimist than a strategy analyst (and rightly so) and therefore may even have unintentionally painted a more positive picture than the one provided by the analyst.

The firm's CEO may subsequently doubt the quality of the assessment. No matter how balanced the analyst's report is, based on multiple well-researched and validated OSINT-sources, the result may create a credibility issue for the analyst. Additionally, no matter how well prepared and balanced an OSINT-based analysis is, when such analysis does not lead to an investment choice the CEO may wish to pursue, the report may still be questioned or ignored.

An excursion into the beautiful world of politics may illustrate this point. There is a great story about the pressure that US intelligence officers were facing in Vietnam in the period 1965–1968, during the Johnson administration. All reports that had a pessimistic tone – and/or that showed that the fundamental beliefs underpinning the US policy were incorrect – were either stopped from circulating or polished up (Weiner, 2008b):

> *"LBJ liked the agency's (the CIA's) work only if it fit his thinking. When it did not, it went into the wastebasket. 'Let me tell you about these intelligence guys,' he said 'When I was growing up in Texas, we had a cow named Bessie. I'd go out early and milk her. I'd get her in the stanchion, seat myself, and squeeze out a pail of fresh milk. One day I'd worked hard and gotten a full pail of milk, but I wasn't paying attention, and old Bessie swung her shit-smeared tail through that bucket of milk. Now, you know, that's what these intelligence guys do. You work hard and get a good program or policy going, and they swing a shit-smeared tail through it.'"*

The suppression and falsification of intelligence reporting on the war in Vietnam remained a constant in the 1960s (Weiner, 2008d). The pressure was high and the truth was the victim.

Weighing evidence that the decision-maker himself collected will generally lead to failure. The OSINT-related message is that even the most solid and balanced piece of OSINT-based analysis may still face a credibility issue or an unimpressed and biased decision-maker. To my fellow analyst I say: let this never discourage you. When your work is, objectively speaking, correct it is not your fault when management decisions you have recommended against do not deliver on the business case expectation.

## THE COUNTRY PROFILE

Preparing a country profile, as input for a market-attractiveness-based geo-expansion strategy for a particular line of business, is typically an OSINT application. Multiple sources, some of which are listed in Appendix 2, will offer extensive details. Data are endless. What matters most is to define what makes a country attractive to do business in – or unattractive for such purposes. Especially when investments are considered in politically and/or socially less stable countries (e.g., in parts of Africa or in parts of Central Asia) the quality of such country profiles may determine whether or not business plans will be approved. Since so many OSINT sources of high quality are available online and offline, a country profile is among the most fail-safe strategic analysis deliverables. Or isn't it?

The strategic analysis indeed may as such be flawless. That, however, doesn't mean that Keegan's Law does not apply when OSINT-sources are good and plentiful. Keegan helps us remember that intelligence is only as good as the use that is being made of it. This, unfortunately, is a universally applicable law. Preparing a country profile can easily be done in splendid strategic analysis department isolation. It would be a mistake to forget, however, that the user of the profile is a human being rather than an emotion-free automaton.

The decision-maker for whom such profiles ultimately are made may well be biased prior to receiving the country profile. Biases may originate from as trivial a thing as the decision-maker having had her purse stolen in a particular, profiled country when visiting the country as a student. The decision-maker's view on the country may also be outdated. The view is nonetheless real to the decision-maker. Perception is reality. No matter how well OSINT has been used in preparing a balanced profile, such biases, which may well be unconsciously present, are thus not automatically put aside by decision-makers.

What does this mean? As was shown, strategic analysts can in this case objectively prepare an OSINT-based analysis without other inputs. It may, however, still be highly useful to interact with the designated user prior to starting the project. When the designated user is asked to provide the most important indicators *he* wants to see in a country profile (and preferably told why), the result, even when it challenges his perceptions, may be accepted more easily. The latter increases the chance that the country profile is usefully applied in decision-making. Getting the output of strategic analysis work *actually used* should at all times be the foremost aim. The morale is that even when OSINT sources are so plentiful and rich that no other input is required to prepare a good analysis, the ultimate quality criterion is user acceptance and not analysis sophistication. Getting user acceptance remains priority one, even when having irrefutable evidence for a case based on solid OSINT.

# 6.4 ATTENTION POINTS WHEN USING OSINT AS COLLECTION METHOD

This section is dedicated to the multiple opportunities for obtaining inaccurate or downright wrong data when applying OSINT as a collection method. Below some characteristic issues are discussed that regularly occur when executing OSINT. The list is not exhaustive. It has more than once been stated above that OSINT is the most common collection tool. Usually it works out fine in terms of accuracy and completeness, but its value may be clouded by one or more of the issues below.

## RELIABILITY

Diagram 3.1 shows that OSINT, more than any other collection method, ranges from high to low reliability of the underlying sources. Certified OSINT sources tend to be highly reliable. Database sources that are fee-based are generally reasonably reliable. The internet, however, is a big data pool that may be completely unreliable.

## INFORMATION OVERLOAD

The perils of information overload, or to use a more fashionable term, 'infobesitas', have been well documented (Dean, 2011; Zeldes, 2007). These perils mainly concern the analyst who should restrict the analysis deliverable. If not, the decision-maker/principal who is downstream in the process will also suffer from information overload.

Information overload also matters in the collection phase of strategic analysis. Everyone in strategic analysis knows how to define information overload. Think of the sheer, amount of data available. There seems to be no directional trend or emerging pattern in sight that turns these heaps of data points into knowledge or intelligence that supports decision-making. Moreover, through the 'internet of things' and the explosion of recorded data, the speed with which the volume of globally available data grows over time, is much higher than the speed with which analysis can grow to ever make sense of it all. Information overload can be intimidating and frustrating.

Information overload sometimes just happens. It may, however, also be the result of:

- an insufficiently focused strategic analysis briefing
- a too broad analysis project scope
- a poorly designed search query

Worst of all, it results from a combination of the above factors. Writing a good brief prior to starting an analysis is critical, but how to do so is out of scope in this book. Getting the scope of an analysis briefing to a manageable level from an information overload perspective is not always within the analysis department's own hands. It is crucial that the analyst expresses concern when a brief is too broad to be reasonably turned into an analysis project. "Tell me all about processed cheese" should as a brief simply be rejected by an analyst. The principal has to be more specific, leading to a more focused brief, less information overload and hopefully a deliverable that enables the principal to take meaningful decisions. In this way the analyst creates an opportunity to receive a manageable scope. Such scope avoids excessive information collection and processing that doesn't lead to action-enabling conclusions.

A classic example of the third common origin of information overload is poorly defined queries on web-based general search engines. Preventing this pitfall requires rigorous application of the recommendations given in the query definition section earlier in this chapter.

## ADDICTIVENESS

(Internet) searching is addictive. Too often, even when using good queries, the internet is not willing to provide its secrets too easily. Query upon query is typed into the search engine. Time and again, tiny, not-so-relevant puzzle pieces are retrieved, but the treasure trove that is sought is still missing. Another query is written. Again, results are unsatisfactory, even after having read some of the lengthy documents that had been found. Any data collector will probably recognize the above. The belief that it *must* be possible to find what is looked for on the web is so strong that, before the search results have been fully reviewed, the next search query has already been typed and entered. When the above concerns a hobby pastime, this is not a problem. In professional work, however, time tends to be limited. This is either because of the analysis project's deadline or because of that other common nuisance: the need for an analyst to get at least some sleep.

There is a second nasty result of not finding what is being looked for. This is that something that is not being looked for is discovered, which – surprise, surprise – is interesting in itself. There are few more rewarding activities than to follow internet search-generated leads that distract from the topic searched for, only cater to a curious mind that is unconsciously or consciously losing precious time.

To mitigate the risk of search addiction and/or distraction, OSINT specialist Reuser recommends the time-tested strategy of dedicating only a proportional amount of (professional) time to locating a single puzzle piece (Reuser, 2012). He recommends using a classic hourglass. In advance, you are advised to define the time finding the puzzle piece is worth. Set the hourglass appropriately. Stop searching when the hourglass tells you that time for collecting this puzzle piece is up. Discipline is needed in this final step. Sticking to this discipline will help you avoid missing a project deadline or providing an unbalanced analysis product because of having lost time in collecting a particular detail. Discipline is difficult, but as with any addiction, the consequences of not being disciplined are worse.

## TRACEABILITY

A common issue in OSINT is that as a data analyst you 'have seen something' and you are not able to retrieve it later when it becomes of interest. The straightforward solution to mitigate the risk of not being able to relocate information is to file *everything* that may ever become of interest directly into your filing system. This may at times be tedious and boring work. Filing only makes sense when a well-structured filing system is in place that allows you to retrieve its treasures. It is not the aim to go into details on filing in this chapter. Having said that, rule No. 1 of filing is as follows:

> *"The first and most relevant attributes of anything that is filed are the source and the date."*

Do not trust the internet as a reliable filing cabinet. Sources on the internet are beyond your control. They may be there today but can disappear tomorrow. It may be (perceived as) tedious and old-fashioned but download what you *may* need in the future *when you see it now* and do not wait until you *need it*.

It is acknowledged that it is impossible to *know today* all you *may* need to know in the future. It requires your expert opinion, as it does with setting the right radar frequencies for monitoring your business environment, to select those files for which 'seeing = filing' applies. It is recommended to make a too-broad rather than too-narrow topic selection for securing future access to what you see. Once downloaded, file your data properly and ensure you add at least the metadata tags 'publication date' and 'source' to it.

My possibly old-fashioned opinion is that it does pay to download whatever you see when you see it. Numico in the Netherlands used to be a listed company with a well-designed investor relations website that was well accessible. You may think, why is it necessary to download and store their annual report files on an internal server, rather than quickly go to the Numico site? But in July 2007, in a process that took three weeks, Numico was bought by Danone and as a result delisted. Almost immediately all the Numico history was removed from the web. This was logical: in a sense Danone, had become Numico's single investor. No other investors had to be informed anymore. Danone aggregated the former Numico figures into their reporting. As a result, relevant business details from a competitive strategy perspective that Numico used to provide were lost. If only as an analyst you had scheduled your annual leave in these three fateful weeks in July 2007… you might have enjoyed the sun on the beach but upon your return, suddenly, your entire Numico history files had been lost.

An adjacent, common issue is not being able to retrieve the source or the publication date (or even worse, both) of data that you otherwise have available. Data without source and publication date is still useful, but less so than with it. Compared to not having the data at all, as was discussed above, this is the lesser of the two evils. Usually, the data you have still happens to be on the net, often in combination with the missing metadata. A simple search query like 'full title of the article', is likely to allow you to retrieve the metadata.

## LANGUAGE AND CULTURE

At first sight, English looks to be the lingua franca of the world. For successful strategic analysis work, starting a search in the English language domain is the best thing to do. This approach will lead to a high success rate, but it will be below 100%, especially when English is not the first language for the competitor or market that is researched.

To make matters more challenging, the role of English is changing in an increasingly globalized world (Mercado, 2009b). English is gradually declining from the world's dominant language to merely a language that has become 'first among equals'. The implications of this for OSINT are captured in a catchy phrase (Mercado, 2009b):

*"Put simply, English is best for monitoring nations where English is used".*

It is strongly recommended for any analyst, to where possible, search OSINT in the language of the competitor. Online dictionaries and online translation services may come in handy, but are not yet a substitute for mastering, as an analyst, the relevant foreign language yourself. This is not always possible. Matters get more difficult when the search focuses on countries or companies operating in countries where a non-Roman script is used.

Many examples exist: you need only think of Mandarin (China), Arabic, Japanese, Korean, Russian and Hindi (India). It pays to remember that these six languages together are spoken and written by over half of the globe's population.

This fact may require analysts in global companies to rethink their OSINT collection efforts. Outsourcing of tailored collection assignments to well-connected, local-language-mastering third party teams may be an effective answer. Such third parties could both collect OSINT for bespoke projects as well as permanently monitor the OSINT that is out there and turn it into a weekly local-language news digest.

Market intelligence agencies like M-Brain, although Europe-based, already employ half of their staff, mainly locals, in cities like Shanghai, Hong Kong and Singapore, to ensure the relevant local languages are no barrier to OSINT collection and interpretation.

OSINT collection and first-line analysis executed by local staff based in non-Western countries may provide an additional advantage. Language is more than words. A lot of cultural messages may be hidden between the lines.

These messages might be just as relevant to pick up as the plain, translated facts that the collected non-Western OSINT message brings. Extracting the culturally-relevant subtext is also facilitated by having a knowledgeable local source to collect and analyse the matter.

A first step for an English-language based analyst may be to switch search engines. Using the same query in google.com often gives different results than in google.it (for Italy). When I want to understand Italian cheese market dynamics and use the internet as a source, I would always start with google.it

To summarize this sub-section's message: English is great. When, striving in OSINT collection for completeness on non-Western countries, companies, markets or other topics however, create options to get sufficient access to non-Western-language OSINT as well. When possible, do include the cultural perspective.

## SEMANTICS

All OSINT search strategies start with a definition of the data need. Even when cultural and language issues, as discussed above, do not play a role, a good information need definition does not automatically lead to the capturing of all relevant sources. The latter also requires that the search terminology is unequivocal. That is not always the case. Several dimensions exist in semantics, where things may go wrong (Reuser, 2012). Two of these are culture and language. These have been discussed above. The other dimensions are covered in the next intermezzo.

## INTERMEZZO: ON SEMANTICS IN OSINT COLLECTION

Keep several dimensions of semantics-based issues in mind when defining OSINT search queries (Reuser, 2012). Performing web-based searches with more than one version of a search term may deliver significantly better results. For the table below I have been inspired by the work of Reuser.

| DIMENSION | CHARACTERISTIC EXAMPLES |
|---|---|
| SPELLING | Danone, Dannon; it is the same company, but it operates under a different name in different parts of the world<br>Nestlé, Nestle; search engines may be sensitive to the difference<br>Organisation: Organization; it is even the same word, but the US-English spelling differs from the UK-English spelling |
| SINGULAR, PLURAL | Analysis, analyses |
| ACRONYMS | DMK – 'Deutsche MilchKontor'<br>FAO – 'Food and Agricultural Organisation (or Organization)' |
| JARGON | EBITDA, EBIT, earnings or returns: all refer to a definition of profit<br>GOS: galacto-oligosaccharide<br>Lactose: milk sugar |
| HISTORY | Numico: now Danone<br>Nordmilch or HumanaMilchunion: now DMK<br>Campina: now FrieslandCampina<br>Campina Melkunie: now FrieslandCampina<br>Melkunie: now owned by Arla (the brand name, that is)<br>Czechoslovakia: now either the Czech Republic or the Slovak Republic |
| SYNONYMS | Holland: the Netherlands<br>Infant formula: infant nutrition (but not babyfood, as the latter is broader) |
| QUASI-SYNONYMS | Vevey: Nestlé head office<br>England: Great Britain or United Kingdom (not all the same but often mixed up)<br>Great Britain: UK (again not the same, as the UK includes Northern Ireland)<br>Dubai: UAE (often mixed but again not the same: Dubai is one of the seven Emirates)<br>Milk, dairy (not the same, but often mixed up) |

TABLE 6.1 ▶▶▶ SEMANTIC CHALLENGES WHEN APPLYING OSINT

## LEAVING TRACES

The most convenient OSINT searches are those in fee-based structured databases of known reliability. Such searches tend to be convenient and fast, provided that what is searched for is covered in the database. They have a significant disadvantage. The (commercial) database provider will be able to trace all the search queries.[7] A search query set may reveal more than is meant to be shared with the outside world. Trusting the discretion of external parties is good, but control is better. There is no way to prevent a fee-based database provider from 'seeing' what is searched for. There are, however, always ways to prevent them from creating a revealing pattern. The solution is simple: do not try to contractually assure that they will act upon the pattern they see. There is no way to ever reveal an infringement of such an agreement.

I would prefer a smarter but more tedious approach. Do regularly search for off-strategy topics, to obfuscate the real direction of the strategic queries. In doing so, you ensure there is no causal relation between what you searched for and what you will act upon later (such as in in mergers and acquisitions). This would be the case if what you searched for was, for example, a particular company that indeed was later a target of your M&A bid, but it was one among so many others that it was still impossible to tell upon which company you had actually been working.

This is inconvenient, for sure, but inconvenience is a common feature of safety measures.

CHAPTER 7

# PICTURES: COLLECTION OF DATA FROM IMAGES

# 7.1 INTRODUCTION

A picture is worth a thousand words, or so the saying goes. That is probably why, ironically, this chapter has no pictures and thus needs over four thousand words. In strategic analysis, pictures are in contrast to data rarely the core matter, but pictures can be a source of data and insights that are impossible to get to in any other way. In this chapter I again follow military intelligence parlance by using the term IMINT, which as I shared before is short for '**Im**agery **Int**elligence'. In this book IMINT is defined as 'the intelligence obtained by legally collecting and analysing pictures or human observations of (usually) competitor products, activities or (fixed) assets.'

IMINT differentiates itself from other collection techniques by focusing on legal observation. This is either of a static or moving image, or for example of a competitor engaging in an action that may contribute to understanding the competitor's competences, intent and or its plans to surprise.

As we saw in previous chapters, HUMINT, in contrast, focuses on listening – potentially involving direct contact with a competitor. HUMINT revolves around the spoken word even when during HUMINT activities all the non-verbal communications that come with a conversation are offered as a bonus. Admittedly, this may not always be the case. HUMINT can be an answer from a human source on a collector's question written down in an email. OSINT focuses on *reading*, even when OSINT may include images that need to be analysed separately. Finally, extracting intelligence from products or MASINT focuses on *dissecting* tangible (competitor) products – possibly including software code – which, to complete the human sense repertoire, may include smell and taste. It is the nature of the source that determines the typology and not the medium through which the data or information reaches the analyst.

IMINT, provided that it is executed professionally, like OSINT and MASINT, leaves almost by definition no traces for the competitor that can be observed, listened to, studied and dissected. The boundaries between MASINT and IMINT are not sharply defined. When electron microscope images are produced of submicron particles in a competitor's product, strictly speaking the method should be defined as IMINT, where in practice it is more likely to be part of a MASINT-based analysis. Similarly, as indicated above, OSINT sources such as a competitor's annual report may contain images that require analysis by an IMINT expert. When observing the speech of a competitor's CEO, the CEO's body language is strictly speaking IMINT, whereas the text and the intonations are HUMINT. The definitions of the boundaries are not critical. Hair-splitting is not useful. This book is and remains a practitioner's text; it has no pretense to be an academic treatise.

I started this chapter with the age-old adage, a picture is worth a thousand words. This is also true both in defense and counterintelligence contexts – in selecting such images in company communications that avoid giving a competitor any more information than strictly needed. Studying images of such things as competitor plants and/or products is often an underrated part of data collection efforts in support of strategic analysis. To assist the application of IMINT in strategic analysis, this chapter will first discuss the anatomy of IMINT. In doing so, I will use five of Kipling's usual six honest service men: why, where, who, when and how. *What* IMINT exactly is, has already, been defined above.

# 7.2 WHY ANALYSE PICTURES?

The key reason for analysing pictures is literally to observe (usually a competitor or its actions) through either static or dynamic images. In government intelligence and increasingly in law enforcement, image collection through cameras has become routine. In the UK alone, a 2011 study estimated that 1.85 million cameras are in operation, 92% of them privately owned. That equated to one camera for every 35 citizens. Most of these surveillance cameras were either operated through a stationary orbit (military) satellite or in the shop next door, and serve a pre-emptive and sometimes deterrent goal. The thinking seems to be that when all that is done on earth is visible at all times, it may lead to less behaviour that can't stand the test of view.

## CUBA REMAINS A STRIKING HISTORIC EXAMPLE OF PICTURES THAT CHANGED THE WORLD

In military intelligence, no pictures have probably been more relevant to the world than those related to what became known as the Cuban Missile Crisis. On Sunday, 14 October, 1962, an American U-2 reconnaissance aircraft, operated by Major Richard Heyser, shot pictures over Cuba of unusual military building activities and vehicles (Dobbs, 2009e). On Tuesday 16, October 1962, at 11.50 a.m., the chief photo interpreter for the CIA, Arthur Lundahl, and US President Kennedy, surrounded by multiple advisers, discussed the pictures.

On the table was irrefutable evidence that the Soviet Union, in contrast to all statements regarding Cuba it had made, had installed Medium Range Ballistic Missiles which could potentially carry nuclear warheads at bases in Cuba. These were placed at less than 100 miles firing range from the US coast.

The key corroborating evidence was that the rocket's lengths visible in the photos taken overhead were calculated to be equal to those photographed during a Moscow Red Square May Day parade.[1]

The pictures revealed the stage of the operationalization of the rockets. The analysis was feasible because the defector Oleg Penkovskiy had delivered to the US military the operations manual of the SS 4 Missile (Bruce, 2008a). This piece of information allowed the US to estimate the most likely time that was needed for the rockets to become operational. It was estimated – later proven correct – to be 13 days. This intelligence from these different sources allowed President Kennedy to negotiate toughly with the USSR leadership. During these critical 13 days, the world was brought to the brink of nuclear disaster.[2] That is not to say that intelligence prevented the world falling into the abyss. Credit, I believe, should go both to the Politburo (the principal policymaking committee in the USSR) and the Kennedy Administration for both backing down timely and wisely. It is, however, fair to say that imagery intelligence markedly improved the quality of the decision-making. This after all is what intelligence efforts are at all times intended to do, even in a less dramatic context.

## PRIOR TO TAKING ACTION, INTELLIGENCE FROM PICTURES NEEDS TO BE VALIDATED

What happens when action is taken based on hypotheses which have not been validated by IMINT has been described in detail (Hoffman, 2011c). Hoffman reproduces the fateful conversation between a Russian military interception pilot, Gennadi Osipovich, and ground control just prior to the Russian plane shooting off two rockets to destroy the Korean Airlines (KAL) operated flight 007. KAL 007 was flying from Anchorage to Seoul on 31 August, 1983. On its way, it lost its course and entered Soviet air territory. (In this context it does not matter whether the flight entering Soviet air space did so intentionally or not, which is still a matter of dispute.)

Russian ground control radioed to the pilot: "If there are four jet trails, then it is an RC-135." The RC-135 was a US spy plane regularly used to test Soviet defense systems by provoking them into action. KAL 007 was a Boeing 747. This plane also has four engines and thus also produces four jet trails. The first hypothesis was incorrectly validated. Ground control requested: "Can you determine the type?" The pilot responded: "Unclear." Osipovich indicated he could not identify the plane because it was still dark; he only saw a shadow. The pilot came alongside the plane realizing it wasn't an RC-135, as the latter is much smaller than a Boeing 747. Still he couldn't determine the type as he 'lacked a good image.' Running out of fuel, he did not have much time left. In distress, he decided to obey the order to destroy the 'target' anyway, leading to the loss of 269 innocent lives.

In business, IMINT cases with such impact are not to be expected. The Cuba and KAL 007 examples, however, show profound truths that relate to strategic analysis just as much as to military intelligence:

- Pictures indeed are worth more than a thousand words and are generally much more impactful in communicating a message than a written text.
- There is no point in collecting imagery intelligence when there is no follow-through. It is critical to strategic success both to be permanently vigilant and to act immediately upon threats revealed through intelligence collection and analysis.
- Never act on non-validated imagery; that may make matters worse, not better.

# 7.3 WHO AND WHERE SHOULD INTELLIGENCE COLLECTION FROM PICTURES BE APPLIED?

In the military, IMINT collection and analysis are typically separate disciplines. As a general rule, in business an answer to the *who* question for the collection is relatively simple. Anyone that can operate a photo or video camera can collect images. It has a merit when in a planned IMINT mission the IMINT collector in advance connects with the IMINT analyst – if it is not the same person – to ensure that the pictures, where possible, capture the most relevant features the analyst looks for. In the context of strategic analysis, especially when it comes to taking and analysing pictures of a competitor factory, for instance three golden rules apply:

- Pictures can only be taken from public roads or other publicly accessible territory. Trespassing onto a competitor factory site is never an excuse for getting a good shot.
- When being invited to visit a competitor site, pictures can only be taken with the explicit prior approval of the host, assuming the latter has the authority to approve this. Similar to recording conversations without asking for approval, taking pictures without approval is ethically (and possibly even legally) inappropriate and should thus at all times be refrained from.
- The IMINT *analysis* is not everybody's job. Expertise in interpreting what is being seen is critical.

To ensure full compliance with your firm's code of ethics, it is recommended not to outsource IMINT collection activities to third parties, unless they are trustworthy enough not to violate your firm's ethics code or in any other way harm your firm's reputation. Even when paparazzi operate legally, the ethical code displayed by most of them still does not make (most of) them acceptable as your firm's suppliers.

The answer to the *where* question is usually determined by the location of the object to be photographed or observed. In strategic analysis, static IMINT collection targets usually include (list not necessarily exhaustive):

- The outside of competitor factory sites – to get a clear picture on the scope of their assets.
- New competitor products for example those on display on trade shows.
- Images from competitor or general websites displaying products or other relevant assets of the competitor.
- TV or internet commercials and/or print or outdoor billboard ad campaigns.

Moving targets of observational IMINT may include (list not exhaustive):

- The number of trucks leaving and/or arriving at a competitor's factory site, to estimate the factory's capacity and/or utilization.
- The location where a truck that left the competitor's factory site delivers its products, to map the competitor's customer base and related downstream supply chain
- Interviews with or live speeches by competitor, supplier or customer staff to be able to later observe their non-verbal communication when being asked particular questions, as in a conference setting.

IMINT in strategic analysis resembles HUMINT. It is often location-determined by the possible touch points with the competitor and/or its activities. This makes part of the IMINT collection by definition time-consuming and costly to execute.

## 7.4 WHEN TO APPLY INTELLIGENCE COLLECTION FROM PICTURES?

IMINT is used when the images allow the strategic analyst to reach conclusions that would have been impossible to draw otherwise. For this reason, IMINT collection, however costly and time-intensive, will be an even more specific information-need driver than OSINT.

As was said, OSINT collection activities may result in obtaining endless numbers of relevant images. OSINT should therefore always get priority over IMINT field missions. Good OSINT may allow IMINT-collection work to be avoided. As some images or observations can really only be obtained through IMINT fieldwork however, the latter should not be shied away from when needed. It can't be repeated too many times – a picture that is timely taken is indeed worth a thousand words.

# 7.5 HOW TO APPLY INTELLIGENCE COLLECTION FROM PICTURES?

In IMINT, like in HUMINT, the information need determines the search approach. In IMINT, like in parts of HUMINT collection efforts, the second determining factor is the occasion. The opportunity for collection of relevant data is determined by the competitor and its operations. Given a particular information need, the timing is on the competitor's side, but the turning of an opportunity into a success is on your side.

Collection occasions may include:

- The timely visit of a trade fair.
- Monitoring/photographing/filming the new products presented by the competitor:
  - collecting their brochures
  - observing which customers visit the competitor's site and how warmly these are welcomed
- The photographing of a competitor's production site, just when a big new piece of equipment is being hauled in. Once the equipment disappears behind the walls, the opportunity for studying it is gone (as will be discussed in more detail in the next section).
- The observation of which customer site a competitor's truck drives to from their own plant.
- The observation during a scientific conference of a competitor's scientist being questioned by his academic peers. The question and answer session potentially reveals more on the competitor's R&D competencies and insights than the competitor's powerpoint slides that are formally presented (and that may have been vetted by a consciously careful corporate communication department).

All the above collection occasions and methods are perfectly legal, even when some may not always feel ethically appropriate. Apart from ethical considerations, cost/benefit considerations play a role in IMINT as well. Following a truck (or having an intern follow the truck for you) that leaves a competitor's site all the way to the drop-off point at the customer plant or warehouse is:

- Time-consuming, tedious and costly.
- Delivering only a limited piece of data following a major effort.
- May be detected and thus risks breaking collection rule number one, which is to leave no traces during intelligence collection efforts.

## MAXIMIZE THE INTELLIGENCE VALUE OF CAPITAL OR EFFORT EMPLOYED

The effort and cost in IMINT, as in any collection technique, should thus be matched with the expected value/benefit of knowing the data have high accuracy. As the resources available for strategic analysis tend to be limited, this calls for maximizing the returns spent on the resources.

To maximize returns, creativity is a necessity. This is nothing unusual. The ancient Greek philosopher Theocritus remarked that "poverty is the greatest driver of creativity." For IMINT this means that defining and measuring proxy indicator images may be useful. In cases where direct observations are impossible, indirect indicators may ultimately reveal the same data. Below are a few examples of such proxy indicators:

- Counting the number of cars in a competitor's factory parking lot in some remote industrial zone at 3 a.m. is such a proxy indicator. The indicator is used to assess the size of the factory's night shift. The size of the night shift is an indicator of factory utilization, where the number of cars is almost by definition proportional to the number of staff during the night shift, as neither car pooling nor public transport use is logical given the factory's remote location and the start and finish times of the night shift.
- Counting the number of illuminated windows at a competitor's factory at 3 a.m. is another proxy indicator. This indicator is a proxy for which parts of the competitor's factory are being used. This indicator gets extra value when through other sources (as with OSINT – the checking of public records for an environmental permit) it has been become clear how the competitor's factory has been laid out.

- Counting, the number of facings of a competitor's product (range) as a percentage of total facings in a given category on a supermarket shelf. In the absence of expensive market share data or when such data are not available due to inadequate coverage of the market share information provider, the percentage of facings is often a nice first market share indicator – at least for the respective channel that is under review. This is a gross simplification. In the absence of better data, however, it is a better-than-nothing start, especially when a sufficiently large number of supermarkets are checked.

These are just three examples of proxy indicators. There are many others; there are in fact countless ways to translate an information need into a collection plan.

OSINT often is a rich source of images. In Google Maps/Streetview and Google Earth (or similar web-based databases) satellite images of many locations in many countries are just a few clicks away. Reliability of the data, however, is not guaranteed, so viewer beware. The Streetview picture of the author's house, until recently, is at least four years old and did not show a major reconstruction.

## 7.6 ATTENTION POINTS WHEN USING IMAGERY INTELLIGENCE OUTPUT

IMINT is a useful collection method but it has its its share of shortcomings. Below a few classic pitfalls are briefly touched upon (list not necessarily exhaustive):

- **Experts** are great resources to interpret images. Most experts, however, only see what they know but rarely admit what they don't know.
- **Images** may have lost value or may even be misleading as they may no longer be accurate. The images don't always show when they were made.
- In image-making it is a common bias to zoom in on the pear in the box of apples. This bias could be called the 'look at this' type of bias. The focus on the pear may distort the representativeness of the total image, and thus any conclusions and decisions that are taken based on the image.
- **Images may have been changed intentionally.** Multiple software packages are available to change images. Long before digital image processing was available, the Soviet leadership under Stalin 'removed' disgraced former comrade Leon Trotsky from images where Trotsky was at the side of Lenin (University of Minnesota, 2013). The conclusion is simple. When the source of the image is not a fully trusted 'owner' collector, be aware that the image may intentionally have been changed for purposes of deception.
- **Images may not be clear enough** to make a proper assessment but are used anyway. The fate of KAL flight 007, discussed above, is a tragic reminder of the relevance of ensuring a clear and validated picture is available prior to drawing conclusions and acting upon those conclusions.

## CHAPTER 8

# PRODUCTS: COLLECTION OF DATA FROM THINGS

# 8.1 INTRODUCTION

In the context of strategic analysis, MASINT, an acronym for Measurement And Signature INTelligence, is defined as:

> *"The intelligence obtained by collecting and analysing or reverse-engineering (competitor or customer or supplier's) physical products or equipment."*

MASINT has been proudly positioned at the summit of data reliability (see diagram 3.2 in chapter 3). The output of MASINT analyses is after all not subjected to human memory frailty as may be the case for data delivered through HUMINT collection.[1] The reason for the high reliability of the output is that the output is generated in validated and calibrated tests in a laboratory environment. This is an environment where a physical product (or possibly a software code) is taken apart by proven methods with a known accuracy. In doing so, MASINT will directly meet an information need specified in a strategic analysis project brief.

MASINT is the final collection method discussed in this book. In MASINT, as to some extent in IMINT, collection and analysis are more strongly interlinked than in HUMINT or OSINT. The actual collection in MASINT, provided the collection is strictly legal, is often not the most difficult part. In the case of FMCGs (fast-moving consumer goods) made by competitors, MASINT is simply collected by buying the competitor's product from a retailer. There is no collection activity more legal than buying a product in a shop. For most MASINT activities, collection doesn't need to be more difficult. For this reason, this chapter will touch on some MASINT *analysis*-related attention points. Strictly speaking this is not consistent with the fact that a collection method is discussed in this chapter. As the MASINT analysis-related attention points are so specific to MASINT the choice has been made to discuss these here.

In this chapter, sections 8.2 to 8.5 will dissect MASINT itself, using five of Kipling's six honest service men: why, where, who, when and how. Selected applications of MASINT in strategic analysis are covered in section 8.6. These are illustrated with some public domain examples of MASINT from government intelligence literature. Section 8.7 looks at attention points when using the output of MASINT in strategic analysis.

# 8.2 WHY TO BACK-ENGINEER AND ANALYSE PRODUCTS?

Back-engineering is the art of taking apart a competitor's product in order to understand that product and possibly also the production technologies behind it. The key reason for back-engineering and analysing competitor products (or MASINT) is that MASINT, in principle, can answer any or at least most questions that arise related to a physical product (or software code) produced by a competitor. Among the scariest things in business strategic analysis is being surprised by new customer-relevant features of competitor's products, based on superior but unknown technologies. This explains why, for example, defense industries undertake great efforts to keep secrets. After all (Hoffman, 2015):

> *"The most secret of all technologies is the one that the other person doesn't suspect exists."*

Monitoring a competitor's products frequently and thoroughly may help in understanding the competitor but may not automatically *allow the use* of the so-obtained knowledge.[2]

There are limits to what MASINT can contribute to strategic analysis. A number of requirements have been listed below (the list is not necessarily exhaustive), that have to be met to apply MASINT successfully.

### PRODUCT AVAILABILITY

- For an FMCG, or even a durable consumer product, the collection step is as simple as buying the product in a shop, be it a brick and mortar storefront or online. In the FMCG industry, specialized research agencies focus on new product spotting. They, at a modest extra cost, even deliver products to their subscribers. For a producer of nuclear power stations, ordering the delivery of an off-the-shelf nuclear power station from a competitor to take it apart is not so simple, so product availability may be easier in some cases than in others.

- Firms in a business-to-business (B2B) environment may deter a competitor from buying a product directly by refusing to sell their product to any unknown customer they suspect is a cover for a competitor planning a MASINT project. This presupposes that the firm controls the relevant sales channel(s).

## BUDGET AVAILABILITY

- A budget is needed to carry out the often expensive and time-consuming product analyses and subsequent (R&D) expert evaluation.
    - either the budget may not actually be available or
    - the upside potential of knowing the answer on the MASINT question to the firm may not justify spending the budget on the analysis,
- Acquiring the product itself may be too expensive in comparison to the upside potential of the value extracted from the product-related MASINT work.

## ANALYTICAL TECHNOLOGY AVAILABILITY

- Competitor products may be so fundamentally different from the firm's own products that the in-house laboratory may lack the skills to properly analyse and evaluate the product. The analyst who is warned in advance by the in-house laboratory that this is the case is a lucky person. Laboratories, excited to do something that is non-routine, will often start trying anyway. They may end up with decisively wrong results. It will be hard and most of all painful to discover the errors later when incorrect MASINT output was used to deliver the wrong recommendation to management.

## THE PRODUCT NOT REVEALING ITS SECRETS

- An example may serve to illustrate this point. Take two batches with all the relevant ingredients used to produce chocolate bars, only using different types of sugar. Do not change anything else – in the other components of the recipe or in the production process. The taste of the two identically produced bars will differ markedly. Using classic destructive testing to find the cause for these taste differences will not really (likely) succeed. The difference leading to the different taste

> is not a traceable signature. To trace the difference to its root cause, experts need to get involved. This type of assessment would probably require multiple tests. They may ultimately be able to deduct the factual physical difference (i.e., the different initial size distribution of the sugar crystals) that is so easily tasted by the candy-eating public.
>
> The point is that the subtle difference in the crystal size distribution of the sugar may lead to unsubtle analysis cost with an uncertain chance of success.

Even though these limitations are real, MASINT remains a powerful collection and analysis tool, though its value may well be underrated in strategic analysis versus seemingly more exciting HUMINT.

# 8.3 WHO AND WHERE TO APPLY PRODUCT BACK-ENGINEERING?

MASINT analysis is usually either in-sourced in an in-firm laboratory or outsourced to a (preferably certified) trustworthy third party analytical service provider. The advantages and disadvantages of in-firm analysis or outsourced analysis are summarized in table 8.1. However, biases may occur during the analysis of the results, in particular during an in-firm analysis. A typical example of a bias that may occur in this context is the ethnocentric bias. This happens when a laboratory may unknowingly or unconsciously be expecting a competitor's product to have been made in a similar way to the products they routinely analyse from the firm's own production. In such a scenario, the laboratory may incidentally use measurements and techniques that are tweaked to the firm's own technology, but give wrong results when applied to the competitor's product. The strategic analyst should make a point of personally speaking with the chemical or physical analyst to learn what methods are being used and how universally applicable these methods are, prior to accepting laboratory results at face value.

| | ADVANTAGES | DISADVANTAGES |
|---|---|---|
| IN-FIRM | Close connection between strategy department and analysis team, allowing for easy interim result evaluation and steering of MASINT.<br><br>Usually cheapest route for routine analysis.<br><br>Usually fastest route for analysis. | Risk of expert bias.<br><br>Risk of confirmation bias.<br><br>Risk of culture bias.<br><br>Expertise may lacking for non-routine analysis. |
| OUTSOURCED | Neutral and unbiased.<br><br>Trustworthy source for lawsuits, when MASINT may be used to prove patent infringement by a competitor, or a competitor not complying with applicable product-related law (e.g., violating food law standards). | Usually more costly.<br><br>Usually more time-consuming.<br><br>Normally less easy to make 'on-the-fly' changes during the research, based on interim outcomes, as the third-party laboratory will only deliver complete reports (as per their internal quality policy). |

TABLE 8.1 ▶▶▶ ADVANTAGES AND DISADVANTAGES OF IN-FIRM AND OUTSOURCED MASINT ANALYSIS

# 8.4 WHEN TO APPLY BACK-ENGINEERING?

MASINT is used both in strategic and in tactical decision-making. In tactical marketing and sales plans, both in business-to-business (B2B) and in business-to-consumer (B2C) contexts, MASINT should feature. In section 8.6 some examples are provided to illustrate how MASINT can be integrated in commercial planning.

MASINT can be executed as a one-off analysis to paint a picture of a certain performance feature of a competitor's product in comparison to the firms own competing product. Commendable as this is, it is still a one-off approach. The picture may fade the moment a competitor launches a product update, especially when such update is not communicated to consumers or customers and thus fails to attract our attention. From that moment on, any decisions in the firm's commercial area are based on outdated information.

In FMCG categories, it is strongly recommended to periodically dissect competitor's product on all potential relevant composition and/or property dimensions, including, in the case of food products, sensory testing. This is particularly so when those functional product benefits matter to consumers. This allows the strategic analyst to know the functional properties that the competitor's product delivers to the customer/consumer at all times. This knowledge is required in order to persuade the competitor's customer base to switch to your firm's products. Especially in B2B or highly-functional FMCG sales this knowledge plays a critical role. When the functional benefits of all offerings are fully understood by our sales force, the best informed and most successful pitches can be made to win the hearts and minds of current non-buyers.[3]

MASINT, especially when the analysis is carried out by reputable third-party certified laboratories, is often cited as evidence in lawsuits between firms. Such cases may relate to one firm aiming to prove infringement of intellectual property, usually patents, by their competitor. Similarly, a firm may use MASINT to convince regulatory authorities that a competitor is not in compliance with applicable legal product standards.

# 8.5 HOW TO APPLY BACK-ENGINEERING?

MASINT typically delivers individual puzzle pieces that fit together in a larger jigsaw puzzle. Applying MASINT may involve considerable out-of-pocket cost. Therefore, at all times the call should be made in advance whether the money spent on MASINT is justified by the applicability of the MASINT output. In the end, the MASINT output has to at least to earn back the analysis cost and preferably much more than that.

The latter judgment call essentially points to the core question of any strategic analysis collection effort, referred to here as the Law of Keegan (Keegan, 2003c):

*"Intelligence is only as good as the use that is made of it."*

Before a strategy department goes all-out on a costly MASINT-analysis initiative, it must ensure that the project principal not only fully understands what is planned, but is even so committed to the topic that he will act on the results. This means commercial choices will indeed be based on the output. If not, MASINT output may end up being a nice to know, but a waste of money in the long run.

# 8.6 APPLICATIONS OF BACK-ENGINEERING

This section provides examples of MASINT applications, good and bad, from corporate and military sources. The examples serve both for illustration and to elucidate some of the possibilities and challenges of MASINT.

## GUCCI VERSUS HERMÈS

It may be amusing to share an example of how to use MASINT in an unusual category (Montgomery, 2012b). MASINT played a role in the strategic turnaround of luxury goods firm Gucci. In the process of redefining Gucci's market, and especially price positioning, Domenico de Sole, Gucci's CEO, ordered key competitor Hermès' handbags to be taken apart. This piece of MASINT work (just imagine: destructively analysing an exclusive high-fashion handbag just bought for thousands of Euros) led to two key conclusions:

- Gucci in terms of quality still met the standards of competitor Hermès.
- Gucci's cost of goods sold, however, were far too high.

Addressing the latter point – and subsequently transferring most of these benefits on to its (future) consumers by courageously taking high street prices down by 30% (!) – Gucci regained buzz around their brand for turning it into a good-value offering. Three years later Gucci would be named 'European Company of the Year' by the European Business Press Federation for its successful turnaround. Lesson learned: by applying MASINT through deconstructing Hermès handbags, Gucci in the end bagged big profits.

## SHIPPING A NATO-TANK ENGINE

Victor Suvorov[4] was the pseudonym of a Soviet defector to the West called

Vladimir Bogdanovich Rezun. In his memoirs, he presents a telling example of MASINT collection efforts of the former Glavnoye Razvedyvatel'noye Upravleniye (GRU), the Soviet military intelligence service (Suvorov, 1984). Recognizing that the Soviet Union could not economically compete with the West due to its technological backwardness, the Soviet decided to assess what knowledge they lacked and subsequently to boldly go forth and steal this knowledge. To execute this policy, Soviet Union embassies ran extensive technology collection efforts in Western countries. When an agent of a Soviet embassy in a Western country had got his hands on a technologically interesting item, it was smuggled into the embassy. Sneaking items into Soviet embassies in Western countries could present a challenge in itself, as Western countries sought to stem the flow of technology secrets to the Eastern Bloc. When the delivery into the embassy had been, the item, assuming it was not too bulky, could be safely shipped to Moscow by diplomatic mail. Once in Moscow, it was subjected to careful MASINT analysis.

But what to do when the item of interest weighed more than a ton? GRU agents had succeeded in obtaining an entire written-off NATO tank engine in one of the countries that had bought German Leopard tanks. The engine obviously was of exceptional interest to the GRU. The actual purchase went unnoticed. There was, however, no way to get this bulky item into the Soviet embassy and subsequently to get it shipped by diplomatic mail. To solve the problem, the Soviet consulate in this particular country bought an old cruising yacht. The yacht was refitted to accommodate the engine. After making several pleasure trips with the yacht to avoid the NATO host-country's suspicion, the yacht, loaded with the engine, met up 'by coincidence' with a Soviet trawler. A few minutes later, out on the open sea, the engine had been transferred to the trawler. After the transfer the yacht was kept in use for some more time to maintain its cover… and then quietly sold off.

These illegal cowboy-type of actions to collect competitor's technology are not recommended. The tank engine example only demonstrates the lengths that competitors who choose not to operate ethically may go to in order to obtain proprietary technology.

It would be a mistake to assume that these examples only relate to the military sphere during the Cold War. The Narodnyi Komissariat Vnutrennikh Del (NKVD), the predecessor of the KGB, already active in 1941, started a separate section that was later called Line X. The unit specialized in scientific and technological intelligence operations (Andrew, 2001e). Line X focused on investigating both commercial and military secrets. The best-known former Line X agent is Vladimir Putin, who before becoming President of the Russian Federation was tasked with covertly securing Western technologies (Friedman, 2013).[5]

Line X activities usually related to MASINT. Successful Line X operations included the acquisition of modern Western technology for butyl rubber production from Italy in 1970. Manufacturing butyl rubber efficiently benefited more than the Soviet military; it was a boon to the whole Soviet economy. This valuable acquisition led to the revamping of multiple Soviet chemicals sites (Andrew, 2001f).

The message here is that competitors may include all kinds of covert government agencies, such as the local Food Law audit agencies in emerging markets, which collect trade secrets for their government. The examples I've provided from the former Soviet Union are not intended to suggest that Western democracies or other nations do not operate illegal technology gathering activities as well.

## THE LARGEST NON-NUCLEAR EXPLOSION EVER

KGB Colonel Vladimir Ippolitovich Vetrov, who was involved in Line X, defected to the West in 1981. He ultimately revealed the full extent of Soviet technological espionage in the West (Andrew, 2001g). Vetrov proved to be quite reliable, and this qualified him to become a double agent. The West decided to play dirty by feeding the Soviet Line operation X with intentionally flawed Western technologies (Clark, 2007g):

> *"The most dramatic single event (in terms of Soviet industry setbacks based on flawed Western technologies) resulted from the US providing gas pipeline management software that was installed in the Soviets' trans-Siberian gas pipeline. The software had a feature that would at some point cause pressure in the pipeline to build up to a level far above its tolerance. The result was (...) described as the most monumental non-nuclear explosion and fire ever seen from space."*

Intelligence agencies around the world have been, and currently are, involved in economic espionage. This occurs not only through SIGINT (SIGnals INTelligence – intercepting radio and/or data traffic) but also through MASINT collection and analysis. The above pipeline explosion example is a warning signal that, when applying MASINT, a competitor must be sure that there is no intentional deception at play which would distort the analysis and conclusions (or worse). The typical sample of a new product that is handed out at a trade fair may not be entirely representative for the actual product the competitor plans to sell.

## RECTANGULAR BOTTLES

In a generic review of MASINT in a strategic analysis context, presented by McKinsey staff, the major reason for product teardowns – as they call them – is to spark fresh thinking (Fedewa, 2009). In one example, an FMCG producer takes apart the packaging of a competitor's shampoo offering. In doing so, it identifies four areas for improvement. These include the use of recyclable materials, optimized labelling and an improved volume-to-weight ratio. Most of all, MASINT triggers the redesign of the company's own bottle, from oval to almost rectangular. This contributes to a savings in logistics costs, as rectangular bottles allow for an up to 40% higher packing density than oval bottles. All in all, in this example the packaging cost for a key product had been reduced by 10%.[2]

## PUMP UP THE PROFIT

Another MASINT example concerns a Western FMCG company active in personal care products in emerging markets (Gudlavalleti, 2013). The Western company lost market share to a local competitor. In response, it applied MASINT. It discovered that the local competitor used a recipe that was half as costly as its own, resulting in the same efficacy. The competitor's products were sold in pump-cap bottles and delivered 10% more product volume per pump. In doing so, the pump-cap stimulated more sales per usage occasion. Based on this, the Western company redesigned its product, leading to a 40% margin improvement.[2]

This study provided another useful insight. Industries do not have to restrict themselves to tearing down products sold in their own category and/or being produced by their own competitors. MASINT may thus lead to a spark of creativity, as is shown in the example below.

Multiple factors and many gradual improvements led to the automobile assembly line pioneered by Henry Ford (Lacey, 1986). A key source of inspiration for the main design principle – a moving product object and a static worker – were the Chicago-based slaughterhouses. Here cows on hooks were sequentially disassembled with each butcher having his own tasks in the process. Ford applied the idea to assemble a car rather than to disassemble a cow.

## A PITCH OF SUGAR

This section concludes with an example from a disguised B2B ingredients context. Some ingredients, like sugar, are used in both large-scale B2B applications as well as sold in consumer markets. Believe it or not, plain sugar, like any crystallized product, is a treasure trove for specialists. Studying crystal size distributions, crystal shapes, wear on the edges of the crystals and multiple other physical and chemical (composition) features reveals a lot about the sugar production process. Two chemically-identical sugars may lead to different final products when their physical crystal size distribution is different.

A sugar producer decided to apply a multi-year MASINT program to convince their customers that sugar is not just sugar. The producer's entire sales force and R&D staff mobilized in this drive. Wherever anyone was going, either on a business or on a private trip, the journey would not be complete without buying a consumer pack of sugar. Each obtained sample was analysed as thoroughly as possible. Each sample was linked to an individual producer and, even better, an individual production site. Every analysis was recorded in a dedicated database, including standardized microscopic images of the product.

Sales or technical service staff who visited customers always had to carry standardized sample bottles with them. They had all been trained in sample collection to ensure no sampling-related differences crept into the database. With the permission of the customer, they collected their samples whenever doing a customer site visit, sometimes catching their own products but often also acquiring a competitor's product. Even when the customer didn't share who the other supplier was, back-office MASINT and the use of the ever-richer database often immediately allowed for connecting a product, a customer and a competitor. Over time, over 600 sugar samples populated the database. The database eventually contained multiple samples from many individual competitor's factories. Careful study of the products from a single factory allowed them to monitor the technological changes within that competitor's site. The latter were linked to news items that may have occurred in the trade press, such as of investments in new equipment installed at that particular competitor's site.

In due course, the database became a key resource for every large B2B sales pitch. The sales department knew against whom was pitching and it knew all the functional benefit differentiators of its own product.

It often could even favourably compare those to real customer benefits, such as a lower percentage of 'fines' (dust-like particles) in its own product with that of the competitor. This competitive intelligence helped facilitate the processing of the sugar at the customer's production site as well as reduce the customer's raw material losses and environmental costs and/or hinderances. In the pitch, the benefits could be quantified for the customer based on evidence that was as solid as scientifically possible. When customer benefits of €10/ton were calculated, the sales price would be positioned at €5/ton higher than the expected sales price of the competitor. Rather than talking price, the sales manager delivering the pitch would emphasize the €5/ton lower cost of ownership to the customer, versus the perceived competitor's offer. Even though the price differences look small, when large volumes of products like sugar are sold, such differences easily justify a fully implemented and maintained MASINT system.

## OBSESSED BY CHEVROLET

Prior to becoming US Secretary of Defense during the escalation of the Vietnam War in the 1960s, Robert S. McNamara had been President of the Ford Motor Company. His commitment to understanding his archrival Chevrolet's supply chain and technology through the effective use of MASINT is reflected from the quote below (Halberstam, 1992e):

> *"McNamara never stopped pushing; in those days, he was watching Chevy – how was Chevy doing? The night each year when they got hold of the first Chevy, everyone gathered around in a special room and broke it down, piece by piece into hundreds of items, each one stapled to a place already laid out for it, and they concentrated on it – no brain surgeon ever concentrated more – everyone muttering, wondering how Chevy had done this or that for a tenth of a cent less, cursing them slightly – so that was how they had done it!"*

You may ask yourself where the structural application of MASINT could contribute to the sweetening of your company's profit?

# 8.7 ATTENTION POINTS WHEN USING BACK-ENGINEERING OUTPUT

This chapter opened with good news – MASINT is generally known for its reliability.[6] MASINT data neither lies nor does it deceive. Strategic analysis risks are thus generally not in the collection – provided the collected sample is representative – and measurement in MASINT. They may, however, occur in its interpretation.

At some stage the MASINT data (the recipe or integral cost analysed for a competitor's product) becomes available. The results will be clear, data-rich tables. A premature but tempting conclusion could be that these figures can be used without studying them in their context. The opposite is true. The receiving strategic analysis department would be well advised to open a discussion with their procurement and/or operations departments to estimate the most logical *real* (procurement) cost per recipe component item for the particular competitor in question. This is a subjective step that should be taken with care. Be wary of not taking the competitor's perspective when preparing such estimates and avoid falling into the corporate equivalent of the ethnocentric bias on cost (Johnston, 2005c).

When preparing a cost-price estimation, areas of potential difference between your firm's standard cost price of a product, and that of a competitor, include:

## DIFFERENT RAW MATERIAL QUALITY SPECIFICATIONS

Even when the same raw chemical materials are used, different qualities may be used (for instance, with different specifications regarding tolerated chemical or microbiological contamination[7]). For many firms, guarenteeing the highest quality products requires diligent rejection of lower quality raw material. However, this may not be the case for all firms that produce this product.

To avoid mistakes the firm must work to, reduce complexity, minimize raw material warehouse storage requirements and reduce working capital. A consistently high quality raw material is procured. This quality requirement is determined by the highest minimum quality need of the final product range produced at the factory. Competitors cannot make either the same 'one raw material fits all recipes' choice or have the same range of products and may thus tolerate a lower quality raw material for the same end product.

## DIFFERENT PURCHASING CONDITIONS

Different conditions may be agreed with the supplier. When the competitor is smaller, its bargaining power may be more limited, leading to higher raw material prices per unit for them (including, possibly higher logistics costs as well).

## DIFFERENT COST OF CAPITAL

A local competitor in an emerging market may operate with government-pushed soft loans. These loans may have rather different costs than the weighted average cost of capital that a multinational company would use to price risk for investing in the same country. The multinational cost of capital will almost by definition be higher. For the cost price analysis of an individual FMCG product, this difference is usually irrelevant. A typical FMCG-factory has, for example, an output of 1 billion units/year of €0.50/unit ex-factory price. Assume an investment cost for the factory of say €100 million. This means that the factory's capital turnover is five times the investment, which is not an unusual figure in the FMCG business in emerging economies.

Assume a difference between the multinational and the local firm's cost of 6% (e.g., multinational at 13% versus local at 7%) in favor of the local competitor. In that case, a favourable €6 Million/year or €0.006/unit cost of capital difference is obtained is realized by the local competitor. This is a 1.2% cost disadvantage for the international company's standard product cost price, all other things being equal.

The catch, however, is that this difference is mainly non-cash. As a result, only the debt-related part of the cost of capital, if anything, may appear in the product cost price sheet in the accounting department of the multinational. In other words, determining a company's strategic advantage through it cost-of-capital is critical, even when it seems hardly to matter (or not matter at all) on an individual product basis.

## DIFFERENT LOGISTICS COST

What matters in terms of competitiveness analysis is not the ex-factory price of raw material but the price delivered at the gate of the factory where the raw material is to be processed. When the competitor is much smaller it may have less bargaining power with logistics providers, leading to higher shipping cost per unit.

## DIFFERENT ETHICAL STANDARDS

Large international companies generally at all times comply with all the laws of the land. There is never an excuse not to do so. In the end, a firm's global reputation is at stake. Stringent internal policies are, or at least should be, in place to ensure compliance. Smaller competitors may, however, not be so concerned with compliance. Examples of such companies gaining a competitive edge by cutting legal corners that lead to a lower-than-calculated competitive product cost price include:

- Evading import duties on imported raw materials ('border trade').
- Selling their products to customers or through channels that dodge Value-Add Tax.
- Evading environmental levies, city taxes, etc.
- Cutting product quality corners.

Many countries have a business climate that allows local players to engage in some of these questionable practices. The number of countries where these sorts of practices exist is numerically still the vast majority of all the countries recognized by the UN. Due to the relative growth of global business outside the developed world, the weighted global market percentage where these sorts of practices occur is probably going up. A small competitor's corner-cutting activity that employs one of these tactics usually has a modest impact on its overall competitiveness. When corner cutting becomes the rule and is applied all across the value chain, it can add up to significant differences in local competitor costs and prices versus those of fully compliant multinational companies. Such differences may fundamentally affect the long-term market attractiveness of that product/market combination for multinationals.[8]

## DIFFERENT PURCHASING POLICIES

The competitor may make a different choice in the eternal dilemma of working capital management relative to over- or under-stocking in raw materials that tend to have volatile prices over time. When the volatile prices of such raw materials are low but are expected to go up, overstocking now, even when it comes at a working capital cost, may still pay off overall. Large companies do not tend to do this rather speculative buying, but smaller (for instance family-owned) competitors may. For the latter, this may lead, temporarily, to rather different raw material prices compared to multinationals' in the same market.

Using your firm's internal raw material prices in analysing such competitors generally invites ethnocentric biases to play their ugly role. Such biases may lead to completely missing the point on competitors' market behaviours. An example is a competitor striving to artificially keep prices of its consumer products stable when raw material prices go up. They do this to gain market share and they can afford doing so by de-stocking cheaply and speculatively bought raw materials.

The above list is mainly included for illustrative purposes. For any MASINT collection output, a tailored list of potential bias factors and their potential impact on the conclusion of the analysis should be included. It is only after weighing these factors and their impact on an estimated competitor product cost price, for example, that management decisions should be recommended based on this very MASINT output.

# CHAPTER 9
# ANALYSIS

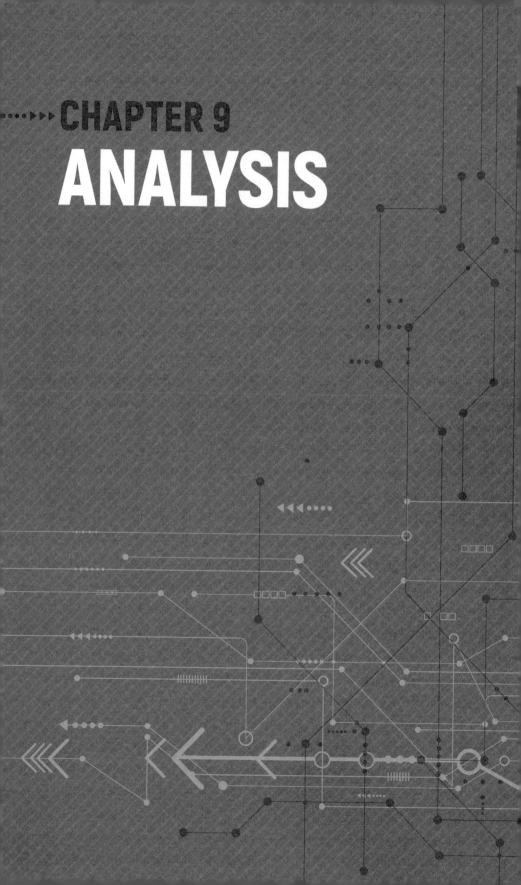

# 9.1 INTRODUCTION

Analysis is a craft that management cannot easily do without. If plain, raw data collection – which in the quote below is summarized in the word *intelligence* – would suffice, why would we need analysis (Davis, 2008)?

> *"When the facts speak for themselves, intelligence has done its job and there is no need for analysis."*

Usually, however, it is not that simple. Data have a nasty habit of not speaking for themselves. Data can often be ambiguous. Different data may be mutually contradicting. Data may be missing. Most of all, data in many instances may not offer the answer the strategic analysis requests (Johnston, 2005a):

> *"Since the facts do not speak for themselves but need to be interpreted, it is inevitable that the individual propensities of an intelligence officer will enter into the process of evaluation."*

The conclusion seems obvious. Data generally need interpretation. By implication, when management needs the answers to strategic or tactical questions regarding the business environment, they will have to build or in-source an analytical capability. Even when the choice is to in-source analysis, at least one individual in the in-house organization will need to know how to brief a third party. Too often the best procurement officer in a particular line of business is a former sales person from that very same line of business. That rule of thumb applies equally to analysis. Management has essentially two options when organizing business environment analysis: either hire a strategic analyst and let them do the work. Or they can hire at least one (former) analyst and let them handle the procurement. In this chapter, I will briefly touch on the discipline of strategic analysis itself.

## DEFINITIONS OF ANALYSIS

The first question is: "What is analysis?" Definitions of the noun 'analysis' vary. The Free Dictionary provides this as one of its definitions (TheFreeDictionary, 2013):

*"The study of such constituent parts and their interrelationships in making up a whole."*

Merriam-Webster (Merriam-Webster, 2013) provides two definitions. The meaning in their second definition comes closer to what I believe to be strategic analysis:

- A careful study of something to learn about its parts, what they do, and how they are related to each other.
- An explanation of the nature and meaning of something.

In sources on (military) intelligence the two definitions below were found (Bruce, 2008a), (Jones, 2007):

*"Synthesized raw information collected from multiple sources, interpreting the meaning of such info in the context of the policymakers' needs."*

*"(analysis is:) a matter of somehow keeping one's head above water in a tidal wave of documents, whose factual content must be 'processed.'"*

The second Merriam-Webster definition, as well as Bruce' definition, probably best cover what analysis actually is in the context of strategic analysis of a company's business environment. The latter definition by Jones will be recognized by many mature analysts. Making sense of data overload is definitely a part of analysis. This book aims to assist analysts in doing just that: making sense of data, even when the data keep coming. The following metaphor may help to elucidate the essence of analysis in synthesizing a strategic analysis function deliverable.

## GLASS PRODUCTION AS A METAPHOR FOR TURNING DATA INTO ACTIONABLE INTELLIGENCE

Common glass is produced by mixing sand (consisting mainly of silicon dioxide), soda ash and lime. Consider the raw materials required to produce glass as data. The raw materials may need to be purified prior to glass production: in strategic analysis, this means the data quality (i.e., reliability) has to be verified and thus assured. Like raw materials in glass production, data that do not meet the predefined minimum quality standards have to be rejected. The different data need to be weighed in terms of relative importance. That is tantamount to the mixing step in glass production. To make glass, one has to follow the recipe. The right amounts of the right quality raw materials have to be mixed to get the right high-quality finished product. Mixing sand, lime and soda ash as powders in the right ratio, at ambient temperature, no matter how intensively the mixture is being stirred, doesn't necessarily lead to the production of glass. Unless other critical factors are taken into account, even when mixed in the right ratio it is still only a mix of powders.

The next step is therefore *processing* the data. In glass production, this happens in an oven. Depending on the required glass quality, process parameters need to be chosen. This has implications for the choice of oven temperature, the type of oven to be used and the length of time the mix of raw materials is left in the oven. In strategic analysis work, the processing happens in the mind of the analyst. Like ovens, some analysts are more suited than others to particular processes. The analyst may choose to be supported by computers and other tools, but the mind matters most. If everything is processed correctly, the output that leaves the oven is glass… or in strategic analysis work, a well-prepared analysis deliverable.

The analysis deliverable needs to be shaped to match with the specific decision-maker's need. Management will not appreciate getting a deliverable that resembles a malformed lump of glass. The deliverable, may meet all the quality specifications but it may not be useful yet. The deliverable, like the glass, will need to be tailored in size, shaped and it will need to be polished and faceted. Finally, the deliverable – like the glass vase that should be ready for Mother's Day, not three days late – will need to be delivered to management at the right time to ensure it is useful for decision-making support.

The analysis step in the analysis cycle is thus meant to process input data, turning it into meaningful output deliverables. The inputs of the process are referred to as data. The process itself is called analysis. The output is generally called intelligence.

# 9.2 ANATOMY OF ANALYSIS

## THE WHERE, WHO, WHEN, WHY AND HOW OF ANALYSIS

Five of Kipling's six honest service men are again employed in this chapter to further flesh-out and explain the concept of analysis – the question-men in this chapter are where, who, when, why and how:

- Where? Analysis is typically a desk research activity. In today's connected world it doesn't really matter where the desk is, as long as it is in a brightly lit and quiet room.[1] The room should be equipped with the right set of tools including (online) newspapers and other database subscriptions and high-speed internet access. The economic laws of increasing and diminishing returns applies to strategic analysis. An analyst who operates in an intellectual vacuum will generally be less effective than an analyst who operates in an organizational environment with peers of at least the same intellectual level.[2] These peers will almost automatically act as a sounding board for the analyst.[3] This will allow the strategic analysis department to produce better quality output.

- Who? An analyst usually relies on the human brain rather than on artificial intelligence, although applying the latter may serve as a helpful tool for the analyst.[4]

- When? The majority of the collection work in a strategic analysis project needs to be finished before meaningful analysis can start. One common analytical bias is premature closing. An analyst or a decision-maker (or both) may prematurely close his mind to new data.

Once a person has seen a meaningful percentage of the facts and based on those facts, has made up his mind, she may not like to see more facts. Needless to say, this phenomenon poses severe risks to the quality of the policy or strategy that, based on the incomplete data set, is subsequently adopted and pursued.

In some projects, iterative loops will occur. Some analysis outcomes will generate new leads for collection, leading to new analytic perspectives etc., Acknowledging this reality, analysts are still advised to finish collecting as many of the facts as possible prior to concluding what it *all* means.

- Why? Analysis is the critical step in *processing* data, information and possibly knowledge into intelligence. Similarly, glass is formed by mixing the right raw materials in the right quantity at the right temperature in the right oven. In the absence of both the oven and sufficient temperature, no glass will be formed.

- How? The *how* question of analysis relates to:
  - The input data and the related individual input data quality assurance – simply put: getting the right individual data inputs into the analysis.
  - The processing of data and information that individually have passed the data quality check.
  - The formulating of multiple hypotheses, the most plausible of which is chosen in the analysis deliverable.
  - The potential use of tools to turn quality controlled data sets into intelligence.
  - The quality control check of the ultimate analysis deliverable – ultimate objective is of course to make the output absolutely perfect.

Diagram 9.1 schematically presents the steps of a common strategic analysis processes.

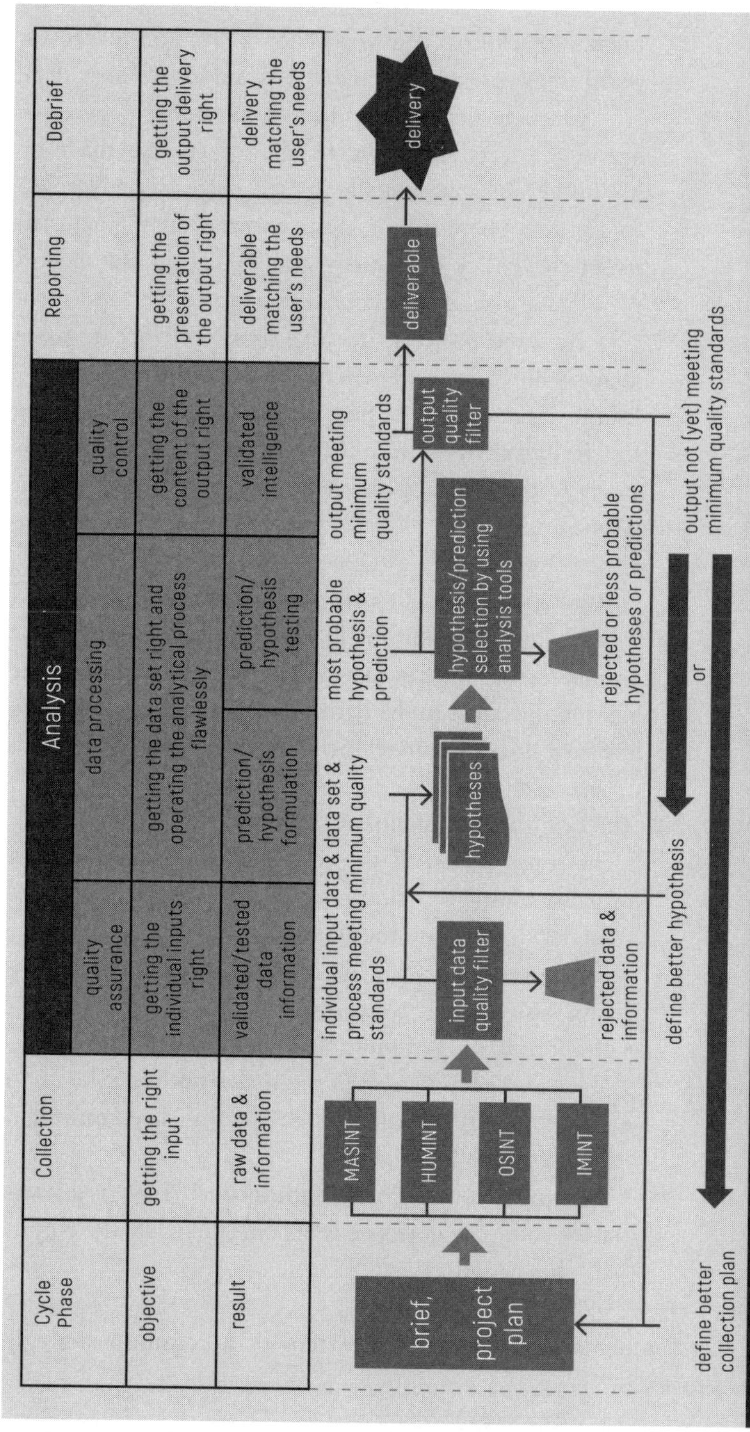
Cycle Phase
objective
result
Collection
getting the right input
raw data & information
Analysis
quality assurance
getting the individual inputs right
validated/tested data information
data processing
getting the data set right and operating the analytical process flawlessly
prediction/ hypothesis formulation
prediction/ hypothesis testing
quality control
getting the content of the output right
validated intelligence
Reporting
getting the presentation of the output right
deliverable matching the user's needs
Debrief
getting the output delivery right
delivery matching the user's needs
brief, project plan
MASINT
HUMINT
OSINT
IMINT
individual input data & data set & process meeting minimum quality standards
input data quality filter
rejected data & information
hypotheses
most probable hypothesis & prediction
hypothesis/prediction selection by using analysis tools
rejected or less probable hypotheses or predictions
output meeting minimum quality standards
output quality filter
deliverable
delivery
define better collection plan
define better hypothesis
or
output not (yet) meeting minimum quality standards

DIAGRAM 9.1 ▶▶▶ STEPS FROM RAW DATA TO REPORTING/DEBRIEFING IN THE ANALYSIS CYCLE

In this chapter, section 9.3 will describe data and their corresponding meta-data. In section 9.4 generic attributes of analysis will be briefly discussed.

# 9.3 DATA AND METADATA

Individual data points come in two dimensions: the actual measurement or data point and the contextual information accompanying the data. The latter are usually referred to as 'metadata'. In the glass production metaphor, data are equivalent to the quantity of sand or soda ash or lime. Metadata corresponds to the date of the shipment, the truck in which the raw material has been delivered, the supplier of the raw material and the silo in which the raw material was stored prior to its use. All metadata taken together, make the shipment of the individual raw materials uniquely traceable.

For strategic analysis work, the following – a somewhat unsavory wartime government intelligence example – will help illustrate the importance of connecting data and metadata. In spite of its slightly dubious nature, the example is used because it nicely illustrates the underlying topic.

During the Second World War, human intelligence source Aiken Sneath informed the British domestic security agency MI5 of a gentleman called Ivor Montagu, a film maker. He stated, without further evidence, that Montagu was "an active fifth columnist" – a communist agent (Macintyre, 2010a).

The measurement or data point in this example is: "Ivor Montagu is an active fifth columnist." The metadata here include (list not exhaustive):

- The source (i.e., the informer), of which Macintyre amusingly remarks that his name was so implausible that it had to be real.
- The timing of the source delivering his message.
- The form in which the source delivers his message (telephone call, formal written document, etc.).
- The recipient of the message at MI5.

- The state of mind of the informer at the time of delivering the data point (agitated, cool, upset, etc.).
- The relation of the source to Ivor Montagu.

Another government-related example below describes how deceiving data points were not sufficiently disputed because metadata were insufficiently valued. Prior to the invasion of Iraq in 2003, an exiled Iraqi source called 'Curveball' indirectly provided the US government intentionally false – or at least heavily distorted – intelligence on Iraq's program to develop and ultimately deploy biological warfare-based weapons of mass destruction. The objective of this source was, through these false reports, to persuade the US government to take action against Saddam Hussein. The data points provided by this source were not corroborated by UN weapons inspection teams' findings. The US government, however, believing the source was reliable, decided to act upon the deception anyway. And, of course, we all know the consequences.

The above is adequately summarized in a statement that strategic analysts may read as a warning regarding data correctness being influenced by metadata (Johnson, 2009a):

*"Who said it is often more important than what was being said."*

This holds true for open source data and especially for human source date. The interim conclusion on data quality assurance is that data points and their metadata information should be validated in totality.

A final word for this section: about two decades after the human source informed MI5 on Ivor Montagu, signal intelligence sources confirmed that Montagu was or had indeed been working for the Soviet military intelligence service GRU (West, 1999). He operated under the code name 'Nobility.'[5] The point is that, in military intelligence, at least, the absence of evidence which negatively affected the credibility of Mr Sneath's data point is not the same as evidence of absence.

What is the lesson from this section? Most of all that metadata forms an indispensable context for a single data point. The analyst must know and record the metadata to assess the correctness of the actual data point. This is the case in the above examples just as much as in handling any data point that an analyst receives as input for her work.

The implication for organizing strategic analysis projects is obvious. Namely, in designing and running any analysis project enough time should be made available to double-check sources and to corroborate findings. In journalism, one source is as good as no source at all. Strategic analysts, as good journalists do, need to organize not only data collection but also data quality validation before formulating conclusions.

# 9.4 ATTRIBUTES OF STRATEGIC (BUSINESS ENVIRONMENT) ANALYSIS

Business environment analysis is, and will remain, a craft in which experience more than learning is determinative. Strategic analysis by its nature has to cope with fundamentally unpredictable (human) behaviour which will never be governed by physical laws that are in most other instances universally applicable. Effective xenocentric strategic analysis predictions should reduce uncertainty in business decision-making. However, no matter how sophisticated the analysis is it will never be able to fully remove uncertainty.

Strategic analysis will thus never be considered a science, as it will never meet the fundamental requirement of science: reliably predictable reproducibility. Still, scientific methods may serve strategic analysis well. The use of scientific methods in intelligence analysis has been strongly advocated (Bruce, 2008c). Bruce proposes that intelligence analysis should use:

- Hypotheses
- Objectivity
- Transparency
- Replicability
- Peer review
- Provisional results

In the remainder of this section I will briefly touch upon each of these attributes. They are all fundamental elements in generally accepted scientific methodology. Apparently in 2008 they were not commonly applied in the US intelligence community, otherwise Bruce's reference would have been superfluous. As I do not believe that Bruce is the king of stating the obvious, the attributes deserve to be discussed in more detail.

Thus, the question is whether scientific methods, and by implication the attributes of accepted scientific methodology are also relevant in business strategy consulting and in strategic analysis as data-provider-to-business-strategy design. I believe they are and in support of that I put forward two suppositions. The first is rooted in my personal experience. In my work, I have benefitted tremendously from my scientific methodology toolkit acquired during my PhD research. The second is that I see business strategy consulting firms, as well as investment banks and private equity funds, recruiting 'quants' (those who specialize in the application of mathematical and statistical methods) with a solid scientific background. Their recruits often hold PhDs in physics, mathematics or engineering. To such staff, scientific methodology is fully embedded in their thinking. I concur with strongly advocating the use of scientific methods, even when the ultimate goal of xenocentric strategic analysis is to think 'like them' and thus to predict what they're thinking. Thus, I believe in organizing a strategic analysis function in a corporate environment in such a way that the scientific methodology attributes as we will discuss below truly matter – and doing so for the better.

## HYPOTHESES

Hypothesis-based strategic plans are becoming the rule rather than the exception in many firms. A strategic analysis function should thus provide strategy designers and other decision-makers with hypotheses.

## OBJECTIVITY

Objective measurement methods are crucial. In physics, every freshman gets to know Schrödinger's cat. This metaphorical feline creature is named after a thought experiment proposed by one of the iconic physicists of the first half of the Twentieth Century, Erwin Schrödinger (1887-1961). Without getting bogged down in the subtleties of quantum mechanics, the point is that a measurement method may not be allowed to interfere with the outcome of the object or phenomenon that is measured. In Schrödinger's experiment the poor cat is locked up for an hour in a room with a radioactive nucleus that may or may not decay during that hour. Upon decaying, the nucleus will release a poison gas that kills the cat. As the timing of radioactive decay of a single nucleus is not predictable, as soon as the cat is locked up in the room it is fundamentally impossible – because the cat cannot be physically seen – to objectively ascertain whether the cat is alive or dead. Unless, of course, the door to the room is opened... but that would represent undue interference.

This example may sound like a bizarre experiment of some mad scientist. If that were the case, Schrödinger's cat wouldn't feature in this text. Unfortunately, this hypothetical cat is a familiar presence in strategic analysis. Answers to questions or even people's responses to probing may be highly dependent on the situation in which the answers are collected. The context of the measurement, to use scientific jargon, may in human source-based collection strongly affect the outcome of the experiment. Objectivity is the aim. Maintaining objectivity requires the collector or analyst to spot Schrödinger's cat in the methodology and scare it away before flawed methodology affects the measurement's accuracy.

## TRANSPARENCY AND REPRODUCIBILITY OR REPLICABILITY

In science, all methodologies need to be documented in detail to allow for reproducibility. In strategic analysis, protection of human sources may hinder this generally preferable approach. Deliverables may, upon request of the decision-makers, have to substantiate all sources behind an analysis. Generally, there is no need to do so proactively. No reference to sources is entirely necessary, unless needed for the decision-makers to understand the background. After all, sources may be too precious to share unless absolutely necessary.

## PEER REVIEW

In science, peers are invited by scientific journal boards to review manuscripts that are submitted for publication. In doing so, a methodology check is executed by experts prior to accepting a manuscript for publication. Peers are entitled to send the manuscript back to the author with questions that need to be answered prior to the journal accepting the paper. Peers may also reject the article altogether when they find it to not meet the required minimum scientific standards, and thus to be 'beyond repair'.

In a strategic analysis function, the process of peer review is a good practice, with neutral yet constructive colleagues operating in peer roles.

## PROVISIONAL RESULTS

In science, "if ugly facts challenge beautiful theory, facts win" (Bruce, 2008b). The beauty of science is that new facts, provided that they are measured objectively and correctly, may (and should!) supersede old hypotheses. This would be commendable in strategic analysis as well but is not so easily implemented. Once the strategic analysis function has developed an output, decisions are based upon the output. If later analysis shows the outputs to have been wrong, then the decisions made based on the deliverables – think large-scale market investments – may not be reversible. So, in strategic analysis the science metaphor is great, but it is not always applicable.

## INTEGRITY

Complementary to the above thinking, the core attribute of analysis, as I see it is captured well in the following quote (Kerr, 2008a):

> *"Integrity is the single most important attribute of solid analysis."*

An analyst may lose a lot, but never – if they are really good at what they do – the perception of their integrity with the decision-makers they serve. McLaughlin mentions four additional attributes of (intelligence) analysis that equally apply to strategic analysis in a business context (McLaughlin, 2008a). The first has already been covered above, focusing on measurement methodologies and Schrödinger's cat. The others speak for themselves:

- Objectivity.
- Civility.
- Balance.
- Thoroughness.

The attributes that management may demand from analysis can perhaps best be summarized as follows (Denrell, 2005):

> *"No managers should accept a theory about business unless they can be confident that the theory's advocates are working of an unbiased data set."*

What matters is the relevance of both data correctness and data set completeness.

I will take this opportunity to repeat the core messages of this section. The key attributes of strategic analysis should be objectivity and integrity. It is critical for a strategic analysis function and its entire staff to be strictly non-partisan in office politics. Any strategic analysis function's organizational design should facilitate operational objectivity and integrity. I had this pitfall in mind earlier, when I introduced Curveball. A flaw in the objectivity of a source (and perhaps a bit of political manipulation) may lead to undesirable outcomes that are to be avoided.

# 9.5 COLLECTOR – ANALYST RELATIONSHIP

The relation between the collector and the analyst, assuming these are different persons, is a topic covered in literature on military intelligence (Clark, 2007a). One question in this field is whether the collector should be briefed on the context of the collection request provided by the analyst. To avoid collector bias, it has been postulated that collectors should only be briefed on *what* to collect but not *why* (Jähne, 2009). The less context they have, the more they bring. However, this is not a universal view (Clark, 2007a) (Jones, 2007):

> *"The key to success with any collection strategy is a close and enduring relationship (of the analyst) with the collectors. Simply writing collection requirements and 'throwing them over the wall' doesn't work. If collectors have access to and understand (...) the problem breakdown, they can respond much more effectively. This usually requires (the analyst) developing and maintaining personal contacts with collectors."*

> *"Intelligence information is typically very ambiguous, with several plausible interpretations. Understanding the context of information, therefore, is a fundamental tool of analysis. It is one reason for housing both collection and analysis capabilities in the CIA. Intelligence collectors are most familiar with the context of information gathered – its reliability, timeliness, relationship to other information and so on."*

In most strategic analysis departments, collectors and analysts work closely together, in fact if the roles have even been separated in the first place. This issue is less relevant in a business setting than in the military context. This does play a role when the collector is an individual in the firm with a lower information security clearance than the analyst.

## COLLECTION AND CONFIDENTIALITY

An example of a collection and confidentiality dilemma is when in contrast to the analyst, the collector is not supposed to be knowledgeable about senior management plans. This could be the case when an analysis for an acquisition is being planned. In such cases, the size of the team in the know is minimized to avoid leakage, with all of the legal and other risks that leaks may entail.

In such a case, the collector must execute his role without knowing the full context of the information requested. Apart from potential suspicions raised in the collector's mind, this shouldn't and generally doesn't generate problems.[6]

Diagram 9.2 gives a schematic, simplified overview along the dimensions of geo-location, timing and personality for the different roles and profiles of collectors and analysts. An 'off-site geo-location' is defined as a location that has no link with the location of the activities or presence of the competitor (or the customer or the supplier, etc.). The collector or analyst need not physically be somewhere (on-site) to execute their work. In diagram 9.2, I use the military intelligence abbreviations for different collection methodologies:

| | |
|---|---|
| OSINT | Open source intelligence. |
| HUMINT | Human intelligence (as from human sources). |
| IMINT | Imagery intelligence. |
| MASINT | Measurement and Signature intelligence (back-engineering of products). |

| dimensions | collection | | | analysis |
|---|---|---|---|---|
| geo-location | critical to understand local culture & language. Need of tenure to build up local network | | | off-site unless cultural specifics, etc., where needed can be 'outsourced' to experts |
| | **collection method** | off-site | on-site | |
| | **OSINT** | mainly | sometimes – e.g., visit to Chamber of Commerce | |
| | **IMINT** | partly via OSINT | partly – e.g., counting trucks at the adversary's site | |
| | **MASINT** | mainly | buying samples of adversary products | |
| | **HUMINT** | telephone & e.g. email questions | interviews, etc. | |
| timing | fixed, especially for HUMINT – e.g., only one conference and one trade fair this year where adversary's staff can be approached | | | more flexible than collection, driven by urgency of decision-makers' needs |
| personality & stereotype | - curious: 'wants to know'<br>- sociable, makes friends easily | | | - fascination: 'wants to understand'<br>- reclusive, prefers to be among peers |

**DIAGRAM 9.2 ▶▶▶ ANALYST - COLLECTOR DIFFERENCES IN GEO-LOCATION, TIMING AND PERSONALITY PROFILE**

Acknowledging the risk of over-generalizing, good analysts are different characters than good collectors. This is especially true for collectors of human intelligence on the one hand and quantitative analysts on the other. In fact this is not a problem at all. When both disciplines respect each other's capabilities, cooperation can be and usually is seamless.

CHAPTER 10

# INPUT DATA QUALITY ASSURANCE

# 10.1 INTRODUCTION

This chapter will focus on the quality assurance of individual input data, both in terms of data correctness and completeness. In diagram 10.1, the material we'll be focusing on in this chapter falls under *input data quality filter.* This chapter is symbolized by the input data quality filter. We will be examining the critical importance of high data quality prior to starting the actual data processing.

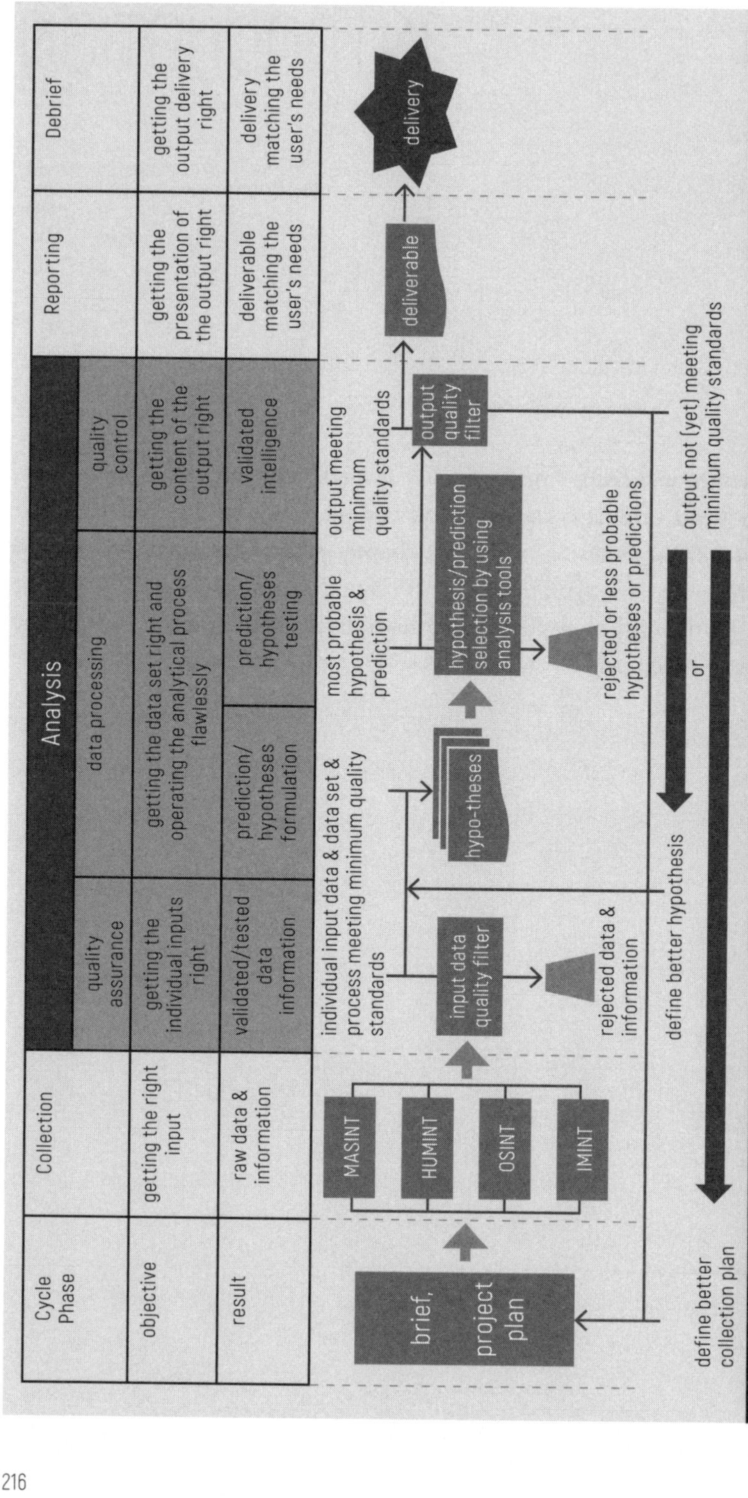
Cycle Phase
objective
result
Collection
getting the right input
raw data & information
Analysis
quality assurance
getting the individual inputs right
validated/tested data information
data processing
getting the data set right and operating the analytical process flawlessly
prediction/ hypotheses formulation
prediction/ hypotheses testing
quality control
getting the content of the output right
validated intelligence
Reporting
getting the presentation of the output right
deliverable matching the user's needs
Debrief
getting the output delivery right
delivery matching the user's needs
brief, project plan
MASINT
HUMINT
OSINT
IMINT
input data quality filter
individual input data & data set & process meeting minimum quality standards
rejected data & information
hypo-theses
hypothesis/prediction selection by using analysis tools
most probable hypothesis & prediction
rejected or less probable hypotheses or predictions
output quality filter
output meeting minimum quality standards
deliverable
delivery
define better collection plan
define better hypothesis
or
output not (yet) meeting minimum quality standards

DIAGRAM 10.1 ▶▶ STEPS FROM RAW DATA TO DEBRIEFING IN THE ANALYSIS CYCLE

# 10.2 INDIVIDUAL DATA CORRECTNESS AND DATA COMPLETENESS

The two most relevant dimensions in individual data quality assurance testing are:

- Data correctness.
- Data completeness.

Diagram 10.2 gives a simple two-by-two matrix, featuring both dimensions. Data correctness is featured from low to high on the horizontal axis. Data completeness ranges from low to high on the vertical axis. Data correctness and data completeness as dimensions show the actual situation. The actual situation in the case of data correctness may be the result of intentional competitor deception or simply of poor analysis or sloppiness during collection work. The same holds true for the data completeness axis. Data may be incomplete due to a competitor intentionally limiting the release of data on its capabilities or intent, or again due to poor collection efforts. In other words, the cause of poor or strong data completeness or data correctness may be internal or external.

## DATA COMPLETENESS ISSUES DUE TO INTENTIONAL DENIAL

In strategic analysis work, for a competitor aiming to limit the data completeness of your strategic analysis the term *intentional denial* is used. The competitor that prevents its rivals from acquiring useful data on its competences and intent can enhance the impact of its competitive strategies. Those strategies are more likely to be executed as unwelcome surprises. Surprise moves (such as unanticipated new product launches) will likely be turned by such a company into a competitive advantage. The objective of denial is to blind competitors' analysts and, through them, their decision-makers.

A blinded analyst will be cautious; he doesn't want to stumble into inconvenient, unseen truths. Subject to his budget constraints, such an analyst will likely intensify his collection efforts in response. In any case, the analyst's conclusions will be cautious. The analyst will (or should) be somewhat anxious about having to build a point of view based on too few data points.

## DATA CORRECTNESS ISSUES DUE TO INTENTIONAL DECEPTION

A company (read: competitor) that intentionally plays with your perception of data manipulates data correctness. In doing so it applies deception. Such companies aim to deceive their competitors by selective and/or misleading information. Legal limits prevent companies from using the deception tricks that the military can apply in wartime. Deception in business is not so common. At times, selectively chosen data – that as such is truthful is intentionally-passed on to you as an analyst to misdirect your company's attention. The objective of doing so of course is to gain or strengthen the sender's competitive advantage.[1]

A competitor that operates a deception campaign delivers the ultimate strategic analyst's test. Seeing through a well-planned and skillfully executed deception is among the most challenging tasks a strategic analyst can face. Several military deceptions over the course of the Twentieth Century have been analysed in detail (Bruce, 2008d). The analysis reveals that 90% of all military deceptions achieved their objective of misleading the adversary into believing a truth different from the actual reality. In some cases this led to serious issues which literally altered the flow of the Second World War.[2] Section 10.3 covers deception in greater detail.

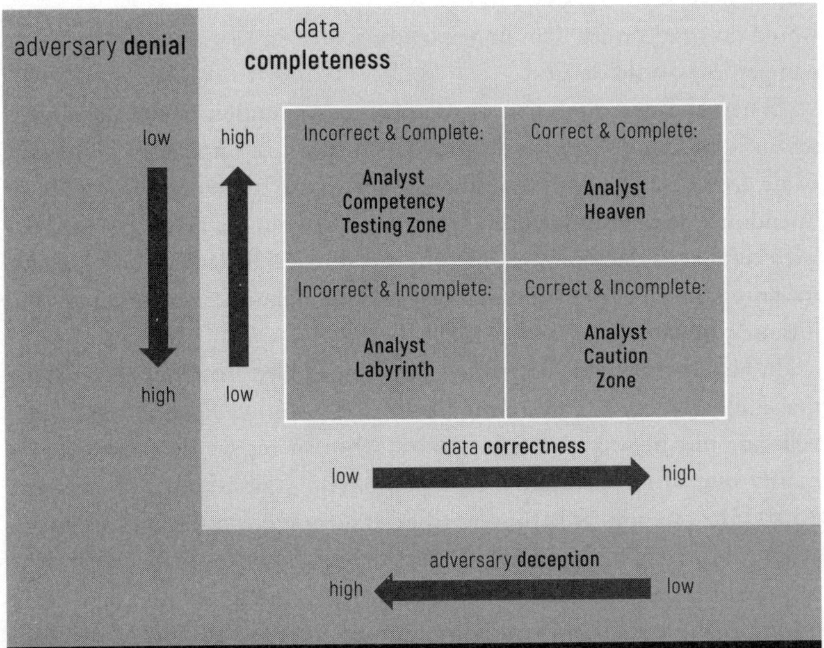


DIAGRAM 10.2 ▶▶▶ DENIAL AND DECEPTION IN DATA QUALITY ASSESSMENTS

The dark grey zone in diagram 10.2 reflects the degree of deception and denial that the competitor intends. Any analyst will see the amount of data available. At first sight, the position on the vertical axis looks clear. Depending on the skills of the analyst and/or the quality of the analyst's sources, a deception either works, or it is partially or completely detected. This determines the position on the horizontal axis.

At the beginning of this section, I already pointed out that diagram 10.2 gives a rather simple view of reality. The complicating matter is that the dark grey zone in diagram 10.2 refers to the degree with which the competitor intentionally deceives the analyst. But what if the competitor has no such intention, and the analyst unfortunately deceives himself?

## DATA CORRECTNESS AND COMPLETENESS ISSUES DUE TO SELF-DECEPTION AND SELF-DENIAL

Self-deception may happen as a result of an analyst applying the wrong (his own, or ethnocentric) logic to a competitor's action. Given certain correct and complete facts on the table, the analyst may, for example, incorrectly predict what we (the company that employs the analyst) in this situation would do next, rather than understanding what in this situation they (the competitor) would do next.

Whether a deception was the competitor's intention or whether it was self-inflicted is not shown in diagram 10.2 because it is irrelevant to the outcome. In both cases, a strategic analysis deliverable based on self-inflicted or intentional deception obviously won't contribute to the quality of the analyst's company's decision-making. The worst reflex any analyst (admittedly, including myself) can have is that 'self-deception may happen to others, but it cannot or will not happen to me'.

In his biography of master-deceiver Kim Philby, Ben Macintyre shows that Philby's success in deceiving his English MI6 intelligence friends into believing that he was one of them (even when spying for the Russians) was mostly due to self-deception among the MI6 establishment (Macintyre, 2014). The old boys at MI6 were all genuine masters in the craft of intelligence. They certainly did not lack the skills necessary to smell a rat if there was one. But they couldn't believe Philby was a traitor because they didn't *want to* believe it. If they couldn't, can we (that is you and I) be open-minded enough not to believe what we so dearly want to believe? In strategic analysis, we'd better not.

What is true for the dimension of deception is also true for the dimension of denial. A competitor may not take extreme care to protect his data (that is, it isn't purposely denying data to the analyst), but the analyst may out of negligence or lack of experience – or for whatever other reason – simply fail to collect the data that are in fact out there.

Succinctly put: the analyst's own perception on data completeness matters significantly. When experience tells them that they are missing much-needed data, their perception of data completeness is low. This will most likely make them cautious in their analysis. They will probably express a lower confidence level in describing 'what it all means' in their deliverable. When an analyst, however, does not know they are missing critical data, they will not look for it either. They will express high confidence in their assessment, unintentionally misleading themselves and the intended recipients of their deliverable.

In the sections below, both the data correctness and the data completeness dimensions will be covered in more detail. Sections 10.3 to 10.5 describe the data correctness dimension: the methods to assess the quality, expressed as degree of reliability of available individual data prior to accepting them as input for strategic analysis.

# 10.3 INDIVIDUAL DATA CORRECTNESS ASSESSMENT

In this section, I will discuss how to execute data quality assessments for individual data points. To return to the glass production metaphor, the quality/purity of the individual raw materials (soda ash, lime, sand) needs to be assured prior to accepting them as input raw materials in the glass oven.

Different reasons may exist why individual data points that arrive at an analyst's desk may not be fully correct (may not give a truthful picture of reality). Speaking from experience, I confess that working in strategic analysis for a long time may result in developing mild symptoms of paranoia when it comes to data quality. In strategic analysis, this is not a bad thing, provided the paranoia doesn't spill over to non-business parts of your life. In strategic analysis for business I believe Aeschylus's 2,500-year-old axiom applies just as well as it does in conflict:

*"In war, truth is the first casualty."*

## SCEPTICISM AS A DESIRABLE ANALYST ATTITUDE

It is the analyst's responsibility to search for the full truth and not for (un-) intentionally distorted truths or half-truths. An analyst has useful weapons at her disposal for protecting the integrity of assessments (Davis 1997). It all starts with testing the quality of individual input data, followed by challenging pre-existing beliefs the analyst may have:

- Scepticism about the reliability of all information, whether from human or technical collection.
- Readiness to challenge and test even well-established assumptions about trends, patterns and cause-effect relationships.

Infusing a healthy dose of skepticism into working processes requires the analyst to assess the data itself and how the data points are received, by both the communication channel and the source.

## A SCEPTICAL LOOK AT COMMUNICATION CHANNELS

In communication, there is a sender, a channel and a receiver. Inevitably, there is noise as well. In the example below, the sender is assumed to be the competitor. For purposes of discussion, he may just as well be a customer or a supplier. The channel consists of one or more chain links between the sender and the analyst. The analyst is the receiver. You should note that the sender is not necessarily, by definition, the source. The source is here defined as the last link in the chain between the sender and the receiver. Diagram 10.3 gives a schematic representation of sender, channel and receiver in individual data point communication.

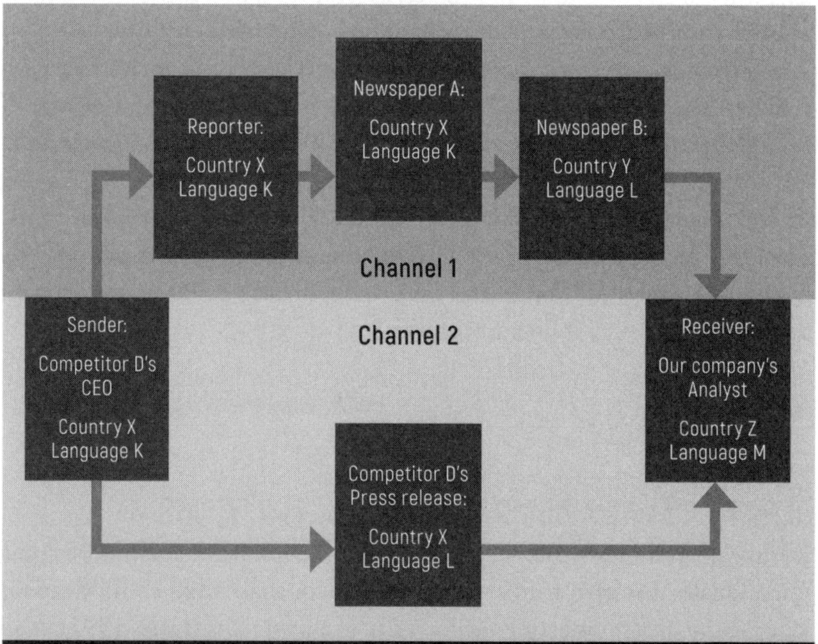


DIAGRAM 10.3 SENDER, CHANNEL AND RECEIVER IN INDIVIDUAL DATA POINT COMMUNICATION

Diagram 10.3 shows two straightforward channels of communication of an individual data point. Channel 1, in the dark grey area, depicts an indirect channel. It is indirect because it covers more than one link in the chain.

In this example, the chain in Channel 1 starts on the day of the release of competitor D's first-quarter financial results. That day, the CEO of competitor D gives an interview to a journalist. The data point may be the expected profit expressed as earnings before his company's interest, tax, amortization and depreciation (EBITDA) in the upcoming full financial year. The CEO and the journalist both speak language K. The journalist truthfully notes the expected full-year EBITDA figure the CEO has given him.

The journalist, however, has to work with an editor at his newspaper. The editor has only allocated the journalist a limited number of words for the coverage of this interview. For this reason, the journalist reports the EBITDA figure in his article as gross profit. A second journalist working in another country for newspaper B (which is published in another language than newspaper A) picks up the news item from newspaper A. He decides to briefly cover the news in his paper, correctly referring to newspaper A as his source. For the sake of convenience and brevity he refers to the gross profit reported into *profit.* By this point, the unintentionally distorted data point in newspaper B reaches the analyst. All other news elements were transferred correctly, but the reasonably well-defined EBITDA figure has been mis-reported as profit. This renders the data point less useless (to say the least) to the analyst.

Fortunately, a second direct channel (Channel 2) existed as well. This channel is considered direct because the analyst uses a source that links directly to the ultimate sender, without intermediate links in the chain. This was the channel through which the press release of competitor D's quarterly results flowed. This document properly offered both the EBITDA actuals for the first quarter as well as the forecasted figure for the full year.

In the above example, complete and correct data were released by the sender. The data were subsequently unintentionally distorted in communication Channel 1 prior to reaching the receiving analyst. In doing so, the data moved to the left along the horizontal axis of diagram 10.2, losing part of their correctness... and thus their usefulness.

## MAKING SCEPTICISM ACTIONABLE THROUGH ASKING QUESTIONS

Using diagram 10.3 and taking the communication flow as a starting point, the following analysis questions emerge as a first quality assurance check on individual input data points:

- What is the nature of the individual data point?
- Who is the source?
- Through what channel did the data come in?
- Who is the sender?

Each of these four questions, plus the question 'What is my situation?' are elaborated upon below. At the individual analyst level, they illustrate four principles that can prove helpful in protecting yourself against deception. Applying these principles should reduce the chances of falsely accepting flawed individual data points as correct or rejecting correct individual data points as flawed. The principles are (Bruce, 2008e):

- Know your competitor (the ultimate sender).
- Know your channel.
- Know your situation.
- Know yourself.

The importance of knowing the competitor (or customer or supplier) and knowing the channel have already been covered in diagram 10.3 as your starting point. Knowing the situation is the final *external* factor – along with the nature of the data point, the source, the channel and the sender – that the analyst has to include in the assessment. These five external factors in the individual input data quality assessment are covered in this section.

The final principle concerns the analyst, whose mind, whether they like it or not, may be a source of deception. This is an internal factor that may affect the individual input data quality assessment. Section 10.4 will cover the individual analyst's potential psychological reasons for introducing bias in the assessment of individual input data.

## WHAT IS THE NATURE OF THE INDIVIDUAL DATA POINT?

In table 10.1, a checklist of questions is provided to assess the nature and thus correctness of an individual data point. A tick in the box specifies for which collection method the question is most relevant (using, again, the military intelligence abbreviations for human source, imagery, measurement and signature and open sources).

| | ADVANTAGES | HUMINT | IMINT | MASINT | OSINT |
|---|---|---|---|---|---|
| 1 | Does the individual data point look credible? | √ | √ | √ | √ |
| 2 | Does the data point confirm existing - implicit or explicit - hypotheses on the underlying topic? | √ | √ | √ | √ |
| 3 | When the data point is quantitative, do the unit and the quantity match? | √ | √ | √ | √ |
| 4 | Does the data point distinguish (what is presented as) facts from conclusions (which may be presented as facts)? | √ | | | √ |
| 5 | In summary: What does the above all mean? What observations/conclusions can be drawn regarding the individual data point? Do you accept the data point, use it with caution or reject it? | √ | √ | √ | √ |

TABLE 10.1 ▶▶▶ QUESTION CHECKLIST ON THE NATURE OF INDIVIDUAL DATA POINTS

## HUMANS LOOK FOR CONFIRMATION, NOT FOR TRUTH

Questions 1, 2 and 3 force the analyst to check the new individual input data point with earlier data points of a similar nature. This may be called a confirmatory check. No matter how objective and principled the analyst is, or at least aims to be, when judging data they will inevitably use their personal frame of reference. Any data received will be compared, with data previously received and/or analysed. So, when a newly received individual data point confirms the analyst's expectations for this type or class of data, the data point may be considered correct. It does not raise suspicions. Research found that as much as 90% of all data that is searched for has been collected to confirm pre-existing views (Makridakis, 1990).

The confirmatory check can, at times, be a good trait. There is a good reason why, in physics and engineering classes, students are taught to estimate the outcome of a calculation, prior to executing the calculation. This is done only to make an informed guess on the approximate size of the result. When, for example, calculating that the height of a new stack at a large oil refinery needs to be 1,500 metres tall, the student should know immediately that the answer is incorrect. Implicitly, a student with only a bit of common sense knows that a stack at a large oil refinery measures some 150 (+/- 75) meters. The absurd initial height figure strongly suggests something was wrong with either the calculation method or with the inputs used. The same would be true when as result a stack height of 1.5 meters would have been calculated.

The significant benefit of a confirmatory check is that obvious (although perhaps unintentional) distortions in data are filtered out. In the example in the previous section, the analyst would likely have *assumed* the expected 'profit' figure that reached him through Channel 1 to be an EBITDA figure. Compared to last year's EBITDA figure for company D, the figure cited in the news articles would mean an increase of 6%. That would in fact relate to the historic performance growth of company D over time. Even when the exact figure would not have reached the analyst through Channel 2, at least through Channel 1 the analyst had a data point with a perceived sufficiently high correctness for the expected EBITDA at company D.

Similarly, when we think about the MI5 analysts in the example in section 9.2, they may have done a confirmatory check on Ivor Montagu by reviewing the membership list of the Communist Party of Great Britain.

Finding Montagu on the list may have added to the credibility or even probability of the *fifth columnist* data point being correct. It should be emphasized, however, that both data points as such are strictly disconnected.

The membership data point adds nothing to the correctness of the communist party affiliation data point.

This example shows that what was intentionally and deceptively called a confirmatory check for the first three questions in table 10.1 in fact was only a rejection check. New individual input data points are perceived to be correct when the new points confirm the analyst's *existing* beliefs or expectations.

## CONFIRMATORY CHECKS MAKE ANALYSTS VULNERABLE TO (INTENTIONAL) DECEPTION

This is a good place to share a quote that I really like, which applies to both intentional and inadvertently self-inflicted deception (Johnson, 2009b):

> *"The basic principle underlying deception is to tell your target what he wants to believe."*

Jan Hatzius, chief economist at investment bank Goldman Sachs, similarly frames the human tendency to confirmatory checking as follows (Silver, 2013a):

> *"I do think that people have the tendency, which needs to be actively fought, to see the information flow the way they want to see it."*

The implication of this is that when people, including analysts and corporate decision-makers, hear what they want to hear they lower their guard relative to the actual data correctness. The risk of the 'rejection check' is that new individual data points that reach an analyst and that are not rejected as unlikely, but rather accepted as credible, are therefore not automatically correct.

To make intentional deceptions succeed, a sender needs to include just enough truth and credibility in the information that is provided to the receiving analyst to catch the analyst off-guard. The bamboozled analyst will not realize that although all the individual data points received are true, together they do not make up the full truth. Doing so exploits in the analyst the all-too-human inclination to – mix up credibility with correctness or completeness. By stressing some truths – and in doing so, muting and thus denying the analyst other important truths, the intentional deception is legal.

An analyst always aims to avoid being deceived. When an analyst has direct interaction with the human source providing the individual input data points, the analyst may, where needed, assess the truthfulness of the source on the spot. There are methods for the analyst to assess whether human sources may be intentionally, or unintentionally, deceiving (Houston, 2012a). The method is more sophisticated than what is suggested by the indicators below. The indicators were selected for their applicability in a strategic analysis context. They may serve as warning signals of deception by a human source, especially when the source answers questions in a less-than-straightforward way. This is not to say that a single indicator signaling an alarm justifies rejection of all that the source says as inaccurate. To justify concerns over data accuracy, multiple indicators should be taken into consideration simultaneously. Table 10.2 focuses on hearing the source, and table 10.3 on seeing the source.

| WHAT THE ANALYST **HEARS** FROM THE HUMAN SOURCE | WHAT THE ANALYST MAY CHECK | DISADVANTAGES |
|---|---|---|
| Fail to answer a question or pretend not to understand a simple question | - Has the source understood the question?<br>- Does the source fail to come to a point?<br>or<br>- is the source using deflecting words or pretending to avoid a clear answer? | "What I do know is"(followed by facts that do not answer the question) |
| Fail to deny a fact that may have negative consequences for the source when admitted | - Does the source know the answer?<br>or<br>- Is the source applying a strategy to avoid giving a clear answer? | "I would never say that" (rather than the source firmly saying "no") |
| Refuse to answer a question | - Does the source know the answer?<br>or<br>- Is the source attempting to avoid answering the question? | "I am not sure I can answer that"<br>"I'm not the right person to ask that" |
| Repeat a question | - Has the source understood the question?<br>or<br>- Is he buying time to polish the story he is making up? | "So what I think you're asking me for is"... |
| Give a non-answer statement | - does the source know the answer?<br>or<br>- Is he buying time to polish the cover story he is making up? | "That's a good question" |
| Provide inconsistent statements in the light of earlier data/remarks | - Does the source really not know this?<br>or<br>- Is he getting confused in the cover story he made up prior to the interview? | |
| Go into attack mode | - Does the source believe he is losing face?<br>or<br>- Is he intimidating his way out of a question he aims to avoid answering? | "Why don't you trust me"? |

TABLE 10.2 ▶▶▶ INDICATORS JUSTIFYING ALERTNESS REGARDING HUMAN-SOURCE INPUT DATA ACCURACY

| WHAT THE ANALYST *SEES* THE HUMAN SOURCE DO | WHAT THE ANALYST MAY CHECK | EXAMPLES OF EVASIVE ACTS |
|---|---|---|
| Provide overly specific answers | - Does the source have a knack for detail?<br>or<br>- Does the source hide details by overly providing details on irrelevant matters? | "bla bla bla bla." |
| Provide referral statements | - Is the source rightfully impatient?<br>or<br>- Is he using this argument to dodge answering a direct question? | "What I said during our last meeting."<br>"What I wrote in the memo." |
| Take a pause | - Does the source test his memory?<br>or<br>- Is he buying time to polish the cover story he is making up? | The source suddenly takes much more time to answer a question than with all (comparable) previous questions. |
| Hide mouth or eyes | - Does the source have an itching lip?<br>or<br>- Is he trying to hide his mouth with his hand or his eyes by closing them to avoid exposure to the analyst? | People unconsciously try to hide themselves when telling a lie, by putting their hand in front of their mouth or by suddenly closing their eyes. |
| Clear throat or swallow | - Does the source need some water?<br>or<br>- Does he get an uncomfortable feeling from the question? | When a throat is cleared after the answer there is no issue, but when it is done ahead of answering this may suggest the source is buying time or dressing up the answer. |
| Make anchor-point movements | - Does the source need to change position because he is getting stiff?<br>or<br>- Does a question make him feel off-balance and is he looking for stability in a trying situation? | For a person who's is standing, his feet are anchor points. When a person in response to a difficult question suddenly looks to his feet or moves his feet, he may display an unconscious an unconscious search for stability. Rubbing hands together is another indicator, even when that has a slightly different physiological cause. |
| Make grooming gestures | - Is a string of hair suddenly irritating so much that it needs to be put behind an ear?<br>or<br>- Is this a grooming gesture that inadvertently shows discomfort with the question that is being raised? | In response to difficult questions, people may suddenly make grooming gestures (hair, tie, skirt). They may also start tidying things up in their immediate environment. Such (often unconscious) moves may indicate a person is uneasy with the questions being asked. There may be a reason for this, and it may reflect on the accuracy of the data that are in the answers. |

**TABLE 10.3 ▶▶▶ ADDITIONAL INDICATORS JUSTIFYING ALERTNESS REGARDING HUMAN-SOURCE INPUT DATA ACCURACY**

Deception becomes illegal when intentionally false statements are published or uttered to misdirect the analyst's and his company's attention for a competitive advantage. Illegal acts in this field may fall under the jurisdiction of competition law. The latter are known in many countries for the high fines that can be imposed upon offenders, up to a maximum of 10% of the global net sales of the ultimate mother company. Sentences can include jail terms for individual corporate executives.

A strategic analysis function should at all times steer clear of breaching competition law. Intentional deception is thus at all times off-limits, and it pays to be alert to the possibility of such tactics being used against you as analyst. The intermezzo at the end of this section discusses the phenomenon of intentional deception in business, and thus in strategic analysis in further detail.

## DISTINGUISHING BETWEEN FACT AND ANALYSIS AS INCOMING DATA POINTS

Question 4 in table 10.1 centres on the question of whether the new individual input data point presented to the analyst is a (raw) fact or the output of an analysis based on underlying but non-disclosed data points. In that case the new data point is itself the output of a previous analysis, which may be or is being presented as a fact.

There is an important difference between the two. In his biography of former US Federal Reserve President Alan Greenspan, Bob Woodward stresses Greenspan's obsession with raw data (Woodward, 2001). Greenspan did not want any pre-cooked analyses. He only wanted raw data, and insisted upon doing the modelling and the analysis himself. Doing so, he believed, ensured that no unintentional analytical flaws or biases crept into his view. Regardless of how history rates Greenspan's presidency, this is in principle a good habit for an analyst.[3]

However, there is a catch. For the quality of the ultimate strategic analysis deliverable to be top-notch, the fact remains that the analyst processing the raw data should be less biased than the sources who prepared the assessment of the raw data. This may depend on the degree of access the analyst has to contextual, often qualitative, information that accompanies the raw data point. The question of whether the analyst is better placed than the original source to make sense of what the raw data mean is applicable both in the case of Greenspan, where he could choose between raw data and some pre-cooked analysis, and that of MI5, which had no such choice. In chapter 11, this topic will be covered in more detail.

Another potential issue is that the analytic conclusion is put forward by the strategic analysis department but the underlying raw data are lacking. This was the example of Aiken Sneath in section 9.2. He presented no raw data but he did present a conclusion. The underlying evidence was not made available for analysis and possibly even unknown by the source (Macintyre, 2010b). In terms of dynamics, the phenomenon of lacking the raw data but reaching a conclusion is commensurate with having insufficient data to draw conclusions. In section 10.5 I will discuss what to do in such a case.

In conclusion, I would at all times recommend meticulously checking the nature of new individual input data points that are provided to analysts. It is a great way to prevent 'garbage in, garbage out.' Using the tables 10.1 to 10.3 may assist you in doing so. Executing these checks is the analyst's responsibility. The analyst is the ultimate gatekeeper in this process step.

## WHO IS THE SOURCE?

In section 9.3 on data and metadata we examined the relevance of the source of a data point (Johnson, 2009a):

> *"Who said it is often more important than what was being said."*

In this section I will elaborate a bit more on why and how sources matter to data points.

## SOURCES MAY HAVE VESTED INTERESTS

The Iraq weapons of mass destruction dossier showed that an individual source (code name 'Curveball,' as referenced earlier) can have a vested interest that is so strong that it enables him to deceive even the US government. Making the latter hear what they wanted to hear, the US set significant actions in motion. In strategic analysis, the psychological dynamics of individuals or groups striving to further their goals – or in business all too often, aiming to achieve their personal bonus targets – are identical to those in politics. Sources generously provide data to make their case or shine a spotlight on themselves, whereas they deny access to data that presents the risks of executing their proposed plan or that illustrate their failures. For a strategic analysis department to deliver objective assessments, the relevance of assessing the source and his personal interests is thus at least as important as it is in military intelligence. Strategy development in business often relates to power. Data are a means to influence strategy. So, data may at times be selectively used as a means to acquire or expand power.

## IDENTIFYING UNKNOWN SOURCES AND SENDERS

The material above implicitly presupposes that the data or information that reach the analyst's desk indeed have both the source and the sender as metadata. This, unfortunately, is not always the case. In this section, the first point of attention is therefore to identify a source that is not available. Once the sender and the source have been determined, a checklist of questions is provided to assess the source and/or the sender.

In instances where the channel, the sender and/or source of data or information are unknown, strategies to identify (part of) the channel, the sender and/or the source tend to vary according to collection method. Table 10.4 provides common steps to uncover metadata for data that reaches the analyst's desk without a proper sender/source signature. Table 10.4 also gives typical strategic analysis examples where metadata may be as relevant as the data itself.

| METHOD | STEPS TO TAKE TO IDENTIFY METADATA WITH A DATA POINT | RELATED EXAMPLES |
|---|---|---|
| IMINT | - Involve a reliable, unbiased subject matter expert; run an internet search on images of the subject matter looking for commonalities/hints; identify parameters within the picture that narrow down the range of possible source/metadata options.[4] | Picture of an unknown (competitor) product such as one acquired at a trade show. |
| MASINT | - Compare the outcome of the 'unknown source' sample against known samples, looking for fingerprints | Unknown product sample from a trade show. |
| HUMINT | - Depending on the nature of the relation with the last source in the communication channel, identify human sources to obtain (more) metadata with your data, including original sender and channel<br>- Proactively feed the new data or information to other (HUMINT) sources to elicit validation or at least reactions, or to get (more) metadata indirectly | Validating data (rumours) on upcoming transactions alluded to by sources who are either secretive and/or may have a bias. |
| OSINT | - Check a website's registration at www.whois.com<br>- Verify the credibility of the web address (URL); does the presented organization match with the address (for example, Governor.BankofTogo@hotmail.com is suspect).<br>- Check the professionalism and writing style of the site with that of the presented organization.<br>- Involve a reliable, unbiased subject matter expert. | Validating documents and websites that do not have a clear originator/owner or may have a different originator than it is purported to have. In other words, check for fakes/deceptions. |

TABLE 10.4 ▶▶▶ STEPS TO UNCOVER (DATA-RELATED) METADATA INCLUDING SOURCES AND/OR SENDERS BY COLLECTION METHOD AND RELATED EXAMPLES

## HOW TO TREAT A SINGLE RUMOUR AS A SOURCE

It is undoubtedly tempting to base an analysis on a single HUMINT source who passed along a rumour, for which the communication channel from the sender is not clear. This approach is not without risk in OSINT. One newspaper or online article that conveys a rumour data point may easily be perpetuated by another newspaper or online article, even when the second newspaper comes in a different language. The fact is, both are based on a biased or downright wrong root source.

There is a cultural dimension to this. Wina Wiroreno points out that presumably reputable print media in Indonesia, as an example of an emerging economy, may actually be less reliable when it comes to data correctness versus rumors. 'Print media,' she once said smiling, 'can be controlled (i.e. manipulated); rumors cannot,' (Wiroreno, 2008). Strategic analysts (and journalists) in Western cultures are in general advised to refrain from acting upon single unverified sources until additional corroborating evidence is available from an independent second source. In emerging countries, a case-by-case assessment of a rumor is highly recommended.

## ASSESSING THE SOURCE OF AN INDIVIDUAL DATA POINT

Assume for the remainder of this section that the data arriving at the analyst's desk either have a known source/channel/sender, or at least that some metadata have been obtained using the above approach and/or tools. This still necessitates considering the source's or sender's objectives for releasing the data. Table 10.5 provides questions (list not exhaustive) that are useful as a checklist to assess sources and their motives, prior to acting upon the data they provide. The table is based on work by Noble (Noble, 2004).

| | QUESTION | HUMINT | IMINT | MASINT | OSINT |
|---|---|---|---|---|---|
| 1 | What is the source's competency in the subject matter? How does the source see her own competency? | √ | | | √ |
| 2 | What is the relation between the source and the sender? | √ | √ | | √ |
| 3 | What is the source's track record in delivering new individual data points that proved to be correct? | √ | | | √ |
| 4 | What if any is the source's personal vested interest in this? | √ | | | √ |
| 5 | What interest does the source's organization have? | √ | √ | | √ |
| 6 | What is the reason the source had access to the data? | √ | √ | | √ |
| 7 | What if any bias could the source have? | √ | √ | | √ |
| 8 | What legal implications could working with this source have? | √ | √ | √ | √ |
| 9 | In summary: what does all of the above mean? What level of trustworthiness[5] could be attached to this source? | √ | √ | √ | √ |

**TABLE 10.5 ▶▶▶ QUESTION CHECKLIST ON ASSESSING THE SOURCE OF INDIVIDUAL DATA POINTS**

Question 1 is among the most relevant considerations in table 10.5. When a source has no competency in the subject matter, chances are that data will unintentionally get distorted, as a result of the source's ignorance. This is a sad truth but it is an inescapable fact of life for an analyst: treat the data with caution; the source/collector may have missed a point or two.

Counter-intuitively, the opposite case carries just as much distortion risk. When the collector/source is an expert in the subject matter, undesirable expert bias may creep in. What is presented as data may be bias. Thus, the analyst may find it challenging to discriminate facts from opinions or pre-cooked collector/source analysis. Even worse, the analyst may be accused of being dumb and/or stubborn (usually both) when not accepting the expert-provided data as 100% reliable and the best thing since sliced bread.

The analyst is advised to keep calm and professional, treating the expert with the utmost respect. In doing so, the expert may get well-deserved recognition. Once this positive attention has registered in the expert's mind, she may become increasingly open to accepting the analyst as an expert. Expert meets expert, with each possessing different expertise: analysis versus the subject matter at hand. Experts in the discipline of strategic analysis cannot do without rigorous data validation, no matter how high-grade the new individual data point inputs are. Thanks for understanding, dear fellow expert. In chapter 12, expert-related biases in strategic analysis will be covered in more detail.

## WHAT IS THE CHANNEL?

Diagram 10.3 depicts two channels through which data may travel from sender to receiver. For purposes of this book, the last chain link before the receiver is called the source. Validating the risk of data distortion as a consequence of the channel through which data travelled is a relevant feature of input data quality assurance. Table 10.6 provides a question-based checklist for assessing the risk that individual input data may be distorted specifically due to the data travelling through a specific channel between sender and receiver. Potential input data quality distortions that are attributable to the sender or the source, for example are not covered below but are examined in the respective related sections.

| | QUESTION | HUMINT | IMINT | MASINT | OSINT |
|---|---|---|---|---|---|
| 1 | Is the full channel between sender and receiver known? What steps make up the channel? | √ | √ | √ | √ |
| 2 | What possibilities for data distortion may result from this channel? Think of:<br>- Text translation: error risks from sender to receiver.<br>- The number of links in the channel (more links correspond with a higher data distortion risk) .<br>- Metadata that got lost in the transfer of the data, perhaps through irony in a remark by or body language of the sender. | √ | | | √ |
| 3 | In summary: What does it all mean? What data quality distortion risk was introduced through the way the data reached the analyst? So what channel-related reliability risk if any is to be used during the analysis? | √ | √ | √ | √ |

TABLE 10.6 ▶▶▶ QUESTION CHECKLIST FOR ASSESSING INPUT DATA DISTORTION RISK DUE TO CHANNELS

Specifically, for OSINT, it is possibile to trace the route between an individual computer and a website (in a Microsoft environment, at least). This sort of route-tracing may reveal relevant metadata for a sender/source that may assist in assessing individual input data or information quality. Similarly, dedicated web-based software tools are available that facilitate the evaluation of websites, for things like hoax detection. It is outside the scope of this book to discuss route-tracing and hoax detection sites in more detail, as these things are seldom relevant in strategic analysis for business, in contrast to law enforcement or business fraud detection.

## WHO IS THE SENDER?

Sender and source are not necessarily the same link in the chain from sender to receiver i.e., the analyst. A sender may be a company that is publishing its an annual report. An annual report may generally be viewed as representing the balanced opinion of the management of the company it describes. A sender, however, may also be a representative of the company whose role is to spin a business story in a certain direction. When an individual (who is not the CEO) speaks for an organization, a balanced opinion is no longer guaranteed. When reading an interview with an executive, he will likely highlight his own successes and will be deny or downplay information on parts of the business under his responsibility that have performed poorly.

In companies – in some more than in others – strategy formulation tends to have a political dimension. In a politicized atmosphere, externally accessible media may also be used as a channel to further personal interests. Assuming that the company's legal and/or communications department have vetted the interview, then all data in it *should* be true. So, the legitimate question should be whether the data make up the full truth.

It is also possible that an individual may not even have a representative picture of his current organization. Such an individual might be a representative of a company that is talking to its competitors. In such a case, he will not be able to share representative data, even when he would want to (Friedman, 2010a). The implicit message here is again one of caution. Cherish the virtue of doubt. As an analyst, keep your sceptical attitude towards sources – especially senders, with their vested their interests – prior to accepting their data as the truth, the full truth and nothing but the truth. Table 10.7 provides a checklist of questions to consider when assessing individual input data points in relation to their sender.

| | QUESTION | HUMINT | IMINT | MASINT | OSINT |
|---|---|---|---|---|---|
| 1 | What is the relation between the sender and the source? | √ | √ | | √ |
| 2 | What interest does the sender's organization have? | √ | | | √ |
| 3 | How representative is the sender's view of the view of the sender's organization? | √ | | | √ |
| 4 | How much does the sender know of the total picture of the organization she represents? | √ | | | √ |
| 5 | What would be the sender's personal intent? | √ | | | √ |
| 6 | What might the underlying intent of the sender's organization be? | √ | | | √ |
| 7 | What if any bias could the sender have? | √ | | | √ |
| 8 | What degree of reliability did previous data points issued by this sender have? | √ | √ | | √ |
| 9 | What could potential legal ramifications could result from working with this sender? | √ | √ | √ | √ |
| 10 | What does this all mean? What degree of trustworthiness can be attached to this sender relative to this individual input data point? | √ | √ | √ | √ |

TABLE 10.7 ▶▶▶ QUESTION CHECKLIST FOR ASSESSING THE SENDER OF INDIVIDUAL DATA POINTS

Let me suggest a word of caution regarding question 6 in Table 10.7. When assessing the intent of the sender's organization the analyst inevitably introduces the risk of ethnocentric bias, as we've discussed in previous chapters. Chapter 12 delves into ethnocentric bias in more detail and examines how to avoid delivering flawed analyses because of it. Here's a sound piece of expert advice (Bruce, 2008e):

> *"Being able to put yourself in the mind of the adversary (i.e., the competitor and sender) is the counterdeception analyst's most effective weapon."*

## WHAT IS MY SITUATION AS AN ANALYST?

Before touching on internal factors that may prompt the analyst to incorrectly assess individual input data, a final external factor is worth mentioning (Bruce, 2008e). External situational factors may affect an analyst's judgment when it comes to assessing individual input data quality. These considerations have been translated into questions in table 10.8. As the questions are truly situational, they apply to all data collection methods.

| | QUESTION | SUBSTANTIATION |
|---|---|---|
| 1 | How much has time pressure affected the data quality assurance process? | Time pressure may, to a certain extent and for some individuals/analysts, positively correlate with concentration and productivity. Overall, time pressure tends to correlate negatively with accuracy. In section 10.6, handling time pressure is also discussed in more detail. |
| 2 | How high were the stakes associated with the issue underpinning this strategic analysis work? | High stakes tend to be proportional to input data quality risk. When the return may be high - in the form of recognition for the analyst's contribution to a large project - an analyst with a high recognition need may be prone to letting down his guard on data quality, if only to show off with his work. |
| 3 | What power relationships surrounded the analyst in relation to the individual input data? | In the case of asymmetric power relations between a junior analyst and a senior company subject matter expert, an analyst doubting the expert or the director is culturally often unheard of. In such case expertise is all too easily mistaken for objectiveness. Chapter 12 covers the relation of analysts working with experts in more detail. Chapter 16 covers the analyst/decision-maker relation in more detail. |
| 4 | What is the risk profile for assessment mistakes due to the external factors affecting the analyst? | |

TABLE 10.8 ▶▶▶ QUESTION CHECKLIST ON SITUATIONAL RISK FACTORS FOR WRONGLY ASSESSING INPUT DATA

## INTERMEZZO: DECEPTION AND STRATEGIC ANALYSIS

Literature on deception in military intelligence may have its relevance for strategic analysis in a business environment. Prior to diving into deception as such, I would first like to share a quote, attributed to J.W. von Goethe, that may puts the notion of deception into perspective (Jervis, 2010d):

*"We are never deceived, we deceive ourselves."*

In other words: an adversary may feed us incorrect or intentionally incomplete data, analysts who mislead themselves have only themselves to blame for incorrect conclusions. What I refer to as 'deception' is the way in which an adversary feeds the analyst data, prompting the analyst to draw the wrong conclusions from these data.

I came across some insightful material that identifies four principles of deception (Bruce, 2008e). Deception not only relates to espionage and to military ambushes, but it's also at work when one tries to decipher corporate financial statements. There are so many ways to tell the truth and yet hide what really matters. Without becoming overly paranoid, knowing these principles may be an asset to an analyst:

- Truth – all deception works within the context of what is true.
- Denial – denying the target (for our purposes the analyst) access to selected aspects of the truth is the prerequisite to all deception.
- Deceit – all deception requires and utilizes deceit.
- Misdirection – deception depends on manipulating what the target (the analyst) registers.

Any deception requires the idea of *embedded truth* to work out well. Truth is critical in confirming the expectations of an analyst one may wish to deceive. In doing so, the deceiver builds up credibility with the analyst.

Denial is the second key element in deception. Denial in combination with sharing only selective truths results in the analyst getting parts of the truth, but not – repeat *not* – the full truth. Denial is covered in some detail in section 10.6 below.

It is perfectly legal for a company to put selective emphasis on some truths while, through selective denial, withholding others. No company is forced to tell the full truth as long as all that is being communicated is true.

Deceit is the third inevitable element in deception. Deceit might involve the analyst receiving individual data points that the sender intentionally distorted. Intentionally spreading false company data is a criminal offense. Distribution of untruths, even when done through obscure channels, will in the end be traceable and may lead to criminal prosecution. This makes deceit an operation that decent companies rightly shy away from at all times. As a result, deception as it is known from military history is rare in business (Macintyre, 2012), (Macintyre, 2010c).

Or is it?

Imagine two sales representatives Alan and Brian working for competing companies P and Q, respectively. Alan and Brian vaguely know each other from university, so there is some rapport to start with. When Alan and Brian happen to meet each other in the context of an industry association meeting, off the record information may casually be exchanged. Assume that neither Alan nor Brian is operating a voice recorder in their pocket. As a result, both correctly assess that there will be no documented trace of the conversation that is about to start. Lack of traceability is no guarantee that their subsequent conversation will not result in issues related to competition law issues later. In competition law, absence of evidence does not equate to evidence of absence.

Fortunately, P and Q are both decent companies. Therefore, Alan and Brian have been properly trained – and trained again – in compliance with applicable competition laws. Alan and Brian will therefore be unlikely to discuss prices, individual customers or other topics that are explicitly forbidden under competition law. So far, so good.

During occasions like this, Alan may in spite of his training say to Brian, "we are going to launch product XYZ in Canada next year." Let's assume product XYZ competes with a product line that company Q sells in Canada.

Technically, Alan's statement may be a breach of competition law, which in most countries would apply when a statement has not yet been made public in a press release or similar publication by company P. The moment Alan says this to Brian, the legal damage is done. In an attempt to control the damage, Brian's training led him to reply that he doesn't wish to discuss commercially sensitive issues with Alan. Once Brian has said this, company Q's legal counsel Simone should have a reasonable expectation that Brian will immediately terminate the conversation.

The statement, however, is still on Brian's mind when he returns to his office. Upon his return, Brian first goes to see Simone in the legal department to report the incident. Subsequently, he also goes to see company Q's strategic analyst Karl-Heinz, who works on the same floor, to share the news. As you would expect, Karl-Heinz also completed the compliance training.

Karl-Heinz cannot resist the temptation to show off with this competitively-significant news. He therefore wrongly believes* that he only needs to disguise the source to be legally sound. Naively, Karl-Heinz thus reports in writing in his next strategic analysis newsletter to top management that, "rumor has it that company P intends to launch product XYZ in Canada next year."

This anecdote shouldn't sound familiar in most companies, but unfortunately it probably does. That is why competition law training is a critical element in strategic analysis (and beyond).

In response to this rare early warning, company Q now prepares plans to avoid losing customers to company P's product launch in Canada. The strategic analysis department will be told to be on full alert for corroborating evidence of company P's preparations for the launch. The local sales office is directed to secure long-term sales commitments for product XYZ as quickly as possible. The sales staff, aiming for volume rather than value share, start to offer their best customers attractive discounts in exchange for long-term contracts. Their priority is to try to retain sales, ahead of news reaching the market of company Q starting sales operations in Canada, or even worse, of company Q actually approaching potential customers.

While company Q's defensive preparations in Canada proceed diligently and even run ahead of plan, company P's CEO is featured in a press release announcing that a new sales office has been opened in Mexico and that sales will commence there within the next few weeks.

This is what in deception is called 'deceit' and 'misdirection'. Sales representative Alan most likely provided sales representative Brian deliberately with false information, to compel company Q to focus on Canada. Whilst focusing on Canada, company Q's sales team in Mexico was not on top alert allowing company P to (more) quietly prepare its launch there.

Sales representative Alan certainly lost sales representative Brian's trust. The next time they met at the trade association, Brian grumpily approached Alan and expressed his dislike of having been steered in the wrong direction. Alan replied with a simple, "A few weeks after we met our Board changed the plans…" leaving Brian puzzled over whether Alan's deception was intentional or not. This proves that (Moore, 2007a):

*"It is easier to lead a target astray than to change his mind."*

* In fact, Karl-Heinz shouldn't have reported anything at all. Reporting non-public statements of adversaries on future plans that may affect markets may under some conditions be liable to scrutiny by anti-trust authorities. There are exceptions to this rule. Exceptions include cases where information on future investment plans may be shared between competitors. Such cases require the information to be shared under explicit non-disclosure agreements between companies for the exclusive purpose of assessing, for example, an M&A transaction. Caution is your mantra here. Involve legal counsel rather than act naively or overconfidently. Do not underestimate the impact that sentences in competition law cases may have on companies and even on individual company executives.

# 10.4 WHO AM I AS AN ANALYST?

In section 9.1 I already emphasized that in analysis the human mind matters most. Yet, regardless of the extraordinary capabilities of the mind, it is essential to remain critical of its outputs. What the mind observes via the senses is determined by the observer, almost as much as it is determined by an objective truth. In analysis, the lovely feline creature we met in chapter 9 is virtually omnipresent. Schrödinger's cat showed that some experiments theoretically can't be done because the measurement tools required for doing them would fundamentally affect the outcome of the experiments. In strategic analysis, a key measurement tool is the analyst herself. The need for individual analysts to recognize themselves as critical analysis tool is essential. How can you as an analyst attempt to understand the behaviour of others when you do not understand yourself (Heuer, 1999a)?

By now it has been scientifically accepted that internal biases do unconsciously affect human assessments of data or situations. Biases thus also apply to an analyst making assessments regarding individual input data correctness. Biases are systematic errors (Kahneman, 2011a). This in a way is good news, as systematic errors are predictable and by implication may even be preventable.

The root causes of an individual analyst's biases may be (Bruce, 2008e):

- Personal
- Cultural

Below I will briefly look into both of these influences. It is up to you as analyst to determine to what degree you can relate to this.

## PERSONAL BIASES HAVE THEIR ROOTS IN INDIVIDUAL EXPERIENCES AND NEEDS

Personal biases relate to personal experiences, needs and beliefs formed by the individual. These biases may relate to experience-based unique knowledge possibly gained over decades of working on strategic analysis projects. The latter knowledge is often of a tacit nature. Patterns of phenomena that in the analyst's personal experience have always been influential are among the hardest for the analyst to unlearn. In other words (Jervis, 2010e):

> *"It is perhaps the most confirmed proposition in cognitive psychology that once a belief or image is established, new material will become assimilated to it, with discrepant and ambiguous information being ignored or fitting into the established views."*

An experienced analyst is thus exceptionally valuable because in their memory they have built up multiple patterns that allow for fast and often correct processing of seemingly unrelated data. Over the course of the evolution of mankind, premature closure of one's mind proved an energy- and time-saver when facing previously experienced problems (see also in chapter 12). Analysts, however, by implication are also remarkably vulnerable when situations in the external environment change in such a way that previously built-up patterns no longer apply. These patterns may be referred to as mindsets. Mindsets have a role in allowing the human mind to treat multiple independent data points efficiently by clustering them. But it's important to recognize that human mindsets, no matter how valuable, are not free of bias (Heuer, 1999a):

> *"(Mindsets) tend to be quick to form but resistant to change."*

Moreover, mindsets that have been formed in human memories are normally not retroactively reorganized in response to new information (Heuer, 1999c). Once a mind-set is part of one's memory, it values data that support the mindset higher than data that do not do so. As a consequence, data that do not fit the original mindset do not become more memorable when the mindset changes in response to new data. Once rejected, data will always remain hard-to-find or even get lost in the human memory.

Table 10.9 presents a checklist focusing on personal biases. The list may not be exhaustive due to my own potential unconscious biases. The questions in table 10.9 are also not 100% mutually exclusive from the questions mentioned in table 10.8. The situation analysts find themselves in may determine who the analyst is or dares to be. Any overlap between questions in these tables hopefully only reinforces the relevance of identifying and countering the potential biases described.

| | QUESTION(S) | SUBSTANTIATION | SOURCE |
|---|---|---|---|
| 1 | What are the deep opinions that I am (un-) consciously holding as a person that may affect my assessment of this data point?<br><br>For example: What perceptions of supposed greatness do I have on my own company's performance and relatedly on a competitor's or customer's supposed weaknesses that may affect my assessment of this data point? | Once opinions have been formed in the mind, the mind is wired to keep them. The result is that data that confirm existing opinions unconsciously receive a higher reliability grading than those that challenge them.<br><br>*Truth only reveals itself when one gives up all preconceived ideas. Japanese proverb* | (Capozzi, 2011)<br><br>(Bradley, 2013)<br><br>(Houston, 2012b) |
| 2 | - What have I written before on this topic?<br>- How could this data point affect *earlier conclusions* that I wrote on this topic?<br>- Do I dare to change my stated opinion if I consciously feel the data point suggests I should? | Once an analyst has communicated a conclusion to customers, altering such conclusion the moment new data come in may induce feelings of failure and uncertainty. | (Johnston, 2005b) |
| 3 | What inferences do I make regarding this topic given this data point? | The more incomplete the data, the more readily the human brain often unconsciously fills in the gaps of a narrative, even in the absence of evidence to support doing so.<br><br>Optical illusions belong to the same inference category. The mind adds 'information' that is not present to match known patterns. | (Sinclair, 2010)[10]<br><br>(Kahneman, 2011b)<br><br>(Kahneman, 2011c) |
| 4 | What patterns do I automatically look for when seeing this data point? | *Humans are extremely good at finding patterns, even when there is none: you rarely find what you are not looking for and usually do find what you are looking for?* | (Cooper, 2005a) |

TABLE 10.9 ▶▶▶ CHECKLIST ON PERSONAL BIASES THAT MAY UNCONSCIOUSLY AFFECT ASSESSMENTS

## CULTURAL BIASES ORIGINATE FROM AN ANALYST'S SOCIAL ENVIRONMENT

In addition, cultural biases may affect an analyst. An analyst acquires cultural biases as an inhabitant of a specific social environment. Culture may both mean the organizational culture the analyst has to operate in, or the broader cultural norms of the society in which the organization at large operates. The culture of a society at large also determines methods of problem solving that may be applied by analysts. In an Asian context, group-based methods of problem solving may, for culture reasons, be preferred over individual methods.

The opposite may be the case in Western cultures, which are more individualistic, where and individuals generally preferring to take all the credit for an analysis – and indeed assuming all the risk when such analysis proves flawed. Six common factors tend to contribute to cultural biases (Bruce, 2008e):

- Knowledge
- Morals
- Beliefs
- Customs
- Cognitive styles
- Habits

As culture hides itself best from its own participants, at times it is hard to see where seemingly objective knowledge has been culturally determined. Being aware that culture matters is is indeed valuable, but that recognition is unfortunately no guarantee against making culturally biased assessments.

## KNOWING AND RECOGNIZING BIASES DOES NOT PROTECT AGAINST HAVING BIASES

Being aware of biases does unfortunately not protect against being seduced by biased thinking (Kahneman, 2011d):

*"Teaching psychology is mostly a waste of time."*

Kahneman seems to me to suggest that increasing the awareness of an individual's potential failures in their assessments doesn't mean that such awareness helps these individuals subsequently minimize their own biased thinking.

No matter how sober this conclusion seems to be, I do not believe that the above observation justifies ignoring biases. On the contrary, I am definitely positive on the value of doing so. Even when little can be done against internal biases, it remains remarkable how well awareness of biases can help the analyst recognize the biases of others (Kahneman, 2011e). This recognition, when looking at the business environment of a company, will always be a core task for a strategic analyst. Recognizing the flawed logic of a competitor's strategy undoubtedly is a great analyst asset.

## AN ORGANIZATION'S CULTURE MAY LEAD TO BIASED ASSESSMENTS

Cultural biases indirectly relate to individual data point correctness assessments. Rather than looking at the data point as such, an analyst may wonder about the impact in the organizational culture of accepting the new data point as reliable. When reliable, analyst should ask herself:

- How could this new data point affect earlier conclusions that I wrote on this topic?
- How does doing so resonate with my customer?
- How does doing so make me look among my peers?
- How would the strategic analysis function head react to my conviction that this new data point is reliable?

Once an analyst has communicated a conclusion to customers, altering such a conclusion the moment new and presumably more reliable data become available may for organizational reasons be challenging. The easy way out for the analyst – depending on the culture of the organization – is simply to question the reliability of the new data, and after doing so to ignore the new data point. A strategic analysis function and a company at large that has developed this behaviour may very well be able to significantly reduce its strategic analysis expenditures.

In such an organization, intelligence will only be used when it confirms existing views. Analysis will never dare to challenge... and that is not a healthy situation. An analyst should feel safe when expressing a contrary view based on new data. Whether the new data require the company to revisit decisions is another thing, but at least that option should never be ruled out in advance.

# 10.5 SYNTHESIS ON INDIVIDUAL DATA CORRECTNESS ASSESSMENT

In section 10.3 we described quality assurance checks related to external risk factors and individual input data. Section 10.4 concentrated on questions that the strategic analyst should ask himself relating to an internal origin of individual input data quality issues. In the daily practice of strategic analysis, a pragmatic balance is needed between following procedure and (sufficiently fast) progress. It obviously doesn't make sense to ask all of the questions in the above sections for each and every data point. Rather, the questions on internal and external origins of individual input data quality issues are provided as checklists. An experienced strategic analyst is likely to have embedded the above questions in their analytic mindset. They may even have thought of some other questions that are relevant to a particular case. The objective of the above sections is to inspire the analyst to internalize an analytical mindset. Thinking of these questions should become automatic – the analyst should trust neither individual input data nor her own perception of individual input data at face value.

Diagram 10.4 summarizes the result of the individual input data correctness assessment. The diagram depicts four situations: two where the analyst correctly assessed the quality of the input data and two where the analyst did not do so.

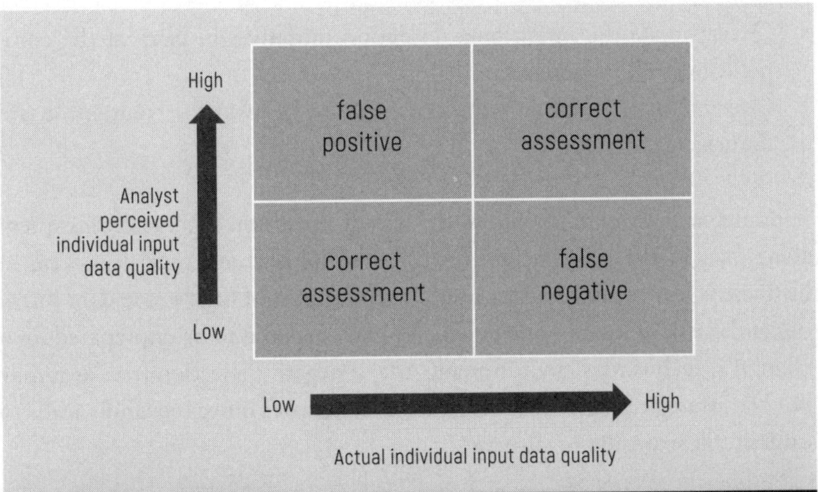


DIAGRAM 10.4 ▶▶▶ INDIVIDUAL INPUT DATA PERCEPTION VS. CORRECTNESS ASSESSMENT

When the analyst has meticulously applied the questions from the lists provided in the above sub-sections, individual input data of poor quality should have been rejected (bottom left in the matrix) and, high-grade data should have been accepted (top right in the matrix).

## FALSE NEGATIVES: IGNORING A CORRECT SIGNAL

In strategic analysis a false negative is defined as a conclusion that input data are false and can thus be rejected, when in reality they are actually correct. Rejecting high quality input data is a serious but not uncommon failure in strategic analysis work (bottom right in the matrix). In military intelligence examples, the rejection of high grade intelligence has been documented and analysed.[6] With the outbreak of both the First and Second World Wars, high-grade intelligence had been ignored, with dire consequences.

The risk of false negatives thus makes it imperative that the analyst uncover the root causes and ascertain how these flaws crept into the process. Additionally the analyst needs to explore how to prevent them from happening in the first place.

When rejecting high-grade intelligence as too good to be true, the receiving side might:

- Underestimate the quality of its own collection organization and efforts.
- Overestimate the professionalism of the data protection in place at the competitor or military adversary.

- Overestimate the intentional deception initiatives in place at the competitor or military adversary.
- Overrate its own (often ethnocentric) view of what the competitor will do next.

In strategic analysis for business, the fear of deception is generally less prevalent than in the military, given that intentional competitor deception in business is less common. As a result, the rejection of high-grade data introduces the risk of leaving one's own company exposed to or unprepared for a change in its business environment. A false negative rejection (rare as it may be) of a strategic analysis warning on a competitor's move inevitably leads to undesirable exposure to surprises.

## FALSE POSITIVES: PERCEIVING EITHER NOISE OR ABSENCE OF NOISE TO BE A SIGNAL

False positives in strategic analysis are more common (top left in the matrix). Overestimating the value of a data point is not uncommon in our line of work. False positives come in two flavours:

- Mistaking noise for a signal.
- Mistaking the absence of noise for a signal of absence.

## MISTAKING NOISE FOR A SIGNAL

The most common occurance of false positives when a source believes that something is about to happen when in fact it isn't. Sounding a warning about such false positives is known in the trade as 'crying wolf'. In this case, the strategic analysis department that was misled by the source may send out a warning signal to management about something that's never really going to happen. Crying wolf can:

- Waste the analyst's company's preparation time and efforts for the wolf (that never came).
- Reduce the analyst's or the strategic analysis function's credibility with management.
- Lead management to ignore the analyst's next, possibly correct, warning.

The potential consequences of false-positive fatigue can be seen in the US military's complete and utter surprise at Pearl Harbor in 1941 (Wohlstetter, 1965a):

*"Admiral Kimmel[7] and his staff were tired[8] of checking out Japanese submarine reports in the vicinity of Pearl Harbor. In the week preceding the attack they had checked out seven, all of which were false."*

## MISTAKING THE ABSENCE OF NOISE FOR THE SIGNAL OF ABSENCE

The opposite is also a logical possibility but is less common: that a source has it that something will not happen and it happens nonetheless. This misinterpretation can also have a negative impact on your company: you can find yourself unprepared for something that is going to happen.

The relevance of individual input data quality assessment becomes apparent when you realize that false negatives by definition lead to surprises for which your company is not prepared. False positives can produce their own unpleasant surprises, when the incorrect input data have it that nothing much is going to happen. A false positive, however, may also lead to an organization being over-prepared for a wolf that never shows up. This is obviously also undesirable. As trust comes on foot but goes on horseback, the strategic analysis function cannot afford too many false negatives or false positives as compared to its number of correct assessments.

The best way to avoid either false positives or false negatives is to make 'foxy' predictions, which I will discuss in chapter 12. Ideally, data of perceived doubtful quality are neither over-valued, leading to false positives, nor rejected altogether, leading to false negatives. This is a fine balance that each analyst will have to find – preferably in an open discussion with the decision-maker (see chapter 16).

# 10.6 DATA SET COMPLETENESS ASSESSMENT

A complete data set without known unknowns – and especially without the even uglier unknown unknowns – is a dream scenario in strategic analysis that rarely comes true. It may well be impossible to do strategic analysis work without the peril of unknown unknowns. Regardless, it is imperative in strategic analysis to minimize unknowns.

## THREE ATTRIBUTES OF STRATEGIC ANALYSIS WORK GUIDE DATA-COMPLETENESS EFFORTS

An analyst may at a particular moment in time be pressured to deliver a view on a topic. In such cases it is necessary to balance the desire for data completeness, for timeliness and for high analytic quality. From a quality-assurance standpoint, data completeness is often but not always a boundary condition. In strategic analysis, the function head assigning projects for execution (and providing the necessary funding) should stress the importance of three non-content project attributes:

- cost (read: cheap)
- speed (read: fast)
- quality (read: top-quality)

An experienced function head may emphasize combination of two of these three attributes, but should in that case de-emphasize the third attribute.

A project can be done quickly and cheaply, but in that case with that slap-dash approach, quality-control will inevitably suffer. It can be done quickly and be of top-quality, but this will have interesting cost implications. Finally, it can be done cheaply and be of top-quality (and be based on an almost complete data set), but in that case it may take unreasonably long to complete. The latter compromises or completely eradicates the usefulness of the project deliverable. In summary, the logical assumption is that upon heavily emphasizing two attributes, the third by definition cannot be obtained.

The function head must require a workable compromise between these three attributes. For every project a match is needed between the specific project's demands regarding delivery time requirements (when management must reach a decision) and budget constraints, whilst at least allowing for minimum strategic analysis quality standards. The latter almost by definition relates to a minimum degree of data set completeness.

The three attributes – time, quality and cost each matter – but time generally matters most (Kirkland, 2010); (Bryan, 2009). This is true even when a possible data set is not yet complete. The importance of an analysis deliverable's timing is illustrated in the quote below (McLaughlin, 2008b):

> *"Because analysts are almost always dealing with incomplete information, there is a natural tendency and desire to wait for the latest data. An assessment that is correct and complete in every way but arrives too late to affect the policymakers' decision is one of the most regrettable outcomes in the analytic profession."*

There are times when being able to rapidly make decisions is more important than delivering analytically solid and balanced reports. In such cases the analyst would be well advised to deliver a 'situation report' in a timely manner than a thoroughly thought-through analysis that is delivered too late. In the analyst reporting'… (McLaughlin, 2008b):

> *"…it is (in the meaning of: remains) critical for the analyst to distinguish between what he or she knows and does not know and then to spell out what he or she thinks in the light of that"*

In short, meeting project deadlines is of utmost importance. The need for timeliness overrides other demands. The overriding objective – with delivery timing being a given – is to optimize budget and quality. Normally the budget for an individual strategic analysis project tends to be proportional to the value upside of the business issue at stake. This boundary condition further narrows down the freedom to specify quality standards, as now a timing deadline and an upper limit for the budget are clearly laid out.

The strategic analysis function therefore has to adjust cost and efforts for data collection, analysis and reporting to meet both a project's budget and time requirements. This is to be done whilst maximizing data set completeness, as the latter tends to be linearly proportional with the deliverable quality.

## THE MERIT OF DATA-COMPLETENESS MAY DIFFER IN DIFFERENT PROJECTS

A complicating factor is that incomplete data and/or lack of tangible complete evidence does not always have to be an analytical problem. Good old Mr Sneath (introduced in section 9.3) made a judgment regarding Ivor Montagu, in the absence of complete evidence. In other words, his was an analysis based on an incomplete data set. Recall that Sneath was ultimately proven right, even though his accusations weren't validated until two decades later. The data, even when incomplete, happened to be solid enough to act upon. The missing substantiating data – the hard, cold evidence – was apparently not critical.

In contrast, the 'solid evidence' that the US government presented on Iraq's WMD program prior to the invasion of Iraq in 2003 proved incorrect (Pillar, 2012). Critical data points were missing. This led to Rumsfeld's proverbial 'unknown unknowns'. These examples only serve to show that there is no silver bullet regarding what to do in the case of incomplete data. Rather, the question becomes how to minimize critical input data set incompleteness. If the latter is inevitable because of time and/or budget constraints the analyst must figure out how to manage a critically incomplete input data set. This is a data processing topic which I will discuss in chapter 11.

Let's now look at intentional and unintentional (competitor) denial of data leading to data set incompleteness. A synthesis on data set completeness will be presented in section 10.7.

## INTENTIONAL DATA DENIAL

There are countless opportunities for competitors to engage in intentional data denial. A company, any company really, permanently faces a dilemma. On the one hand, stakeholders[9] call for the company to become increasingly open and transparent. On the other hand, the company knows that the more information it releases, the more easily its competitors will predict its next moves, knowing its competences and intent through the highly detailed public documents and records that it needs to publish. Openness generally erodes a company's competitive edge and ability to surprise. Especially for listed companies, or for companies aiming to issue bonds on public markets, strict transparency is mandatory… so there is not really a choice. Privately-owned and/or family-owned companies and companies below a certain net sales size have lower requirements regarding the release of data into the public domain.

Smaller companies often only publish a balance sheet, but no profit and loss accounting, in their chamber of commerce records. In such cases, even company data providers like Dun & Bradstreet cannot offer detailed records, as they depend heavily on publicly released information. A general rule is that small and private companies have more options for denial, making strategic analysis of them tougher. This is for them a competitive edge.

There is a catch, though, even when data looks complete in company-published records. For highly transparent, listed companies, this relative openness should not be confused with objectivity. A competitor's company, especially in its communications to shareholders, will always emphasize its successes and strengths and understandably much less so its failures and weaknesses. A presentation to the financial analyst community by a public company will only contain truths, loads of them, but will rarely present the full truth. *Caveat emptor* (let the buyer beware). The upbeat propaganda of corporate statements may convince investors but also intimidate competitors. Propaganda may be true; it is usually not the full truth.

## UNINTENTIONAL DATA DENIAL

Unintentional data denial has two common origins: one is rather straightforward while the other is more understated.

In the straightforward version, the origin is that the competitor or any other sender provides the data in the public domain but the analyst or his collector is for some reason or another unable to find the data. This should not happen, but it does. Despite time pressure, at least the critical issues should be surfaced. Data collection should subsequently be focused on finding those data that are key to resolving the critical issues.

In the subtler version unintentional data denial is referred to as selection bias. In statistical language, selection bias could be defined as basing conclusions on characteristics of a group of data generated by a non-representative sample of that group of data. Put simply: when you want to understand what motivates a group of people, you get a selection bias when you only interview males. No matter how diverse the group of males that you interview, you will by definition overlook what motivates females. This is a simple example. In reality, a selection bias is a trap that is difficult to avoid (Denrell, 2005).

Selection bias typically occurs in management books that compare sets of companies; think of *In Search of Excellence* so to speak. As poorly performing firms have failed and disappeared, such publications tend to be biased in their reviewing of companies. The companies that are reviewed are more successful than average, thanks to their very existence, as those that failed no longer feature in the data set.

Reviewing the attractiveness of an industry, any industry, by looking at its current set of players and their (financial) performance thus almost by definition yields an overestimation.

This is perhaps the most striking difference between business strategic analysis on the one hand and military intelligence on the other. Failures in military intelligence, like 9/11 and Pearl Harbor, are well documented. Successes, however, are kept confidential to prevent the methodologies or sources that underpinned them to become known and thus useless. Uninformed observers (most of us), may end up with the impression that such services are delivering dismal performance, based on intentionally denied data on successes. In business, the exact opposite seems to be the case. Common failures in business, except for the spectacular ones like Enron, are not widely publicized. Failed run-of-the-mill businesses have neither news value nor aspirational attractiveness to anyone but those most closely involved.

This results in the question: how to value an industry where eight out of ten companies make decent returns and two fail, either through going out of business or by being acquired for a song? There is no magic formula for correcting the missing data due to selection bias. When estimating the relevance of the missing data becomes challenging, the analyst can do nothing much more than add a firm disclaimer, however unsatisfactory that solution may be.

# 10.7 SYNTHESIS OF DATA SET COMPLETENESS FACTORS

Similar to the synthesis in section 10.5 on data correctness, this section will provide a synthesis of data completeness factors. Diagram 10.5 summarizes the meta-result of the data set completeness assessment. The diagram depicts four situations: two where the analyst correctly assessed the completeness of the input data set and two where the analyst did not do so.

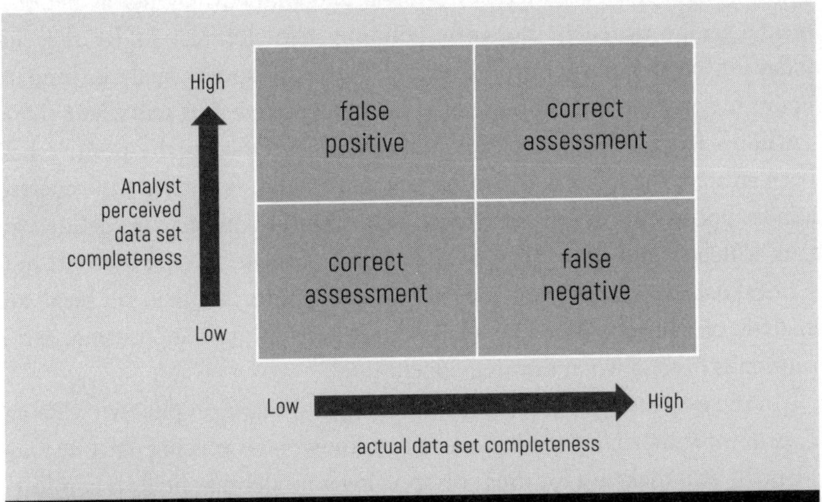


**DIAGRAM 10.5 ▶▶▶ DATA SET COMPLETENESS ASSESSMENT**

## FALSE POSITIVES

False positive outcomes are generated when either collection efforts were flawed or the analyst failed to properly brief the designated collector (or both). False positive outcomes may point at overconfidence by the analyst (Silver, 2013b). The analyst may think he has a complete data set when it in fact simply his perception of what the solution of the puzzle should look like. Such perceptions are based on patterns.

Human craving for recognizable patterns in their environment goes back to the Stone Age (Silver, 2013c). In the absence of natural defenses, human survival depended on outsmarting natural predators. Timeliness of the results of life-and-death threat analysis in the Stone Age determined survival, as facing a predator may not have allowed for the luxury of a lengthy analysis. In the evolutionary survival-of-the-fittest sub-species of the human race, the dimension of analytical speed may have mattered: the faster the analysis, the higher the chance of survival.

To me the commonality of this phenomenon with strategic analysis work is striking: timeliness trumps perfection (Kirkland, 2010). The human ability to recognize a pattern in a threat and immediately act as per the mental recipe stored in the corresponding mental threat folder may in today's information age introduce flaws. Wired for speedy analysis, human brains may see patterns in noise or at least incomplete data sets where there are none. In that case, we create a false positive. Once a false positive has been created, the reflex is not to continue searching. As a result, the analyst almost unconsciously misses critical data. Critical data may be defined as data which would have changed the analyst's conclusions (Frank, 2011a). Critical data are diagnostic – they are the data points that make or break an analytic conclusion. When an analyst knows critical data are missing, extra caution is needed when drawing conclusions.

In the next chapter I will address the topic of managing known missing data in more detail. Even when an analyst knows he is missing data, he may mentally still make up for them by applying a model that he feels comfortable with. The mind is more of a machine made for jumping to conclusions than for balanced considerations. Thus, the analyst's model may barely fit the scarce data that are available, but it does fit them enough for the analyst to see what he wants to see. Again, the delusion of recognizing a false positive pattern plays a part. Confidence comes with positive experiences: being right builds confidence. That is why experts are a special risk category in this context. Experts have so often been right in the past that it turned them into experts in the first place. Being right many times over may have contributed to their overconfidence. How to work with experts as sources in strategic analysis is covered separately, in chapter 12.

## FALSE NEGATIVES

At the other end of the spectrum is the false negative. This phenomenon arises when the analyst has the critical data in his set but possibly being afraid of unknown unknowns, fails to reach actionable conclusions. Forecasters (including strategic analysts within a firm) may well be compared with chess players. Research points out that (Silver, 2013d):

> *"Amateur chess players, when presented with a chess problem, often frustrated themselves by looking for the perfect move, rendering themselves incapable of making any move at all. Chess masters, by contrast, are looking for a good move – and certainly if at all possible the best move in a given position – but they are more forecasting how the move might favorably dispose their position than trying to enumerate every possibility."*

Assessing data set completeness thus requires striking a balance between the unjustified fear of not making the perfect analysis and the overconfidence of unjustified *déjà vu*, whilst actually looking at something new.

The chess masters teach a lesson to strategic analysts here. Rather than wait for the final piece of data to come in and for it to be too late for your deliverable, use techniques developed in and for forecasting to manage the uncertainties – and report in a timely manner.

With this conclusion, I close this chapter on input data quality assurance. The next chapter focuses on what to do when data are lacking or when different data sources deliver input data that happen to contradict each other.

CHAPTER 11

# DATA-SET PREPARATION

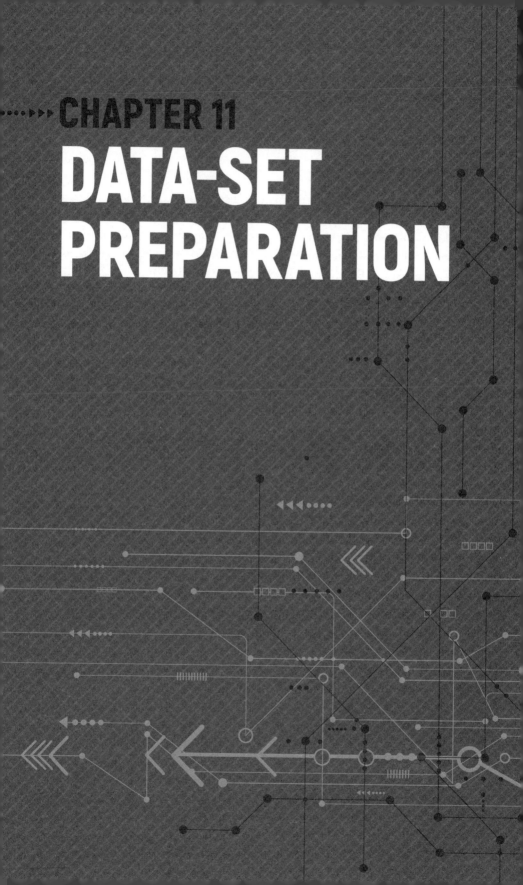

# 11.1 INTRODUCTION

In the previous chapter, I focused on getting the individual input data right. Thus, I discussed at quite some length how to filter out incorrect data from the output of data collection efforts. In the previous chapter I also covered data set completeness. Implicitly it seemed the availability of enough data-points was a given. If only we could grab the rotten apples that may even be fruits of (self-)deception from the basket, we could then assemble a nice basket of data apples. This basket is in fact what we've been referring to as a data set. Having thus created a data set, we could actually start processing the data in an analytically sound way. There are, however, at least two questions the previous chapter does not answer:

- What if we do not have enough data in the first place?
- What if we have conflicting data in our data set, but we cannot tell which are the correct data and which are not?

Prior to discussing data set processing at large in chapter 12, I will give some answers to the above two questions in this chapter.

# 11.2 MANAGING INCOMPLETE DATA SETS

## CAUSES FOR INCOMPLETE DATA SETS MAY BE INTERNAL AND EXTERNAL

Through analysing eight military intelligence failures it has been concluded that denial has a positive correlation with intelligence failure (Bruce, 2008d). Not surprisingly it pays off for companies, or countries, to protect their secrets. The absence of data serves as a prompt for analysts to fill in the data points with assumptions. The failures that have been observed resulted not so much from wrong data but from incorrect assumptions. This results in:

*"...the triumph of faulty assumptions over the absence of needed information."*

In the absence of enough high-quality data, getting the analysis right becomes increasingly difficult. Understandably, when collection for whatever reason fails, analysis becomes more challenging. A country's efforts at denial are the analyst's worst enemy, but self-denial may be just as effective in preventing good analysis.

Causes of self-denial may vary. Creating a list of such causes isn't likely to be exhaustive due to the analyst's lack of the imagination. It is and remains hard to make a list of things that you have not imagined. These unimagined hindrances might include:

- Weak briefings, leading to poor collection plans.
- Poor information sharing among analysts, or between analysts and the organization at large.

- Lack of imagination concerning future competitor (or customer or consumer or supplier or NGO) plans, leading to overlooked collection topics; the most common cause is ethnocentrism (see chapter 14).
- analyst complacency – such as failing to collect enough data, when the first data that come in seem to validate a particular view. This is premature closing (see chapter 12).

Denial may thus negatively affect the analytic output; having to fill in the blanks obviously carries more risk than working with a largely complete and correct data set. Knowing the power of denial makes an even better case for a company (your company in particular) to:
- Deny critical data to the public, and to competitors where legally possible.
- Deny competitors access to your data by protecting your organization as effectively as possible against competitor intelligence collection efforts.

When, possibly as a result of denial, data are known to be missing, a characteristic strategic analysis dilemma emerges. In the case of known missing data, two approaches form the extremes of the analysts' options:
- The overcautious approach.
- The overconfident approach.

## THE OVERCAUTIOUS APPROACH

When an analyst takes an overly cautious approach, the resulting deliverable sticks to known facts, limits the analysis to a minimum and acknowledges, if not emphasizes in the deliverable, what is known to be unknown. When as a result, however, no decision can be taken by management on the matter at hand, it renders the strategic analysis function rather unhelpful. Management (often unconsciously) thinks that it pays for results rather than explanations, so being offered data rather than conclusions has its drawbacks for the analyst.

## THE OVERCONFIDENT APPROACH

The over-confident approach for a strategic analysis department is to analyse "too much from too little" (Bruce, 2008e). Even when data are limited or even random, perceived known solutions to the question at hand may be favoured by the analyst. In the latter case the analyst may implicitly overrate the chance of having found a possible known solution.

In section 10.7 I described the strong human urge to recognize patterns in random data. When an analyst fails to recognize a pattern, he blames himself for not understanding the data, rather than acknowledging that the data may be random or unrelated (Heuer, 1999d). In practice, no matter how limited the data set, an analyst will go to lengths to find a recognized pattern. With the pattern a narrative and a conclusion will follow, offering management, most of all the analyst themselves, the comfort of results rather than explanations.

In analysing too much from too little, analysts may in the process also overestimate the consistency in the thinking (or the execution quality) of the outside company whose next steps they aim to predict. Decisions in companies are taken by groups of humans. Such groups are neither always consistent, nor always rationally acting in their group's best interest. They may simply make mistakes. Luck, either good or bad, may affect the outcome of their decisions. Strategic analysis, no matter how professionally executed, will never be an exact science when it tries to predict the probabilities of fundamentally unpredictable events.

In conclusion, whether a pattern really applies will only become clear when sufficient and critical data is made available. In analysing too much from too little, the analyst may be able to initially please management with firm conclusions. The pleasure, however, may not last when conclusions later prove to be wrong. So, what to do?

## THE SITUATION REPORT

When the proverbial fog of war is still thick, an analyst should stick to situation reports (McLaughlin, 2008b). Such reports emphasize what data are known rather than what those data mean, although the latter should be included as well. Situation reports should also contain add-ons – that we'll categorize as the late, the possible and the impossible forms of add-ons – to the data set:

- **Late**
  A timing roadmap that spells out when facts/analyses will be available to management; for example; MASINT analyses from a laboratory that may still take time to complete.
- **Possible**
  A list of perceived critical unknown data that so far have proved impossible to find. Indicate why data have not been found and what options are being pursued to find them. Also indicate the chances of a positive outcome and, when applicable, provide the related cost.

- **Impossible**
  A list of what perceived critical unknown data are unlikely to legally become available at all.

The combination of known facts, a sense of when additional data will be available and a sense of how the analyst intends to collect missing data provides management with the relevant choices they face at that moment in time. The decision-maker is thus put in a position to do exactly what she is supposed to do: make a decision. On the question at hand, management may choose to either make a decision now or to wait for more data to become available. The latter may require allocating budget to intensify collection efforts – perhaps by buying a report that may contain perceived critical, yet previously unknown data.

With both overcautious and the overconfident approach, the data set as such remains unchanged. Data-sets, however, may in some cases be expanded by an analyst, provided the expansion is well-documented and is executed methodically. In doing so, the analyst starts to fill in the blanks.

## FILLING IN THE BLANKS

Filling in the blanks means that the analyst thinks he has a reliable model of the truth of the matter at hand that can be safely applied to describe the reality. With the output of his model firmly in hand he (often implicitly) believes it to be accurate. Or, at least, accurate enough to allow the model to generate data that may replace real but missing data without jeopardizing the quality of the subsequent analytical output. It is obvious that modelling phenomena that are by definition not fully understood is not without risk (Box, 2005):

*"All models are wrong. Some models are useful."*

Models are at best predictive constructs of reality, but never represent reality itself.[1] Filling in the blanks as a method to combat data denial has its inevitable risks. These risks vary along two dimensions: interpolation or extrapolation, and quantitative or qualitative data sets. Table 11.1 summarizes both the opportunities and the risks of filling in the blanks. Filling in the blanks in a data set and forecasting are methodologically comparable and are for practical reasons discussed simultaneously in this section.

| | QUANTITATIVE DATA SET | | QUALITATIVE DATA SET | |
|---|---|---|---|---|
| | Opportunity | Risk | Opportunity | Risk |
| **EXTRAPOLATION** (FORWARD PREDICTION OR FORECASTING) | Multiple statistical methods are available. | For phenomena that change gradually, models may be useful, provided they are not used 'out-of-sample' (Silver, 2013a). | Understanding past successes and failures of top executives in competitor organizations may be remarkably predictive for their future choices. | Multiple pitfalls are covered in Chapter 14.<br><br>Bias awareness and a 'fox-like' attitude may mitigate risks (Silver, 2013e) |
| **INTERPOLATION** | Multiple statistical methods are available. | Risks are generally moderate when the phenomenon that underlies the data changes gradually.<br><br>Risks are unknown when this is not the case. | Interpolating qualitative data occurs in strategic analysis when reconstructing past decision-trees in competitor organizations as input to assessing their future choices. | |

TABLE 11.1 ▶▶▶ OPPORTUNITIES AND RISKS ASSOCIATED WITH FILLING IN THE BLANKS IN INCOMPLETE DATA SETS

Consider a quantitative data set such as that given below. This data set may represent net sales of a competitor over time in (€) millions. Assume it is now July 2013. The year-to-year sales data would look like this:

| | |
|---|---|
| 2008 | €174 million |
| 2009 | €183 million |
| 2010 | ... |
| 2011 | €196 million |
| 2012 | €209 million |
| 2013 | ... |
| 2014 | ... |

For the interpolation of the 2010 figure it looks like a safe bet to use a linear growth model. It should be recognized that this is done in the absence of contextual data. This makes it risky: the bet may look safer than it is. In this case, the 2010 net sales are estimated at €190 million (183 + (196-183)/2, rounded off). However, the forward prediction of the net sales for 2013 and 2014 will be even less straightforward. To discuss extrapolations, I would like to take you on a trip to the wonderful world of mediocristan and extremistan, created by Nicholas Taleb (Taleb, 2007a).

## DISCERNING BETWEEN MEDIOCRISTAN AND EXTREMISTAN REQUIRES CONTEXTUAL DATA

For foward-looking predictions, we first have to distinguish between mediocristan and extremistan. In mediocristan, change is gradual. A great example of mediocristan is the population size of a country. It will neither shrink by half nor double from one year to the next, lacking large-scale disasters, or fertility or migration booms. For extremistan, there is no such certainty. In extremistan, a parameter may change by any percentage up or down the next year. Share prices of some companies typically dwell in extremistan. They may shrink by half or double the next year, subject to unpredictable investor appetite – or a sudden investor dislike – for the stock. Parameters in extremistan are unpredictable as models. Company shares, like commodities, are traded on markets. Most of these markets are firmly situated in extremistan. This may relate to the fact that price developments at these markets are dominated by herd behaviour. The herd may move, but it is hard to say whether there will be movement, and if there is, when it might occur. However, once it does, the whole herd will move. This herd phenomenon I believe to be part of the human condition. It has been described by the Nineteenth Century writer Mackay (Surowiecki, 2005a). To put it mildly, Mackay did not hold the collective judgment that is driving the herd in high esteem:

> *"Men, it has been well said, think in herds. It will be seen that they go mad in herds, while they only recover their senses slowly, and one by one."*

It is this madness in extremistan that fundamentally makes it impossible to predict herd-related phenomena using models. Or, to use another metaphor, madness is the root cause of the proverbial black swan that may variously bring good luck or bad luck [Taleb, 2007b].

The first question for the forward prediction of the net sales of the competitor is now: will the competitor in 2013 and 2014 be in mediocristan or in extremistan? Predicting the net sales is straightforward when assuming mediocristan, but much less so when assuming extremistan.[2]

Statistical tools are great, but qualitative contextual data are in these cases critical for choosing the prediction to be made, based on the assumptions and tools. The relevance of such contextual data is commonly stressed (Pollack, 2004]); (Makridakis, 1990); (Guszcza, 2012):

> *"Context is crucial to understanding any intelligence assessment. No matter how objective the analyst may be, he or she begins with a set of basic assumptions that create a broad perspective on an issue; this helps the analyst to sort through evidence."*

> *"In cases where the data are messy, incomplete, ambiguous and/or of limited quantity, considerable institutional knowledge, domain expertise and common sense is needed to effectively make sense of it."*

Another way to describe the critical need for contextual data in strategic analysis and business strategy development is to refer the soft underbelly of hard data (Mintzberg, 1998):

> *"Much information important for strategy making never does become hard fact."*

The message is thus that in strategic analysis, quantitative data can be reliably predicted only when qualitative contextual data are presumed to be reasonably well known and when these data are not affected by biases.[3] Too often, forward predictions are implicitly assuming mediocristan. Without elucidating the implicit assumptions, the prediction is purely like-for-like, to use the accountancy term. Unfortunately, like-for-like or mediocristan is rare in most human activities (Taleb, 2007c).

The relevance of obtaining contextual qualitative data, even for quantitative predictions, has been stressed (Silver, 2013f). As a forecaster, Silver always looks for a mix of quantitative and qualitative contextual data, with the latter being highly valued. The broader he can source qualitative contextual data, the more he is able in his forecasting profession to develop a broad consensus view. This is a smart approach in strategic analysis. Broad is here defined as 'multi-disciplinary', rather than as an increase in the number of different but comparable specialists being consulted.

In the latter case, when looking at, for example, forward sale predictions of listed companies, reviewing the opinions of different financial analysts working at different investment banks has clear merit. Doing so provides what could be called a 'specialist consensus'. Alas, the financial press understandably, but still erroneously, tends to refer to this as the 'consensus forecast'. It is not that financial analysts do not tend to take a relatively uniform view on the companies they cover. Still, in their lives they probably have accumulated relatively similar experiences (education, job environment, culture, etc.), over time. Therefore, regardless of the investment bank they work for, they all may have a similar personal bias profile (see section 10.4). For strategic analysis predictions, there may be less safety in numbers when reviewing a large set of financial analyst's assessments, rather than when contextual data have been made available from a broad range of people with markedly different backgrounds and experiences.

## ON FOXES AND HEDGEHOGS

In table 11.1, inspired by Silver, I suggest the importance of always being on the lookout for fox-like forecasters (Silver, 2013e). Foxes implicitly also play a positive role in the work of Pareto.[4] The author Silver has borrowed his fox analogy via Tetlock and Tolstoy from the ancient Greek poet Archilochus:

> *"The fox knows many little things, but the hedgehog knows one big thing."*

In section 10.7 I already pointed to the commonalities between forecasting, extrapolations and strategic analysis of a business environment. This merits reviewing why foxes are better forecasters than hedgehogs. The fox and his antipode the hedgehog are described by Silver both in the quote below and in the intermezzo at the end of this section:

> *"Foxes [...] believe in a plethora of little ideas and in taking a multitude of approaches toward a problem. They tend to be [...] tolerant of nuance, uncertainty, complexity, and dissenting opinion. Foxes [...] are gatherers. Hedgehogs [...] believe in Big Ideas – in governing principles about the world that behave as though they were physical laws and undergird virtually every interaction in society."*

In other words: the fox is pragmatic and the hedgehog is ideological and principled. Having one's own principles and beliefs take centre stage, whilst ignoring a xenocentric view of the competitor is a recipe for trouble when filling in the blanks in a data set. This applies to filling in the blanks for both missing quantitative and missing qualitative data. The risk of a being a hedgehog not only plays a role in filling in missing data, but it unfortunately applies broadly in strategic analysis, and even beyond strategic analysis in generic decision-making (Dörner, 1996a).

Silver stresses that a fox is not only a smart gatherer, sourcing a broad a spectrum of sources, a fox also displays his pragmatism in the nature of his forecasts or deliverables and in his attitude towards those forecasts (of filled-in blanks). A fox recognizes that forecasts like hypotheses in science last until they are proven wrong. In communicating his forecast, he stresses rather than disguises this fundamental truth.

## COMMUNICATING AS A FOX REQUIRES LINKING PROBABILITIES TO FILLING IN THE BLANKS

A foxy way to communicate is to offer a probable estimate in a forecast. By weighing all the evidence, chances of the following outcome materializing are x%. In military intelligence, this is common practice, but it is less common in strategic analysis of a business environment.

There are issues related to factoring out probabilities. When communicating a fixed number as a percentage, unjustifiable and thus disputable accuracy may be implicitly suggested. On the other hand, qualitative statements like 'most likely' or 'likely' may be interpreted differently by the customer of the analysis compared to the reporting analyst. Subject to customer needs, percentage ranges (for example 30-50%) may be a way out of line.

Stated probabilities not only serve as a disclaimer to refer back to when outcomes differ from forecasts,[5] but also as a reminder to decision-makers that new, critically different data may always materialize and change previously held views.

Having communicated the forecast with such a disclaimer, the fox can subsequently adapt his forecast and communicate a possibly changed update to management without losing face. This is a better practice than to mute and reject the data in order to deny them and spoil the earlier forecast – and even worse, the analyst's credibility with it. In summary, filling in the blanks – and predicting in general – is thus a feasible process in strategic analysis, but it is not one without risks and flaws, most of which are manageable when taking the above considerations to heart.

## MISSING DATA AS A BLESSING

Medina gives an elegant twist to missing data (Medina, 2008). She portrays analysis as the craft of making sense of data sets that are fraught with missing and possibly partially incorrect data. When correct, critical data are available in full, the capabilities of an analyst would not be tested. As a result, actually the analyst may lose interest in the job. In conclusion, the analyst should rejoice in missing data.

Analysts, however, do not need to worry any time soon that missing or incorrect data will no longer occur, if not prevail in typical data sets (Bruce, 2008c). Always recognize that some countries, by definition, will be impenetrable. Think of North Korea or some African countries that as nations have so clearly failed that they are countries in name only. Think also of secretive, family-owned companies, some of which have perfected denial.

Predicting the intent of state actors will remain challenging in the foreseeable future. The same is true for non-state actors like NGOs, whose plans may not always be friendly to business. Data collection in such cases will remain difficult. Think of obtaining reliable economic statistics regarding emerging countries or market sizes, or even worse, market share data, that pertain to such countries. The available data may be, and in most cases will almost certainly be, of undeterminable quality.

To properly fill in the blanks the analyst must thus take a xenocentric view. With a xenocentric view, the analyst pays particular attention to the stranger's data, and carefully scrutinizes what the stranger will do next, and why. The better the capabilities/competencies of the stranger's data are known, the easier it is to take their hand of cards and play it. That is: play it their way, living in their shoes and imagining having their wallet in your pocket.

## INTERMEZZO: ON FOXES AND HEDGEHOGS

Table 11.2 below is reproduced in full from the literature as it so elegantly and usefully describes foxes and hedgehogs in analysis and forecasting (Silver, 2013e).

| HOW FOXES THINK | HOW HEDGEHOGS THINKS |
|---|---|
| **Multidisciplinary:** Incorporate ideas from different disciplines, regardless of their origin on the political spectrum. | **Specialized:** Often have spent the bulk of their careers on one or two great problems. May view the opinions of 'outsiders' skeptically. |
| **Adaptable:** Find a new approach – or pursue multiple approaches at the same time – if they aren't sure the original one is working. | **Stalwart:** Stick to the same 'all-in' approach – new data is used to refine the original model. |
| **Self-critical:** Sometimes willing (if rarely happy) to acknowledge mistakes in their predictions and accept the blame for them. | **Stubborn:** Mistakes are blamed on bad luck or idiosyncratic circumstances – a good model had a bad day. |
| **Tolerant of complexity:** See the universe as complicated, perhaps to the point of many fundamental problems being irresolvable or inherently unpredictable. | **Order-seeking:** Expect that the world will be found to abide by relatively simple governing relationships once the signal is identified through the noise. |
| **Cautious:** Express their predictions in probability terms and qualify their opinions. | **Confident:** Rarely hedge their predictions and are reluctant to change them. |
| **Empirical:** Rely more on observation than on theory. | **Ideological:** Expect that solutions to many day-to-day problems are manifestations of some grander theory or struggle. |
| **Foxes are better forecasters** | **Hedgehogs are weaker forecasters** |

TABLE 11.2 ▶▶▶ ATTITUDES OF FOXES AND HEDGEHOGS

# 11.3 MANAGING CONFLICTING DATA IN A DATA SET

The equally dreadful opposite of managing incomplete data sets is managing over-complete data sets. Over-completeness is not defined as having more data than needed. That is almost by definition the case in strategic analysis. Over-completeness is defined as having conflicting data in a data set.

## OVER-COMPLETENESS IN QUANTITATIVE DATA SETS

In quantitative data sets, conflicting data may occur when, for example, two different sources report different net sales figures for what looks like the same company, and for what looks like the same financial year. In sections 10.3 to 10.5, individual input data quality has been discussed. The first recommended step is to distinguish between probable reliabilities of the different available sources. When an original company press release is one source, and the other is a press clipping showing a different figure, the latter figure may safely be rejected and ignored. Primary sources generally outweigh secondary sources in terms of reliability.

When sources at first sight have similar reliabilities, e.g. two press clippings of expected similar reliability it is recommended to think of root causes that may explain the difference, prior to manipulating the data or randomly rejecting a source. In this rather common example, root causes for finding different figures for what looks like the same thing may include (list inevitably not exhaustive):

- Different legal entities e.g. a parent and a group figure *of the same company.*
- Different reporting periods (a quarter or year).
- Differences in the scope of business consolidation, for example reporting only 'ongoing businesses' in one source and all businesses in the other. A common difference is that net sales in the annual report of year x differs

from net sales for year x reported in the annual report covering year x + 1. In such a case, in the report for year x + 1 the year x net sales figures have been *restated,* allowing comparison with the year x +1 figures (generally used to making the company look better, otherwise the re-statement would usually not have been executed).

- To an incongruous book year that in one of the two sources has been made to fit like-for-like with a calendar year.
- Different accountancy standards being used. Nestlé, for example, adopted new corporate accounting standards in 2012, making all Nestlé sales comparisons with the years before that essentially impossible, except when analysing it, diving into the fine print of their reports.
- Different definitions of sales. Lactalis in its limited public disclosures always reports *gross* sales. In a successful bid to further increase confusion, a 2012 prospectus by Lactalis to potential bond investors reported their net net sales (this is neither a typo nor a joke).
- Currency changes. One source may have translated the sales figure in a different currency (without specifying this). Another source may have used the end-of-book-year currency exchange rate, whereas yet another source has used a year-average exchange rate.

Checking one's own assumptions as an analyst always has merits. A *New Strait Times* press clipping reporting $200 million net sales will probably refer to Singapore dollars, not US dollars as might have been expected. Similar discrepancies are also possible between US, Canadian, New Zealand and Australian dollars. The Cape Verde currency, to mention an exotic example, is also represented by the '$' symbol. In Cape Verde, however, the symbol is put behind the number to help avoid confusion.

When there is no indicator pointing to higher reliability of the one or the other source, the ultimate way to reconcile the issue is to choose one of the two figures, to use a range bordered by the two figures, or even more pragmatically, to use the average of the two figures. There is no single best approach, apart from at all times keeping note of potential reliability issues associated with this data point.

## OVER-COMPLETENESS IN QUALITATIVE DATA

For qualitative data, reconciling conflicting input data in a data set is also required. In this case, a typical example is one source postulating that company ABC will sell its business line PQR, whereas another source postulates that business line PQR is strategic to ABC.

This example also calls for a reliability assessment of both data points, taking into account the source, the channel and the analyst's own perspective. All questions proposed in the respective sections of chapter 10 will be needed. A good analyst will intuitively review his own assessment biases, as described in section 10.4, to ensure the comparative reliability assessment of both sources is done without inadvertent personal or cultural bias.

By the end of this section, the quality assurance tests of the individual data points or raw materials have been completed. Let us revisit the glass production metaphor we used earlier. Begin with the assumption that batches of input data or raw materials that did not meet the test have been rejected. The data set is sufficiently complete. Missing blanks data in the set have, where needed, been filled in by sufficiently high quality replacement raw materials. Superfluous, conflicting data inputs have been removed. The processing can begin; the oven can be fired. During processing, however, analysis may still run into issues, even with tested individual input data and with a data set that is neither incomplete nor over-complete. The next chapter describes some common issues in data processing and how to prevent them from happening in your analysis.

CHAPTER 12

# COMMON ISSUES IN DATA SET PROCESSING

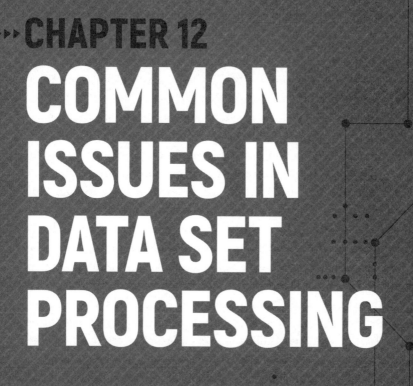

# 12.1 INTRODUCTION

Behaviour and psychology are intrinsically human, no matter what environment an individual works in. That is great news. This very fact allows for the psychology of human biases to be studied, regardless of the professional field those being examined are active in. A lot of work has been dedicated to the study of biases in relation to military intelligence (Clark, 2007d). In this chapter, I attempt to both summarize these experiences, as well as to apply them to the world of business. Biases are a real and present danger in analysis. In my view, the awareness of biases is invaluable in helping the analyst avoid falling prey to biased thinking.

So much for the good news; there is some bad news as well. I urge you not to overestimate the value of reading this section if you are professionally employed as analyst, either in business or in the military. Being aware, or not aware, of cognitive biases is unfortunately not related to being able to deliver better assessments (Heuer, 1999d). Below I've provided a quote by one of the fathers of intelligence analysis, which also illustrates that *awareness of* is not the same as *immunity to* biases (Jervis, 2010a):

> *"The main difference between professional scholars or intelligence officers on the one hand, and all other people on the other hand, is that the former are supposed to have had more training in techniques of guarding against their own intellectual frailties."*

# 12.2 WEIGHING DATA BASED ON VIVIDNESS OF DATA RECEPTION

We all have vivid memories of particular moments in our lives. The actual memory may range from your wedding day to a near-miss car crash. Whatever it was, you still remember it as if it was yesterday. This is great fun in your daily life, but it also may affect your views when you are working in data analysis. This is because the vividness with which you experienced collecting data may tend to affect your judgment as to how relevant a particular data point is in comparison to other data collection which may not have generated such vivid memories. The bias that may thus creep into your analysis is called 'vividness weighing'. Consider this observation about the potential distorting influence of vividness weighting (Clark, 2007d):

> *"The phenomenon that evidence that is [experienced] directly is the most convincing."*

Vividness weighting can in three related ways distort a balanced weighing of all data in a data set:

- Personal experience resulting in a personal impression of a case.
- Mixing up persuasiveness with data quality.
- Treating an individual case as separate from a class of similar cases.

In each of these situations, the result is an unbalanced assessment of the question at hand. Below I will discuss these three scenarios in a bit more detail.

## PERSONAL EXPERIENCE

Vividness weighing may both affect the individual analyst or the strategic analysis function at large, as well as the decision-maker. An uncomfortable but common situation is that the analyst feels that his decision-maker/customer suffers from vividness weighting.

Think of a solid and thorough analysis on anticipated moves by a competitor. The analysis has been sent as a report to the CEO. Think of a CEO who has personally met his counterpart in this competitor organization. Guess what? No matter how intentionally deceiving the counterpart has been, in the CEO's mind the counterpart's message will be seen as the data point with the highest reliability in data sets on this competitor. Strong and dynamic leaders are particularly vulnerable to deception. Think of characters like Roosevelt, Churchill and Kissinger (Clark, 2007d). This is exactly the sort of personality profile many a supervisory board member may consider for their CEO. Once a Churchill-type character has made up their mind, it will take very strong evidence indeed to make them change it. An extra complication is the asymmetric power relationship between the CEO and the analyst. Who is the analyst to speak up against a larger-than-life leader?

After the Cold War ended, many studies reflected on why US President Ronald Reagan, who had dubbed his Soviet adversary 'the evil empire' only a few years earlier, had come to amicable terms with his Soviet counterpart, Mikhail Gorbachev. Vividly obtained impressions apparently had been key in bringing about this change, more than just intelligence assessment (Yarhi-Milo, 2014c):

> *"Reagan, like Shultz [Foreign Secretary George Shultz], would base his judgment on his interactions with Gorbachev and Shevardnadze. Gorbachev's behaviour in Washington would loom larger in their minds than any number of intelligence briefings."*

Reagan proved right, regardless of what hawkish CIA briefings told him. Gorbachev wanted genuine change. Together they ended the Cold War. No matter how deceptive and dangerous the vividness bias may be, an analyst should remain humble. Admiral Stansfield Turner, director of the CIA under US President Carter, remarked (Yarhi-Milo, 2014c):

> *"Sometimes they [decision-makers] have better information than you do. I mean, whenever I briefed President Carter, I always had to keep in the back of my mind that 'he met Brezhnev last week'. I'd never met with Brezhnev, so if I nterpreted what Brezhnev was going to do tomorrow differently than he interpreted what*

*Brezhnev might do tomorrow, I had to give him credit that may he understood Brezhnev better than me."*

Humility is not the same as complacency. Strategic analysis should always be vigilant and provide business leaders with a second opinion that is based on an objective analysis of (other) facts.

I will discuss the relevance of this in greater detail in chapter 16. It relates to leadership in business who requires an overdose of optimism in a leader's character. Optimism and success may breed overconfidence. The result is that an overconfident leader that has vividly experienced a phenomenon will all too easily extrapolate the applicability and ramifications of this phenomenon beyond the boundaries of its actual validity over time or on all occasions. Such a leader is all hedgehog, no fox, to return to the metaphor of chapter 11. When the hedgehog raises its prickly head, bad decision-making is just around the corner. Analysis of spectacular business failures indeed revealed *lack of doubt* among top executives as a root cause (Surowiecki, 2005d):

*"The remarkable tendency for CEOs and executives [...] to believe that they are absolutely right, and the tendency to overestimate the quality of managerial talent by relying on track record, especially in situations that differ markedly from the present [...]"*

If anything is vividly experienced by a senior leader, it is the leader's own career, which has allowed for the building of that track record. Obviously, some CEOs are more benevolent than others. Even when the CEO encourages an analyst to speak their mind, the analyst, mindful of the hierarchy, may at times still be excused for approaching the invitation with due caution. A smart jester may bank on being granted absolution when he made jokes about the CEO's strategy, but the harshest jokes consistently had to be on themselves, if they didn't want to end up in misery or worse.

The remedy is to be a foxy analyst and hold tight to one's self-confidence. The analyst now knows that the CEO may, at that moment, have an unbalanced view of the competitor. In response, it would be prudent to lie low. They collect all new incoming factual data about the competitor. When they're right, as facts gradually emerge showing that the CEO had been deceived, they dutifully report all facts as they come in. No manipulating is allowed at any time, and certainly not when it will impact trust with a top executive! The CEO will, over time, see the facts and will undoubtedly draw their own conclusions, adapting their view to a more balanced one. Analysts should never try to say 'I told you so,' but if the urge is too strong, consider thinking it – if that is any relief. If not, the analyst should consider becoming a CEO themselves.

Obviously, an unbalanced view in and of itself is not detrimental, but actions based on an unbalanced view – which has not yet been adapted by thoughtful intervention by the strategic analysis function – may be so.

For an analyst in this situation, the first strophe of the Serenity Prayer by Reinhold Niebuhr, first written in 1943, may be helpful:

*"God, give me grace to accept with serenity*
*the things that cannot be changed,*
*Courage to change the things*
*which should be changed,*
*and the Wisdom to distinguish*
*the one from the other."*

Putting one's faith in a prayer is by no means an excuse for an analyst or a strategic analysis function to throw up their hands and step back. It is, however, essential to realize that responsibility and authority are connected. Taking the right decisions is at the end of the day management's responsibility and theirs alone. They are authorized by their board to do this. Management also has the sole responsibility to act on balanced data, even when the strategic analysis function does not perceive the data to be balanced. Providing them with the right data to take decisions is the function's overriding responsibility. For this the function is authorized to use a budget. Mixing up the function's responsibility with that of the decision-makers is useless. It only unnecessarily increases stress within the function.

## PERSUASIVENESS VERSUS DATA CORRECTNESS/QUALITY

As was discussed above, the impact of personally experiencing a conversation with a competitor's representative may, even unconsciously, increase the relative value attached to a given data point in a data set on this competitor. This is a sub-set of a more general phenomenon. Metadata quality may generally affect, (increase or decrease) the relative value of data points in a data set, or of single conclusions in a range of conclusions.

Metadata can include the source. Source-related weighing is covered in the next section, as it is not related to vividness. Experience-related metadata in the mind of the analyst or the decision-maker are stored in a way that directly links to the form in which data are presented. Persuasiveness, and by implication the vividness of the experience, links clearly with the format of reporting (Clark, 2007d). The following sequence shows how, for the same data, different presenting formats increase in persuasiveness:

- Statistics
- Abstract (general) text
- Concrete (specific, focused, exemplary) text
- Static images
- Videos with moving images

Professional service companies, think of advertising agencies, investment banks and management consultancies, understand the above better than anyone. All too often, your firm's management may be offered a briefing, or contract a professional services provider to brief them on the business environment. Imagine that in the same meeting the in-house function is also scheduled to present it own strategic analysis findings and recommendations. It's highly likely that your company's in-house strategic analysts have analysed more data and have produced a more balanced and objectively more correct view than the outsider. Still, the threat of arrogance is an ever-present danger. Professional service companies may have HUMINT access to other companies that is denied to competitors analysts so, they may have more, and possibly unique, sources.

The professional service company, however, will almost certainly outperform the in-house analysts in terms of their aura of expertise, perceived impact and overall persuasiveness. Using slick slides with strong imagery, and leveraging overconfidence as presentation power and being a fresh new, outside source (see next section), they will, at the end of the joint session, likely have captured 90+% of top management's confidence and buy-in. This may even be the case when the professional services company has been working from a weaker data set.

The good news is that even when the in-house strategic analysis function feels that it has been overshadowed, outperformed and generally bulldozed by the professional service provider, isn't necessarily a show-stopper or an issue that cannot be resolved. Chapter 15 (on reporting) provides tips on persuasive reporting, including the importance of using impactful imagery at all times. Moreover, the function should remember that the professional service firm may bring to the table less-than-desirable attributes in the mind of top management. Such attributes may include exceedingly high cost, arrogance, etc. Management's expectations for these competing advisors – the in-house analysts and the outside consultants – can be very different in such meetings. That, however, is never an excuse for the in-house function to deliver a less-than-stellar presentation. Training in presentation skills is always advisable for a corporate strategic analysis function.

It is advisable, however, to remain cautious in this context. Professional service providers usually share data most openly when they pitch for a project. The quality of the pitch determines whether they win an order. Facts or opinions shared in such pitches tend to be neither balanced nor neutral. That is understandable: the pitch serves a purpose other than neutrally informing management – namely, the firm's pursuit of a lucrative consulting contract. It is certainly in the in-house function's interest to make management aware of whatever incorrect or incomplete data may have been provided by the third party. There is no loss of face here; this is just regular strategic analysis function hygiene.

## TREATING AN INDIVIDUAL CASE AS SEPARATE FROM A CLASS OF SIMILAR CASES

There is a common human psychological inclination to equate the particulars of an individual case – that often has been vividly experienced – with that of a class of more or less similar cases. This leads to ignoring the statistics available for a group of cases when generating an estimate on an individual case (Kahneman, 2011g).

This bias applies, for example, in the medical profession. Medical professionals, rather than consulting an expert-system database with image analysis techniques, prefer to judge every individual patient's X-ray images themselves. Their reasoning is that 'every case is different'. In doing so, they rely solely on the vividness of their personal impressions of a particular case, rather than on a much more neutral, statistically balanced approach with objectively proven better results. Strategy analysts, especially those with many flight hours under their belts, face the same risk. Even when you have seen a lot, it still requires an open mind to see the particulars of an individual case, just as it requires an open mind to prevent conflating the characteristics of a bigger group of cases with a unique specific case.

'This company will never issue new shares' may be an analyst's opinion based on a vividly remembered discussion with a top executive in that company. Still, in 9 out 10 cases, companies in the same liquidity stress situation as the company in question did eventually issue new shares. Weighing the vividness of the particular case heavily biases the analysis. The odds are stacked against the analyst and against the existing shareholders: the new shares may already be at the printer's.

In summary: to protect themselves against vividness weighing, analysts should ask themselves whether personal impressions, persuasive presentations or over-rating the importance of individual cases have affected how appropriately they have weighted the data in their data set. In section 12.12 the related issue of having too small a sample size to justify conclusions is covered.

# 12.3 WEIGHING DATA ON THE SOURCE

Different sources may, consciously or not, be valued differently by the analyst or the decision-maker. This may lead the analyst or, even worse, the decision-maker to attach more or less value to what could even be precisely the same data provided by different sources. It gets even more complicated when different sources provide conflicting data.

US intelligence officers and senior Bush Administration officials, to cite a difficult example, had strongly differing opinions on the quality of the sources pertaining to Iraq's WMD programme, prior to the invasion of Iraq in 2003 (Pollack 2004):

> *"The worst fights were those over sources. The Administration gave greatest credence to accounts that presented the most lurid picture of Iraqi activities."*

The above quote demonstrates the underlying data set assessment bias that mattered most in this example. This is unfortunately a common bias in strategic analysis and in military intelligence: implicitly or explicitly cherry-picking data that suits what the analyst or the decision-maker wants to see (see chapter 17). The sources listed in table 12.1 are ranked, from top to bottom, by perceived decreasing value in both strategic analysis for business or military intelligence (Clark, 2007d).

In the boxes of table 12.1, common considerations are given that may be behind the perceived differences in value attached to different sources.

| SOURCE | STRATEGIC ANALYST | DECISION-MAKER |
|---|---|---|
| Results of the decision-maker's own collection efforts | Maintaining a job contract has priority over downgrading the data the decision-maker collected (see chapter 17 on Yesmanship). | Nobody beats me in understanding my business. |
| Top-notch professional service firm | When you filter out the jargon and correct for the glossiness, you only see data from a common fee-based syndicate subscription we also have<br>Gov't. example: US failure to predict the Iranian Revolution in 1979, with the US relying on the Shah's own biased security service (Bruce, 2008c) | Have worked with these guys for years – they really understand my challenges in this business. |
| Hard to obtain HUMINT (Mercado, 2009a) | Talking to that person was a real hit (ignoring the fact that the person may not have had a complete picture). | We have inside sources, disregard open sources (Johnston, 2005c)<br>Military intelligence example: Indian nuclear test as surprise to US (Bruce, 2008c). |
| Any strong narrative that dresses up the bare data | The story is so good, I identify with the logic and thus 'buy' the data: it is too persuasive to be doubted (Lovallo, 2010a). | (Same view as the strategic analyst). |
| Anything expensive | Have to visibly use this material to justify this expenditure; so better take it serious. | Should be good, can't tolerate the thought we wasted money. |
| Fee-based syndicate OSINT | This is what everyone who matters in this industry already has, so it will not offer a competitive edge. | This is what the experts say. |
| Free OSINT | This is the base, anyone has it; it will not make a difference. | No major feelings on this. |

TABLE 12.1 ▶▶▶ PERCEIVED VALUE OF DIFFERENT SOURCES FOR WHAT COULD BE THE SAME DATA (FROM HIGHEST IN THE UPPER ROW TO LOWEST IN THE BOTTOM ROW)

There are different columns for the analyst and the decision-maker for the upper two sources. In the previous section, it was made clear that relative weighing differences may not only occur in the mind of an analyst or in that of a decision-maker. It may also happen simultaneously with both parties, but with different weighting as a result. Inevitably, when that happens, the process and outcome of the analysis gets more political.

The moral of table 12.1 is that the awareness of these often-implicit considerations assists in reaching a more balanced view on weighing sources before conclusions are drawn.

## 12.4 WEIGHING DATA ON ACTUALITY

Analysts have a tendency to rank the most recent data as the most highly valued in a given data set (Clark, 2007d). This boils down to mixing up actuality with relevance and/or value. Analysts are not alone in this behaviour, (Tversky, 1973). Tversky's study amongst other things covers the topic of favouring the most recent data in a data set. It refers to research on the occurrence and severity of floods:

> *"Men on flood plains appear to be very much prisoners of their experience. Recently experienced events appear to set an upper bound to the size of loss with which managers believe to be concerned."*

What applies to the population living on a flood plain also applies to financial traders. Research on trading decisions by the University of Chicago points in the same direction (Fenton-O'Creevy, 2000),(De Bondt, 1985). The outcomes of experiments demonstrate, to put it simply, that stock price fluctuations that result from buying/selling decisions are disproportionally affected by recent news and under-proportionally by fundamental underlying values of the stock (e.g., dividend pay-out). This is a clear example of mistaking the noise for the signal.

Psychological barriers apparently compel humans to imagine more than what was recently experienced – to favour the most recent data and/or to overweigh highly memorable events. These barriers have also been referred to as the saliency bias (Lovallo, 2010a).

Such barriers may be a root cause (next to convenience) for a rather visible phenomenon in strategic analysis outputs purchased or obtained from multiple third-party service providers. Rarely do such third-party reports look back more than a few years in, for instance, the history of a company that is being discussed. This statement holds true regardless of whether it concerns quantitative or qualitative data. Most reports are all about recent results and recent transactions. Mixing up actuality with relevance leads to not looking back long enough during collection in the first place. This inevitably results in a higher risk of compiling an incomplete data set. The question is whether the root cause for this is the authors of such short-term view reports. The blame may lie more plausibly with the customers who order them. In management, anything older than a few years, and certainly anything older than the tenure the manager herself has in their current job seems ancient history. It is usually ignored. Management is, so to speak, very much in the moment. With employee job tenures gradually declining in most countries, corporate institutional memory is rapidly dwindling.

Strategic analysis, I believe, needs to take a different view, when time and budget reasonably permit. In the case of qualitative data, taking a long-term view is most relevant when reviewing family- or privately-owned companies. Such companies tend to be less dynamic and less prone to management or strategy changes than their listed and often larger equivalents. Developing an accurate picture of the competences and intent of family-owned companies may require studying a relatively long historical track record. These companies may be seen to have slow dynamics, with just few critical data points available per year. In such cases, a long history is required to reach a balanced data set that allows for solid strategic analysis or for well-reasoned forecasts.

In the case of listed companies, it is rarely necessary to look back more than five to seven years. The maximum relevant time span to look back may be the tenure of the current CEO, when that period is longer than five to seven years. Especially large market cap-listed companies could be viewed as having high dynamics, where more critical data points are available per year. In these cases, a shorter history is sufficient to reach a balanced data set for strategic analysis.

Overvaluing recent evidence is most risky when reviewing the fundamentals of financial performance of a company that operates in a profoundly cyclical industry. This is especially true when the business cycle tends to have a long cycle time (over three years). The risk is to mix up the noise of day-to-day changes with the signal of the longer-term business cycle.

In summary, when in strategic analysis it comes to choosing a historical time-window for data collection that is long enough to avoid valuing only the recent data, qualitative contextual data matters most. In chapter 11, on managing incomplete data sets, you'll recall that we placed significant emphasis on contextual qualitative data. This should not come as a surprise, as ensuring a sufficient timeframe for data collection in strategic analysis can help you avoid an unintentionally incomplete data set.

# 12.5 WEIGHING DATA ON SEQUENCE OF RECEPTION

Several challenges accompany the first data that come in on a new issue:

- The first data that come in may be overvalued in the subsequent analysis.
- The first data usually neither form the true nor the complete story.
- The decision-maker may receive some bits and pieces of data prior to the strategic analysis function and may already have made up his mind.

## OVERVALUING THE DATA THAT FIRST COME IN ON AN ISSUE

An analyst may have the reflex to take the first data that come in on a new matter – through whatever channel – as an anchor. Additional data that trickle in later on this topic will be viewed against it. Once the first data trigger an impression, the impression tends to persist; even when later data justify modifying or changing such a first impression (Heuer, 1999k). This is again a common psychological phenomenon, once humans believe they have seen a pattern in the first data, it is hard to erase the weight they place on that impression. That's why in human contact making a good first impression is critical. This potential bias has some similarities with the potential bias of 'premature closing' which will be discussed later in this chapter.

## THE FIRST DATA USUALLY NEITHER FORM THE TRUE NOR THE COMPLETE STORY

The issue here is that, especially in breaking news events, the first report is not likely to capture the true story in its entirety (Stewart, 2013). In quickly making sense of myriad detailed data on a breaking event, Stewart recommends trying to look for a pattern as quickly as possible. This recommendation doesn't need to be pushed: it is what humans naturally do. The analyst's challenge is to look for a pattern without overvaluing the first data.

Questions that may help to do so include:

- Which data that have come in match with a possible hypothesis x, what with hypothesis y? What data necessitate rejection of hypothesis x or y?
- Which of these hypotheses most likely applies?
- If that hypothesis applies, what evidence that normally is also present in such case now appears to be lacking?
- What does this event have in common with earlier events in a similar context?

Analysts develop such patterns as the result of analysing multiple breaking events – be they security issues, or management briefings/situation reports on competitors or customers.

## MANAGEMENT SEES THE NEWS BEFORE THE ANALYST

Breaking news may have reached the decision-maker's desk (or electronic device) earlier than the analyst's. The article or broadcast story, as is often the case with first news, may provide data points that neither are fully correct nor fully complete… but the decision-maker has by now received and absorbed it. She may start to make up her mind on the topic (also see below on premature closing) (Cooper, 2005b).

News services and the internet at large pose an ongoing challenge to in-house analysts in a company that strives for a balanced picture. Decision-makers, should they wish to, may become their own analyst. An analyst trying to change a decision-maker's first impression once it is formed is pulling the wrong string. My suggestion is not to try to change that impression. Make the decision-maker change his own mind by feeding him more balanced facts once they are available. It may take more time. Still, this is the more effective form of change management. Let the manager himself change his view rather than having the analyst try to push him to do so.

Having breaking news come in first to an analyst may create an urge to distribute it – with perhaps a dose of tentative 'what does it mean'? This has its risks. It may lead to drawing unbalanced conclusions based on erroneous first impressions. These first reports that might later prove wrong may in time hurt the credibility of the strategic analysis function. The first report, as we've said, is never the true story. Rather, it's best to avoid competing for speed and stick to objectivity and balance in reporting.

# 12.6 CHALLENGES OF WORKING WITH EXPERTS

*"On the big issues, the experts are very rarely right."* This quote is taken from Peter Wright's book *Spycatcher*. This book was upon its release in 1987 – still during the cold war – as controversial as this quote is provocative (Wright, 1987). The book was initially published in Australia, as the UK Government had banned its publication. Wright, a former MI5 counter-intelligence officer, points to the complex relation between experts and military intelligence. As is so often the case, what is true for military intelligence is true for strategic analysis in business; the relevant issues may be different, but not the human dynamics. Wright's bold assertion may be exaggerated but it holds some truth. Experts, to their deserved credit, are generally useful and tend to be great sources in strategic analysis work. Experts can interpret (combinations of) data that only people with an in-depth knowledge of a subject can. Such interpretations may create new insights that the analyst could never have obtained otherwise. Experts, however, often not only introduce knowledge but also bias (Clark, 2007d). In this section, the usefulness of experts is taken for granted. It is the biases that I wish to focus on next. Knowing the biases, analysts can work with experts even more effectively. A foxy analyst works with many experts rather than with one expert alone, if only to get as balanced an assessment as possibe of what data in a data set may mean.

Common issues in working with experts include:

- Meeting an expert but working with a hedgehog.
- Underestimating the capabilities of other parties.
- Overestimating predictability, even with a good track record of prediction.
- Overestimating the value of expertise in meaningful decision-making.

- Deceiving by narrative.
- Self-fulfilling expert prophecies.

I will now briefly cover, each of these issues.

## MEETING AN EXPERT BUT FACING A HEDGEHOG

There are beautiful historic examples to illuminate this bias (Jeffery, 2011c). Jeffery describes how MI6 (formerly the Secret Intelligence Service) before the First World War had inserted well-placed agents into German naval circles. As a result, the UK Admiralty started receiving valuable technical intelligence on innovative German navy concepts. Unfortunately…

> *"The impact of this work was less than might have been hoped. […] the resistance which much of this reporting encountered in the Admiralty, where the preconceived ideas of some experts led them to question intelligence which stressed the great importance of German developments in torpedoes, submarines, mines and aircraft."*

If, 25 years later, the German naval warfare was to have one edge, it was their submarine fleet.

Analysts themselves may also start to consider themselves subject matter experts. This too has its risks as it may result in hedgehog attitudes. This has been referred to as the 'mindset trap' (George, 2008a):

> *"The more expert the analyst, the more prone an analyst becomes to the 'mindset' trap – that is, believing that his or her view of the problem is the best explanation for all behaviour. Yet as many intelligence failures have demonstrated, intelligence experts can become too complacent about their knowledge and too resistant to alternative explanations and thus miss important changes in the international environment or in the attitudes of […] adversaries"*

George urges analysts to not become complacent, but rather to keep on testing multiple analyses. Car maker Henry Ford, himself possibly a hedgehog, uttered more generic reservations on experts (Freedman, 2013d):

> *"If ever I wanted to kill opposition by unfair means I would endow the opposition with experts."*

The lesson from Ford's quote is that the analysis customer himself is a hedgehog; consider not adopting an expert hedgehog as your ally if you'd like to get your message across more clearly and credibly. Experts have a habit of either really liking or really hating each other. Indifference seems less common. In the former case, the confirmatory bias may come in to play, leading to groupthink (see chapter 17). In the latter case, nothing gets accomplished. Think before using experts as a (personal) source – love them or hate them, success in decision-making is not guaranteed.

## UNDERESTIMATING THE CAPABILITIES OF OTHER PARTIES

This bias could very well be characterized by the sentiment: "I am an expert; if I can't do it it can't be done." To illustrate this bias, I am pleased to introduce the British Second World War scientific military intelligence manager Reginald V. Jones. Similar to during the First World War submarine example, the Second World War, Jones had serious trouble persuading the British rocket experts that the highly innovative German V-2 rocket – the first ballistic missile ever – could actually work (Jones, 1978b).

Again, innovative German military engineering, even when developed for dreadful purposes, was underrated by less-than-capable experts.

In response, Jones defined the 'principle of impotence'. When a scientist has performed an experiment and failed to achieve a result, the erroneous but comforting expert conclusion is often that 'it can't be done' rather than 'I couldn't do it'. In strategic analysis, the fact that your company failed to launch an innovative concept in a difficult market does not mean that a competitor may not be able to do so successfully. Granted, that may be the strongly-held opinion of the marketing director who failed to get the product sold in this market in the first place).

## OVERESTIMATING PREDICTABILITY, EVEN WITH A GOOD PREDICTION TRACK RECORD

Taleb doesn't claim to be an expert (Taleb, 2007c). He does, however, offer opinions on a broad range of topics, not the least on prediction. In that context, he provocatively suggests a segmentation of selected disciplines where experts, in his opinion, do indeed exist and other disciplines where those claiming expertise are by definition suspect (Taleb, 2007f). According to Taleb, individuals who tend to be legitimate experts include chess masters, astronomers, accountants, physicists and mathematicians, as long as they don't do empirical work. So-called authorities who tend not to be bona fide experts include stockbrokers, councilors, economists, financial forecasters, personnel recruiters, clinical psychologists and intelligence analysts.

Taleb's central thesis is that experts can only reliably predict matters in mediocristan, the quiet country defined in chapter 11. As soon as a discipline enters extremistan, on the other hand, forward predictive expertise is suspect if not a downright illegitimate.

There are indeed worrying results of empirical research in which expert predictions were tested against the reality that later emerged. In predicting future political events, experts had barely done better than random guesswork, regardless of their occupation, experience or sub-field (Silver, 2013e); (Peterson, 2008). Interestingly enough, some experts did better than others. An inverse proportionality seemed to exist between experts who were cited most frequently in the media and the quality of their predictions. This research led to the segmentation of forecasters into hedgehogs and foxes, as was presented in chapter 11.

Taleb could have written the mandatory disclaimer in consumer advertisements for financial services like investment funds: 'Returns obtained in the past do not provide a guarantee for the future.' What is true for investment services is just as true for experts' or anyone else's predictions of the future. A strong track record of successful past predictions may not, in itself, be an indicator of the upfront credibility of new predictions by the same (expert) source for events that are yet to come. Doing so in and of itself is a bias – when an expert insists upon the reliability of a prediction about future events based solely on her previously-good track record, it is called the 'Champion Bias' (Lovallo, 2010a). Having an expert with, a good track record may be a relief to an analyst, but strategic analysis for business is not about an analyst's personal sense of comfort and relief. Former Intel CEO Andy Grove put it well in a quote that is directly applicable to strategic analysis (Grove, 1996b):

*"Success breeds Complacency; complacency breeds failure; only the paranoid survive."*

## OVERESTIMATING THE VALUE OF EXPERTISE IN DECISION-MAKING

This bias is illustrated well in a spectacular business failure by one of the best companies in the FMCG space: the 1985 introduction of New Coke. Long-time American business executive Donald R. Keough was president of the Coca-Cola Company through the New Coke disaster. Following that dreadful experience, he is understandably reluctant to praise experts and their vaunted advice. In his book *The Ten Commandments for Business Failure*, experts have earned a chapter (Keough, 2008b). Keough postulates that when failure is the objective...

*"Put all your faith in experts and consultants."*

He suggests, with a potential bias, that all the blame for the New Coke disaster was due to an unquestioning (albeit surely uncomfortable for the illustrious old brand) reliance on so-called experts' assurances about how well the new-tasting Coke would be accepted by consumers. As we now know, the New Coke debacle went down in history as one of the biggest business fiascoes of all time..

In retrospect, it's clear now that Keough and his leadership team should have asked the inverse analysis question, "Why shouldn't, rather than why should, a great company like Coca-Cola launch New Coke?"

## DECEIVING BY NARRATIVE

Experts might better be defined not as people with extraordinary subject matter, but rather as people who are able to come up with a superior, more credible narrative than non-experts, even when data availability is limited (Guszcza, 2012). Here's one way to look at the power of senior-level business experts' story-telling abilities:

*"Their seniority lends them an air of authority, and indeed part of their success might be attributable to their charisma and ability to convince their colleagues with their narrative accounts."*

The above narrative skills may explain why some experts are highly appreciated in the media. An interesting question is whether the better storytellers, who may appear prominently in the media, have less success with their strategic business predictions, as mentioned earlier in this chapter. The implication would seem to be that more capable storytellers, due to their persuasive strengths, tend to be more self-confident. As a result, even if they start out as a fox they may end up as a hedgehog. This speculation might be an avenue for further research. For the analyst, the conclusion is that however good the experts' narrative is, the self-proclaimed expert will always remain foxy.

## SELF-FULFILLING EXPERT PROPHECIES

There is another relevant bias that relates to expert predictions. This bias deals with the self-fulfilling nature of some of their predictions.[1] When an expert inspires a herd of people to follow him – based on an irresistibly appealing prediction – that prediction may, through sheer power of persuasion, actually come to pass.

Moreover, the relationship between experts and analysts may vary culturally. This adds a final dimension to consider in this section. In Japanese culture,[2] and possibly German/Austrian culture, experts are, or at least have been, treated with more respect than, for example, in the Anglo-Saxon culture, where business success may well be valued higher than subject knowledge. Foxiness works in all cultures. So does respecting experts when they deserve it.

# 12.7 MIXING UP DATA QUANTITY AND DATA QUALITY

## MORE DATA DOES NOT MEAN BETTER DATA – ONLY FEW ARE EITHER USED OR NEEDED

Intuitively one would suspect that, in theory, more data should lead to better predictions (Silver, 2013h). Empirical evidence, however, suggests otherwise (Makridakis, 1990):

> *"More information merely seems to increase our confidence that we are right without necessarily improving the accuracy of our decisions."*

Analysts, by nature, tend to overestimate the number of data points that they should ideally use in an analysis. Even in a large data set, only a limited amount of data are really used to reach conclusions (Heuer, 1999j). Moreover, data over-abundance has its intrinsic practical limitations. It is easy for strategic analysts – and any of us, really – to not see the forest for the trees. Data overload has in the past elegantly been referred to as (Wohlstetter, 1965b).

> *" [an] embarrassing riches of data."*

Wohlstetter also refers to the signal and the noise in data.[3] Signals are data that point to a competitor's (or customer's or supplier's) planned or already-executed action, or to a latent or explicit customer need that your company may be able to serve in a better way than your competitors. Think of noise as extraneous data points that may distract you from making sense of the data that truly matter to your work.

As you focus on customer needs, try to separate relevant signals from confusing noise by asking 'Essential Questions' (Frank, 2011c). The proposed questions focus on asking what might go wrong.

So, noise is defined as the background clutter data that may be irrelevant, inconsistent and/or pointing in the wrong direction. At the very least, noise is distracting. In the cases of Pearl Harbor and the Cuban Missile Crisis, the signals were there. They were, however, hidden amidst an abundance of noise. Some noise had deliberately been sent by the adversary, some simply was there, but some had also been inadvertently created within the US intelligence community itself. Inadequate modelling of Japanese and Soviet behaviour prevented analysts from better distinguishing the important signals from the overwhelming amount of noise. The same applies to the tragedy of 9/11 (Bruce, 2008c).

The flow of the intelligence assessment – fortunately for the world – worked well in the Cuba Missile Crisis (Wohlstetter, 1965c). The intelligence chief with final responsibility for the assessment was Lieutenant-General J.F. Carroll, head of the US Defense Intelligence Agency (DIA). From a staggeringly overabundant data set he ultimately synthesized a hypothesis based on only three or four (!) data points of evidence. This nicely corroborates the above statement that analysts, regardless of how many data they have, actually use a small number of data-points. Carroll had this hypothesis tested by having aerial reconnaissance flights scheduled over an area that he postulated to be a possible Soviet rocket-launching base in Cuba. The photos proved him right: a Soviet rocket launch base was indeed under construction. The photos also proved a point that is even more important to this book. Carroll possessed a great skill – the ability to filter critical data out of noise and the persuasiveness to make the relevant intelligence customer (President John F. Kennedy) decisively act upon them.

For an analyst, the lesson is that even when one has abundant data, a small, crisply focused sub-set is generally all that's necessary. This scary fact may resonate with you as reader. If you are fair to yourself, ask how many data you really use to draw a conclusion, irrespective of how many data you have or can get.

Filter the critical data out of the abundance and ensure to use these critical data. This brings me to the question, what are critical data?

## CRITICAL DATA ARE DIAGNOSTIC

Today, having many data does not equate to having actionable data (Frank, 2011b):

> *"At some point in almost any business project, you'll be confronted with far more data than you need. The data you want, however, should lead to clear, actionable information with no ambiguity."*

The challenge of extracting good data from a large data set also matters in another civilian area that only require critical data: administration of justice. The parallels with strategic analysis and the administration of justice may look less obvious at first sight. Yet, in the latter, the defense attorney may also face a tremendous data set. Some data points may incriminate the accused; others may be noise and thus irrelevant. If only the defense attorney can find a single critical data point in the evidence, she can seed reasonable doubt of guilt in the minds of the jury.[4]

This is why it matters to identify the critical data in your data set (Bruce, 2008e). Critical data, in line with the criminal-justice example, are those pieces of evidence in a data set that when removed make a theory crumble to pieces. Such data may also be called 'diagnostic'. A warning is needed here. It is great to have distinguished critical, diagnostic data in a data set. However, when attempting to build a theory on only a few data points, the analyst needs to be sure of the quality of these selected points, otherwise critical analytic failures are just around the corner.

Analysts should not overestimate their ability to filter critical data out of a data set (Makridakis, 1990). In empirical research, subjects too often use the irrelevant data in a data set, overlooking those that matter the most.

Examples of critical data being overlooked due to information overload have been vividly described (Gladwell, 2005). One particularly striking example concerns predicting the duration of a couple's marriage. Knowing a couple for a long time does not make us better predictors of the chances of divorce. No matter how much we think we know from observing a couple's behaviour, we have only seen what they wanted to show and heard what they wanted us to hear.

A selective information reduction strategy of only monitoring and categorizing occurrence and frequency of the couple's standardized facial expressions when they have a conversation on a topic of potential mutual conflict proves to be a much better predictor of the marriage's longevity. This is due to the fact that human facial expressions cannot be controlled – they are reliable indicators of underlying emotion – whereas speech can be as deceptive as it is smooth. What people say is actually a weak indicator. It is information overload, whereas the facial expressions people generate are a strong indicator. When love has faded, people may unintentionally and perhaps even unknowingly show it, even when they still verbally express their passion.

In strategic analysis in business, the ideal situation is to know the strong indicators predictive value that cannot be intentionally distorted. Once the critical data are known, the task is to subsequently filter those indicators – or critical, or diagnostic data – out of the data overload.

In chapter 13 I offer a tool for defining and assessing multiple hypotheses. This tool assists in uncovering diagnostic data. For diagnostic data and for diagnostic data alone, this can help you work through various input data quality assessment questions provided in section 10.3. For an analyst, a sceptical mind is a joy forever.

## HAVING MORE DATA MAY NOT MEAN HAVING MORE DIFFERENT SOURCES

There is an additional warning that relates to data quantity. This bias relates to so-called 'cumulative redundant evidence' (Clark, 2007d). Let's assume that two sources provide largely or completely overlapping data. The analyst may receive these multiple, overlapping data-sets from a single sender… and that sender may be hard at work trying to intentionally deceive the world. The sender, however, is also being quoted by different, often reliable sources. When separate sources deliver the same message, they may erroneously build the analyst's confidence in the data. In strategic analysis, it is obviously great to be confident, but it is infinitely better to be right.

## TODAY'S DATA QUANTITY REQUIRES FILTERING TOOLS TO EXTRACT CRITICAL DATA

Critical data matters. The ablity to filter critical data out of large data sets has been described as the essence of intelligence (Wolf, 1998):

> *"Intelligence is essentially a banal trade of sifting through huge amounts of random information in a search for a single enlightening gem or an illuminating link."*

In Wolf's DDR days, in East Germany, the sifting was accomplished by the allocation of massive human resources to the task. In strategic analysis in the world of business, that is not economically feasible. It wasn't in the DDR days either, but that's beside the point of this book. What to do?

In a remarkably prescient article, Luhn in 1958 pointed out that information overload was a key issue in business decision-making (Luhn, 1958). After all, many data did not automatically mean good or actionable data. Luhn – working for IBM – unsurprisingly concluded that rather than using large numbers of human resources, automation was essential to manage information overload:

> *"Undoubtedly the most formidable communications problem is the sheer bulk of information that has to be dealt with. In view of the present growth trends, automation appears to offer the most efficient methods for retrieval and dissemination of this information."*

Although most of the examples in this book concern military intelligence, the above quote shows that business decision-making in the 1950s was also affected by data overload.

Today we face an exponential rise in data quantity. An intriguing metric has been defined for this: the number of data available per decision (Edward, 2014). Diagram 12.1 shows the trend over the course of time. The horizontal axis shows the progress of time, and the vertical axis the number of data per decision. The attractive element in this diagram is the link that is being made with the capabilities of human short-term memory (Heuer, 1999k). Essentially, we cannot handle more than five independent, unconnected data points at the same time. What Luhn in the 1950s had predicted was that people, especially analysts, need data-processing tools and strategies.

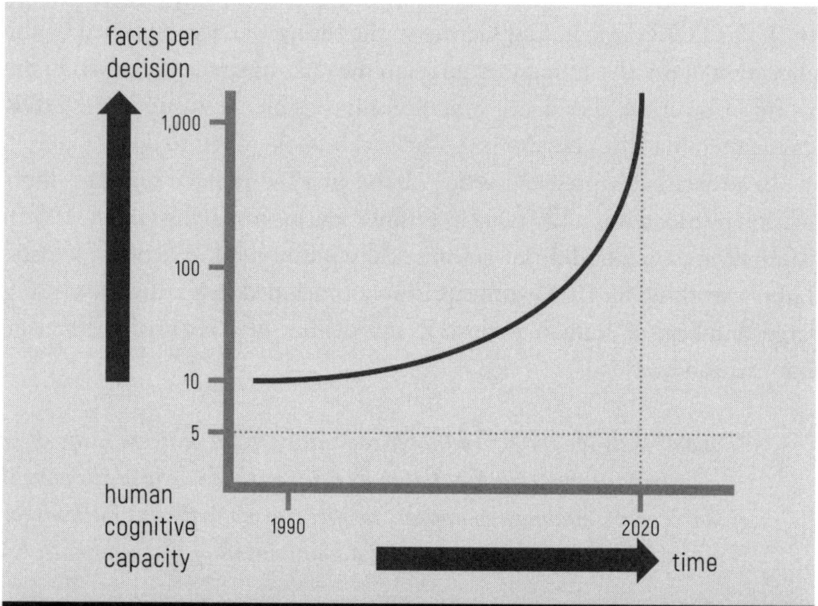


DIAGRAM 12.1 ▶▶▶ THE EXPONENTIAL INCREASE IN OVER TIME OF DATA AVAILABLE PER DECISION

In conclusion, getting our hands on copious amounts of data is usually not a problem. Having a lot of data, however luxurious it looks, does not equate to having critical data. What matters most is the ability to filter the signal from the noise. It is a rare but essential accomplishment to be able to extract critical data from a data set with thousands of individual data points, most of which are irrelevant. Asking the right questions is the first step:

- What data matter most in relation to the issue at hand?
- Why?
- What data may disprove the hypothesis at hand?

In the next chapter, I will describe the analysis tool that, with competing hypotheses, assists in identifying critical or diagnostic data. After all, for management, making sense of data overload remains one of the key roles of strategic analysis. An analyst that masters this capability does not need to worry about long-term employment.

## 12.8 CONFUSING QUANTITATIVE DATA WITH QUALITY DATA

The valued intelligence output attributed to objectiveness is unfortunately not by definition synonymous with quantitativeness (Silver, 2013i). Quantitative statements may have a deceiving aura of exactitude. There is truth in the clever saying that 'figures don't lie but liars do figure'. Sharing figures is dangerously persuasive, as fascinatingly sufficient figures record much better than qualitative arguments in people's (executives') minds. Once an analyst has provided an executive with estimated net sales figures for a secretive competitor, all the disclaimers on data quality and accuracy are instantly forgotten. Except for the figure – the figure will definitely be remembered. There are examples from the history books of how persuasive advisers, knowing the power of figures in psychology, used figures into intimidate others to following their proposed course of action. Reportedly Robert S. McNamara, US Secretary of Defense in the Johnson administration during the Vietnam War, was a wizard with figures that he used to drive his agenda (Halberstam, 1992c):

> *"McNamara was a ferocious infighter, statistics and force ratios came pouring out of him like a great uncapped faucet. He had total control of his facts and he was quick and nimble with them; there was never a man better with numbers, he could characterize enemy strength and movement and do it statistically.*
>
> *Poor George [George Ball – a State Department official] had no counterfigures; he could talk in vague doubts, lacking these figures, and leave the meetings occasionally depressed and annoyed. Why did McNamara have such good figures? […] One of the reasons was that McNamara had invented them."*

Beware as an analyst of those sources only adept at pushing figures. There are more risks connected with how well quantitative data register in the human mind. In mergers and acquisitions (M&A) negotiations, the worst thing to do, unless you are the lead negotiator and you really know what you're doing, is to mention a figure. When the seller of a business has heard a figure, say €80 million, as the price that the buyer is considering paying for his company, going forward the price will have to be at least €80 million. No matter how many conditions were mentioned in the same sentence, and no matter whether the seller has even the slightest inclination to meet these conditions, the only thing that the seller registers is the figure. In M&A parlance this is called 'anchor pricing'. The anchor is stuck on the price.[5]

Based on the same psychological phenomenon, anchoring to figures clearly undermines strategic decision-making. Countering anchoring is best done by postponing the introduction of figures in a meeting, if possible (Lovallo, 2010b). Another approach to preventing getting hooked onto an anchor thrown out by the other party is to focus on the lowest offer the other party may accept (Kahneman, 2011d).

The anchoring of the mind to a figure is a bias that may also affect analysts with a data set consisting of quantitative and qualitative data. The fact that data are quantitative by nature does not make them more correct or accurate than the qualitative data that accompany them in the set. The fact that humans apparently remember figures well does not mean that quantitative data enthusiastically offered up by a source should automatically make it into the strategic analysis deliverable. In chapter 10, multiple tests to assess input data quality were proposed. These cautionary notes should be applied as rigorously to quantitative as to qualitative data.

# 12.9 MISPERCEIVING EVENTS THAT TOGETHER FORM A STORY

A set of separate events or data in an analysis often have to be interpreted in conjunction with each other. Such sets could be called a story. Biases may raise their ugly heads when it comes to interpreting such stories (Taleb, 2007g). Taleb refers to the *triplet of opacity*, sounding in his book remarkably enough four rather than three warnings.[6] Two of these warnings have a direct relevance to strategic analysis for business:

- **The illusion of understanding** a set of events – originating from underestimating the complexity or randomness of the events that are analysed. This links to the confirmation bias discussed in chapter 10. The illusion of understanding may lead to premature closing (covered in a later section in this chapter). A narrative of understanding may create a 'halo effect' (Freedman, 2013e). Business narratives of historical success are created where success is attributed to a set of antecedent and present factors. All too often such narratives, no matter how smooth, are not based on proper research. Too often an analysis fails to point out whether the same factors were also present in cases of failure. In other words, the factors may not at all be relevant to the success. A lot of business hero-worship is based on this sort of sloppy thinking.

- **The retrospective distortion** – originating from the fact that events only allow sound interpretation sometime after their occurrence. At the time of their occurrence, events – or at least what is known about the events at the time of their happening – tend to look much less connected than with the benefit of hindsight, when often more or most data regarding the events have become available. This 'fog of war' problem is inevitable. It boils down to the 'incomplete information dilemma' that was described in section 10.6. In the event of a highly incomplete data set, any attempt to analyse what is available is fraught with high risk. In such cases, it is recommended for an analyst to stick to situation reports and refrain from premature analysis.

If only analysts were not so very human. How much easier it would all be if they didn't need to fight the all-too-human desire to create histories. How nice it would be if business analysts didn't constantly find themselves immersed in trying to make sense of and find causal relations between what essentially may be unconnected data or events (Kahneman, 2011i):

*"It is easier to construct a coherent story when you know little, when there are fewer pieces to fit into the puzzle. Our comforting conviction that the world makes sense rests on a secure foundation: our almost unlimited ability to ignore our ignorance."*

The above quote in my view imparts an important message: think twice as an analyst before accepting causality in a history, no matter how well the narrative sounds or is being told.[7]

An illustrative example of the illusion of understanding has been provided in the book *Blind Man's Bluff*. The book describes the history of US submarine intelligence collection (Sontag, 1998a). The time is April 1968. US submarines patrol the coast off the Russian Far East. To their surprise, the US submarines discover that Soviet submarines are intensively, and rather casually, using active sonar to look for something. The conclusion they correctly arrived at was that the Soviets lost a submarine. For a submarine to get lost, essentially two things had to have happened: the submarine encountered an autonomous problem that had proved to be fatal or it had collided with another submarine and had been lost as a result. The first narrative was unthinkable. The Soviets were convinced that such a thing simply couldn't occur, given their rigid naval safeguards, controls and procedures. Soviet submarines did not and could not have autonomous problems. And so, Soviet military intelligence started to look for evidence to substantiate the second narrative. A few days after the Soviet submarine disappeared, a US submarine moored in Yokosuka harbor in Japan. In principle that US submarine could have been at the location of the hypothetical Soviet submarine collision to, at the time of the collision. The Soviet Navy needed the collision validate their narrative. In addition, the American submarine (the USS *Swordfish*, SSN-579) pulled into port with visible damage to its sail and periscope. This damage was of course the missing puzzle piece. According to Soviet military intelligence, it unquestionably linked the Swordfish to the USSR's missing boat and the collision scenario. The US Navy took a different view (Sontag, 1998a):

> *"They [Soviet military intelligence] would add two and two and come up with thirty-six."*

US underwater research later provided the real narrative. The Soviet ship did have an autonomous problem that proved fatal and the Swordfish, completely unconnected, had simply hit a small iceberg.

# 12.10 PREMATURE CLOSING

In strategic analysis, an analyst may be tempted to make an assessment of a particular set of data prior to having evaluated or even collected all the data that should have underpinned the assessment. The analyst, upon observing the loosely available data, is satisfied with the first pattern that their brain comes up with to make sense of the data. In doing so they prematurely close their mind to the possibility of anything else.

The term commonly used for this bias is 'satisficing'. Let me make this less abstract. Imagine that you, as an analyst, observe some data. For example, in the Seventeenth Century, in northern Europe, you observe only white swans. The combination of data suits a pattern that you already know or are easily able to generate. In this case, the simple pattern is that the swan is a white bird. The implication is that when I see a swan, it is either white or it is not a swan. Every white swan you see afterwards strengthens your belief in this pattern. You are not aware that non-white swans exist and do not feel the urge to know this as your pattern suits your observations. This in analysis relates to the so-called 'availability bias'. The only data that are available are being used in an analysis, not all the data that could have been made available. With the available data, an analyst – often unknowingly – prematurely closes his mind, rather than choosing the best fitting pattern when all the available data had been used. There are several psychological drivers that seem to explain the human urge to draw conclusions and act upon them prior to having all available data properly collected and/or analysed.

Below I will briefly discuss the drivers for premature closing in relation to pattern recognition and decision-making:

- Less data favours rather than hampers pattern recognition.
- Less data favours rather than hampers the human propensity to act.

- Time pressure drives the human propensity to act.
- Once a pattern match has been recognized, the human brain switches off.

## PATTERNS EMERGE EASIER WITH FEWER DATA AVAILABLE

In psychology, it is the consistency of information in a data set that matters for the credibility of the information, not its completeness (Kahneman, 2011a). The often-lazy brain tells the analyst:

> *"Knowing little makes it easier to fit everything you know into a coherent pattern."*

With fewer data, inconsistencies have a lower chance of occurring. It is all too easy to lay out a straight line when you only have two points to connect. This phenomenon thus favours the risk of premature closure based on incorrect analysis.

## TAKING ACTION IS EASIER WHEN LESS DATA ARE AVAILABLE

Humans act much faster and more confidently when they (believe that they) recognize a pattern than when they feel uncertain about a situation, as was discussed in more detail in chapter 9. Psychological experiments indeed reveal that there is an inverse relationship between information gathering and the urge to act (Dörner, 1996b):

> *"The less information gathered, the greater the readiness to act. And vice versa."*

If this factor in itself wouldn't be alarming enough, there is a psychological catalyst that may increase the risk of premature closure. The catalyst relates in particular to executives. Executives are driven (and want to be seen to be driven) to act. The combination of these two factors makes the risk of premature closure very real. The urge to act may itself also be catalyzed by a third factor: time pressure.

## TIME PRESSURE FURTHER INCREASES THE RISK

Premature closing has also been referred to as 'early closure'. Early closure forms an all-too-human way out of the uncertainty that analysts or executives experience when they have to make sense of too much data under the gun of time pressure (Wohlstetter, 1965b). The point here is that an analyst will favour a hypothesis that comes to mind first and/or suits a personal or political purpose best (Rumelt, 2012b):

> *"Under pressure to develop a way out of the difficulty, that first idea is a welcome relief. Thank goodness, here is something to hang on to! It feels much better to get oriented. The problem is that there might be better ideas out there [...] But we accept early closure because letting go of a judgment is painful and disconcerting. To search for a new insight, one would have to put aside the comfort of being oriented and once again cast around in choppy waters for a new source of stability. There is the fear of coming up empty-handed. Plus it is unnatural, even painful, to question our own ideas."*

The relief one feels when fitting together the puzzle – even when the fit is incorrect – has been mentioned before (Makridakis, 1990). In a complex world, intentionally underrating uncertainty is an understandable coping mechanism.

## ONCE A PATTERN MATCH HAS BEEN MADE, THE HUMAN BRAIN SWITCHES OFF

For the analyst, another trigger for this bias might be that the data he has seen so far may confirm his pre-set expectations. This may be due to a confirmation bias but this does not need to be the case. The analyst may not in advance have looked for a particular pattern to be confirmed. Upon analysing the data set, they may simply perceive themselves as having discovered a known, fitting pattern or an analogy.[8]

Subsequently, the analyst's timesaving modus starts up:

- The pattern has been recognized.
- The implication of what the data mean is now clear.
- There is thus no need to collect or even see more data.
- The analyst selects a frame he knows and applies it to the new data, extrapolating the expected future truth in his analysis to fit his mental model. This is his tried-and-true 'script,' which has been collected and built over years of analysis experience.

The mind, after all, is a 'machine for jumping to conclusions' (Kahneman, 2011b). This message should be taken seriously. Efficiency is critically important in strategic analysis but it should not come at the cost of analytical quality.

## WHAT IF NEW DATA PROVE PREMATURELY-CLOSED MINDS WRONG?

New data come in. Inconveniently, they have proven an existing analysis of a particular situation wrong. The output of any analysis should preferably, as in science, always be seen as a theory. Sound science demands changing a theory when new data come in that invalidates a hypothesis that was based on an untenable theory. A hypothesis is after all only valid until the opposite has been irrefutably proven. In science, revisiting theories is the golden standard. Science as a whole, however, is impersonal. One scientist posts a theory-derived hypothesis, carries out experiments, validates the outcomes and – assuming the outcomes confirm the hypothesis – validates the theory. Another scientist, however, may do another experiment that leads to results that falsify the theory. As was stated in chapter 2, in the face of ugly facts even a beautiful theory has to be rejected (Bruce, 2008b).

A key difference between intelligence and science is that in quantitative or exact science hypotheses are indeed falsifiable, where in intelligence the foreknowledge element by definition is not (Bruce, 2008b).

What is common in science, strategic analysis and military intelligence is that revisiting one's own theory in the face of new facts is not easy (Heuer, 2008):

> *"At a [...] meeting, the last thing the author of a report wants to hear is a new idea."*

For an analyst, this can pose quite a challenge. When the analyst has earlier issued a firm conclusion, now issuing data that questions that conclusion may affect their credibility – in their own eyes or in those of peers or decision-makers. They have to admit to themselves or to other stakeholders that their earlier assessment of the situation had not foreseen the possibility that the new data seem to suggest. There is, however, a way out. They may reject and discard the new data for legitimate or entirely made-up quality reasons. This may save face, at least for a short time, even when it poses a risk to their company. The analyst has now intentionally withheld relevant data from their company.

The analyst's dilemma is clear. The solution, of course, is never to withhold data or to reject it on false grounds. The key is, as described earlier in this book, to be a foxy analyst. Unfortunately, foxiness doesn't eliminate the possibility of premature closing. Foxiness may work for an individual analyst. They may, however, be part of a broader strategic analysis function. When the new data come in and the theory, usually referred to as output of the analysis, has to be reviewed, it is not only an individual analyst's credibility that is at stake, but that of the whole function.

When the business issue at hand is significant enough, the fallout will likely reverberate up to the head, including the head of the function. This dramatically raises the stakes. Chances are that the new data will be scrutinized across all data quality dimensions. The new data may be put on trial, with the function head, like a suave defense attorney, ripping the evidence apart to save the theory (read 'his reputation and/or career').

In comes the decision-maker. Where foxiness normally works for the analyst and may work for the strategic analysis function as a whole, it does not work for the decision-maker. This executive may have expressed opinions and/or have substantiated decisions based on an analysis that now proves to have been constructed on an incomplete and incorrectly analysed fact base. The analyst may obviously have a hard time getting the decision-maker to embrace new facts that prove their earlier opinions or decisions wrong. Examples from the military show that even undisputable new facts may not alter the opinions of decision-makers' prematurely closed minds.[9]

## PREMATURE CLOSING ESPECIALLY MATTERS IN ANALYSIS FOR STRATEGY DESIGN

The process dynamics of designing a business can open the door to premature closing. Premature closing may affect both analysts and decision-makers. Getting a strategy executed effectively requires more than an analytically correct conclusion based on a cognitively solid process. During the analytical process it also requires securing the buy-in of key stakeholders. Once part of the analysis has been finished by the analyst, tentative (read 'premature') strategic elements are often shared with stakeholders. The latter may include senior managers who are not part of the team designing the new strategy. These managers will not only test the strategy process on its analytical correctness, but possibly with even more interest also look for what is in it for them, once the new strategy is executed. Strategy changes may after all have an impact on organization structure. Structural changes can in turn lead to changes in senior management job status, responsibilities and authority.

The premature closing can stem from decision-makers, based on analyses that are tentative and may not incorporate complete data sets, already lobbying key stakeholders. "When you get this position, will you then support the approval of this strategy?" (Bower, 1979). A decision-maker who assembled a hard-won coalition to support adoption of the new strategy won't take kindly to an analyst who suggests a revised analysis that renders the earlier strategy design sub-optimal.

Premature closing would not be a big problem if it wouldn't tend to occur so naturally. The intermezzo at the end of this section summarizes of a historical, well-documented example of premature closing from a military intelligence context. The example in the intermezzo allows to better grasp the potential real-life dynamics of this bias.

## TIME MAY BE AN ALLY IN PREVENTING PREMATURE CLOSING

The most effective way to prevent premature closing is to postpone judgment calls until all data are available. When the collection phase delivers all data more or less at the same time to the analysis team, there is at least a synchronous review of all data. By simply being aware of the bias and reminding themselves that, until all facts are available, assessments are at best tentative, analysts may help prevent premature closing even when the condition of synchronous data delivery is not met. The delivery of all data and conclusions to decision-makers at once, the analyst helps ensure uniform, up-to-date executive review. No matter how obvious this solution, it will not always be easy to execute. When decision-makers have part of the data and have prematurely made up their mind on key conclusions the analyst should avoid a heated debate on the matter. The analyst should simply share the additional data with the decision-makers and render an informed opinion on the reliability of the data. Finally, when possible, the analyst should return another day to discuss implications and conclusions, and work on guiding the decision-maker to a favorably conclusion. Still, the decision-maker may not change direction until, in her heart of hearts, she's convinced it's the right thing to do... which may not happen until well after the analyst suggests that she do so.

## INTERMEZZO: AN EXAMPLE OF PREMATURE CLOSING FROM THE SECOND WORLD WAR

Examples of premature closing have been described by several authors. The example below illustrates the characteristic flow of premature closing. Some data are too good to resist, they allow a politically acceptable solution to the issue at hand, and thus new data that may question the outcome are no longer searched for. When they come in they are either twisted, as in the example below, or rejected on (possibly false) quality-assurance grounds.

For those who love the history of intelligence I recommend reading the full account of Operation Mincemeat (Macintyre, 2010f). It recounts the incredible story of MI6 intentionally deceiving the German High Command during the Second World War. The message the Germans were made to believe was that the Allied invasion in the Mediterranean would take place in Sardinia and Greece, rather than in Sicily, which in fact was the real plan. The deception used an actual human dressed up as a British officer, with a suitcase containing highly confidential but misleading documents. The corpse was to be disembarked from a British submarine just off the coast of Spain. The corpse and the satchel of documents would fall via neutral Spanish sources into German hands. The deception plot was not without its flaws. For several reasons the execution of the operation had been delayed. The corpse, taken from a London mortuary, was of a person who had passed away months earlier, and it was in an advanced state of decomposition. In the end, the person had passed away months before the actual operation took place. Meanwhile, the Germans were meant to be believe that the officer had drowned at sea, in a plane crash that at best had happened a few days before the body washed up on the shore. Based on theatre tickets with recent dates put in one of the officer's pockets, the condition of the body needed to convey that the officer had died just days earlier.

Despite this complication, everything worked according to plan. The body was found by the Spanish and the suitcase with the documents made its way to German intelligence staff in Spain. The local German intelligence chief believed he'd made the find of his life. He was convinced that the suitcase contained the highest-grade intelligence. Berlin had to be notified immediately. However, he had to polish away the conflicting evidence that a Spanish autopsy concluded that the body had been dead for at least eight days, even when the theatre tickets suggested less:

> *"The Abwehr had decided, from the outset, that the discovery was genuine, and moulded [sic] the evidence, despite obvious flaws, towards this belief."*

Once this fox had turned hedgehog, there was no turning back.

A final note: this is not just amusing to read. I would suggest that any one of us, under the right circumstances, could have fallen for such a deception. This intermezzo is meant as a warning, and a lesson... not as a distraction.

# 12.11 CONFUSING CAUSALITY AND CORRELATION IN A DATA SET

At this stage one may wonder whether there are still more biases to come. Unfortunately, the answer is yes. Reaching correct conclusions from a data set is not easy. So, I hope you will join me on this voyage of discovery into the biases that can influence the processing of data sets.

The next potential bias I would like to discuss is that of confusing causality and correlation in data set analysis (Denrell, 2005). Data do not always come as single facts. Often facts and partial (pre-cooked) analysis put forward by a source reach the analyst bundled together as a new data point. In such partial analyses, data may have been to some extent causally linked. Denrell mentions the example of culture and company performance. Consider studying a set of companies. When data analysis reveals a proportionality between a strong culture in individual companies and the outperformance (in profitability) of the strong culture companies, the easy but incorrect conclusion may be that a strong culture is imperative for being or becoming an outperforming company. In some cases, the proportionality may be inverse: it's the strong-performing companies that can truly afford to build a strong company culture. These costs may even be a drag on the outperformance. Two independent variables may correlate perfectly, but do not need to be causally related.

The credibility of Curveball, one of the most relevant sources of 'intelligence' on Iraq's alleged pre-2003 biological WMD programme was based on precisely this confusion (Jervis, 2010h). This narrative is so bizarre that it has to be true. Curveball provided data on Saddam Hussein's secret weapons programme. These data corroborated largely with the picture that US intelligence analysts themselves had been able to construct – through connecting multiple bits and pieces from public (such as internet) sources. This added greatly to Curveball's credibility. It also inflated the analysts' self-esteem. Now they heard from the horse's mouth – from the Curveball informant – what they so painstakingly had collected and analysed themselves. In the subsequent euphoria, the analysts failed to see that Curveball had access to the very same public sources and had used these to creatively build the picture that he 'sold' to the intelligence community. For the analysts it also made Curveball all the more compelling of a source for additional intelligence.

Such correlations – one public source, two similar stories – quite often reflect that the situations have a common cause but are nonetheless unrelated.

An example of such unrelated phenomena that correlate convincingly is given below. In the polarized 1990s the Dutch Chemical Industry Association informally lobbied the Dutch government for the prohibition of ice cream sales. Substantiating evidence for this lobby was the strong proportionality, portrayed as a causal relation, between the number of people drowning on a given day and the sales of ice cream on that day. Given the apparent correlation, the lobbyist argued, prohibiting ice cream sales should help reduce the number of drownings. The two phenomena of course had a common cause but nothing to do with each other. The industry used this ironic example to help spotlight, in the industry's eyes, similar flaws in upcoming environmental legislation. In strategic analysis, root cause analysis should be part and parcel of the analyst's tool kit. There is catch, though. Causal relations in business and in life may be less common than they look to the observer (Taleb, 2007h):

> *"We are explanation-seeking animals who tend to think that everything has an identifiable cause and grab the most apparent one as the explanation."*

Let me repeat this warning: beware of jumping to causality conclusions. Keep wondering. Do these phenomena correlate, because they have a common cause, or is the one phenomenon indeed the cause of the other? Could there be feedback loops, where phenomenon two indeed interferes with phenomenon one? All too often, good corporate performance is related to managerial excellence rather than to favourable market conditions. The opposite (poor performance) is all too often blamed on unfavourable market conditions, which management conveniently insists were beyond its control and were thus the root of all evil.

As a rule, correlations occur much more frequently than causal relations. Beware of the human tendency to see a (simplified) pattern of logical links that the reality of a situation does not justify.

# 12.12 UNDERESTIMATING SAMPLE SIZE REQUIREMENTS

The next topic I wish to discuss regarding issues in data set processing focuses on the common problem that 'statistics' is easier to spell right than to do right. Statistics is not an intuitive science. It is all too common to underestimate the size of a data set that is needed necessary to responsibly and correctly draw conclusions.

An obvious example relates to smoking. Knowing a single person who consistently smoked 20 cigarettes a day and yet turned 90 in good health does not justify denying or in any way minimizing the risk of health issues due to smoking. A causal relation between frequent smoking and health issues has been statistically proven beyond any reasonable doubt, based on millions of cases that have been studied. It would be foolish to think that the 90-year-old heavy smoker is anything but an exception, and to disregard the statistically valid conclusions that relate to the population at large (Heuer, 1991).

In strategy analysis, the same phenomenon plays a role. Knowing a company that has successfully consumer-branded a line of previously generic products does not allow one to ignore the lack of marketplace traction suffered by other generic products. Before making a call on the feasibility of consumer-branding a product, at least a dozen peer cases should be reviewed, rather than one compelling example being overemphasized.

Statistically correct analyses are understandably more time consuming than intuitive analyses. When in the strategic analysis function the quality of the outputs is rated high, sample sizes in analyses should always err on the edge of being too large and never on the border of being too small. It always pays to study multiple cases prior to drawing generic conclusions. Every case may offer yet another insight as rarely are two cases in business really similar. Balanced conclusions underpinned by multiple cases add to the function's credibility and the management acceptance of its deliverables.

# 12.13 USING FLAWED ANALOGIES

Instant and correct pattern recognition when confronted with a new event is a hallmark of expertise in many professional settings. The beauty of this is that it allows for fast and often flawless decision-making in the management of emerging issues. Once a particular pattern has been recognized, the brain instantly suggests the most appropriate course of action, aligning that action with one that worked in the earlier instance where the patterned behaviour was recognized. The mind suggests a course of action that is based on an analogy. The observed event is believed to be analogous to a previously, probably vividly experienced event. Paradoxically, a pattern is recognized faster when less data are available. Pattern recognition is a great human asset but it is not flawless.

As a result, seeing an earlier sequence of events as a reliable predictor of how a new sequence of events will roll out may seem undeniably reliable. This prediction, however, may happen to be flawed. The analogy may not apply – and the observer may, as a result, respond inappropriately.

## ANALOGIES MAY BE FLAWED IN THE MINDS OF BOTH THE ANALYST AND THE DECISION-MAKER

Harvard Professor E.R. May in the 1970s analysed a number of US foreign policy decisions that were underpinned by flawed 'historical analogies' – in May's words, 'lessons of the past' (May, 1973a). He identified four pathologies in the use of history-based analogies that are also applicable to strategic business analysis work:

- The first anology that comes to mind is chosen.
- Once an analogy has presented itself, it is common not to search more widely.
- Analogies are not tested for fitness or deception.

- Current trends that one uses an analogy to illustrate are projected forward, without checking whether the underlying phenomena that caused the trend are continuing over time.

Choosing the first analogy that comes to mind, and subsequently searching no further, can contribute to overvaluing the most recent data, and can prompt premature closing. Professor May also observed that analogies are invariably chosen from the analyst's lifetime experiences, and not from an analogy pool that pre-dates the analyst (May, 1973b). This resembles the bias of vividness weighing. For an analyst, the challenge in data processing is thus to avoid carelessly choosing a historical analogy that may not be predictive for the future development of the new case at hand. Analysts should at any rate avoid using superficial and thus flawed analogies (Gavetti, 2005). The key message is first to scrutinize the validity of the analogy relative to the new case, and then to keep monitoring whether an analogy remains applicable once the course of action addressing the event has moved to the execution stage. The moment analogies no longer apply, adaptations to the analagous course of action are immediately necessary.

Even when analysts are professional enough to avoid the trap of the flawed analogy, the analyst still faces the challenge of convincing her customer that analogies may or may not apply. This is not necessarily easy. Decision-makers, in this case US President Franklin D. Roosevelt, can at times get (May, 1973c):

> *"(...) captivated by a single conception of the future, based largely on beliefs of a recent past."*

Let me share a few historical examples on flawed analogies to illustrate the point. I start with the post-Second World War recalibration of the US-USSR relationship. During the war, the countries had been uneasy allies against Nazi Germany. Now that the war was over, the US reviewed its former ally's policies in Eastern Europe with an increasing concern. This is where the analogy comes in.

The US decision-makers felt that ignoring Nazi Germany – a totalitarian state – in the late 1930s had in retrospect been a huge mistake. They realized that their inaction had led to unimaginable sacrifice, death and destruction – namely, years of global conflagration that literally consumed the planet. After WW II, as the US saw a new adversary emerge that seemed to display 'totalitarian characteristics' – the Soviet Union, with its authoritarian behaviour in Central and Eastern Europe – they felt compelled to act strongly (May, 1973d). As a result, the Truman administration was so forceful against Stalin's Soviet Union that the Cold War probably became much colder than was necessary. The US only used confirmatory evidence of the parallels between Hitler's Germany and Stalin's USSR, not the differences between the two regimes. The latter phenomenon may be generalized. When events are perceived as analogous, all other rationale loses relevance (May, 1973e). When that occurs, we observe a classic example of the confirmation bias – even when not all the available data support the comparison.

This USSR example does not stand on its own (Clark, 2013b). Clark also describes Russian pre-First World War diplomacy. This example first describes a single, unfortunately flawed but credible narrative:

> *"Russia had always been the docile, peace-loving neighbour and Germany the duplicitous predator, bullying and humiliating the Russians at every opportunity. Now the time had come to stand firm."*

As this narrative spread in St Petersburg – even though it was wrong – it felt so good that it considerably limited Russian policy options. It contributed to Russia's belligerence towards Germany and its decision for a full military mobilization in 1914. This example speaks for itself: flawed analogies leading to credible narratives may seriously deceive decision-makers or limit their flexibility.

A flawed analogy also seriously affected US policies towards Vietnam in the early 1960s (Halberstam, 1992a). Based on extensive experience in the Korean War, a top US military adviser saw more analogies than differences between a possible future military conflict in Vietnam and what the US had experienced in Korea in the early 1950s. As we saw above, one key criterion for finding parallels had been met: the Korean conflict happened in the adviser's lifetime. A second criterion for flawed decision-making was also met – differences between the two cases were overlooked or ignored. Think of the climate and the terrain: tropically humid jungles in South Vietnam versus the harsh winters in the plains of Korea. Most of all, think of the difference between a war amongst two standing armies (US and Chinese-backed North Koreans) in Korea versus an insurgency in South Vietnam, where a civilian farmer in daytime could be a Vietcong insurgent by night. By implication, a standing army's competitive advantages were wiped out by the very fact that there was no enemy willing to fight on the standing army's terms. It almost sounds like having a great brick-and-mortar retail outlet, but no consumer willing to buy holiday airline tickets, hotel stays and other merry-making through retail outlets anymore. The enemy is online, rendering your advantage of high street visibility irrelevant. You may wonder why I associate the fate of old-fashioned travel agencies with Vietnam, but back to Vietnam. In short, the US military in 1961 quite inaccurately assessed South Vietnam as (Halberstam, 1992a):

*"(...), not an excessively difficult or unpleasant place to operate."*

Flawed analogies leading to credible but incorrect narratives should thus be watched out for. The analyst and the decision-maker both are recommended to be alert to statements:

*"X happened before, so X is likely to happen again."*

*"Y is a regular pattern, X is an illustration."*

This type of narrative should alert the analyst that a flawed analogy is being presented or is at least in the making. Chapter 16, on analyst – decision-maker interaction describes how an analyst may consider handling an untested or flawed analogy presented by a decision-maker.

To avoid closing off this section too negatively it should again be stressed that recognizing and using analogies based on experience-based pattern recognition is a powerful tool. Great business examples of analogies inspiring innovations in products and business models have been described for your further reference (Gavetti, 2005). Smartly using analogies is the key behind the strategic approach to looking for repeatability of models as a driver of growth (Zook, 2012a).

It remains relevant for the analyst to try to at all times ensure that the analogies used *really* apply rather than only are seeming to apply.

CHAPTER 13

# HYPOTHESIS FORMULATION AND TESTING

## 13.1 INTRODUCTION

In the previous chapter I focused on how weighing evidence within entire data sets may affect the quality of analysis. This chapter focuses on the tool of using hypotheses in an analysis. My objective is to describe how to formulate hypotheses in support of an analysis. In Section 13.2 I will cover the formulation process, beginning with a brief examination of theories and predictions. In section 13.3 I will introduce an efficient method for testing hypotheses.

# 13.2 ON ANALYSES, THEORIES, PREDICTIONS AND HYPOTHESES

In previous chapters analyses, assessments, theories and hypotheses have been referenced in passing. So far I have not taken the trouble to properly define these terms. To avoid confusion, simple definitions are provided below.

## DEFINITIONS

Analyses create knowledge and ultimately intelligence by processing and combining data that are usually obtained empirically. Analyses may be supported by mathematical modeling tools or by applying logic. Data usually concern events that happened in the past. In such cases the analysis leads to an interpretation of events. When on the basis of assessing past events the analysis generates a future-oriented output, it is referred to as a forecast or a prediction. I use the word 'analysis' and interchangeably the word 'assessment'.

The output of an analysis may be a theory, vividly presented as a narrative. A theory *describes* a phenomenon, either based on (preferably) rational/logically consistent thinking and modeling and/or on empirical data. Generally, the best theory chooses the simplest explanation that fits the data at hand. This heuristic is known as Occam's razor, or the law of parsimony (Silver, 2013g). A theory may not always be tested experimentally. In physics, some theories in quantum mechanics could only be experimentally verified decades after they were postulated, simply because measurement methods were not available any earlier. Validation was logically possible but not feasible (and here I use 'validation' interchangeably use with 'verification'). Let's also think back to chapter 2, and Schrodinger's cat, which warned observers that objectivity in measurements is critical. The core principle there was that the measurement method shall not affect the outcome of the measurement as such. Thus, to test a theory, measurement methods should be available that are both feasible (i.e., do not affect the outcome) and objective.

To test a theory experimentally, a hypothesis may be generated. I define a hypothesis as:

> *A statement based on a theory that is consistent with all available data or knowledge regarding the phenomenon that underpin the theory at that moment, and that predicts a future outcome of that phenomenon that has not yet been experimentally verified.*

The key attribute of a hypothesis is that the outcome of the experiment should allow for the hypothesis to be either accepted or rejected. And, be aware that it is possible to falsify a hypothesis.

In science, a four-step approach is commonly used to stretch the borders of existing knowledge:

i. A phenomenon is observed.

ii. Literature research is carried out in an attempt to understand the phenomenon and most of all to find the boundaries of current knowledge. In other words, (all) existing knowledge is sought. In strategic analysis parlance: science starts with OSINT. This step is finalized by defining a theory that is consistent with all available knowledge. Such a theory allows us to define a hypothesis to be tested.

iii. The hypothesis predicts the outcome of an experiment that has never been attempted.

iv. The experiment that has not yet been attempted is designed in such a way as to provide an objective outcome that allows to irrefutably reject the hypothesis or to confirm the hypothesis *for now*. This means that the hypothesis is perceived to be correct for as long as no experiment has been executed that proves the hypothesis to be wrong.

In chapter 1, I showed that a hypothesis may be developed on a theory that is based on empirical data and inductive knowledge: swan 1 is white, swan 2 is white, swan 3 is white, etc. (Taleb, 2007e). In such a case, a theory may be postulated that states 'swans are white birds'. The next step is to formulate hypotheses. Two possible hypotheses for this theory are:

- All swans are white.
- All swans are not black.

Such hypotheses allow for verification. Every new swan that is being observed may be checked against this hypothesis. When the bird is white the observation confirms the hypothesis. As more white birds are counted, the more confident the observer may become that the hypothesis is correct. In medical science, there are four gradations given to scientific evidence that underpins a hypothesis (from low to high):
- Unlikely.
- Possible.
- Probable.
- Convincing.

If the evidence to support the acceptance of a hypothesis is weak, the sobriquet 'unlikely' is adequate. With an increase in the strength of the evidence, the rating gradually moves up from possible to probable to convincing. After having spotted untold thousands of white swans in seventeen different European countries over 1,600 years, the evidence to support the hypothesis 'all swans are white' had become quite convincing… until the first Western explorer sailed to Australia and discovered a black swan.

## PEARL HARBOR AS AN EXAMPLE OF FAILED HYPOTHESIS GENERATION

At Pearl Harbor, as we all know, the Japanese Imperial Navy launched a surprise attack on the US Fleet and Air Force. Pearl Harbor is commonly perceived as a major US intelligence failure. Before we examine Pearl Harbor more closely, be aware that for analysts -- and all of us, really -- it can be dangerous to define through example (Johnson, 2005d):

> *"Each case is contextually unique and can be argued ad infinitum."*

Having said this, examples do serve a purpose as illustration for a particular point to be made. I will continue to use narrative examples in this book, while acknowledging that I lack sufficient in-depth knowledge regarding individual examples to comprehensively highlight all relevant dimensions. Let us now review the American intelligence failure that allowed the Japanese to succeed in their sneak attack on Pearl Harbor:

i. **US-observed phenomenon:** The Japanese government has built a strong navy, executes an aggressive expansionist policy in north-east China and colonizes Korea.

ii. **Available knowledge:**
   - Nations historically do not seek war with adversaries that are much stronger.
   - Japan launching a surprise attack on Port Arthur, Russia, in 1904 was no exception to this rule as Tsarist Russia was not perceived as a stronger adversary at that time.
   - Economic sanctions are a non-military means to force nations to retreat from occupying foreign territories.

iii. **Theory:**
   - Sanctions will make Japan retreat.
   - Japan will not attack the US.

iv. **Hypothesis:** sanctions will be effective.

v. **Implication:** There is no need to place US troops on high alert status at Pearl Harbor.

vi. **Experiment:** Economic sanctions can be tightened.

vii. **Outcome:** The Japanese government went to war with the US rather than retreat.

This example elucidates the critical flaw in the American hypotheses. In section 14.2, the ethnocentric bias will be discussed. This bias is, in knowledge and hypothesis generation, among the most destructive (and common) sources of prediction failure. In the greatly simplified example above, the US military, following American ethnocentric logic, reasoned that the Japanese would take a rational view of the economic and industrial status of both countries prior to doing anything as staggeringly monumental as starting a war. Doing so would inevitably and correctly have led the Japanese to conclude that their chances of winning a war with the US were negligible. The Americans just couldn't imagine that the Japanese would be so stupid as to start a war with the US. Admiral Isoroku Yamamoto, one of the leading Japanese naval strategists and a Harvard University graduate, held this view, but failed to persuade the Japanese government to maintain peace with the US.[1]

The Japanese government, however, most members of which had not seen the US with their own eyes, may have insufficiently realized the economic power of the Twentieth-Century America. They therefore may not have been convinced by what Yamamoto postulated based on empirically obtained and vividly experienced knowledge. They just couldn't imagine that American power could be unleashed against them, in their own geopolitical sphere, over such a long distance. The above reasoning presupposes that the Japanese decision was based on rationalism. This may also be doubted as irrational emotions like pride and overconfidence may also have played a role. It's likely that an overwhelming cloud of groupthink among Japanese government and military leadership banished any possibility of logical decision-making (see chapter 17).

In short, had the Japanese thought like the Americans, they may not have attacked Pearl Harbor. Had the Americans thought like the Japanese, they may not have been surprised by the disastrous surprise attack. Previously in this book, we've seen how failure to imagine the next move of an adversary (i.e., the failure to think xenocentrically) has been a common feature in multiple intelligence failures. What applies to historical military examples just as well applies in business, the same logic applies. This book does not provide an abstract historical analysis for the sake of it. The very same logic is applicable in a daily business context. Thinking xenocentrically is an essential and potentially highly valuable tool to make business predictions on a variety of competitor actions. Doing so successfully requires the same vivid imagination to put the other 'xeno' (fundamentally strange party) truly front & centre in one's analytical deliberations.

## INSTRUMENTS AND TOOLS TO THINK XENOCENTRICALLY

The implications of all this present a paradox in strategic analysis. Truly xenocentric hypothesis or prediction generation in strategic analysis requires analysts, selected for their rational deductive reasoning capabilities, to be imaginative. Here's one way to think about it (Smith, 2008):

> *"Deterministic or reductionist analytics do not promote or proliferate hypotheses; instead, analysis narrows focus and eliminates hypotheses. Hypothesis generation is the 'art' of science, the domain where intuition and imagination can and must play an indispensable role."*

To mobilize imagination as input for taking a xenocentric view in hypothesis generation, the following instruments may be useful (Bruce, 2008c):

- Run war games.
- Run contingency 'what if' analyses.
- Imagine black swans – high-impact/low-probability events (Taleb, 2007c).

These tools may also be called 'challenge analysis' – methods to challenge the logic of the analysis and in doing so either find flaws in that logic and/or generate alternative and more xenocentric perspectives (Davis, 2008).

In addition, the following complementary methodologies may be applied (Heuer, 2005):

- Appoint a devil's advocate to challenge assumptions and group-consensus.
- Scenario analysis.
- Brainstorming.

Bruce emphasizes that a single theory may be tested with multiple hypotheses. Above, the hypotheses that all swans are white and that all swans are not black both matched with the Sixteenth-Century European knowledge about swans.

The hypotheses themselves are markedly different. As noted, the nullification of these hypotheses came when European voyages of discovery revealed the existence of black swans.

Two other useful methodologies to validate hypotheses are together called 'externally structured analysis' (Davis, 2008). Externally structured analysis includes the analysis of competing hypotheses and signpost analysis – both of which will be covered in the next section – and argument mapping. These methods can help to mitigate the risks of unbalanced weighing of data in a data set. The methods are not difficult to put to use, but as far as I know are infrequently applied in strategic analysis-related decision-making. Analysts who've gained the trust of their decision-makers may further improve their standing by not only being known for the best collection, analysis and reporting of market intelligence, but also by providing their senior management with a rich toolbox of strategic analysis decision-support tools.

## ON HYPOTHESES AND PREDICTIONS

In strategic analysis, generating a theory does not always mean that experimental validation of that theory is (immediately) possible. Objective measurements may be lacking for some theoretically-based predictions. For example, a theory may be that the competitor suffers margin pressure due to rising input cost. The prediction may be that the competitor will increase prices next week. It is called a prediction rather than a hypothesis because this statement cannot be empirically tested and thus cannot be debunked, with the latter being a key attribute of a hypothesis.

The prediction, and thus the theory, can only be validated after the event. Analytic validation after the event is crucial for accumulating knowledge to make better hypotheses or predictions next time, and is therefore indispensable.

In the above example, a hypothesis may be that the competitor will raise prices after your firm has raised prices. This is a hypothesis, as in this case empirical validation is possible. The difference between a hypothesis and a prediction has only been emphasized for consistency. Only in cases where our firm acts first, or in scientific jargon, 'does the experiment', is defining a hypothesis made possible. A hypothesis thus always forecasts the marketplace response to a firm's action.

When, in contrast, a theory postulates the next independent move of another actor in the market, it is called a prediction. In intelligence literature, the above definitions are not always as strictly adhered to. Hypotheses that are not refutable – and that should be called predictions – are still referred to as hypotheses.

For generating imaginative theories, hypotheses and predictions, teamwork is crucial. In business, the best teams embrace diversity, are multi-functional and generate mutual trust (Lencioni, 2002). Diversity of team members includes more than gender or age; it also should include backgrounds, roles, risk aversion profiles and interests. A meritocratic atmosphere is critical: expertise rather than rank matters most (Lovallo, 2010b). The more perspectives on a data set that can be turned into theories, hypotheses or predictions, the more likely the (correct) xenocentric view is developed.[2]

A common approach will be to articulate not only a confirmatory prediction but also opposite views:

- The competitor will increase prices next week.
- The competitor will keep prices stable next week.
- The competitor will decrease prices next week.

Strategic analysis, it should be repeated, does not fully resemble science. Where generally in science one hypothesis is to be accepted, or rejected, in strategic analysis, this approach is too limiting. The real question in strategic analysis is: which prediction or hypothesis has the highest probability to materialize?

Articulating three different, preferably opposite predictions, and subsequently, in a team effort, listing all data evidence or codified knowledge and all tacit knowledge (see chapter 1) in favour of and in opposition to each of these predictions may lead to remarkable xenocentric insights. These insights will unleash more imagination and will, as a result, generally have superior predictive power than even a team discussion on a single prediction would have generated. The best participants in such team discussions are critical thinkers. The desirable competencies of critical thinkers are listed below. This summary list relates to the various analysis steps covered in the chapters 9-14 (Moore, 2007b):

- Recognize problems or questions and find effective means of solution.
- Engage in meta-cognitive activities that identify assumptions, biases and performance as solutions are developed.
- Interpret data, appraise evidence and evaluate statements in order to recognize logical relationships between propositions.
- Infer warranted conclusions and generalizations from evidence.
- Test generalizations and conclusions by seeking out contradictory evidence that enables them to judge the credibility of claims.
- Convey sound, well-reasoned arguments.
- Focus on the process of reasoning with the intention of improving the process.

# 13.3 TESTING PREDICTIONS AND HYPOTHESES

By now you have certainly noticed that I've build this work on the thinking of multiple authors. In the field of intelligence analysis a few authors stand out for their valuable contributions to the field. One of them is R.J. Heuer Jr, author of the seminal work *Psychology of Intelligence Analysis*, which was first introduced in section 3.4. He is also known as the preeminent author in the field of prediction and hypothesis testing. He developed a methodology referred to as 'analysis of competing hypotheses', commonly known by the abbreviation ACH (Heuer, 2005); (Heuer, 2008). The ACH methodology is equally useful in analysing predictions; where Heuer writes hypotheses one may also read predictions. The input of ACH is a set of hypotheses such as described in the previous section; the output is the most probable hypothesis, which is a key input to downstream strategy or policy decision-making.

There are three key benefits to ACH over conventional intuitive analysis:

- ACH avoids the risk of conveniently confirming an existing theory by only looking for evidence that is confirmatory.
- ACH determines which evidence forces you to accept some but rejects other hypotheses; this is called the 'diagnosticity of evidence'. Such evidence may also be referred to as critical.
- ACH forces you to refute weak hypotheses by focusing on the critical evidence that leads to rejecting rather than accepting such weak hypotheses.

ACH allows us to determine which individual data points in the evidence are critical. Subsequently, it is good practice to double-check the accuracy of those particular individual data points. As was demonstrated earlier on Cuba, only a few critical data points in a sea of noise made the difference.

These data points must be of unquestioned reliability to enable the selection of a most probable prediction or hypothesis. A key point in ACH is that the most probable hypothesis is the one with the least evidence against it. It is explicitly not the hypothesis with the most evidence in favour of it. The same logic is used in table 13.1, which summarizes the arguments for and against a hypothesis (Noble, 2004).

| ARGUMENTS SUPPORTING A HYPOTHESIS | ARGUMENTS OPPOSING A HYPOTHESIS |
|---|---|
| - Confirming evidence.<br>- Lack of alternative hypotheses able to explain the evidence. | - Conflicting evidence.<br>- Alternative hypotheses able to explain the data.<br>- Available data that the hypothesis cannot explain.<br>- Data expected if the hypothesis is true, but that were not obtained. |

TABLE 13.1 ▶▶▶ QUESTION CHECKLIST ON THE NATURE OF INDIVIDUAL DATA POINTS

## SIGNPOSTS MAY PROVIDE EARLY WARNING SIGNALS

The last bullet point in the right column is an especially critical test. The test could be called the 'phase two analogy' test (Von Baeyer, 1993). An analogy may be recognized between an unfolding phenomenon that is now, being studied, and another phenomenon that is fully known and understood. In such a case, it may be possible to predict the next step in the development of the current phenomenon by an analogy that refers to what happened when the other phenomenon unfolded.

When, for example, the hypothesis is that a company in a geo-expansion drive is aiming to start selling products in a new country, normally it is to be expected that, by drawing a parallel with similar previous cases, the company will follow a known standard operating procedure (SOP) or script:

- Air-time for TV or radio commercials is bought.
- Outdoor advertising space is rented.
- An advertising agency is retained.
- An office is rented.
- Products may be registered at the appropriate food law authority.
- Product listing plans are discussed with major retail companies etc,.

When one or more of these usual analogous signposts are not registered by strategic analysis, either the geo-expansion plan will be innovative – that is, it may contain unknown unknowns – like a launch that entirely depends on e-commerce initiatives – or the hypothesis may have to be rejected (for now). The better SOPs or scripts of competitors are understood, the easier it is to test hypotheses, provided the SOPs still apply.

As always, there is a dark side to signpost analysis. This type of analysis is looking for the evidence of a script to unfold, but if a competitor's product launch employs an unexpectedly innovative approach, the expected evidence may never actually appear. To paraphrase Taleb, signpost analysis is a brilliant tool in mediocristan but gets you nowhere in extremistan. Signpost analysis will thus not spot disruptive innovation and should be used with care (Christensen, 2000). This will be illustrated in more detail in section 14.8, when we examine 'conventional wisdom'.

## ACH SOUNDS MORE COMPLICATED THAN IT IS

ACH, as such, is simply executed by preparing a table. In the far-left column, the various hypotheses are written, one in each row. In all others except the far-right column, the various pieces of evidence are listed. The cells in the table analyse the match of the evidence (confirming or +, neutral or 0, discarding or -) with a particular hypothesis (or prediction). Table 13.2 shows an ACH template.

| HYPOTHESES (OR PREDICTIONS) | DATA POINT *p* | DATA POINT *q* | DATA POINT *r* | DATA POINT *s* | ACH-RESULT |
|---|---|---|---|---|---|
| ***a*** | - | - | - | - | least probable |
| ***b*** | + | 0 | + | - | most probable |
| ***c*** | + | + | - | - | less probable |

TABLE 13.2 ▶▶▶ ACH TEMPLATE FOR THREE HYPOTHESES AND THREE DATA POINTS

In table 13.2, data points *p*, *q* and *r* form critical evidence, or may be called diagnostic. These data points allow one to differentiate between the probabilities of different hypotheses. Data point *s* leads to the rejection of all three hypotheses. As a data point, *s* is not critical; it has no diagnostic value. In analysis, unfortunately, most data points tend not to have diagnostic value (Heuer, 1999g).

Generally speaking having a data point that leads to the rejection of all three hypotheses, should still warn the analyst in charge, as it is never advisable to propose a hypothesis or prediction to decision-makers for which conflicting evidence is available. Hypothesis *b* (not *c)* is considered as the most probable. Both have two data points that favour choosing it, but *b* has the lowest number of data points suggest rejecting it.

As a method, ACH is relatively straightforward; the question seems to be why it is not being applied more often. What may possibly affect the application of ACH is that it is so clinical. It lacks emotion. It also lacks room to manoeuvre for teams that apply it. There is no ambiguity. ACH does not allow management to pretend a formal analytical process has been used, when in actuality a personal, pre-defined preference has simply been elegantly substantiated. For a strategic analysis function, ACH should be a tool to be proposed whenever it fits. Just be prepared for management resistance, especially when a tool may be perceived to limit post-analysis managerial options.

CHAPTER 14

# ANALYTICAL PITFALLS

## 14.1 INTRODUCTION

This is another chapter dedicated to what may go wrong in analysis. Chapter 10 focused both on what may be wrong in individual input data and what could go wrong in the mind of the analyst assessing the data. It also covered potentially erroneous perceptions on data set completeness. Chapter 12 discussed what could go wrong in assessing a data set as a whole. In this chapter, the starting point is a data set which is (perceived to be or in reality) sufficiently complete. Moreover, individual data in the data set have all passed the quality assurance test. What else can still go wrong? The sobering answer is that an awful lot can still go wrong.

Unfortunately, weighing data in a data set in a balanced and correct way is no guarantee of a bias-free overall analysis. In assessing the meaning of data either the individual analyst, the strategic analysis function and/or the decision-makers still have to avoid blunders, and biases. This chapter describes common analytical pitfalls. Which should be watched for in any final quality control checklist. Only when this quality control threshold has been successfully passed it is time to worry about how to report the outcome of the analysis.

# 14.2 COMMON PITFALLS IN INTELLIGENCE ANALYSIS

Quality defects in analytical processing ultimately originate from the fact that analysts are human. Moreover, so are the decision-makers who the analysts report to. When companies fail, it is not the companies themselves that shoulder the blame, it is the leaders of the business (Keough, 2008a):

> *"Businesses are the product and extension of the personal characteristics of their leaders – the lengthened shadows of the men and women who run them."*

When business decisions are flawed – even when complete and reasonably correct, business environment data and possibly even strategic analyses were available – the human touch (in a negative sense) almost always matters most. In strategic analysis, the human touch may negatively affect the individual analyst, colouring an analysis with an ethnocentric bias, for instance. Just as often the analyst may deliver a correct assessment to management, but the latter may either not accept the conclusion or may modify it due to personal preferences, so significantly that it may render the analysis useless. The pitfalls described in the sections below are common. Being on the lookout for these obstacles is no guarantee that they will not haunt the analysis produced. Chances of these pitfalls distorting the work, however, may become less of a threat if a diligent analysts stays on her toes.

# 14.3 ETHNOCENTRIC BIAS

In the context of business environment analysis, ethnocentrism is best defined as the failure to imagine the competitor's moves. Competitor should be read here as 'other party'. This other party could also be a supplier, a customer, a consumer or any other stakeholder who matters to a business. Ethnocentrism can arise when analysts or decision-makers get trapped in the cage of their own rigid mindsets. It is all too human to overestimate the extent to which others share a person's view, belief or experiences (Roxburgh, 2003).

Even when an analyst is aware that he has to put himself in the other party's shoes, this is not always a guarantee of success. In military intelligence, the term for this flaw is mirror imaging (Heuer, 1999f). A sentence like 'if I were the competitor's marketing director…' may still unfortunately hide the fact that the analyst does not know or understand how the competitor thinks. This may be due to a failure to understand the competitor's competences and intent, or an inability to put one's self in the competitor's shoes and act accordingly. Either way, whatever the analyst plugs into the second half of the sentence 'If I were…' may give false confidence, resulting in seriously flawed predictions. 'If I were…'is a good start, though. Truly seeing through the eyes of another, and adopting an insightfully xenocentric view, requires a conscious attempt to really be the other, rather than just to mumble, 'If I were him...'

## "IF I WERE..." IS A GOOD QUESTION WHEN WE BELIEVE WE UNDERSTAND THE OTHER

In military intelligence they tell the story of US Navy Captain Will Rogers III. He prevented the US from getting involved in the Iran-Iraq War in April 1988 by asking the right "If I were…" question (Klein, 1999a).

One clear, bright day, an Iranian F-4 fighter jet 'locked-on' a US cruiser patrolling the Strait of Hormuz. This means that the fighter pilot had locked his weapons guidance system into the ship -- the last step before firing a missile. The pilot was sure the ship's captain would have detected the imminent attack and be preparing for counter-measures, since hostile locking-on is commonly monitored by naval ships and military aircraft. The captain now had to take a decision: do nothing, similarly lock-on and stand ready or immediately fire a missile to destroy the aircraft. Given the rules of engagement of the US Navy, the captain could choose each of these options without having to involve a higher authority. A 'locked-on' ship could at that time proactively defend itself. The captain, realizing his far superior fire power and radar, compared to the F-4 jet, determined that no pilot would have reason to believe that they would get away alive when trying to fire a missile at a naval cruiser. If I were the pilot, the captain reasoned, I may test the cruiser for its response, but that is as far as I would go. The captain decided to do nothing. The F-4 subsequently unlocked and flew back to base – a dangerous escalation had been prevented by the captain asking the right questions and answering them correctly.

The example shows the value of xenocentric thinking and the critical importance of imagining what the competitor will do next and the intent that drives the act. This pilot was clearly teasing the ship's captain (and examining his response). He had no intent to attack. The captain correctly assessed the pilot's intent. No damage was done. It does not always end as well as in this example, as several other examples in this section will show. All too easily, the poorly understood intent of an adversary leads to inappropriate responses and unnecessarily damaging consequences. The scenarios presented here are intended to help you to recognize ethnocentric biases when you see them – by others in your own thinking – and preferably to redress them before it is too late. As I've said previously, although many of these examples originate in the military, the logic and psychology is just as applicable in business.

## THE ETHNOCENTRIC BIAS AS A FAILURE OF IMAGINATION (OF UNDERSTANDING THE OTHER)

When ethnocentric bias creeps into the picture, we can fail to predict the acts of others because, in all likelihood, we fundamentally don't understand them. The competitor may resort to actions that no one in their right mind would ever do. Even extensive wargaming exercises didn't help the US Navy predict that the Japanese would use kamikaze tactics – with airplanes themselves being used as weapons – towards the end of the war. These desperate, suicidal tactics had simply been beyond the imagination of Allied wargame participants.

The result of an ethnocentric bias is either a failure of prediction or that special type of failure of prediction that strategic analysts particularly loath: failure to predict anything is to happen that will negatively affect you (Heuer, 1999c).

The American sociologist Jessie Bernard nicely sums up the qualities required for a strategist, emphasizing the need to embrace xenocentrism (Freedman, 2013b):

> *"Imagination, insight, intuition, ability to put one's self in another person's position, understanding of the wellsprings of human motivation – good as well as evil – these are required for the thinking up of policies or strategies."*

After all, the essence of strategic reasoning is (Freedman, 2013c):

> *"[actors] making choices on the basis of the likely choices of opponents and, in so doing, recognizing that opponents' choices would depend in turn on expectations about what they [the actors] might choose."*

Xenocentrism is thus a critical virtue in intelligence analysis. It obviously requires cultural understanding. But there's more. Xenocentrism also allows a proper weighing of data obtained about or from the other party – be it a competitor or a political adversary. A military intelligence officer involved in understanding the Syrian Civil War in the 2010s warns that, regrettably, xenocentrism remains all too rare (Grey, 2016d):

> *"[…] the inability of people sitting mostly in London or Washington to understand a conversation involving someone like an Islamist is extraordinary."*

Determining our business or political choices on the basis of properly assessing the likely choices of adversaries is what xenocentrism is about. Xenocentrism must take as broad a view as is needed to cover the total scope of the environment in which a business operates. Xenocentrism resembles the target-centric approach to intelligence analysis (Clark, 2007b). The bad news, however, is that imagination and xenocentrism remain rare commodities in human thinking.

## EXAMPLES THAT ILLUSTRATE ETHNOCENTRIC BIAS AND ITS UGLY CONSEQUENCES

Life is full of examples of unwelcome surprises. The examples below characterize adversaries as categorical *enemies*. What is true when one is unable to understand, and thus predict the actions of, enemies is just as true when it comes to difficulty in understanding and thus predicting future customer or consumer needs.

In each of the following examples, ethnocentric bias prevented an understanding of another party's next steps, with often regrettable consequences:

- 9/11/01.[1]
- Pearl Harbor, 1941.[2]
- Cuban Missile Crisis, 1962.[3]
- The Soviet biological weapon programme in 1989/1990.[4]
- The Soviet invasion of Afghanistan, 1979.[5]
- The Israeli Defense Force's strike at a Libyan civilian airliner that, losing its way in a 1973 sandstorm, crossed into the Israeli-controlled Sanai desert.[6]
- The Soviet invasion of Czechoslovakia, 1968.[7]

In each of these instances, there are strong indications that – perhaps due to ethnocentric bias – military analysts tried to work through a challenging situation in an entirely wrong state of mind.

It bears repeating that ethnocentric bias is not limited to the military. It is just as common in business. A B2B example concerns an ingredients company that once improved one of their products. The innovation was properly protected with patents. By using the improved ingredient, the company's FMCG customers in turn improved the features of their consumer products. The end-products were upgraded with meaningful benefits that were known to appeal to consumers. There was, however, a caveat. In order to use the new and improved ingredient, the consumer-facing FMGC product companies has to slightly re-tool their factories. Once adapted, the factories could only handle the innovated ingredient. The ingredient manufacturer's business case for the reformulated offering looked airtight. There was no technological concern on the customers' side. The payback time was a matter of months. Yet, much to the chagrin of the ingredient manufacturer, not one of its consumer-product company customers even entertained the thought of trying the innovative new offering.

All the convincing figures in the business case that the B2B company's sales staff presented could not hide one fact. After switching, the customer would become solely dependent on one supplier. No FMCG company's procurement department was willing to tolerate such vulnerability. The ingredient manufacturer's ethnocentric bias was that, for R&D and marketing and sales, all looked rosy for everyone involved. In a textbook case of woefully myopic ethnocentrism, the procurement problem that the manufacturers would face just hadn't been taken into consideration.

## THE ETHNOCENTRIC BIAS IS NOT CULTURALLY DETERMINED

The US-related examples do not mean to suggest that American analysts are particularly prone to this bias; the examples have simply been chosen because they are well-documented and they well illustrate the bias. The ethnocentric bias occurs in all cultures. It also infected the French army in 1940 when it failed to counter the German Blitzkrieg.

The French Chief of Staff, General Doumenc, is honored by military strategist Liddell Hart with a beautiful quote, which perfectly captures the essence of ethnocentric bias (Liddell Hart, 1991a):

> *"Crediting our enemies with our own procedure, we had imagined that they did what we would have done"*

The Germans, however, didn't do as the French would have done, as Germany had between the world wars adopted an entirely new military doctrine (Guderian, 1999).

The ethnocentric bias starts with thinking that *they* think like *we* think. Similarly, this final example provides a potent example of Israeli ethnocentric bias underpinning the intelligence failure of the Yom Kippur War in 1973 (Bruce, 2008c):

> *"Analytically impaired with faulty assumptions, Israeli (and US) analysts did not succeed in understanding the Arab mind, to which the 'rationality' of the improbable invasion made perfect sense."*

For the record, let me state that these references are not meant to in any way judge the character or actions of the parties involved. They are simply historical references that help illustrate some of the concepts we're exploring in this book.

In the past, US analysts often struggled to think like the enemy (Kerr, 2008b). Kerr uses a remarkable phrase, which is, probably unintentionally, loaded with ethnocentricity:

> *"They [the Western analysts] frequently failed to understand how those decision-makers [on the Soviet side] could miscalculate or reason differently than Western analysts."*

Read in a way in which Kerr likely didn't intend, it was not the analysts who failed, but the adversary's decision-makers who were just miscalculating. They made the mistake of reasoning differently than our analysts. A former CIA official described a joke that circulated around the agency to defuse embarrassment when the CIA failed to predict the Soviet invasion of Afghanistan in December 1979 (Friedman, 2012):

> *"The analysts got it right, and it was the Soviets who got it wrong."*

To conclude this section there is a bit of good news as well. Some parties have found a way out of ethnocentrism. Call it 'immersion'. Here is yet another example from the military. In the second half of 1942, the Japanese Navy faced a formidable US enemy in the Pacific theatre. In preparation for battle, the Japanese admiralty organized wargames. In a wargame, a percentage of your participants, for at least part of the time, have to play the adversary – and, ideally, to do so as xenocentrically as possible. This is what the Japanese did (Perla, 2011):

> *"To obtain the best possible players for the Red (United States) side, the General Staff arranged for participation by the most thoroughly informed Japanese officers with the most up-to-date contacts with the United States. They found them among some outstanding Japanese Naval Intelligence Officers who had been assigned to duty in the Japanese Embassy in Washington, and who had been interned with all Japanese nationals in the United States when war broke out. In August 1942 arrangements were completed to repatriate internees, with a mutual exchange of Embassy personnel."*

In other words: exposure to 'the other' enables thinking like the other.

## INTENT IS HARDER TO IMAGINE THAN COMPETENCES

Kerr makes another important observation. He shows that US intelligence consistently had greater difficulty in predicting Soviet political and leadership issues than predicting the state of the Soviet economy. Sir John Scarlett, the former head of MI6, concurs with this view and adds an additional dimension: the smokescreen of propaganda may blind outside observers to the real logic that underpins an adversary's decisions (Corera, 2012a):

> *"What we were less successful at is getting into the mindset of the Soviet leadership [...] It was very difficult to get into that mindset because there was so much propaganda and jargon around."*

In this context, I would like to introduce what in military intelligence circles is known as the threat analysis equation:

*Threat of Attack = Competences + Intent + Surprise*

Kerr's observation seems to suggest that the relatively rational matters like competences (economic or financial performance, etc.) are easier to predict than emotional matters, such as how leadership issues are resolved. The latter are likely to be more culturally linked. This becomes evident in the example where ships carrying troops to Cuba had been identified, but the culturally linked (lack of) options for the Soviet military staff to discuss the conditions during their trip had been missed. As a result, the number of troops was grossly underestimated.

In business, Michael E. Porter similarly noted that assessing the intent of a competitor is harder than assessing their competencies (Porter, 1979):

> *"Most companies develop at least an intuitive sense for their competitors' current strategies and their strengths and weaknesses. Much less attention is usually directed at understanding what is really driving the behaviour of a competitor. These driving forces are much harder to observe then is actual competitor behaviour, yet they often determine how a competitor will behave in the future."*

The reason why ethnocentrism is covered as the first analytical pitfall in this chapter is that it may well be the most perfidious pitfall of all. It comes so naturally to take one's own logic and context of thinking as the implicit reference. The word implicit is key here. A key attribute of culture is that culture hides much more than it reveals… and what it hides, it hides most effectively from its own participants (Trompenaars, 2007).

When moving towards countering the ethnocentric bias, I believe it all starts with an open mind (Shulsky, 2002):

> *"[…] open-mindedness to be able to imagine that the adversary has adopted different solutions to common […] problems and that his solutions may well be appropriate for his circumstances and resources or even superior to one's own."*

## COUNTERING THE ETHNOCENTRIC BIAS

Ethnocentrism tends to go unnoticed. The opposite of ethnocentric is, of course, the neologism xenocentric: putting the other party whose next steps are to be predicted at the centre o the analysis. There is a catch, though – ethnocentric and xenocentric together are not collectively exhaustive. Not being ethnocentric means we do not look from our own perspective. That does not automatically mean we take a view on the perspective of the right other. When we take the wrong other in mind, even when dissimilar to ourselves and our culture, we still fail.

In chess, taking the xenocentric view is easy because there is only one other and the game's rules are fixed. Chess master Garry Kasparov, describing how he vanquished rival Viktor Korchoi, talks of adopting a xenocentric view (Coutu, 2005):

> *"I put myself in his shoes long enough to lure him into fighting the game on my territory, and so I won."*

In the same interview, Kasparov warns against ever underestimating the adversary. This respect for an adversary's unknown capabilities and intent is infinitely preferable to arrogance and complacency.

## RED TEAMING HAS BEEN ESTABLISHED TO PREVENT ETHNOCENTRISM

In a (US) military context, lessons learned from failures to predictively assess competitor's next moves have led to the development of an assessment methodology called 'red teaming' (Tradoc, 2010). The definition below shows that red teaming has a much broader scope than combatting an ethnocentric bias, but rather preventing that bias to distort analysis is part of red teaming. As defined below, red-teaming is designed to prevent bias from distorting critical analysis by – once again – putting one's self in an adversary's shoes. The red team in effect *becomes the enemy.*

> *"[…]a function executed by trained, educated and practiced team members that provides commanders an independent capability to fully explore alternatives in plans, operations, concepts, organizations and capabilities in the context of the operational environment and from the perspectives of our partners, adversaries and others."*

Again, the need for a xenocentric view is emphasized. Inwardly-focused mirror imaging is a persistent but unwelcome habit that negatively affects analysis.

> *"When a Red Team is formed or is part of the intelligence staff, they help the unit avoid mirror-imaging by ensuring that intelligence estimates are made through the perspective of the enemy's goals, intent and culture – an old lesson continually rediscovered by intelligence professionals. Red Teams challenge the assumptions made by the intelligence staff about the enemy, other stakeholders on the battlefield (for instance, tribes, major factions, neighbours) and the other critical variables found in the operational environment. During wargaming, the Red Team guards against wishing away the enemy or subscribing to unrealistic motives, goals or capabilities."*

Red teaming is a catalyst to challenge your thinking. What xenocentrism in the end boils down to is a proper appreciation of what is referred to as the 'otherness of the enemy'. The most important way to properly appreciate the other party is to interact with them. Open source intelligence cannot do this. This is where HUMINT comes in, both for ourselves as analysts as well as for our decision-makers (Grey, 2016e):

> *"The point of having […] human intelligence in general, was to have real people with deep insider knowledge of cultures and events abroad who could talk back, who could quietly correct a politician's misunderstandings of the world."*

For an analyst who may double as a human intelligence source in business, it is not easy to question too many ideas and views that may already exist in an organization concerning a competitor or customer. It may be a good idea to start by questioning your own views first.

# 14.4 WISHFUL THINKING

Another pitfall – wishful thinking – is a deceptively easy one to succumb to. No analyst, decision-maker – or even worse, team of decision-makers – wishes to think it may affect them. This in itself is perhaps the best example of wishful thinking. The reality of the situation can in fact be quite different. A great example of wishful thinking relates to the Israeli intelligence failure prior to the October 1973 Yom Kippur War, which was referred to in the previous section (Friedman, 2012):

> *"Documents [...] reveal that the Israeli intelligence community believed that the country's superior military power would deter its Arab neighbours from initiating a war."*

The Arab neighbours, however, were undeterred and initiated the hostilities. The key word in the sentence above is 'believed.' Wishful thinking happens most often when data sets are incomplete. Rather than realizing that unknown unknowns and possibly known unknowns hamper a necessary analytic judgment call, a set of assumptions is created which may feel good but happen to be based on (often ethnocentric) quicksand. 'Faulty assumptions' preceded the Yom Kippur War intelligence failure (Bruce, 2008c).

Another classic example of wishful thinking in military intelligence was the bombing campaign that the US government unleashed on North Vietnam in the mid-1960s. The wishful thinking was that the North Vietnamese government would respond by realizing there was no point in further supporting the Vietcong guerrillas in the South, and agree to a negotiated ceasefire in the South. The opposite happened:

the bombing strengthened the resolve of the North to continue their insurgency in the South. Another decade of war would follow, until the North had achieved its strategic objective on its own terms.

Wishful thinking also happens when decision-makers are not ready or willing to handle the challenges put forward by an intelligence-based warning. The first Persian Gulf War that started with Saddam Hussein's invasion of Kuwait provides a great example of this type of wishful thinking (Clark, 2007c). On 25 July, 1990, the CIA issued a warning that estimated a 60% chance of an Iraqi attack against Kuwait. Neither the US nor Kuwait was prepared for the attack when it came one week later. US policymakers believed didn't believe Iraq would attack, and rather than prepare (wishfully thinking), they stuck to their belief despite the CIA's warning. A similar example: the UK's refusal to believe that Germany would invade France in 1940.

In a business context, wishful thinking has also been referred to as the 'optimism bias' (Makridakis, 1990). The optimism bias is frequently observed in business plans. Businesses that for years have shown a low single-digit growth rate in net sales value are suddenly projected to grow in double digits with the approval of a particular capital expenditure. In business, such plans are known as 'hockey stick' for the dramatic, nearly vertical upward swing that illustrates the phenomenon on a chart. Cash first sinks to the dip of the stick but afterwards cash returns are projected to go sky-high. Such hockey stick-shaped forward projections of sales and profits are not uncommon in investment memoranda, issued by the sellers of companies. Buyer beware. In such cases, remember to look for the 'faulty assumptions'.

It is not a coincidence that the Yom Kippur War example features both in this section and in the previous section. Analytic pitfalls, as described in this section, are not mutually exclusive but often happen to come in pairs or groups. Different pitfalls may indeed strengthen each other.

As an analyst, a skeptical attitude to organizational beliefs is therefore essential. Do not unconditionally join in the belief that a single capital investment fundamentally changes the profit pool of an industry or the growth rate of a market. Do not just share in the belief that a customer will remain loyal to your company when a new entrant arrives on the scene. Formulate questions like 'what do we need to believe to see the profit pool increase?' 'What do we need to believe to expect customer retention when a new player enters the market?' As in the case of ethnocentric bias, it's usually a case of too few questions are being asked, not too many! To combat wishful thinking most effectively, get your data and get them right (Sunstein, 2015a):

> *"Nothing seems to inject reality into a discussion and banish wishful thinking and biased speculations as well as empirical evidence, especially in the form of data and numbers."*

# 14.5 STATUS QUO BIAS

Another common analysis pitfall is the 'status quo bias', with 'status quo' being defined as the existing state of affairs. A fitting description of the status quo bias is given here, linking the comforting, warm *fuzziness* of the status quo to complacency (Friedman, 2010b):

> *"The worst sin of intelligence is complacency, the belief that simply because something has happened (or has not happened) several times before it is not going to happen this time."*

It was complacency of this type that resulted in the fateful decision to no longer watch out for Japanese submarines close to Pearl Harbor in December 1941, following seven 'cry wolf' false negative signals, as described in chapter 10.

The status quo bias relates to fear (Roxburgh, 2003). People generally are more concerned about the risk of loss than excited by the prospect of gain. As long as stability is preserved, all is under control. With this mindset, warnings of change, such as those provided by new intelligence may be, underrated or downright rejected.

Great examples have been published that illustrate this phenomenon (Hoffman, 2011b). Let me share one I particularly like. In February 1985, in the weeks before Mikhail Gorbachev took power in the USSR, the CIA discredited all signals that Gorbachev would significantly change Soviet policy. Gorbachev could not be all that different. The Soviet system was a monolith. One individual that could drive change according to the CIA's deputy director of intelligence, would ever be able to rise to the top of that system. That wasn't consistent with the system's thinking. Gorbachev was known to have been mentored by hardliners such as Suslov and Andropov. The CIA's deputy director is reported to have said (Hoffman, 2011b):

*"They [Suslov and Andropov] would not take a wimp under their wing."*

In what may well have been a yet undiscovered example of groupthink (see chapter 10). The CIA in this case had an ally in the White House. In his memoirs, US President Ronald Reagan wrote (Yarhi-Milo, 2014a):

*"I can't claim that I believed from the start that Mikhail Gorbachev was going to be a different sort of Soviet leader [...]. He will be as tough as any of their leaders. If he wasn't a confirmed ideologue, he would never have been chosen by the Politburo."*

Despite growing evidence – and as trusted allies like Margaret Thatcher tried to convince them otherwise – the CIA and the American President held steadfastly to their status quo bias. The president changed his opinion but only in response to vividly and personally experiencing in several face-to-face meetings that Gorbachev indeed was different.

Again, the same fawning devotion to the status quo is all too prevalent in business. In 1973 the world faced what it is now known as the first oil crisis. In response to political issues in the Middle East, global oil prices shot up. In the preceding quarter-century, up to 1973, global oil refining demand and capacity had steadily increased by 6% per annum. Despite the oil crisis, the 1973 oil price shock, which actually resulted in a drop in global refined oil demand, the oil industry maintained its capacity growth momentum for another two years. It took another six years before refinery capacity expansion ceased – a full eight years after global demand dropped (Heijden, 1997c). This period is obviously much longer than the time needed for refinery equipment contractors to finish work that had already been planned before 1973. The status quo bias belief in the need for continued 6% per year capacity expansion was so strong that it took the industry eight years to 'unlearn' its heuristic rule.

The above examples show that people, including analysts, love to change their views or working processes but most hate it when external circumstances force them to change. Everyone knows that the oil industry has the right to grow 6% per annum in volume. A price hike will not change the apparent inevitability of that growth – the price hike is a temporary effect, right?

For new intelligence that may challenge such strong views to actually change stubborn minds, it must, almost by definition, be accompanied by a positive attitude. Think back to the fox and the hedgehog you first met in chapter 11. Hedgehogs are more susceptible to status quo bias than foxes. Both the CIA and the oil industry apparently had their share of hedgehogs. As an analyst, it pays to be foxy.

# 14.6 HERDING INSTINCT

There is safety in numbers, or at least that's how the saying goes. It is a natural instinct to feel comfortable among like-minded people. Most people are most comfortable when their opinions and behaviours conform with those exhibited by the larger societal group (Roxburgh, 2003). Analysts are human, so by deduction, this heuristic applies to analysts as well.

## HERDS FOLLOW LEADERS

The confirmatory (opinion) desire of a person – and thus that of an 'average' analyst – usually gets stronger when certain behaviours are observed in those in leadership positions by those aspiring (leadership) positions. For this to happen, there is no need for a personal connection between the analyst and the leader. The leader may be a thought leader, such as a reputable and inspirational business school professor. Warren Buffett's status as an investment wizard is such that herds of investors follow his every move by making the same investment bets as Buffett makes. As long as this belief holds and the herd remain sizeable enough, the herding instinct phenomenon retains its own forward momentum.

The herding instinct affects most financial markets. If certain large, successful investors simultaneously reduce their asset portfolio exposure in India, for example, many investors suddenly believe they have to upgrade the risk of investing in India. In response, they may leave India in droves, and suddenly the Indian Rupee drops, as was the case in the second half of 2013. With the right put-options in place, the first movers may make a quick buck on such self-fulfilling herd instinct moves. Given the convergence of strategies in most industries, herding also affects strategy development (Bird, 2009). When aspirational or leading players in an industry make moves (like strengthening their market-geo portfolio mix so that it's top-heavy with developing economies), droves of second-tier players in the same industries will follow, as a herd, if only to avoid missing the boat. This generally leads to asset inflation, which increases up to a point where the asset returns in what initially looked to be a great opportunity is actually no longer better than those in the initial markets in which these industries were active. At that moment, a new equilibrium is established and the herd takes time for grazing (and debt servicing). That is, until the next big thing… and the herd gains momentum again, following the leaders.

## IN CONTRAST TO GOOD ANALYSTS, HERDS ARE NOT SKEPTICAL

Strategists should always be wary of the social herding instinct to think everything is OK because everybody says it is (Rumelt, 2012a). Rumelt emphasizes taking a broad look at times and places where other heuristics applied, prior to reaching pre-emptory conclusions. Where herd-based beliefs like '50 Million Elvis fans can't be wrong' overshadow the facts, analysts should step back – even when risking an often-temporary decline in the popularity of their views.

Chapter 9 mentioned objectivity and integrity as the most important attributes of analysis. These values do not match well with following the herd to find safety in numbers; they may, however, fit well with leading the herd.

When there is a personal connection between the analyst and the decision-maker, with the latter pushing to follow the herd, the analytic pitfall of writing reports that validate the herd mentality can quickly devolve into fainthearted yesmanship. This pitfall is covered in chapter 17.

# 14.7 OVER-RELIANCE ON PREVIOUS JUDGMENTS

This bias relates to the inertia of thinking along particular lines. Once an analyst fits a data set into a particular pattern, the image that emerges from the pattern moulds the decision-maker's overall opinion on the matter. Even when individual data points prove to be outdated or incorrect in the first place, or new data points have appeared, the inclination is to stick to an opinion or maintain an impression once it has been taken (see diagram 10.4).

The inertia increases when an analytic product moves up the organizational ladder (Cooper, 2005b). Over-reliance on previous judgments may already be in play at the level of the individual analyst. It will, however, get more important once a strategic analysis function has issued a view on a topic to a company's executive board. It gets even stronger when that executive board has reported this view to its supervisory board (assuming a two-tier board system).

Once in the above process, previous judgments turn into 'habit of thought' knowledge, then the bias of conventional wisdom creeps in, which is discussed in the next sub-section. To combat an over-reliance on previous judgments, the analyst should remain open to new data, patterns and insights, however challenging that may be. There may be some merit to using diagram 10.4 as a screensaver/reminder on your computer.

# 14.8 CONVENTIONAL WISDOM

Prior to discussing when conventional wisdom is a pitfall, it is essential to first emphasize that conventional wisdom is usually right. I define conventional wisdom here as choosing a conclusion that is plausible given the data currently available. The quote below describes the ambiguity of conventional wisdom: it is usually correct, but usually is not always (Jervis, 2010f).

> *"Of course, in science and in intelligence, being strongly influenced by plausibility can be criticized as being closed-minded or assumption-driven. But this is a powerful and legitimate habit of the mind, necessary for making sense of a complex and contradictory world, and [...] most of the inferences it produces are right. [...] the implicit theories of the world that we bring to cases usually are correct and most of the time we are better off being guided by them rather than adopting exotic alternatives, we will be misled and surprised when the other's behaviour is extraordinary."*

The fact that 'wisdom' is part of the term is deceiving – for the strategic business analyst, conventional wisdom can be deadly. In practice, it is neither actually conventional nor any longer wisdom, as both the conventional and the wisdom part are outdated by the time it becomes a pitfall. It resembles, to put it prosaically, interpreting today's events with last week's newspapers, without knowing that quite a bit has changed since then. Conventional wisdom often has its roots in 'habit of thought' knowledge. Chapter 1 covered methods of knowledge generation and mentioned the characteristic drawbacks of 'habit of thought' knowledge. This source of knowledge has an intrinsic resistance to change and it tends to fail in anticipating discontinuities (Bruce, 2008b).

In analysing the Cuban Missile Crisis, a characteristic example of the tyranny of conventional wisdom is evident (Dobbs, 2009a). CIA analysts tried to identify where the Soviets had hidden the nuclear warheads that were to be mounted on the Soviet missiles smuggled into Cuba. A CIA source reports his bewilderment with the situation:

> *"The experts kept saying that nuclear warheads would be under tight control of the KGB. [...] We were told to look out for multiple security fences, roadblocks, extra levels of protection. We did not observe any of that."*

What the analyst did notice was a rickety fence around an unidentified munitions storage site that was not even protected by a closed gate. Absence of the right (conventional) signposts of evidence was mistaken for evidence of absence. This led to an incorrect assessment of what was the major nuclear warhead storage site. In chapter 13, in discussing hypothesis testing, I already warned that conventional wisdom may be extremely useful in mediocristan but leads to failure in extremistan. Looking for signposts as indicators of phenomena is most useful, when an analyst is lucky enough to consistently encounter signposts that actually do point to analytically valuable phenomena. But, a missing signpost should not be construed as a missing phenomenon – and a spotted signpost is not necessarily a guarantee the relevant phenomenon is lurking around the next corner.

During the Cuban Missile Crisis, the US authorities were convinced that the Soviets' policy and practice would not lead them to create a secret missile emplacement in Cuba. The resulting assessment predicted that the chances of the Soviets doing this were negligible (Bruce, 2008c). Conventional wisdom predicted the mediocristan behaviour of an extremistan-type leader like Nikita Khrushchev. This example again illustrates that the biases described in this chapter are not mutually exclusive. The view on Khrushchev was too ethnocentric: if we as Western analysts had been Khrushchev, we would never have installed rockets at Cuba – but we failed to be Khrushchev. When did you last fail to 'be' your competitor or your customer, leading to a nasty surprise?

Apart from an element of ethnocentric bias in these examples, this incorrect logic fits well with the limits to using decision models (Rosenzweig, 2014). The moment the behaviour of small numbers of humans is to be predicted, models become weak. Small numbers of people are intrinsically unpredictable. Only when truly large numbers of people are involved – think of millions – predictive models have a chance. This corroborates Taleb's *Black Swan* logic: predicting the birth rate of a population is feasible, predicting an individual pregnancy is not (Taleb, 2007c).

Large numbers of people, however, may also defy conventional wisdom. Western analysts failed to predict the fall of Shah of Iran in 1979 exactly because of that (Jervis, 2010c):

> *"At bottom most observers [...] found it hard to imagine that the Shah would fall. The idea that one of the world's most powerful monarchs could be overthrown by an unarmed mob of religiously-inspired fanatics was simply incredible. Furthermore, it probably would have been incredible even had observers grasped the depth of popular discontent in Iran."*

The above examples show the wisdom of two classic strategic tests (Liddell Hart, 1991b). To defy conventional wisdom and deliver surprise a strategy has to:

- Attack the line of least resistance.
- Operate along the line of least expectation.

Lucky is the strategist who can make her competitor believe what the competitor wants to believe. With the competitor cherishing its conventional wisdom, they may mistakenly persist in looking for the signposts along the line of highest expectation, until the surprise becomes a fact.

# 14.9 SYNTHESIS

At the end of an elaborate multi-step data collection and analysis process a data set, quality checked along the dimensions described above, looks ready to either be used in analytic tools or to be reported to the project principal. Without wanting to spoil the joy of having finished a process, there may be merit in doing a final quality check on it prior to feeding the tools or delivering the results. The short checklist below, adapted from a US government document, may be helpful in doing so (ODNI, 2007).

Any analysis to be documented in a deliverable should:

- Properly describe quality and reliability of underlying sources.
- Properly caveat and express uncertainties or confidence in analytic judgments.
- Properly distinguish between underlying intelligence and analyst's assumptions.
- Incorporate alternative analysis where appropriate.
- Exhibit consistency of analysis over time, or highlight changes and explain rationale.

These points may provide a framework for reporting. Not surprisingly, reporting is the topic of the next chapter.

# CHAPTER 15
# REPORTING

# 15.1 INTRODUCTION

Good reporting is as challenging as it is rare. All too often, presentations are given that…

- Take refuge in details, and in doing so avoid to deliver a key message.
- Contain too many unexplained abbreviations or jargon and scare off the intended recipient.
- Are poorly structured and prevent the audience from getting the key message.
- Provide data that is irrelevant to the key message.
- Provide so much data that the key message drowns in the volume.
- Provide data in chronological order of collection, rather than in a logical sequence, which is needed to substantiate the key message.
- Take refuge in too many slides that focus on the structure of the presentation, rather than on the key message.
- Have so many messages on a slide that the forest is lost for the trees.
- Have visuals which confuse rather than clarify the slide's message.
- Have slide titles that do not capture the slide's content and vice versa.
- Have slides with such small text fonts that they are not meant to be read but only to be admired as abstract modern industrial art.
- Are so complex that they are not only new to the audience but also seem to be new to the presenter.

About 30 years of office life easily would have allowed an extension of this list, which was inspired by Frank and Magnone (Frank, 2011e). The list in the example above was meant to deliver two implicit key messages. Good reporting is:

- not easy
- all about getting a (key) message across to a recipient decision-maker

To manage expectations, a third key message of this chapter is that the art of good reporting easily deserves its own book. This book focuses on strategic data analysis, not on reporting, so reporting is covered only briefly. This chapter assists you as an analyst with some tips and tricks but is by no means a replacement for thorough training in reporting. The chapter at best scratches the surface of reporting as part of human communication.

## REPORTING IS MORE THAN WRITING

Reporting is defined here, in a broad sense, as encompassing all forms of communication that an analyst may use to deliver a message to a decision-maker. Obviously, written reports constitute a large part of that communication, but other forms also matter, from elevator pitches to phone calls, video messages and body language.

This chapter is complementary to chapter 16, which focuses on the psychological dynamics of the interactions between an analyst and a decision-maker.

This chapter aims to implicitly address common questions of balance in reporting, like how to strike a balance between:

- Details versus key message.
- Methodology versus subject matter content.
- Main storyline versus back-up.
- One large report versus multiple small reports.
- Need-to-know versus nice-to-know.

Section 15.2 will briefly discuss the process of reporting, as writing and reporting often are synonymous. Section 15.3 focuses on defining the aim of reporting. The pros and cons of different formats of reporting (oral, written, etc.) are covered in section 15.4, for times when the key message is unambiguous. In section 15.5, generic requirements of reporting, focused on strategic analysis of the business environment, are covered. Section 15.6 concludes this chapter with some thoughts on developing reporting capabilities as a form of lifelong learning.

# »»» 15.2 THE PROCESS OF REPORTING

As in the previous section, reporting is defined as the delivery of one or more messages to one or more decision-makers by the analyst, in some shape or form. The process discussed below applies in principle to all forms of reporting, even when in practice a lot of reporting – when measured in quantity – will be in a written format. When measuring persuasiveness or impact, it may be that oral, personal delivery will actually be the most important form of reporting.

In the analysis cycle discussed in chapter 1, clear sequential steps have been defined in the development of a strategic analysis project: brief, collection, analysis and reporting are followed by a debrief. As was indicated before, this cycle oversimplifies the realities of strategic analysis work. The oversimplification doesn't make the cycle useless, but it makes it necessary to briefly discuss the strategic analysis project process as it would work in reality. Doing so helps to position reporting in the overall process.

## STRATEGIC ANALYSIS PROJECTS ARE DESIGNED BACKWARD AND EXECUTED FORWARD

In simplest terms, an analysis project begins with a brief. Assume that the analyst is experienced. The experienced analyst will, upon receiving of the brief, almost unconsciously and intuitively form a clear script for the project flow. This is the fruit of experience. Scanning the brief, the analyst will quickly recognize the nature of the project's challenge, matching it with a pattern of similar projects she executed previously.

Based on this so-called 'recognition-primed decision-making' in the analyst's mind, key messages to be delivered to the decision-maker as the outcome of the project might take the form of hypotheses. (See chapter 16 for a more in-depth discussion of recognition-primed decision-making.)

Working backwards from key messages or conclusions, to hypotheses, experiments (also known as analyses) to validate these hypotheses, analytic methodologies, data needs and, ultimately, to sources for these data needs, a project script emerges in a split-second in the analyst's mind. The analyst, in doing so, designs the real project from the debrief backwards to the brief. This may sound weird, but it is once again the inevitable and fruitful consequence of experience. Moreover, as will be discussed in more detail in the next chapter, recognition-primed decision-making is both more efficient and more effective than other forms of decision-making. Once the analyst is comfortable with the mentally crafted script, which may be seconds after the reception of the brief, the real project definition starts. The real project follows the sequence of the analysis cycle from defining the brief to delivering the debrief. The project definition guides the execution.

Recognition-primed decision-making matters to reporting because the strategic analysis project and the reporting by an experienced analyst starts with the message(s) to be delivered to the decision-maker, and not with the format ... and certainly not with the data or the analytic methodology.

## STEPS IN THE ANALYSIS CYCLE ARE OFTEN BLURRED

An academic description of the real-life sequence of a strategic analysis project's design, is too rigid when it describes the different steps in the cycle as truly independent. In practice, there is for example some blurring between collection and analysis. It is only when the analysis has been carried out that it becomes clear whether enough data have been collected to distill undisputable messages. Analysis outcomes may thus in an iterative way trigger more data collection. The same is true for the interface between analysis and reporting.

The best test for an analyst to check whether they fully grasp an analysis is to force themselves to report it to somebody else. When analysis allows the definition of a coherent and solid narrative, an analyst may start to feel comfortable that the key messages are properly and logically substantiated – and thus valuable and robust enough to share with the decision-maker. When not, more analysis is needed to develop the coherent narrative, which may even trigger more collection work. This process clearly involves multiple iterations.

The question now is when to stop the iterations. There is no silver bullet answer to this question. The most correct answer is: 'It depends on the project, the decision-maker and the analyst'. This answer is as useless as it is true. In practice, a good measure to stop iterating is when the marginal improvement of another round of iteration no longer significantly alters the key messages. Stopping too early may trigger premature closing (see chapter 12), which is to be avoided. Stopping too late may trigger inefficient tinkering or the missing of deadlines, both of which are also to be avoided. Finding the right balance between speed and superficial quality is the analyst's prerogative.

## PERFECTIONISM IS GREAT BUT SHOULD NOT LEAD TO INSIGHTS NOT BEING SHARED

It may sound strange, but even when far-out deadlines allow for marathon work sessions, there is a limit to perfectionism. The Nineteenth Century composer Franz Liszt left music lovers a treasure trove of compositions. The truth, however, is that he wrote possibly four times more music than what we today know, as most of his work he believed not to be good enough to be played. He trashed them. From a music lovers' perspective that is a tremendous waste. Do not follow Liszt's example in your firm's strategic analysis function. Even analyses that may not be perfect may still offer insights that enlighten decision-makers and enable better decision-making.

## REPORTS ARE ALSO DESIGNED BACKWARDS, USING A STORYLINE AS GUIDE

Recognition-primed decision-making leads to a message-driven design of good strategic analysis projects. By implication reports, as deliverables of reporting, are designed backwards. Starting with the (hypothesized) key message, a tested method to turn a management brief into a logically sound deliverable is to first develop an overall storyline. A storyline forms the logical backbone of any strategic analysis project report. Good storyline writing is helpful, regardless of whether the reporting takes the shape of a two-minute call or of a 40-page slide show. The example below elucidates what is meant by a storyline. (See the intermezzo at the end of this section for a brief description of storyline writing, called 'The Pyramid Principle'.)

Management brief:

What happens to the competitiveness of yoghurt drink manufacturers in Yololandia when competitor Yosmurf opens its new plant?

Storyline of the reporting:

(i) Yosmurf's plans for setting up a plant in Yololandia have been reconfirmed.

(ii) Yosmurf is rumoured to be planning a plant that will open Q2 of the following year in Yogadishu.

(iii) Supplier YotraBloc informally shared that it has leased six filling lines for the plant; the terms of the leasing arrangement will likely hurt Yosmurf's competitiveness.

(iv) Yosmurf is expected to produce 125, 250 and 500g portion packs of yoghurt drinks; these do not directly compete with the current firm's 1000g packs.

(v) Yoghurt drink consumers in Yololandia have limited inclination to substitute 1000g packs with smaller portion packs, as the latter are perceived to deliver poor value for the money, serving an impulse rather than a family's in-home consumption needs.

(vi) The yoghurt drink market in Yogadishu is already highly competitive, as Yogadishu is also locally supplied by local market leader and global player, Yonone.

(vii) In addition, Yogadishu's number-three yoghurt drink producer is called Yodidit. It specializes in portion packs; the entry of Yosmurf will most likely target Yodidit's market position.

(viii) The impact of Yosmurf's market entry to your firm's competitiveness will by implication likely be modest and indirect at best.

(ix) It is recommended not to immediately increase your firm's Yololandia-based unit's advertising and promotion budget to defend your drinking yoghurt market share in Yololandia pro-actively.

An analyst's best practice is to dissect the management brief into manageable sub-briefs through asking questions. Once the experienced analyst receives the brief, they will instantly come up with how they will operationalize the definition of competitiveness. They'll likely break down the overall brief into key questions that may be answered individually. The answers to these questions guide the analyst in constructing a logical storyline. In the case of the example above, some questions may include:

- What determines the competitiveness of your firm's position?
  The current and future competitive environment.
- Who are already playing in that environment?
  Yonone and Yodidit.
- What positions do they take in today's markets?
  Yonone is no. 1, having a full range of packs; Yodidit is no. 3 specializing in smaller portions.
- How is the market segmented (by pack type, by channel, by user need, etc.)?
  In-home users buy liter packs, impulse users buy portion packs.
- What do we know about the entry plans of Yosmurf?
  Leasing YotraBloc machines, which are only able to produce up to 500ml unit packs.

Assume for the sake of simplicity that a written presentation is being prepared. The above storyline consists of answers to the following three questions (Frank, 2011b):

- What? i – vii
- So what? viii
- Now what? ix

These three questions are an analyst/story-liner's best friends, next to Kipling's six honest service men: what, where, why, when, who and how.

Each of the elements above, i – ix, may justify a dedicated separate slide with the above text as titles. The slide provides through a balanced mix of visuals, quantitative data and text the must-know substantiation for its concluding title. Using the above storyline, the sum of the slide titles makes up the overall conclusion. This also doubles as the executive summary.

In the collection phase of this project, undoubtedly a lot of press coverage will have been found regarding the recent, rather turbulent management changes at Yosmurf. None of this will find its way into this report, unless it matters to the analyst's answering of the key question.

Preparing storylines is like strategic analysis at large: an art rather than a science. In a strategic analysis department, a senior analyst may in a team effort focus on the briefing intake and the storyline preparation, while a junior analyst collects and visualizes the data within the storyline. In their cooperation, the junior analyst gradually gain on-the-job experience until he possesses sufficient briefing intake and storyline writing skills.

One final thought: do not underestimate how time-intensive preparing a good storyline may be. Preparing the storyline for this chapter took about 20 hours, using 18 handwritten A4 pages (I know I am a bit old school). Over that period, the section titles were first defined, followed by a colouring in of each of the sections in the storyline by digesting and ordering all material on reporting that I had available and deemed useful. In addition I collected material that answered questions that remained, but for which data were not yet available. The major advantage of rigorous storyline-based development, next to deliverable quality, is efficiency. On almost any topic there is too much data out there. Sticking to a storyline will prevent drowning in information overload (Frank, 2011b).

## REPORTING IS A SOLITARY ACTIVITY

A reporter aims to achieve two things in parallel: defining their ideas by finding the right words and subsequently conveying those ideas to others through carefully chosen words – utilizing gestures, tone of voice etc. (Sinclair, 2010). This is not always easy.

For reporting to achieve high standards, the analyst thus needs to be able to concentrate (this is why noisy office gardens for staff in analysis and reporting roles are such a brilliant invention). Preparing for reporting or simply writing is a lonely business. Solitude pays off in terms of both quality and efficiency of writing, but it has a downside, as it precludes team interaction. A balance thus needs to be found between solitary analysis and reporting on the one hand and teamwork on the other.

## INTERMEZZO: THE PYRAMID PRINCIPLE FOR GENERATING STORYLINES

The aim of reporting is to get a message across. The reporting should be clear, compelling and devoid of any confusing material so that it delivers the message to the intended recipient in an unambiguous and thoroughly convincing way. The implication of this is that a storyline in business reporting should have a logical, well-thought-out flow. Let's assume the strategic analysis function regularly communicates to the same recipient decision-maker. If so, the consistent use of a familiar flow will reduce cognitive strain, as the recipient will presumably be familiar with the presentation's look, feel, style and voice.

Barbara Minto has introduced the pyramid principle in writing as a generic methodology to help one achieve effective flow. The familiarity/

comprehension correlation can be helpful in business reporting (Minto, 2008). Minto postulates that a recipient has lower cognitive strain while trying to grasp messages when they:

- Are organized as a pyramid under a single point.
- Focus on answering a question existing in the recipient's mind.
- Obey a limited number of logical rules.

The pyramid principle methodology consists of three separate elements. The upper element in the pyramid in Minto's parlance is the SCQ-overview: S stands for situation, C for complication and Q for (key) Question. SCQ relates well to the 'What?', 'So What?' and 'Now What?' questions that I consistently used in this book to structure illustrative storylines.

The middle element in Minto's pyramid consists of the MECE-requirement. MECE stands for mutually exclusive, collective exhaustive. MECE works as follows. A car manufacturer launches a new model. It is available in three colours: red, green and blue. There are no bi- or tri-colour cars offered for sale. As a result, a car is either red OR green OR blue. A car being red excludes it from being either green or blue. Red and green and blue are mutually exclusive. As there are no cars sold in colours other than red, green or blue, together the colours red, green and blue are collectively exhaustive.

The MECE-requirement is indispensable in many logic arguments, as it shows that the analysis exhaustively looked at all options within a dimension (in this case: red, green and blue) whilst ensuring the options do not mutually overlap (not a single bi- or tri-coloured new car has ever been produced and sold). Strategic analysis work generally has to meet three basic attributes: it needs to timely, accurate and complete. Embracing the MECE-requirement ensures this last attribute.

The third and final element in Minto's pyramid is logic. Logical reasoning relates to what as discussed in chapter 1: how logic allows the generation of knowledge. The true value of using the pyramid principle in reporting is not the use of logic as such but the fact that doing so allows *the structure of the logic* to be easily grasped by the recipient. This is not about logic; this is about convenience!

When applying the pyramid principle, the key message in reporting is to feature the conclusion on top. (In slide preparation this is often the headline; see the second intermezzo later in this chapter). The key message is substantiated by arguments concerning, in this case, three main topics: A, B and C (mutually exclusive and collectively exhaustive). Each of these is further substantiated by key facts or supporting analyses (again, the substantiation needs for topic A, B and C to be mutually exclusive and collectively exhaustive).

Some useful rules apply to pyramid principle work:

- In the original set-up of pyramid principle working *the most important* issue from the SCQ-step should be covered *at the top* of the pyramid. In this book, we refer to the statement at the top of the pyramid as the key message.
- Any supporting arguments at a lower level of the pyramid substantiate the message one level above in the pyramid.
- The different supporting arguments at any level in the pyramid, except for the top, should at all times be mutually exclusive, collectively exhaustive.
- The supporting arguments that are presented at each level of the pyramid are mutually of the same order, meaning:
  - The level of detail is comparable.
  - The nature of the argument is comparable; facts versus facts, not facts in one substantiating branch and actions in another substantiating branch.
- The supporting arguments are structured following the logic of the reasoning that has been applied. A simple check is that a lower level in the pyramid answers the question 'why?' for the statement given one level up
- People are known not to be able to grasp or memorize more than seven arguments in parallel. By implication, never use more than seven parallel substantiations.

Diagram 15.1 provides a simple example of a pyramid principle-based report to illustrate the above rules and summarize this appendix.

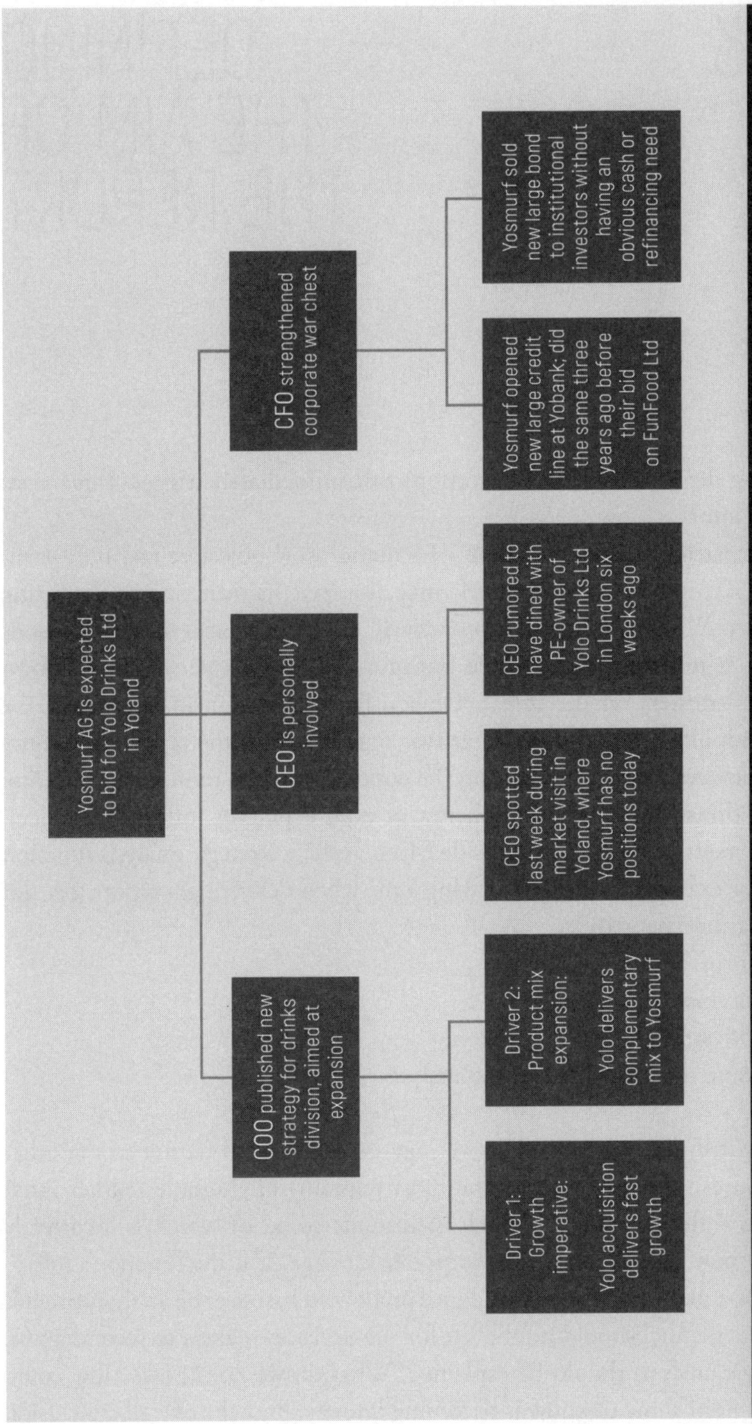


**DIAGRAM 15.1 ▶▶ EXAMPLE OF A PYRAMID PRINCIPLE REPORT**

## 15.3 DEFINING THE AIM OF THE REPORT

Writing the word 'aim' in this section's title immediately triggers a question: whose aim?

A strategic analysis function – no matter how objective and non-partisan in a corporate environment – may also have its own aims in delivering a report. When the function proactively observes what it sees as a serious threat, it not only has the role but also the duty to persuasively inform decision-makers on the threat. Obviously, the decision-makers retain the responsibility and authority to act (or not) based on the report. The function, however, through choosing the content, format, timing and phrasing of the threat, may indeed implicitly, or even explicitly, influence the decision-makers' choices. Putting aside Machiavelli, a strategic analysis function may for example have the following aims when delivering a report (list not necessarily exhaustive):

- Inform.
- Convince.
- Motivate/persuade to decision.
- Ensure the proper use of the analysis.

The fourth aim mentioned above may be different in nature to the other three aims, but may well be the most relevant. High-grade market intelligence – the meaning of which is misunderstood or which is incorrectly used – may cause tremendous corporate damage. It is the function's role to provide a manual that gives guidance on how to best use the analysis provided. This manual should not be left for the decision-makers to second guess. Strategic analysis should be explained. What do we not know? How could the result of some unknowns becoming known affect the overall conclusion that is based on all currently available intelligence? Strategic analysis is (usually) probabilistic rather than predictive. Strategic analysis is not omniscient. Its conclusions, as in science, tend to have a tentative nature: they are true until conflicting-yet-solid evidence emerges. Good strategic analysis reduces uncertainty but even the best analysis does not ever entirely remove it. Explaining strategic analysis in reporting should be genuine. It should not be perceived as just covering the analysts' back.

## THE AIM IDEALLY DEFINES THE DELIVERY FORMAT AND THE REQUIREMENTS FOR THE REPORT

Setting an aim for a report ideally precedes choosing the report's format. The aim also defines the specific requirements for the content of the report. Sometimes a format is an inevitable given. No matter how much an analyst would like to have more time from a decision-maker, that time is simply not available, or not granted, prior to when the decision-maker should receive the report. That may not be ideal, but the world is not always fair: the analyst has to make do with it.

The point is that format, aims and requirements are not truly statistically independent dimensions. Certain formats facilitate some aims and requirements better than others. Persuasiveness as an aim is in some cases greatly assisted by a personal meeting but harder to achieve by sending an e-mail. An oral briefing without visuals rarely succeeds in meeting the general requirement that reports should be memorable when the topic is a complex technical issue.

An experienced analyst therefore chooses an ideal mix of reporting formats and requirements – one that best suits achieving the function's aim. When needed and when the compromises would render achieving the aim no longer feasible, the analyst either accepts the compromises or escalates the matter to a higher managerial level.

Even when formats and requirements are not statistically independent, the sequence of discussing either formats or requirements is arbitrary. The next section covers formats.

# 15.4 FORMATS OF REPORTING

Reporting, as I said earlier, is a form of human communication. People send and receive communication signals through five senses. For reporting, three dimensions of sensing seem to matter most: vision, sound and touch. Smell and taste are normally less relevant. The three relevant senses are statistically independent. As a result, eight permutations are possible when combining these three dimensions ($2^3=8$). This means that reporting can take place in a situation when all the senses of both sender and recipient are able to connect in real-time (so: yes, yes, yes). An example of this is when two people meet for dinner. The other extreme is when reporting takes place when none of the senses of the sender and recipient are able to connect in real-time communication (so: no, no, no). This is, for example, the case when one person sends an e-mail to another person.

Of the eight possible permutations of real-time connected reporting, only four are relevant. Touch without sound and/or without vision may, for example, apply in silent dark, rooms... but that is not the type of setting where strategic analysis work is generally reported to decision-makers. The four relevant permutations are shown in Table 15.1. As expected, all four are commonly used in strategic analysis reporting and intuitively we all know their pros and cons.

| REPORTING FORMAT | REAL-TIME VISUAL INTERACTION | | REAL-TIME AUDIO INTERACTION | | REAL-TIME PHYSICAL INTERACTION | |
|---|---|---|---|---|---|---|
| | yes | no | yes | no | yes | no |
| Personal meeting | √ | | √ | | √ | |
| Video conference | √ | | √ | | | √ |
| [Conference] call | | √ | √ | | | √ |
| Video briefing (movie), recorded audio briefing, written document, image | | √ | | √ | | √ |

TABLE 15.1 PERMUTATIONS OF REPORTING FORMATS FOR HUMAN REAL-TIME INTERACTION

Table 15.1 carries two implicit messages. The first message is how much variety is still possible in formats within the 'no, no, no' reporting format. The second message is that in the 'no, no, no' format the reporting stands on its own. It is as hermetically independent as North Korea. Once the reporting is out there, there is no possibility for adjusting it based on implicit or explicit recipient feedback. It has to be so strong in order to come across on its own merits. The high demands put on a written report may well be the reason why in professional organizations, written reporting skills are included in training programmes.

Below we take a closer look at each of the four relevant reporting formats, starting with the personal meeting (yes, yes, yes).

## PERSONAL MEETINGS ARE POWERFUL WHEN THE ANALYST IS PERSUASIVE

It is not a coincidence that the personal meeting is referred to here by its coordinates (yes, yes, yes). When an analyst gets the opportunity to deliver reporting to a decision-maker, their immediate reaction should be 'this is a yes, yes, yes occasion!' Personal meetings can be bilateral, as can larger meetings where the analyst and the decision-maker are simultaneously present. A personal meeting gives the analyst an opportunity for direct interaction, hearing not only the decision-maker's questions and considerations 'live', but also being able to observe his other communication (tone-of-voice, body language, etc.). The latter make up the vast majority of any person's communication so seeing and hearing real-time, with as added bonus a handshake, has tremendous communication value. This of course applies both ways. A decision-maker is much more inclined to accept the work of one who is highly persuasive than an analyst that radiates uncertainty.

To orchestrate successful personal meetings, the analyst has several upfront choices to make. In the context of reporting, we focus on two dimensions: the use or non-use of visual support materials, and when using visual support materials, the choice of when to distribute these. Table 15.2 summarizes these choices.

| USE OF VISUAL SUPPORT MATERIALS | DISTRIBUTED IN ADVANCE OF AND (PARTLY) PRESENTED DURING THE MEETING | DISTRIBUTED AT THE BEGINNING OF OR PRESENTED DURING THE MEETING | (PRE-PLANNED) EMERGING DURING THE MEETING |
|---|---|---|---|
| Yes | Pre-read (may include written slide show, tables, audio, video, samples, etc.) | Pre-print (may include written slide show, tables, audio, video, samples, etc.) | Whiteboard/flip chart |
| No | Nothing | Nothing | At most a symbolic object |

TABLE 15.2 ▸▸▸ CHOICES OF VISUAL SUPPORT MATERIALS FOR REPORTING IN PERSONAL MEETINGS

The most important choice is whether or not to use any form of visual support materials. The fact that presenting slides is so easy and so common does not, by definition, mean using slides is suitable on all occasions. One may wonder whether, if Martin Luther King had had the choice in his time, whether he would have used slides when he gave his 'I Have a Dream' speech. Similarly, it's hard to imagine Winston Churchill clicking though a slide presentation when he proclaimed that 'even when the British Empire would last for a thousand years, they would still say that this was its finest hour.' Using slides may serve many purposes, but doing so is not linearly proportional to creating impactful reporting.

The most important disadvantage of using slides when delivering a personal speech, even with the best laid-out slides, is that the audience's attention splits between the speaker and the content of the slides. The more attractive and numerous the slides, the more difficult it is for the speaker's personal communication to be impactful due to the distraction caused by the simultaneous slide show.

## CREATIVITY PAYS OFF WHEN CHOOSING TO USE VISUAL SUPPORT MATERIALS

There is no general rule governing when to use which visual support materials, as it depends on the aim of the reporting. Creativity, however, tends to pay off in any case. A business unit management team wanted to make clear to top management that customers really wanted to see 'one face to the customer' rather than four different sales representatives covering one product each.

In order to substantiate their plea for this organizational change, they prepared a video message shot featuring three of their most important customers. Each of the customers called for this change, in no uncertain terms. The persuasive quality of showing a larger-than-life customer's face projected in the board room, calling for your firm to change certainly had its impact, convincing top management to realign the organization.

## PRE-READS ACCELERATE DECISION-MAKING

When a strategic analysis function delivers a debrief of a larger project to a group of senior decision-makers, a best practice is to distribute a pre-read about a week in advance. Ensure this pre-read has a brief, one- or two-slide bulleted summary. It may be beneficial to call the individual recipients a few days after sending the presentation, but before the meeting, to ask whether they have any questions or preliminary comments. It is amazing how such well-planned stakeholder management initiatives can contribute to the ultimate success of your presentation.

At the beginning of the meeting, hand out a hardcopy of the pre-read you'd sent around, and tell your audience you'll now be expanding upon it all and will of course address any of their thoughts or concerns. Avoiding the hassle of presenting slides, let alone slides that have not in advance been shown to the decision-makers, may have unexpected merits. Showing complicated new slides to decision-makers almost by definition leads to unanticipated questions. These questions may not be instantly answerable and can delay decision-making. The fact that investment bankers in their pitches to top management rarely use slides but invariably pass around slick, pre-printed material should tell you something. They seem to understand that people connect better with other people than with slides.[1]

## VIDEO-CONFERENCING SAVES TRAVEL COST AND HASSLE

The difference between a video conference and a personal meeting is that during a video conference no physical interaction is possible between a report's sender and its recipient. The major advantage, of course, is whilst real-time video and audio connectivity allow one to pick up most of the non-verbal communication, the sender and the recipient do not have to be present at the same place. This potentially saves travel time, associated costs and a whole lot of hassle. As video conferencing becomes technically better and better, it is an increasingly useful alternative to personal meetings, especially when the sender and the recipient already know each other. If they haven't in fact met before, video conferencing will not easily build trust between sender and recipient to the extent that would be possible during a personal meeting.

What is harder to do is to have a video conference and at the same time try to collaboratively view, absorb and discuss a slide show. Though the use of three screens, advanced video conferencing facilities allow you to simultaneous see the other party, the other party's view of you ,and your slide presentation. This is the best option. Still, the recipient's attention is continully pulled back and forth between the slide show and the presenter. All of these factors combine to reduce the effectiveness of the virtual meeting, versus the impact you could have made in a direct, face-to-face dialogue. The same is true for a WEBEX, another great and efficient tool that again, is most useful when sender and recipient already know each other.

Another common meeting option is of course the voice-only phone call. Multi-party conference calls save tremendous time, effort and travel costs... but the downsides referenced above tend to become even more pronounced. Disembodied, echoing, half-understood commentary that drones on over remotely-viewed slide presentations can be disappointingly ineffective.

Still, the strategic analyst must accept that a long-distance discussion with the decision-maker, no matter how awkward, is always preferable to delivering no reporting whatsoever. Decision-maker airtime in reporting, even in a call, is precious. Cherish it – and most of all, make it worthwhile for the decision-maker.

## REPORTING OPTIONS EXIST WITHOUT REAL-TIME VIDEO, AUDIO OR PHYSICAL INTERACTION

When none of these three avenues for interaction between sender and recipient are available in real time, the chance for misunderstanding between participants multiplies exponentially. To prevent these communication breakdowns -- and deliver your best possible presentation -- choose your setting, form and format carefully and prepare, prepare, prepare.

In chapter 12 we pointed out that persuasiveness of various reporting formats differs, with videos/moving images being most persuasive, while the same data presented in tables can be significantly less so. Because video of questionable quality and effectiveness may affect the analysis function's credibility, there is a role for many different 'no, no, no' reporting formats (Sinclair, 2010).

A fair conclusion of this section is that the written reports are the most labour-intensive whilst potentially having the lowest impact, whereas personally delivered (elevator pitch) messages tend to be most persuasive and require the least preparation time. Top consultancy firms for this reason train their staff to at all times have an elevator pitch ready, if only to ensure that when they have an occasional encounter with a decision-maker, they are prepared to deliver a short and sweet message. And what works for top consulting firms will, in this case, work well for strategic business analysts.

# 15.5 REQUIREMENTS OF REPORTING

## REPORTING STARTS WITH PUTTING THE RECIPIENT FRONT AND CENTER

Any form of reporting should focus on the personal needs of the decision-maker, who shouldn't have to adapt to the form or content of the reporting. This is rule number one; it is the single most important requirement. Put yourself in the decision-maker's shoes and proceed with that all-important xenocentric perspective. The scenario below may elucidate this.

Imagine having two CEOs within the same company. The first insisted on getting a 40-page slide deck that covered every conceivable detail surrounding a strategic analysis topic. Co-CEO #1 read every word, and the next morning appeared at the analyst's desk and asked a probing question about the footnote at the bottom of page 37. Meanwhile, Co-CEO #2 had a reputation for not really reading anything at all. Some wondered whether this individual actually could read, but that wasn't really fair. The fact was that Co-CEO #2 preferred receiving intelligence in staccato, two-minute bursts, delivered verbally, that delivered the key message with as little embellishment as possible. Both were unquestionably successful in their roles. This brings us to a recurring theme in this chapter: in reporting there is no silver bullet. Human peculiarities drive choices.

To summarize the above, we can say that a report must have:

- The delivery form that best appeals to the decision-maker as recipient.
- The content (e.g., amount of detail) that best suits the decision-maker's needs.

The analyst's job is to focus on how the evidence, argument and presentation will appeal to and ultimately convince the intended audience... not how it appeals to the analyst herself (Macintyre, 2010d).

Table 15.3 provides insight into a typical decision-maker's contextual perspective, his motivation and needs, and the implications to reporting strategic analysis work. In the decision-makers' column, a segmentation has been made between the functional and the emotional side of the context, the decision-makers' needs and the implications for the reporting. In the implication column we identify several requirements for reporting. As so often, this segmentation is not based on sound science, but rather on heuristic office rules, gathered over many years behind a desk. The table aims to elucidate why reporting has different requirements and how effectively meeting those requirements can satisfy decision-makers' needs.

| | WHAT? | SO WHAT? | NOW WHAT? |
|---|---|---|---|
| | Decision-makers' context: what they face... | Decision-makers' needs: what they look for... | Implications: reporting should thus be... |
| Functional dimension | time pressure | efficiency | - concise<br>- complementary knowledge<br>- remarkable |
| | many questions, few answers | solutions, not problems | - (immediately) actionable<br>- straight and simple<br>- need to know |
| | today's results pressure | actuality<br>winning insights<br>forward-looking focus | - timely<br>- cost-efficient<br>- purpose-oriented |
| Emotional dimension | uncertainty | assurance<br>association | - memorable<br>- convincing<br>- reproducible |
| | hierarchy | respect<br>status/power<br>recognition | - humble |

TABLE 15.3 ▶▶▶ DECISION-MAKERS' CONTEXT AND NEEDS FOR REPORTING

Each of the thirteen requirements identified in table 15.3 will be discussed below. At first sight, the emotional dimension may be less tangible than the functional dimension; it is certainly not less relevant. When a report does not meet the emotional needs of a decision-maker, the functional side of the report, no matter how solid, is unlikely to be compelling enough to make her act upon it. A report that is perceived as arrogant or talking down to the decision-maker will rarely motivate her to accept the conclusions, let alone take the actions that the report may recommend. Another sure-to-fail approach is to issue a report that implicitly (or even better explicitly tells the decision-maker how wrong she is), disparaging her carefully-considered policies and positions.

Chapter 16 will discuss in more detail how to handle the challenges of creating and having to deliver strategic analysis work that questions current corporate strategies and policies. The remainder of this section focuses on the requirements of reporting as such, building on work by McLaughlin (McLaughlin, 2008c).

## BE CONCISE

Reporting should generally be short and to the point. Reporting on some topics at times may require and justify sizeable deliverables. As long as you keep the needs, desires and attention-span of the decision-maker in mind, a long report may be perfectly acceptable, provided it has a concise, razor-sharp executive summary, a good index and good content structure. When the executive summary is crystal clear and easy for the decision-maker to grasp, it's likely that the rest of the report will be equally well executed. This is not a new insight. French scholar Blaise Pascal in 1657 quipped:

> *"I have made this letter longer than usual because I lack the time to make it shorter."*

## COMPLEMENTARY KNOWLEDGE

A great way to make a decision-maker ignore your deliverable is to focus their attention on facts and analysis she already knows. Savvy, well-informed business executives tend to know the headlines of a story and the general, underlying situation (Davis, 2008). Do not bore them with things they already know, or even worse, dare to lecture them on matters they obviously know much more about than you do. The impact of missing this message may be substantial. President John F. Kennedy sacked CIA Director Allen

W. Dulles, whom he had inherited from the previous Eisenhower administration, because, among other things, the President disliked Dulles' briefings (Talbot, 2015):

> *"[Kennedy] was not very impressed with Dulles's briefings. He did not think they were in much depth or told him anything he couldn't read in the newspapers."*

What decision-makers need is intelligence, not news. Interpret the news. Clarify what the news reports offer on new or expanded capabilities or intents of a competitor or new insights on opportunities or threats in markets. There is no point in trying to beat a news agency in being the first to have the news, but there is value in interpreting and contextualizing the news of the day in a way that helps enable confident decision-making.

## MAKE IT REMARKABLE

Another decision-maker's constant is information overload. The analyst's material competes with countless other demands on the decision-maker's precious time and attention: other emails, reports, elevator pitches, etc. Some questions an analyst should ask include: why would anyone pay attention to this reporting? How does this report stand out above the clutter? What makes this reporting so remarkable that it grabs the decision-maker's attention? How can I prevent the decision-maker from intellectually 'disconnecting' from this report once they look at it?

The xenocentric approach to remarkability of reporting starts with considering the recipient decision-maker. Why should he need to know this? Which of this decision-maker's emotional needs does this analysis implicitly, or perhaps even explicitly, meet? Why does paying attention to this report assist this decision-maker in meeting their (bonus) targets? Do not shy away from innovative delivery formats. Why not present short video messages instead of dull slides? Instead of using a standard presentation, present the outcome of an analysis in a personal meeting, in a tag-team dialogue format, where – standing in front of the decision-maker – one analyst asks the most relevant questions and the other answers with a memorable narrative. These and other ambitious, creative approaches can transform your reporting from stale and predictable – and unlikely to yield great results – to truly remarkable.

## ACTIONABLE

Reporting is considered actionable when it prompts forward movement on a decision… and helps a decision-maker to make the *right* decision. Actionability is an indirect requirement. For a report to be actionable it has to meet some of the other requirements mentioned in Table 15.3. The reporting, most of all, needs to be simple (easy to grasp), timely, purpose-oriented (answering the *real* questions that the decision-maker has) and convincing.

## STRAIGHT AND SIMPLE

Reporting in a straight and simple way sounds more simple than it is. It is hard to overestimate the virtue of simplicity in reporting. When the aim is to report a persuasive message, the first rule is to keep it simple. Anything that reduces cognitive strain on the recipient will help in achieving this aim (Kahneman, 2011f). A smart, experienced executive will see through the pretension of grandiose *purple prose* in an instant (Kahneman, 2011f):

> *"Couching familiar ideas in pretentious language is taken as a sign of poor intelligence and low credibility."*

Since we now know that simplicity is a virtue, the next question is: How can simplicity in reporting be achieved? Below we'll look at that question in three dimensions: language, reporting format (in writing) and storyline.

A xenocentric view in using *language* is to preferably report in the mother tongue of the recipient, or at least in a language the recipient is highly familiar with. Never put yourself in the position of facing an insurmountable language barrier between you and your audience. Even when reporting in the recipient's mother tongue, there is no guarantee that the analyst and the decision-maker *speak the same language*. The terminology and jargon used by the analyst should be calibrated to those of the decision-maker. Believe me, an executive's eyes will glaze over thirty seconds into an insider's master class on strategic analysis jargon. Using unfamiliar jargon violates the golden rule of reporting: always try to minimize, and never amplify, your audience's cognitive strain. Otherwise, your recipient is bound to get irritated by the effort required to follow along, and will probably lose the thread of the storyline. In summary: avoid unfamiliar jargon.

Over-the-top language, over-elaborate visuals and impenetrable statistics can also shut down your audience. Taleb has almost made it a life's calling of warning against intuitive but incorrect conclusions based on statistics

(Taleb, 2007c). If the cunning and duplicitous Machiavelli had been an analyst he would likely have turned Taleb's evidence into his advantage. He would have used figures and statistics to create misleading reports, inviting wrong interpretations by the recipient that in the best Machiavellian style would serve his self-centred interest. As noted earlier in this book, figures do not lie, but liars do figure. Avoid ambiguous, let alone misleading reporting, that abuses figures for political purposes.

Here's another thought on using ambiguous terms in reporting (Heuer, 1999e). Words like 'may' or 'can' are expressions of uncertainty. Uncertainty in strategic analysis is not uncommon. In section 10.6, I discussed the uncertainty that stems from having to make do with too many known unknowns. Such qualifying words should be used with care. Alone, these terms have no clear meaning. As a result, the recipient of your analysis will be forced to fill in the meaning. The recipient, however, can be expected to already have at least some degree of familiarity with the matters covered in the report. The recipient will thus unconsciously fill the term 'may' with his own meaning, matching the knowledge she already has. The risk of this is twofold. First, the recipient feels she has not read anything new in the report. The second is that the word 'may' conjures up two entirely different things in the minds of the analyst and the decision-maker. With written reporting, the recipient 'may' (oops, forgive me!) thus act on a different view of reality than the analyst aimed to convey. Using terms like 'may' can at times be inevitable. When this occurs, it puts extra responsibility on the reporter to avoid any possible misunderstandings caused by introducing ambiguous uncertainty.

In choosing a reporting format, the first rule is to distinguish facts, methodologies and messages as clearly as possible. To a decision-maker facts and messages normally matter much more than methodologies. Cater to the needs of the decision-maker, no matter how innovative you may think your methodologies are. Sharing methodological best practices is great among peer analysts but rarely a best practice when presenting to decision-makers. In reporting formats the second rule is to use standard, well-recognized formats when delivering periodical (standard) reports. Once the decision-maker is familiar with them, standard presentation formats will help reduce cognitive strain and ease his grasp of your key messages. What is true for standard formats also applies to standard colours. If your firm's primary branding/presentation colour is magenta, always use magenta in charts that detail your company's performance data... and use other colours to represent competitors' numbers. Doing so reduces cognitive strain and sparks instant recognition of the underlying logic (Frank, 2011b). 'Magenta – that is us, right?'

Typography is another instrument to facilitate easy reading. Use bullet points, sub-bullets, bold face and italics. No matter how much there is to say about a topic, keep the summary succinct and provide it in a layout, look and feel that invites reading. The intermezzo at the end of this section gives a few hints about slide writing that may also prove useful.

A final element that contributes to simplicity in reporting is providing a storyline with a compelling and sound logic.

## NEED TO KNOW

The requirement 'need to know' applies along two dimensions. First, it helps ensure that the strategic analysis work gets to the right person and not to others who aren't logically involved and shouldn't be privy to such strategic analysis. Second, it is essential that the right person receives the deliverable at the right time along the project timeline continuum. The timing element is further discussed below. Another need-to-know consideration is ensuring that material is properly classified, labeled and secured to prevent exposure to those who shouldn't be seeing it. How to classify data and documents is outside the scope of this book.

## TIMELY

Arguably the most critical requirement for strategic analysis is timeliness. What is true for strategic analysis at large is certainly true for the reporting phase of the analysis cycle. Taking the xenocentric view, the decision-maker's agenda drives the project. There is simply no substitute for good timing, as the quote below illustrates (Bryan, 2009):

> *"Much of the art of decision-making under uncertainty is getting the timing right. If you delay too much, opportunity cost may rise, investment cost may escalate, and losses can accumulate. However, making critical decisions too early can lead to bad choices or excessive risks."*

## COST-EFFICIENT

Decision-makers intuitively tend to put a cost price tag on most initiatives they encounter in business. This is a healthy habit. Indifference to cost as a rule does not correlate with building a better business. Whatever is offered to decision-makers is always related to a cost. When the output of strategic analysis is directly actionable, cost is rarely a topic of discussion. When it isn't directly actionable, inconvenient questions may come up. A strategic analysis function might even consider putting up a poster with a message that was displayed in a US R&D centre of Akzo Nobel in the '90s:

*"We pay for results, not for explanations."*

## PURPOSE-ORIENTED

In a drive to best serve decision-makers, the strategic analysis function should perfectly match the analysis deliverable with the intelligence the decision-maker needs to make a reasoned decision. Less is more. Stick to what the decision-maker needs and get it to her when she needs it. Purpose-oriented reporting is easier in reactive work – such as work ordered by a decision-maker with a purpose – than in pro-active work, instigated by the function to signal, for something like a new opportunity or threat to the decision-maker.

In pre-planned, periodical reports (like a monthly business environment newsletter) getting the format right by designing it well in conjunction with the designated decision-makers pays off. Subsequently, over time, proactively solicited recipient feedback may lead to further improvements in appropriateness of the topics covered and efficiency (by avoiding reporting things that may be nice to know but are really only of interest to the analyst and her brother).

## MEMORABLE

The next two requirements are memorability and convincingness. Being memorable and convincing as requirements of reporting are not statistically independent. A memorable message may, also be more convincing.[2] This means that tricks to increase the memorability of reporting may also implicitly and positively contribute to convincingness.

Both the print style of a written report and the actual language that is used for conveying the message may contribute to memorability. Print style factors that increase add to memorability  are, for example, the selective use of bold font to emphasize messages, the use of colours to highlight to highlight a key point, the presentation of separate narratives in text boxes or the use of intermezzos.

Language itself is probably an even more powerful tool in driving memorability. Psychological experiments indicate that at least three features of the language used in reporting may contribute to memorability (Kahneman, 2010f):

- Rhyme.
- Alliteration.
- Narrating quality.

The use of rhyme to facilitate memorizing texts dates back to antiquity. Kahneman points out that a rhyming sentence like 'Little strokes will tumble great oaks' is more memorable than 'Little strokes will tumble great trees'. How often do we capitalize on such simple yet fundamental human insight in strategic analysis reporting?

What is true for rhyme also applies to alliteration. Horrid Henry is a famous UK children's book character.[3] Henry's overachieving but dull brother is Perfect Peter. If the author of these books had called the boys Horrid Peter and Perfect Henry, the publishing house would probably never have rolled the presses. How often do we in strategic analysis spot an 'obvious opportunity' instead of a 'great opportunity'?

Finally, when it comes to memorability, nothing beats a good narrative. The particular case of an individual *with whom the recipient of the story can identify* is as strong as it gets when it comes to achieving memorability and convincingness of a message. Journalists use casuistic (overly subtle) narratives all the time. When an earthquake flattens a city and takes 1,000 lives, the story of the caring mother with the disabled son who lost her husband and economic livelihood will catch and keep the newspaper reader's attention. This individual case will hands-down beat in memorability any objective analysis of percentage of houses collapsed in which part of the town.

Take the cases that are taught in business schools. The scripts of these cases almost by default start by introducing an individual manager who faces a dilemma to be resolved. The students connect with the manager in the narrative – as a person to be empathized with – prompting them to think through what they would have done in the manager's situation.

The golden rule of a convincing and memorable narrative is that it follows a consistent storyline (Kahneman, 2010f).

Consistency does not require a storyline to be complete. Consistency overrides completeness. Consistency is a fundamental human need in enabling efficient decision-making. When the mind discovers consistency, it allows for fast (and possibly erroneous) recognition-primed decision-making. When the recipient's brain receives enough puzzle pieces to assemble a puzzle that matches a known pattern in the recipient's psychological pattern library, completeness will gently be overlooked. (See chapter 16 for a more detailed discussion of this phenomenon.)

The obvious flaw of a casuistic narrative is that it may be a good story, but it may not be representative of the situation at large, no longer be relevant or for some other reason not apply to what a decision-maker needs to know to come to a balanced decision (Taleb, 2007d). A strong story told to a decision-maker may trigger vividness weighing, an awfully distortive bias that we encountered in chapter 12.

If Machiavelli had indeed been an corporate analyst reporting his analysis to management, telling strong narratives would be among his favorite tools to manipulate decision-makers. For a decent strategic analysis function, strong narratives can help ensure that their key messages reverberate, and that the recipient sees the forests in spite of the many trees. Good storylining is a must-have capability for a strategic analyst.

## CONVINCING

In this book the words convincing and persuasive are defined as having complementary meanings. For purposes of this book, we'll use the word convincing in this way, 'The evidence is convincing.' In contrast, we'll use the word persuasive in a way that implies action, as in: 'The salesman persuaded me to buy this car.' The test for whether evidence is convincing should be whether it is objective and neutral – the narrative that the salesman used to make me buy that used car is probably not objective but personal; it was tailor-made for the occasion and the recipient. The narrative may not have worked with other people or on another occasion, whereas in the ideal case any judge would (independent of how others may judge it) have found the evidence to be convincing.

Assume we define the word convincing as we do above. The output of both data collection efforts and of data analysis must be independently convincing. This will help ensure the recipient that the report supports sound decision-making.

The output of collection efforts are usually data, or information or knowledge, usually from HUMINT sources that need to fit into a bigger picture. To report data convincingly, the first step is to provide clarity to the recipient on what data are known. Diagram 15.5 is generically applicable on the clarity question, using four permutations of unknown-known (horizontal axis) and unknowns-knowns (vertical axis). Providing clarity on data availability is a professional obligation of a good analyst (Davis, 1997)

When applicable and relevant, data (or evidence) should be graded for reliability to add credibility to the work (Jeffery, 2011a). All in all, when reporting data the analyst should strive to report the truth, the full truth and nothing but the truth. The logic virtue of this legal statement is that it is all-encompassing. Reporting that meets this gold standard is at least complete.

| | | |
|---|---|---|
| KNOWNS | (Serendipitous) data that may be unlocked in HUMINT-collection efforts in your firm that are still to be completed (ready by...) | Data that are available for this analysis, such as... |
| UNKNOWNS | If only we knew | Data that we know we need but have not identified a legal source for... (collection efforts will be finalized by...) |
| | UNKNOWNS | KNOWNS |

DIAGRAM 15.5 ▶▶ REPORTING A CONVINCING REVIEW OF DATA AVAILABILITY

The implicit call for completeness has not been made to suggest that all data that are available should be pushed onto the decision-maker through the report. Backup slides, appendices and even literature references have their role in reporting. The purpose of reporting is not to impress but to enable better decision-making. Data that do not directly contribute to improving the quality of decision-making do not belong in the main body of a report.

On the contrary, sometimes an analyst has to make a call to provide an analysis that is understandable to non-expert decision-makers, simplifying matters beyond what experts would find sufficiently weighty and probing. The real art is in intelligently conveying all the necessary detail, context and subtleties, but not bombarding an overwhelmed executive with more than she can handle.

The analysis should allow the decision-maker to almost effortlessly reach the right conclusions. The logic of the analysis should be so compellingly (and simply) narrated that the message is grasped instantly. The decision-maker will only admire the depth of thinking that went into the work when he can, through the quality and the brilliant simplicity of the narrative, to understand it. When a decision-maker cannot connect the dots from data conclusions, he will feel as though he is being made to manage while blindfolded.

To convince a decision-maker, we as analysts will have to provide guidance. Implicitly answering the following questions may help when delivering reports (based on Heuer, 2008):

- What alternative explanations or hypotheses exist, other than the one presented as most credible?
- Why have other hypotheses or explanations been discarded?
- What signposts, when observed in the future, will suggest a change that may necessitate revisiting hypotheses or explanations?
- How do we monitor those signposts, how frequently do we do so and how much delay is there between the signal we pick up and the fluidly changing situation that it highlighted?
- How much of the conclusion is based on undisputed data and how much on reasoning?

The ultimate question is not what methodology or analysis has been used, but what does the executive need to understand about methodology or analysis to be enabled/assured in his decision-making?

## REPRODUCIBLE

Reproducibility is the single most relevant requirement in reporting any scientific inquiry. When another set of researchers, acting completely independently, can on the basis of the scientific report follow its procedures to the letter, but not reproduce the findings, the report does not qualify as science. In business decision-making, supported or not by strategic analysis, this requirement is rarely asked for. That is not to say that decision-makers' minds do not unconsciously consider this requirement.

The reproducibility question may very well pop up in the guise of the question of repeatability. A report that shows a trend, illustrated with multiple, clearly independent examples is infinitely more convincing than a report that describes what could still be seen as an individual anomaly.

## HUMBLE

Strategic analysis is a service business. The customer is always right, even when technically he is not – a CEO should not be embarrassed and humiliated by intellectually superior analysts. The following rule may be helpful: report to inform, not to impress, let alone intimidate.

To conclude this section, let me stress that humility is the last but not the least requirement in reporting. Humility correlates with easy, simple-to-grasp language. There is a catch, though. Humility should not compromise the need for your reporting to be smart, insightful and truly meaningful. Second World War-era UK Director of Naval Intelligence Admiral John Godfrey eloquently summarized the need to reconcile balanced, humble, business-like reporting with remarkability when he wrote (Macintyre, 2010d):

> *"Elegant trimmings should have no place in the intelligence officer's vocabulary. On the other hand the man who cannot tell a good story is a dull dog."*

# 15.6 REPORTING AS LIFELONG LEARNING

Reporting, like strategic analysis, is a craft. It seems that in reporting the rule applies that true expertise only develops when an individual dedicates at least 10,000 hours to that craft. One of the easy, obvious ways for an analyst to get better at reporting is to seek feedback from one of her actual executive decision-makers.

Reporting tools are not static. As a strategic analysis function, do not hesitate to incorporate new media and/or tools as they become available. Anything that contributes to making the strategic analysis function more remarkable – in a positive sense, that is – will help burnish the function's credibility and reputation in the eyes of senior leadership.

I will close with two final remarks on reporting. First, seek inspiration from great communicators. Whether Barack Obama may say what you want to hear or not is immaterial to the fact that he knows how to get a message across. What communication tricks can you pick up from him and put to use in your next verbal report? Think of tricks like using:

- Silence between key words to build up tension and focus audience attention.
- Face and body expressions that fully match the words spoken, to add to persuasiveness.
- No body movements at all, to minimize audience distraction from what is being said.

Misunderstood or overlooked reporting is a key risk factor in strategic analysis. After all, the entire analysis effort has been wasted when the report fails to get the messages across to the decision-maker.

## INTERMEZZO: TIPS ON SLIDE WRITING

Writing slides is a sub-discipline of writing, which itself is a sub-discipline of reporting. All best practices that relate to reporting by implication also apply to slide writing. For slide writing the pointers below may be helpful:

- Match the slide design to its purpose: live presentation or reading
- Minimize content: less is more
- Be consistent: consistency creates clarity
- Be persuasive: use visuals
- Provide only one message per slide keep it simple
- Give every slide an action title grab their attention
- Ensure a good storyline reporting is storytelling

## AD I. SLIDES CONVEY YOUR NARRATIVE, BUT THEY'RE RARELY 'ONE SIZE FITS ALL'

Slides are a great tool but only when used properly. A slide that is meant to be presented to a large audience during a live meeting serves another purpose than one appearing in a document intended for a solitary reader.

Slides that are targeted at large audiences who aren't familiar with the subject matter should help illustrate the storyline delivered by the presenter. People connect to other people, and generally not to slides. We say they should help *illustrate* the storyline because the presenter – through her verbal delivery, eye contact, facial expressions and gestures – should be the primary vehicle. The worst presentation slides are those that contain so many messages and so much text that the presenter feels compelled to read them aloud, word-for-word, to the audience. As there is so much text that it would be impossible for the presenter to recall it all, so they have to turn their back to the audience and look at what's projected on the screen. Now it is the slide show that presents with the presenter.

In summary: slides for live presentations are meant to illustrate, not to do the talking.

When the messages are unavoidably complex, it may be advisable to distribute a stage-setting pre-read to the audience in advance. You could even consider passing out copies of the entire slide presentation, but as we said in an earlier chapter, that introduces the risk of attendees becoming so absorbed in the handouts that they don't pay attention to the speaker, lose the thread and drift away.

## AD II. SLIDE CONTENT SHOULD BE AS SUCCINCT AS POSSIBLE

In slides intended for use in live presentations, less is more. I previously emphasized the critical importance of minimizing cognitive strain. Cognitive strain and superfluous or unclear content are linearly proportional. The 'cognitive strain avoidance check' should be the final checkpoint with any presentation intended for an unfamiliar audience.

And again – at risk of being terribly repetitive – I can't overemphasize the importance of keeping it simple. For an analyst/presenter, the perceived knowledge gap between the audience and himself should determine the weight and heft of the slides. The larger the gap, the less complexity is allowed.

## AD III. CONSISTENCY CREATES CLARITY

Three other instruments that can help reduce the recipient's cognitive strain:

- To brand deliverables published by the strategic analysis function.
- To build credibility by quoting reputable sources.
- To report in a consistent format.

Branding serves as an endorsement of quality. When the strategic analysis function has built a solid reputation, the decision-maker will automatically know that anything the group presents to him will be of the highest quality. This will go a long way towards reducing the recipient's cognitive strain. When the decision-maker sees the facts and sees the conclusions, and both more or less match his expectation, he will rarely bother to dive into the nuts & bolts methodology that led to the analyst's conclusions. The strategic analysis function's reputation therefore not only has value for the function but also for the decision-maker. In the end, the function in the corporate environment is what it knows (Davis, 1997). The totality of what it knows and how it turns what it knows into insights helps it rise above.

What is true for the reputation of the function also applies to the reputation of the sources used in its reporting. This is why consistent reference to reliable, undisputed outside sources should be a standard element on a slide. Sources like the IMF, the World Bank, the Economist Intelligence Unit and the McKinsey Institute (to name a few) serve as beacons of credibility. The scholarship of an individual analyst may also bolster the material's credibility when the decision-maker is not yet familiar with her. If the analyst's education and professional credentials are impressive, be sure to sufficiently highlight them on a presentation's title page.

As mentioned previously, the use of a consistent design template – for slides as well as other documents and deliverables – can be reassuringly familiar to a harried business executive. The essential benefit is of course that the form and format becomes transparent, allowing the recipient to effortlessly zero-in on the content.

The benefits of format consistency are as follows:

- Standardization drives the consistent use of solid analytic methodology embedded in a standard format. Standardization contributes to output quality.
- Standardization drives efficiency as it is easier to transfer slides across different analysis deliverables. Reusing slides across multiple presentations becomes effortless.
- Standardization also drives efficiency as storylines and presentations can be mass-customized, eliminating the need to create everything from scratch, every time a new presentation has to be made.

CHAPTER 16

# ANALYST DECISION-MAKER INTERACTION

# 16.1 INTRODUCTION

Turning a management briefing into a management report may be less difficult than delivering a debrief in such a way that the principal acts upon it. Strategic analysis should enable the principal to become a decision-maker. Unfortunately, not all intelligence – no matter how timely, accurate, strategically significant and actionable – translates into action (Treverton, 2008):

> *"The typical problem at the highest level of Government is less often the misuse than the non-use of intelligence."*

Management consultancy firms are generally well acquainted with the dynamic of the interface between the analyst or consultant and the decision-maker. A common maxim in consultancy is:

Impact of a consultancy product = Quality * Acceptance

Previous chapters have predominantly focused on the 'quality' element in the above formula, whereas here we will consider the 'acceptance' element. This chapter is neither a scientific treatise on organizational psychology nor a study of decision-making under uncertainty. Rather, it is intended to provide you as an analyst with some thoughts to help improve the acceptance of your deliverables. The ideas here can be found in literature on psychology, but for the most part they come from my personal, day-to-day professional experience as an analyst. It is empirical knowledge.

In section 16.2 I revisit the objective of strategic analysis: reducing management's uncertainty on a firm's business environment. I will first discuss the phenomenon of uncertainty. Section 16.3 looks at decision-making as such. Section 16.4 examines how analysts work towards decisions and how they tend to cope with uncertainty. Section 16.5 briefly discusses how business leaders make decisions, especially when facing uncertainties. Section 16.6 looks at common challenges in analyst/decision-maker interaction. Finally, in section 16.7, I aim to provide thoughts on how an analyst can maximize executives' acceptance of analysis deliverables. Along this continuum – as she learns, grows and progresses through her career – an analyst gradually moves up the the organizational influence hierarchy from data cruncher to an executive's trusted sounding board and advisor.

# 16.2 ON UNCERTAINTY

As we've been stressing, a prime objective of the strategic analysis function is to reduce management's uncertainty regarding the business environment. Gary Klein vividly describes the problem of uncertainty in his book *Sources Of Power*. His work has clearly inspired this chapter and I will make several references to it, because its narrative is so compelling for analysts. Klein's chapter covering uncertainty is amusingly called *Why Good People Make Poor Decisions* (Klein, 1999b). This, I believe is exactly the problem that analysts try to prevent both to ourselves as well as to the business leaders we serve.

Klein reviews four potential factors that contribute to poor decision-making: biased thinking, stress, uncertainty and expertise versus superstition. He concludes that decision biases do not seem to entirely explain poor decisions. Similarly, stress is not a factor in poor decision-making as such, unless stress leads to the choice of overlooking critical data. Expertise may lead to less than optimal decision-making when the domain of decision-making is dynamic and the executive's own obtained experiences are in actuality less relevant than they are perceived to be by the executive. Most poor decisions may result from having inadequate knowledge and expertise.

Implicitly both analysts and decision-makers may rightfully worry that inadequate knowledge and expertise are risk factors in their work. And that's bound to lead to uncertainty, which is likely to impact decisiveness. As Klein put it:

*"Uncertainty is doubt that threatens to block action."*

## UNCERTAINTY RELATES TO INFORMATION

Klein identifies four sources of uncertainty. Although his book covers decision-making in the broadest sense, each of the four sources of uncertainty he identifies factor heavily in corporate strategic analysis. Those sources of uncertainty are (Klein, 1999b):

- Missing information. Information has not been received or has been received but cannot be located when needed.
- Unreliable information. The credibility of the source is low, or is perceived to be low even though the information is highly accurate.
- Ambiguous or conflicting information. There is more than one reasonable way to interpret the information.
- Complex information. It is difficult to decipher and integrate the different facets of the data.

How to handle the above sources of uncertainty, from a qualitative standpoint, was extensively discussed in the chapters 10-14. Those chapters focused on the relationship between the analyst and the content. In this chapter the perspective changes: we'll imagine a more or less confident analyst and her interaction with the decision-maker. The analyst offers up her deliverable. The decision-maker, however, has not gone through the analysis cycle. The decision-maker still lacks the background, perspective and insight the analyst gained in working through the cycle. It's now up to the analyst and her hopefully well-prepared deliverable to get the executive up to speed and on track to make a decisive, well-reasoned decision.

To do so, the analyst again needs to apply xenocentric thinking. This time, however, it is not the adversary that is the xeno (or strange) element that needs to be dealt with. This time it is the business leader.

## UNCERTAINTY NEEDS TO BE SPLIT IN ENVIRONMENTAL AND EXECUTIONAL UNCERTAINTY

There is one attribute of uncertainty that is specific to strategic analysis and has not been covered by Klein. In strategic analysis, I believe there is more than one type of uncertainty.

So far in this book, the word uncertainty has been used to describe the inevitable difficulties in predicting future developments in the business environment. This type of uncertainty is a fact of life in strategic analysis, and a well-executed piece of analysis can to some extent help reduce this type of uncertainty. But no matter how good the analysis, the perils of so-called 'environmental uncertainty' can never be completed ameliorated. In the remainder of this chapter we will address this challenge.

A decision-maker may not feel any uncertainty regarding what the future holds in his industry environment. Yet he may still feel uncertain whether he and his team are up to the challenge of successfully executing the moves he plans to make. In this chapter we will refer to this type of uncertainty as 'executional uncertainty'. The analyst ideally understands the doubts, qualms and hesitancy an executive may harbor. As I will show, dealing with this special brand of uncertainty may not always be easy. 'Executional uncertainty' in organizations more often than not is a taboo. It is rarely openly discussed. Hence we again identify the need for an analyst to take a xenocentric view, this time towards the business leader. Additionally, for an analyst, uncertainties that are not articulated can adversely colour the decision-maker's reaction to her deliverables.

The next section provides some background on decision-makers and uncertainty. The good news is that analysts can use awareness of this knowledge to improve deliverable acceptance.

# 16.3 ON DECISION-MAKING STRATEGIES

Human decision-making is fascinating. People say that they do things they actually don't do, people also do things they they say they'd never do. This is the world the analyst works and lives in. For the analyst, understanding some basics about human decision-making can pay big dividends, particularly when it comes to optimizing the acceptance of her deliverables. Human decision-making is mind-bogglingly complex; it can make rocket science look like child's play. Everyone on the planet makes countless decisions daily, which is why describing and codifying human decision-making is so tremendously difficult. One reason may be that human decision-making – out there in the real world – is not intuitive.

An intuitive take on human decision-making would be that before taking a decision on an issue:

- Experts on the issue compare options and choose the best.
- Novices to the issue can only think of a single option and will apply it.

Research shows that exactly the opposite happens in practice (Klein, 1999c). It seems that novices encountering a particular problem that is new to them initially take better decisions – if only because they are uncertain and extra inquisitive going into the process. But when they become more and more familiar with an environment or a type of situation, they increasingly begin to make decisions based on a mental model they have developed in their neophyte phase. Usually that mental model is still incomplete, and often incorrect, but that does not stop slowly-evolving novices from often acting over-confidently, instead of acknowledging their limitations, asking questions and easing into their expertise (Dörner, 1996c). This research shows how treacherously rapidly the bias of premature closing creeps into decision-making.

Our initial hypothesis is thus to be rejected. Novices will start a mental voyage of discovery to create options. They will subsequently compare these options in choosing the best course of action to resolve the issue. In contrast, experts will instantaneously choose a single option for the course of action to resolve the issue. Experts will quickly apply their own, time-tested criteria, plow through the viable choices and make a decision. Experts dedicate their thinking time foremost to a situation assessment of the issue at hand, looking for a pattern they recognize. Pattern recognition is based on:

- Seeing relevant cues.
- Having clear expectancies.
- Having plausible goals.
- Knowing typical actions.

Once an expert recognizes a known pattern in the situation awareness phase, a script emerges in his mind. When particular cues are present that match with what this situation seems to show to him, the expectancies become predictable. When plausible goals have clearly been set for resolving the issue, actions automatically come to mind that in previous issues with a similar pattern worked satisfactorily to achieve the expert's goals.

A common illustration of pattern recognition concerns chess as the game played by masters. In chess, the number of possible moves and counter-moves is nearly infinite, but in a given game only a few moves are truly good. If ever there was an abundance of distracting noise – of possible but irrelevant or ineffective moves – it is in a game of chess. Picking the truly good moves resembles filtering out the valuable signals, in the midst of abundant noise, in analysis. In an interview, former chess world champion Garry Kasparov in 2005 revealed that he had analyzed the playing histories of great chess players since about the year 1800 (Coutu, 2005). Kasparov says:

> *"I found something very interesting. It was often at the very toughest moments of their chess battles – when they had to rely on pure intuition – that these great players came up with their best, most innovative moves. Ironically, when the games were finished and the players had the luxury of replaying them at leisure and analyzing them for publication, they typically made many more mistakes than*

*they did when actually competing. To me the implication is clear: What made these players great was not their analytic prowess but their intuition under pressure."*

The hallmark of a first-class chess player is having in their memory a large store of chess game patterns – perhaps as many as 50,000 patterns. This store has often been built up over decades of competition and study. Based on pattern recognition from this rich store, the chess master's mind selects the next move so quicky that an observer cannot but conclude that intuition is at work. And decision-making that from an external perspective is based on intuition is not the exclusive domain of chess players. Research tells us that an astounding 95% of human behaviour is not based on conscious decisions.

## RATIONAL OR RECOGNITION-PRIMED DECISION-MAKING LINKS TO ISSUE FAMILIARITY

H. Simon, a Nobel Prize laureate in economics, has described the above pattern-recognition decision-making strategy as 'satisficing' (Klein, 1999c). An expert on an issue will tend to select the first action option that *satisfices* the attributes an action needs to minimally fit in the pattern script he recognizes. A small set of independent cues may be enough for an expert to register with an individual pattern in his library. Consider a financial expert seeing a company with:

- A low solvency (equity as % of total assets) at the last published balance sheet.
- A negative free cash flow in the last published reporting period.
- One or more hybrid instruments (like perpetual, sub-ordinated bonds), showing as 'equity in name only' on the balance sheet.

This expert recognizes enough cues to determine how likely this company is to get into future financial trouble. In Simon's terminology, the independent cues satisfy this expert's implicit mental requirements for imagining the insolvency script as feasible. As a result, the expert decides to advise any overly risk-adverse investors to steer clear of a new debt bond the company is planning to issue.

This approach to decision-making is called 'recognition-primed decision-making'. It is fundamentally different from what is called a rational choice strategy: collecting information, analyzing and comparing options and choosing the most suitable option to resolve an issue.

Experts by definition focus on a particular subject. That is the area in which they have greater than usual expertise. Interestingly, people with expertise on a given subject tend to only apply recognition-primed decision-making to issues in their own field of expertise. These same experts apply a rational choice strategy when they face issues that are outside their area of specialization. The differentiating attribute for people to choose either recognition-primed decision-making or rational choice strategy is thought to be familiarity with the matter.

When a executive feels sufficiently familiar with the issue, his confidence will be strong enough to make him rely on pattern recognition in his decision-making. It is for solving unfamiliar issues that an analytic approach will tend to be chosen.

## TWO HUMAN BRAIN SYSTEMS OPERATE IN DECISION-MAKING

We know that the brain consists of two distinct sub-systems (Kahneman, 2011l). Kahneman describes them as follows:

> *"System I operates automatically and quickly, with little or no effort and no sense of voluntary control.*
> *System II allocates attention to the effortful mental activities that demand it, including complex computations. The operations of System II are often associated with the subjective experience of agency, choice and concentration."*

The output of System I may be superficially summarized as intuition. System I handles no-brainers. The output of System II may be summarized as analysis. The intermezzo at the end of this section gives examples of actions that are attributed to System I and System II, respectively. Kahneman explicitly mentions that finding the best move by a chess master (a classic example of recognition-primed decision-making) is an output of System I. This seems to imply that decision-makers who consider themselves expertly familiar with the matter at hand will automatically rely on System I for a decision they have to make.

The benefits to a decision-maker of using System I are probably only partly experienced consciously. What matters to busy business leaders is that System I is fast, it takes little mental effort and, as Kasparov pointed out, above also generally leads to better decisions. Moreover, there is an additional benefit that should not be overlooked here: System II is lazy and loves to be kept in peace. System I operates as follows when a new issue emerges that needs to be resolved:

- Issue is familiar to the decision-maker.
- Issue shows common, relevant cues.
- In issues of these types, expectations are predictable to the decision-maker.
- Goals set for the business confronted with this issue are unambiguous.
- Pattern is recognized and known, typical actions can 'confidently' be taken

System I is kind to System II. As the decision-maker has confidence in his approach, there is no need to mobilize System II. There is certainly no need to do a full-blown analysis of competing hypotheses to guide actions. Such analysis (and the waking up of System II) is normally only triggered in the decision-maker's mind when he:

- Feels unfamiliar with the issue.
- Faces (too much) conflicting evidence with existing patterns.
- Does not detect relevant cues that are normally present.

Klein provides this view of conditions under which real-life decision-makers tend to use System I or System II (reproduced in Table 16.1) (Klein, 1999c):

| TASK CONDITIONS | RECOGNITION-PRIMED DECISIONS | RATIONAL CHOICE STRATEGY |
|---|---|---|
| Greater time pressure<br>Higher experience level<br>Dynamic conditions<br>Ill-defined goals | More likely | |
| Need for justification<br>Conflict resolution<br>Optimization<br>Greater computational complexity | | More likely |

TABLE 16.1 ▶▶▶ BOUNDARY CONDITIONS FOR DIFFERENT DECISION-MAKING STRATEGIES

The key message that Klein and Kasparov convey to us is that people may effectively and efficiently engage in decision-making without using a formal rational choice strategy. Still, the fact that rational choice strategy underpins most of the methodology of strategic analysis does not mean that it is an indispensable and essential action for good decision-making. A cow is an animal, but an animal is not by definition a cow. The analysis of competing hypotheses as discussed in chapter 13 is a great tool for analysts. Analysis of competing hypotheses, however, may not automatically appeal to decision-makers who feel familiar with an issue.

An analyst, no matter how much he cherishes rational choice strategy or analysis of competing hypotheses, should be sufficiently xenocentric to realize that executives may prefer recognition-primed decision-making to rational choice strategy at times when they feel familiar with an issue. After all, using recognition-primed decision-making saves time. An analyst also should realize that she is the one to adapt to the decision-maker; expecting or demanding otherwise may be less effective.

In the following two sections, we look at how analysts and decision-makers think and act, respectively when facing uncertainty.

## INTERMEZZO: ACTIVITIES ATTRIBUTED TO BRAIN SYSTEMS I AND II

Kahneman illustrates the different roles that the brain's Systems I and II play with examples of how the automatic activities attributed to System I and the thought-through activities attributed to System II (Kahneman, 2011l).

Typical instances where the brain's System I kicks in would be situations where you:

- Detect that one object is most distant than another.
- Orient to the source of a sudden sound.
- Complete the phrase 'bread and…'.
- Make a 'disgust face' when shown a horrible picture.
- Detect hostility in a voice.
- Answer 2 + 2 = …
- Read words on large billboards.
- Drive a car on an empty road.
- Find a strong move in chess (if you are a chess master).
- Understand simple sentences.
- Recognize that a 'meek and tidy soul with a passion for detail' resembles an occupational stereotype.

On the other hand, typical instances where the brain's System II comes to life would be times when you:

- Brace for the starter gun in a race.
- Focus attention on the clowns in the circus.
- Focus on the voice of a particular person in a crowded and noisy room.
- Look for a woman with white hair.
- Search your memory to identify a surprising sound.
- Maintain a faster walking speed than is natural for you.
- Monitor the appropriateness of your behaviour in a social situation.
- Count the occurrences of the letter 'a' in a page of text.
- Tell someone your phone number.
- Park your car in a narrow space.
- Compare two washing machines for overall value.
- Fill out a tax form.
- Check the validity of a complex logical argument.

## 16.4 STRATEGIC ANALYSTS AND UNCERTAINTY

Table 16.1 shows that at least three of the four task conditions that make people more inclined to use a rational choice strategy are common analysts' tasks. Analysts often have to provide justifications for major decisions. They are regularly involved in optimization projects. And yes, they tend to be selected because they can handle projects of greater computational complexity. Thus, by the nature of their work, analysts will often apply the rational choice strategy method. For parts of an analyst's work, recognition-primed decision-making is often simply less suitable.

This is not to say that analysts do not use recognition-primed decision-making. Like grand masters in chess, highly experienced analysts will easily recognize a pattern that to a novice would simply appear to be a random, unconnected assortment of data. Recognition-primed decision-making may allow them both to react instantly when being confronted with new facts – and often to intuitively recommend smart responses.

Especially experienced analysts may, as a rule, thus perceive their own judgment to be better than it actually is. Overconfidence, which also affects decision-makers, may therefore just as well affect the analyst. The difference between decision-makers and analysts may be that the best, most foxy analysts in contrast to decision-makers will never feel certain. They cherish the virtue of doubt. Sir Francis Walsingham, head of English foreign intelligence under Queen Elizabeth I in the 1580s, adequately summarized the feelings the best analysts naturally have when he said (Alford, 2013a):

> *"There is less danger in fearing too much than in fearing too little."*

Similarly, but more recently, an analyst has been defined as (McLaughlin, 2008c):

> *"Someone who smells flowers... and then looks for the coffin."*

Analysts hopefully have learned their share of lessons, having been tricked too often by realities that unfolded differently than they had anticipated.

As a result, even when she is vulnerable to overconfidence, the best analysts will cherish the uncertainty that remains at the end of the analysis. An analyst works to reduce environmental uncertainty in decision-making, but will and should not shy away from highlighting the remaining environmental uncertainty.

## THE ANALYST HOPEFULLY STIMULATES RESPECTFUL LEARNING

Regardless of whether the environmental uncertainty is significant or not, the analyst may be asked for advice by decision-makers. In his book *The Quiet Leader*, David Rock urges leaders to be mindful of how they give advice (Cramm, 2013). Rock suggests giving advice as infrequently as possible, but when it is necessary he advises analysts to:

- Making it **xenocentric** rather than autobiographical. The needs and experiences of the recipient should be central.
- **Tackling the root cause**, rather than the issue that is initially put forward. The latter issue may be what the recipient believes is the issue. Respectful questioning may reveal that the real issue is different. Once the real issue has been revealed, advice may be useful but may even no longer be needed. Often, defining the problem with the would-be recipient cancels the need for advice.
- **Accepting** rather than rejecting. Even when the analyst upon hearing a problem immediately discovers the solution (recognition-primed decision-making), the worst thing to do is to recommend it over-forcefully. Doing so will make the other party lose face and feel stupid. How could the other party have been so stupid not to see it? The analysts does not want to be the one publicly upbraiding a senior executive, asking how he could have been so ignorant. The other party, however, is not likely to take take this sort of humiliation lying down. No, he'll probably get defensive and suggest that the analyst's proposition can't possibly be

> correct. This may especially be the case when the recipient has a higher rank than the analyst. Rather, the foxy analyst should ask the recipient a thoughtful set of questions to help guide him to the realization that the analyst's conclusions are in fact correct and true. In taking this more diplomatic approach, the analyst will achieve her objective while subtly strengthening her relationship with the executive.

Rock's approach may help drive acceptance of an analyst's recommendations, and give the decision-maker a greater appreciation for her knowledge and insight. Too often decision-makers scorn environmental uncertainty, blaming the analyst for inevitable known and unknown unknowns. The next section will look at how decision-makers typically deal with both environmental and executional uncertainty.

# 16.5 DECISION-MAKERS AND UNCERTAINTY

## DECISION-MAKERS ARE OPTIMISTS AND THUS HAVE A NATURAL COMPETITIVE ADVANTAGE

Decision makers in general tend to be more optimistic than the average person (Kahneman, 2011m). Optimism has its advantages. Richard Wrangham, a biological anthropologist at Harvard, explains (Gladwell, 2009a):

> *"An exaggerated assessment of the probability of winning increases the probability of winning. Winners know how to bluff. And who bluffs best? The person who, instead of pretending to be stronger than he is, actually believes himself to be stronger than he is."*

An exaggerated assessment of the probability of winning sounds quite like optimism. Optimists have a natural competitive advantage: their abiding self-assuredness helps them win beyond what their fundamental talent or means would suggest. The inevitable conclusion is that it is hard to underestimate the value of optimism in business (or in the military for that matter). Optimism and optimists should be cherished – hire them, retain them and promote them.

Kahneman also sings the praises of optimists. However, he also expresses a nuanced hypothesis in which he distinguishes between optimism (generally desirable) and overconfidence (often risky). In calling for a prudent balance between the two, he warns that optimism has a dark side – it can blind the beholder to the risks of unfettered arrogance (Kahneman, 2011m):

(Praise:) Optimistic individuals play a disproportionate role in shaping our lives. Their decisions make a difference. They are the inventors, the entrepreneurs, the political and military leaders – not your average people. They got to where they are by seeking challenges, taking risks and conquering the insurmountable.

(Hypothesis:) The people who have the greatest influence on the lives of others are likely to be optimistic and overconfident, and are ready to take more risks than they realize.

(Conclusion:) Evidence suggests that optimism is widespread, stubborn, and – despite its benefits – costly.

## OPTIMISM CORRELATES WITH OVERCONFIDENCE

Although optimism may lead to overconfidence in the population at large, some groups are more vulnerable than others. Corporate CEOs and other leaders are especially vulnerable. The typical CEO, by virtue of her achievement and exalted stature, is inevitably a confident person… and it's not uncommon for a CEO's confidence to tip over into overconfidence.

In addition, more powerful people tend to rely disproportionately on System I for decision-making than on System II (Kahneman, 2011m). Power thus seems to correlate with an inclination to use recognition-primed decision-making rather than rational choice strategy in decision-making. A possible explanation for CEOs' propensity for overconfide and their tendency to more than proportionally rely on System I in decision-making may be that power is based on success. Their success has bred overconfidence. Success may also have bred a CEO's exaggerated view of his own capabilities, ability to effectively juggle multiple complex issues, and of their skills and talents in general. The latter three factors, as per Table 16.1, correlate with a preference for recognition-primed decision-making over rational choice strategy, even when that propensity is not objectively justified. In business, this overconfidence has its price. A CEO's overconfidence can ultimately contribute to exacerbate and perpetuate corporate underperformance (Kahneman, 2011m).

Risk forms the connection between overconfidence and corporate underperformance. In the context of strategic analysis, risk may also be defined as ignoring or underestimating environmental uncertainties.

Overconfidence leads an executive to tolerate higher than healthy risks, as overconfidence is:

- A powerful source of illusions (Lovallo, 2010a).
- A common source of (self-)deception, especially regarding environmental uncertainties or the complexity of the issue at stake (Bruce, 2008e). Telling a target what he wants to believe after all remains the most successful form of deception (Johnson, 2009b). Deceiving an overconfident executive into believing he can manage the risks he may encounter in an endeavor will fuel his hubris. This is exactly the tone of voice I have heard so often from investment bankers when they recommend a too-expensive acquisition. Really, Mr Executive, you can do this. Guess what: that feels good to everyone involved.

In contrast, the analyst who emphasizes to an executive that the organization's previous strong performance is no guarantee of future success has a fair chance of being ignored. That message may not feel good to the overconfident optimist, even when the analysis objectively is correct.

Overconfidence may thus negatively affect the acceptance of strategic analysis work. When an analyst understands the drivers behind an executive's overconfidence, he may become more effective in working towards better acceptance of his deliverables. Three common drivers of an executive's overconfidence are discussed below:

- Her implicit need for safety.
- An ingrained bias for action.
- A gnawing fear of displaying or admit executional uncertainty.

## WHEN UNCERTAINTY BUTTS HEADS WITH THE HUMAN NEED FOR SAFETY IT ALWAYS LOSES

An unbiased appreciation of uncertainty is a cornerstone of rationality (Kahneman, 2011m). In this sentence uncertainty can be both environmental and executional. A balanced view is not always in high demand. This is true neither for people at large nor for executives in large organizations. Just one example from another part of society may suffice to illustrate this point. Patients of medical doctors favour those doctors who do not express (environmental) uncertainty. For the patient who seeks two opinions, but the doctor that brims with confidence about the high success rate of a proposed treatment is preferred over the doctor who expresses a more pragmatic view of its efficacy. A doctor who 'sells' hope is preferred over one who 'sells' a more balanced, sensible view. Many people have a need for safety – not a need for involuntary environmental uncertainty. Ignoring environmental uncertainty may be a way to cope with it. When you cannot *be* safe, you can at least try to *feel* safe.

What is true for patients applies equally to investors. When two competing plans with similar expected returns on capital are proposed to a decision-making board, the plan proposed by the most 'confident' management team tends to get the cash to execute it.

## UNCERTAINTY LEADING TO PROCRASTINATION IS A ROOT OF CORPORATE EVIL

There is another dimension to this discussion (Lovallo, 2010a). Decision-makers tend to show an action-oriented bias: execution takes centre stage in their comfort zone. Activity, after all, may foster an illusion of competence (Dörner, 1996d).

In contrast, inaction – or even worse, procrastination – makes them restless. Environmental uncertainty leading to procrastination simply cannot be tolerated. Impatience may lead an executive to push for a decision, even when environmental uncertainties are unclear. True, making a snap decision can help the executive regain that safe, confident feeling of being in execution mode. For most executives few things are worse than giving in to what is perceived as analysis paralysis (Kahneman, 2010):

> *"We associate leadership with decisiveness. That perception of leadership pushes people to make decisions fairly quickly, lest they be seen as dithering and indecisive."*

## DECISION MAKERS' EXECUTIONAL UNCERTAINTY, EVEN WHEN PRESENT, IS CONVENIENTLY HIDDEN

Executives know they need to show confidence and act assured, no matter what. They can't show a hint of uncertainty, even in situations where their confidence tumbles.

We already discussed why investors select optimistic and confident leaders – and for the right reasons. In execution, confidence clearly boosts staff morale and productivity. Why would anyone agree to be led by an hesitant, uptight leader? Showing executional uncertainty, either regarding the why or the how of any mission, is a clear no-go in executive behaviour.

There is a military equivalent of the corporate taboo against executional uncertainty (focusing on the 'why' question) which applies equally in business (Friedman, 2009):

*"The question of whether the war is worth fighting [...] is not asked — and properly so — in the theater of operations."*

Along similar lines, this quote could almost apply more to decision-makers than to strategists (George, 2008a):

*"Strategists can ill afford to show doubt about their policies."*

## ADMITTING UNCERTAINTY TAKES COURAGE BUT IS THE SMART THING TO DO

Professor Schoemaker of the Wharton Business School calls for leaders to stop denying uncertainty. He recommends admitting ignorance in today's complex world (Schoemaker, 2009). He believes that leaders should embrace uncertainty, not unlike the recipe given for foxy analysts and predictors by Nate Silver in previous chapters of this book:

*"It takes courage to admit (...) ignorance because it conflicts with our common notion of leadership, which prizes omniscience. However, our world is too complex for the heroic leadership of the past where a great leader rides up on a white horse and points the way to the future. A better approach now is to embrace uncertainty and examine it in detail to discover where the hidden opportunities lurk."*

For the time being, Schoemaker's call for change remains relevant. Too often executives still display an attitude of omniscience, fiercely hiding any executional uncertainty they may have – and some executives likely have more of it than others. Outwardly, the insecure executives may appear to be control freaks; inwardly they may be praying no one senses how uncertain they really are in their day-to-day job work.

This omniscient attitude – the 'I know' demeanor – is a leadership blind spot (Malandre, 2009). You can see it in the executive who's quick to interject a terse 'I know' sort of retort after almost any statement. Such executives never openly tolerate even a smidgeon of doubt. This type of person cannot tolerate the thought that they may be seen as not having the best ideas, at all times. Given their control focus, they will review everything and indeed know a lot. They are often also among the hardest workers on the team – and as a result they often exhibit exemplary performance. Not surprisingly, this sort of executive is often on the fast-track, and is promoted upward through the organization. As a result, they often become the prominent decision-makers to whom the analyst community presents. 'I know' executives are among the most common types of people that analysts look to for approval for of their deliverables. Before discussing some of the common challenges faced by an analyst in such situations, let me briefly briefly summarize.

## OPTIMISM CAN BE A DOUBLE-EDGED SWORD

At this stage I believe we can acknowledge the advantages of optimism in executing decisions. Similarly, we can now also see how an overblown sense of optimism can be a mixed blessing (Kahneman, 2011m).

And what does that mean?

- Executive decision-makers need to have an above-average inclination towards optimism; in decision-execution, optimism correlates with success.
- Confident decision-makers tend to be impatient and action-oriented: why wait with your decisions when you know what you want to do and how you want to do it?
- Executive decision-makers (and medical doctors, and others) who express confidence rather than environmental uncertainty meet the often implicit needs of their investors (or patients, etc.).
- It is this optimistic, impatient character that gets hard-charging executives elected to corporate boards and acclaimed in other highly visible ways.
- Optimists tend to underrate environmental uncertainty as they make critical choices, potentially leading to a less than optimal risk-reward balance in business decisions.
- Executive decision-makers see decisiveness as a virtue and doubt as a weakness, so they will suppress their own doubts – when they have them – in front of their subordinates and superiors. They will generally also have a limited tolerance for executional uncertainty in others.

I would suggest that executives who deliver in terms of execution tend to underestimate or underrate environmental uncertainty in business decision-making and suppress their own executional uncertainty. In doing so they implicitly serve the needs of their investors or bosses.

A generalizing conclusion of the sections 16.4 and 16.5 is that analysts and executives may well have different preferences in decision-making. The analyst will most often adopt rational choice strategy as her methodology, whereas most executives make decisions based on recognition-primed decision-making. Where the analyst preferably cherishes the uncertainties, the decision-maker is and should be the optimist, believing that he and his team will make the difference. Knowing this, the analyst needs to be xenocentric, rather than to expect the decision-maker to change to the viewpoint of the analyst, solely for the analyst's comfort. Getting executive acceptance for solid strategic analysis work that improves corporate choices is the analyst's responsibility. Acting upon solid analysis is the decision-maker's responsibility. How the analyst can achieve such acceptance is the subject of the next section. We'll look at common challenges an analyst may bump up against in her interaction with the principal decision-making executive.

# 16.6 CHALLENGES IN ANALYST/ DECISION-MAKER INTERACTION

For analysts, working with overly optimistic decision-makers may at times be quite challenging. Similarly, decision-makers may dislike working with analysts. Where analysts are likely to have some tendency to distrust optimism, decision-makers often dislike cynical pessimists. Frantisek Moravec, the head of military intelligence in Second World War Czechoslovakia, was called a 'professional pessimist' by the president of the Czechoslovak government-in-exile (Moravec, 1975b). The mutual prejudices inherent in relationships like theirs existed then, exist now and will continue to exist.

The tension between what decision-makers need and what analysts provide has been captured well in the quote given below (Jervis, 2010g):

> *"Decision makers need confidence and political support, and honest intelligence unfortunately often diminishes rather than increases these goods by pointing to ambiguities, uncertainties and the costs and risks of policies. In many cases, there is a conflict between what intelligence at its best can produce and what decision-makers seek and need."*

In spite of these prejudices and tensions, the analyst still needs to get a decision-maker to act upon the intelligence she delivers. Below I suggest different options she may wish to consider.

Consider an analyst who has just finished a solid piece of work. She is ready to deliver her finished analysis of an issue or opportunity to the key decision-making executive. Once the work reaches the executive, he will of course formulate both an opinion about and a response to the finished work. The analyst may want to think about how the decision-maker will react to her deliverable in two ways:

- The executive's expectation regarding the outcome of the analysis.
- The impact the executive thinks the issue will have on his firm.

Expectation links to the confirmation bias. Often unconsciously, as we've said earlier, both analysts and decision-makers look for data that confirm an existing view. The dimension of expectation may be split into three possibilities: the deliverable may confirm an executive's expectations; it may conflict with his assumptions; he may not have had any expectation whatsoever.

The dimension of perceived impact leads to the executive inevitably anticipating either a positive or a negative impact on the firm. The response option for a neutral impact will generally be indifference; it has been left out of Table 16.2.

The dimensions of expectation and perceived impact are independent. As a result, six possible responses are possible. The response options listed in Table 16.2 are generalized, common options that I encountered in multiple occasions, involving many different types of personalities as recipients of deliverables. They are not based on solid organizational psychology research. The response options are only provided to stimulate an analyst to pre-empt typical possible responses by executives to his deliverables. These responses are used to suggest how an analyst might work through the various executive response scenarios. An analyst normally aims to have the executive not only accept the facts but also the conclusions and recommendations from an analysis. Turning recommendations into actions is, after all, the analyst's ultimate objective. The analyst is bound to encounter different sets of challenges as she seeks executive acceptance in difference response option scenarios.

| INITIAL EXECUTIVE EXPECTATION | LIKELY EXECUTIVE RESPONSES UPON RECEIPT OF DELIVERABLES? | | INFLUENCE ON EXECUTIVE'S VIEW ON ISSUE |
|---|---|---|---|
| | PERCEIVED NEGATIVE IMPACT: A THREAT TO THE FIRM | PERCEIVED POSITIVE IMPACT: AN OPPORTUNITY FOR THE FIRM | |
| Confirming | **1. Weariness**<br>Bad news but expected. Already 'calculated in' in executives' mind. Probably limited excitement. | **2. Positive**<br>Indifference.<br>Good news but not unexpected. Already 'calculated in' in executives' mind. Probably limited excitement. | Solidified |
| Absent | **3. Irritation**<br>What do we pay analysts for when we can't avoid these sorts of surprises? What other risks are we exposed to that we so far overlooked? What do we need to improve to prevent this from happening again? How can we minimize the impact? | **4. Delight**<br>Pleasant surprise, but why didn't we see this coming? Give me more facts and analysis. What opportunities may this offer beyond this particular occasion? How quickly can we grasp this opportunity? | Enriched |
| Conflicting | **5. Anger**<br>Why don't we recruit analysts who understand this business? What other risks are we exposed to that we also overlooked? What do we need to improve to prevent this from happening again? And finally, how can we minimize the impact? | **6. Disbelief**<br>What's new here?<br>Can we trust these sources? Can we trust this analysis? Can you get this reconfirmed from other sources? What do other executives say about this? | Challenged |

TABLE 16.2 SIX POSSIBLE RESPONSE OPTIONS WHEN AN EXECUTIVE RECEIVES A DELIVERABLE

## FOR ANALYSES THAT CONFIRM EXPECTATIONS, ACCEPTANCE IS INCONSEQUENTIAL

Obtaining acceptance for an analysis that confirms the decision-maker's initial expectation is easy. This is true regardless of whether the perceived impact of the issue is positive or negative for the firm. Delivering an analysis that confirms an executive's expectation is a win-win. The far-right column of Table 16.2 shows that this analysis not only confirms the executive's expectation but also allows him to comfortably maintain his view on the issue. The confirmatory nature of the analysis will likely solidify his view. The System I function of the executive's brain will handle this matter; System II will continue to snore. The upper boxes in Table 16.2 are friendly territory for an analyst.

An analyst who seeks executive acceptance more than he seeks truth may be seduced into yesmanship, as we'll explore in the next chapter. Telling the executive what he wants to hear rather than providing a balanced approach is a low-resistance, high-reward strategy, but it will usually conflict with a company's longer-term strategy.

Assume the analyst will provide a balanced analysis. The first reason why a decision-maker may easily accept an analysis is that the deliverable confirms his existing view. Such analysis does not require the executive to change his mind; it solidifies it.To the executive, acceptance is a no-brainer.

Moreover, an executive easily accepts an analysis that confirms their expectations, and may be additionally pleased with analysis that does not require difficult, costly action. Executives may, as we have seen above, be action-oriented. Still, most are impossibly busy, so they won't be searching for extra work to do. The reason that action is probably not required is that the outcome of the analysis had been expected. If the outcome required executive actions, these actions probably had already been taken. In the absence of a need for an executive to turn acceptance of an analysis into action, to change his mind on the issue it is as easy as it is inconsequential for the executive to accept the analysis. So far so good, but we have four more boxes to work through in Table 16.2.

## OBTAINING ACCEPTANCE WHEN ACTION IS NEEDED TO GRASP AN UNEXPECTED OPPORTUNITY

What is true for the upper boxes in Table 16.2 is not true for the middle (no expectation) and lower (conflicting expectation) boxes. These boxes describe situations where an analysis may first trigger the need for the executive to enrich or challenge his existing views on the issue. Subsequently, the analysis will probably need to trigger the executive to take some action. It's no longer entirely inconsequential for the decision-maker to have to accept the analysis for the middle and lower box situations in Table 16.2.

For an analyst, offering an executive a upbeat, easy deliverable (box 4 in Table 16.2) still is relatively easy. A smart analyst will focus on the opportunity this analysis opens up for the firm. When the analyst smartly frames his communication, the upside potential of the issue in the decision-maker's mind will overshadow the fact that the outcome had not been anticipated. The upside potential does the talking. It will seduce the executive by enriching his view. Subsequently, the analyst may capitalize on the executive's action-oriented bias when an upside presents itself. This is an elegant form of upward delegation, with acceptance becoming implicit and natural. Again: so far, so good.

For an analyst, to offer an executive a 'disbelief' deliverable (box 6 in Table 16.2) requires empathy. The executive is, after all, normally hierarchically superior to the analyst, even when the analyst is not a direct or indirect report. This is a classic example of the perceived lower-rank analyst delivering a message – even when it has a positive upside for the company – that proves the higher-ranking decision-maker wrong.

In these cases, the nature of the analysis itself may mean a difference between immediate acceptance or plain and simple rejection by the executive. When the analysis is a situation report that focuses on facts, acceptance may not be too difficult to obtain. Again, the upside potential of the matter provides the key. Consider a message like:

*"Adversary XYZ has announced that it will not participate in the auction of an attractive M&A target to our company."*

Last week, our company's executive may have met his counterpart from adversary XYZ, who at the time seemed keen to buy the company. XYZ's withdrawal is not what the executive expects. The information conflicts with what had seemed to be highly reliable market intelligence. The convincing nature of the previous intelligence may have resulted in the executive overrating the source. The analyst should, however, not miss this great opportunity to *shut up*. Uttering a 'vividness bias' message to the executive will likely make him feel intellectually challenged, if not disrespected, by a lower-ranking staff member.

Rather, the analyst should in this case literally refrain from analysis. The data shows the opportunity; why add unsolicited analysis?

A great way for an executive to reject a conclusion is to dispute the data upon which it's based. The more stressed executives are about the success of the firm, the bigger the chance that subordinates serving up unwelcome data will be chastised (Collins, 2009). This is an executive escape route from rejection that an analyst, summoning all of her powers of tact and persuasion, should block. To accomplish this, the analyst should be prepared to answer any conceivably question or challenge the decision-maker may have on her data's reliability. For example:

- What is the source?
- What is the track record of the source in terms of reliability?
- How many sources do we have?
- Are different sources believed to be independent or simply copying the findings of a single source?
- What steps have we already taken to search for additional validation of this news?

Here's an additional question that intentionally hasn't been listed above is: Why do we think the adversary has pulled out of the auction? Asking, and daring to suggest an answer to such a question in advance may well be perceived by the decision-maker as an attempt to push an opinion beyond the facts. An executive whose view on an issue is challenged does not need 'smart ass' opinions. He has enough to think about. Teeing up this sort of provocative, unsolicited opinion could make the executive angry, which is the last thing an analyst wants. What the analyst should hope and prepare for is that the executive does ask the 'why' question spontaneously… but calmly and rationally. That is a win-win. And that would be the analyst's golden opportunity to modestly present his point of view. The executive, having taken the initiative, will at this point be more likely to listen receptively to a rational answer. Starting the answer by implicitly recognizing the decision-maker's disbelief may even help gain acceptance: "I have been wondering about that as well. It is not immediately obvious. Our competitor may…"

## REJECTION TRIGGERED BY A SINGLE WORD

In the case of an unexpected opportunity – but even more in the case of an unexpected threat – subtlety and finesse are essential in analyst's report to executives. I once had the experience of a single word triggering the rejection of an entire analysis. Literally hundreds of hours of work were wasted, because a single word set a tone that the executive was not prepared to accept. One single word – the word was 'commodity' – sealed the fate of the whole report. The executive's angry response:

> *"How could you as analyst be so stupid as to think that the term commodity applied to this business I believe we should buy? If that is what you think, I don't need to see the rest of that work. I am now concerned about how poorly you understand this business!"*

There are cases where threatening surprises are more difficult to control when they originate from third parties. These are discussed below.

## OBTAINING ACCEPTANCE WHEN ACTION IS NEEDED TO MANAGE AN UNEXPECTED THREAT

Boxes 3 and 5 in Table 16.2 form the perilous territory where the analyst is tested most. The analyst's dilemma has been well captured in the following quote (Weiner, 2008f):

> *"It is not enough to ring the bell, you've got to make sure the other hears it."*

It takes courage to provide an executive with an unexpected and threatening message in an analysis that surprises or downright challenges his firmly-held view. This book does not purport to provide a balanced treatise on how to deliver such bad news. There is no single, 'one size fits all' method for doing this. Choosing the best approach depends on the personality of the executive, the self-confidence of the analyst, their professional relationship and experience, the culture in which the analyst and executive operate, etc.

In preparing to deliver bad news, an analyst may benefit from a classic model of how people at large react to such information. It's well worth repeating this old adage: All models are in some way wrong, but some of them are useful nonetheless. The benefit of this particular model is twofold: it is both simple and straightforward, and when all is said and done it leads to 'acceptance'. This latter is what analysts aim for. If the analyst takes this approach to heart, she can remove considerable difficulty and angst from the delivery process and hopefully improve her changes of gaining acceptance.

In 1969, Kübler-Ross postulated a model describing the five phases of emotion that people tend to go through when facing 'bad news' (Kübler-Ross, 1973). Table 16.3 lists the five sequential phases. For each of those phases you'll see a decision-makers potential emotional states and the corresponding responses he might give to an analyst's suppositions.

| PHASE | EMOTION | CHARACTERISTIC / INDICATIVE EXECUTIVE EXPRESSIONS IN THIS PHASE |
|---|---|---|
| I | Denial & Isolation | - 'Don't believe **you**, why do you bother me with this?'<br>- '**Your** source must be wrong.'<br>- 'Are you sure you can trust **your** source?'<br>- 'Are **you** sure we are talking about the same thing?'<br>- '**Young man**, they wouldn't dare.' |
| II | Anger | - 'Why didn't **you** see this coming?'<br>- 'Why do **you** never provide the intelligence I need?'<br>- 'Why are **you** bringing important information to me so late again.'<br>- 'When I did **your** job, this never happened to me.'<br>- '**Intelligence** always drags my plans through the dirt.' |
| III | Bargaining | - 'What can **we** do to delay this?'<br>- 'Who else is hit, that may be **our** ally to reduce the impact of this?' |
| IV | Grief | - 'How will we ever cope with this loss?' |
| V | Acceptance | - '**As we can't change it**, we might just as well accept it; and so what are we going to **do** about it?' |

TABLE 16.3 ▶▶▶ EMOTION PHASES IN RESPONSE TO BAD NEWS AND RELATED EXECUTIVE EXPRESSIONS

Expressions of guilt are exceedingly rare in the business world, and senior executives may try to show that they're above this natural human emotion through displays of overconfidence and bravado. This may be done by minimizing the impact of the bad news with a brash pronouncement like: "You know, these lightweights can't really hurt us". They may not believe what they're saying, of course but it may be the only thing they feel comfortable saying. By verbalizing it, they may actually start to believe it, and regain their psychological balance… which will allow them to move on to phase IV: Acceptance.

In Table 16.3 we see that in phases I (Denial) and II (Anger) the analyst will likely get the blame. Apart from pleading that the angry decision-maker not kill the messenger, there is little that can be done about it. Expect it, be prepared for it and stick to your opinion. When you as an analyst don't trust your own opinion, do more research. Once you have reached your well-researched opinion and you're not confronted with new facts or insights, stick to it. Executive who are simmering in the noxious territory of phases I or II may not like you to do so. On the other hand, a decision-maker who sees an analyst waver under fire will conclude that the analysis was shaky in the first place, even when the hard, cold data suggests otherwise. What future credibility is left for such an analyst? Sadly, if she folds once too often she becomes fated to a future of cowardly yesmanship.

In phase III (Bargaining), the decision-maker may be less emotional but normally is not yet open to rational analysis. In phase IV (Grief), the executive may start to belittle the threat, out of concern that any sign of sorrow or grief telegraphs a lack of optimism, confidence and decisiveness. It is only in phase V (Acceptance) that an executive is once again open to rationally coming to terms with bad news and, ideally, even turning it into an opportunity.

The reason for sharing this model, especially in the cases of an analysis that ends up in boxes 3 and 5 in Table 16.2, is that the analyst should think xenocentrically, not only about the impact of the content of her message but also its emotional impact.

The analyst should anticipate that the executive will need to process through these emotional phases. By now the analyst – who has collected, assessed and more or less come to terms with the bad news – will have taken a deep breath and returned to a calmer state of rational acceptance. This means the analyst is four phases ahead of the executive. She's already thinking ahead to the formulation of pragmatic recommendations and actionable next steps. When the news is really bad, the analyst may even feel impatient for action and show in her body language that she would like to see decisive executive action. Expecting the executive to somehow skip over the emotional phases is insensitive and naïve. Rarely will an experienced decision-maker take immediate action following receipt of a bad-news analysis. Executives are likely to ask for rapid confirmation and a preliminary impact assessment, but they'll almost surely rely on System I (automatic response) instincts and recognition-primed decision-making.

An analyst therefore may consider a two-step approach to pre-empt losing acceptance for sound analysis that happens to contain bad news. In step I the bad news is dropped off at the executive's desk, with the analyst making a quick exit to avoid compromising the relationship by coming across as impudent or rude. Still, at this sensitive early stage in the process, avoid a request for action, do not explain the methodology, do not attempt to argue that the research was executed as well as it could have been, do not mention having impeccably reliable sources, do not give excuses. Resist the natural urge to do any of that. Bear the brunt of the executive's denial and anger while saying as little as possible – and beat a hasty retreat!

A few days later, the analyst may ask the executive at the proverbial coffee machine what he thinks about the issue. Is there anything the executive would like to have worked out in more detail? Does he have additional thoughts or questions? What have they learned in their network about this issue? By that time, the executive and the analyst are probably once again in the same emotional phase. Allowing a cooling-off period and then engaging in an informal hallway conversation will invariably yield better results than immediately pressing the executive – while he's still recoiling from the bad news – for an intensive, hour-long war-room session.

## SUMMARY OF APPROACHES AIMING FOR EXECUTIVE ACCEPTANCE OF ANALYSIS

In the above sections, we at length discussed approaches for working towards executive acceptance of analysis. The proposed approaches partly depend on the degree of expectation of the conclusion by the executive and on the nature of the anticipated impact of the issue covered in the analysis. In Table 16.4 the approaches are summarized.

<table>
<tr><th rowspan="2">INITIAL EXECUTIVE'S EXPECTATION</th><th colspan="2">LIKELY EXECUTIVE RESPONSES</th></tr>
<tr><th>PERCEIVED NEGATIVE IMPACT:<br>A THREAT TO THE FIRM</th><th>PERCEIVED POSITIVE IMPACT:<br>AN OPPORTUNITY FOR THE FIRM</th></tr>
<tr><td>Confirming</td><td colspan="2">1. Weariness & 2. Positive indifference<br><br>Approach:<br>Low-key, low-excitement, emphasize confirmatory nature.<br><br>Executive action:<br>Probably not needed, actions likely already in place.</td></tr>
<tr><td>Absent</td><td rowspan="2">3. Irritation & 5. Anger<br><br>Approach:<br><br>Stage 1:<br>Offer plain data, weather the storm, avoid defensiveness or meekness, refrain from analysis, stick to opinion.<br><br>Stage 2:<br>Seek rational reconciliation between relationship and content; pro-actively offer assistance.<br><br>Executive action:<br>Provide sufficient time for executive to assess data, size-up risk, take appropriate action.</td><td>4. Delight<br><br>Approach:<br>Focus on upside potential.<br><br>Executive action:<br>Triggered automatically by size and feasibility of upside.</td></tr>
<tr><td>Conflicting</td><td>6. Disbelief<br><br>Approach:<br>Focus on (reliability of) facts, and sources; avoid emphasizing analysis.<br><br>Executive action:<br>Provide sufficient time for executive to absorb data, gauge upside potential, and act.</td></tr>
</table>

TABLE 16.4 ▶▶▶ APROACHES TO GAINING EXECUTIVE ACCEPTANCE

## 16.7 TOWARDS TRUSTED ADVISOR

In the previous sections I discussed decision-making strategies, uncertainty and the handling of uncertainty by both analysts and executives. Linking elements from these discussions, we developed approaches to gain acceptance from executives with different initial expectations for your analyses. And this brings us to the final section of this chapter, where we'll look at the make-or-break dynamics of the analyst/decision-maker relationship.

As an introduction the ins and outs of this interaction, it let's revisit Machiavelli's early Sixteenth Century guidance on how to work with advisers, as recalled by Powell (Powell, 2011a):

> *"Effective leaders have to get the balance right between trusting their staff too much and too little. Machiavelli writes that 'The new Prince should not be too ready of belief, nor too easily set in motion; nor should he himself be the first to raise alarms; but should so temper prudence with kindliness that too great confidence in others shall not throw him off his guard, nor groundless distrust render him insupportable'."*

It is the analyst's role to find that balance in the relationship with the decision-maker. A good decision-maker will also search for that balance, but the lead is with the analyst. He realizes, after all, that the executive is the customer to be served, not the other way around. This section discusses a number of factors that may contribute to turning analyst/decision-maker relationship into one invested with balance, trust, interdependency and respect. Factors that come into play in this dynamic include governance, distance, culture and pragmatism. Such interaction obviously involves countless other factors, both realized and subliminal, but these four predominate. Recognize them, understand them and use them to your advantage.

## GOVERNANCE: RESPECT THE ROLE OF THE DECISION-MAKER AND BE RESPECTED AS AN ANALYST

Gaining the respect of a senior executive may indeed be the analyst's consummate achievement. Respect starts with recognizing two defining dimensions that separate the analyst and the decision-maker: role and responsibility.

As an analyst I always try to respect the fact that the decision-maker has the responsibility and the authority to make a decision. The decision-maker has the last word. Full stop. As an analyst, I may be invited to advise, and may have the opportunity to suggest options in the decision-making process... but the final decision does not reside with me. The decision-maker should respect that as an analyst and a professional I have my own role to play, and that it includes remaining objective. US President Kennedy, in the midst of the Cuban Missile Crisis, is reported to have cited a brief poem that illustrates that advice may be helpful but responsibility is the indisputable realm of the executive (Dobbs, 2009c):

> *"Bullfight critics row on row crowd the enormous plaza full, but only one is there who knows, and he is the one who fights the bull."*

Respect also includes the decision-maker knowing what to reasonably expect from a strategic analysis function. A respectful executive understands the difference between a puzzle and a mystery (Steinberg, 2008). The puzzle can be solved when enough pieces have been collected, scrutinized and organized. Analysts are responsible for collecting what is 'out there' and for turning it all into a meaningful road map to decision-making. The analyst does not want to present the decision-maker with an inscrutable mystery, because a mystery is – well, a mystery.

## DISTANCE: A KEY TO AVOIDING POLITICIZATION

As a professional, the analyst should at all times aim to be neutral. The analyst may help a decision-maker as a sparring partner, but should at all costs avoid becoming politicized and refrain from preaching policy to the decision-maker. The following quote talks of the need for analysts in the military intelligence community to resist being sucked into the quagmire of politicization (Gannon, 2008):

*"Pressures to distort analysis are an occupational hazard in the intelligence business, a recurring problem to be managed by rigorous adherence to the best tradecraft, by analytic courage and integrity, and by the timely intervention of responsible managers."*

An analyst who respectfully but stubbornly sticks to his guns may indeed at some stage need support from a superior. But there are certain tools and techniques an analyst can employ to help mitigate the risk of politicization (Treverton, 2008). There are different approaches when dealing with policy-makers, for instance. Take the example of two former CIA Directors: Richard Helms and Bill Casey. Helms on one occasion delivered a briefing to policy-makers and then left the room prior to the start of the subsequent policy discussion. Helms, who was known to place a particularly high value on objectivity, put it this way (Robarge, 2007):

*"Without objectivity, there is no credibility, and an intelligence organization without credibility is of little use to those it serves."*

After Casey delivered a briefing, he remained in the room and by default got involved in the ensuing policy discussion. A confident, principled analyst must assess risks of politicization in each and every briefing and decide when he wants to be Helms and when he wants to be Casey. An analyst who detects the winds of politics and tries to play Helms may, despite her best efforts, find herself inexorably pulled into one camp or the other. The good news is that when management teams do not agree on an approach, the last thing they want is to argue among themselves in the presence of outsiders. In such a case, it is incumbent upon the analyst to follow Helms out of the room before even contemplating rolling up her sleeves and following Casey into the fight.

## CULTURE: MERITOCRATIC DECISION-MAKING IN TEAMS, COMMITTED EXECUTION

As has been emphasized above, the best decisions are reached in meritocratic teams that are open to multiple opinions. Paraphrasing Nate Silver: foxy teams take great decisions. An objective analyst flourishes in such a give-and-take culture. It is in this atmosphere that an analyst can most effectively surface, frame and collaboratively work through any dilemmas that arise in the analytic part of his work. One dilemma that comes to mind is how to balance between false negatives (ignoring good sources) and false positives (taking bad sources serious), as was discussed in chapter 10. An analyst should not try to export the problem to the executive's desk by asking what the executive thinks. Rather it should be that the executive asks the questions and the analyst answers them. What the analyst can do, however, is openly present and discuss the criteria used to identify false positives and false negatives and mention the environmental uncertainties that may have crept into the analysis. An analyst who has built such a relationship with his decision-maker – a relationship that allows for such discussion – should consider himself fortunate.

The success of the meritocracy model is not new. Persian ruler Cyrus the Great, in the Fifth Century BC, already embraced decision-making in a remarkably foxy way (Bower, 1979):

*"Diversity in counsel – unity in command."*

Cyrus' quote not only stresses the relevance of a broad sourcing of facts and opinions, but also conveyed that once a decision has been taken, commitment to execution by all involved is essential. An analyst cannot be seen whining that this stubborn executive did not want to listen, resulting in a disastrously uninformed decision. The analyst only has himself to blame if his analysis, or the way he reported it, was not persuasive enough. Don't blame another actor for your ineffectiveness.

## REALISM: EVEN PERFECT ANALYSES MAY NOT BE ACCEPTED

Above I have argued that executives may prefer recognition-primed decision-making, but are open to a rational choice approach when the circumstances convince them to do so. Once in rational choice strategy mode, the analyst and the executive may psychologically at least both operate in a System II frame of mind, which probably favours a discussion on the merits of the analysis. This may contribute to the analysis being accepted and subsequently acted upon. The analyst knows that for an executive to switch from System I to System II, the executive has to:

- **Admit unfamiliarity** with an issue, which may not come naturally as doing so challenges the notion of executive omniscience.
- **Accept conflicting evidence** regarding an issue that may not fit perfectly into his currently known and understood patterns in the firm's business environment.

- **Admit that relevant cues are lacking** in the current evidence pertaining to an issue, to make it fit with his currently known and understood patterns.

Making the switch from System I to System II may be more or less of a stretch to an executive, depending on how overconfident he has become, how much time is available, how sensitive and or important the issue is, whether the executive trusts the analyst to discreetly handle the executive's unfamiliarity with the issue, etc. Normally, an executive will neither want to nor have to switch from System I to System II when the above criteria have not been met.

An analyst may capitalize on the above knowledge. She may benefit from assuming a xenocentric view – from the executive's perspective – when in her analysis she illustrates:

- That the business environment has become **unfamiliar** to the executive.
- **Evidence** of a highly reliable nature has emerged that doesn't fit known patterns.
- **Relevant cues are lacking** that should normally be present when known patterns apply.

A perfectly calibrated pitch that's intended to guide the decision-maker into System II thinking may, for any number of reasons, still not work. No matter how good the new intelligence seems to the analyst, some decision-makers have simply become mentally incapable of change (Bower, 1979); (May, 1973g). May references this phenomenon, which is often evident in companies or governments that aren't doing particularly well, in the following passage:

> *"A change in policy commenced with the dislodgement from power of those men who had staked their careers on the course of action that had failed."*

In the face of failure, patience may be an analyst's most valuable virtue. He can wait for real change to occur... or if that seems unlikely, and the situation becomes particularly desperate, he can of course choose to abandon the sinking ship.

## THE TRUSTED ADVISOR

The most coveted position an analyst can assume is to be seated at the right hand of a senior executive, as his trusted advisor. In the best of all possible worlds, she becomes so trusted for her instincts, skills, knowledge and wisdom, that she and the decision-maker seamlessly engage in joint decision-making. At the end of his magnum opus on political power, A.A. Berle wrote two profoundly insightful lines that I'll close this chapter with (Berle, 1969a):

> *"In sum, power is a tired politician on one side of the table with a trusted friend on the other [...] in camps and courts, though personalities vary, the essence is always the same."*

And so, the game-changing question becomes: how can the analyst build a track record of achievement and respect that leads the executive decision-maker to consider him a truly trusted friend and adviser?

# CHAPTER 17

# SOCIAL BIASES IN DECISION-MAKING

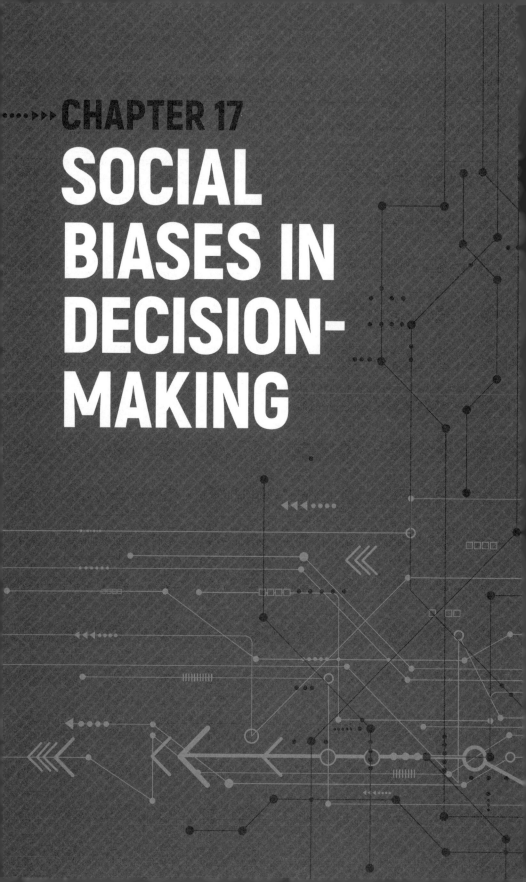

# 17.1 INTRODUCTION

Analytic pitfalls (see chapter 14) tend to penetrate analysis and decision-making relatively stealthily. Suffering from an ethnocentric or status quo bias is not a conscious choice. Wishful thinking, following the herd, over-reliance on previous judgment and falling back on conventional wisdom may reflect flaws in critical thinking, exhibited by either analysts or decision-makers, that intentionally distort an analysis.

This is where social biases vary from analytic pitfalls. Social biases relate to intentional behaviour exhibited by either analysts or decision-makers. When this occurs, the person adapts his behaviour to a perceived socially desirable norm, even when doing so distort the conclusions of a piece of analysis. And, as you might imagine, that can wreak havoc with the quality of an organization's decision-making.[1]

Below we'll take a look at three common social bias phenomena, each of which was briefly mentioned earlier in this book.

The first bias is that of selectively cherry picking data from a data set for political purposes. Cherry picking may either happen at the desk of the analyst, elsewhere in the strategic analysis function or in the corner office of the CEO.

The second social bias is 'yesmanship'. Yesmanship in its most common form is saying what the audience wants to hear, regardless of what you as analyst have discovered through your research and know to be true.

The third bias is groupthink.[2] This is in fact an umbrella term for several factors that may or may not together occur in group dynamics. Groupthink is a negative phenomenon. It may lead to flawed data set analysis, which can result in less than optimal decision-making. We noted in an earlier chapter that groupthink can pop up in M&A deliberations. The M&A sector is a major employer of strategic analysis resources, so analysts working in that space should certainly be on the lookout for creeping groupthink.

Cherry picking, yesmanship and groupthink are just some of the factors that can lead to sub-optimal outcomes, even when well-rounded data sets are available to support decision-making.

The research on groupthink shows that there is no inevitable causal link between this phenomenon, wrong executive choices and poor outcomes (Janis, 1982c). An executive who finds herself surrounded by groupthinkers, and the murky waters they engender, may still succeed in making the right decisions (Janis, 1982d). However, once an organizational dynamic becomes infected with groupthink, executives generally underestimate the risks entailed in executing their chosen strategies.

# 17.2 CHERRY-PICKING FROM A DATASET

Cherry picking is an extreme form of premature closing (see chapter 12). In cherry picking, the analysis starts or at least almost starts with a pre-cooked analytical conclusion. In 2002 the US government gradually moved towards a decision that a war with Iraq was necessary.

In the aftermath of 9/11, any evidence that pointed to a new threat to the US homeland was understandably treated extremely seriously. Without this context, the so-called Iraqi aluminium tube intelligence failure of 2001/2002 cannot be understood. Australian intelligence discovered that the Sadaam Hussein regime was procuring a large batch of a particular type of high-grade aluminium tubes, to be shipped into Iraq (Albright, 2003)[3]; (Clark, 2007d). Under the Iraq military technology ban program that existed at that time, the country was not allowed to procure these tubes, even when they had civilian uses, as they also had known military applications, including a use in short-range ground-to-ground rockets. From a US perspective, the tubes shouldn't have been destined for Iraq; that much was clear.

The CIA, however, believed the tubes could serve yet another use. They could be used as ultracentrifuges to allow the Hussein regime to separate natural uranium into a weapons-grade component part (a fraction rich in isotope $^{235}U$) and waste (a fraction depleted in the isotope $^{235}U$). These tubes could be a missing link in a possible Iraqi program to acquire its own nuclear weapons. Saddam having WMDs was a no-go in the George W. Bush administration. The tubes were confiscated at the Jordanian-Iraqi border. All evidence (size, material specifications, coating) pointed to the tubes being suited for conventional rocket applications. Using them for ultracentrifuges required considerable, and rather improbable, extrapolation of the facts and knowledge. In layman's terms: it required a lot of imagination to conclude that they were planning to use them for nukes.

The CIA, however, had already accused Iraq of trying to develop nukes and stuck to its prematurely closed position. A balanced, verifiable view was apparently not what the administration needed. National Security Advisor Condoleeza Rice, in a CNN interview on 8 September, 2002, used the following text, even while admitting that there was uncertainty over how long it would take for the Iraqi government to have a working weapon:

*"We don't want the smoking gun to be a mushroom cloud."*

Once the decision-making moved beyond the point-of-no-return for starting the Iraq War, any data that questioned the substantiation for that decision were vigorously smeared, as this quote from a senior Pentagon official shows (Grey, 2016a):

*"It wasn't intelligence, it was propaganda [...] They'd take a little bit of intelligence, cherry-pick it, make it sound much more exciting, usually by taking it out of context, often by juxtaposition of two pieces of information that don't belong together."*

Reliable data showed that the tubes were in fact useless for uranium enrichment, but the disinformation became so overwhelming that those findings were ignored (Pollack, 2004). There seems to be a proportionality between the acceptability by decision-makers of intelligence data confirming chosen policies and the degree to which data are used in policy design and execution (Treverton, 2008). Inversion is the ultimate risk: the data are framed as leading evidence for a decision, starting with the decision and scrambling backward for the facts. This example helps illustrate how dramatically a highly politicized dynamic can skew the decision-making process, and how serious the consequences can be. And it can happen in business as easily as it did in military intelligence, with facts and figure cherry picked to sell completely erroneous conclusions.

## CHERRY PICKING OCCURS IN BOTH GOVERNMENT AND BUSINESS

Think of a executive who may similarly have rallied relevant stakeholders in a large company to support a major capital expenditure. The similarities with the Iraq War story are clear. Once the mental commitment to the investment is there, any evidence that changes in the market could negatively affect the business case is suspect. The tendency of some business leaders is to subsequently discredit this type of new data. The leader has passed the mental point of no return – anything that could halt the investment approval is to be firmly rejected.

This means that for the new data to be accepted, the condition is now that these data have to substantiate the business case the executive is championing. In any other case, the correctness of the data or the source or the sender, or all of them at the same time – must be questionable. When all other arguments fail, the data may be dismissed as a plant: an intentional deception by an adversary. Fortunately – or so the company line goes – the deception was unmasked just in time, allowing for full implementation of the planned strategy. In competitive corporate cultures such deception could even originate from a colleague who's after the same limited corporate investment budget for his own pet project.

This bias, however, not only applies to the business leader. The filtering of data leading to questionable but undebatable conclusions, may also occur in the analyst's mind. In strategic analysis, correctly informing decision-makers about what will happen next adds the most value. This indeed turns an analyst into a special breed of forecasters, making the quote below applicable both to to the sweep of strategic analysis in general and to the phenomenon of cherry picking we're examining in this section (Silver, 2013c):

> *"A forecaster should almost never ignore data [...] Ignoring data is often a tip-off that the forecaster is overconfident [...] that she is interested in showing off rather than trying to be accurate."*

Managers, as I discussed in chapter 16, have been selected for their confidence, and in most cases rightfully so. The analyst, on the other hand, was chosen for her objectivity (among other attributes, of course). It goes without saying that objectivity does not go hand-in-hand with a proclivity for cherry picking.

# 17.3 YESMANSHIP

The social bias of yesmanship can be triggered by the real or imagined desire of a hedgehog decision-maker (Lovallo, 2010a). In chapter 16 we got a glimpse of the overconfident business leader. It is the type of leader who rarely requires strategic analysis on his competitors. He already knows them all. Moreover, he certainly knows them better than his strategic analysis function could ever know them. (This is to some extent actually true out in the real world... but to some extent is true only in his own mind.)

Yesmanship starts with a given fundamental: an asymmetric power relationship between a decision-maker and his analysis staff. In the world of public policy, a particular paradigm, first postulated by Lowenthal, applies (Yarhi-Milo, 2014b):

> *"Policymakers can exist and function without the intelligence community, but the opposite is not true."*

What is true in public policy equally applies in business. An analyst may not be blamed too much for being tempted to reason that whoever finds their bread and cheese determines the tune to which they dance – especially in a difficult labour market. Given the asymmetry of the relationship it is the self-confidence of the decision-maker and by implication how tolerant he is of opinions other than his own that determines the *freedom of speech* enjoyed by the analyst.

Some leaders may simply not appreciate or allow that freedom. They may prefer their staff to express opinions resembling their own. That is where the negative impact of yesmanship raises its ugly head (Surowiecki, 2005b):

*"One of the things that get in the way of the exchange of real information (...) is a deep-rooted hostility on the part of bosses to opposition from subordinates."*

Yesmanship is typically a phenomenon that intensifies when management is under stress. During the second half of the Johnson administration, the US – despite continuously increasing its military commitment – got nowhere nearer to achieving its political and military objectives during the Vietnam War. American political leadership came under increasing pressure to show results. Expenditures on the war went through the roof, body bags came back in ever-larger numbers, public approval for the war took a nosedive and there was no sign of success on the horizon. In this atmosphere, as illustrated in the long quote below, yesmanship became the rule in the White House (Halberstam, 1992b):

*"[US President Lyndon B. Johnson] was in an office isolated from reality, with concentric circles of advisers who often isolated rather than informed, who tended to soften bad judgments and harsh analyses, knowing that the President was already bearing too many burdens, that he could not accept more weight, that it would upset him, and also knowing that if they became too identified with negative views, ideas and information, their own access would diminish (a classice example of the two problems would be Bob McNamara [US Secretary of Defense] telling Arthur Goldberg midway through the escalation, when Goldberg raised a negative point to him, that it was certainly a good point but would he please not raise it with the President, it would only upset him)."*

As discussed earlier in this book, McNamara's behaviour as US Defense Secretary, and earlier, as president of Ford Motor Company, reinforces my view that the yesmanship bias is equally present in business and wartime government. The following passage makes direct reference to its business-government ubiquity (Halberstam, 1992c):

*"[McNamara] believed in what he did, and thus the morality of it was assured, and everything else fell into place. It was alright to lie and dissemble for the right causes. It was part of the service, loyalty to the President, not to the nation, not to colleagues, it was a very special bureaucratic-corporate definition of integrity; you could do almost anything you wanted as long as it served your superior."*

The behaviour of the president and his advisers is all too human. A stressed executive who is about to lose control of events is as difficult a customer as you can find. I believe these McNamara anecdotes describe a dynamic that that can be evidenced in any culture, although some are probably more vulnerable to yesmanship than others. Leaders with a larger-than-life profile, who inspire such acquiescence may simply be more common in some cultures than in others.

Yesmanship clearly stands perpendicular to the professional values of an analyst: it is impossible to reconcile it with integrity and objectivity. Sir Winston Churchill links yesmanship to inevitable failure in a characteristic statement that the conscientious analyst may consider tacking to her office door (Jones, 1978a):

> *"The temptation to tell a Chief in a great position the things he most likes to hear is the commonest explanation of mistaken policy. Thus the outlook of the leader on whose decisions fateful events depend is usually far more sanguine than the brutal facts admit."*

Yesmanship is part of a broader set of social biases in strategic analysis and intelligence that we touched on earlier – 'politicization' (Treverton, 2008). Politicization may have different causes, including those mentioned below. Cherry picking (as discussed above) and groupthink (discussed below), fall under the politicization umbrella:

- *Direct pressure:* Decision-makers push for conclusions they like to see, regardless of whether the data set and the analysis support such conclusions. Giving in as an analyst or business function to such pressure is the most open form of yesmanship.
- *The house line:* The strategic analysis function (head) has a particular view on a topic and rejects other conclusions to be distributed, even when the data set suggests that doing so is justified. The origin of the 'house line' may be a pitfall resembling conventional wisdom.
- *Question asking:* The smoothest politicization starts with a tailored brief delivered by a business leader to the strategic analysis function that ensures fitting and 'useful' conclusions will follow from the requested work.

Military literature gives other examples of yesmanship.[1] Below are some additional military examples in which the analyst may see parallels with the business environment.

## THE ANALYST'S CHALLENGE IS TO POLITELY WITHSTAND DIRECT PRESSURE FOR YESMANSHIP

German military intelligence during the Second World War had little choice but to fall back on yesmanship, if only to save their own analyst's skins (Macintyre, 2010e). Over the course of a war that was gradually being lost, German military intelligence over time developed a vulnerable position under the paranoid Nazi political leadership. Bad news was not welcome. Knowing this, British intelligence started to exploit Berlin's hunger for good news as a basis for deception: generating false propaganda that German intelligence wanted to believe. The confirmatory bias that this triggered helped guarantee that the bogus intelligence was passed up the chain of command, which proved most damaging for the the Axis powers.

And the Germans weren't along in demanding slavish yesmanship. American hero General Douglas McArthur by the end of his career no longer tolerated divergent opinions.

At the beginning of the Korean War in 1951 his relationship with his intelligence organization was described as follows, and I believe this quote to be a great illustration of yesmanship (Halberstam, 2009c):

> *"[...] MacArthur's key intelligence chief [was] a man dedicated to the proposition that there were no Chinese in Korea, and that they were not going to come in, at least not in numbers large enough to matter. That was what his commander believed, and McArthur's was the kind of headquarters where the G-2's (military intelligences') job was first and foremost to prove that the commander was always right"*
> *There was an arrogance to Willoughby [McArthur's intelligence chief] that was completely different from the uncertainty – the cautiousness – you associate with good intelligence men. It was as if he was always right, had always been right. [...] Worse, you couldn't challenge him. Because he always made it clear that he spoke for McArthur and if you challenged him you were challenging McArthur. And that obviously wasn't allowed."*

Dire were the consequences of the consistent rejection of reports on the build-up of the Chinese military in Korea by the top of US military intelligence.

Due to the underestimation of its adversary, the difficulties America faced during the Korean War tainted its superpower reputation.

However, direct pressure to tell executives what they want to hear is not limited to military intelligence. R.J. Fuld, the former (and last) CEO of Lehman Brothers – the investment bank whose failure catalyzed the 2008 global economic crisis – also had a reputation for demanding yesmanship (McDonald, 2009):

> *"There were mind-blowing tales of Dick Fuld's temper, secondhand accounts of his rages and threats. It was like hearing the life story of some caged lion."*

It would be impossible for a strategic analysis function to prevent yesmanship in such a corporation. There is an inevitable temptation to serve characters like Fuld with what it's thought they want to hear. The temptation is only mildly reduced by being aware that characters like Fuld may in response to biased strategic analysis take less than optimal decisions, with all the risk that involves. Yet even when direct pressure may at times be strong, the incompatibility of yesmanship and proper analysis is obvious.

Choosing objectivity, however difficult that may be and no matter how much courage it may take, is the better option. The quote below, related to a senior CIA manager, puts a fine point on this (George, 2008b):

> *"It was never difficult to respond to political pressure by saying that the CIA supported the president best when it provided the best and most comprehensive analysis possible."*

There is much to be said for being incorruptible: as an analyst and as a strategic analysis function, you are obligated to do your best to withstand pressure from anyone who aims to interfere with the objective outcome of an analysis. It may not be easy, but given the analyst's *raison d'etre*, there is no alternative.

## 17.4 GROUPTHINK

The best collective decisions are the product of disagreement and contest, not of consensus and compromise (Surowiecki, 2005c). When group-based consensus and compromise appear the quality of decision-making is at risk, no matter the quality of the input data that is supplied to the group. Groupthink is appropriately defined as 'collectively uncritical thinking' (Janis, 1982c). The size of the collective matters here: this is an instance where small is not beautiful (Surowiecki, 2005c):

> *"Small groups can exacerbate our tendency to prefer the illusion of certainty to the reality of doubt."*

> *"Juries deliver verdicts each individual juror would disapprove of."*

Fortunately, the phenomenon of groupthink has been analyzed in quite some detail. In the classic study of groupthink, several US government policy fiascoes that resulted from this phenomenon were analyzed, vis-a-vis various political group decision processes that had successful outcomes. The central theme of the analysis is (Janis, 1982d); (Janus, 1982f):

> *"The more amiability and esprit de corps among the members of a policy-making in-group, the greater is the danger that independent critical thinking will be replaced by groupthink, which is likely to result in irrational and dehumanizing actions directed against out-groups. [...] Members of any small cohesive group tend to maintain esprit de corps by unconsciously developing a number of shared illusions and related norms that interfere with critical thinking and reality testing."*

The groupthink research from the 1980s has since been reviewed and criticized. One criticism is that the research was not sufficiently based on a randomized trial of cases (Sunstein, 2015c). In other words: the outcome may suffer from the availability bias discussed in section 12.10. As we have only seen white swans, we prematurely conclude that all swans are white.

Despite methodological criticism of the 1980s study, a 2015 meta-analysis of subsequent research into group decision-making revalidates the 1980s research's worrying conclusions. More recent research adds an extra dimension. When individuals, be they analysts or business leaders, enter a group decision-making process with a bias, the group decision tends to be more biased than if each of the decision-makers had individually been biased prior to the decision being taken. In other words, group deliberations *amplify* the biases (Sunstein, 2015d):

> *"The larger point is that with group discussion, individual errors are often propagated and amplified, rather than eliminated. When individuals show a high degree of bias, groups are likely to be more biased, not less biased, than their median or average member. Here, then, is a major reason that groups fail."*

These observations should send a loud and clear warning signal to us as strategic analysts. Given that the 2015 conclusion reconfirms the 1980s study about the risks of groupthink to decision-making in groups, I have decided to ignore the methodological concerns regarding the 1980s study. After all, as I've said earlier, I believe that all models are wrong, but some models are useful (Box, 2005). To assist in our understanding of groupthink dynamics I therefore continue to rely on the models and schemes of the 1980s research. I believe those still to be sufficiently useful to our chapter's purpose to share them below in more detail. Admittedly, I may be deceived by the quality of the 1980s' narrative, but what a good narrative it is.

The relevance of groupthink to strategic analysis in business is significant. Strategic analysis stands for integrity and objectivity, resulting from neutral and independent critical thinking. Being corporate custodians of critical thinking, analysts who encounter the social bias of groupthink may well face group pressure. Group dynamics may for example pose a challenge to analysts when a cohesive group of executives collectively (sometimes implicitly) agrees to a particular view – regarding a competitor, for example. Getting these executives as a group to accept a fact-based and rational, yet different, outlook on the competitor in question may be a daunting but, possibly to some readers, familiar task. This is no new phenomenon.

Paradoxically, enough business leaders normally do not even exhibit groupthink to favour their personal agenda. Resistance to change is what an analyst bearing new news will often face, even when the change is for the better (Reger, 1994):

> *"Even beneficial change is often resisted by loyal [group] members who sincerely want what is best for the organization."*

Since analysts often encounter the challenge of presenting change, and often have to present their findings to groups of decision-makers, it seems justified to discuss groupthink in more detail. Janis developed a generalized dissection of the conditions that lead to and the symptoms and consequences of, groupthink. This is reproduced in its entirety in diagram 17.1 (Janis, 1982g).

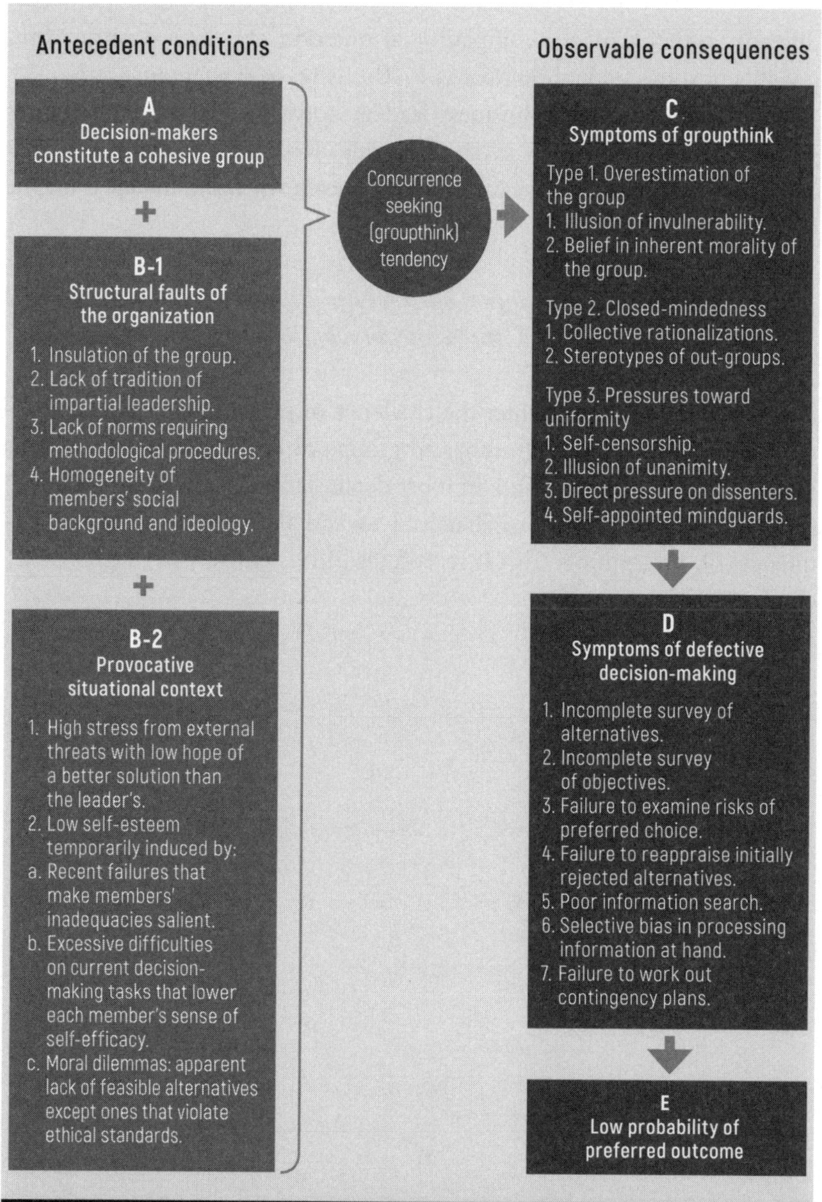

Antecedent conditions
Observable consequences
A
Decision-makers constitute a cohesive group
+
B-1
Structural faults of the organization
1. Insulation of the group.
2. Lack of tradition of impartial leadership.
3. Lack of norms requiring methodological procedures.
4. Homogeneity of members' social background and ideology.
+
B-2
Provocative situational context
1. High stress from external threats with low hope of a better solution than the leader's.
2. Low self-esteem temporarily induced by:
a. Recent failures that make members' inadequacies salient.
b. Excessive difficulties on current decision-making tasks that lower each member's sense of self-efficacy.
c. Moral dilemmas: apparent lack of feasible alternatives except ones that violate ethical standards.
Concurrence seeking (groupthink) tendency
C
Symptoms of groupthink
Type 1. Overestimation of the group
1. Illusion of invulnerability.
2. Belief in inherent morality of the group.
Type 2. Closed-mindedness
1. Collective rationalizations.
2. Stereotypes of out-groups.
Type 3. Pressures toward uniformity
1. Self-censorship.
2. Illusion of unanimity.
3. Direct pressure on dissenters.
4. Self-appointed mindguards.
D
Symptoms of defective decision-making
1. Incomplete survey of alternatives.
2. Incomplete survey of objectives.
3. Failure to examine risks of preferred choice.
4. Failure to reappraise initially rejected alternatives.
5. Poor information search.
6. Selective bias in processing information at hand.
7. Failure to work out contingency plans.
E
Low probability of preferred outcome


DIAGRAM 17.1 ▶▶▶ THEORETICAL ANALYSIS OF GROUPTHINK

## ANTECEDENT CONDITION FOR GROUPTHINK: AN EXTERNAL THREAT TO A HOMOGENOUS GROUP

Upon analyzing different policy-making cases, Janis identified three antecedent conditions that may lead to groupthink. The most important condition, labeled 'A', is that the group is intrinsically cohesive. Non-cohesive groups do not develop groupthink. Decision-making in non-cohesive groups may lead to an even lower probability of a preferred outcome, but that is beside the point and out of the scope of this discussion.

The second antecedent condition, labeled 'B1', relates to structural faults of an organization. Faults include the group not having established fundamentally sound working processes such as a serious review of multiple options prior to decision-making. That is not to say that in groups that succumbed to groupthink no working processes existed. In two of the groupthink cases described by Janis,[4] sticking to decision-making protocol was put before improving the quality of decision-making. Evidence for this, for example, was denying external (i.e., out-group) experts an opportunity to participate in meetings. In other words, self-censorship within the group led to a misuse of existing working processes to ensure group cohesion. In contrast to this, in the example that Janis provides of a group that did not develop groupthink, meetings were held that resembled brainstorming (Janis, 1982h). Even when the President of the United States attended the meetings, no formal agendas were used.

Other structural faults relate to the composition of the group. Overly homogeneous groups that intentionally do not allow consideration of multiple views are more susceptible to groupthink than less homogeneous groups.

The third concurrent antecedent condition, labeled 'B2', is that the group must face a provocative situational context. When a cohesive, overly homogenous, insulated group is exposed to high levels of stress caused by external factors, options to resolve the issue are few. When in such a situation the group's leader offers a clear solution, the probability of groupthink becomes significant. In three of the cases described by Janis,[5] the perception of time-pressure by the decision-makers was a stress-enhancing factor. Similarly, the need for strict secrecy was used in two cases[6] as an excuse to prevent competing hypotheses from being tested. Secrecy requirements may thus be both a cause of groupthink and an instrument or excuse to protect a cohesive group against challenging outside views.

The homogenous, insulated members of the in-group may start seeking concurrence – obtaining strength from the idea that they are at least in this together and that together they can work miracles.

## SYMPTOMS OF GROUPTHINK INCLUDE THE ILLUSION OF INVULNERABILITY

Symptoms of groupthink are listed in box C. Rather than seeking multiple options, the in-group may develop shared illusions of invulnerability and moral righteousness – as opposed to the vilified out-group, which is stereotyped based on collective (and normally erroneous) rationalizations. Whereas moral righteousness probably relates more to a government context than a business environment, illusions of invulnerability apply to business just as well. A characteristic illusion of invulnerability is wishful thinking, which we discussed in chapter 14. In three of the cases described by Janis, wishful thinking became dominant – partly because accepting the reality of the situation had become too painful.[7] Stereotypes and ethnocentric biases are close neighbors. In all four of the cases related to US foreign policy failures described by Janis, ethnocentric biases mattered. Due to the closed-mindedness of the in-group, these ethnocentric biases could neither be challenged by reviewing solid neutral data nor by inviting external experts.[8]

Once a group has developed its convenient set of stereotypes, members may even start to suppress each other's expressions of doubt in the chosen option. In trying times, revisiting ideas, options and choices represents heresy.

## THE KEY SYMPTOM OF GROUPTHINK IS THAT ALTERNATIVES ARE NOT PROPERLY WEIGHED

As a result of groupthink, decision-making will no longer be sound. Box D represents symptoms of defective decision-making. These include the incomplete surveying of alternatives and objectives, a lack of interest in new data and the biased view of new data that comes in unsolicited. The bias of premature closing comes to mind here. New data are unwelcome or challenged to ensure the shared illusions are not compromised by new facts. Finally, box E represents the result of groupthink: a low probability of a favoured outcome of the decision-making. As it becomes more pronounced, groupthink is a phenomenon where multiple biases may concurrently play a role. As we've repeatedly shown, groupthink is as likely to occur in a business environment as it is in the military and other branches of government. A 2014 study demonstrated that an overabundance of workplace cohesion is a potent catalyst for groupthink. (Palmquist, 2015).

## GROUPS MAKE BETTER DECISIONS THAN INDIVIDUALS

Prior to reflecting on the interface between groupthink occurring in decision-making and the strategic analysis profession, a few remarks need to be made. The first is that Janis is anything but subtle when he starts his groupthink book. Janis opens with a well-known quote from Friedrich Nietzsche (Janis, 1982i):

> *"Madness is the exception in individuals but the rule in groups."*

Janis, however, also points to the unmistakable fact that groups tend to make much better decisions than individuals. This implies that abandoning group decision-making to prevent groupthink is not an option (Janis, 1982d). That would be like calling on Beelzabub to drive out the devil; hardly a comforting thought for those hoping to improve fact-based decision-making. Secondly, it makes sense to review the susceptibility of individuals to groupthink. Although Janis exclusively researched US-based cases in detail, he also points out that groupthink is not likely a culture-linked phenomenon to which only US-based business leaders are susceptible (Janis, 1982j). Third, the publication of Janis' book in 1982 did nothing to suppress the existence of gropupthink.[9] Awareness of groupthink, like awareness of psychology, is no guarantee of people acting differently because of such awareness (Janis, 1982k):

> *"[…] none is immune to groupthink. Even individuals who are generally high in self-esteem and low in dependency and submissiveness are quite capable of being caught up from time to time in the group madness that produces the symptoms of groupthink."*

In particular, people with an affiliation need prefer not to be rejected by group members. This is probably most true in trying times. In such cases, these people prefer to concur with a group position. They may develop into mind-guardians, even when they personally have doubts about the decisions at hand. I don't want to jump to conclusions and I admit that I have not done or read solid scientific research to prove this point, but groupthink versus sound decision-making seems to compare well with the proverbial hedgehog versus fox personalities in forecasting, as discussed in chapter 11.

When the antecedent conditions as described above are present, a group may gradually swing towards groupthink, and in doing so display hedgehog-like behaviour. Like a hedgehog in its most defensive, rolled-up stance, the groupthink-infected collective aims to expose itself as a sphere with the smallest possible interface per unit volume to the outside world. The group dogmatically closes its mind, takes on a defensive veil of secrecy and self-censorship and endeavour to obtain its information only from like-minded sources. In the comfortable womb of mutual in-group admiration, the group cherishes the negative stereotypes heaped on the out-group, knowing that they are so much better than the others. Janis uses the word 'doctrines' (Janis, 1982l), whereas Silver, talking about hedgehogs, refers to 'ideologies' (Silver, 2013e).

## XENOCENTRIC GROUP PROCESSES MAY PREVENT GROUPTHINK

As foxes outsmart hedgehogs, good group processes may prevent groupthink tendencies from occurring in cohesive groups. Such processes, when operating properly, allow groups to remain the best fora for sound decision-making. Janis proposes both major criteria for sound decision-making[10] and proposes three of what he calls tentative inferences to counteract groupthink tendencies (Janis, 1982m):

- The group leader should actively encourage all group participants to openly voice their doubts and objections. This must be reinforced by the leader's acceptance of criticisms of their own judgments. The latter must be genuine and to the team members safe and not career-damaging. If the team members doubt this, the leader will see them begin soft-pedaling their disagreements or not voicing them at all.

- The group leader should not prematurely shut down policy or strategy discussion by letting their personal views be known. Briefings to a strategy-developing team should be neutral and limited to the scope of the problem and the availability of resources.

- An organization may consider setting up multiple, parallel groups acting under different leaders but focusing on a similar assignment. As a result, truly independent courses of action may be developed, which may later be competitively tested as hypothetical options.

Janis' work strongly underpins one of my core beliefs. Sound decision-making requires unbiased, broadly sourced intelligence that is developed with a xenocentric view. When commenting on decision-making by the Kennedy administration at the time of the Cuban Missile Crisis, Janis says this about one of the key drivers for the peaceful resolution of the most threatening episode of the Cold War (Janis, 1982o):

> *"The wording of the President's letter [that defused the crisis] clearly conveyed the emphatic view of the members of the Executive Committee toward the Russian leaders, reflecting their efforts to project themselves into the role of their counterparts in Moscow [...]. Had the President and the Executive Committee thought about the enemy leaders in the usual stereotyped way, without considering how they would react if the roles were reversed, the necessary restraint probably would not have been achieved. [...] Robert Kennedy [the President's brother and Attorney General at that time] said 'A final lesson of the Cuban missile crisis is the importance of placing ourselves in the other country's shoes.'"*

## RECOGNIZING AND HANDLING GROUPTHINK IN M&A PROJECTS

Having reviewed these additional government examples, let's once again turn our attention to the world of business. Table 17.1 provides an overview that correlates the antecedent conditions to groupthink in Janis' model with business strategy practice. The table elucidates the potential applicability of the groupthink theory to an M&A team that may be supported by a strategic analysis function. In the case of M&A projects, the antecedent conditions are strongly present.

As a result, symptoms of groupthink can be quite apparent in M&A project teams. Table 17.2 relates the symptoms of the groupthink theory to the same M&A team example, which again may be supported by a strategic analysis function, justifying this in-depth discussion. This table shows that in line with the antecedent conditions being present across the board, symptoms of groupthink may develop in M&A teams.

Table 17.3 relates the symptoms of defective decision-making due to groupthink to the roles and responsibilities of a strategic analysis function and an M&A team. As in the case of the antecedent conditions and the symptoms of groupthink itself, table 17.3 also shows that symptoms of defective decision-making are commonly observed in M&A processes.

Customers of strategic analysis, such as M&A teams, may be prone to groupthink tendencies as is shown in the tables 17.1-17.3. The M&A team is only used as an example. This is not to suggest that M&A teams' susceptibility to groupthink is much higher than that of other groups of corporate decision-makers. Similar tendencies may be observed in teams preparing major capital expenditures, those gearing up for new product launches, in management teams or on executive boards.

| (SELECTED) ANTECEDENT CONDITIONS | TENTATIVE ASSESSMENT OF SUSCEPTIBILITY TO GROUPTHINK IN A BUSINESS CONTEXT |
|---|---|
| **A** Decision-makers constitute a cohesive group. | Effective business leadership teams tend to be cohesive.[11] The cohesion factor may increase when the leader has the longest tenure in the team and has hand-picked his team members. |
| **B-1** Structural organizational faults. | Groupthink antecedent conditions are worked out below for a particular business setting: an M&A project team, as for such a team, all antecedent fault conditions do matter. What is true for an M&A project team just as well applies to a strategy project team preparing a plan for a major capital expenditure or a major new product launch. |
| 1. Insulation and secrecy. | Secrecy is particularly relevant in M&A projects where share price – related information is available. To minimize risks of leaking and of insider trading, information flows are limited to as small a group as possible. This may induce an inevitable, strong 'in-group' feeling among the team members – the happy few to whom the information is entrusted. |
| 2. Lack of tradition of impartial leadership. | M&A teams do not tend to start with a neutral briefing; they start to win a deal and they know the project principal and top executive want that deal. |
| 3. Lack of norms for methodological procedures. | M&A teams are formed for the occasion and may not have established processes in place. Time pressure, especially when the target company is offered in an auction process, is such that no time will be available to agree to methodological procedures for sourcing and weighing all necessary strategic data to do a proper valuation and really take a balanced look at rewards and risks of the potential transaction. Risk areas are an overestimation of market growth and market value in the future – which both relate directly to strategic analysis work – and underestimation of post-merger integration issues and value risks. |
| 4. Social and ideological homogeneity of the group. | M&A teams may also be relatively homogeneous, being overpopulated by staff with financial and legal backgrounds and often a similar educational/social background – Ivy League MBAs who started their careers in dogmatic top-end services firms (consultancy, law, investment banking), most of them working 70 hour-plus work weeks in their early 30s. Moreover, most members of the team probably share the same overriding motivation: we want this deal to happen to obtain our success fee or bonus. |
| **B-2** Provocative situational context. | |
| 1. High stress – no alternative to the leader's initial idea. | In an M&A project team, high stress due to external threats (i.e., other bidders) is inevitable. M&A teams may develop tunnel vision, becoming singularly focused on 'if we don't win this deal we never will be able to enter this market'. Such vision implicitly subscribes to the antecedent condition proposed by Janis that there is no alternative to what the leader proposes: buy that company! |
| 2. Low self-esteem. | In an M&A project team low self-esteem is probably uncommon. A cause for collective low self-esteem may be that one or more previous deals were lost to adversaries, whilst the pressure from top management to grow the business through acquisitions grows ever-stronger. |

**TABLE 17.1 ▶▶▶ GROUPTHINK ANTECEDENT CONDITIONS APPLY TO M&A PROJECTS**

| C (SELECTED) SYMPTOMS | TENTATIVE ASSESSMENT OF SUSCEPTIBILITY TO GROUPTHINK IN A BUSINESS CONTEXT |
|---|---|
| Overestimation of the group | |
| 1. Illusion of invulnerability | Gordon Gekko in the movie Wall Street was a caricature of an M&A professional who believed he could win all and everything. A book like Barbarians at the Gate, describing the fight for control of RJR Nabisco in 1988, may be highlighting an extreme case (Burrough, 1991). Still, the illusion of invulnerability may infect M&A teams and their principals. This may result in M&A transactions closing too high, which possibly leads to M&A having a modest success rate in corporate value creation at large. This is not to suggest that M&A teams and processes due to groupthink (alone) realize less than optimal outcomes. Academic research on business may be necessary to prove that. It does, however, suggest that the sorts of people who become successful in M&A tend to display higher than average self-confidence. A group of such players may develop an illusion of invulnerability. |
| Closed-mindedness | |
| 1. Collective rationalizations | M&A teams may develop collective rationalizations of the type: "The target operates in a sustainably strong market with a tremendous potential" or "This currency will no longer devaluate due to the maturing of this economy, so the weighted average cost of capital can safely be lowered" or "This is the only feasible option". |
| 2. Stereotypes of out-groups | In corporate M&A, two out-groups play a role. The first consists of those business leaders who see one of their peers command massive resources for a deal. In so doing this peer reduces the M&A budget available for other (read: their) deals. To avoid internal competition for resources, these peers are excluded from the in-group information on the deal at hand.<br>The second group consists of the interlopers who are to be beaten in the bidding process. |
| Pressure toward uniformity | |
| 1. Self-censorship | An M&A team may at times doubt the wisdom of a high valuation, but may not always easily call it off because of that, when the team feels a principal badly wants the deal. |
| 2. Illusion of unanimity | The M&A team may have hearted but useful internal disputes at times, but in the presence of the principal will (understandably) always speak with one voice. |
| 3. Pressure on dissenters | An M&A team may have dissenters, but in the presence of the principal it is not common practice that a dissenter loudly voices why a deal should not be pursued or a valuation is excessive. Once 'deal fever' sets in, doubt is out. |

TABLE 17.2 ▶▶▶ GROUPTHINK SYMPTOMS APPLIED TO M&A PROJECTS

| D<br>SYMPTOMS | TENTATIVE ASSESSMENT OF SUSCEPTIBILITY TO GROUPTHINK IN A BUSINESS CONTEXT |
|---|---|
| 1. Incomplete survey of alternatives | M&A teams will always and possibly rightly blame corporate strategy departments for insufficient guidance on what to buy and why. Ideally a target has indeed been identified, and based on thorough criteria-based screening has been selected by corporate strategy. Still, even when an individual target has been singled out, multiple alternatives are possible in a transaction. These may at times not be completely surveyed, even though when it comes to term sheets and deal structures, M&A teams normally cover multiple alternatives. |
| 2. Failure to examine risks of preferred choice | The M&A team is neither responsible for the market estimates that are used in the business case nor for post-merger integration. The risks involved in getting things wrong in either area may indeed be underestimated. |
| 3. Failure to reappraise initially rejected alternatives | Once rationalizations such as 'this is the ideal target' have become embedded in an M&A team, the tunnel vision of groupthink may develop. In such cases, alternatives are overlooked. When in the process the going gets tough (or expensive or both), the earlier alternatives may no longer be revisited. |
| 4. Poor data search | In the ideal case, the M&A team depends on the quality and quantity of its external (market) data intelligence. This is the role of strategic analysis in M&A. When due to excessive secrecy the M&A team decides to collect market information themselves, such as through the back-office of an investment bank involved the threat of poor information search is just around the corner. |
| 5. Selective bias in processing info at hand | Even when M&A teams fully depend on strategy analysts for their data supply and analysis, the outcome of the analysis may due to inherent yesmanship still be skewed to achieve a particular desired outcome. The increase in a target's valuation when increasing the target's anticipated key market value growth with only 100 bps is often remarkable and may just make the difference between getting or not getting board approval for a deal. |

**TABLE 17.3 ▸▸▸ GROUPTHINK-BASED DEFECTIVE DECISION-MAKING APPLIED TO M&A PROJECTS**

The analyst, once valued for her neutral contribution and subsequently having been integrated into an M&A team, for example, may not remain immune to groupthink. This again is not new. Analysts at MI6 struggled to find an appropriate distance from a group of positive and encouraging executives who in wartime fought for a common cause with the intelligence staff (Jeffery, 2011b):

> *"It was constantly argued (with reason) that close coordination was highly desirable between the producers and consumers of intelligence. Only then could the intelligence agencies fully understand what was required and thus meet their customers' requirements. But if the relationship were too close, and the understanding too complete, then there was a danger that the intelligence sought and provided might merely reflect the preconceived needs of the consumers."*

There is undisputed value in analysts and executive cherishing two-way data and intelligence traffic (Steinberg, 2008). Teamwork always beats the work of a lone wolf. Still, for the analyst working in a multi-disciplinary group, a delicate balance needs to be found between objectivity and distance on the one hand and trust and understanding on the other. This applies both for the relationships the analyst builds with individual executives and with teams. An analyst who values her reputation for objectivity and integrity will intuitively manage this dilemma. That is not to say that analysts will always be in a position to correct social biases. That would be a naïve suggestion. Being well-aware of what these biases look like – from antecedent conditions to outputs – may, however, assist analysts to propose appropriate steps, as would outside counsel, to combat groupthink tendencies and/or forced yesmanship effectively.

CHAPTER 18

# ETHICS AND COMPLIANCE

# 18.1 INTRODUCTION

Collection is the most sensitive activity in strategic data analysis when it comes to legal compliance. Collectors may be tempted to collect 'just a little bit more', even when that technically means exposing their employer to huge litigation and reputation risks. Proactive collectors do exist who (believe it or not) sometimes even bribed the sales staff at a competitor to come up with the other company's marketing plan.

To prevent such things from happening, as a strategic analysis department, it is critical to ensure that everyone in your firm knows that compliance and ethics rank above creativity or creatively navigating the grey zone in collection. Therefore, it's important that your collectors are trustworthy – they make the difference, either in a good way or, heaven forbid, in a bad way. If only all cases were so black and white and simple. Some may be less straightforward. When is elicitation – the collection of data from unsuspecting people during seemingly innocent conversations – still ethically acceptable? When is it certainly not? What to do with competitor data that is unsolicited, perhaps received through a wrongly addressed email which you couldn't help but receive? Plainly asking for data may be illegal; asking while exercising coercion – better known as interrogating – is clearly illegal. Especially but not exclusively in HUMINT, there are a large number of collection methods that are clearly off-limits. As always in HUMINT, care is to be taken to steer clear from ethically treacherous waters. But what to do if a (former) employee of a competitor simply comes along and without being probed blurts out some data? Moreover, what actually is the law when it comes to trade secrets?

This chapter tries to answer some of the above questions. We first look at ethics and compliance as such, and briefly discuss relevant US legislation in this field. In the following section I will urge the reader to control the collectors and control them again – if only to ensure thorough compliance both with the law and with any company-specific ethical standards that may apply. We will also look into some collection methods that unfortunately are known to be use in strategic analysis but that I, writing as an experienced strategic analyst, consider unethical, if they are not necessarily illegal, I realize my ethical norms are my own – they are not universal. I cannot and do not want to make a call for anyone else on ethics. To prevent ethics from becoming too much of a subjective personal matter, some companies fortunately have solid codes of ethics in place that may even cover strategic analysis. Because such codes have been phrased so broadly, strategic analysis by default is covered. For those companies where that's not the case, I conclude with some ideas on how to rely on a company's code of ethics for guidance.

# 18.2 COMPLIANCE IS MANDATORY, ETHICS IS A QUESTION OF IDENTITY

Any decent company will at all times strive for full compliance with applicable law. This holds true for any business discipline, including strategic analysis. Ethics, however, is less straightforward than sheer compliance. Ethics relates to identity. Who do you as an individual strategic analysis practitioner want to be? Similarly, what is the identity that you as a company that has a strategic analysis practice want to have?

Let me share a personal note. Strategic analysis, sometimes also referred to as competitive or market inteligence, has become my professional passion. Yet, the public image of intelligence work has long prevented me from writing about market intelligence or strategic analysis. Let me share two quotes to illustrate my point. This is what US naval intelligence officers say about their work (Sontag, 1998):

*"The second oldest profession in the world, one with even fewer morals than the first."*

*"... the new director of Naval Intelligence, Frederick J. 'Fritz' Harlfinger II [...] who had been the Defense Intelligence Agency's assistant director of collection (called intelligence), a polite word for theft."*

The moral in military intelligence apparently is or at least has been: the other party's secrets are fair game. Stealing them is a means more than justified by the end of serving the national interest. The more advanced the intelligence collection methods, the worse the public perception. This does not only concern the headlines about the NSA in 2013. In the late 1950s US public opinion on intelligence was already negative when an illegally operating

KGB colonel who had been betrayed and caught red-handed had to be defended in court (Donovan, 1964):

> *"A man who steals the truth by sophistry is worse than a common thief."*

As intelligence is mainly known for collection, I realize that as a strategic analysis practitioner I may be held guilty by association in the public's eyes. Writing about strategic analysis may thus inadvertently taint my reputation.

## A SOLDIER IS NOT BY DEFINITION A WAR CRIMINAL

I have never been involved in illegal or unethical market intelligence activities. In a sense I am a soldier, but not a war criminal, just as a soccer supporter is not by definition a hooligan. Still, my clean sheet is immaterial. Changing the public perception of intelligence and by association market intelligence is a quixotic task. As I saw it, I had two options. I could accept the perception, refrain from writing and proceed with ethically and legally correct strategic analysis work as usual. Or, I could start writing and emphasize that as a strategic analyst soldier I am not by definition a war criminal, even when some soldiers intentionally or in extraordinarily trying circumstances have crossed the line and some in the future will.

I chose the option to start writing about what I believe good strategic analysis soldier-ship to be. In this section I will therefore emphasize that a good strategic analysis soldier has a chivalrous code of ethics that guides his collection behaviour. Living up to the standards of the code protects the strategic analyst's personal reputation, that of the company and also that of their professional community, even when the latter may sound idealistic.

Every person has their own ethics. Business, however, increasingly seems to hew to a global definition of integrity. Consumers hold businesses accountable to what they promise and to a minimum standard of ethical behaviour. These implicit global ethical standards by implication apply to any market intelligence professional, regardless of the professional's personal ethics. This makes ethics less of a legalistic topic.

It does not matter whether one is compliant. It matters whether one is seen to be 'doing the right thing'. Gilad once phrased a key question to be asked prior to starting out any strategic analysis (or market intelligence) collection effort:

*"What if this market intelligence methodology would make tomorrow's headline in a business newspaper?"*

This should be the minimum guiding question for any matters beyond compliance. In a globally connected internet world, unethical behaviour on one occasion and in one country may be known and frowned upon across the world in a matter of minutes.

Let me share an example. Nestlé hired a market intelligence service firm. On behalf of Nestlé, the firm 'infiltrated' an NGO with anti-capitalist leanings by planting an informant (Just-food, 2013). This informant reported confidential information from the NGO to Nestlé in the period between 2003-2008. Using intelligence parlance: at some stage the operation was blown. In court, Nestlé and its service firm were ordered to pay financial compensation totaling CHF 27,000. The amount is of course peanuts to Nestlé, but the reputation damage is not. A Nestlé spokesperson stating that "incitement to infiltration is against Nestlé's corporate business principles" didn't matter much. What matters is not what you state as principles, but, indeed, what you do (and not only what you are seen doing!).

In the past, corporate values like 'quality' and 'safety' have become mainstream. Today, 'integrity' is developing into a corporate must-have. Not surprisingly, again following 'safety' and 'quality', the first studies have appeared showing that high-integrity corporate cultures actually generate superior returns compared to their less integrity-focused peers (Doty, 2014).

# 18.3 RELEVANT LEGISLATION

The US government takes the view that business should be competing fairly and on a level playing field. Fair competition is ensured in many countries by anti-trust laws: companies are for example forbidden to execute pricing agreements with competitors to extract unfair value from their customers. This is where the governments limit companies' freedom of action. On the other side, in the government's view, companies own trade secrets that enable them to compete. Governments do not protect trade secrets as such. Trade secrets do not equate to intellectual property. Governments, however, indirectly offer protection by punishing those that steal trade secrets. Below I will discuss the link between strategic analysis – particularly data collection – and both anti-trust law and trade secret protection law. Later I will also briefly touch upon copyright law.

## ANTI-TRUST LAW IS TOUGH AND COMPLIANCE IS STRICTLY MONITORED

Anti-trust law will only be covered briefly as data collection tends to be a back-office discipline that does neither directly interact with customers nor with competitors when it comes to pricing, etc. Strategic analysis staff are strongly encouraged never to connect directly with competitors on prices, market developments, market trends or any other topic that may in some way or another be construed as limiting (the fairness of) competition. Regulatory bodies that monitor anti-trust compliance often break price cartels or similar anti-competitive connections between what should be competing companies by encouraging one cartel participant to 'talk'. Keep that in mind when, as strategic analysts, you may be tempted to 'talk' with your competitors. You see it as just some chit-chat. Questions may include things like:

What do you think will happen at customer XYZ now that they have a new boss? What do you think the oil price will do and how will that affect your company's pricing?

At first sight these questions seem to be innocent enough. But, they are not. When you competitor-friends' bosses or legal counsel find out, they may report these talks to the authorities. In doing so they leave you with the task of providing evidence that your discussions were harmless. The anti-trust bodies have the authority to take your computer, and check all your files and email. They may also check all your telephone records (metadata), to verify when you talked with whom. When they connect the dots between a call between your friend at the competitor and yourself, and a similar commercial step by both companies, it is up to you to explain that there was no link between the two events. In the anti-trust law of most Western nations, you are now guilty unless you can seed reasonable doubt that you are not, instead of the other way around. Do not underestimate the cost of non-compliance. Sentences include personal imprisonment and draconian fines. Often in anti-trust compliance training former inmates who believed making price agreements with competitors wasn't a big deal tell their stories. The inmates know better now and deliver a personal warning.

Another approach that may work to build awareness and strengthen compliance is to do what could be seen as an anti-trust mystery shopper test. Hire a law firm in the coming month to to do an unexpected raid on your office, similar to what a real anti-trust authority would do. Give them all the authority an anti-trust authority has: confiscating files and computers, checking emails, etc. The law firm's raid will subsequently reveal whether all your office staff, from the receptionist to the managing director, acted as per the training script. In addition, the law firm's raid will nicely reveal any non-compliant files and behaviours. The only cost will be the law firm's hourly rate – a small amount in comparison to the penalties an anti-trust authority may impose if they'd done the raid and discovered the non-compliance.

## THE US ECONOMIC ESPIONAGE ACT IS NO DEAD LETTER

Let's look for a moment at the US Economic Espionage Act, signed 11 October, 1996, by President Clinton. The law is an example of legislation that countries use to protect trade secrets. Strategic analysis practitioners should at all times involve legal counsel to check what relevant legislation is applicable to their (collection) efforts[1].

The act, the EEA for short, is a six title act of Congress, of which only the first title matters to data collection.[2] The first title is called Protection of Trade Secrets; it has appeared in scientific literature in full (EEA, 1997). This law was updated in January 2013. The update included amongst other measures an increase in the fines that can be assessed against individuals or companies found violating this law. In the 1996 edition, an individual could be fined a maximum of $500,000. This amount has been increased to $5,000,000. The EEA law has two sections:

- 1831 Economic espionage (Agent of Foreign Power).
- 1832 Theft of trade secrets (Commercial Espionage).

Segment 1831 enables the US government to punish foreign intelligence services or their agents caught in the act of economic spying. This is not a dead letter. An individual acting on behalf of the People's Republic of China was sentenced to a sixteen-year prison sentence for stealing US company-owned technology secrets. This segment obviously does not relate to data collection in strategic analysis.

Segment 1832 has led to convictions of individuals stealing trade secrets such as technology blueprints. Similarly, this part of the law is no dead letter.

## FOR TRADE SECRETS IN THE EEA, INFORMATION PROTECTION MEASURES ARE TO BE TAKEN

The definition of trade secret in the EEA is broad:

Trade secrets are all forms and types of financial, business, scientific, technical, economic, or engineering information, including patterns, plans, compilations, program devices, formulas, designs, prototypes, methods, techniques, processes, procedures, programs, or codes, whether tangible or intangible, and whether or how stored, compiled, or memorialized physically, electronically, graphically, photographically, or in writing if:

(a) the owner thereof has taken reasonable measures to keep such information secret; and
(b) the information derives independent economic value, actual or potential, from not being generally known to, and not being readily ascertainable through proper means by the public

Given this definition of a trade secret, the EEA makes it (Halligan, 1997):

> *"... a (US) federal criminal offense to receive, buy, or possess the trade secret information of another person knowing the same to have been stolen, appropriated, obtained or converted without the trade secret owner's authorization."*

A company *using* anything that could meet the above definition of a trade secret from another company is not by definition at fault (Horowitz, 1997). It doesn't matter what the trade secret consists of. What matters is that for a trade secret to be a trade secret it should not be available by legal means. Horowitz cites a paragraph from the Restatement of Torts (1939) to illustrate the government's thinking behind this:

> *"The privilege to compete with others includes a privilege to adopt their business methods, ideas, or processes of manufacture. Were it otherwise, the first person in the field with a new process or idea would have a monopoly which would tend to prevent competition."*

In plain language: anything, no matter how sophisticated, that is not secret and has not been protected as a secret is not a trade secret. A simple example may illustrate this point. Buying a competitor's product from the shelf in a shop is legal. Anything that careful analysis of that product reveals through MASINT to a strategic analyst about, for example, the competitor's production processes or technologies is not a trade secret. By offering the product for sale, the competitor did not take reasonable measures to keep the information secret. This does not mean that the processes or technologies to make the product may not be protected by patents, but that is a separate matter. This means that when a competitor is negligent with data protection and inadvertently and accidentally loses a secret customer list in a public parking lot, that list ceases to be covered by the EEA. The same holds true for a wrongly addressed email with sensitive information. Or an email invitation to the opening of a new office by a competitor where a competitor's negligent employee puts all addressees in the CC rather than the BCC. In this real-life case, the office worker revealed the entire commercial and professional service companies' network to the competitor. What a company does with a competitor's information that inadvertently has ended being secret is a question of ethics. This will be discussed later.

# 18.4 SCOPE OF COMPLIANCE AND ETHICS IN STRATEGIC ANALYSIS

For systematically defining the scope where compliance and ethics in strategic analysis normally matters most, the questions when, where and who are answered below.

## LEGAL COMPLIANCE MATTERS IN COLLECTION AND IN FILING

Within the realm of strategic analysis at large, the legal and ethical sensitivities tend to be in collection efforts executed by humans or HUMINT. In the next section, I will therefore discuss various ethically gray or downright illegal collection methods to stay away from, many of them involving HUMINT efforts.

In filing data, potential legal issues relate to copyrights. Strategic analysis departments often work with third party data providers that provide data for a price. The price tag for the data almost by definition is proportional to the number of users who post-transaction can get access to the data. For a strategic analysis department, it is tempting to buy a single-user copy and distribute it to more than one user. Nobody will notice, right? But it is illegal. Some data suppliers are truly tough on their customers' compliance with their contract provisions (and rightly so). Their detection of non-compliance happens more frequently than one would think. Every report this supplier sends out encourages the customer to call the supplier  in the event that the customer has any questions. What if a user doesn't realize they are not supposed to have the copy of a certain document and therefore shouldn't be asking about it? So they call. The recommendation here is to comply. My recommendation is to buy a corporate subscription and exercise your right to share it as widely as you like.

This is even more strongly the case with 'barter'. Let's say the strategic analysis department at company A calls their peer department at company B. "Have you seen these two new reports that data supplier X has just released? Good. I'd imagined you'd be interested as well. What if you buy one and I buy the other? We know each other well enough; this stays between us. Thanks, always good to have a friend." No point stating that this is illegal. That is obvious. The chances of being found out, however, are not to be ignored. Data suppliers mark their reports. There may be a bar code on the front with a customer number. That is a simple mark that is easily avoided in illegal copying. Upon copying you just take out the first page in the PDF file you share.

Smart data suppliers go a step further. They include a customer specific typo on a random page. Just one letter may be missing. Seems like an innocent typo. It is not. That one-letter typo appears on a coding list in the supplier's office. It connects the report to the customer who paid for it and to whom the report was originally sent. Whenever a copy of the report with that particular typo appears visibly to the supplier at anyone but the legal owner's desk, legal proceedings can start. Legal proceedings in companies usually are handled by legal affairs departments. That is typically the type of department that has a very low threshold access to a company's board. The fact that you as strategic analyst have been held liable for data theft may hurt your reputation more than dozens of great analyses offered to this same board can compensate for. What better way to lose the board's trust than being sued for stealing?

## CONTROL YOUR COLLECTORS AND CONTROL THEM AGAIN

Apart from respecting copyrights, the real ethical and potentially legal concerns are, as I said, in the area of collection. Which brings us to the question 'who'. Who is collecting? There are two groups of collectors: your own strategic analysis staff or third parties to whom collection may have been outsourced. In the Nestlé NGO-infiltration case, it was a third-party collector that did the work, but the collector of course got the assignment from someone within Nestlé who apparently had both the authority and the budget to assign this task to an outside party. Nestlé's spokesperson, whom we quoted earlier, also remarked (Just-food, 2013):

> *"If it turns out that a Nestlé employee has acted negligently, we will take appropriate action."*

That's not to say that Nestle should be blamed as a company. Nestlé is a highly professional company that I deeply admire and respect. This is just to illustrate how it works. What the spokesperson implicitly and understandably states is what any spokesperson of a large company would say. The company has procedures in place to prevent these sorts of things from happening. A company, however, cannot at all times and in all places control all its employees' zealous acts. The company will take appropriate action towards this individual. The action, albeit late, will serve as an example.

There is, however, a cynical side to this. In intelligence parlance, this is called 'plausible deniability'. It doesn't matter if the employee was under top management's orders to take that action. The point is that the employee has to be portrayed as a zealot. They need to be sacrificed by termination of their contract or through other disciplinary measures. The terminated employee will normally get enough severance money, but that payment is provided subject to the condition that the only narrative that survives this issue is that he acted on his own. This is not to blame top management for doing this. I wish to emphasize that I would not in advance condemn any large company's management for doing this. There may be cases in which I might lay blame, but not by default. It's imperative for the company to continuously require top management to take tough decisions at all times. Company continuity also has its ethical advantages, after all, like offering continued employment to its staff and returns to its investors. This may just be a case where a tough and at first sight unfair decision has to be taken. Without wanting to go deeper into the ethics of company continuity, I think this narrative for us as strategic analysis carries two lessons:

- A strategic analysis department that for legal or ethical reasons causes a scandal and as a result causes corporate reputation damage will normally not go unpunished (and rightly so).
- Outside data collectors are an above-average risk factor, as the strategic analysis department at the end of the day carries the responsibility for what they do, but can't see how they do it.

In the next section I will cover some 'how they do its' that should contractually at all times be blocked, no matter whether the collection work is internal or has been in-sourced.

# 18.5 ETHICALLY UNACCEPTABLE METHODS IN DATA COLLECTION

The listed methods below, although unethical or downright illegal, should be seen as a warning of the tactics competitors might use against your firm. The list is certainly not complete. It provides examples (in no particular order) of unscrupulous moves that a principled practitioner should steer clear of.

## FAKE JOB OFFERS

When a company wants to burrow down into its competitors' industries or plans, what better cover story to choose than to suggest they have well-paid jobs to offer? When candidates from competing companies proactively apply, interviews are aimed at understanding the competitors rather than at recruitment. In literature, these have been referred to as 'phantom interviews' (Ehrlich, 2006). Organizing phantom interviews to extract trade secrets may well be called fraudulent. Fraud is a crime. It may lead to significant punitive damages.

## FAKE INTERNS OR STUDENTS OF FALSE FLAG JOB SEEKERS

It's also unethical and fraudulent to send interns or students on a 'trade secret hunt' to a competing company.

Similarly, using students to interview competitors on product properties during, for example, trade shows is ethically off-limits, even when anything that the competitor provides in terms of *convention center* data is no longer a trade secret. The reason for data thus losing its status as a trade secret is simple: the moment a competitor shares data with a student, for instance, the company surrenders the data's protected status. What is said to a student in the middle of a bustling trade show is anything but a secret?

As a rule, do not ask anyone to pretend she's applying for a job with a competitor for the purpose of collecting information.

## INFILTRATION OF OUTSIDE STAKEHOLDERS

The Nestlé example demonstrates a common government intelligence collection technique when it comes to monitoring terrorist or other activist groups. Place a mole and tap that group's conversations. The Nestlé example also shows that this should not be done.

## COERCION OF FORMER COMPETITORS' FORMER EMPLOYEES WHO ARE NOW ON YOUR FIRM'S PAYROLL

Once a a competitor's former employee has joined your firm's ranks, it may be tempting to debrief that person. Normally such an employee has a legal obligation not to disclose their former employer's trade secrets, or at least an ethical obligation not to do so. Either way, as we already discussed in chapter 4, extracting data that is not in the public domain from a former competitor's employee is off-limits.

## CULTIVATING THE DISAPPOINTED CURRENT OR FORMER EMPLOYEES OF COMPETITORS

There are times when some people simply want to talk. P. Sichel, former CIA station chief in Berlin, illustrates that some sources are looking for a sympathetic ear, regardless of the risk involved (Delattre, 2006):

> *"Good intelligence sources are usually those who, for ideological reasons, do not agree with the policies of their government. [...] Only rarely are 'agents' recruited through subterfuge of the offer of money or blackmail. Ideology is still the great motivator [...]."*

The same human psychology applies to sources who proactively and intentionally share business data. An employee who feels bad about what their previous employer (who happens to be your competitor) has done to them is eager to talk, even when the only thing they are getting in return is 'a shoulder to cry on'. In some countries, however, intentionally encouraging such an outpouring of anger (and insider business information) would be unethical and illegal.

Post-acquisition turbulence is a typical occasion when the acquirer's top management may put new rules, policies and strategies in place new strategies (and place new players in key positions) in the acquired entity. At that point the acquired company's management may no longer recognize their beloved company, or know where they fit into the picture. They may feel that their loyalty to their company is no longer being reciprocated. And so, understandably, they won't feel so keen on remaining loyal to the old, virtually unrecognizable organization. From a strategic analyst's data collection perspective this situation might seem rife with opportunities.

Still, she should be careful about offers of documents or other sorts of competitive intelligence. As long as active solicitation and probing are not being used, the data obtained may be perfectly legal (listening is not a crime). Still, it is essential to at all times avoid touching stuff, even when it only reaches us in an audible form, that simply shouldn't be in your hands/ears.

## MISUSE OF INFORMATION MEMORANDA

Companies that are offered for sale need to disclose a lot of information to allow potential bidders preparing a first non-binding offer. Investment banks that assist in such sales processes compile an 'Information Memorandum,' or IM. Such IMs are only distributed to candidate buyers under the condition that the information is only available for the purpose of evaluating the possible transaction. When a buyer company decides not to make an offer, or loses the deal in the bidding process, the buyer is usually legally obliged to delete all IMs (except for one copy to be filed in the corporate legal department). Non-compliance is clearly illegal and usually – when exposed – and carries heavy fines that normally will have been stipulated in a non-disclosure agreement.

## ACQUISITION 'FEELER' MEETINGS THAT ONLY SERVE FOR INFORMATION COLLECTION

When a company is interested in new markets or new products, it may approach an established player to suggest that it's interested in looking at what value that player could offer. Sometimes a non-disclosure agreement between parties has been agreed upon in advance. But that still doesn't reveal whether the visiting company really wants to buy the player, or if it only wants to 'look'. This practice may not be illegal but it is unethical.

## TOLERANCE FOR WRONGLY ADDRESSED MATERIALS

People make mistakes. As we noticed above, some office workers are smarter email users than others. Emails may be sent to the wrong people.

The question is not whether these things happen; it's what we do with data obtained in this way. Strictly following the definition of a trade secret, these data have not been properly protected and therefore aren't a trade secret. Ethically, however, the only proper reaction when tempted by data obtained in this way may be to immediately send it back. Most companies' emails even carry a disclaimer to the effect that when an email inadvertently arrives in the wrong inbox, the sender should, as a standing precaution, have pre-emptively tagged the contents as a trade secret not to be revealed. Legal ramifications notwithstanding, it is always advisable to stay away from these 'finds'. An organization that is known to troll for such gems may encourage staff to proactively start 'finding' stuff – and end up in serious legal trouble.

## DUMPSTER DIVING

In 2000, a well-known case involved consumer goods company Procter & Gamble sending out third party collectors to go 'find stuff' (Mark, 2002). P&G had their service firm collect waste at a Unilever site.[3] Technically, waste that is placed on a sidewalk can no longer be considered a trade secret, as the material is in the public domain. Anyone can pick it up; it is not protected as a secret. But ethically, the purposeful, stealthy collection of a competitor's discarded paperwork is a different thing. In the P&G case, Unilever demonstrated that the collectors had most probably trespassed on Unilever's property, which turned waste collection into theft. P&G settled with Unilever – and sustained a big ethical hit.

## COLD CALLING

Strategic analysis staff (or even worse, their data collection contractors) sometimes simply call competitors and ask them for data. The data may, for example, be product specifications. These queries are perfectly legal when the caller states clearly and honestly which company they are calling from. The competitor may assist by providing public domain data. The tricky part is asking questions that may be construed as limiting competition between different players in a market. This is a very serious criminal offense in most countries. Questions related to things like pricing, price strategies (discount programs, timing of upcoming changes, etc.), future product launches and future investment plans for industrial plants all are strictly off-limits.

Competition law is so strictly enforced and defined that cold calling is to be actively discouraged. A third party data collector may present itself as a market research firm doing a study for a customer. This may still be legal, even when the third party is a cover for a company that never intends to buy from its competitor but is only after its data.

As a strategic analyst, it is important to control all-too-eager contractors in their quest for data. Make clear that cold calling by contractors isn't acceptable by stipulating this in the contract. When allowing a third party to call a competitor, agree to the contractor's questions – or better yet, draft the questions yourself – prior to approving the work order.

## BRIBERY OR COERCION

This seems so obvious. Bribery is a criminal offense – so serious that you wouldn't think anyone in their right mind would resort to it for purposes of corporate data gathering. There is outright cash-in-an-envelope bribery, as well as more subtle varieties.

For example, when a company asks a supplier for some sensitive information about a competitor, the management of the supplier faces a dilemma – reveal sensitive information about his former customer to win new business, or clam up and watch the new order evaporate. This is a form of coercion. Like bribery, coercion also is forbidden by law in most countries, but its outlines are much hazier, especially when nothing is committed to writing.

Suppliers should never give in to coercion, but if the order book is looking particularly empty, they may be tempted. Your strategic analysis department should always do its part to steer data collection suppliers away from coercive situations. Remember, providers who do it once are apt to do it again… and their next victim could be you.

## DUBIOUS TRADES WITH SUPPLIERS

A true wilderness of mirrors[4] – where it's unclear who's playing with whom – is present with the often smaller professional service firms that work for several competitors at the same time. Large, highly reputable firms like McKinsey & Co. keep their various clients segregated behind impervious Chinese walls. Even when concurrently working for competing companies they ensure that trade secrets do not pass between their teams. Small service firms simply do not have the luxury of maintaining sufficiently large, highly qualified teams to do this. In the best of all possible worlds, such firms will ethically choose to only work for one customer in a sector at a time. After having made their choice, they conclude an exclusivity agreement with their customer. In legal parlance, when another company in the same sector calls the service firm, the service provider is conflicted. The less ethical among these providers will start to play games like: 'Do you want to understand the market for product XYZ in South America? We happened to come across some valuable insight into this recently… We can make you a good offer.'

In essence, they attempt to sell the same insights at least twice – and may throw in details on the original customer's plans for good measure. Working with such 'traders' means that anything they learn about any firm will likely be passed on to any other firm. The moment one signs up to work with a company with such questionable ethics, you're teetering on the edge of a very slippery slope. There are no good reasons to be there.

## HACKING

Internet sourcing of information is almost always legal, as the internet is by definition public domain. Hacking or any other form of cybercrime, however, is obviously illegal. The grey zone in between is populated by sites like SlideShare. Files that are available through this popular slide hosting site can contain remarkably interesting data. The question, however, is how those files got there. Were they simply cut and pasted from a company's public website? Were they lifted from a firm's restricted internal system and posted by a disgruntled employee? Or is an entity, for whatever strategic reason, disseminating information on itself in a way that intentionally looks like the disclosure of company secrets?

## INTENTIONAL EAVESDROPPING

Strategic analysis departments will not use classic eavesdropping techniques like telephone tapping (or SIGINT – signal intelligence – in intelligence parlance). There are, however, technically legal examples of eavesdropping on competitor conversations that are still to be avoided. A widely rumoured, but probably fictional, example is of a market intelligence service firm that made a legal visit to the boardroom of a client's competitor. In doing so, it checked the brand and type of wireless PA system that the board used during their meetings. From there, it was easy to find the frequency of the signal. The signal was strong enough to be picked up and recorded in a car parked in a public spot across the street. The boardroom PA system clearly did not use encryption, so collecting the signal was de facto copying of the board meeting transcript. This method is not covered in the Economic

Espionage Act, as a signal captured in the public domain that has not been encrypted cannot be characterized as a protected secret. But let's face it: this collection method, however imaginative, remains deeply unethical. Just imagine the headline, 'Company Y tapped company X's boardroom conversations'. What would that do to company Y's reputation or share price? Let me reiterate: even 'grey area' practices that are technically legal should remain strictly off-limits.

Having said that, the time may come when a competitor's employees are overheard talking shop. The classic example is when two employees from a competing company sit next to you. Maybe after hours, in a friendly local drinking establishment... after multiple drinks.They can't contain themselves, and – as yet another round is ordered – the information begins to flow. Anything you and your colleagues innocently overhear is fair game. When the newspaper headline reads: 'Company X loses secrets through loud conversation at McGinty's Pub', company Y cannot be blamed – Company Y took no intentional steps to collect information. It simply happened.

What is true for barroom conversations is just as true for someone in the seat next to you on an airplane enthusiastically working away on her laptop. All too often, eager beaver employees believe they cannot afford to waste a minute, even when crammed into a torturously narrow economy class seat. So, after take-off, there they are, at your elbow, proofreading confidential documents. Although sideview-protection screens for laptops are cheap and easy to get, most companies don't provide them as a standard accessory. Truth be told, I don't have one either. Not having one allows me, however, to indulge in reading books while flying... using the great excuse that airplanes are too data-insecure a place to work.

Some regularly-scheduled flights are so frequently used by particular companies that not finding one of their executives on-board would be the exception. Buying a ticket as strategic data collector to gain exposure to competitive intelligence may sound more far-fetched than it is. Public companies announce for example board meetings and their locations in advance. Some unethical collectors may try to predict what flight a competitor's top executive will take, hang out in the business class lounge, and nonchalantly look and listen. He may even approach the executive and try to chat him up, pretending to be someone he isn't. This brings us to another serious offence in data collection: misrepresentation.

## MISREPRESENTATION

Misrepresentation comes in many shapes and forms. Common places you might encounter this would be at a trade show or a factory opening day. Someone trying to get a competitor's staff to open up might cover his ID badge or, worse yet, actually registering under a false name and be given false credentials. A really deceitful cover is to pretend to be a journalist, encouraging a competitor to share some powerful insights for press coverage (Kalitka, 1997). And we touched earlier on using fresh-faced students to ferret out information.

Sometimes factory visits or an executive briefing are part of an industry sector conference. Here misrepresentation is considerably tougher and some delegates for competitive reasons are simply not allowed to participate. When allowed in, ethics still require the visitor to be a good guest. This includes only taking pictures when allowed, not wandering through employee office space, and certainly not trying to poke around a mail room or copy center.

Cold calling while pretending to be a customer prospect also is a common form of misrepresentation.

Horowitz logically points out that under certain conditions misrepresentation can open one up to prosecution under US EEA trade secret law (Horowitz, 1997):

- *"Trade secret law protects the holder of a trade secret from someone who misappropriates that trade secret, i.e. obtains that trade secret through improper means. [...]*

- *Trade secret law considers misrepresentation an improper mean*

- *Case law has interpreted misrepresentation to apply to situations where:*

  i *one has induced another to violate his duty of confidentiality to his employer*

  ii *one has violated a confidential relationship with another*

  iii *one has acquired a trade secret from another knowing that the other had misappropriated the trade secret or that he had violated his duty to keep the information secret."*

Horowitz points out that fraudulent misrepresentation only applies when one party has the legal duty to tell the truth. The law as such does not ask for the intentions of misrepresentation. However, intentional misrepresentation is without question a serious ethical issue. Imagine the news headline when you get caught doing that; it won't be pretty. Bottom line: don't do it.

There is power in repetition. Therefore, to summarize, there are two questions that must be asked prior to approving any strategic data collection effort. The first is simply 'Is this legal?' The second is 'How would this look as a headline on the web or in a newspaper?'

No decent company should want to employ methods like those discussed above. This may be well understood within a company's strategic analysis department but that's not good enough. The strategic analysts should ensure everyone involved in data collection lives up to the minimum of ethical standards at all times. To accomplish this, two aims are to be set: standards need to be defined; the second aim is to ensure awareness of the standards. Everyone involved needs to know them. I will now discuss how to work towards achieving these necessary safeguards.

## 18.6 DEFINING AND IMPLEMENTING A CODE OF ETHICS FOR STRATEGIC ANALYSIS

Ethics are a company-specific topic (McGonagle, 2008). Rather than adopting a standard code of ethics, such as the one compiled by the Society of Competitive Intelligence Professionals,[5] it makes sense to tailor a program that's perfectly suited to a company's unique strategic analysis needs. Doing so serves two purposes:

- Upon writing, the in-company strategic analysis team and their legal advisers make choices what legally acceptable collection methods are also ethically tolerated and which are not.
- The firm also gets an ethical code that matches its needs.

And how do you go about crafting a suitable company-specific code of ethics? One way is to study those that have been developed by other companies. There are many published, readily available examples of ethics codes developed for corporations that have an in-house strategic analysis practice (Fehringer, 2006). The same source provides twelve codes of ethics developed within market intelligence service firms. Having evaluated these codes, it appears that a code of ethics for most organizations will consist of at least the following three sections:

- **Scope**
  What are trade secrets? To whom does this code matter? How does this code relate to other legal/ethical initiatives – for instance, competition law or a general code of conduct? Who should be contacted in case of questions? Who should be alerted to cases of unethical or illegal practices?

- **Appropriate conduct**
  What practices are illegal? What practices may be legal but do not pass the 'newspaper headline test'? The section above provides a clear but not exhaustive list of in-score topics. For reasons of clarity, it may be useful to segment appropriate conduct for market intelligence collection by type of sources and potential settings where these sources may be encountered:
  - Proactive collection initiatives focused at competitors (trade shows, applying to a job offer without having the intention to join the company, cold calling, etc.).
  - Former competitors' employees.
  - Current competitors employees (job interviews).
  - Regular suppliers (equipment, banking, consultancy, raw materials, etc.).
  - Market intelligence suppliers (such as service firms).

- **Sanctions**
  High-ranking company staff (like the chief legal counsel or a board member) should endorse the code. This makes it clear that complying with this code is a mandatory condition of employment.

In any company, management will need to adopt and implement a paragraph on data collection in its code of ethics. It will be necessarily to clearly define the legal, ethical and compliance requirements, issues and implications (Herring, 2006); (Pooley, 1997). I would recommend the following approach:

- **Define legal boundaries**
  What laws are in scope, applying to which countries? This requires the analysis team to work closely with the corporate legal department, amongst others, to align guidelines specific to data collection with existing corporate compliance and ethics codes or similar initiatives.

- **Develop ethical guidelines**
  This can all serve as a guiding framework, but formulation of corporate ethics standards is not a desk research exercise. To craft the bests possible covenant, and secure company-wide buy-in, have relevant players meet early on to collaborate on its drafting. Legal affairs should participate

to ensure alignment with other corporate governance and help create a legally sound protocol.

Outside facilitation of such a workshop is recommended. This is a round-table topic. The definition phase is not to be perceived as something 'corporate' imposes on a decentralized team of in-company strategic analysis practitioners around the globe.

- **Formalize the guidelines**
  Once the strategic analysis community and the legal affairs team agree on the final wording of the guidelines, ensure adoption by the company's executive board, through legal affairs. Board certification makes the guidelines' seriousness clear to employees and broadcasts a strong, no-nonsense ethical image to the outside world. Then – if an ethics-related lawsuit or government regulatory action arises – the company will be seen as having made every reasonable effort to ensure exemplary behaviour. An unethical employee will be seen as having flaunted company rules, and that will shape the regulatory and legal outcome of such a case (Fine, 1997).

- **Implement the guidelines**
  Implementation has two sides. There is the soft side that involves training relevant staff to secure their personal commitment and compliance. On the hard side, in-scope employees will be required to sign a compliance agreement that spells out the consequences of non-compliance (Kindler, 2006). Make no mistake, considerable time and effort will be required, but with a firm commitment from the top of the organization you'll come away with a solid – and altogether necessary – code of ethics.

  What is, much more difficult is to subsequently keep this code alive and ensure compliance. Staff will come and go, leadership will chance, and company's priorities, strategies and budgets will change from year to year. Through it all, the code of ethics should remain etched in stone. Kindler recommends keeping the code alive by planning a review with the key stakeholders at least once a year (Kindler, 2006).

  It will be helpful to piggyback as much as possible on corporate compliance programs that are already in place, most likely overseen by the corporate legal department, such as competition law training and compliance. A complication may be that target groups do not overlap, but procedures do. Don't fret, synergy may be just around the corner.

It makes sense to include the code of ethics in a corporate manual, if the company has one (Tyson, 2006). A corporate manual spells out tasks, responsibilities and span of authority by functional discipline, as a practical reference guide for everyone operating in a complex hierarchical organization. When a strategic analysis department is part of a bigger corporate strategy or corporate marketing department, the code will contain a distinct sub-set of considerations, rules and responsibilities for analysts. The corporate department responsible for keeping the corporate manual up-to-date (probably internal audit, legal affairs or risk management) may also be in charge of monitoring compliance. Strategic analysis could ally itself with that group to keep the guidelines alive and relevant. Still, any way you look at it, creating, implementing, monitoring and complying with this covenant will be hard work for all involved.

## 18.7 CONCLUSION

As we've made clear, professional compliance and ethics are not a luxury for the analyst community. They're an absolute necessity, and must be taken very seriously. With even a minor indiscretion, hard-earned reputation and trust can be gone in the wink of an eye.

CHAPTER 19

# DATA MANAGEMENT AND RETRIEVAL

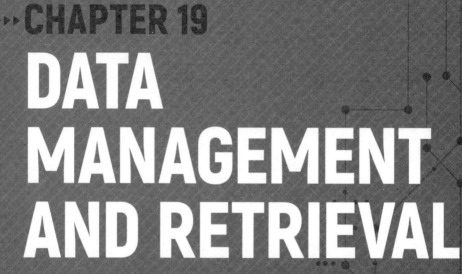

# 19.1 INTRODUCTION

Filing is perhaps the most underrated step in strategic analysis. The work of the former Dutch Security Service, BVD, was once described as looking for needles in haystacks. Thus, it was decided to collect haystacks (Engelen, 2007). Finding a needle in a haystack is tedious by any standard. With a proper filing system in place, after having gone through the haystack once, the next query will be more efficient and effective. Setting up a good filing system may well be the single most critical factor in creating an efficient strategic analysis function. Empirical evidence suggests that high-performing organizations have significantly more advanced tools and capabilities to work with unstructured data than their lower-performing peers (Brown, 2016).

Surowiecki summarizes the two imperatives that a good filing system needs to reconcile (Surowiecki, 2005e). Regarding the human dimension, he correctly points out the need for:

> *"Making individual knowledge globally and collectively useful (as we know it can be), while still allowing it to remain resolutely specific and local."*

This chapter will cover filing as an instrument to enable this reconciliation, and show how the logic of filing forms the bedrock for setting up an automated database for both quantitative and qualitative data points in support of strategic analysis. In the sections below, filing will be discussed using all of Kipling's six honest service men: why, what, how, when, where and who.

# 19.2 WHY ORGANIZE DATA MANAGEMENT?

Filing is key because, amongst many others, three particular things tend to get lost over time: people, the truth and files.

## PEOPLE

The history of the British secret intelligence service shows that poor filing and people changing positions led to one of the British Empire's worst intelligence failures: the fall of the colony of Singapore during the Second World War. Singapore, for those unfamiliar with the story, was attacked from the land, where it was not defended, rather than from the strongly defended sea. This followed the Japanese invasion of the Malay Peninsula, which commenced one hour before the attack on Pearl Harbor in December 1941 (Jeffery, 2011d). The military intelligence failure was due to a:

> *"...lack of any scientific system of collation. Owing to frequent changes of officers, information which had been filed was soon forgotten."*

The sobering truth is that all too often companies know what they need to support great decision-making, but unfortunately vital intelligence is not known and thus not available to the right people, who as a result cannot make the right decision at the right time. This may indeed sometimes be due to people changing positions and not passing on their tacit or codified data and knowledge to their successors. 'If only we knew then what we know now' too often summarizes corporate executive astonishment when knowledge management initiatives do prove their worth.

This art and discipline, however important, has proved more difficult to implement than is suggested by many a consultant preaching the knowledge management gospel. The systems were there to be leveraged, but a certain percentage of employees resisted changing their personal habits for a common good. After all, IT systems don't make a difference... people do.

The experience of organizations with knowledge management initiatives points to a classic people-related issue that, in itself, strengthens the case for setting up such a system for strategic analysis. There is an all-too-human tendency to think 'my info = my power = my future in my job'. This reflex tends to block selfless contribution of facts, knowledge and insights into a common filing and sharing system. Making everybody responsible for an open file sharing system tends to invite free-rider behaviour. Even when people are passionate users of such common open-source repositories, they themselves may still not actively contribute, either because of a lack of time or simply because others do so anyway. So why bother? And still, hugely popular websites like Wikipedia keep calling for contributions from their users. The numbers of users vastly outnumber their eagle-eyed gatekeepers, fact-checkers and editors. Even within Wikipedia's community of registered editors there is a long tail. It has been reported that a miniscule 0.04% of registered editors (1,050 people) are responsible for 50% all English-language Wikipedia content (Baeza-Yates, 2014). In other words, many will take but few will give.

The implication of this for setting up a corporate data filing system is as follows. Such systems only work well when lines of authority are clearly defined – who is allowed to file what material and who is responsible for keeping the system up-to-date and administratively squared away. Given the tendency for freeloading behaviour, this systems management won't happen automatically. In the sections below, we'll look at creating this sort of system in more detail.

## TRUTH

I came across a fascinating anecdote the other day that contains a number of important lessons on data management (NSA, 2007):

> *"One of the most famous stories about libraries tells of the Tenth Century Grand Vizier of Persia, Abdul Kassem Ismail, who in order not to part with his collection of 117,000 volumes when travelling, had them carried by a caravan of 400 camels trained to walk in alphabetical order. However charming this tale may be, the actual event upon which it is based is subtly different. According to the original manuscript [...] the*

*great scholar and literary patron Sahib Isma'il b. 'Abbad so loved his books that he excused himself from an invitation by King Nuh II to become his prime minister at least in part on the grounds that four hundred camels would be required for the transport of the library alone."*

The first lesson is that stories have a remarkable tendency to change when they are not properly documented and filed away when they're freshly available. Everybody knows the famous kindergarten game involving putting ten six-year-old children in a line next to one another. As the story is whispered from one child to another, it is remarkable to hear how different is has become when told back by the child standing at the other end of the line. Unfortunately, this distortion phenomenon applies to, shall we say, children of all ages. Stories have a remarkable tendency to change, more so over time and more so the longer the line is. The good news is that stories also tend to get better over time, but that is beside the point. In summary: the bleakest ink is better than the best memory.[1] Recording and filing data at the time it becomes available is not a luxury. Rather, it is a basic starting point of any strategic analysis function worth its name.

## FILES

The second lesson of the story of the Grand Vizier is that parting from your library is something that professionals cannot afford to do, not even when the prize is to become prime minister of Persia. This is a truth across all ages (although as a bibliophile I may be biased here). A more contemporary source essentially says the same. Amazon.com founder and CEO Jeff Bezos refers to the depth, breadth and historical value of big data when he says (Davenport, 2014a):

*"[at Amazon.com] We never throw away data."*

This statement says it all. For a strategic analysis function, throwing away data should never be a first reflex... or, for that matter, an option at all. Having to look for data that had earlier been in your possession ranks among the more frustrating tasks in this profession. Cost should never be an argument for throwing away potentially useful data. The cost of (soft-copy) memory storage is so low that holding on to what you already have is the beginning of all wisdom, especially when – through your well-maintained data management system – the data are available in a structured form that facilitates efficient retrieval.

There are countless examples of 'old files' coming to the rescue when a badly-needed puzzle piece just wasn't available anywhere else. The internet, no matter how useful it is as source for strategic analysis, simply isn't a structured data management system. Data on the web come and go – that is the nature of the beast. It is outside the analyst's control.

There is, however, at times also a case to be made for throwing data away. The key question is: how long do data on a file remain relevant? In science, the concept of a 'half-life time' is used to indicate how much time it takes for decaying radioactive material to emit 50% of the radiation it emits at the start of the measurement. For data on competitors, the half-life time of data value varies by topic and most of all by what purpose the data have been or are to be used for.

For operational decisions and for most tactical considerations, information older than one year, perhaps two, tends to be of limited use. Market share data that are more than three years old are sold by companies like Nielsen at a big discount because they have lost value for most (tactical) marketing applications. So, the half-life for this type of data is probably a year. In contrast, for strategic reviews of competitors, especially for analysis of how competencies at the competitor have developed over time or what past successes the competitors' current leadership has enjoyed, ten-year-old data may still be relevant. In that case the half-life time is easily ten years.

A discerning view on what data to keep and what data to discard is needed. As a rule, the more structured and thus retrievable the data are in the filing system, the lower the incentive to ever remove them. When in doubt, refrain from cleaning out your closet and abide by the Bezos Rule: never toss data!

# 19.3 WHAT DATA TO MANAGE?

What to file should exclusively be determined by the current or expected future demand for data in defined strategic analysis projects or in permanent (early warning) monitoring processes. This links to a fundamental utilitarian condition: data are only worth filing when they'll be put to use. Fortunately, it is in advance often clear whether data will only be useful in one particular project or in a future one as well. Hence, filing data that may have multiple uses is a no-brainer, whereas filing data that probably will be used once should be given a second thought. But again, always keep the Bezos Rule in mind.

In the case of qualitative data – think of news clippings or press releases issued by competitors – the recommended default step is really to file everything in a single structured data management system. Computer memory, after all, is cheap. Moreover, it is virtually impossible to predict in advance whether a particular data point that is embedded deep in a qualitative file (say a clipping) may not become relevant in some future analysis project. Obviously, a 'filing it all' approach is only useful when the system is designed for efficient file retrieval. How to create a structure in the system that facilitates efficient retrieval will be covered in the next section.

In the case of quantitative data, a more differentiated approach is recommended. Quantitative data that forms a firm's backbone of understanding the business environment deserves to be filed in a well-defined, highly structured data warehouse.

Such quantitative data, relating to the industry in which a firm operates, may include:

- Key financial data of competitors (net sales, gross profit, EBITDA, EBIT, etc.).
- Sizes of key markets (by product, by channel, by volume, by value, etc.).
- import/export statistics of key product classes for key markets (volume/value).
- Key weather statistics where applicable (e.g., rainfall in agricultural areas as a predictor of agricultural yields in the next harvest by region/country).
- Key commodity product quotations (metals, crude oil, diesel, etc.).
- Relevant economic statistics (such as various countries GDP, CPI, GDP growth forecasts, etc.).
- Demographic statistics (population sizes by country or even better by city).

Quantitative data that have been collected for a single project, like the income distribution of women of a particular age in a particular city, may be less desirable for filing. Doing so would make the warehouse unnecessarily complex and expensive to maintain.

Deciding whether or not to set up a structured filing system for quantitative data is akin to assessing whether to undertake full-blown analysis projects. Diagram 19.1 depicts the dilemma. Line A represents the approach of setting up a folder containing individual quantitative analysis project files. When an individual, one-off project is complete, the file usually goes into a hibernation state. It may sleep in a more or less common project file directory or in the individual data file storage area (the 'C: drive,' so to speak) of the project leader or a designated member of the project team. Such files tend to get lost forever when the file owner changes jobs. Line B in Diagram 19.1 represents the approach of setting up a well-designed data warehouse for quantitative data. This approach can initially be costly and time-consuming, so it pays to be clear on whether the data will be relevant – and used by a sufficient number of users, across multiple analysis projects – well into the future.

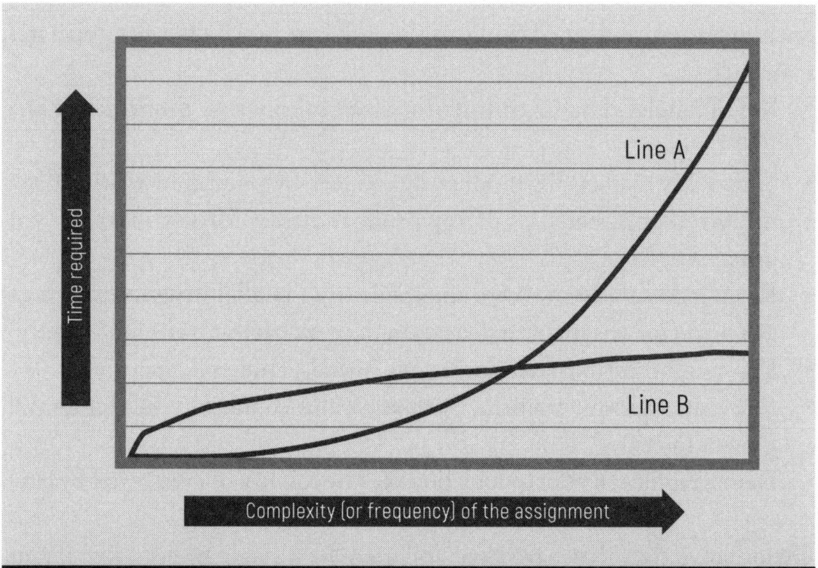


DIAGRAM 19.1 ▶▶▶ WHEN TO SET UP (B) AND NOT TO SET UP (A) A QUANTITATIVE DATA WAREHOUSE

To summarize, setting up a quantitative data warehouse is an exercise that requires a discerned view on which quantitative data may be used for multiple assignments and which may not. Individually generated, non-central Excel files can do the job. Accepting that such files (and the data in them) form the backbone of an analysis and yet may over time get lost is part of the deal. For qualitative data, it's highly advisable to always set up a single company-wide data management filing and retrieval system, provided that is well designed to make data retrieval efficient and reliable.

# 19.4 HOW TO ORGANIZE DATA MANAGEMENT?

The ultimate objective of data management is efficiency in retrieval. It only makes sense to tuck your needle into a haystack if it's pre-threaded for easy extraction. As we've established, the two main categories of data for filing are quantitative and qualitative data. About 80% of all data used in companies is of a qualitative nature (Fillié, 2010). Both data types need their own management.

## QUANTITATIVE DATA

Quantitative data comes in various shapes and forms. Common quantitative data for strategic analysis have been listed in the previous section. Each of these categories of data in itself may have a clear structure, but almost by definition there is limited common structure among them. The only common independent variable that may link the data is time.

Thus, even though in practice most data sources tend to use the 10-digit numeric system, variation in definitions between different data categories may still prevent data across categories from being used in comparative analyses. A simple yet common example is that in continental Europe, 1.000 means one thousand whereas Anglo-Saxon sources depict one thousand as 1,000. In Arabic-language documents entirely different symbols for figures may be used. This adds an extra challenge to manually, and certainly automated, source-to-data warehouse transfer processing. These minor differences tend to complicate automated processing of data categories into a single- or common- structured file. Data that represent the same physical entity (for example, the physical length of a rail line) may also come in different units, such as miles versus kilometers. Financial data from different companies are even more challenging to compare as they may come in different currencies that over time have fluctuated in value against each other. Moreover, different accounting standards may result in the same numeric values but those values do differ in meaning. For example, $1,000 net profit reported under US-GAAP may not be equal to $1,000 net profit reported under IFRS. To make comparing data across companies even more daunting, some companies still have financial book years that do not correspond with calendar years. New Zealand dairy giant Fonterra, to name just one example, starts their financial year 1 August and ends it, for good reasons, 31 July of the next year.

When the sole purpose of a filing step is to create a file that the strategic analysis function itself controls – and to put on record 'data as is' – these differences may not create too much of a problem. In filing 'data as is' the quantitative data are at least stored, and thus secured, for future reference and analysis. Due to peculiarities in the definitions, however, they remain relatively unstructured.

Even so, in strategic analysis there is merit in building a 'data as is' file for many of the categories. Such a file can be simple. It stores 'data as is' in columns and rows for each topic category. This means that the strategic analysis function would create one file for each company that is or may in the future be of interest. The rows usually contain the different years (or another relevant time period) of the database, whereas the columns contain the different quantitative dimensions that are to be filed. This would help clearly reflect net sales, e.g. net sales in the corresponding year, in the original reporting unit and currency and under the originally used accounting standard. In doing so, by default, a common structure across such individual files for different companies is neither possible nor really desirable. A common layout for company-specific files, let alone a common file across different companies, may only deceive users when they use data from categories where different definitions are 'hidden' in the data. One never wants to compare apples with pears.[2] A professional analyst prefers to work with original data wherever possible. Avoid using pre-processed data offered by some data providers where the processing steps have not been fully documented. You just do not know what processes the data have been through.

Small inaccuracies, due to different definitions of data from different sources, do not by definition result in problems. When high accuracy is not imperative for drawing a conclusion and time is short, reasonable comparability may well be good enough. What matters to the analyst is to recognize when complete accuracy is necessary and when that's not critically important.

The implication of the above, especially when high accuracy is required, is that all too often the collection and filing of quantitative data is time consuming and involves manual, hard-to-automate work. The time and therefore human cost element in collection and filing of quantitative data also means that this part of analysis will likely remain 'Small Data'.

To allow graphic representation or analysis of data from different companies, rules of translation to a commonly defined data analysis warehouse need to be set. The strategic analysis function may choose to set such rules themselves. It makes sense, however, to at least align such choices with the function's main customers. It is imperative that these choices are fully documented in any data warehouse that is made available to users who weren't privy to the ins and outs of the translation process.

Setting up such a database will require time and investment. There are two main value drivers underpinning the business case for building this kind of data warehouse: creating a single, living corporate truth, and creating a resource to facilitate better fact-based decision-making.

## A SINGLE, LIVING CORPORATE TRUTH

Two steps need to be taken to arrive at one truth for the entire company when it comes to quantitative data. The first step to take is to work through the one-off history-building exercise in the database. This step builds the base data set that will serve as a starting point for analyses. The second step is the process of keeping the data up-to-date. The first step is a project; the second is the design and execution of that process. The second step – and especially tackling the execution and ongoing maintenance considerations – is the hard part. If sufficient resources to design and build a robust, updateable data base aren't allocated up front, it's not really worth embarking on this journey. A snapshot may be nice, but a full-length feature film with Dolby surround-sound and subtitles is so much better. Building a continuously updatable data base not only creates a single, living corporate truth, it propagates and evangelizes that truth. The permanently actualized quantitative database will then guide all decision-making across a firm that uses quantitative business data.

Allowing company-wide 'read-only' access to the database empowers anyone in the firm looking for quantitative data to build a business case, a marketing plan, an investment approval request, etc., to use a validated, permanently actualized 'single living truth' source. Moreover, business leaders who develop plans and take action based on data residing in this repository will know they're working with the best available market intelligence. This can reduce the need to cherry-pick data to polish up a plan. It will never fully eradicate this all-too-human habit. And, perhaps unfortunately, having a bullet-proof, supercharged quantitative database at your disposal may limit the integration of gut-feel stories into fact-based decision-making.

## MOVING TOWARDS FACT-BASED DECISION-MAKING

The first step is to get the data warehouse in place and continuously maintained. This repository, made accessible to all relevant users via an intranet application, should now proactively distribute periodical reports and facilitate one-off report making. The fact that the organization is now empowered with permanently updated data, at everyone's fingertips, lowers the barrier to entry. Gone are the days of labouring through tedious data collection and structuring work. The only task that remains to be done by a business team is to do the tailored analysis for their business plan. The time savings alone will be substantial. It also will raise quality bar for internal plans. From that point forward, a plan that is not solidly based on quantitative data extracted from the *one living truth* database will start to look rather lightweight. The data warehouse will thus drive professionalization across the firm.

The next stage for a strategic analysis function is to agree with their colleagues of corporate finance and administration on common MI/BI (market intelligence/business intelligence) reports for senior management that show the firm's internal structured data compared with similarly structured data out in the marketplace. MI/BI deliverables might include comparisons with peer companies that show quarterly volume and net sales growth by geo-territory and category.

Such deliverables offer top management not only a view of how the firm itself has performed but also what net sales growth their business partners and competitors reported in the same period, category, geo-territory and currency. This adds a potentially valuable extra perspective to a firm's competitive analysis, strategic planning and go-to-market tactical actions.

Diagram 19.2 summarizes how setting up a data management system is critical to unlocking value from what initially looked like 'unstructured' quantitative data. In the diagram MI stands for 'market intelligence'.

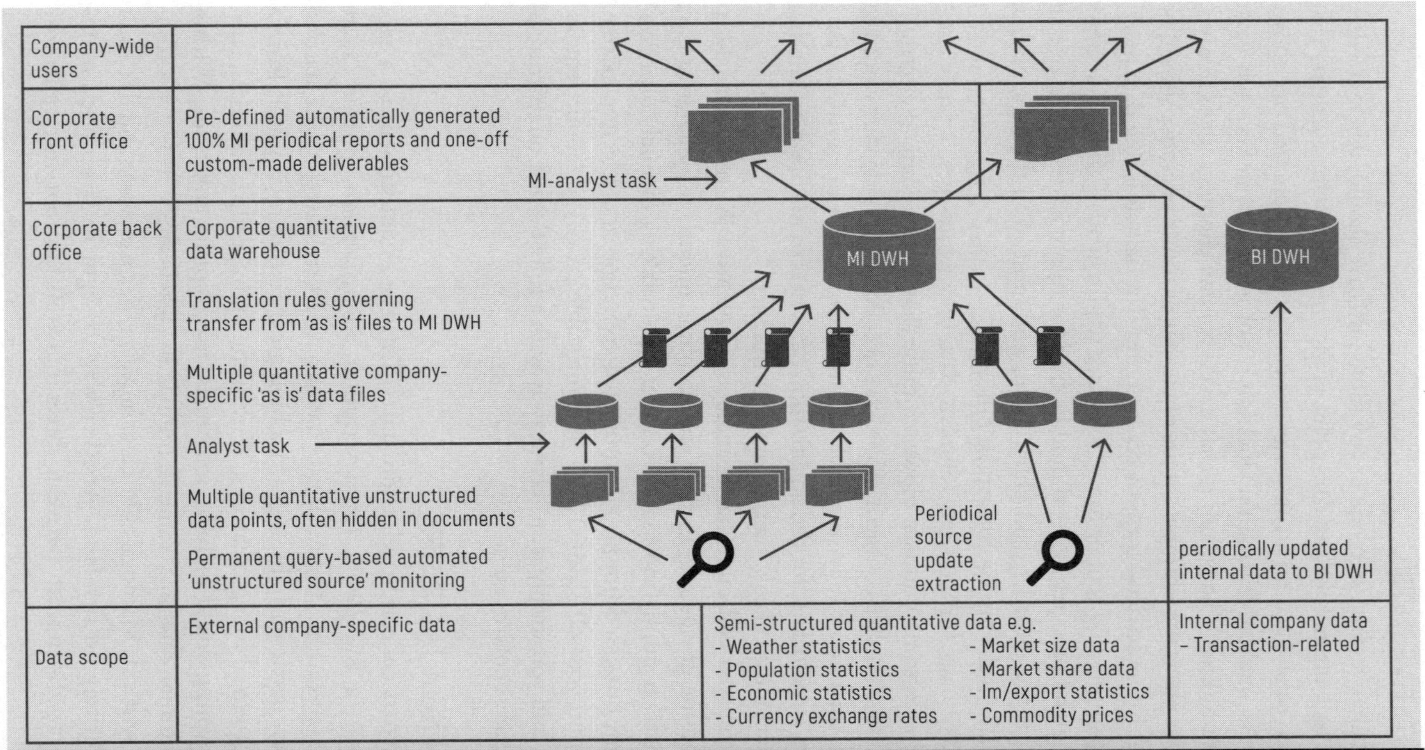


DIAGRAM 19.2 ▶▶▶ A PROCESS FOR COLLECTING, FILING AND DISSEMINATING QUANTITATIVE EXTERNAL DATA

## QUALITATIVE DATA

For qualitative data, step one of any filing initiative should, where needed, be full digitalization of any data point (a file containing whatever data that has been catalogued on a company or a category). As I pointed out above, relative to qualitative data, the question is not what data to keep but what data not to keep. The default is that data (i.e. news clippings, press releases, etc.) that meets the simplest criteria of current or future relevance should be filed for future retrieval for projects to come.[3] The default is that data meeting the simplest current or future relevance requirements – things like news clipping and press releases – should be filed for future retrieval. The overall process is thus broader than filing. Filing, and most of all the logic of data management, forms the core of the process.

Today most business environment data (news messages, reports, etc.) arrive in electronic formats. However, those that do not come in electronically – however, like competitors' brochures collected at trade fairs – need to be processed into a fully searchable electronic equivalent to ensure the data in them is 'unlocked' for the organization (the users of the filing system that is to be made accessible via the corporate intranet).[4]

Automated collection has become an imperative in strategic analysis. The volume of ongoing in-flow and absolute amount of qualitative data 'out there' is simply too big to consider a painstaking manual collection/selection process. Without an automated collection and selection system, you'll find yourself saddled with unmanageable costs and labour requirements, and you simply won't come away with a fully fleshed-out picture of the business environment.

## DEFINING A TAXONOMY

Automated collection/selection starts with the establishment of a taxonomy – a framework for description, identification, nomenclature and classification. The notion of taxonomies originated in the natural sciences, particularly biology. In a biological taxonomy, animals form a main group of living creatures. Within the main group of animals, sub-main groups would include, mammals, fish, reptiles and birds. Within the mammal category, some mammals live exclusively in the sea (dolphins, whales). Mammals like cats, however, despise water and live their lives entirely on dry land. Another way to segment land-based mammals is to distinguish between those that walk on four feet and those that walk on two. Yet another segmentation dimension for mammals distinguishes between those species that hibernate in winter and those that don't. Likewise, another dimension is to categorize mammals that are indigenous to Africa apart from those that are exclusive to Europe and so forth. In short, setting up a taxonomy means defining multiple segmentation dimensions to structure loose data.

The periodic table of elements is a most elegant example of a taxonomy (Johnston, 2005a). By structuring the highly disparate information available on the building blocks of nature, Mendelejev turned chemistry from an empirical into a structured science. Librarians, of course established taxonomies long before digital technology was available. The fundamental thinking underpinning taxonomy definition and application processes has never really changed (Fisher, 2008). A firm's business environment can be segmented in a similar, multidimensional way, to unlock the value hidden in multiple unstructured data points.

Prior to going into the detailed dimensions of a business environment taxonomy, it should be emphasized that a taxonomy is an instrument of strategy, not a descriptive goal in itself. For a biologist, taxonomy offers a way to segment nature into logical classes of creatures with common habitats, habits or features. For a strategic analyst, taxonomy is not an instrument to describe the nature of the business environment as such. Rather, a strategic analysis taxonomy is a tool to facilitate selecting/collecting, filing, retrieving and even the proactive dissemination of data, segmented in a way that's determined by your firm's strategy. A taxonomy allows one to structure data in a way that facilitates understanding or analysis of the business environment that may affect a firm's strategy. Your own firm's strategic segmentation (e.g., categories, value drivers) determines how the business environment, through a matching subservient taxonomy, is defined.

There may be merit to emphasizing here that a data point as mentioned above both consists of the actual fact (company X will change its management structure) and the contextual data or metadata that accompanies it (who said it, when, through which channel did the information reach us, etc). Facts in the absence of metadata lose a lot of value, so combining both is critically important in order to provide value by sharing data (Jones, 2007).

## DEFINING THE MAIN GROUPS OF A BUSINESS ENVIRONMENT TAXONOMY

The recommended main groups of a business environment taxonomy in a qualitative database might include the following common dimensions. This list is not necessarily exhaustive and depends on the key dimensions of your firm's strategy.

- Source type (with sub-types being news clippings, press releases, annual reports, etc.)
- Date (with possible sub-types being publication and upload date)
- Language (with a non-limitative number of languages as sub-types)
- Company (with a non-limitative number of company names as sub-types)
- Category (with a limited number of clearly defined types, with each possibly having sub-types).
- Territory (with continent, country, city as different type levels).
- Channel (hypermarket, supermarket, when relevant).
- Discipline (M&A, HR, marketing, etc.).
- Secrecy unrestricted, classified, secret (see section 19.8 below).

In addition, for each data point (such as a clipping), the full title might be stored as a separate field in a database, connected to the main body of the text, as well as perhaps the first 100 words of the main body of the text, usually referred to as the *teaser*.

In conclusion: the use of a taxonomy allows one to file loose data in a structured way. What initially for example was a random, one-in-a-million news clipping is now a segmented data point in a multi-dimensional data warehouse for which the firm's strategy-based taxonomy structure forms the street plan. The different terms selected from the taxonomy together form the metadata of an individual data point – the information that adds structure to that data point. Consider the following hypothetical example of a data point and the corresponding possible metadata, originating by dimension from the taxonomy.

*Cheesefreaks acquires Freakcheese*

*The Cheese Times, London, June 6, 2014 – US-based Cheesefreaks Ltd. yesterday signed an memorandum of understanding to acquire Freakcheese BV from the Netherlands. Closing of the transaction is subject to regulatory approval. No terms and conditions for the deal were disclosed. Freakcheese BV produces low-fat Mozzarella for the food service channel. The Freakcheese range of products complements the cheddar produced by Cheesefreaks Ltd. Mr Colby Cheesehunter, CEO of Cheesefreaks Ltd, said: "This acquisition allows us to create synergies in sales and distribution, with Freakcheese's excellent Dutch logistics organization offering a great platform to sell US cheddar in the Dutch food service market." Adds Mr Edam Jones, CEO of Freakcheese BV: "Selling our company to Cheesefreaks is both a great way to create value for our shareholders and create exciting new opportunities for our staff – It really is a win for everyone involved – particularly our customers."*

The metadata for the above clipping, collected from a fictional taxonomy-based thesaurus, could look something like this:

| | | | |
|---|---|---|---|
| • | Source type | newspaper clipping | |
| • | Date | publication: 6 June 2014 | |
| • | Language | English | |
| • | Company | Cheesefreaks, Freakcheese | |
| • | Category | main category: | Cheese |
| | | sub-category: | Mozzarella, Cheddar |
| | | sub sub-category: | Low-fat |
| • | Territory | main category: | North America; sub-category: US |
| | | main category: | Europe; (sub-category: Netherlands) |
| • | Channel | Food service | |
| • | Discipline | M&A | |
| • | Secrecy | unrestricted | |

Once the metadata have been added[5] and assuming compliance with applicable copyright laws,[3] the loose clipping can be stored in the qualitative database. Retrieval of this data point from the database is now possible through well-designed software tools. For this at least three clearly different methods are available:

i. By searching the database with a free-text search engine.
ii. By searching the database along one or more taxonomy dimensions.
iii. By searching the database along taxonomy dimensions whilst adding free-text search terms.

A typical free-text search in the database could be on the search string 'Cheesehunter'. Let's say Colby Cheesehunter, the CEO of Cheesefreaks Ltd., approaches your company for a meeting. In preparation, your chief executive asks his strategic analysis team for a detailed profile of Mr Cheesehunter. No matter how enormous the database, a search for a name like Mr Cheesehunter will for sure to generate relevant hits.

If an outlook on the dynamics of the mozzarella market in the Netherlands is the topic of the project, a typical taxonomy-based search could be on the terms 'mozzarella' in the cheese category dimension and 'Netherlands' in the Europe territory dimension.

Now let's say your company is approached by Edam Jones, CEO of Freakcheese BV. Unlike a search for a distinctive name like 'Cheesehunter', a database search for 'Jones' isn't likely to yield such focused results.. Searching in a large database on a free-text search string 'Jones' won't be too successful. The name Jones is obviously far too common. A more promising approach would be to search for 'Jones' in combination with the taxonomy term 'Freakcheese.'

Even more advanced text structuring approaches allow for more refined structuring, and thus searching, of text (Noble, 2006). In the practice of strategic business analysis there is generally no need to apply such approaches, unless a truly big data context requires it. The above example highlights three key elements in data point collection and selection in a well-designed qualitative data management process. It shows:

i. What a taxonomy-based thesaurus is.
ii. How to apply a taxonomy-based thesaurus to add metadata to a data-point.
iii. How a thesaurus-based database allows efficient retrieval of a data-point, either by using free text, metadata dimensions or both.

Most of all, it demonstrates that the usefulness of a qualitative data management system fully depends on the definition of the taxonomy, which provides the structure that projects your company's strategy into a filing system. When a company has a clear strategy, setting up the data point database to guide and monitor execution of that strategy is merely a question of disciplined effort.

## AUTOMATION OF ADDING TAXONOMY-BASED METADATA TO DATA-POINTS

The above example starts with implicit assumptions regarding four highly labour-intensive steps involved in the data management process. In this example it is assumed that:

i. There is a (relevant) clipping.
ii. There is a way in which the metadata are chosen from the text and the context of the clipping.
iii. There is a way in which the metadata are added to the data-point in the database.
iv. There is a way to file the clipping with the metadata in the database.

In the distant past, government intelligence departments employed hundreds of clerks to execute these sorts of tasks. They filled in thousands of cards prior to filing them in countless grey filing cabinets. In business, competitive intelligence expert Kirk Tyson as late as 1992 still had this to say about filing (Tyson, 1992):

> *"A manual inventory list of available competitive information and manual card index can keep track of the information. [...] commercially available [computer] packages that will work for the intelligence process are not yet available."*

Fortunately for us, Twenty-First Century information technology facilitates automation of the data management process. Even a modestly ambitious strategic analysis function can make a compelling business case for setting up a qualitative database along the lines of the one described above. Once that decision has been made, designing a smart automated process is almost inevitable. As Diagram 19.1 shows, when an assignment is often recurring, setting up a first-time-right automated solution generally pays off. The automation should thus accomplish three tasks:

i. Involve initial, up-front selection of data that is now, and will be likely in the future, relevant to your business. The criterion of relevance for a data-point is the frequency of occurrence of taxonomy terms.
ii. For each data point 'out there' that sufficiently matches pre-set taxonomy-related search criteria, add the metadata and the context info (for instance the publication date) to the data-point file.
iii. Store the data-point file in the qualitative database as per the taxonomy-based structure. All of the above three steps are possible and are applied in practice.

## CATCH THE RIGHT FISH (AND IGNORE THE OTHERS) THROUGH BUILDING QUERIES

To facilitate pulling the relevant fish from the sea, it makes sense for a strategic analysis function to work with a dedicated web-based news search company. There are simply too many sources out there to monitor them all on your own. A common approach is to discern what sources to follow directly such as relevant, industry-specific news providers, and which to follow indirectly through a news search company like general newspapers.

There are examples of companies that monitor general newspapers and magazines. Their search query normally operates as a net in the great, sea of open source that's data published every day, catching only those fish that match predefined criteria. The criteria and the queries to catch the fish that match those criteria – and ignore those that do not – are based on the company's strategy-derived taxonomy.

A simple query word would be Nestlé. This company's name is so unique that false positives are unlikely to occur. There will also not be many false negatives, as Nestlé on a corporate level is not known under different names. But in the case of Hewlett Packard (HP) for example, the full name forms a selective query that is unlikely to deliver many false positives. In contrast, a query for text strings with HP may result in news related to engines with a certain amount of HorsePower. HP as a query may thus yield a lot of false positives. To avoid such false positives, it may be helpful to specify in the query that directly before HP no number may be present. A news article in which the string "150 HP" occurs would thus be rejected as hit. This, however, may also result in false negatives, as in instances where a number rightfully appears before HP in an article about the IT company. A news article featuring a sentence like "in 2012 HP announced it was updating its strategy" would no longer have been selected. An even more advanced query would thus specify that all text strings containing figures before the HP-text string should be excluded, except those mentioning figures that clearly represent years – for instance, from 1939, when Hewlett Packard was founded, through a year perhaps a decade or so into the future, to prevent the need for annual updating of the parameters. As this example shows, a query that delivers a minimum number of both false positives and false negatives can easily get rather complicated. With the emergence of ever more powerful computers, this sort of 'query language' can get more sophisticated without the search processing time becoming unduly long. The ultimate results of developing these types of query language scripts are algorithms that increasingly seem to *think* like humans. The scientific term for this technology is 'natural language processing'. Also known as NLP, these programs (Davenport, 2014b):

> *"[...] may involve counting, classifying, translating, or otherwise analyzing words. [...] Virtually every large firm that is interested in big data should have someone available with NLP skills [...]."*

However, Davenport cautions not to expect too much too soon from NLP (Baker, 2014):

> *"You need to figure out how to structure all that [big] data and get it in a format where you can analyze it, and it takes a lot of time and effort to get the data into useful rows and columns. Even once it is structured, it is not easy to analyze, for example, the meaning of people's comments on social media or in blogs or customer reviews. [...] computers are totally incapable of detecting sarcasm."*

Search queries, however troublesome they may be to get right, should not be static in time. Every-day patterns appear in the output batch file of the query delivered by the automated news search through the external provider. Repeating patterns of particular false positives may invite further refinement of the query. A typical ratio between valuable data points and false positives would be 1:10. This means that the query search initially uncovers ten times more results than are ultimately sorted out for filing in the database.

Part of the reason for this high ratio is the dispersion of news. A press release issued by a large competitor may easily be picked up by ten or more newspapers. To avoid information overload in the system, only the most relevant and differentiating press coverage will be included in the database along with the original press release. The other hits do not add additional value and will not be covered. For this reason alone, a fully automated system that populates a qualitative database without human involvement is not yet believed to be economically feasible. What does already work relatively well to reduce the 'query-output to database inclusion ratio' are NLP queries related to unique names – those of companies, countries, brands, chemical compounds, etc. What is more challenging still is to minimize false positives that relate to taxonomy terms that are more descriptive.

NLP is also increasingly applied to extract patterns for social media-sourced sentiment analysis, for research related to corporate reputation or to brands. From a corporate perspective, these are relatively defensive applications: such tools are designed to provide early warnings of sudden marketplace sentiment issues that, when not acted upon immediately, may go viral and affect a company's reputation. The use of such early-warning tools is technically possible in a strategic analysis context, for example for ongoing tracking of a competitor's brand performance. In my experience, it has proven extremely challenging to turn data obtained in this manner into actionable corporate intelligence. That may of course change in the future.

## ADDING METADATA TO SELECTED DATA-POINTS

The taxonomy-based thesaurus provides the search terms for the online search query described above. As a result, a hit that is caught as a potentially valuable fish in the output of the query process is immediately linked to the thesaurus-based metadata that occurred in the text of the data-point that caused the hit in the first place. The benefits of the consistency that the thesaurus provides are obvious. IT solutions allow titles, publication dates, teasers and to some extent source types to be extracted from a data-point, filling the corresponding qualitative database metadata fields for this data-point automatically.

## FILING A DATA-POINT WITH A METADATA SET IN THE QUALITATIVE DATABASE

At present, I believe a human touch is still needed to approve an automatically collected/selected data point (like a clipping) to be included in the qualitative database for sharing on the corporate intranet. The automatically generated metadata (including title, source type, publication date, etc.) are (or certainly should be) automatically added to the corresponding database file.

There are four more features of an integrated qualitative database system that are based on the same taxonomy thesaurus. The system should:

i. Permanently disseminate email alerts based on tailored user-defined alerts.
ii. Permanently update 'insight' excerpts from the database, featured in the knowledge management system that serves as the database's user interface.
iii. Create intra-company 'human source' suggestions.
iv. Create intra-company 'common interest communities.'

## AUTOMATICALLY ALERTING USERS TO NEW NEWS

As the taxonomy has been defined with corporate strategy, its dimensions align directly with assigned responsibilities of individual staff. When, for instance, a sales manager is responsible for a key account and for a category, taxonomy-based data-point segmentation allows selection of all new data points that match the responsibilities (and thus likely the interests of) that manager.

Turning this feature into a user benefit, a good database system allows all users to select metadata that represent the news that they need in an unlimited number of self-defined queries. The functionality to install new, and edit or delete existing, user queries is self-explanatory and would typically appear on the home page of the intranet-based system.

A side benefit of having set up such system is that news subscription costs may also be reduced. Although that may be a nice side-effect, this has never been the key driver for setting up this process.

## CREATING AND PERMANENTLY UPDATING PREDEFINED SEARCH REPORTS

On the one hand, a user can extract their own need-to-know data points (clippings, reports, etc.) from the database by using taxonomy terms, possibly in combination with free-text search terms. This was presented above when the deal between Mr Cheesehunter and Mr Jones was discussed.

On the other hand, having a taxonomy in place also allows for another feature to be added of the qualitative database: the creation of permanently updated predefined, clearly displayed reports. The system, using predefined searches, in that case offers continually updated 'standard' reports. An example of a set of standard reports would be a feature called, 'company insight'. Here a user could select any company that is covered in the system as a taxonomy term, such as:

- Carrefour
- Tesco
- Walmart
- Auchan
- Nestlé

If Nestle were chosen the system would automatically generate several parallel database search results. Each search would give a list of individual data-points in the database, presented with the most recent one featured on top of the list:

- News — newspaper, magazine, trade journal articles where Nestlé is a metadata term.
- Press releases — press releases issued by Nestlé (including those of companies that Nestlé acquired, like Purina or Wyeth Nutrition).
- Reports — annual reports issued by Nestlé (including those of companies that Nestlé acquired in the past).
- Analyses — third party analyses of Nestle, as well as the company's own, internal analyses, provided they don't reveal confidential information.[7]

The system, based on the taxonomy, does not only offer such 'insight' pages for companies but also for countries, categories, etc.

These pre-set, continually updated 'insight' pages offer additional convenience to the user, guided as they are by the strategy-based taxonomy.

## CREATING INTRA-COMPANY HUMAN SOURCE SUGGESTIONS

A pre-condition for analyzing news alerts from individual staff is ensuring compliance with applicable privacy laws and the explicit consent of the contributing employees. Assuming both have been secured, it is acceptable and potentially useful at the strategic analysis function level to see which users have subscribed to which taxonomy-related 'news preference' terms.

Implicit in a user requesting ongoing updates on a particular topic is that such news is of particular importance to that person. The user's interest itself may prove to be a gold mine from a strategic analysis perspective: people usually want to know a lot about things they already know a lot more about. Employees who explicitly request regular news feeds on a topic may in fact be great sources of data on that topic.

In settings where a knowledge management system struggles to get people to dedicate time to actively contribute knowledge, the selection of taxonomy terms for the intra-company news service leaves a great footprint of an individual's interests, needs and desires and by default the possibility that they're a source of valuable knowledge.

Subject to privacy law compliance and the concerned individual's consent, the taxonomy-based thesaurus thus also unlocks in-company sources to be tapped for strategic analysis purposes. Fillié reports that the 'Who Knows What' feature is indeed a recent addition to many qualitative data management systems (Fillié, 2010).

## CREATE INTRA-COMPANY 'COMMON INTEREST COMMUNITIES'

After identifying employees with knowledge on specific topics, the analysis staff might make contact with them, and as they become aware of common interests elsewhere in the company, make people aware of like-minded co-workers. The strategic analysis function may do so by creating 'common interest communities' across different business units, lining similar interest and expertise profiles. There is much to be gained in connecting people for their expertise.

One approach could be for the strategic analysis function to create such a community as a spin-off of a specific demand-driven project. For example, when a profile of a firm that competes against several of your company's business units is going to be updated, a taxonomy-driven email alert could be used to invite the relevant community of common interest to a planning session. When, during such a meeting staff from different business units discover each other's expertise, the connections will be secured. Following that initial bonding experience, employees will invariably reach out on their own to others who'd demonstrated their interest and expertise in a given area.

To conclude this section, Diagram 19.3 visually summarizes what's involved in maintaining an integrated qualitative data management system and the roles such a database plays in news distribution and file retrieval. The analysts' tasks that are depicted are recurring; another recurring analyst task is the ongoing improvement of the taxonomy-based query in the 'unstructured sources'. The tasks related to the one-off definition of the taxonomy and the system at large have not been depicted.

The substantial, continuous 'fresh' data-point inputs flow in at the bottom-left of the diagram. At the bottom-centre the 'industry-specific sources' news and information flows in. In the bottom-right the 'dropbox' is depicted, where internal staff can drop data points that they want included in the system. All three in-flows are filtered (manually) by an analyst. The output of the filtration step forms the input of the metadata tagging step. The output of the metadata tagging step is then fed into the 'robot' that checks whether a new data-point that entered the system matched a predefined user search query. If so, the involved user will receive an automatically generated email. Once the 'robot' has been passed, those data points for which copyright-based distribution rights have been acquired are, depending on the copyright agreement, temporarily or permanently stored in the database. The database is the core of the system, generating the permanently updated 'latest news' as well permanently actualized 'insight reports'. It is also the port of call for user search queries, involving taxonomy-based searches, free-text searches or mixed searches. Based on the database of user email alert profiles, potential human sources may be identified by taxonomy term. Users with common search interest may be connected in communities. In the following diagram, MI stands for market intelligence, the currency of strategic analysis.

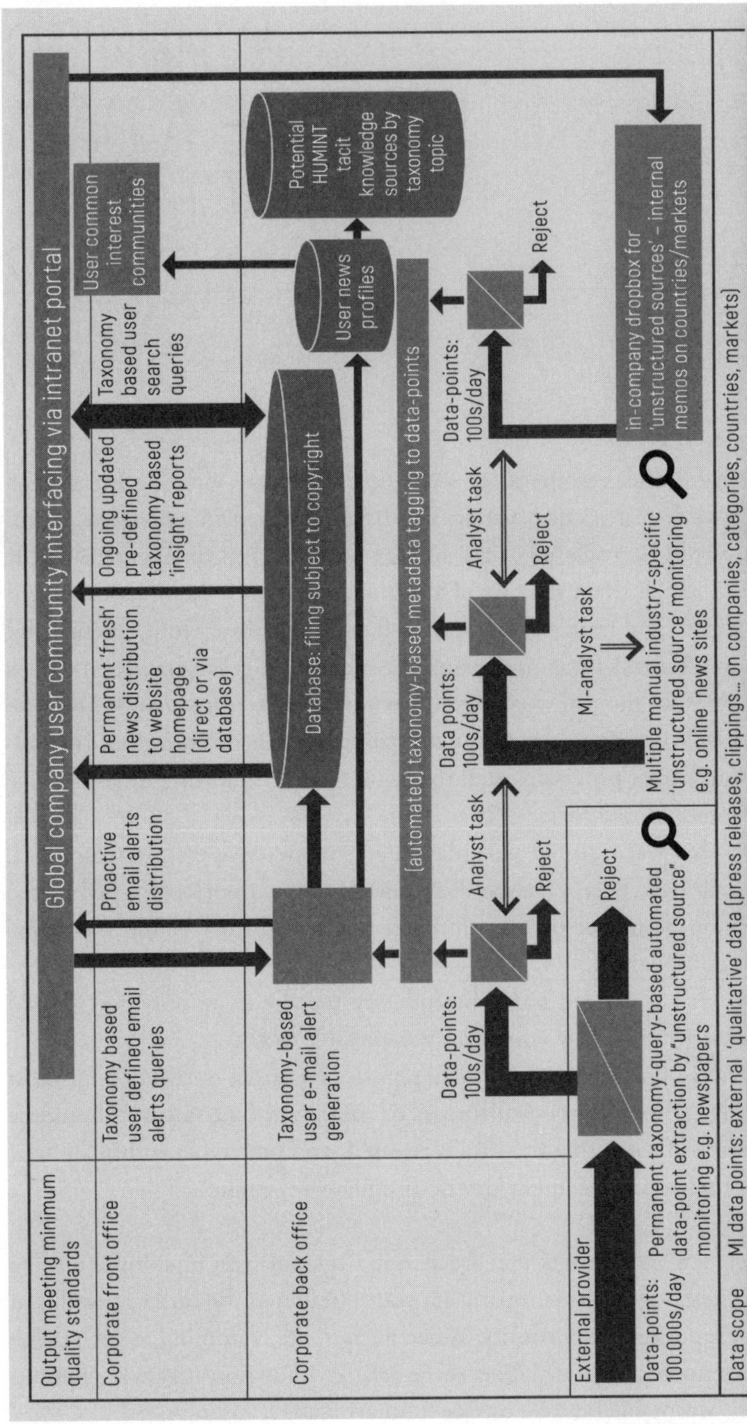


**DIAGRAM 19.3 ▶▶ PROCESSES ASSOCIATED WITH OPERATING AN INTEGRATED QUALITATIVE DATA MANAGEMENT SYSTEM**

# 19.5 WHEN TO OPERATE A DATA MANAGEMENT SYSTEM?

In an ideal world, resources for strategic analysis are virtually infinite. In such a world, this section would not have appeared in this book, as resources would be available to file all data-points in real time, especially the large numbers of them that are of a qualitative nature. The function would simply recruit and train enough staff to handle peak load requirements, and be able to offer real-time intelligence the moment it get its hands on a mass of data. Alas, in the real world resources are far from infinite and the above scenario is but a pipe dream. What a company can do, however, is to recruit enough data-processing staff to ensure that the following time-sensitive quality standards are met:

i. News that was featured yesterday in general newspapers and magazines, and will have been a Yahoo! headline before you got out of bed in the morning should be on your intranet bright and early (subject to copyright compliance).
ii. News that is offered today by industry-specific news providers should likewise be posted by you as early as possible today.
iii. Quarterly, half-yearly and annual reports of a dozen or two of your most important competitors, customers or suppliers of a company should be out the same day that the data is released (and preferably within an hour after their announcement-day news embargoes expire).

All other new data points that reach a strategic analysis function are to be filed and released to the company via your intranet at the earliest possible at the earliest possible opportunity. When analysts are cramming to get a deliverable out under a tight deadline, some delay in filing non-urgent data points is usually acceptable (and let us face it, unavoidable).

## 19.6 WHO IS TO RUN THE DATA MANAGEMENT SYSTEM?

This question of where to host a quantitative or a qualitative data management system has two possible answers: *roll your own* or outsource it. There is no right or wrong answer.

### QUANTITATIVE 'SMALL DATA' USUALLY START OUT BEING HOSTED INTERNALLY

Especially in a start-up phase of a strategic analysis function, the best option for filing quantitative data from multiple sources is usually a do-it-yourself solution, designed by the function itself. The first quantitative data warehouse is likely to be a spreadsheet, stored in a corporate SharePoint-based intranet environment to facilitate collaborative use of the most recent version, accessible by multiple employees simultaneously. The function has exclusive administrator rights, offering 'read-only' access for a select group of need-to-know users, whilst maintaining 'read-and-write' rights to the function's analysts. The Excel program has multiple options to analyse data that will usually meet all such needs.

There are two reasons to move beyond the off-the-shelf spreadsheet to a higher level of professionalism, which may include outsourcing the quantitative data warehouse to a specialized web-based IT provider.

The first catalyst would be that your data warehouse content morphs from small to big data. Sharepoint is a great environment for sharing very small data, and spreadsheets work well with medium-sized data, but neither program was designed to handle moderately large (say 100GB) to very large (nosing up into petabyte territory) data.

This first reason usually is not the most urgent one, as an analysis function strives to become more professional and the quantity of data crunched in its analyses skyrockets. The more common reason to justify a move to a tailored quantitative data warehouse tool (that might be outsourced) is that your customers start being offered to – or, better yet, begin requesting – online quantitative reports.

The graphics update functions of mass-market spreadsheet tools may not meet a increasingly professional function's standards. Dedicated tools, both for the data warehouse as such, and for enhanced data visualization may be needed. The latter requirement alone may justify outsourcing quantitative data warehouse hosting.

## QUALITATIVE DATABASES ARE AVAILABLE OFF-THE-SHELF, INCLUDING OUTSOURCED HOSTING

When a strategic analysis function takes the initiative to set up a permanent news (and background info) monitoring and filing process, the information-sharing tool to support it is critical. Rather than start with some home-built Sharepoint application, it makes sense to immediately turn to a third-party vendor.

A Sharepoint application may satisfy your initial needs, but the time will quickly come when Sharepoint limitations related to database size start to kick in. Sharepoint has an additional drawback. Building versatile user navigation capabilities into the database is feasible in Sharepoint, but such tailoring may not automatically be version-upgrade compliant. That means that with every (major) Sharepoint version upgrade, the user interface may need to be redefined as well, which can become rather costly. For this reason, some corporate IT departments in companies don't even allow tailored solutions on top of Sharepoint. With an abundance of off-the-shelf tools in the marketplace, there is readily available technology that would allow an analysis function to buy straight into a learning curve rather than work up through it. Moreover, such suppliers usually also offer to maintain the news content for their customers, even further lowering the threshold to set up and operate a qualitative (market intelligence) database.

## 19.7 WHO SHOULD BE PROVIDED WITH ADMINISTRATION RIGHTS?

It is important to carefully select the person or persons to whom writing and filing into the database is entrusted. A brief excursion into government intelligence history proves that point. A sole filing clerk caused what may well be the single largest leak in Soviet KGB history (Andrew, 2001c). For twelve years, by being his inconspicuous self, Vasili Mitrokhin fooled the KGB security system when, whilst working at the archive, he smuggled copies of KGB files of up to the highest secrecy classifications home with him. Mitrokhin had become disillusioned with the system. He wanted to show the West how thin the thread of peace had been during the Cold War. The files ultimately where delivered to British intelligence and became known as the Mitrokhin archive. Disillusionment with the system, either corporate or political, often drives a shift in peoples' loyalty.

The message here is that there is merit in treating the strategic analysis function staff entrusted with the responsibility for data processing very well. Such staff members have seen all there is to know about the industry the firm is operating in. Losing them to a competitor entails losing invaluable industry insights that may well underpin a firm's competitive edge.

It pays for a strategic analysis function to clearly define a governance structure for filing qualitative and quantitative data. Table 19.1 below lays out a possible structure. In Table 19.1 five different classes of company staff are differentiated, each with a different authority level. These include the:

- Data processing staff with administrator rights.
- Strategic analysis function head.
- Super-user.
- Top executive.
- Regular user.

The data processing staff and usually the function head have full 'writing' rights. These staff members have the clearance to approve a data-point for inclusion in the database. One or two data processing staff even have a higher authority level: they have as administrators the right to change other staff's authority levels. Selected super-users of the database may have partial yet exclusive 'writing' rights. These super-users are often strategic analysis staff themselves. They have for example the exclusive right to add or change metadata details to particular data points concerning their speciality. They may, however, not have the right to upload new data-points. The latter may sound unduly bureaucratic but does help to keep a database as clean as possible, by at a central level preventing the entry of double data-point records. Facing the prospect of crippling data overload, restricting the unbridled uploading of data is not a luxury. Rather, it is the core thought behind building one's own database: to minimize false positives and beat just 'Googling' for data by offering more relevant, accurate and complete hits to any search run on the database. The regular user, not even the CEO, gets authority to write in the database; consistency before rank.

| STAFF CATEGORY | AUTHORITY TO CHANGE OTHER STAFF'S AUTHORITY IN THE DATABASE | AUTHORITY TO UPLOAD NEW DATA-POINT RECORDS | AUTHORITY TO SELECTIVELY ADD METADATA TO EXISTING DATA-POINT RECORDS |
|---|---|---|---|
| Administrator (often also data processing staff) | √ | √ | |
| Strategic analysis function head | | √ | |
| Super-user | | | √ |
| Top executive | | | |
| Regular user | | | |

TABLE 19.1 ▶▶▶ POSSIBLE AUTHORITY STRUCTURE FOR MANAGING (QUALITATIVE) DATABASES

# 19.8 WHO TO ADMIT ENTRY?

At least some of the data points in the strategic analysis function's possession inevitably need a secrecy classification. Even when strategic analysis is concerned with the business environment of a firm and is working solely on publicly available data, some analyses may reveal sensitive conclusions that your company does not want widely disseminated. Unless consciously deciding otherwise, analysts should consider defaulting to a secrecy classification on all data, and particular the qualitative variety.

Classifying data-points into different secrecy categories has at least one similarity with defining taxonomies: it came in use long before data-points were digitalized. The SIS (the predecessor to the British foreign intelligence service MI6) in 1922 defined a classification system (Jeffery, 2011e). The SIS linked secrecy to potential value and expected reliability of the data that was classified.

In general, the value of knowledge dissemination is not to be underestimated (Silver, 2013j). The extraordinary global economic growth that started in the Eighteenth Century was certainly linked to the invention and distribution of the printing press and to the Industrial Revolution. Silver's thesis is that in the absence of knowledge sharing, value creation is impeded. This thesis supports the call for setting up data management systems that are openly shared across a company. Taking this thesis one step further, it also calls for a restrictive attitude towards unduly classifying data as secret.

As a result, it's difficult to find a reasonable balance between the need for secrecy and creating value by facilitating data flow through a company. How do you gauge how much commercially sensitive data to share with how many people on your staff, when you know that a percentage of them will eventually pursue greener pastures with your fiercest competitors?

In the corporate strategic analysis practice, three secrecy classification levels are generally enough to address this challenge. The following classification levels are recommended:

i. Secret: circulation limited to need-to-know staff and top executives only.
ii. Classified: wider circulation than secret, but not unlimited.
iii. Unrestricted: free flow within the company, in principle to all company staff.

Table 19.2 provides recommended authority levels for different in-company staff.

| STAFF CATEGORY | AUTHORITY TO CHANGE OTHER STAFF'S AUTHORITY IN THE DATABASE | AUTHORITY TO READ 'SECRET' DATA POINTS | AUTHORITY TO READ 'CLASSIFIED' DATA-POINTS | AUTHORITY TO READ 'UNRESTRICTED' DATA-POINTS |
|---|---|---|---|---|
| Administrator (often also data processing staff) | √ | √ | √ | √ |
| Strategic analysis function head | | √ | √ | √ |
| Super-user | | | √ | √ |
| Top executive | | √ | √ | √ |
| Regular user | | | | √ |

TABLE 19.2 ▶▶▶ AUTHORITY STRUCTURE FOR READING IN (QUALITATIVE) DATA MANAGEMENT SYSTEMS

CHAPTER 20

# ORGANIZING A STRATEGIC ANALYSIS FUNCTION

# 20.1 INTRODUCTION

The aim of strategic analysis is to deliver quality deliverables that are accepted – and acted upon, with positive results – by decision-makers. When it achieves this goal, the analysis function can contribute significantly to the company's fortunes. In doing so, it also secures its own continuity, but that should never be a leading consideration. Analysts are still human, for the time being anyway, and some effort needs to be invested in organizing for analysis. According to recent research, getting the organization right is a challenge.

In a 2015 McKinsey survey, 519 executives representing the full range of regions, industries and company sizes reported that organizations pursue data and analytics activities for a variety of reasons (Brown, 2016). But:

> *"[…]companies have found mixed success: 86 percent of executives say their organizations have been at best only somewhat effective at meeting the primary objective of their data and analytics programs, including more than one-quarter who say they've been ineffective. […] the low-performer executives say their biggest challenge is designing the right organizational structure to support analytics."*

This conclusion should not come as a surprise. Harvard Business School icon Michael Porter pointed out in the 1980s why organization in strategic analysis should not be neglected (Porter, 2004):

> *"Analyzing competitors is too important to handle haphazardly."*

Reading this chapter will allow you to avoid just that: creating a haphazardly organized strategic analysis group. In this chapter we'll take a look at which sorts of organizations stand to best serve your company's analysis needs. In the end, the very nature of your firm's strategic analysis needs will define how you set up your analysis function.

# 20.2 HOW TO GET STARTED?

## THE GO-AHEAD: SETTING UP A STRATEGIC ANALYSIS FUNCTION IS A LONG-TERM CHOICE

Strategic analysis as a function in a company is normally established when:

- A management team identifies business environment analysis needs that are perceived to be unmet; the team faces challenges it lacks the information and insights to cope with.
- A decision is made to create an analysis function internally, rather than outsourcing it to a vendor.

The need to set up this function often arises out of the execution of a formal strategy process, for example the writing of marketing plan where a lack of understanding of the business environment is discovered. Strategic analysis after all is a specialized discipline that cannot just be undertaken by any marketing executive. In response, a decision is taken to structurally execute strategic analysis tasks within a company. Subsequently, the responsibility for the task is assigned to one or more individuals, sometimes only as a part-time role. In response, a strategic analysis department is born. All this talk about the need for an analysis group may sound exaggerated when, in the beginning, the work probably only takes a single employee a few hours a week to polish off. Technically, however, the amount of resources dedicated to strategic analysis is immaterial to the fact that it is recognized as a must-have function in a company, or in a sub-section of a larger unit of the company.

A management team choosing to embed strategic analysis as a function in their organization is advised to take a long-term view. Strategic analysis is not an undertaking to set up one year, run for a second year, shut down in year three, and have a new management restart it again in year four. If you'll pardon the cliche, an analysis group can be like a fine wine; it gets better when given time to mature. To a management team that in essence only has a one-off (or short-term) strategic analysis need, outsourcing the requirement is almost by definition the better option.

Research firm M-Brain reported in a survey of 989 respondents, evenly distributed around the world, that 76% of all surveyed companies/units had a strategic analysis function in place (GIA, 2011). This suggests that most larger companies have progressed beyond an initial kickoff phase with their strategic analysis program. The survey was perhaps slightly biased towards companies that already had some basic function in place. Even so, a substantial number of companies have not yet established such a function.

## START WITH DEDICATED STAFF ASSIGNED TO STRATEGIC ANALYSIS

Shared responsibility is no responsibility, as no single individual can be held accountable. This universal truth is applicable to organizing a strategic analysis function. When the size of the business does not immediately justify appointing a full-time equivalent staff member, the responsibility for strategic analysis may well be combined with the responsibility for other back-office tasks. A common approach is to combine strategic analysis with consumer (market) research, with internal or external communications or with public affairs. These functional disciplines require a similar type of personality and have similar job dynamics. In these roles, control over the agenda is relatively more in the hands of the individual staff person than is the case in front-office functions. In contrast, in sales the ethos is entirely target-driven, with the prioritization and timing of everything continually set and re-set by demanding customers.  In the hit-and-run world of sales, you live and die monthly numbers.

Allocating strategic analysis to someone as a part-time role alongside a demanding front-office job (such as sales or customer service) is a sure-to-fail choice. The high priority (but relatively low-importance) tasks of day-to-day sales administration and sales ops will constantly disrupt the lower priority (but strategically more important) analysis work. As a result, the strategic analysis output will rarely amount to more than situation reporting. Moreover, a person who gets his adrenaline rush from hit-and-run sales work will rarely be a discerning, uncertainty-loving analyst, working quietly on a complex puzzle.

This also means that a competitor-monitoring gatekeeper model in a business team is neither desirable nor effective. A business that faces ten major competitors should not disperse the responsibility to 'keep track of' these competitors across ten different operational managers. Below are just a few of the reasons why it's less than optimal to have each of those ten managers half-heartedly track a different customer and report back once or twice a year on developments:

- When such managers do a fine job with their primary responsibilities, but ignore the competitor monitoring, no senior executive will truly push them to do their strategic analysis homework. In other words, they will get away with ignoring it
- Even when the gang of ten all start with the same template for monitoring a competitor, chances are they will each deliver different outputs in terms of quality, interpreting template topics differently, etc. Their wildly differing outputs will likely be so informal and unstructured and as to render them unactionable.
- None of these executives spends enough time on strategic analysis to become truly good at it, so no matter how effective they may be in their day jobs, most will be amateurs in strategic analysis. Tenure tends to positively correlate with strategic analysis output quality.
- No cross-competitor insight will be gained because ten uncoordinated players will each be focused on a single competitor, rather than collaboratively cross-referencing their find.

Strategic analysis is a functional specialty, just like HR, finance or law. A company wouldn't spread its ten most pressing lawsuits across ten managers, each responsible for a single case, right? Research by M-Brain indeed indicates that in 2005, about 90% of all their globally surveyed companies had appointed a dedicated staff member to strategic analysis (GIA, 2005). This is a global best practice. When starting your journey in strategic analysis I recommend you adhere to it.

## CHERISH CHAMPIONS TO GET STRATEGIC ANALYSIS THROUGH THE DIP

In the early phase of setting up a strategic analysis function, its cash flow will be negative. Money will be expended, but tangible outputs that lead to actionable intelligence or help mitigate risks opportunities or mitigating or controlling risks will yet be few. This period forms the fundamental of a management team's commitment to maintain the function.[1]

The dynamics of starting up an analysis function in an organization have been well described (Godin, 2007). Godin phrases it so well:

> *"At the beginning, when you first start something it's fun. You could be taking up golf or acupuncture or piloting a plane or doing chemistry – doesn't matter; it's interesting, and you get plenty of good feedback from people around you. Over the next few days and weeks, the rapid learning you experience keeps you going. Whatever your new thing is, it's easy to stay engaged in it. And then the Dip happens. The Dip is the long slog between starting and mastery. A long slog that's actually a shortcut, because it gets you where you want to go faster than any other path. [...] At trade shows, you see dozens of companies trying to break into an industry. They've invested time and money to build a product, to create a marketing organization and rent booth space – all in an attempt to break into a lucrative market. A year later, most of them don't return. They're gone, unable to get through the Dip."*

## TAKE YOUR TIME

The previous section emphasized the need to deliver results quickly and to build a solid base of champions for the analysis function. However, building such a group doesn't happen overnight. Don't expect enthusiastic support or exuberant contributions early on. This is especially true when building a network of human sources, both within and outside the company.[2] Requesting that others in your firm embrace strategic analysis requires them to accept the notion that this new function is in place and that it now delivers analyses. Change happens in phases. It starts with awareness. So in the first few months, awareness-building work is key. Why will strategic analysis allow your colleagues to arrive at better decisions, and do so faster? What will strategic analysis contribute and by when? And, just as importantly, what won't it contribute? What instruments need to be used to make people aware of all the good you can do? Who has to be talked to first? Who is an opinion leader, whom once in the camp of strategic analysis, will be the ambassador to tout your message. Strategic analysis may initially be perceived as another overhead function that promises to conjure up insights that managers intuitively already had.

There is a catch here: don't over-communicate. There is a need to search for balance. It is great when strategic analysis awareness covers your firm like an oil spill. The film, however, shouldn't be spread too thin. Awareness that you've arrived on the scene should be backed up rapidly with a library of case studies demonstrating concrete, tangible, immediate contributions of strategic analysis work to business decision-making. Filling up that library also should be on the calendar. There is no magic ratio for the time spent on building awareness and building up your case library. The ratio depends on the size of the company and the scope of the strategic analysis function that is being introduced. In a relatively small, organizationally flat company, based in a single country, awareness-building may be relatively straightforward. In a diversified, organizationally complex, truly global business, it will take more time and considerably greater effort.

## PROPOSE A REALISTIC BUDGET

The ultimate proof of commitment in a corporate environment is budget allocation (more later on executing your new group's first-ever strategic analysis plan). Many managers will pay lip service to how relevant strategic analysis is in an organization, but how many are really prepared to earmark a tangible figure in their budget for the out-of-pocket cost and staff expenses?

The previously mentioned M-Brain survey also touched on the size of corporate analysis budgets (GIA, 2011). The conclusion was that a company's median budget was €357,000 per year (including staff cost), whereas the weighted average was about €1 million (including staff cost). The median net sales of the surveyed companies was some €2.5 billion/year and the weighted average was €11 billion. This suggests strategic analysis requires a typical budget of 0.01-0.02% of net sales.[3]

For a smaller company, there is a minimum threshold below which any spending is probably not useful. A unit of a company, or a smaller company, should not start strategic analysis work when it is not prepared to dedicate at least 0.4 full-time staff member to it, with at least about €100,000 a year to spend on buying subscriptions to news services, journals, reports, key web databases, etc. Spending less will unlikely lead to actionable strategic analyses of sufficient quality.

The history of MI6 as told in public literature presents two views. When Winston Churchill in 1919, facing the aftermath of the First World War, learned about a budget cut proposal for MI6, he reacted as follows (Milton, 2014):

> *"With the world in its present condition of extreme unrest and changing friendships and antagonisms...it is more than ever vital for us to have good and timely information."*

This quote is immediately applicable to today's business world, or so it seems. In the corporate environment, however, overhead cuts are just as common as government budget cuts intelligence are in the military, are after a war. A level-headed view of intelligence budgets remains helpful (Jeffery, 2011g):

> *"[there are] twin permanent and unchanging truths about intelligence: that, no matter what the circumstances, there is never enough money; and equally, no matter how much information is provided; there is never enough of it."*

The ideal tone of the pitch for a strategic analysis function to 'sell the budget' depends on the personal needs of the executive who ultimately would provide the funding. Some executives are more risk averse. They may feel better when spending on strategic analysis is positioned as paying for fire insurance for your corporate cash flows. Others may be more entrepreneurial. They may be triggered to sign off on the decision by focusing on the opportunities strategic analyses may discover, or conversely the opportunities lost when strategic analysis is not being executed. The rationale and tone should of course match with the initiatives planned for the new year. The best strategic analysis budget is the one about which executives only wonder: 'is that enough?'

## UNDER-PROMISE/OVER-DELIVER

In laying the groundwork, subtly map the group's initial needs (and projected ability to help with) the specific needs of key budgeting executives. But tread lightly; in order to quickly build a happy initial customer base there's serious risk in over-promising too many people too much too soon. One of the most widely applicable versions of Murphy's Laws reads: 'if you try to please everybody, nobody will like it'. When business executives mention strategic analysis problems they would like to see resolved, the problems are more than likely to be more complex than they look. Had these problems been easy, they would have already been resolved. Underestimating complexity equates to underestimating the upcoming workload of the strategic analysis staff. With a fixed number of strategic analysis staff, this either means underestimating the time of delivery or timely delivery of a sub-par deliverable. The best deliverables are timely, accurate and complete. When you are still in the first year of building the function's reputation, it makes sense, as possible, to only take on work from customers that can reasonably get done in a timely manner. I would also only offer quality standards that are (realistically) attainable. When the deliverables subsequently are provided before agreed deadlines and the quality of the deliverables consistently exceeds expectations, the function's reputation gradually builds. Manage expectations from day one – and regularly exceed them wherever possible.

## LOOK FOR SYNERGY IN THE STRATEGIC ANALYSIS PORTFOLIO

When toiling under the constraints of a tight budget, it can be both challenging and, in a way, exciting to make the most of every dollar spent. The trick is to create a portfolio of assignments and a structured data and analysis-filing system that allows for the creation of internal cost synergies. In summary: collect once, use (sell) thrice and do not reinvent the wheel.

In carefully plotting out a new analysis function's initial portfolio of projects, be sure to populate the calendar with activity that:

- Addresses a direct (burning) business need.
- Is opportunity/upside-driven rather than geared towards risk-mitigation.
- Is realistically doable, with a high probability of success.
- Promises to deliver a result reasonably quickly.

The first projects that are executed make or break the perception of the analysis operation's value. Ensure the projects work out well not only for the your internal customers but also for the department's image.

## START SMALL, THINK BIG

Building on the previous recommendation of maximizing output per unit of input, let me repeat how important it is to begin with the end-game in mind. The foundations of the back-office collection and filing flows (see chapter 19) in particular need to be designed correctly right out of the starting gate. Ensure that any system solution that is chosen is scalable on the key content dimensions. At the start, it is hard to imagine that one day the system may contain over 100,000 different documents that all need to be easily retrievable based on either a metadata profile, or through searching for a text string, or be mined using natural language processing.

For strategic analysis projects, the recommendation for the first year is most of all to learn by doing. Consider engaging in pilot projects with a limited scope and a single customer first. Once the learning curve has been surmounted alongside an understanding and positive customer, a flawless roll-out of the project to less understanding and less-than-positive customers is the next step.

## INTEGRATE AND CONNECT

No man is an island. Thus, the back-office strategic analysis department should not become an island. When setting up your operation in a country- or category-organization of a larger company, or in a decentralized company, ensure that it becomes integrated into the rest of the organization. In a country or category unit, strategic analysis in most cases will connect best with the sales and marketing staff.

An easy first step for a strategic analyst is to get invited to regularly-scheduled sales or marketing meetings. As the analyst, listen in on the discussions. Learn where your firm competes with which competitors for what orders. Understand the benefits and features that allow your sales colleagues to win and how competitors gain an upper hand. What makes the difference? Why? How can your analyses help further your company's advantage?

Being present in a low-profile way allows you to monitor the business environment as the sales and marketing staff see it. Apart from one-on-one discussions with the company's senior-most executives, there's no better way to flesh-out an analysis team's project portfolio. Come to be seen as a smart, trusted, collaborative partner who's there to help the sales and marketing organizations win. With that trust in place, the function becomes the focal point for tacit knowledge collection, analysis and, most of all, dissemination. This may sound simple, but don't underestimate the time, study, planning and effort necessary to build bridges, gain trust and become a valued member of the bigger team.

Forging the human connection is critical to gaining trust. Trust precedes sharing. Tyson emphasizes that a strategic analyst may easily spend 80% of his time on the people side of connecting and sharing and perhaps 20% on the IT systems side of sharing (Tyson, 1995).

Sharing unfortunately may be counter-intuitive in a great many organizations. The paragraph below explains why getting people to share isn't always the easiest thing to accomplish(Cusack, 2010):

*"Access to information is the currency of intelligence. Both analysts and organizations are sometimes reluctant to share an insight with others not in their fiefdom because it may be replicated with credit and they could lose their perceived value (and funding). Only strong leadership can overcome a basic psychological bias: sharing often requires more work without direct personal reward."*

As a rule, as a strategic analyst you have to give tenfold to sales colleagues what you can reasonably expect to receive back. Don't start to whine about this. Paradoxically, this is actually a good thing. Sales staff should not as a reflex give things away freely. Sellers have been recruited to provide a good or service for a price. Your company can find itself in big trouble if giving comes all too easily for a sales person. Conversely, a predisposition toward giving should be second nature to a successful analyst. Empower the front office staff with easy-to-locate, tailor-made, relevant news and analysis (see chapter 19). An additional benefit is that once the sales staff knows the analyst behind the system, the system insert may actually be trusted and thus used more effectively as well.

The value to the analyst of connecting and sharing is twofold. First, it allows the analyst to build a picture (as complete as possible) of the environment, by encouraging human connections to deliver their tacit knowledge. Second, as an analyst it enables you to connect the dots across business disciplines or even categories/countries. Suddenly, the jumble of data-points that made no sense begins to assemble itself into insight that can drive real, meaningful change. Failing to share facts has been identified as the root cause of significant government intelligence failures.[4] This learning should also apply in business, especially in larger companies. When an analyst can position her group as an internal knowledge broker, its value will grow exponentially.

This reasoning on the relevance of connections is confirmed by research in business. Networking and sharing are even more important than having a bigger budget (GIA, 2011):

*"The best market intelligence programs are not better resourced than the rest but they are closer to management, more networked and more effective."*

It shines a light on the importance of an analysis team being outwardly focused, networked, and truly tapped into the larger organization's goals, methods and activities. With this approach, those outside the analysis group who contribute facts and analysis to the system are consistently recognized. This is indeed good practice. However, the best way to get sales staff to proactively contribute their insights to your analysis work is to deliver analyses that really and truly help them win in the marketplace.

## BUILD A BRAND BUT DO NOT OVERDO IT

It is good practice to support awareness-building by branding your strategic analysis function and its deliverables. Consider defining a creatively playful yet distinguishing small logo that consistently appears on every one of your function's deliverables. Branding helps to build the identity of your function around the key promises that speak to your internal customers. Think of promises like timely, accurate and complete. In FrieslandCoberco Dairy Foods I started off by branding the internal knowledge management system with the tagline *Dairy News and Analysis*, or 'DNA'. The logo was of course a stylized double helix, suggesting that without DNA an organism (in this case, the company) has no future. We went live with DNA in October 2001. By 2015 the system had logged roughly 50,000 discrete visits (on a user base of approximately 8,000) with a typical monthly average of around 1,700 unique users. The consistent but low-key marketing efforts paid off nicely.

In another large food company, the competitive intelligence unit used a picture of a fashionable lady in a trench-coat, wearing a typical 1930s spy hat, wearing sunglasses and carrying binoculars. Clever as that sounds, such type of 007-bravado imagery is probably best avoided. When ethics and compliance are the true, underlying values of a strategic analysis function, as they should be, even a playful hint at espionage tradecraft is inadvisable.

As you've seen throughout this book, strategic analysis in business and government intelligence have multiple methodologies and best practices in common, but legally non-compliant or unethical collection practices are not among them.

## WHEREVER POSSIBLE, CHOOSE YOUR PROJECT BATTLES

As we've made clear, it is important to quickly establish both the credibility and the value of the strategic analysis function. To do this, it is preferable to attract projects that have a quick-win impact and to ensure a balanced portfolio of tasks and projects. Some projects may not have an immediate pay-off but once finished will have disproportional relevance and value. A strategic analyst needs to at all times watch out for 'the tyranny of current intelligence' (Moore, 2007c). This term refers to working exclusively on making sense of current news in support of tomorrow's orders. Happy are the analysts who operate in an environment where executives are hungry for strategic analysis also to look beyond this week's deal-close and the end-of-month revenue roll-up.

## SET YOUR RADAR FREQUENCIES RIGHT

Two pivotal tasks for a new strategic analysis function are to build awareness and help deliver successes. The latter is often linked to solving the initial problem that management faced, which triggered the creation of in-house strategic analysis function in the first place. The initial data and information needs required to execute the first projects drives the search and selection of the first sources. But too often, the process runs in the wrong direction. A subscription-based information source seller stresses the relevance of their offerings. The vendor will position itself as the proverbial hammer, and the analyst as the overwhelmed carpenter with many nails to be pounded. The service provider will convince the analyst that not buying the biggest, best hammer will be downright irresponsible. The vendor will argue that all your competitors are armed with veritable sledgehammers, and that if you aren't sufficiently equipped, you'll be embarrassingly out-hammered. Listen, rookie, have you ever tried to hit a nail with your bare hands?

Buyer beware: information needs, both for projects and for general business environment monitoring, always precede the source selection. Over time, a right-sized network of useful data sources and information collection for both process and project purposes will sort itself out. Don't be talked into buying what you don't need; the right hammer will eventually find its way into your toolbox. Gradually it will also become clear what to look for in a continuous monitoring process (the right radar frequency); this too will come through trial and error.

## ACTIVATE AND PROTECT YOUR SOURCES

Most information sources are not free. And, as I've noted internal human sources (like sales staff) may need to be given ten units of data before they give one piece back. Most external (public) sources may first require payment of a subscription fee. As the analyst goes about her business, networking externally through conferences and elsewhere, she'll connect with a whole host of sources. The protection of these sources is critical. Therefore, as a best practice, a report may contain the cloaked term 'team analysis' as its source. This can be a useful euphemism for a source that may not wish to be connected to a particular data-point. As long as all applicable laws and professional standards are being complied with, a good rule of thumb is to almost always keep your human sources anonymous.

Deutsche Telekom provides a good case study on establishing a human source network for insight into technical innovation (Rohrbeck, 2006). This model might be applied when a set of external human sources is identified that can be helpful with specific structural data monitoring needs.

## MAKE A PLAN

The strategic analysis function needs a plan. It should summarize the function's areas of responsibility over a given period of time (normally a year), its main scheduled activities and, where applicable, the related budget breakdown. Table 20.1 gives an example of a plan for a typical corporate or centralized analysis group. I've called out the following routine responsibilities:

- Permanently monitoring your company's business environment (the radar).
- Disseminating all relevant radar blips as actionable insights.
- Developing and running a project portfolio of strategic analysis tasks and projects. (As discussed above, priority projects must be identified and sufficiently defined before the plan is drawn up.)
- Developing the organizational capability.
- Servicing the organization as a strategic analysis expert in multiple assignments.
- Procuring multiple subscription-based sources.

Demonstrating a track record of early successes and effectively wooing management stakeholders (with one presumably leading to the other) will obviously be critical factors in getting the function's plan approved. As discussed, establishing the relevance of projects to key decision-makers – 'playing to your audience' – will be helpful.

| RESPONSIBILITY AREA | MAIN ACTIVITIES & PLANNED DELIVERABLES | BUDGET INVOLVED IN K€ | KPI | CUSTOMER |
|---|---|---|---|---|
| Monitor business environment | - Quarterly quantitative peer review<br>- Half-yearly qualitative peer review<br>- Continuous updating of news and filing in quantitative/qualitative data warehouse | 400 for data subscriptions<br><br>200 for IT services | y/n | Exec Board All intranet users |
| Execute analysis projects | - Deep-dive on competitor ABC (ready Q2)<br>- Deep-dive on competitor PQR (ready Q4)<br>- Deep-dive on market XYZ (ready Q1)<br>- To-be-determined ad hoc projects | 50 for outsourcing & travel | y/n<br>y/n<br>y/n<br>tbd | BU X<br>BU Y<br>Category Z<br>tbd |
| Develop strategic analysis capabilities | - Deliver four training sessions; include advanced open source data collection<br>- Chair 'best practice exchange forum' in quarterly meetings | 50 for travel and materials | y/n<br>y/n<br>80% of invitees attend | 4 BUs |
| Offer professional services | - Run three wargames | 30 for travel and materials | Average appraisal >4 out of 5 | 3 BUs |
| Coordinate global source subscriptions | - Conclude and sign three-year corporate contracts with yet-to-be-chosen suppliers | | No cost increase | Global company |
| Others / HR / compliance monitoring | - Recruit one junior analyst, ready to start 1 January; update Corporate Code of Ethics for data collection | 30 for recruitment | y/n<br>y/n | |

TABLE 20.1 ▶▶▶ SNAPSHOT OF A STRATEGIC ANALYSIS FUNCTION ANNUAL PLAN (COVERING ONE YEAR'S ACTIVITIES)

## ESTABLISH YOUR POSITION

Once the strategic analysis plan has been approved and the function's position in the organizational chart has been established, it is the analyst's responsibility to maintain, and where needed defend, its position. Although this may sound more aggressive than it is meant to, it's just a kind reminder that responsibilities and authority have been given to the function – and the function should be ready to be held accountable. This may not become an issue, but in a competitive corporate environment questions about various groups' competence, relevance, roles and responsibilities do arise. As a relatively new function, strategic analysis may become embroiled in debates over territory, and who's responsible for what. For example, when does signalling changes in the regulatory arena become a monitoring responsibility for strategic analysis, and when does it remain within the realm of a public affairs department? Similarly, when do changes in consumer trends stop being purely a marketing responsibility and cross over in the analysis group's jurisdiction? And so on.

Before you run for the trenches, consider a lesson I've learned the hard way over the years. To a senior executive, it is usually immaterial who does the work. The executive simply wants the work to be done, and preferably now. Whatever you do, try to always first solve the executive's problem. Once the problem is solved and the time pressure is off, consider how to agree on competency border issues with other departments to avoid the same misery once the next urgent call comes up. There are a few neighbourly ground rules that can help fend off petty disputes with the team down the hall:

(i) Beating a competitor is more useful for value creation (and continued employment) than fighting a colleague.

(ii) Management means getting things done through other people (Peter Drucker).

(iii) Make friends before you need them (as per former NATO Secretary-General Jaap de Hoop Scheffer).

Rule (i) speaks for itself. Competency fights seldom create value – and senior management generally frowns upon all the brawlers, no matter who started it. Rule (ii) is also simple: when a business issue with a strategic analysis dimension can be viewed through different lenses, cooperate with other departments and work together as a team to deliver a common viewpoint. A multi-disciplinary team almost by definition delivers a better deliverable than a one-man band. This links automatically to rule (iii): ensure you develop good relations with other departments before you urgently need them. This is a logical part of the awareness-building work that the strategic analysis function should drive anyway. The time spent on this is bound to pay off well.

## ESTABLISH A MANAGEMENT CONTROL CYCLE

Once the function's plan has been approved, ensure the function not only produces content deliverables but also shows an activity progress report to its sponsors. A well-organized manager will cycle through some version of a *plan-do-check-act* loop. Apply this loop within the function as well. Develop a simple one-page progress report that is, for example, issued quarterly, showing what activity was scheduled for the year, what progress was made, what issues may have emerged, etc. Included in such a report can also be performance measurement statistics reflecting use of internal and external information technology systems (number of unique users per month, total visitors per month, etc.).

## 20.3 STRUCTURE FOLLOWS STRATEGY

Once strategic analysis has been firmly established established in a firm, its usefulness is likely to generate a growing need for analysis. To satisfy such a need, more execution resources may be required. And that can fuel organic growth in both outsourced solutions and the in-house organization itself.

Growth is a great thing, provided it is managed well. As we've discussed, strategic analysis may start with a single individual's part-time work. It can grow over time as that sole provider that forges links with other part of the business, informally building a network of experts, self-starters and self-appointed analysts. Such informal networks can quickly jump borders and go truly international.

Organizational growth goes in stages. Each stage requires a different management focus – and possibly a different management team personality profile. Rarely is the CEO of a large multinational able to drive the growth of a new start-up and vice versa. What applies to organizations at large also applies to organizing the growth of strategic analysis within an organization.

The analyst-pioneer who nurtured a fledgling effort through its baby steps, built initial awareness and realized a first success or two may not be the natural-born leader needed to manage a 10-person strategic analysis department. The world of start-ups is littered with awkward geniuses who don't survive the journey from their cluttered basement workshops to the glass & walnut of the corner office.

What is true for a function leader is equally true for the organization itself within a firm. The structure that worked well in the start-up phase may not be the ideal construct for a mature corporate organization.

## THE RIGHT ORGANIZATIONAL STRUCTURE ENABLES THE MOST EFFICIENT/EFFECTIVE EXECUTION

In 1962, Chandler launched a paradigm that remains useful to this day. He suggested making structure follow strategy (Chandler, 1962). This also applies to setting up and running strategic analysis in a company. Chandler defines strategy as what you aim to do, but most of all what you don't want to do. In enabling you to do what you set out to do, strategy becomes the guiding principle for allocating execution resources. In other words, once the choices have been made (responsibilities, span of authority, deliverables), the structure should enable the work to be executed efficiently and effectively.

In the function plan described in the previous section, the structure for execution has intentionally been kept open. This is partly due to the fact that the quality specifications for the deliverables have not been spelled out. A deep-dive into a market may require anywhere between 150 hours to 1,500 hours of work, subject entirely to the quality specifications set for the effort. Even so, the overall plan may still be executed with equal success through different organization structures. The whole plan may be driven through a central team, servicing various business units as well as the executive board. Similarly, business-unit-specific projects might be executed by decentralized staff who are at best loosely connected through a platform that facilitates the exchange of best practices.

## CENTRALIZED AND DECENTRALIZED STAFF BOTH HAVE THEIR MERITS

To organize strategic analysis in a corporate environment, an almost infinite number of structures is imaginable. An easy way to begin working through structural planning is to sketch out two extreme forms, and an intermediate form, of large company organization models. That exercise might look like this:

- Central — All staff form a single team (often located in a single office) that offers deliverables to the global company.
- Pip — 'Primus inter pares' (abbreviated to pip) is Latin for 'first among equals'. There is a central organization where the most experienced/senior analyst operates: the *primus*. In parallel, there are analysts employed in business units who don't report into the central function's team but reside in a line of the business: the *pares* or peers. The peers are loosely connected to the central team, perhaps through sharing procurement budgets for collection, or through training.

- Decentralized Analysts are appointed in business units as and when the need arises; there is no 'central' coordination and no organized mutual exchange within the company's informally-organized analysis community.

Choosing the right structure for your company's analysis function depends first and foremost on the nature of its analysis needs. Below we will first share a few design principles and subsequently discuss the pros and cons of a centralized or decentralized structure model.

## DESIGN PRINCIPLES FOR CHOOSING YOUR BEST STRUCTURE

The three design principles below may assist in deciding the structure of a strategic analysis function in a firm:

- Follow the money.
- Minimize the distance.
- Need to know.

**Follow-the-money** speaks for itself. Management that pays for strategic analysis as a function has the say over where it is physically based and can prioritize its activities. M-Brain in its surveys of best company practices found that strategic analysis is in most cases set up under strategic planning (GIA, 2005); (GIA, 2011):

| | 2005 | 2011 |
|---|---|---|
| • Strategic planning/business development | 55% | 38% |
| • Sales and marketing | 28% | 37% |
| • Technology and R&D | 10% | 14% |
| • Others | 7% | 11% |

Strategic planning/corporate strategy/business development may over time seem to be losing some of its lead as the most dominant organizational port of call for strategic analysis. Yet, there remains a logical connection.[5] When strategic analysis has a more long-term/strategic focus, corporate strategy prevails; with a shorter-term/tactical focus, the, sales and marketing group is a more logical harbour for the function. Logically speaking, one or the other of these corporate functions would be the natural home for a strategic analysis function.

**Minimize the distance** is another relevant design principle. General Patton stated that plans should be made by those that will execute them (Axelrod, 1999). A strategic analysis plan should be executed as close to the plan makers as possible. Distance should be minimized in at least three dimensions: time, physical presence and psychological connection. A function that is present – as and when the business environment of a company changes – is also front-and-center when senior leaders think on their feet and formulate plans on the go in response to changes. Being there in real time enables strategic analysis to be part of the team, to help address a problem or grasp an opportunity, and thus by default to be part of the business solution. Even in an internet-connected world, physical presence may still make the difference in understanding what a business really needs in terms of analysis, resulting in deliverables that are actionable and that are being acted upon. Being close to the decision-makers may also contribute to the building of psychological trust. This not only leads to the function becoming more of a trusted advisor, but also puts the analysts where they'll hear the rumours the business hears; the staff become part of *us* (in the line business or the functional team) rather than one of *them* from corporate.

**Need-to-know** is another key element to consider. Lines of business may not wish corporate staff departments to know all the details of their operational wrangling, because the moment corporate functions know, control is lost. Corporate may start to think for itself about what the data mean for that unit (and may: may start to interfere in that unit's decision-making). Line managers may not have been recruited for their control-freak tendencies but may at any time become intrusively heavy-handed. A decentralized analysis outfit with a reporting line within the organizational unit is within such a unit's scope of control. A decentralized team may again be perceived as *one of us*. This positive sentiment eases the sharing of data and analysis between the unit's management and its dedicated staff, enhancing the probability that the deliverables are being acted upon. The embedded unit will truly get all the need-to-know data it requires for its work. There is a limit, though. Still, a too-chummy relationship can lead to one of those dreaded psychological biases: groupthink.

In contrast, a corporate strategy-based small analysis unit, a bit detached from the line organization, may more objectively review strategic issues in the light of the holistic interests of the entire company, rather than the parochial interests of an individual business unit. Such a corporate-linked unit may also have a different need-to-know base. This central department may for example be privy to the corporate M&A funnel and plans, which would never be need-to-know if the analysis team resided in a line of business.

## CENTRALIZED FUNCTIONS ARE EFFICIENT, DECENTRALIZED ONES ARE FAST AND ON TOP OF DETAILS

Centralizing and decentralizing staff both have their respective merits. Table 20.2 summarizes the pros and cons by key responsibility (Canadian Land Forces, 2001); (Tyson, 1995); (Philips, 1999); (Gilad, 1988).

| RESPONSIBILITY | CENTRALIZED STRUCTURE | DECENTRALIZED STRUCTURE |
|---|---|---|
| Monitor business environment | - No duplication, efficient.<br>- Critical mass to ensure permanent review of actuality in filing.<br>- Scale to justify IT-systems' cost.<br>- Scope to justify monitoring global trends/competitors. | - Speed of issue identification and issue response due to rapid priority review of staff.<br>- Capture decentralized, tactical human-sourced based news.<br>- Focus on local unit's precise needs based on in-depth understanding (including unit-specific sources).<br>- No language barriers.<br>- No cultural barriers.<br>- Local staff facilitates trust-building with local principals and customers. |
| Execute projects | - Objectivity, limited groupthink risk.<br>- Global scope of thinking, applied to local issue .<br>- Central team may have more diverse and stronger talent pool. | |
| Develop capabilities | - Economy-of-scale (procurement).<br>- Experience in developing tools for multiple contexts. | - Tailor-made for unit's real needs rather than compromise solution that pleases nobody. |
| Offer professional services | - Economy-of-scale.<br>- Experience through frequency of using tools in multiple contexts.<br>- Neutral facilitator: not one of 'us'. | |
| Procure source subscriptions | - Economy-of-scale (procurement).<br>- Contract standardization. | - Tailor-made for unit's real needs (cheap single pop rather than costly corporate subscription). |
| Compliance | - Single undisputed code of ethics. | - Code of ethics harder to develop and implement due to 'loose' structure. |

TABLE 20.2 ▶▶▶ MERITS OF CENTRALIZED AND DECENTRALIZED ANALYSIS STRUCTURE BY RESPONSIBILITY AREA

In conclusion, there is no ideal one-size-fits-all structural model for organizing strategic analysis in a firm. Where synergies arise by combining different analyses – as when different units within a firm have the same competitors or serve the same customers or consumers – it almost by definition calls for shared resources. When lines of business within a firm have highly specific product-market combinations, strategic analysis should be local and tailored. To achieve synergies, it certainly makes sense for methodologies, capabilities, tools, procurement and preferably the sourcing and filing system to be centralized and standardized. Empirical evidence corroborates this assessment: a hybrid pip-model often delivers the best overall results to a company (Brown, 2016).

Execution of projects, however, remains a service to the business principal. Serving the principal's needs is critical to maximizing strategic analyses being used for the furtherance of the goals of the business the analyst serves.

# 20.4 ORGANIZING FOR A GOOD STRATEGIC ANALYSIS TEAM

The evidence that teams outperform individuals is irrefutable, provided a single condition is met: it has to be a good team. First, let's define the word 'good' in this context. The first dimension is behavioural. Having a strong cohesive team may still result in poor decisions if it doesn't capitalize on the diversity of its skills, as it may lapse into groupthink.

A team has good behavioural dynamics when it gets the best out of all members (Lencioni, 2002). The behavioural dimension is truly important.[6] However, covering this fascinating topic in more depth is outside the core scope of this book. Assuming the team's behavioural interaction is positive and strong, there are two other dimensions that need to be managed: the personal and the functional diversity aspects. The section below will elaborate on both.

## DIVERSE MEMBERSHIP STRENGTHENS A TEAM

Let's face it, depending on the age, race, gender, upbringing, cultural background and socio-political disposition of a reader, any discussion of diversity will carry its share of sensitivities. Any normative statement in this field is probably, on some level political. Having acknowledged that, the section below looks at generally accepted views you're likely to find inside a contemporary Western-headquartered company. For that matter, most of this is probably also valid globally. Personal diversity dimensions include:

- Gender.
- Nationality/race.
- Language/culture/religion.
- Age.
- Personality (e.g., introvert versus extrovert).

Functional dimensions, specifically relevant for strategic analysis, include (Philips, 1999):

- Analytic versus collection skills.
- Deliverable content quality versus deliverable acceptance orientation.
- Qualitative versus quantitative orientation.

Two general statements apply. Heterogeneously composed teams tend to outperform teams of homogenous composition. Separately, in most cases teams outperform individuals. A diverse flock of decentralized and independent thinkers who work together will in most cases outperform both a team of groupthinkers and a set of dispersed individuals (Surowiecki, 2005f).

Diversity along the personal and the functional dimension is a must in a strategic analysis team that serves a large (global) company. This applies both when the team is centrally located and when it is decentralized. To build a diverse team, staff with different educational backgrounds should be recruited. Since specific training in strategic analysis is rarely taught in university curricula, recruits may include economists, econometrists, sociologists or anthropologists, political scientists, historians and engineers or scientists. The latter are preferably subject matter experts specializing in business lines the firm operates in.

Diversity along the personal dimension may be accomplished by having at least two long-term senior staff members that have amassed extensive mental libraries of business patterns for quick recognition, interpretation and action. One long-tenured executive is too few; it would make the firm too vulnerable. In parallel, having younger staff is critical in ensuring that the team doesn't miss out on how younger generations think and act. In a multinational company, an equally multi-national team is critical to ensure that language and cultural differences don't create analysis barriers. Collection staff, especially those who are to gather data from human sources need extroverted, sociable attitudes. In contrast, back-office analysts may be introverted, if not even a bit reclusive, and still do a brilliant job. The department head or functional leader has the privilege and the responsibility of defining the diverse team that serves her company best, given its industry sector, geographic reach, business environment and resource constraints.

## TENURE CAUSALLY RELATES TO JOB EXCELLENCE, REQUIRING SMART HR INCENTIVES

Given the fact that strategic analysis is a holistic discipline that sources insights and skills from many different scientific disciplines, it remains a bit of a craft. A craft is learned through experience. There is solid evidence that a longer tenure in this craft leads to objectively better forward-looking intelligence assessments (Economist, 2014); (Mandel, 2014). Experience does build excellence, and excellence breeds success.

Given the importance of experience and craftsmanship, so the importance of building a pupil-master on-the-job training model in a strategic analysis team is evident (Cooper, 2005c). The seniors in the team will not only work on the department's more complex assignments but are also to be held accountable for continuously educating the next generation of collectors, analysts and reporters.

To encourage tenure of the best staff members, a good department head has to convince HR of the need to align personal incentives with long-term company tenure needs. A dual career ladder needs to be defined, similar to that in R&D. In R&D a senior scientist does not need to have many direct reports to still achieve a decent (read: high) job grade. How nice it would be if this were done more often in strategic analysis as well, to help build and sustain crack analysis teams. These last few lines sound simple. This may sound logical enough, but securing attractive compensation and career opportunities for analysts is never a cakewalk (Brown, 2016):

> *"The most significant talent challenges that companies face, according to respondents, are a lack of structured career paths (especially at larger companies) and the inability to compete effectively on salary and benefits."*

A strong strategic analysis leader is a critical asset to not only ensure that the function creates great deliverables, but also that the company creates a context within which great analysts can make it all happen.

## STRATEGIC ANALYSIS IS NOT A NUMBERS' WAR

Strategic analysis not only is a craft, it is also in many ways a competition. Good analyses enable a firm to outsmart its competitors. M-Brain reports that a typical strategic analysis team consists of 13 staff (GIA, 2011). A diverse team of highly qualified staff, does not need to be larger than that to outsmart their competitors. A military example may be helpful to illustrate this. British Second World War military scientific intelligence chief Reginald Jones beautifully summarizes from his experience why I believe a strategic analysis head is to ensure that her department does not get too big (Jones, 1978c and 1978d)

> *"[…] keep the staff to its smallest possible limits […], because the larger the field any one man can cover, the more chance there is of those fortunate correlations which only occur when one brain and one memory can connect two remotely gathered facts. Moreover, a large staff generally requires so much administration that its head has little chance of real work himself, and he cannot therefore speak with that certainty which arises only from intimate contact with the facts. Do as much as the actual Intelligence work yourself as you can; you will find that you can then speak with increased confidence at the highest conferences, which you will certainly be required to do. The fact that you have done much of the work yourself will give you a great advantage."*

There are two messages here. The first message is the relevance of exposure to multiple-source dimensions simultaneously. This text, written more than 70 years ago, implicitly describes what is now known as recognition-primed decision-making. The second message is that a leader of professionals, such as a strategic analysis function head, should aim to do the work themselves. Professionals often have a nasty habit of being meritocratic. For them, reporting to a department head who really and objectively is (among) the best in the discipline is easiest to accept. A boss that is just a boss but isn't seen by the staff as an intellectual peer is going to have a hard time of it. To principals and decision-makers, a strategic analysis function head who is a highly respected professional also adds to their confidence in the function's work, which increases the probability of the function's output being acted upon. (And think of the implications in terms of budget perpetuation, salary hikes, all-around respect and admiration, etc.)

Jones wrote an epilogue to his book, *Most Secret War,* where he reiterates his key messages (Jones, 1978d) as a recommendation to management regarding future intelligence professionals:

> *"Intelligence depends more than anything else on individual minds […], and your organization should only provide a smooth background on which these can operate."*

Creating a diverse team of brilliant individuals is the functional leader's ultimate assignment.

# 20.5 FUNCTIONAL AND BEHAVIORAL ANALYTIC COMPETENCY BUILDING

## FUNCTIONAL AND BEHAVIORAL COMPETENCIES DESERVE TRAINING

As we've alluded to, in contrast to physics or chemistry, strategic analysis is a craft. But the foundation of science is reproducibility. Every experimenter who repeats this methodologically and correctly will observe this physical phenomenon, regardless of the place or time where this it's carried out. Science curricula are an elegant mix of facts and hypotheses that are considered enduringly true – as long as new experiments do not prove them incorrect – and methods to reconfirm these truths and expand the body of truths. The scientists has at her fingertips a painstakingly accumulated, endlessly reassessed, historically sweeping base of scientific knowledge.

In strategic analysis there is no such thing as an accumulated base of knowledge, because almost by definition reproducibility of 'experiments' is impossible. Strategic analysis only knows facts: the observed acts and reported resulted of companies, the size of markets, consumer yoghurt-eating habits in the kingdom of  of Yololandia. Data in strategic analysis, however, cannot upgrade to knowledge. Consider the following example. Company X acquired three distributors in foreign countries in the past two years. In an interview two years ago, Company X's CEO indicated he was looking for acquisitions to drive his company's products global distribution. Afterwards, he bought three foreign distributors. Still, this does not in any way guarantee that more deals will follow. There is no reproducibility or forward predictability of a sort that definitively says: this happened, so it will happen again. An answer to a strategic analysis question that was correct two years ago may now be incorrect. This means that while strategic analysis has to store data, there is no point in teaching them, as historic facts do not have universal value. As a consequence, in strategic analysis only methodologies are worth teaching. Methodologies are best split in two main segments: those aimed at strengthening an analyst's functional and those intended to enhance his behavioural competences.

In short, the answer to the generic question 'what to train?' is simply functional and behavioural competences. The proverbial five honest service men – why, who, where, when and how – help us to further define strategic analysis training as part of an in-company an analyst's function's responsibilities.

## TRAINING OBJECTIVES RELATE TO BOTH IMPROVING DELIVERABLE QUALITY AND ACCEPTANCE

Let me start by elaborating on the why question. Training is a means. The end goal of training is to upgrade the functional or behavioural competences of the different strategic analysis stakeholders and/or strategic analysts. This ladders up to the two real needs served by training in strategic analysis.

The first may be to improve the competency level on the supply side – that is within the function. This is realized by upgrading the skills and expertise of the in-house staff to meet the demands put upon them by the (increasing) complexity of the function's portfolio of assignments. Junior staff (in terms of experience) may also require training because senior staff (in terms of experience) can move on to other jobs or retire. Even when this training often proceeds whilst on the job, formal trainings focusing on specific topics in tailored settings may be needed and quite useful. This can do wonders to improve the quality of deliverables and elevate their executive acceptance rate.

The second need relates to improving the competency level on the demand side of strategic analysis. This involves the subtle art of helping executive decision-makers get better at articulating their needs and calibrating their expectations. Having better-educated, more realistically level-set senior leaders will in turn lead to better all-around performance by the analyst.

The question 'why train?' thus gets a straightforward answer: to improve competences in order to improve required quality or acceptance on the demand and/or the supply side. Implicitly, this also answers the 'who' question regarding; both your analyst team supply side and your decision-maker customer demand side. There is another relevant answer to the 'who' question which concerns whether the participant volunteered to do the training or were directed to. The answer to this question may affect a participant's buy-in to active participation in the training. Discussing participants' buy-in in great detail is out of scope in this book. What is obvious, however, is that a participant who voluntarily or proactively applied is likely to have a much higher commitment to the training than a participant (read: victim) forced to attend. The volunteer wanted to change, whereas the employee who was told to show up has been forced to change.

In summary, strategic analysis training relates to, at a minimum, the following independent dimensions:

| | | | |
|---|---|---|---|
| What? | functional | and | behavioral |
| Why? | deliverable acceptance | and | deliverable quality |
| Who? | demand (i.e. customer) | and | supply (i.e. analyst function staff) |
| | volunteer participant | and | victim participant |

## ON-THE-JOB TRAINING IS THE PREFERRED FORMAT; IT PUTS NEW SKILLS TO IMMEDIATE USE

Of the three remaining questions (where, when and how) the questions where and how do not represent fully orthogonal dimensions, as the choice where to train partly defines how the training is delivered. The question when represents a separate dimension. First, we'll discuss when.

Trainings has the highest impact in competency building when the learned skills are immediately put into (daily) work practice by the trainee. Providing training to teach a skill that is not put to use by the participant until some time later is almost by definition useless. This is a generic truth. The answer to the question 'when to train?' thus links training to the work agenda of the participants. The work agenda determines the training needs. Consider a management team trying to articulate its business environment analysis needs for the next year. Why not deliver a training session that generically explores what strategic analysis can do for them (and what not!). Conclude the training with a final exercise that lets the management team actually create a working draft of an analysis needs portfolio for the year ahead. This means that you as the strategic analysis function both train and apply the training in one fell swoop, compelling your executive students to put their lessons into immediate action.

In this way, on-the-job training isn't limited to junior staff; it helps drive skills development all the way up the chain of command.... and greases the skids for your day-to-day work with senior decision-makers going forward.

## SETTING DETERMINES THE CONTEXT, CONTEXT AFFECTS ACCEPTANCE

Table 20.3 provides a non-exhaustive list of where/how options that are common in training strategic analysis. For the sake of simplicity, I have used an individual-participant scenario as the basis. Simultaneous, group training is usually done in classroom sessions at your office location, or classroom sessions conducted at an outside venue.

| VENUE LEARNING METHOD | AT PARTICIPANTS' HOME | ON-THE-JOB | IN-CLASS OFFICE VENUE, IN-COMPANY | IN-CLASS OUTSIDE VENUE IN-COMPANY | IN-CLASS OUTSIDE VENUE, OPEN |
|---|---|---|---|---|---|
| Delivery: non-personal e-learning | √ | √ | | | |
| Delivery: personal In-group Individual | | √ | √ | √ | √ |

TABLE 20.3 VENUES/OCCASIONS AND LEARNINGS METHODS OF EMPLOYEE TRAINING

Table 20.3 at first sight looks all too simple. Group training is conveniently delivered in a classroom setting. First of all, in-class comes in three different forms: in-the-office with colleagues; in an external venue but still exclusively with colleagues, and in an open enrollment program; and where your firm's participants mingle with peers from other companies with a similar training need. These are very different approaches even when objectively the same learning materials are offered through (possibly) the same trainer. The different venue alone may strongly affect whether participants absorb and retain the material, and put it to use when they return to their desk.

Venues are all about context. In his book *The Tipping Point*, Gladwell describes the underestimated relevance of context to human behaviour (Gladwell, 2000b). He shows that the very same people with the very same personal needs act profoundly differently in different settings. We may see a commonality here. What applies to strategic analysis deliverables may just as well apply to strategic analysis training. As one might imagine, the training's success is directly related to the quality of the classes and the participants' buy-in, attention and participation level. In the final analysis, getting participants to sit up and pay attention may be just as critical as the quality of the course materials and its delivery. Not entirely unlike trying to teach geography to a classroom full of teenagers, I suppose.

Unwilling victims in a workplace venue – like the conference two doors down from their regular office – are the worst. Stuck in that setting, they are encouraged to constantly think of the emails they cannot attend to because they have to be in this stupid training they don't believe they need. A strategic analysis function that chooses an appealing venue for its training may may soften the blow somewhat. The hotel is nice, and the breakfast spread was OK, but all-in-all he'd rather be somewhere (anywhere) else.

Training the same stuff in another context may result in both different participants behaviour and in creating a different impact.

The strategic analysis function should put some thought into what venue suits which learning objective for which group. When the group is believed to consist mainly of victims, investing in the appropriate venue may be a lever (however meager) for group buy-in and ultimate impact.

Expecting victims to run e-learning courses at their homes is wishful thinking. When they do, it is because of the black mark they fear on their annual performance appraisal if they skip out of school. If they do sleepwalk through an online course, it is not because they believe they should learn something. Genuinely interested volunteers, however, may not care about having to do it in a less-personal way and at home: they are eager to learn. They believe the training supports them in their career development.

In conclusion, for a strategic analysis function, choosing the 'where' and the 'how' of training depends on the answers given to the question of 'who'. The individuals' and groups' motivation and attitude will help determine what setting promises to work best.

## PARTICIPANTS' (INDIVIDUAL) NEEDS SHOULD DETERMINE THE LEARNING METHOD

There is one more dimension to the question 'who'. This relates to the personal learning preferences of the participant. Some may strongly prefer to be personally trained and coached in learning a new competence. Others may simply want to quietly study using written or audio/video materials, doing so individually in a silent, well-lit room. Those participants preferring to be personally coached may either benefit most from working in-class or being taught by a more experienced colleague, in on-the-job training mode. Results may vary, but if you embrace employees' preferred learning styles, this can be an effective way to upgrade staff competencies.

## CONTENT OF THE TRAINING MODULES MAY BE FIXED OR TAILOR-MADE

Classes should not only be tailored to teaching methodologies your students are comfortable with, but you'll obviously need to deliver the right material at the right time. In-house, on-the-job training of a junior function staff member by a senior team member comes closest to this ideal of pure tailor-made training. This presumes the senior staffer feels appreciated for offering this form of training. It also helps if both team members have developed a personal rapport that stimulates a mutually fruitful exchange of ideas.

Even so, even the best longtime employee can neither be a specialist in all sub-disciplines of strategic analysis nor have unlimited time to dedicate to training due to what is known as the tyranny of current intelligence. This wonderful term refers to the constant need to deliver analyses. So, in some cases, training may need to be outsourced to specialists, perhaps to a corporate education and training firm.

A strategic analysis function head may choose to in-source a tailor-made analysis curriculum, meeting a particular competency-building need related to a specific project. He may also buy an off-the-shelf, fixed content training package from a third-party supplier, which can be company-specific or made available to multiple companies through an open enrollment program. In the latter case, there is next to no possibility of changing the curriculum in the former case, a co-design of the curriculum and agenda may to some extent be possible. Either way, the start of any competency-building initiative in intelligence begins with the set-up of a common and indisputable taxonomy (Fisher, 2008). Words in strategic analysis should have only one meaning. In chapter 19 I discussed taxonomies at some length, as they are also critical to filing. Once such a taxonomy has been defined, the most practical way forward for a function head is to define a set of modules that can act as coursework building blocks, which can be used as they are delivered mixed and matched for at least some degree of flexibility and variation.

Table 20.4 gives an example of what a strategic analysis training module collection could look like. In this table the focus is on analysts, so not suitable for training the analysis functions' internal decision-maker customers. As mentioned, those internal customers may benefit from introductory training on what strategic analysis can and cannot do, built up from (parts of) the modules below. Such training may introduce strategic analysis as discipline, focusing on collection and analysis and the related methodologies, techniques and tools. We've noted that the training may be completed by having the customer – your business leader – apply the concepts she learned

| DISCIPLINE | BEHAVIORAL COMPETENCE MODULES | FUNCTIONAL COMPETENCE MODULES |
|---|---|---|
| Project definition & management | | - Project management skills/Project portfolio management<br>- Time management |
| Collection | | - Open source data collection<br>- Interview techniques<br>- General collection skills<br>- Compliance (anti-trust, etc.)<br>- Languages |
| Analysis | - Dealing with uncertainty | - Counter-deception<br>- Creativity<br>- Finance for non-finance types<br>- Statistics<br>- Strategy and analysis tools for business<br>- Psychology for analysts<br>- Industry-specific subject matter courses<br>- Analysis tools (executive profiling, etc.) |
| Reporting | - Personal effectiveness | - Storylining (pyramid principle)<br>- Slide writing<br>- Visualization |
| Filing | | - Software-tool related skills<br>- Information management |
| Interaction with decision-makers | - Persuasion skills<br>- Personal effectiveness<br>- Leadership | - Stakeholder management<br>- Meeting facilitation<br>- Consultancy skills |
| Counter-intelligence | | - Counter-elicitation<br>- Counterintelligence program design and implementation |
| Compliance & ethics | - Dealing with integrity | - Ethics and strategic analysis<br>- Anti-trust and competition law |

TABLE 20.4 ▶▶▶ A PORTFOLIO OF POSSIBLE TRAINING MODULES FOR STRATEGIC ANALYSIS STAFF

to an exercise that actually begins shaping her analysis needs plan for the following year by defining their analysis need portfolio for the next year.

## COMPETENCE LEVEL AMBITION TARGETS MAY VARY BY DISCIPLINE

An additional dimension to training is the capability level that a participant needs to have achieved once all is said and done. There is a wide gap between having elementary awareness of and becoming subject matter expert in a discipline. The needs of the participant, by discipline, determine how intensive training should be to yield varying levels of competence.

Jähne summarized the escalating ladder of competence levels (Jähne, 2009):

- Understand
- Apply.
- Correlate.
- Adapt.
- Teach.
- Develop.
- Inspire.

Happy is the strategic analysis function head who sees his staff voluntarily move up this ladder, mastering multiple sub-disciplines.

## UNIVERSITY ACCREDITATION IS THE GOLDEN STANDARD

Larger companies tend to have an in-house training department that may facilitate training (participation recruitment, venue management, etc.) that may include strategic analysis training modules in a broader corporate training program. Some companies even ensure key training is delivered in cooperation with universities. Such training is thus formally accredited. This option also allows an employee to add a university-level training and education credentials to her resume.

# 20.6 TOWARDS A WORLD-CLASS STRATEGIC ANALYSIS ORGANIZATION

Rome was not built in a day. Similarly, it will take time, patience and a lot of hard work to grow your analysis function into the respected, game-changing powerhouse it can become. A previously published schematic titled 'World Class Market Intelligence Roadmap'[7] can be both inspirations for newbies and helpful to functions still working their way up the professionalization curve(Hedin, 2011). In the next chapter we will define strategic analysis as a profession that entails lifelong learning. Taking the lifelong learning perspective implies that the World Class Market Intelligence Roadmap may be useful to any strategic analysis staff or function, regardless of its stage of development.

The Roadmap distinguishes five levels of progressively increasing professionalism. For each level, the Roadmap indicates the nature and sophistication in six MI dimensions. The dimensions include:

- Intelligence scope: the function's project portfolio.
- Intelligence process: the collection and filing process.
- Intelligence deliverables: the analysis product portfolio.
- Intelligence tools.
- Intelligence organization.
- Intelligence culture: this dimension relates to how well strategic analysis has been embedded in an organization at large.

The five levels are given below, in diagram 20.4.

| | Informal MI | Basic MI | Intermediate MI | Advanced MI | World Class MI |
|---|---|---|---|---|---|
| **Main role** | Fire fighting | Fire fighting and some pre-planned assignments | Delivering refined output; coordinating the MI cycle | As with advanced analysis and tools used | Sophisticated broad view of current and likely future business environment |
| **Key feature** | MI-staff person appointed | First MI-plan executed | MI recognized as valuable for business continuity | MI becomes part of strategy design | MI (through Strategy Dept.) is trusted C-level and/or board advisor |

**DIAGRAM 20.4 ▸▸▸ FIVE LEVELS OF PROGRESSIVELY INCREASING STRATEGIC ANALYSIS DEPARTMENT PROFESSIONALISM**

The competence levels, using the authors' original term 'market intelligence' (MI), relate well to the competence levels mentioned in the previous section. In strategic analysis one starts with understanding that the professional discipline exists and that it has a value. This leads to level one – informal MI. Pick the fire that burns most ferociously and start fighting it, and in doing so, make friends who allocate the budgets that can help move the MI function beyond only changing the oil in the fire engine.[8] Applying discipline and order to the analysis function allows you to move from fighting unexpected brush fires to implementing a well thought out prevention and emergency-response plan. In doing so, we reach level two. Upon correlating and adapting strategic analysis to meet the tailored needs of its widening group of the core audience of executive decision-makers, we move towards level three – intermediate MI. To reach level four, you need to teach business leaders and staff to embed analysis in strategy design and execution. At level five, MI-based strategies inspire boards and shareholders to invest in the future of the firm.

I'll say it again: Rome was not built in a day. Patience has its virtue. In 1999, at FrieslandCoberco, we started the strategic analysis journey, taking off barely at level one. This book reflects much of what was encountered during a 17-year journey. Over time we enjoyed some fine successes and developed a passion for lifelong learning. We will indeed keep moving. Hopefully this book contributes to your passion for moving forward with strategic analysis competency-building as well.

CHAPTER 21

# PROFILE OF A STRATEGY ANALYST

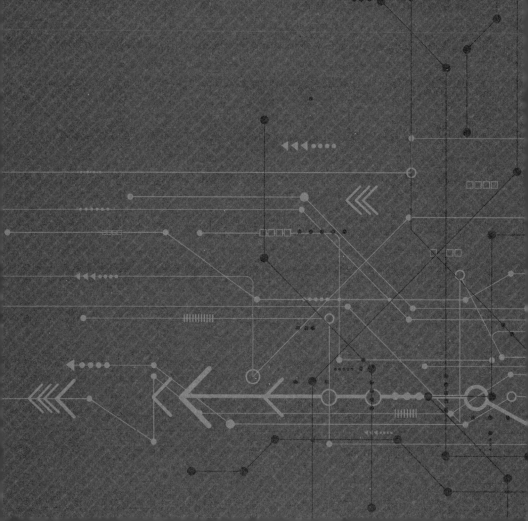

# 21.1 INTRODUCTION

After having worked well over 35,000 hours in strategic analysis, I believe the single question I've been asked most frequently has been: "What should I look for when I want to recruit my own strategic analysis staff member?"

The question always left me a bit embarrassed, even when I delivered some off-the-cuff answer. I felt I never had a single authoritative source I could point to in response to this question. And so, I decided to give this some serious thought, seek out inspirational new sources and, in this final chapter, synthesize my conclusions. Among other things, I combed through public domain sources from the world of strategic intelligence. This proved helpful, as there is overlap in the nature of their task-work, and thus the required experience, skills and abilities. With this chapter I share the well thumbed logbook of a practitioner's voyage of discovery. Think of it as a meta-analysis of strategic analysis.

## GOOD PEOPLE MAKE ALL THE DIFFERENCE

Strategic intelligence thought leader Sherman Kent wrote this in the 1960s (Heuer, 1999m):

> *"Whatever the complexities of the puzzles we strive to solve and*
> *Whatever the sophisticated techniques we may use to collect*
> *The pieces and store them, there can never be a time when the*
> *Thoughtful man can be supplanted as the intelligence device supreme."*

The 1960s saw the start of widespread computational support for business analysis. Fifty years later these computational tools have improved beyond what anyone could have imagined. The analyst, however, is still the determining success factor in strategic analysis. No matter how advanced the computer technology, I dare to predict that solving strategic analysis problems will forever require a human touch. Having said that, we continue to search for the right mix of human skills and attributes – the secret sauce that produces the very best strategic analysts.

In this chapter I will first break down the functional competencies an analyst must possess. I'll lay out what an analyst needs to physically do in the workplace, on a day-to-day basis, and the competencies necessary to effectively perform those duties. We'll also look at the ideal (or, at least, desirable) behavioural profile an analyst should embody. Based on these two dimensions – cognitive skills and behavioural traits – I'll then attempt to map out the characteristic and abilities needed for sequentially higher levels of strategic analysis work. These are summarized in an intermezzo at the end of this chapter.

# 21.2 FUNCTIONAL COMPETENCIES

## INTELLECT IS IMPERATIVE BUT NOT ENOUGH

A strategic analyst is a knowledge worker and a professional. Academic training and credentials are critical to a professional's success. Analysis involves seeing real patterns and signals where others only see randomness and noise. The fewer pieces an analyst needs to solve a puzzle, the better. After all, in strategic intelligence, as in business in general, reliable puzzle pieces are by definition in short supply (Heuer, 1999o):

> *"This ability to bring previously unrelated information and ideas together in meaningful ways is what marks the open-minded, imaginative, creative analyst."*

In the world of military intelligence, the best intelligence professionals take counter-intuitive thinking as an article of faith (Grey, 2016g). An analyst thus at all times has to be intellectually and psychologically able to recognize and fight the all-to-human tendency to look for confirmation of their existing beliefs, and in doing so turning a blind eye to change.

In strategic analysis, the decision-maker/customer focuses all too often on content and the subsequent decisions that will be made based on that content. It is, however, the analyst who collects the data efficiently and subsequently unlocks insights lurking in that data. When the legendary R.V. Jones, who successfully ran the British scientific military intelligence practice during the Second World War, was asked to write his operational plan in 1940, he included this (Jones, 1978e):

> *"The size of the staffs […] should be kept as numerically small as possible, and that quality was much the most important factor."*

Admiral John Godfrey, the head of British naval intelligence in the Second World War, in the same context stated (Macintyre, 2010g):

> *"It is quite useless, and in fact dangerous to employ people of medium intelligence. Only men with first-class brains should be allowed to touch this stuff. If the right sort of people cannot be found, better keep them out altogether."*

It is easy to dismiss the above two quotes as dating back to other times, situations and needs. The world of the business decision-makers that strategic analysis serves today, however, still seems to be governed by people competing with each other. This after all is also Clausewitz's definition of war. Parallels between the intensity of 1940s wartime efforts and today's cutthroat global competition may well be drawn. For those in business who fail to outsmart through superior analysis, through smarter strategies and through (most of all) better execution, the threat of formidable, costly, head-on competition looms large.

There is a catch here. Intellect should not be overrated. After all, intellect as measured by IQ matters only up to a point (Gladwell, 2009a):

> *"Once someone has reached an IQ of somewhere around 120, having additional IQ points doesn't seem to translate into any measurable real-world advantage."*

Once an analyst meets the threshold of about 120 IQ points, success or failure are largely determined by behavioural traits. It is for this reason that most of this chapter has been dedicated to behavioural competencies that can contribute to an analyst's success.

## IMAGINATION AND ANALYSIS RARELY GO TOGETHER; CREATIVITY MAY BE IN-SOURCED

Too often a lack of imagination has been the root cause of (military) intelligence failures. The best analyst xenocentrically not only understands what a competitor has done in the past but also why. The analyst also can imagine what the other party will (most likely) do next. Imagination is not an analytical skill. It is a creative skill. Imagination does not correlate with analytic skills in people; the skills are orthogonal (Gladwell, 2009b). When a strategic analysis department head has to choose between a candidate with an IQ of 150 who exhibits low creative skills and one with an IQ of 120 but extraordinary creative skills – all other things being equal – the latter individual is the obvious choice.

When there is a distinct lack of imaginative thinking in a strategic analysis department, dare to acknowledge this internally. Where necessary, address this shortfall by in-sourcing creative talent to complement the rest of the staff's skills and experience in a particular assignment. Provided these staff get the right briefing and context, the freelance creatives may imagine a competitor's next moves in a way that rigid, run-of-the-mill analysts may fail to see. Strategic analysis departments should have a tolerance for individual eccentricity. In reviews of the success of the British Second World War code-breaker units in Bletchley Park, the eccentricies of a large number of extraordinarily bright staff features again and again as a critical factor.

## RESEARCH SKILLS ARE A HOUSEKEEPING MATTER

An analyst's research proficiency is a basic matter of business skills hygiene. Profound knowledge of disciplines such as mathematics (especially statistics), experimental design, where applicable physics or chemistry or another science specialty may round out an analyst's research toolkit. This is not to say that anthropologists, students of law, historians or economists can't develop into good analysts. They very well might, providing they develop a sufficiently strong understanding of quantitative methodologies that reside at the core of strategic analysis.

## BUSINESS ADMINISTRATION KNOWLEDGE HELPS WITH UNDERSTANDING THE CONTEXT

In serving senior executives, mastery of the language of business management is essential. An analyst should be well versed the classics of business strategy. Understanding company financials goes beyond knowing the difference between the top and bottom line of a profit and loss account. It includes grasping the meaning of footnote 34 to a balance sheet that appears on page 527 in a company's information memorandum.

The small print in a competitor's report often brings the greatest joy to a curious analyst: that's where an illuminating link has been buried that may tell the company's real story.

## LANGUAGE SKILLS ASSIST IN TAKING A XENOCENTRIC VIEW

Language skills have long been highly valued as intelligence collection and analysis assets (Deacon, 1982c). In collection, mastering the language of a competitor's documents is of immediate value – even when tools like Google Translate have made an analyst's life a bit easier. In personal face-to-face contact, mastering another party's language is even more important, as sharing a language usually increases trust and breaks down barriers. Understanding a competitor's language in analysis assists in better grasping the competitor's culture and through the culture its possible and impossible next moves. It can also help an analyst assess a competitor's culture, and its predisposition toward certain tactics and strategic moves. Literary critics were among the most effective British and American counter-intelligence officers in the Second World War (Johnson, 2009d):

> *"(they were) trained to look for multiple meanings, to examine the assumptions hidden in words and phrases, and to grasp the whole structure of a poem or a play, not just the superficial plot or statement. So the multiple meanings, the hidden assumptions, and the larger pattern of a counter-intelligence case were the grist for their mill."*

A multilingual analyst is for most international companies a valuable asset.

## CONCENTRATION AS A VIRTUE

An overwhelming amount of noise (or, as it is also known, information overload) is linked to attention fragmentation (Dean, 2011). Attention fragmentation is to be avoided. It is detrimental to analytic thinking, learning and the quality of decision-making:

> *"[Uninterrupted time is needed] to synthesize information from many different sources, reflect on its implications for the organization, apply judgment, make trade-offs, and arrive at good decisions."*

An analyst with a natural ability to concentrate has a distinct competitive edge in her profession.

## CONSULTANCY SKILLS

For an analyst, a basic mastery of consultancy skills is imperative; it is a basic housekeeping matter. Consultancy skills, for example, include:

- Process management, including managing for stakeholder acceptance of deliverables.
- Storylining and slide writing, including mastering visualization tools.
- Communication skills: including situational application of various approaches (tone, content, medium, timing, etc.).

An analyst, however, is not by definition a good consultant, and vice versa. An analyst is first and foremost a subject matter expert, focused on creating timely, accurate, high-quality deliverables. It goes without saying that the deliverables should be accepted by executive decisions-makers; otherwise they're essentially worthless, academic exercises. Gaining executive acceptance of your hard work is where consultancy skills come in most handy. When strategic analysis is part of a corporate strategy department, the analyst and the strategy consultant will likely team up to ensure both quality and acceptance.

For an analyst who operates in a solo capacity and does not have the luxury of working with a consultant peer, consultancy skills that are often tightly interwoven with communication skills are even more relevant (Davenport, 2014c).

# 21.3 BEHAVIORAL COMPETENCIES

## CURIOSITY IS ESSENTIAL FOR AN ANALYST TO SUSTAIN JOB SATISFACTION

It is hard to overrate the relevance of curiosity as an attribute in a good analyst. In English strategic intelligence in the Elizabethan Age (second half of the Sixteenth Century) Sir Francis Walsingham – who led the equivalent of MI6 in his time – is reported to have said in defense of his work (Alford, 2013b):

> *"I protest before God that as a man careful of my mistress's [i.e. Queen Elizabeth I] safety I have been curious."*

This wording is truly elegant. In Alford's estimation the value of the word curious can hardly be overstated:

> *"This was a masterful piece of wordcraft, for though 'curious' meant in one sense attentive and careful, it also gave a meaning of something hidden and subtle. After many years of fighting a secret war against an unforgiving enemy, Walsingham captured his profession in a single adjective."*

Walsingham in this respect is an example to any analyst in the Twenty-First Century. True analysts should be as passionate as Walsingham was to want to know everything about their competitors. The tagline for a strategic analysis department may well be 'We know it all – or else we know how to get it'.

This passion for knowing goes beyond the search for knowledge for the mere sake of it. There is a remarkable confluence of interests in a company's and an analyst's shared urge to satisfy burning curiosity. Through obtained fact and knowledge-based analysis, the company will benefit from solid market intelligence as input to value-creating strategies. At the same time, the analyst benefits emotionally from what an extra puzzle piece may bring (Moore, 2007b):

> *"Successful intelligence analysts are insatiably curious. Fascinated by puzzles, their high levels of self-motivation lead them to observe and read voraciously, and to take fair-minded and varied perspectives. This helps them to make the creative connections necessary for solving the hardest intelligence problems. Finally, the emotional tensions created by problems, and the cathartic release at their solution, powerfully motivate analysts."*

## TOLERANCE FOR FRUSTRATION IS THE HALLMARK OF ALL RESEARCHERS

They also know that, more often than not that release never comes. At times, issues appear that look like puzzles but happen to be mysteries. On these occasions, the analyst does not solve the mystery, a solution is not at hand... and the analyst comes away understandably frustrated.

We're not going to try to identify all possible frustrations that an analyst can encounter in her daily work. That would be too depressing. We will take a look at two common sources of frustration that arise with some frequency. A natural ability to handle both is a critical strategic analyst competency, so I'll briefly touch on how to manage them.

The first such annoyance is the simple lack of sufficient data to solve a puzzle in a timely manner. This frustrations may have two root causes: time is too short (given the resources available) or the issue is too unfamiliar. In such situations surfacing and focusing on the critical issues is the best approach when handling assignments under intense time pressure. When data available for analysis lacks solve the critical issues, the only option left is to acknowledge that you're unable to solve the mystery, admit defeat and to stick to situation reporting. No matter how unsatisfying that may be, it is the analyst's role and obligation to be totally open with the principal about what is known and what is not known. The analyst must then shake off the sting of a missed deadline and advise the executive of when the next data are expected to arrive, and how you can all re-set for the now-delayed decision/action.

A possible second source of frustration is that the market intelligence developed is high grade, but management's reaction was lukewarm at best. To make matters worse, the decision-maker may not take timely action on your recommendations, or ultimately never take any action whatsoever. This does not only happen in the business world, as these cynical and frustrated remarks by former US intelligence analyst Robert S. Ames makes clear (Bird, 2014):

> *"You have this notion that all you need to do is get the right facts before the policy makers – and things would change. You think you can make a difference. But gradually, you realize that policy makers don't care. And then the revelation hits you that U.S. foreign policy is not fact-driven."*

A strategic analyst who feels the need for action following a task, as a basic requirement for job satisfaction, has sadly chosen the wrong job. In this profession, the analyst simply must learn to keep dissatisfaction at bay when things that are clearly beyond his control go cockeyed. In this field, anyone who's susceptible to being badly shaken by things he can't control is at risk of a range of psychological problems. When recruiting an analyst, look for some who's thick-skinned, rolls with the punches and knows how to choose his battles.

## PERSUASIVENESS

It is not always the other guy's fault. The analyst always has to look how she can improve in her performance. This starts with realizing that even high-grade intelligence needs to be persuasively communicated. The following example puts a sharp point on that.

In the early 1970s Henry Kissinger was National Security Adviser to US President Nixon. At some stage an intelligence analyst offered him new, high-grade intelligence. Kissinger did not act upon it. When the intelligence later proved to have been correct, Kissinger is reputed to have said to the analyst (George, 2008b):

> *"Well, you warned me but you did not convince me."*

The message here is simple. Look for an analyst who not only delivers a prescient report, but also can compel the recipient to promptly and thoughtfully act upon it. The recipient may still choose to do nothing, but at least he gave the report appropriate consideration. It was not unfairly discounted.

## HUMILITY

An analyst must be confident and persuasive but must never tip over into arrogance or start talking down to the principal. The analyst's ego must be checked at the door (Lauder, 2009). Strategic analysis serves the senior business leader. Anyone out there who goes into business out of a desire to lead and decide, rather than discover through collection and analysis, should consider becoming something other than a strategic analyst. When looking for an analyst, avoid hiring a person with a strong *people power* need.

## PERSEVERANCE

At times analysis work requires sifting through large amounts of random information in search for some illuminating links (Wolf, 1998). If ever a job required stamina and perseverance, it is data collection and analysis. An individual seeking employment in the analysis game should have the word perseverance underlined on her resume.

From the company's standpoint, this persistence and determination do not come free of charge. Perseverance links to time spent on an issue. For a firm that over time hopes to develop knowledge of its markets and business environment to increase its competitive edge and deliver value, investing in go-getter analysts will yield high returns provided… a critical condition is met. Namely, the output of the strategic analysis department should seamlessly inform corporate (strategic) decision-making. When recruiting an analyst, look for an individual willing to go the extra mile, but who remains focused on getting the better decision taken.

## TENURE IS NEEDED TO BUILD UP A LIBRARY OF PATTERNS...

Strategic analysis is a craft, not a job. It is a specialist capability that one needs to extensively practice and gradually master. Implicit in the idea of craftsmanship is the notion that a young apprentice will be guided/coached by a senior craftsman in learning the trade, ideally on the job (Cooper, 2005b). This organizational model equally applies in business. Once mastering a craft, it does not need to be practiced for many years and still will not be lost. Javers points to Vladimir Putin, who as president of the Russian Federation remarked in 2005 (Javers, 2011a):

> *"There is no such thing as a former KGB-man."*

This statement, absent the dark pride that is concealed in it, also applies in strategic analysis. Once an analyst, you will always remain one. Even after many years of doing different jobs, a person that has worked as an analyst still instantly will recognize strategic patterns, still will view data presented with a healthy skepticism and will still by default double-check superficial conclusions.

Former CIA Director Allen W. Dulles once told Congress that intelligence (Robarge, 2007):

> *"...should be directed by a relatively small but elite corps of men with a passion for anonymity and a willingness to stick at that particular job."*

The willingness to stick at a particular job is critical to the process of learning a craft. Sticking at the job is therefore imperative if one hopes to become truly good in strategic analysis. Being an analyst is one of those professions where the so-called '10,000 hour' rule applies. The idea is that a person requires 10,000-hours of concentrated practice before true excellence in a craft can be achieved (Gladwell, 2009c):

> *"In study after study, of composers, basketball players, fiction writers, ice skaters, concert pianists, chess players, master criminals, and what have you, this number [10,000 h] comes up again and again. [...] No one has yet found a case in which true world-class expertise was accomplished in less time. It seems that it takes the brain this long to assimilate all that it needs to know to achieve true mastery."*

The 10,000-hour rule undoubtedly applies to strategic analysis. The importance of an analyst building up a library of patterns for future reference and instant pattern recognition is critical (Heuer, 1999b). Tenure is the only way in which to build up such a library (Klein, 1999d).

More recent research confirms this view. Researchers conducted a geopolitical forecasting tournament, assessing the accuracy of more than 150,000 forecasts from 743 participants (all of them analysts) relating to 199 events occurring over two years (Mellers, 2015). The key finding was that the best forecasters were:

- Better at inductive reasoning.
- Pattern detection.
- Cognitive flexibility.
- Open-mindedness.

The best forecasters:

> *"...viewed forecasting as a skill that required deliberate practice, sustained effort, and constant monitoring of current affairs."*

When selecting an analyst, look for individuals who see analysis as a career, not a job where second-guessing and doubt – particularly haunting doubts about one's own conclusions – are daily companions.

## ...BUT TENURE HAS ITS RISKS AS WELL

There are two common downsides of long employee tenure. First, building up expertise through multiple years of pattern recognition is only possible in a relatively stable or even a regulated environment (Kahneman, 2011n). The stability of the environment is critical. In the absence of stability, the accumulated patterns in the mind of the analyst would not be valuable as building blocks for handling future cases. Such stable work environments include firefighting (where Laws of Nature apply, and chess or poker, where rules are fixed and statistics matter (Klein, 1999d) or possibly in relatively stable industries such as food processing).

The second potential downside concerns sustaining staff motivation. In business, long tenure is sometimes associated with organizational sclerosis: comfortably settled-in employees who do just enough to get by and who may resist innovation and change. Convincing research, however, shows that (McNulty, 2013):

> *"[...]high [business] performance standards can keep people motivated for decades."*

Strategic analysts almost by definition set high performance standards for themselves; that is the true nature of the beast. Rather, analysts too often tend to be overly perfectionist. Tenure in strategic analysis, in a relatively stable industry setting, is therefore an asset by any measure.

## COURAGE

An analyst needs at times to be prepared to challenge the status quo by boldly expressing original thinking, and going to the mat to defend those ideas. Yesmanship may be an easier approach for an analyst who wants to retain his credibility and his reputation for objectivity. Respectfully but persistently sticking to a well-substantiated analytic conclusion that may not be entirely popular with a company's leadership requires courage. Analysts should have such courage, trusting their intellect and their employability.

Courage is not universally defined. It differs by culture. Assuming a respectful but challenging position with a decision-maker may be common and perfectly acceptable in some cultures, whereas in others exactly the same behaviour may considered bravery. The Dutch psychologist Geert Hofstede suggested a quantitative yardstick to measure attitudes toward hierarchy. He called this indicator the 'Power Distance Index'. The ethnic theory of plane crashes is based on this work (Gladwell, 2009c). The more a culture values and respects authority, the larger the Power Distance Index and the more courage it takes to speak up to authority. In cultures in which speaking up is not the norm, plane crashes occur more frequently, because flight crews don't offer up their own observations, suggestions and warnings, relying instead entirely on the exalted pilot. Don't emulate the airline with the tight-lipped crew when hiring strategic analysts; look for those who are willing to speak up when they need to.

## BEYOND COMPLIANT

Strategic analysis staff relate to spies as shop customers relate to shoplifters. Spies are at times assigned to steal information, whereas analysts are assigned to legally collect and process information. An analyst who duly shops and pays for the goods acts ethically and legally. A scoundrel who goes to the shop and takes the goods without paying clearly does not. A collector or analyst – often the same person in a business setting – must possess a natural inclination to steer clear of ethically (let alone legally) shady practices. An analyst who can't suppress the urge to steal cannot be hired to do your shopping.

## SYSTEMATIC

An analyst must not be chaotic. Markus Wolf, quoted earlier, emphasized that in intelligence work, the analyst searches for illuminating links in a set of seemingly random data. Doing so requires a systematic approach to data management – both in an individual's work and in a strategic analysis department.

## QUALITY FOCUS

An analyst needs to be able to balance intrinsically conflicting factors in his work. For instance, there are always more questions than resources to answer the questions. An analyst must sense why some work deserves more priority and more effort than other work, intuitively linking the work to the urgency and relevance of having the answers available to the firm. Quality starts by doing the right work.

Quality also requires doing the work right. Good analysis work has three attributes: it is timely, accurate and complete. All three attributes together make up the quality of the work. An analyst needs to manage dilemmas that may occur when timeliness cannot be sacrificed, even when a deliverable is neither accurate nor complete.

An incomplete and inaccurate assessment, however, may do more harm than good. Hire the analyst who can figure out how to navigate such conflicts, even when best choices may differ case by case.

## EMPATHIC - XENOCENTRIC - SOCIABLE

An analyst who doubles as a collector requires the skills specifically required for collection. Especially for collecting data from interviews, sociability is a plus. What truly matters is that an analyst has a fundamental interest in people. Strategic analysis is a craft that sources skills from multiple disciplines. Having a quantitative analyst with a passion for anthropology may be rare, but may just be what an analysis department needs. Xenocentrism cannot be executed through filling out and filing spreadsheets only.

## DISCREET

An analyst should set out to gradually develop a trusting relationship with her senior executives. Over time, through those high-level relationships, an analyst may become privy to a company's secrets as well as get a sharper view of the personal needs and vulnerabilities of its decision-makers. Developing such insights will greatly enhance an analyst's effectiveness. To become a trusted advisor to senior leaders, one must also exercise discretion. Bragging to peers or subordinates about what friends in high places have confided is a critical mistake.

## INNOVATIVE AND CHANGE-ORIENTED

The analyst profession over time has changed and it continues to change, requiring the analyst to be innovative and at times to lead change. An analyst can be seen as a violin player in a symphony orchestra, with the decision-maker being the audience and the strategic analysis department head (or the head of strategy) being the conductor. Gradually, however, the analyst role in parallel also evolves into that of a conductor of his own orchestra, with his own players being computers and models. See diagram 21.1, on analyst-computer interaction (Edward, 2014).

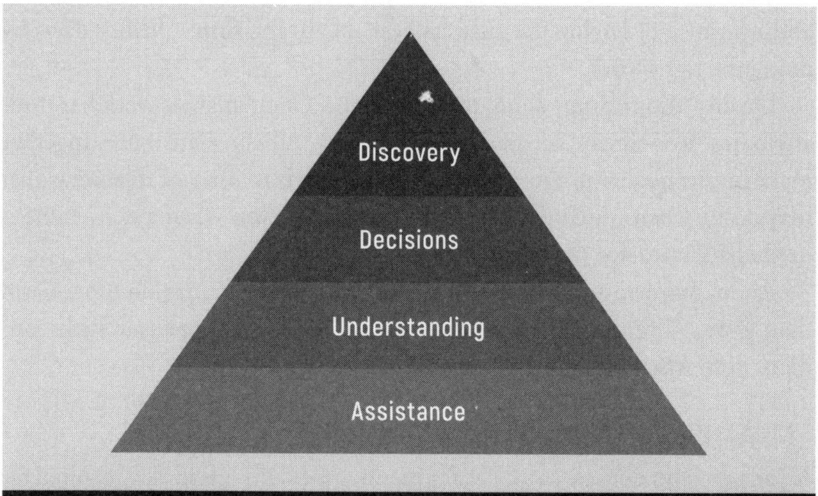


DIAGRAM 21.1 ▶▶▶ FOUR LEVELS OF ANALYST – COMPUTER INTERACTION

At the bottom of the pyramid is level one – assistance. Any analyst uses the computer as a channel to the Internet, for assistance, as an on-demand encyclopedia encompassing the knowledge of humanity. Nothing new or innovative here: using a computer in an assistance role is a basic, underlying necessity for functional competency.

## 'UNDERSTANDING COMPUTERS' AS A CURRENT BACKBONE SUPPORT TOOL

Level two is called 'understanding'. At this level, behavior skills matter at least as much as functional skills for the analyst. In strategic intelligence, no analyst can dream anymore of reading all available materials by himself (Medina, 2008). Collection is so cheap and data are so abundant that making sense of it all becomes a bottleneck. Moreover, the information avalanche is such that a single expert cannot cope with it.

There are two ways to cope with this challenge; each involving a behavioral innovative skill of an analyst. The analyst has to feel comfortable to:

- Work in teams and divide the workload, even when doing so is resource-intensive.
- Program computer algorithms to spot (combinations of) key words, to filter critical data and information pieces out of the clutter (Natural Language Processing).

The latter approach is by its nature no longer the traditional, anecdotal form in which data reach an analyst's desk. Rather, it is holistic. The output is not a single story on an issue but it may reveal patterns and patterns may, for example, reveal social media attention to an issue. To return to Markus Wolf's search for illuminating links: in his former East German life, filing cabinets with hardcopy cards were needed, with the card being appropriately coded with metadata in multiple dimensions. In today's world, a single well-defined search algorithm may generate an inflow of potentially relevant news stories to a strategic analysis department, with the computer having read and understood thousands of clippings daily. Today, the computer finds the links and the analyst's role is to focus on making sense of these links.

## INTELLIGENCE MAY NOT MATCH WITH AUTOMATED DECISION-SUPPORT SYSTEMS

Level three is called 'decisions', which is shorthand for direct decision support. An example would be analyst-computer interaction using expert systems that assess patient x-rays and based on the assessment suggest treatment options to a medical specialist. The computer algorithm is based on accumulated learning of medical professionals on things like bone fractures. What are typical cues for a typical type of fracture? What evidence should be present and what should not be present? The medical specialist, in making a judgment on what is seen and by implication what to do, not only uses his own accumulated library of mental bone fracture cases, but in parallel may check what his electronic peer recommends. A classic similar example is chess. IBM's Deep Blue actually beat the chess world champion. What does this level III interaction mean for strategic analysis?

Heuer argues that while analysts may benefit from building a library of business cases, the rules of business or politics are fundamentally different from those of chess or bone fractures (Heuer, 1999p). Chess is guided by fixed rules. Within a wide legal framework, however, business thrives when it innovatively changes the rules. No disruptive innovator after all ever started out complying with all the rules of an existing business model. Attempting to automate direct decision-support in strategic analysis may therefore have a fundamental flaw.

The strategic analyst who one would preferably hire will be wary of trusting expertise claimed in fields that are not governed by natural laws or fixed rules (Taleb, 2007f). This may equally apply to market intelligence and digital decision-support expert systems. Heuer even warns analysts to never put too much trust in their accumulated library: rules that in the past may have applied in politics or in business, may no longer apply. As a result, the patterns the library may be woefully obsolete. Unlearning established patterns may well be harder than coming to understand new patterns. Being eager to engage in an ongoing, open-ended process of learning and unlearning is thus a critical analyst asset.

## DISCOVERY IS ALL AROUND US

Level four is called 'discovery'. Discovery is making a computer algorithm look for connections that nobody knew existed. This is a capability that is under rapid development. Retail chains using bonus card systems may discover patterns in human in-store behaviour that even the shoppers themselves may not consciously know they're exhibiting. This applies both to classical brick-and-mortar retail and probably even more so to online retail merchandising. Every click can be measured, reflecting often implicit human behavioural patterns. When either through a bonus card database review or through on-line site interaction analysis a pattern is discovered, the retailer that capitalizes on it has an opportunity to deliver better offerings to its customers. As the dynamic unfolds, the seller's offerings map increasingly well to a customer's individual (sometimes unconscious) needs, desires and buying patterns. The retailer gains a bigger share of the customer's spending and more profits, allowing it to further optimize its buying pattern analysis and targeted selling, etc. This is where Big Retail may turn (or is turning) into Big Brother. This technology is ready, it's out there, and is being applied. Algorithm-oriented data analysts who feel ethically comfortable using their brains to work in this sub-section of data processing will likely find ready, willing and eager employers.

## 21.4 STRATEGIC ANALYSIS AS A PROFESSION OF LIFELONG LEARNING

When recruiting strategic analysis staff, behavioural competences – from curiosity to courage to compliance – matter most once a candidate demonstrates a certain baseline level of intellect. Intellect and experience are independent of one another (Klein, 1999e), but both matter in selecting an analyst. In a craft like strategic analysis, practiced in a more or less stable environment, experience matters because a library filled with relevant patterns will enable much faster and generally better decision-making. The ideal analyst has both a sufficiently high intellect, at least the beginning of an experience-based library with relevant patterns, and the willingness to (over a longer period of time) continue in to trade enrich that library. A twist of eccentricity in an analyst may be indicative of a creative spark that enables her to find the unconventional, creative solution to a strange new puzzle. I believe the quote below sums it up, matching my personal experience and that of some of the brightest analysts I've had the privilege to work with over the years (Freedman, 2013f). Strategic analysis is:

> *"...the domain of the strong intellect, the lifelong student, the dedicated professional, and the invulnerable ego."*

I hope I've effectively portrayed strategic analysis as a craft that has rightfully earned its place as a valuable functional discipline in the world of business. We've seen how, from their origins in the military and government, a wide range of data collection and analysis methodologies – applied with a bit of effort and a little imagination – can make a real difference in the world of business. For those of you embarking on a career in strategic analysis, it is my hope that these observations and insights will help send you on your way, and enrich your experience as you live and learn this fascinating trade. For those seasoned, long-term practitioners among you, I hope my thoughts and advice will ring true and complement your own experience, skills and expertise. Above all, I sincerely hope your endeavors in this field bring you the same sense of fulfillment and pleasure I've felt through my long career as a professional strategic analyst.

## INTERMEZZO: SKILLS AND ACCOUNTABILITY

For both the individual analyst and the broader strategic analysis department, functional and organizational accountability is spelled out in Table 21.2 and 21.2:

| ACCOUNTABILITY | KEY ACTIVITIES | RESULTS |
|---|---|---|
| **Functional**<br>- Collection<br>- Analysis<br>- Reporting<br>- Delivery | - Set up network of sources<br>- Develop standard methods/views<br>- Produce ad-hoc & periodical reports<br>- Periodic presentations to management | A xenocentric view on the business environment:<br><br>- No relevant 'missed' news<br>- Set of analysis tools/practices<br>- Periodical & ad-hoc deliverables<br>- Embedded output in decisions |
| **Organizational**<br>- Budget<br>- Staff<br>- Training/tools<br>- Work portfolio | - Set up annual budget for strategic analysis discipline<br>- Recruit and train balanced team<br>- Define training in portfolio/tools<br>- Manage time/ resources/budget | A department delivering output that management acts upon<br><br>- Clear cost/benefit overview<br>- Motivated, professional team<br>- Portfolio ready to use for projects<br>- Accurate, complete and timely output |

TABLE 21.1 ▶▶▶ FUNCTIONAL AND ORGANIZATIONAL ACCOUNTABILITIES OF ANALYST/DEPARTMENT

| COMPETENCY LEVEL | COMPETENCY DESCRIPTION |
|---|---|
| 1.<br>Fact collector: diligent, resourceful | - Able to collect basic competitive data (news, launch announcements, background on products, customers, suppliers, etc.)<br>- Able to clearly report key findings in response to a given management brief<br>- Able to understand and use basic economic data (GDP, etc.)<br>- Grasps the importance of and ensures secrecy<br>- Has basic interaction/communication skills |
| 2.<br>Junior analyst: reliable facts, basic analysis | - Able to periodically update and where needed proactively inform senior mgt. on key developments in the your company's business environment (facts only)<br>- Able to superficially analyze several separate facts to prepare a bigger picture view for decision-makers<br>- Able to directly liaise with outside information suppliers (AC Nielsen, Planet Retail, etc.) when directed to do so<br>- Able to understand basics of business strategy theory<br>- Able to understand own firm's strategy and business drivers<br>- Has well-developed reporting and persuasive communication skills |
| 3.<br>Experienced analyst: trusted source of facts & interpretation | - Able to collect all data and map a competitor, using a pre-defined format, through desk research, including analysis of competitor's perceived strategy and assessment of possible implications for your firm's strategy execution<br>- Able to independently manage a portfolio of assignments and set priorities matching business needs and upside potential<br>- Able to (and trusted to) network with competitors, customers, etc., remaining wary of their attempts to elicit intelligence on your company<br>- Able to capture HUMINT; knowing the basic HUMINT rules<br>- Able to organize and (periodically) run 'competitor review' workshops to collect, analyze and codify 'tacit business environment information'<br>- Understands need for full compliance with applicable laws and ethical considerations<br>- Able to explain and convince stakeholder beyond content-driven arguments; understands and applies xenocentric view |
| 4.<br>proactive experienced professional: from analysis to foresight; trusted adviser | - Able to execute tailored, self-defined collection and analysis missions, even in new markets, new geo-areas (incl. interviews)<br>- Able to understand own firm's corporate strategy – brands and supply chain – and implied unit choices and options; credible MT sparring partner<br>- Able to write full 'business environment analysis' chapters for strategic plans, budget books, acquisition or investment plans<br>- Able to independently innovate collection and analysis methodologies; must have state-of-the-art knowledge of best practices and track record in applying various collection and analysis tools; recognized expert in the field<br>- Able to train/educate/coach and manage junior staff where needed<br>- Able to raise secrecy awareness and persuade management to employ counter-intelligence initiatives<br>- Able to proactively generate M&A proposals based on business environment trends; liaise with investment banks/lawyers on M&A teams<br>- Able to embed xenocentric view in strategic analysis<br>- Able to enforce full compliance with applicable laws and codes of ethics<br>- Able to persuade based on content and personal reputation/track-record<br>- Has courage to report news and analysis that goes against the party-line. |

TABLE 21.2 ▶▶▶ FOUR STRATEGIC ANALYST COMPETENCY LEVELS IN A SEQUENCE OF INCREASING COMPLEXITY/JOB RANK

# ACKNOWLEDGEMENTS

This book is based on my personal experience working in the offices of Akzo Nobel, the Dutch multinational paints, performance coatings and specialty chemicals company, and the Dutch dairy cooperative Royal FrieslandCampina. Many esteemed colleagues guided me in my voyage of discovery in strategic analysis, and for that they have my eternal gratitude. Special thanks goes to the Cheese, Butter & Milk Powder Business Group team at FrieslandCampina. My valued friends and colleagues Bas van den Berg, John Habets, Yves van Coillie and Sandra Vendel have consistently encouraged and supported my passionate writing hobby. Together with AartJan van Triest and Jan-Willem ter Avest, they gave flight to my dream of making this work available to a truly global audience.

Many friends have proofread parts of this work, through various stages of its development. My special gratitude goes to Godfried Wessels, Wim de Koning and professor Bob de Graaff for their encouragement and helpful suggestions.

The editorial team at LID Publishing, especially Sara Taheri, deserves my gratitude for their patiently editing the manuscripts, and for turning opaque language into clear messages. It has been a pleasure!

Three more individuals deserve special thanks. Hans Steensma, as co-founder of Military Formats In Business, opened up his larger-than-life network and connected me with multiple valuable sources, some of whom developed into great friends. Hans, knowing my strategy work experience, convinced me that I should write this book. About six years after his initial exhortations to do so, it is a published work. Without your encouragement, Hans, this book may never have been written.

Last but not least, two people deserve my greatest expression of thanks and gratitude: my patient wife Marieke, who had to make do with my solitary writing… and my daughter Louise, to whom I have dedicated this book, as a way to compensate for the many games of chess we could have played had I not been cloistered away in my writer's garret.

# APPENDIX

## APPENDIX 1: CONVERSATION TECHNIQUES IN DATA COLLECTION

Elicitors use conversational techniques methods to avoid asking overtly probing questions and still draw information from their target. The list of techniques below, adapted from an FBI brochure, is not necessarily exhaustive (FBI, 2014). Each of the techniques mentioned is referred to by its specific trigger. An example of a statement is provided for each trigger. A superficial analysis is made of what human psychological or social norm-induced behaviour this trigger appeals to. For some triggers the risks of use are included. It has been stated before in this book: this is practitioners' guide, not a scientific study. The author does not pretend to have an in-depth understanding of psychology. The aim is to illustrate, and most of all to warn, but certainly not to explain.

---

### TRIGGER 1 MAKE SUGGESTIVE STATEMENT

Example:

*"I bet you got over 100 new customers because of this innovation."*

Appeals to:

- Target's (human) tendency to correct others.
- Subtly addresses recognition need through mild flattery.

---

The FBI brochure suggests using leading questions with a similar purpose (FBI, 2014). Using questions in in general – particularly leading questions – is to be avoided at all times.

---

### TRIGGER 2 BRACKETING

Example:

*"Sales because of this innovation must be between € 5 – 15 Million?"*

Appeals to:

- Target's (human) tendency to correct others.

---

### TRIGGER 3 'REPEAT – A – WORD'

Example:

Target: *"We have lots of new customers due to the innovation."*

Elicitor: *"Lots?"* [accompanied by smart body language & intonation]

Appeals to:

- Target's (human) tendency to correct others.
- Target's need to get recognition.

Risk:

Target may get suspicious when using 'Repeat-a-Word' more than once

---

## TRIGGER 4 BE A GOOD LISTENER AS A TARGET COMPLAINS

Example:

Target: *"There is no f***ing way I pick up wireless here to let me check the web."*

Elicitor: *"I am sorry; do you want to use my 3G on my iPad?"*

Appeals to:

- Target's showing strong dislike of something.
- Target's openness during trying circumstances.
- Target's response to kindness, which really helped.

---

## TRIGGER 5 INCORRECT STATEMENT

Example:

Elicitor: *"I saw two press releases on FrieslandCampina acquisitions."*

Target: *"What do you mean two? There is only one – the other one is not in the public domain as far as I know."*

Appeals to:

- Target's (human) tendency to correct others, especially when pride in someone's job or capabilities is at stake.
- Target's inability to control emotion: outburst led to indiscretion.

Risk:

This can be a show-stopper if the target realizes he's been triggered; it can put him on High Alert and result in severe distrust. And trust in the elicitor is gone for good.

---

## TRIGGER 6 QUOTE REPORTED FACTS

Example:

Elicitor: *"I saw double-digit value sales growth in your cheese business in the last quarter."*

Appeals to:

- Target's tendency to recognition for his achievements.

Risk:

When feeding the target real facts in 'quid pro quo' way, the elicitor always will ensure that the result of the conversation is that he gained more than that he gave.

---

## TRIGGER 7 GOSSIP/CONFIDENTIAL BAIT

Example (in conspiracy tone, bit hush-hush):

Elicitor: *"Off the record, of course, but I trust you also looked at buying WBD?"*

Target: *"Sure we did, but we just couldn't justify paying what PepsiCo did."*

Appeals to:

- Target's valuing themselves above others.
- Target's need for recognition.
- Target's implicit moral obligation to return the favor given (reciprocity): the elictor gives a secret, now the target gives a secret. This is the bizarre, competitive dynamic of 'who' dares to release the biggest secret?'

---

## TRIGGER 8 PROVOCATIVE STATEMENT

Example:

Elicitor: *"Margins in processed cheese will never exceed 10% ROS."*

Appeals to:

- Target's tendency to correct; this is a strongly developed trait in teachers, professors, experts.
- Target's tendency to show off understanding (recognition).

In the FBI brochure this trigger is referred to as 'criticism' (FBI, 2014). The goal is to make the target upset with his employer, for example, prompting him to release non-public information about the employer. The risk with overly harsh criticism is that the target may simply get annoyed and walk away, or get angry and alarmed that he is a victim of elicitation. Using criticism without directly connected-praise is to be avoided.

---

## TRIGGER 9 FEIGNED OR REAL DISBELIEF

Example:

*"Did you really invest €100 Million in that expansion? Wow."*

Appeals to:

- Target's tendency to value recognition for achievement.

Risks:

The risk of feigning disbelief (or recognition, for that matter) is that the target may see through the elicitor's set-up. The target may get suspicious or plainly recognizes the hypocrisy and dislike her for it. This means the source is 'wasted' on this particular occasion.

A second risk is that the elicitor may themselves start to mentally reject their own behaviour, as the hypocrisy required for satisfying some business info need may increasingly conflict with the elicitor's personal values. Such self-denial of values may be reasoned away by an elicitor when needed to win a war, as the cause justifies the means. But abandon one's principles for a commercial assignment from a business services agency, on behalf of some anonymous corporate client? Such commendable values may make the elicitor functionally less effective.

---

## TRIGGER 10 START A SENTENCE

Example:

*"It is hard to recruit good staff in."*

Appeals to:

- Target's tendency to complete / correct others.

---

## TRIGGER 11 FLATTERY (DISGUISED AS CRITICISM)

Example:

*"We initially didn't consider your acquisition in China a smart move."*

Appeals to:

- Target's need for recognition for achievement.
- Target's tendency to correct others.

Risk:

This can be a risky move, as it might offend and anger the target, and end up shutting him down entirely.

---

## TRIGGER 12 NAIVE STATEMENT

Example:

*"We really didn't understand how you could offer this product so cheaply."*

Appeals to:

- Target's need for recognition (of achievement).
- Target's tendency to correct others.

Risk:

This is also a dangerous weapon because it may hurt the elicitor's credibility (especially if he's a peer and dissuade the target from talking further, as she may view the elicitor as simply too clueless to waste her time on).

---

## TRIGGER 13 REASSURANCE

Example:

*"We operate in different markets anyway."*

Or

*"When we talked to your CFO last month, he shared... [feeding sensitive info]."*

Or

*"Neither you or I work for ABC Ltd., and neither of us understands their business model."*

Appeals to:

- Target's need for safety.
- Target's inability to value the information properly.
- Target's need for social validation; it is no problem when superiors do the same.
- Target's tendency to complete/correct others.
- Target's tendency to show off understanding (for recognition and praise).

---

## TRIGGER 14 PROVIDE BREAKING NEWS

Example:

*"I see here on my iPhone that the CEO of company ABC just resigned."*

Appeals to:

- Target's curiosity, news hunger.

---

## TRIGGER 15 OFFER ETHICAL DILEMMA

Example (knowing that the competitor is operating a business in West Africa):

*"A friend of mine who's a business development director in another industry sector [imaginary of course] recently considered investing in West Africa, as that market shows strong growth prospects, but he just had no clue how to handle the corruption."* [Then either silence, or a question like: 'What do you think?']

Appeals to:

- Target's tendency to complete/correct others.
- Target's tendency to show off understanding (recognition).

Risk:

This is potentially a powerful technique, as it will reveal a great deal of the other party's real intent. There are few better indicators of intent than how a real-life dilemma was handled. The target, however, may see through the objective of the elicitor, and immediately lose trust.

---

## TRIGGER 16 VOLUNTEER INFORMATION

Example:

*"We reported 1% sales growth, when consolidated in €, due to currency headwinds in the last quarter of 2013 in our emerging markets businesses."*

Appeals to:

- Target's tendency to complete/correct others.
- Target's implicit moral obligation to return the favor given (reciprocity) – the elicitor gives a secret, now the target gives a secret. Once again, this is an example of the strange, competitive dynamic of who's willing to release the biggest secret.

Risk:

When pumping the target with real facts as a quid pro quo tactic, the elicitor will always see to it that they gained more than than they give. Moreover, the elicitor ensures that they only give public domain information.

---

## TRIGGER 17 CAN YOU TOP THIS?

Example:

*"We heard the volume growth of Company D's yoghurt sales in Germany was over 30% last year. Just imagine trying to manage that sort of growth."*

Appeals to:

- Target's tendency to show off understanding (for recognition and praise).

---

## TRIGGER 18 'DISCOVER' MUTUAL INTEREST

Example:

*"You also attend this conference often right? Suppose you visited last year as well when it was held in Ireland. So much hot air we heard on the Irish dairy industry remember?"*

Appeals to:

- Target's tendency to belong to a group.
- Target's tendency to complete/correct others.

---

## TRIGGER 19 SILENCE

Example:

*"So that puts me in a tough position..." (accompanied by the elicitor pretending to thoughtfully dwell on his dilemma, with corresponding body language).*

Appeals to:

- Target's tendency to keep talking: silence is uncomfortable.

Risk:

This poses risks because breaking the conversational flow might prompt the target to lose interest and walk away.

---

An elicitor will not use every trigger in every conversation. This is an iterative, on-the-fly process they: test which triggers work to keep the conversation going, whilst ensuring the conversation is focused on capturing the data the elicitor is after.

# APPENDIX 2: SOURCES SEGMENTED BY DATA NEEDS

| INFO NEED | SOURCE DESCRIPTION | SCOPE | COST | UPDATE FREQUENCY |
|---|---|---|---|---|
| General | www.cia.gov World Fact Book & World Leaders Database<br>+ Covering country information in multiple dimensions<br>+/- Western perspective<br>- No forward-looking economic forecast | +++ | 0 | Perpetual |
| | www.eiu.com<br>+ Covering country information in multiple dimensions<br>+ Neutral perspective | +++ | Partly fee-based | High |
| | www.international.loc.gov<br>+ Library of Congress country information; in-depth studies<br>- Neither geographically complete nor up-to-date | + | 0 | Low |
| | www.wikipedia.com or www.wikitravel.com<br>+ Covering country information in multiple dimensions<br>- Accuracy, completeness, actuality not verifiable | + | 0 | Varies by country |
| Political / security/ stability | www.stratfor.com<br>+ Analysis<br>- Non-partisan but US perspective | ++ | Partly fee-based | High |
| | www.controlrisks.com<br>+ Guidance to security Related decisions, (e.g., travel) | ++ | Partly fee-based | Perpetual |
| | www.trustedsources.co.uk<br>+ In-depth political analysis<br>- Limited number of countries covered | +/- | Partly fee-based | High |
| | www.transparency.org/country<br>+ Scoring by country on corruption perception and other human development parameters | +++ | 0 | Annually |
| Economics & finance | www.imf.org<br>+ World Economic Outlook covers most countries<br>+ Looking up to 5 years ahead on GDP, CPI, etc. | ++ | 0 | Quarterly for WEO |
| | www.oanda.com<br>+ Superb database for historic exchange rates for a country's currency against virtually any other currency | +++ | 0 | Perpetual |
| Health | http://www.who.int/countries/and/en/<br>+ Covering nutrition and health statistics | +++ | 0 | Perpetual |
| Development | http://www.worldbank.org/en/country/<br>+ Development programs for poverty reduction | ++ | 0 | High |

TABLE A2.1 ▶▶▶ SOURCES PROVIDING COUNTRY DATA (ECONOMICS, POLITICS, CULTURAL)

All industrialized nations and most developing/emerging countries publish extensive statistics online. For example, for the Netherlands visit www.cbs.nl for general statistics and www.dnb.nl (The Dutch central bank) for monetary statistics, interest rates, etc. For developed and some developing countries, check either www.tradingeconomics.com or www.oecd.org. For the European Union, consider using Eurostat: http://epp.eurostat.ec.europa.eu/portal/page/portal/statistics/themes

Country studies are often carried out by think tanks. Visit the site of Penn State University to find an appropriate entity http://gotothinktank.com/2015-global-go-to-think-tank-index-report/

| INFO NEED | SOURCE DESCRIPTION | SCOPE | COST | UPDATE FREQUENCY |
|---|---|---|---|---|
| General | The company's own website (should always be the first call)<br>+ It may answer all questions<br>- Info provided may be biased, incomplete, inaccurate and or no longer actual (international companies may have multiple websites, in the various countries in which they operate) | Variable | 0 | Variable |
| | www.prnewswire.com<br>This site offers press releases from multiple sources including individual companies. Free-of-charge searchable database. Results include teasers on research reports | + | 0 or fee-based | High |
| | www.thecasecentre.org<br>The case centre is an independent clearing house for, amongst others, company-specific business school case studies prepared at multiple institutions, including Harvard's. | + | Fee-based | Low |
| | www.researchandmarkets.com<br>Internet store that offers syndicate market research reports including company specific analyses | +++ | Fee-based | Variable |
| Financial | www.hoovers.com (owned by Dun & Bradstreet)<br>+ Large database; provides comprehensive profiles | +++ | Fee-based | High |
| | www.dnb.com (the original Dun & Bradstreet)<br>+ Advertised as the world largest company info database<br>+ Provides multiple financial data and ownership info | +++ | Fee-based | High |
| | www.sec.gov (for listed companies in the US)<br>+ Detailed financial filings for listed US companies (10K)<br>- Coverage (unfortunately) limited to listed companies | ++ | 0 | Perpetual |
| | www.standardandpoors.com (for rated companies)<br>+ Financial filings<br>- Only covering companies with a debt rating, which is a small group | + | Fee-based | High |
| | www.thomsonone.com (for selected listed companies)<br>+ Stockbroker analyst reports<br>+ Coverage is limited to selected stockbroker houses; generally, investment analyst reports are a valuable source<br>+ Access is restricted to (institutional) investors as customers of the respective investment banks | + | Fee-based | High |
| | www.bloomberg.com<br>+ The standard site for actual news/data on listed companies<br>+ Free of charge access to news archive | +++ | Fee-based | Perpetual |
| | www.tadawul.com.sa (for listed companies in Saudi Arabia)<br>+ Detailed financial filings for companies listed in Saudi Arabia This is just an example of a site in an individual country, most stock exchanges offer extensive details on listed commercial operations | ++ | 0 | Perpetual |
| | www.bundesanzeiger.de (as a country example)<br>+ Detailed financial filings from government filing site. This is just an example of a site in an individual country, many countries have chamber of commerce equivalents | ++ | 0 | Perpetual |
| Innovation | www.mintel.com (GNPD database)<br>+ Coverage of multiple countries in many FMCG categories | ++ | Fee-based | Daily |
| Mergers & acquisitions (M&As) | www.mergermarket.com<br>+ Coverage of global M&A transactions, news & analysis<br>+ Includes legal and other advisors involved by transaction | +++ | Fee-based | High |
| | info.mlex.com<br>+ Coverage of legal details related to M&A transactions | ++ | Fee-based | High |
| Trademarks & Intellectual property | http://tmview.europa.eu/tmview/basicSearch.html<br>+ Coverage of European trademark registries<br>+ Connected site covers other intellectual property | +++ | 0 | Perpetual |
| | http://www.uspto.gov/trademarks/process/search/<br>+ Coverage of US trademark registries | +++ | 0 | Perpetual |

**TABLE A2.2 ▶▶▶ SOURCES PROVIDING COMPANY INFORMATION OTHER THAN ROUTINE NEWS**

| INFO NEED | SOURCE DESCRIPTION | SCOPE | COST | UPDATE FREQUENCY |
|---|---|---|---|---|
| General | www.marketresearch.com<br>A site that fulfills the role that amazon.com offers for amongst others books: it is a repository that lists syndicate reports written by other market research firms. Broad industry scope | +++ | Fee-based | Regularly |
| Global-geo-scope-sources | www.euromonitor.com<br>Euromonitor is a global market research agency that offers through its Passport subscription access to quantitative and qualitative market information by country by FMCG category. It also offers bespoke analyses to customers. Euromonitor offers company-specific analyses including some that were both detailed and of high analytical quality | +++ | Fee-based | Annually in Passport; actual in bespoke work |
| | www.mintel.com<br>Mintel offers a Food & Drink suite that resembles Euromonitor's Passport. It is best known for its GNPD database (see previous table). Also offers bespoke work | ++ | Fee-based | Regularly |
| | www.datamonitor.com<br>The Informa group operates under several brands: datamonitor, but also marketline.com. Comparable to Euromonitor in types of services. Superior in consumer insights, smaller in quantitative market research. Also offers company-specific profiles (accessible also via ThomsonOne) | ++ | Fee-based | Regularly |
| | www.frost.com<br>Frost & Sullivan is a market research company focusing on multiple non-B2C-industries. It offers syndicate research reports | ++ | Fee-based | Regularly |
| | www.researchandmarkets.com<br>Advertising itself as the world's largest market research store, this site offers an overview of syndicate reports prepared by multiple research companies | +++ | Fee-based | Regularly |
| Global but product-mix focued | http://www.fil-idf.org/Public/ColumnsPage.php?ID=23077<br>The International Dairy Federation is a global sector association that amongst others publishes the most reliable dairy statistics in the World Dairy Situation reports. This site serves as an example of a primary sector- specific global source. As a rule, industry associations have better statistical data than third-party market research companies | ++ | Fee-based for reports | Annually for statistics |
| | http://www.canadean.com<br>Canadean is a sector-specific market research company with a global scope. Its origins and deserved claim to fame are in quantitative (carbonated) beverages markets, but it has expanded its scope. It also offers company-specific analyses | ++ | Fee-based | Regularly |
| | http://www.erc-world.com/<br>Comparable to Canadean, ERC is an FMCG-focused syndicate research company. One focus area is baby food | ++ | Fee-based | Regularly |
| | http://www.fao.org/home/en/<br>The Food and Agricultural Organization of the United Nations is used as an example of a multinational not-for-profit organization that provides statistics on agro (commodity) markets. The above-mentioned oecd.org offers similar services for different industrial activities. | ++ | Fee-based | Regularly |
| Geo-mix and product-mix specific | http://bjboabc.en.china.cn/<br>BOABC stands for Beijing Orient Agricultural Business Consultancy. BOABC focuses on China and on food and agriculture. When looking for a market-specific and geo-specific research report it may pay off nicely to identify the specialist consultancy firm for that geo/product niche, rather than automatically buy the 'big name' report that features on top at sites such as researchandmarkets.com | ++ | Fee-based | Regularly |
| | http://www.imesconsulting.com/<br>IMES has a focus on the Middle East and Arab world and offers detailed reports on multiple FMCG categories. Each region and sector has such specialist agencies | ++ | Fee-based | Regularly |
| | http://www.nielsen.com<br>Nielsen is best known for its retail-scanning data: it registers all FMCG-products sold via supermarket cash registers. The data are sold in multiple formats and for many countries and categories are the standard source for calculating market shares | +++ | Fee-based | Usually monthly or bi-monthly |
| | http://www.iriworldwide.nl/<br>IRI offers services that partly overlap with those of Nielsen | ++ | Fee-based | Usually monthly or bi-monthly |
| Global topic specific | http://www.healthfocus.com/hf/?page=health-studies<br>Health Focus International is a supplier that provides consumer views and attitudes towards health. The syndicate reports are country-based. Tailored, single-client questions can be catered for at an extra cost | +++ | Fee-based | Regularly |
| | http://www.tnsglobal.com/what-we-do<br>TNS is a global market research agency that amongst other things offers 'shopper panel data'. Rather than taking the scanning data from retailers, as in the case of Nielsen, here a representative group of shoppers have scanners at home with which they scan all their purchases. This allows for obtaining category specific intelligence | | | |

TABLE A2.3 ▶▶▶ SOURCES PROVIDING MARKET & CATEGORY DATA

| INFO NEED | SOURCE DESCRIPTION | SCOPE | COST | UPDATE FREQUENCY |
|---|---|---|---|---|
| General news | www.lexisnexis.com<br>Lexis Nexis offers a service that, based on your news need, operates a tailored query, searching multiple online sources permanently to offer you a tailored news feed. LN also offers search functionality in its news database | ++ | Fee-based | Daily news feed |
| | www.factiva.com<br>Factiva reports to be the world largest business news site, covering news from 200 countries in 28 languages | +++ | Fee-based | Perpetual |
| | www.meltwater.com<br>Meltwater offers services similar to those of Lexis Nexis | ++ | Fee-based | Daily news feed |
| Channel or sector-specific news | www.planetretail.net<br>Planet Retail offers a global database on the world of retail: details on every supermarket and country worldwide. PR also offers analyses, country forecasts and pictures | +++ | Fee-based | Daily |
| | http://www.igd.com/<br>IGD has a smaller retail database compared to Planet Retail and is UK-focused. IGD has a separate information business on supply chain capabilities and practices | + | Fee-based | Daily |
| | http://www.kantarretail.com/<br>Kantar retail is another retail-oriented site. Kantar is an expert in shopper marketing | ++ | Fee-based | Daily |
| | http://www.just-food.com/<br>This news provider is focused on the food industry. The owner also offers just-drinks.com | ++ | Partly fee-based | At least daily |
| | http://www.flex-news-food.com/Home.aspx<br>This is a news provider similar to just-food.com | ++ | Fee-based | At least daily |
| | http://www.ihs.com/products/chemical/index.aspx<br>IHS offers market intelligence, including price quotations for multiple industries including the chemical and the consumer/retail industries. It also offers country profiles like EIU. | +++ | Fee-based | Perpetual |
| Quotation and price news | http://www.lme.com/<br>The London Metal Exchange offers prices on metals that are traded at an exchange (similar to a stock exchange on stocks). Every industry has its own undisputed price sources, the LME serves as an example | +++ | 0 | Ongoing during trading hours |

**TABLE A2.4 ▶▶▶ SOURCES PROVIDING GENERAL AND CHANNEL/SECTOR-SPECIFIC NEWS AND ANALYSIS**

| INFO NEED | SOURCE DESCRIPTION | SCOPE | COST | UPDATE FREQUENCY |
|---|---|---|---|---|
| Industry best practices | http://www.executiveboard.com/<br>This group is a membership-based broker of industry best practices featuring multiple disciplines (law, finance, R&D, marketing, and more). It also offers bespoke research. | ++ | Fee-based | Regularly |

**TABLE A2.5 ▶▶▶ SOURCE PROVIDING INDUSTRY BEST PRACTICES**

# APPENDIX 3: INTERNET SEARCH OPERATORS

Next to the common operators AND and OR, the operators covered below are offered by most internet search engines to narrow down the number of search results and increase the relevancy of the search results that are being obtained:

- Adjacency
- Around
- Filetype:
- Intitle:
- Inurl:
- NOT
- Range
- Site
- Truncs

This is but a small sub-set, selected on the basis of their likely usefulness to a business strategy analyst. Search specialists are encouraged to check other sources for more details, for example the 2007 NSA manual (NSA, 2007).

## ADJACENCY

The adjacency operator allows searching for terms in a fixed subsequent order. For the sake of simplicity, the Google formatting for the adjacency operator is used.

It is outside the scope of this work to cover the multitude of available search engine formats. The reader who wants to use other search engines will easily retrieve the specific formats that are actual at the time of searching. Search engines are run by commercial companies that may have commercial reasons to change their formats. Unfortunately and in contrast to scientific disciplines like physics or chemistry there are no global standards. In chemistry the element lead is abbreviated by Pb; that abbreviation is universally recognized in any chemistry lab anywhere in the world. On Google, AND is represented by a space, on Bing it's denoted by the word AND, and Yahoo uses '+'.

In the intermezzo at the bottom of chapter 6 the example of processed cheese is given. The search query "processed cheese" in Google Boolean language means processed AND cheese, as the space is defined as logical AND. Starting and ending the query with quotation marks ("processed cheese") will only give results where the words processed cheese are featured immediately next to each other.

Apart from its use in successive fractions, the adjacency operator is also highly useful to retrieve the source of a particular document. When a hard copy, even a single page, of a document without a source, reaches the analyst, she should try to locate the full document. This is simple housekeeping. The analyst needs at least to establish the publication date, the author and preferably some sourcing context. The adjacency operator is a great help. Statistically the chances of, say, seven words appearing in exactly the same sequence in multiple documents is really small, unless these words form a definition that is commonly used across multiple documents.

The following example will illustrates this. When a one-page hard copy document without a source appears on an analyst's desk with in it the sentence:

*"Pertinent information is highlighted and not obscured by a mass of trivial facts."*

Chances are slight that the search query "pertinent information is highlighted and not obscured" will result in many hits. Running that query (www.google.nl, 21 December 2013) yielded only two hits, of which the first indeed gives the full report in which the sentence appears (Canadian Land Forces, 2001d). The adjacency operator thus offers an extraordinary efficient process to locate data on the web.

The drawback of using the adjacency operator is that the sequence of the terms must be exact. A query aimed at data on "whey derivatives" will not find a report on "whey protein derivatives". In Google, the adjacency search operator has a solution for this.

The search query "whey * derivatives" will retrieve results where a maximum of one word is located between whey and derivatives. "whey * * derivatives" allows for two words in between the two search terms etc.

## AROUND (PROXIMITY)

The proximity operator – in Google featured as the AROUND(x) format – enables to search for different terms simultaneously in no particular order, but they must be close to each other. The x variable in between the quotation marks indicates the number of words that are allowed to appear between the two search terms.

The search query *whey AROUND(2) derivatives* will for example retrieve documents with the text:

- ...derivatives of the whey...
- ...whey protein derivatives...

It will not retrieve a reference to a *whey from casein is the source for multiple derivatives.*

The AROUND operator is much more specific than the AND operator, as it allows retrieval of only those documents where the search terms are close to each other.

## FILETYPE:

In Google, the filetype: operator restricts the search results to a chosen filetype. A common search approach to find original reports on a particular topic rather than news items that stem from those reports is to specify as filetype:pdf.

In the example of the intermezzo that closes out chapter 6 on processed cheese, you saw that the adjacency query "processed cheese" resulted in 1,380,000 hits (at www.google.nl, 21 December 2013). Changing the search query into filetype:pdf "processed cheese" resulted in 41,800 hits. Restricting the output to pdf-files thus only results in a narrowing of the results to about 3% of the original search output.

## INTITLE:

In Google, the intitle: operator searches only for words in the title of a document. Building further on the processed cheese example from the intermezzo in chapter 6, the mix of an adjacency query and intitle: has as (Google-)syntax intitle:"processed cheese". This query yields 17,400 hits. It is critical to not put a space between the double colon and the first bracket of the search string. Using a combination of the intitle: and adjacency operator leads to a narrowing of the results output to about 1% of the number of hits where the intitle: condition had not been specified. The resulting set probably has higher relevancy.

Combining filetype: and intitle: further narrows the results. The (Google-)syntax looks: inurl:"processed cheese" filetype:pdf. This query results in only 489 hits. Adding Netherlands to the search query results in only fifteen hits.

The first two hits provide (fee-based) reports on the processed cheese market in the Netherlands. These reports feature the processed cheese producers I'd looked for as well.

## INURL:

In Google, the inurl: operator searches only for words in the url of a document. For processed cheese the query inurl:"processed cheese" yields 50,800 hits (at www.google.nl, 21 December 2013).

The inurl: operator is particularly useful to select domain name groups. The syntax for Netherlands focused query can be: inurl:.nl. Similarly, work from educational institutions can thus be retrieved by using inurl:.edu etc.

## NOT

In Google, the Boolean NOT operator has a –symbol as syntax. To search for processed cheese that does not originate from France, the syntax reads: "Processed cheese" –France.

This results in 1,240,000 hits, compared to 1,380,000 hits without the limiting condition of excluding France.

The syntax "Processed cheese" -.com only yields results from web sites that do not have a .com domain. This yields 207,000 hits – only 15% of the "processed cheese" hits originate from a non .com domain.

## RANGE

The range operator allows one to select a quantitative range. The syntax is a ... This means that a search query wine 1980...1985 gives results on wines produced in that period. This operator may be useful to locate an older annual report of an company, but for that information this approach is generally a last resort, used when all annual report databases have been exhaustively and unproductively searched.

## SITE

In Google, the site operator allows selection from websites from a particular domain. The syntax is site.

For processed cheese sites that only originate from Belgium, a search query reads site:.be "Processed cheese". This query yields 3790 results; the same query for .nl yields only 1140 results. The site operator is thus a powerful tool in narrowing down results. The question remains whether the country-specific domain names are still used often enough to generate enough *relevant* results on a query.

## TRUNCS

The Trunc operator is useful when the root of a search term is clear but not the whole term. A search on chees? retrieves both cheese and cheesecake.

This operator is also useful when results, both with singular and plural forms, are sought after: for example cheesecake? which retrieves both cheesecake and cheesecakes.

In contrast to (partly fee-based) services like Lexis-Nexis and Factiva, Google searching does not, at the time of me writing this Appendix (December 2013) support Trunc searching.

# NOTES

## CHAPTER 1

1. Data (stimuli in the quote below) ladder up through information, subsequently lead to knowledge – a new insight, new knowledge [Favaro, 2013]:

   *"In 2000, Eric Kandel won the Nobel Prize for showing how humans produce a new thought. [...] Kandel's work also shows the human brain to be the greatest inventory on earth. From birth, your brain takes in stimuli, breaks them down, and then stores them on "memory shelves", which are distributed throughout your brain. When presented with a particular challenge, your brain searches to see if there is any connection with what is already sitting on your memory shelves. When your brain finds a match, your memories combine with new stimuli and you experience "Eureka!" – a novel thought that feels like a flash of insight."*

2. Let me make a slight detour to Cuba in 1962, and military intelligence, to illustrate my point about the critical role of perpetual monitoring. In my experience this role in business is just as relevant as it is in the military... justifying this detour to Cuba [Dobbs, 2009a]:

   *"The Cold War was an intelligence war [...] for the most part it was fought in the shadows. Since it was impossible to destroy the enemy without risking a nuclear exchange, Cold War strategists attempted instead to discover his capabilities, to probe for weaknesses."*

   Massive resources were dedicated on both sides of the Iron Curtain to maintain a reliable image of the adversary's competences and to analyze the adversary's intent. Insisting all the while that it would never do such a thing, the Soviet government had been had been duplicitous [Dobbs, 2009f]. A US-operated Cuban monitoring operation revealed an inconvenient truth: despite extensive American analysis of Soviet capabilities and intent, the Russians had surprised the US with their progress in deploying nuclear missiles a mere 90 miles south of Miami.

   It was a single general's decision to maintain a monitoring sub-process that allowed the US, albeit late in the game, to mount a daring response before the missile systems became operational. Former East German foreign intelligence director Markus Wolf – better known as the man without a face – once postulated that 'vast stretches of intelligence work are very boring' [Wolf, 1998]. The statement most of all applies to the permanent monitoring processes and the related routine analysis work that predominated in the days before Big Data. In the case of the Cuban crisis, monitoring work delivered a timely warning and more than proved worth its tedious effort.

## CHAPTER 2

1. Hammer wrote in the New York Times on Gerstner's changes in IBM [Gerstner, 2003]:

   *"Gerstner decided that sooner is better than perfect – that was anathema to the old IBM. That is the most important change that can come from the top."*

2. McGeorge Bundy, US National Security Adviser to President Johnson during the Vietnam war made a startling admission about the lack of precise objectives set for American involvement in the conflict [Halberstam, 1992f]:

   *"The Administration, Bundy recounted, did not tell the military what to do and how to do it; there was in his words a 'premium put on imprecision', and the political and military leaders did not speak candidly with each other. In fact, if the military and political leaders had been totally candid with each other in 1965 about the length and cost of the war instead of coming to a consensus, as Johnson wanted, there would have been vast and perhaps unbridgeable differences."*

In other words: already in the early briefing phase, an analyst is warned that 'imprecision' may be an indicator of politicization of the topic to be studied – with all the risk that brings to objectivity in strategic analysis.

# CHAPTER 3

1. Further reading on deception is only recommended for intelligence history buffs. For those among you, Martin provides a compelling glimpse of the complications that deceptions caused in the US counterintelligence world, featuring characters like conspiracy-obsessed James Jesus Angleton. You can read more in his book *The Wilderness of Mirrors* (Martin, 2003).

# CHAPTER 4

1. Clearance is jargon for the degree of access to confidential information that a person in an organization has. The higher a person's clearance, the more confidential documents a person can access.
2. The list of roles is not exhaustive.
3. In military intelligence, cover stories are also known as 'legends'.
4. A classic example of intelligence being available in time to be acted upon but still rendered useless due to the greater need of source protection is the Battle for Crete on 20 May 1941. The Commonwealth Force Commander General Freyberg knew exactly when and where the German airborne troops that were planning to invade Crete were to dispatch. Still, Allied High Command placed such importance on keeping the British 'Ultra' code-breaking program under wraps that Freyberg could reveal top his men very little of what he knew about the Germans' assault plans. General Freyberg could not reveal all he knew to his men. His only known public utterance about his access to Ultra intelligence was, upon the German planes arriving where and when expected: "They are dead on time!" (Keegan, 2003b).

# CHAPTER 5

1. The use of leading, negative, compound and vague is out of the question at all times (Canadian Land Forces, 2001b).

   *"Questions must be framed to have the source provide information, rather than 'yes' or 'no' answers that have limited value" (Canadian Land Forces, 2001c.).*

   Asking questions of a target/source, is, perhaps unconsciously, linked to the collector's desire to 'take control' (Jähne, 2009). Asking questions may thus be perceived as aggressive. When asking questions, the target/source may go through the following emotional sequence:

   1. Who are you to ask that question? This makes me suspicious.
   2. Why are you asking? What is behind this question?
   3. How should I respond? Truth, half-truth, deception, lie?
   4. How much should I say? Liars tend to use a lot of words.
   5. How will he use what I say?
   6. What is in it for me when I say A or B or C?

   As becomes clear from statement 2 above: asking questions may reveal the intent of the questioning. This is a no-go territory in elicitation work. If the intent is not immediately clear then it may very well raise suspicion. Finally, asking questions may have legal repercussions. In court, in a corporate espionage case that the target may mount againts the elicitor, the judge may ask: 'Did the elicitor ask for that information'. If the target can truthfully confirm this, it becomes evident that the elicitor was intentionally trying to collect data that was known to be confidential. If, however, the target can only say: 'no, we were talking and in the course of the conversation I shared this but it was unsolicited', the judge may not be able to prove the intentions of the elicitor were ever to collect the data and therefore there is no case for a verdict. Needless to say, that court cases are to be avoided at all times. So, staying away from elicitation and especially from doing so through pointed questioning is the better choice.

2. The Japanese Secret Service considers intelligence collection to be an honourable, patriotic and commendable profession (Deacon, 1982d). As a result there has never been a shortage of volunteers among officers of higher rank to take on intelligence jobs, even when their cover story necessitated them to accept a lowly job, like that of a clerk.

# CHAPTER 6

1. During the Cold War the adversaries of the US heavily relied on OSINT (Mercado, 2009a):

   *"The US aerospace publication Aviation Week, dubbed "Aviation Leak" for its scoops, was a perennial favorite. The journal was among the US technical periodicals that East German intelligence, amongst others, translated to monitor current developments in aerospace."*

2. In the chilly cold war years of the early 1980s, the USSR was obsessed with spotting preparations for a Western first-strike nuclear war. The London desk of the KGB received an order to monitor (Hoffman, 2011c):

   *"...field exercises involving cruise missiles stationed at the Royal Air Force base at Greenham Common. But according to [defector] Gordievsky, the London office had no intelligence sources for this; they sent British Press reports to Moscow instead."*

   The Kremlin, in other words, partly relied on OSINT to receive the critical early warning signals for NATO war preparation they so desperately looked for.

3. Prof. Dr. B. de Graaff estimates that due to the exponential increase of OSINT material available on the internet and as a result of the changed agendas of security services in the Western world, OSINT collection now makes up 95% of the input amassed by these services (Graaff, 2015). During the Cold War, government intelligence on either side of the Iron Curtain was focused on the other party's capabilities. In short, they were counting rockets and tanks. Today's threats are different: Twenty First Century security services are immersed in anti-terrorism activities. Terrorists still do leave traces on the internet that are technically OSINT.

4. An additional challenge is that commercial companies often consist of myriad different legal entities. For each of these companies the full filings need to be retrieved. Reconstructing the financial condition of the different companies is challenging, as internal transfer price systems that have potentially been developed for tax purposes may disguise the profitability of commercial operations. Not being able to untangle such knots may lead to incorrect conclusions on the lines of business that contribute most and least to a competitor's bottom line. It gets really difficult when some of the legal entities are 'offshored' to tax paradises such as the British Virgin Islands, as there's no such thing as a Freedom of Information Act in such countries. This inhibits any sort of clear, reliable view of commercial companies' filings. In response to the so-called 'Panama Papers' revelations, which in 2016 revealed the tax schemes of many high net-worth individuals and companies, international legislation may be forthcoming that would force companies force companies to become more transparent on net sales and real profits by market. From a strategic analysis perspective, such information would be extraordinarily valuable, which is exactly why I do not expect such transparency rules to be put into force any time soon.

5. The exception is a group of industrial activities that from a risk or hazard standpoint are deemed so relevant that the mandate to grant such permits is with the governing province or the state rather than at the individual city level. Nuclear power stations' permits are for example not granted on city council level. From a strategy analysis data collection perspective, the level where the mandate sits does not make a difference to the collection approach.

6. The OSINT manual prepared by the NSA in 2007 and declassified in 2013 is the best example of the fluidity of sources in the internet age. The manual has (only...) a six-page section (pp. 400-405) on using the internet to research companies. Quite a few of the source hyperlinks no longer refer to useful websites. Other references, such as references to to academic business school libraries, are only really relevant to students of such business school as they require the right user id/password. For finding the free sources, one doesn't need such libraries. Other sites that are mentioned as being free are so incomplete that it is almost amusing. http://www.reportgallery.com is referred to as a site offering free annual reports, and does indeed offer free annual reports.

   When looking for dairy companies, this site offered (as of 19 November 2013) three company reports. This apparently was the only view of the dairy industry available there. The three companies on which the reports were offered *together* process less than 2% of the global milk pool. None of them feature in the global dairy industry top ten by sales or milk processing by volume.

7. The same is true for search engine providers like Google. The sheer mass of data these search engine providers access is such that chances are your individual search term and related click behavior will pose less of an information security risk.

## CHAPTER 7

1. Showing off of rockets at May Day parades proved detrimental to the Soviet surprise strategy aimed for in Cuba. The latter is proof of the risk of bravado in a government communications context. Clearly, the impressive May Day parades served to remind the Soviet people that this time, the motherland would not be destroyed by invaders, be they French, German, British or American, as the army stood ready to never again be beaten. Showing off to their own people, however, also offered valuable intelligence to their adversaries. What was true for the Soviet is still just as true in a corporate context. Rallying a company's staff behind a (new) strategy may require revealing more of its competences and intent than a competitor, to whom this information will easily become available, should know. As in the Soviet case this is a dilemma. As with any dilemma there is by definition no satisfactory solution – there will always be the need for compromise. Companies, especially listed companies that also have to convince shareholders, tend to favor openness over being too secretive. Privately-owned companies in particular tend to favour discretion, giving their competitors fewer clues as to their competencies and intent.

   The interesting fact is that Collins in his classic Harvard Business Review paper on Level 5 Leadership, makes the case that high-bravado, movie star-type CEOs tend to correlate negatively with their company's long-term performance (Collins, 2005). This is not a dilemma. Bravado beyond essential corporate communication to make staff and or shareholders literally buy in to a strategy and its implications for them usually only serves a CEO's ego purposes. It usually doesn't build long-term shareholder value when contrasted with more humble and low-profile but no less ambitious CEOs.

2. Soviet military sources point out how close the world had come to nuclear war (Hoffman, 2011d). At the height of the crisis, the Soviet leadership sent out the code word "BRONTOZAVR" to its rocket divisions:

   > *"The word was a signal: switch the command system from peacetime to combat alert status."* Never before had this word been sent, not even in drills. The communication officer recalled: *"It was strangely quiet. I cannot forget the mixture of nervousness, surprise and pain on the faces of each operator, without exception – officers, enlisted men, women telephone operators."*

   Fortunately the crisis was resolved and the "BRONTOZAVR" alert expired.

# CHAPTER 8

1. The frailty of human memory has long been acknowledged (Goleman, 1994):

   *"The lay expectation is that whatever we remember should be true, but memory does not work like a video camera. From the point of view of neuroscience, every memory is a fragile reconstruction of what the nervous system actually witnessed.*

   *The context – the time and place – in which you acquire a memory is the quickest part of the memory to decay and the easiest to interfere with."*

   Given the scientific evidence for the frailty of memory,

   *"...the miracle is that anything we remember is true [...] not that there is distortion."*

   This is a sobering thought and a warning to anyone involved in strategic analysis, where true facts are the basis for any deliverable that ultimately is to underpin a corporate decision. Structured filing of facts as they appear when they appear is probably the best mitigation to the risk of distortion following the acquisition of those facts. In HUMINT collection, however, this doesn't solve any distortion of the truth, distortion resulting from intentional deception or from the frailty of memory.

2. After buying a can of instant milk powder at the supermarket, you become the owner of the can and its contents. Whether you subsequently want to analyze the powder to reverse-engineer the recipe and/or the process technology of the producer of the powder or whether you feed the product to a family member doesn't matter. What does matter if you acquire the product for competitive intelligence purposes is what you do with the information. Knowing how a producer processes instant milk powder, based on reverse-engineering a sample of that powder, does not mean that applying that knowledge in your own factory, is by definition legal. The process technology may be protected by intellectual property rights. MASINT-obtained knowledge may help to understand matters. Care should be taken not to violate legitimate rights upon *applying* knowledge so obtained.

3. In a highly functional and rapidly innovating FMCG category, disciplined, embedded strategic analysis work has in the past contributed to delivering immediate, low-hanging fruit-type value. This was done by providing every sales staff member with an every quarter updated and fully elucidated on-the-market product range review. The review only contained the key facts on all competitor offerings and on our own.

   It was of course highlighting the many differentiators of our firm's offering that made our offering irresistible, but it was most of all factual. It was the size of a credit card. It was nice, colorful and easy to read. It came with a transparent and water-resistant plastic cover. As a keychain it was connected to the sales force car keys set. This ensured there was a large chance the sales staff had the card with them when they needed it. As you can see, this example is a decade old. Today we of course provide a confidential and dedicated permanently updated app.

   The discipline, the follow-through and the continuous attention paid off, drawing the focus of the sales force to the functional benefits that consumer research had told us really mattered to customers. This initiative, along with many others including outpacing competitors in product renewal, allowed for a doubling of the market share from 19 to 38% in three years in a geo-region/product mix combination, where our firm competed against the first- and second-place global leaders in this category.

4. The name Suvorov was undoubtedly ironically chosen, referring to one of Russia's greatest generals:

   *"Suvorov is considered to be one of the few generals in [Russian ed.] history who never lost a battle (63-0). He was famed for his military manual The Science of Victory and noted for several of his sayings, including 'What is difficult in training will become easy in a battle'"(Wikipedia, 2013)*

5. Deacon reports the amusing story that on 6 September 1976 Russian pilot Viktor Belenko defected with his MiG 25, one of the very latest models at the time, landing at the Japanese Hakodate airfield (Deacon, 1982f). The plane was thoroughly inspected by a Japanese team – a task that suited their natural curiosity well. One most surprising find was that the plane was not made of lightweight titanium, but of old-fashioned steel. It was considered to be 'brilliantly

engineered', giving great insight into state-of-the-art Soviet military aviation technology. Eventually, after repeated requests, the plane was sent back to the Soviets in huge crates.

6. There is a catch here. The sample that has been analyzed using MASINT methods must be sufficiently representative. Never place exaggerated faith in small samples (Kahneman, 2011b).

7. Adulteration of raw milk in 2007/2008 in China led to arguably the largest food scandal in history. In China, smallholder farmers deliver their daily dairy farm output of typically 10 litres of raw milk to a middle-man who operates a milk collection centre. In dairy farming regions every village has a few of these privately run milk collection centres. The farmers usually get their milk pay-out check on a weekly basis based on litres of milk delivered and the amount of the two key components in their milk: protein and fat. The latter are analyzed by delivered batch in the presence of the farmer.

   The collection centre subsequently sells their total output, easily 1,000 or 2,000 litres a day to a dairy processing firm, which turns the milk into dairy products, typically either drinking milk, infant formula or yoghurt. The dairy processing firm, like the collection centre, analyses every batch of raw milk procured on three parameters: weight and protein and fat content corresponding to that weight.

   This is the basis for the procurement price. Collection centre managers knew the analysis method used by the dairy factory to analyze the most valuable component in the milk: protein.

   This method is called Kjeldahl-N. It analyzes organically-bound nitrogen as a proxy indicator for protein. Criminally unscrupulous collection managers decided to make a quick buck by diluting the milk with water and compensating the inevitable dilution of protein by adding a chemical substance high in organic-bound nitrogen. This substance, a building block for construction materials, is called melamine. This cheating practice became widespread across China. Melamine thus ended up in infant milk formula. Due to its toxicity to infant kidneys it resulted in the death of several babies and the illness of several hundred thousand more. Needless to say that this adulteration of milk with a poisonous chemical to make a quick buck wiped out the trust of Chinese consumers in the local infant milk industry for at least a decade leading to massive imports of Western-made infant milk formula. To make their point clear that this cheating was intolerable, the Chinese government decided to execute several key culprits, including the CEO of one the largest Chinese infant nutrition producers before this crisis hit.

8. A Western firm has operated in a non-Western country where it shipped finished goods by road over long distances. Due to the country's poor road infrastructure, such deliveries easily took two to three days to reach the warehouse destination, from which the goods were further distributed with local trucks. Every truckload was monitored by authorities and had to comply with the laws of the land. Overloading was prohibited. Every truck had to have two drivers at all times, etc.

   The Western firm's logistics provider informed that local competitors sent their trucks out with one driver and heavily overloaded, operating more than the legally acceptable number of working hours etc. The Western firm's compliance resulted in a cost disadvantage which was hard to earn back. There were only theories regarding how the competitor got away with these violations, but then the country in which the operations took place scored poorly on the Transparency International lists. A multitude of such non-level playing field disadvantages resulted in the Western firm's decision to cut its commitment to this market and divest part of its businesses.

## CHAPTER 9

1. Office gardens do not qualify as suitable work locations for analysis work, regardless of what HR managers say.

2. This is a generalized statement; it is not a rule. Some works of great intellectual sophistication

have been prepared in relative isolation. Think, just to name an example, of Einstein in 1905. As of 16 June 1902 he was employed as technical expert third class at the Swiss Federal Patent Office in Bern – initially on probation, earning SFR 3,500 a year. As of 16 September 1904 his position became permanent. Promotion, however, "had to wait until he mastered machine technology" wrote his boss, adding as an excuse that "he studied Physics". March 1905 he delivered the scientific paper that earned him his Nobel Prize. A month later, on a different topic, his Ph.D. thesis has been approved. His biographer adds (Pais, 1982):

*"No one before or since has widened the horizons of physics is so short a time as Einstein did in 1905."*

The implication of this quote: in analysis, minds are more important than teams. On the other hand, no individual is perfect but a team can be. In my experience teams do outperform in strategic analysis even the smartest individuals.

3. This presupposes the different strategic analysis function staff all have the same clearance when it comes to access to confidential information of each other's projects.
4. 'Big data' are presented as a new chapter in information analysis. Big data allows one, simply put, to find insightful patterns that for example emerge upon analysis of the data of millions of transactions. Big data indeed necessitate computerized analysis. What to analyze, however, remains the analyst's call.
5. There is a remarkable inconsistency between sources related to Ivor Montagu. Nigel West postulates that Ivor Montagu was codenamed 'Nobility' (West, 1999). According to West, Montagu reported into an unidentified GRU-operator called 'Intelligensia'. He was active in Line X: stealing technology secrets. Macintyre claims Montagu *himself* was agent Intelligensia (Macintyre, 2010b).

   As a reader you may wonder why on earth this footnote matters to you setting up or operating strategic analysis in a business environment. The reason is that in this section on data and metadata, data accuracy and quality is a topic. I share this example because I *so far* had taken the well-known, well-published and profilic intelligence history writer Macintyre as a very reliable and compelling source – and who additionally has a good writing style. I am, however, tempted to trust West better here as he studied the labyrinthine Venona cables. The lesson to me was: no matter how good a reputation, dare to doubt.
6. If unavoidable, such suspicions can be prevented by telling the collector a false but credible cover story, to avoid him to start speculations. Telling lies to staff, or to anybody else for that matter, is not the right thing to do at any time. Therefore the cover story solution should only be applied when all other options to prevent suspicions are exhausted and the risk of staff speculations being discussed at the coffee machine is deemed serious. Speculations may indeed cause undesirable staff insecurity and unrest in the firm on what moves senior management are considering or planning to execute, but the question is whether that is a sufficiently strong excuse for a management or strategic analysis department to fabricate stories (i.e. tell lies).

## CHAPTER 10

1. An example of an advantage that a successful deception campaign, without using deceit (!), may generate is the time *bought* for a new product launch to succeed. Earning back innovation-related investments requires time during which the innovating company enjoys exclusivity for its new product on the market. When the launch is successful, in time competing products will be developed and marketed. Therefore, a market is usually best captured as first mover. The longer the first mover advantage lasts, the higher the net present value of the launch likely will be. The entry of multiple companies offering a product similar to the newly launched product will likely result in margin pressure for all market participants.

   In terms of dynamics, a launch in business resembles a military invasion (see note 2 of chapter 10 below). When competitors are being misdirected into preparing for a different market than the one where the launch is to take place, the deception may have an attractive pay-off. This means that even when strategic deceptions in business are not common, tactical and legally permitted deceptions can still occur and may not be ruled out in strategic analysis for business.

2. Two of the Allied Second World War deception operations have been documented in popular literature in great detail (Macintyre, 2010c]) (Macintyre, 2012). Operation Mincemeat successfully deceived the German High Command that the Allied landings in the Mediterranean Sea were aimed at Greece and at Sardinia, whereas the actual landing was planned for Sicily. Operation Fortitude was part of a deception campaign to make the Germans believe the allied invasion would be at Calais rather than at Normandy. Especially the latter deception changed the war considerably.

   German High Command was made to believe that the main Allied invasion would be taking place at the Calais coast. This deception capitalized on the insight that the Germans, all the way up to the Führer, *wanted* to believe that the invasion would be at Calais. At Calais the crossing is only 20 miles. Why choose a longer sea route?

   The deception in addition had it that a smaller Normandy coastal invasion preceding it would be a ruse. This fake invasion at Normandy was only meant to pull German forces away from Calais, prior to the big invasion landing at the Calais beaches. High Command therefore avoided falling in the trap of deploying reserve troops, especially the strong German XV army, located near Calais, in Normandy once the messages of the Allied invasion in Normandy reached German top brass.

   German hesitation to do so bought the Allies precious time. During the famous first twenty-four hours, the longest day of the Second World War, the Allied invasion forces were numerically much weaker than the German defenders in France. Once the German High Command realized they had been duped and that what they believed was a ruse in Normandy, actually was the real invasion, the Allied forces that had landed in Normandy were numerous enough to withstand German counter-attacks. In doing so they liberated North-Western Europe.

   Along similar lines the Soviet deception in the Cuban Missile Crisis has been described (Hansen, 2007). What Hansen's analysis most of all shows is that when intentional deception is operated, no detail is overlooked.

3. Having access to all the raw data may be more relevant in the case of quantitative than of qualitative analysis. This may explain why Greenspan, focusing on the quantitative side of economics, insisted on having the raw underlying numbers.

4. OSINT-expert Reuser recommends specifically for IMINT data quality verification (including video clips) an in-depth analysis to obtain (more) metadata, including (list not exhaustive) (Reuser, 2012):

   - Clothing – check match with season/current fashion.
   - Weather – check match with known weather statistics and apparent weather, link with clothing.
   - Timing within a day, e.g. length of the shadows.
   - Environment: signposts with text, car license plates, buildings, landscape characteristics, etc.

   In strategic analysis in contrast to military intelligence this type of IMINT metadata analysis is rarely needed.

5. The trustworthiness (or reliability) of sources is a topic of relevance in strategic analysis. When it comes to the attribute trust in the context of strategic analysis it should unfortunately be reiterated that 'absence of evidence' does not equal 'evidence of absence'. When there is no evidence that the source is providing incorrect data or information it does not mean that the source actually provides correct data or information.

6. First, two examples are drawn from a study of the origins of the First World War (Clark, 2013a). The example aims to illustrate the occurrence and relevance of false negatives in diplomacy. What applies in diplomacy I believe equally to apply in business:

Prior to the First World War, the Black Hand operated as an ultra-nationalist Serbian (terrorist) organization. Gavrilo Prinzip who would later shoot Crown Prince Franz Ferdinand of Austria in Sarajevo, Bosnia, was a member of the Black Hand. A clearly false negative emerged when the Austrian minister in Belgrade in 1911 reported that the Black Hand's claim to operate outside Serbia was a cover. In other words, a valid statement by the Black Hand about their foreign intentions ("we are going to operate outside Serbia" – which they did in 1914 with such catastrophic consequences) was *intentionally* misconstrued to better fit Austria's interest. The Austrian minister wrote:

> *"Its claim to plan for foreign activities] was really only a cover; its real purpose is to intervene in internal [Serbian] affairs."*

A false negative may and does often originate from wishful thinking. It may also simply originate from carelessness. A known Black Hand member on 21 June 1914, i.e. a week before the assassination of the Crown Prince on 28 June, warned a member of the Austrian government that a visit of the Archduke to Sarajevo would have consequences. The visit was planned on the day of the defeat of Serbia on Kosovo Polje in 1389. The visit as such was disliked but a visit on a sensitive day was in Serbian circles seen as an outright provocation. The Austrian government member *ignored* the warning stating "let us hope nothing does happen".

Another well-documented example of a false negative is the case of Count Jurek von Sosnowski (Bassett, 2005). Von Sosnowski operated as Polish military intelligence officer in Berlin from 1927 to the late 1930s. Through highly unethical practices, von Sosnowski obtained multiple German military secrets, including a substantial part of the original German Blitzkrieg attack plan to overrun Poland. The Polish military staff in Warsaw did not, or rather *could not* believe that the high-grade intelligence they had received through von Sosnowski was genuine. The staff considered that if it was so good, it must have been provided as an intentional deception by their German military intelligence adversary, commonly referred to as a plant or a ruse. The Polish military believed it was better to avoid becoming prey of a German deception. The staff decided not to use the material, leaving themselves possibly more vulnerable than needed on 1 September 1939 when the Second World War in the West did break out and followed the script their intelligence source had provided them with.

It has been analyzed why even now false negatives haunt intelligence analysis (Grey, 2016b).

Three reasons are reported:

- Human intelligence is often the source of unusually high-grade data. The problem, however, is that in military intelligence the sources that deliver these data are not under the intelligence agency's control. Sources tend to be foreign that through providing these data *betray* the country they live in and often the organization they work for. This generates a dilemma of trust. How to trust a person that betrays to not betray you in a scheme you cannot oversee but they can? How do you know it is not a ruse, made up to further the source's interests but not your own?
- High-grade data may provide the receiving end with a so-called 'truth shock'. High-grade stuff rarely confirms existing beliefs. An all too human reaction is to deny that these data are true.
- Human sources may hesitate to give high-grade data too easily, because once given they are no longer in possession of it and by implication their value as a source is gone. So, human sources give small bits – bit by bit – trading their skin for the highest price. Meanwhile, in this imperfect trading environment, the receiving end may only value bits they can verify – which renders them to undervalue the real high grade data.

The above reasons explain why Soviet intelligence had an intrinsic reluctance to belief their best spy assets ever (Kim Philby, Anthony Blunt) were genuine – and by implication that their high-grade data were genuine (Grey, 2016c).

7. Admiral Husband E. Kimmel was a four-star admiral in the US Navy. He was Commander-in-Chief of the US Pacific Fleet at the time of the attack on Pearl Harbor.

8. Exactly the same weariness hit Israeli intelligence in failing to predict the outbreak of the Yom Kippur War. HUMINT sources in Egypt had in the spring of 1973 alone announced a starting date of a war between Egypt and Israel four consecutive times. When another warning came which correctly predicted the war to start 6 October 1973 it did not receive the attention it needed (Shalev, 2014a). Sending multiple false positive signals seems to work greatly as a deception strategy.
9. Such stakeholders may include customers that want to know that they buy from a solid company. This requires the company to release information on its financial health and/or its assets base, etc. Investors or lenders, when applicable, want to know whether they're investing in a solid company. They also demand, often public, release of financial statements. Regulators insist to secure that the company complies with all sorts of legislation. They increasingly enforce openness in multiple dimensions, from detailed ingredients list on an individual packaged food product to public release of detailed environmental pollution records. Similarly, the public at large wants the company to provide for example convincing Corporate Social Responsibility related data.

   In addition, in most countries, companies have a legal requirement to file company records. An additional requirement is that independent accounting firms have to approve such records, providing an extra data quality assurance. Such records contain from the most basic to highly detailed financial statements. The latter are often also giving a clear direction of the company's competences and intent. As investors in a competitor tend to dislike surprises just as much as strategic analysts in a company monitoring that competitor, even forward looking statements are sometimes published.

   Financial regulatory authorities around the globe have over time set rules that strongly limit *public* companies in their possibilities to deny their investors and thus the broader public information. This mandatory transparency did not happen overnight. A lot of public naming and shaming was needed (e.g. Enron, Ahold) to achieve this.

   Especially in the US legislation now links *company's* financial fraud to the company's top executive *personal* jail terms. As a result company's data that are published are now among the most correct data in the strategic analysis universe.
10. The risk of inference has been elegantly illustrated in the example below (Sinclair, 2010):

    > *"In a cognitive science lecture a speaker reads aloud the following sentence:*
    >
    > Mary heard the ice cream truck coming down the street. She remembered her birthday money and ran into the house
    >
    > *Those in the audience conclude that the sentences are about a little girl who is going to buy some ice cream; the speaker notes that this conclusion is based on inference, not on anything explicitly stated.*

# CHAPTER 11

1. A quote with more limited 'spin' value than the quote provided by Box is bit a more nuanced but definitely more precise (Guszcza, 2012):

   > *"Remember that all models are wrong; the practical question is how wrong do they have to be to not be useful."*
2. Two quantitative approaches are logical in this example: taking the linear growth forward based on the most recent data, or taking a longer-term view, using a compound annual growth rate. The quantitative approaches do under such circumstances replace the need to search for a *specialist* consensus forecast based on the work of other analysts and for the collection of qualitative contextual data that should at all times guide a quantitative forecast. The most reckless analyst is the analyst that thinks he can always outsmart all his peers (Silver, 2013f).

A linear growth forward prediction would assume the increment of €13 million between 2011 and 2012 to be the sales growth momentum for 2013 and 2014 as well. This would result in a net sales prediction for 2013 of €222 million (i.e. 209 + 13) and for 2014 for € 235 million (i.e. 222 + 13).

Using a compound annual growth rate-based prediction, first requires to calculate the compound annual growth rate. The formula is: CAGR = ([Sales last year in a data set]/[Sales in the first year in a data set] ^(1/n))-1. In this formula n gives the number of steps, i.e. n = last year – first year.

In this example, CAGR (in %)= (209/173)^(1/n) -1 with n = 2012-2008 = 4. This means the Compound Annual Growth Rate equals 4.84%.

For predicting the 2013 sales, the following formula is applicable: [2013 sales] = [2012 sales] * 1.0484. This means the 2013 sales prediction is = 209 * 1.0484 = €219.1 million. For 2014 the sales prediction is 219.1 * 1.0484 = 229.7 i.e. €230 million.

This example shows that even two simple prediction methods may for 2014 sales already lead to a difference of 2% in the outcome; the linear method is 2% higher at €235 million than the CAGR method at €230 million.

This looks like a meaningless difference. Knowing however that most net present value calculations used to value companies in an acquisition process look ten years ahead, the differences do meaningfully matter in the outcome of such NPV calculations. In the absence of more data it is impossible to say which prediction method is better.

It is very likely possible that in this example 2010 has been a difficult year for the adversary. Sales growth had completely stalled and the unknown net sales figure for 2010 in reality had been €183 million, just as in 2009.

At the end of 2010 the competitor's management had been replaced by its non-executive board and in January 2011 new management had come on board. In that case, two years in a row (2010-2011) and (2011-2012) the net sales increment has been €13 million. Apparently, the new management had made strategic choices that allowed the company now to grow with €13 million per year. The linear method may in such case even still underestimate the company's underlying sales momentum.

The CAGR method would only be safely applicable in mediocristan, whereas the replacement of management is a typical extremistan case. The new management and board, being so confident with the accelerated growth, may even in 2013 decide to acquire a company with say €50 million sales, with as transaction completion date of 31 December 2013. In that case, net sales for 2014 would be of the order of €285 million.

3. To ensure you harvest the significant synergy of doing combined quantitative data and contextual (qualitative) data analysis, I always recommend to add in-company strategic analysts to outside strategy consultants when preparing strategic plans. Where the outside consultants are well-trained in structured number crunching, the in-company strategic analysts provide the essential contextual details to together come to balanced predictions.

4. The Italian philosopher Vilfredo Pareto's has implicitly given a role to Silver's proverbial fox in his views on strategy, where he stresses the need for the fox-like quality to make connections and imaginatively source ideas (Freedman, 2013a):

   *"The impulse to make connections between disparate elements and events, to think imaginatively, encourage attempts to outwit others, maneuver out of trouble, generate ideologies, and form expedient coalitions."*

5. This type of disclaimer is more commonly known as *cover my back.*

# CHAPTER 12

1. I believe the quote below provides a great example where prediction and predictor are not mutually independent. I see it as illustrative enough to reproduce it in full (Keough, 2008b):

   *"It's October and an Indian chief believes it's going to be a cold winter. So he tells his tribe to collect firewood. To double-check his prediction, the chief calls the National Weather Service and asks a meteorologist if the winter is going to be a cold one. The weatherman says, "According to our indicators, we think it might". So the chief tells his people to find extra wood just in case. A week later he calls the National Weather Service again, and they confirm that a harsh winter is headed their way. The chief orders all his people to scavenge every scrap of wood they can find. Two weeks later, the chief calls the National Weather Service again and asks, "Are you sure this winter is going to be cold?" "Absolutely," the weatherman replies. "The Indians are collecting wood like crazy."*

2. The British General Sir Ian Hamilton has been reported to have said: "The Japanese accept what their experts tell them. But the Anglo-Saxons revolt at the very word 'expert'" (Deacon, 1982b). This quote gets extra perspective in the context of the 2016 Brexit vote and the less-than-compelling impact of experts' opinions on this vote.
3. Nate Silver's book title, *The Signal and the Noise*, was inspired by these lines of Wohlstetter.
4. The movie *Twelve Angry Men* provides a superb example of dissecting evidence to find critical flaws in abundant and at first sight reasonably convincing evidence.
5. What applies to a figure like a sales price, equally applies to e.g. a multiple. Mention a buying price that is a multiple of EBIT: e.g. eight times. Eight times EBIT it will be, at least.
6. The human mind tends to overvalue factual information and expertise tend to correlate with bias [Taleb, 2007d]. I disagree with Taleb that overvaluing factual information is an ailment of the human mind. Facts or data points of which the quality has been confirmed are by definition usable input in intelligence analysis. Whether these facts are also *useful* depends on the desired intelligence deliverable.
7. The persuasiveness of narratives in learning and remembering is hard to underestimate (Gladwell, 2000a):

   *"...the narrative form, psychologists now believe, is central to them. 'It is the only way they have of organizing the world, of organizing experience [...]. They are not able to bring theories that organize things in terms of cause and effect and relationships, so they turn things into stories, and when they try to make sense of their life they use the storied version of their experience as the basis for further reflection. If they don't catch something in a narrative structure, it doesn't get remembered very well, and it doesn't seem to be accessible for further kinds of mulling over."*

   The above quote does not concern strategic analysts though. This applies to three to five year old children. When replacing 'They are not able' by 'They do not wish to spend the time' this quote, however, also looks applicable to time-constraint strategic analysts (or decision-makers for that matter). When the analyst faces a credible narrative, chances are that he will remember it and may overrate the value of the evidence, if only because he only needs to invest toddler-level capabilities to remember it.

8. The value of *learning* by defining and/or recognizing analogies is hard to underestimate (Von Baeyer, 1993). When being confronted with a genuinely incomprehensible problem, the analyst may consider looking for an analogy to the problem. The analogy should be an everyday activity that is instantly recognizable. When the analogy happens to shine a light on the solution of the complicated problem, phase one has succeeded. When the analogy is really good, it moves into a second phase. In that case the analogy not only assists in explaining what is observed now but even *by analogy* suggests what to expect next. McBeth has screened R.V. Jones book *Most Secret War* in search of examples on learning-by-analogy in (military) intelligence and comes up with some convincing examples (McBeth, 2002). One of these concerns the relative vulnerability of open societies to intelligence efforts by adversaries, where Jones compares London in the 1940s with Pericles' Athens.

9. The US military have overrated the quality of the Iraqi army in the liberation war of Kuwait in 1991 (Gordon, 1995b). Despite having experienced poorly executed small-scale Iraqi offensive campaigns against the allied forces in Saudi Arabia, the US Army leadership retained its opinion that the Iraqi army, once attacked by the allies, would stand and fight. The Iraqi army, however, did not stand and fight, but rapidly evacuated Kuwait, avoiding most of the losses it would have suffered had it stood and fought. In doing so, it most of all retained its men and materiel to fight another internal war within Iraq: against the Kurds and the Sunni tribes that rose against Saddam when the allied forces attacked the Iraq army in Kuwait. As a result the 1991 war ended much faster than anticipated, but it only partly achieved the allied objectives of both liberating Kuwait and triggering an Iraqi internal uprising that was to topple Saddam Hussein's regime.

# CHAPTER 13

1. Tragically, Japanese Admiral Isoroku Yamamoto was the only Japanese Imperial Navy leader that knew the US well. He feared the US economic/industrial power and knew Japan could only lose the numbers war that Japan was to unleash. He is quoted to have said to the Japanese government prior to the Pearl Harbor attack that "he could run wild for a year or six months" in the Pacific with his fleet, prior to the US regaining decisive and irreversible military dominance in the entire Pacific, allowing them to defeat Japan (Keegan, 2003a). Even when the initial Japanese military successes in 1942 following Pearl Harbor and the defeat of Singapore looked promising from a Japanese perspective, Yamamoto was ultimately proven exactly right: the Battle of Midway, at 4 June 1942 almost exactly half a year after Pearl Harbor proved to be the turning point in the Pacific Theatre of the Second World War.
2. Taking a truly creative approach to formulating hypotheses is reported not to be common in business. Bradley has surveyed business executives to check the hypotheses they used in strategy and planning. The outcome was that nearly eight in ten executives reported that (Bradley, 2013):

   *"The processes of their companies are more geared to confirming existing hypotheses than to testing new ones."*

# CHAPTER 14

1. The concept of turning wide-body passenger jets into self-propelled and guided kamikaze rockets as Al Qaeda did 11 September 2001 proved ethnocentrically hard to imagine. Kamikaze actions with airplanes were, however, already known and so where aircraft hijacking by terrorist groups from the Middle East. The innovation, for the lack of a better word, of hijacking a passenger aircraft to use it for a kamikaze action proved indeed difficult to imagine.
2. An attack on the fleet of the most powerful nation on earth in its own harbor on a quiet yet fateful early Sunday morning in December 1941 proved to be outside what the US ever imagined. The type of attack, however, had been operated by Japan against Russia in 1904 (Deacon, 1982a). In business, all too often, when failing to understand a competitor it retrospectively started with failing to study the competitor's history.
3. US intelligence could not imagine that the USSR would install nuclear weapon-delivering rocket systems just 90 miles off the shore of the US mainland, while in doing so completely tilting the global security balance. For sure the overall Soviet policy had not been imagined by US intelligence, who didn't believe the Soviets would make such a daring step. US intelligence also had the details wrong. They incorrectly estimated the number of Soviet troops that a few Soviet ships to Cuba had carried. Taking US soldier's standards as measure, US intelligence estimated that the troop ships could not have carried more than ~10,000 staff. The ships, however, had carried 41,900 personnel. The difference was caused by the fact that US intelligence *could not imagine* the dismal conditions the Soviet military had to accept during the trip. Even historic facts – see the quote below – at times offer a panacea for avoiding an ethnocentric bias.

Already in 1889 when British and Russian intelligence officers met to discuss both countries' strategies in conquering Central Asia, the Russian officer remarked (Hopkirk, 1994):

> *"the Russian soldier was a stoical individual who goes where he was told, and did not trouble his head too much about transport and support. He looked upon his commander as a child did its father, and if at the end of a grueling day's march or fighting he found neither water nor food he simply did without, carrying on cheerfully until he dropped."*

The permissive attitude of the Russian and later Soviet soldier involved, however, becomes easier to imagine when the alternative offered to the soldier had been imagined had the soldier involved rejected the conditions on board the troop carrying ships. Such soldiers would probably have made a trip to Siberia rather than to Cuba (Hansen, 2007).

The classic phrase of the CIA's National Intelligence Estimate issued on 19 September 1962, i.e. a few weeks before the crisis shows one of the most tangible examples of mirror imaging: a form of ethnocentric bias, properly defined as the believe the competitor thinks like you think (Weiner, 2008a):

> *"The Soviets themselves are probably still uncertain about their future military program for Cuba."*

The Soviets were not uncertain; it was only the CIA that was.

4. The US defense community did not imagine the Soviets building biological weapons while having signed a treaty that stated they wouldn't (Hoffman, 2011a). There is a fascinating element in this example of an ethnocentric bias. In this example, the mirror imaging concerns the organization structure, rather than the choices of the perceived peers at the other side.

   The Soviets built bio-weapons while the US authorities could not accept the thought that the Soviets would do so. This example shows that who is in the "ethno-homogenous" zone may not automatically be clear. In this case, the logical split would have been US versus Russia. That was not the case though. Based on trustworthy sources, the US staff correctly knew that Soviet-Russian military leaders considered biological and chemical weapons useless.

   These weapons were devices of terrorists, not the arms of a highly professional army. They also knew the Soviets to operate a high standard of professionalism in the army.

   In this, US and Soviet military leaders had the same 'ethnic' background: that of professional soldiers. Professional soldiers would never do this. That assessment was correct. The failure of imagination was that the professional Soviet military leaders, in contrast to their Pentagon peers, had no authority in the decision whether these weapons were developed. Soldiers on both sides thought alike, but political systems didn't. What in this case was true for soldiers proves to be true for any professional discipline. Engineers may easily imagine how their peers in the competitor's factory would *like* to operate their factories. It is, however, much harder to imagine what instructions they get to *actually* run them. The very same applies for disciplines like marketing or R&D. A focused exercise like an open-minded wargame may trigger the imagination to better assess the otherness-of-the-enemy.

5. Weiner framed the CIA's failure to predict the Soviet invasion of Afghanistan in 1979 as a failure of imagination, relating it to the CIA lacking a xenocentric view (Weiner, 2008c):

   > *"A lack of intelligence was not the cause of the failure. A lack of imagination was."*

   Similarly, Sontag describes how hard it was to imagine the real Soviet psyche or intent, even where facts on competencies gradually became available through traditional government intelligence collection means (Sontag, 1998c):

   > *"Human agents, satellites, and spy planes, along with subs, all got very good at collecting information about Soviet hardware-what was being built, the technical specifications. It was much harder, however, to get a glimpse into the Soviet psyche. In the end not even the cable taps [US eavesdropping of non-encrypted USSR military communications] could reveal much about what the top Soviet leadership thought or show the true political and economic crises building in a country so closed."*

6. Klein provides a detailed analysis of this sad case, where the wine-drinking French pilots believed they were still approaching their destination airport of Cairo, the IDF pilots that had been sent to intercept them, believed the aircraft had been hijacked and was on its way to be blown up above an Israeli target.
7. In 1968 British intelligence had well-placed assets in Eastern Germany that were (Aldrich, 2011b):

   *"watching the Red Army as it mobilized for a 'major exercise'. The classic question these observers confronted was whether this was an exercise, a bluff or a real invasion. The fabulous anthropological knowledge that [...] had developed over twenty years of watching its subject provided the key warning indicator. It had observed the Red Army going out on exercise countless times, and knew how it behaved. A routine exercise provided an opportunity to leave broken or faulty vehicles in barracks to be worked on by engineers. What marked this out as the 'real thing' was that the Soviets took everything with them. Vehicles were piled high with personal effects, showing that the troops were not expecting to come back for some time. [...] The Soviets were definitely up to something.*

   These data did not convince the UK Joint Intelligence Committee that the Soviets were actually preparing for the crush of the Prague Spring. The cause was most of all an ethnocentric bias:

   *"The chairman of the JIC, a rather lofty gentleman called Denis Greenhill refused to accept the evidence that was staring him in the face. He insisted that the Soviet mobilization was only an attempt to apply psychological pressure, and argued that if he was in the Soviets' shoes he would think the wave of international criticism an invasion would provoke too high a price to pay. In other words, he thought like a British decision-maker, not a Russian one."*

   In 1981, a study commissioned by the JIC again observed (Aldrich, 2011c):

   *"British intelligence analysts tended to suffer from two psychological neuroses. [...] they found it difficult to believe that an aggressor would ever think the use of force acceptable. They tended to think what the British would do when they were in the shoes of their enemies. In fact, the political regimes they were looking at were often unstable, and therefore much more inclined to commit acts of violent aggression."*

   This study preceded the unanticipated outbreak of the Falklands War. As long as ethnocentrism is not effectively countered (e.g. by forcing analysts and decision-makers to have lived and worked for a long time in the countries/cultures they are to report and decide on), adversaries will continue to deliver surprises and intelligence failures will continue to occur.

# CHAPTER 15

1. In the early 2000s there was a Finnish company called Nokia that – for a short period of time – had the highest market capitalization of any European listed company. Its key product, the mobile phone, revolutionized human communication. Its tagline was not: we make the most fashionable phones. That was what they did in terms of product features. The tagline linked to the benefit they delivered: 'Connecting People...' The implicit message of this example: people do prefer to communicate with other people – when Nokia facilitated this, it was rewarded with tremendous sales and profits which lasted until Nokia's competitive advantage was lost to Apple and other players. How much reward would your firm's decision-makers have for your strategic analysis function's next reporting that facilitates them to connect to other (relevant) people?
2. A message that doesn't convince at all may also be memorable to a decision-maker. When the strategic analysis function is the sender of that message, being forgotten may, however, be preferable to being remembered for reasons that may negatively affect the credibility or persuasiveness of future reporting.
3. The *Horrid Henry* books not only amuse children but also offer multiple lessons that are directly applicable in business. One is that the daring, entrepreneurial Horrid Henry usually gets the fun while his obedient brother Perfect Peter gets the blame. In strategic analysis, with the exception of compliance and ethics, asking for forgiveness also tends to be more effective than asking for permission.
4. The word "evidence" has especially a legal connotation and may for this reason be problematic when the strategic analysis work relates to work with a legal context (Davis, 1997); in such case, stick to the word data.

# CHAPTER 17

1. This footnote provides a collection of examples of how intelligence analysts and their function heads faced and often had to succumb to political pressure. High-grade intelligence that did not match the needs of political leaders had to be discredited or at least withheld from a broader audience. I came across these examples during my voyage of discovery in military intelligence – and I believe they serve their purpose of illustration well.

**A cow called Bessie**

The pressure the US intelligence officers were facing in Vietnam in the period 1965–68 during the L.B. Johnson administration is a case in point. All reports that had a pessimistic tone and/or that showed the fundamental beliefs underpinning the US policy were incorrect were either stopped or polished up (Weiner, 2008c):

> *"LBJ liked the agency's [i.e. the CIA's] work only if it fit his thinking. When it did not, it went into the wastebasket. "Let me tell you about these intelligence guys," he said "When I was growing up in Texas, we had a cow named Bessie. I'd go out early and milk her. I'd get her in the stanchion, seat myself, and squeeze out a pail of fresh milk. One day I'd worked hard and gotten a full pail of milk, but I wasn't paying attention, and old Bessie swung her shit-smeared tail through that bucket of milk. Now, you know, that's what these intelligence guys do. You work hard and get a good program or policy going, and they swing a shit-smeared tail through it."*

The suppression and falsification of intelligence reporting on the war in Vietnam remained a constant in the 1960s (Weiner, 2008d). The pressure was high and the truth was the victim.

Similarly, Janis describes President Johnson's communication of the escalation of the Vietnam War in the late 1960's (Janis, 1982b).

> *"President Johnson repeatedly issued unwarranted, optimistic statements to the press, not just because he was temperamentally inclined to oversell his policies but because he was also constantly 'buoyed by the stream of glad tidings coming from his advisers'."*

**The loss of Pueblo due to inter-agency competency issues**

The Johnson administration, while having its hands tied in Vietnam, still in parallel pursued intelligence operations against the Asian coastal defence of the Soviet Union and of North Korea. When a mission to send a practically unarmed small US Navy vessel called the *Pueblo* to go eavesdropping near the coast of North Korea, the NSA was asked for a security assessment of the mission. A young NSA analyst sounded a loud warning (Cheevers, 2014):

> *"Boy, you people have got to be complete blithering idiots to put that ship off North Korea, because all kinds of bad things are going to happen. Therefore, cancel [the mission]."*

The *Pueblo* mission, however, was a Navy operation. NSA top officials did not want to appear to be interfering with the Navy, so watered down the message. The mission was on. When indeed on 23 January 1968 the ship was captured by the North Koreans, resulting in the death of a sailor and the harsh imprisonment in North Korea of the remaining eighty members of the ship's crew, the NSA top officials decided not to mention the warning to anyone outside the NSA. Political pressure sometimes demands warnings to be buried.

**A prelude to Star Wars**

The Nixon administration was no less demanding in requesting to hear what they wanted to hear. President Nixon had planned to build an anti-missile defense system, a prelude to what was later to be called "Star Wars" under President Reagan. To justify the expenses, Nixon needed hard evidence that the Soviets had the intention and the capability to deliver a nuclear first strike. The CIA reported exactly the opposite based on the evidence they had built up (Weiner, 2008e). This was not what the President was looking for. After pressuring the CIA's Director Richard Helms, the latter gave in and trimmed the evidence to meet his customer's needs. The CIA's analysts viewed that Helms had compromised the CIA's (and for that matter any intelligence analyst's) mandate *"to evaluate all available data and express conclusions irrespective of US policies."*

For strategic analysts of a business environment, please read "company policies."

**The rainy season**

Yesmanship flourishes when bad news is unwelcome, as this US example from the Vietnam War shows (Halberstam, 1992d). In the early 1960s, at the beginning of the US involvement in Vietnam, the US Military Advisory Command Vietnam got as new head General Paul D. Harkins. Harkins started off:

> *"very friendly, except of course if a subordinate insisted on providing bad news. A civilian intelligence officer later recalled trying to warn Harkins in 1962 about the growing Vietcong threat in the Mekong delta.*
>
> *'Nonsense, I am going to crush them in the rainy season,' Harkins said (the rainy season, of course, favored the guerrilla, affording him better canal transportation and infinitely more hiding places than the dry season). When the intelligence officer insisted, saying that the situation was about to become irreversible, Harkins pushed him aside. This was not what his own intelligence shop was saying. [...]*
>
> *'General Harkins,' the civilian interrupted, 'your intelligence chief doesn't understand the threat at all. He's an Air Force officer and his specialty is [...] picking nuclear targets, but he doesn't understand this war and he's not going to give you any feel for it.' But Harkins was no longer so genial or so pleasant, nor such a good listener the civilian found. [...] Harkins was comforted by his staff and his statistics, and he comforted his staff as well; those who comforted him and gave him what he was looking for had their careers accelerated."*

**Iraq's WMDs in 2003 were a positive exception**

There is controversy on this topic in the various sources. At least some 'politicization' took place around the decision-making in the US in 2003 related to the intelligence on Iraq's weapons of mass destruction (WMDs). In this case *leading questions* were being asked, but one source suggests there was no evidence of *direct pressure* (Treverton, 2008). Rather analysts wanted to be helpful to the politicians as the following quote illustrates (Jervis, 2010b):

> *"Analysts may also have been influenced by the desire to please policymakers, not so much by telling them what they wanted to hear but by being able to reach a firm conclusion rather than writing in the typical and disliked style of "on the one hand, on the other hand."*

**Political pressure on analysis' outputs are not exclusively a US problem**

Andrew similarly sketches the sheer fear in the NKVD (a predecessor to the KGB) in the Stalinist Soviet years (Andrew, 2001a):

> *Those [intelligence officers] who compiled them [intelligence briefings to Stalin] increasingly feared for their life expectancy if they failed to tell Stalin what he expected to hear. [...] The main function of Soviet foreign intelligence was thus to reinforce rather than to challenge Stalin's misunderstanding of the West."*

Distortion became a hallmark of the Soviet system up to the glasnost years under Gorbachev, according to the last head of KGB foreign intelligence Leonid Sherbarshin (Andrew, 2001b):

> *"[the KGB] 'had to present its reports in a falsely positive light' which pandered to the predilections of the political leadership."*

The impact of decades of flawed views became visible to the world when the Iron Curtain came down in 1989-1991. Politized intelligence and successful decision-making do not tend to go well together.

2. Janis coined the term 'Groupthink'. He chose a term that is of the same order as infamous words like 'doublethink' and 'crimethink' in George Orwell's novel *Nineteen Eighty-four* (Janis, 1982e):

> *"By putting groupthink with those Orwellian words, I realize that groupthink takes on an invidious connotation. The invidiousness is intentional: Groupthink refers to a deterioration of mental efficiency, reality testing, and moral judgment that results from in-group pressures."*

Janis could not realize at the time of his writing this that later research revealed that Orwell's (the pseudonym for Eric Blair) writings had been inspired particularly by Orwell's posting as British colonial police officer in pre-Second World War Burma. The society created in the 1930s in the British Asian colonies must have had the particular dynamics of an in-group of British expatriates versus an out-group of locals.

The all-powerful in-group was, as Orwell observed, undoubtedly taking at times irrational decisions based on shared illusions embedded in groupthink. As such it is ironic that the author that coined groupthink bases his term on Orwell, who, as his more autobiographic novel Burmese Days also suggests, himself in his formative years must have been heavily exposed to groupthink (Larkin, 2005).

3. It is impossible for me to judge whether the source of the assessment is free of bias or whether it selectively presents information to clean the CIA track record in this matter.
4. Janis describes as clear examples of failed policies that at least partly were due to groupthink:
   - Cuban Bay of Pigs: the CIA-backed failed 1961 invasion of Cuba by anti-Castro Cuban militia members.
   - Korean War: the conscious decision to attempt to liberate all of Korea in the Korean War, rather than liberate only the territory of the former South Korea by UN forces.
   - Pearl Harbor: the Navy's lack of vigilance that allowed the Japanese to launch a surprise attack.
   - Vietnam: the decision to escalate the intensity of warfare in Vietnam by the Johnson administration in an attempt to bomb the North Vietnamese into surrendering.
   - Watergate: the Nixon administration staff attempt to cover up the White House' involvement in the break-in in the head office of the Democratic Party.

   In contrast, Janis mentions the Cuban Missile Crisis and the post-war Europe-oriented Marshall Fund as examples where cohesive teams operated sound decision-making processes that resulted in good policy outcomes. In case of both the Bay of Pigs failure and the Pearl Harbor tragedy, protocol was put before decision-making quality.

   Since Janis wrote his groupthink book, the US faced two major intelligence-related failures similar in seriousness to the surprise delivered by the Japanese in Pearl Harbor, the underestimation of the Red Chinese forces in the Korean War and the resilience and determination of the North Vietnamese in the Vietnam War. These failures were 9/11 and the justification of the Iraq War: the presumed possession by the Saddam Hussein regime of weapons of mass destruction. A CIA source postulates that the Iraq War intelligence failure did not originate from groupthink (Lowenthal, 2008):

   *"the intelligence community has correctly argued that the [US] Senate's accusation of groupthink on the Iraq estimate is wrong."*

   When all relevant files have been declassified, historians may need to verify this conclusion. Former French President Jacques Chirac did believe groupthink had been a factor in the case of the Iraq War. In a fabulous quote he describes a typical secretive in-group phenomenon (Aldrich, 2011a):

   *"Chirac was highly suspicious and was among the first who doubted the intelligence reports [on Iraq's WMDs]. He understood how the Western intelligence agencies worked, continually bringing their specialists together and a collective outlook that is often called 'groupthink'. Chirac put it rather well, asserting that the intelligence agencies had tended to 'intoxicate each other.'"*

   The only reason for referring to both failures in this book context is to show that the awareness of the groupthink phenomena may not be enough to protect a group from groupthink tendencies. It should be repeated: when the antecedent conditions are present, nobody seems to be immune to groupthink.
5. In the case of the Bay of Pigs failure, the time pressure had to do with external circumstances. The US anticipated Soviet fighter jets to be delivered to Cuba soon. The US also wanted to plan the invasion before the start of the rainy season in Cuba. In the case of the Korean

War, the US wanted to outpace the Chinese and confront them, based on speed, with a fait accompli. In the case of the Vietnam War, the Johnson administration wanted to 'bring the boys back home' as soon as possible, as Johnson aimed to drive a domestic agenda called "The Great Society" rather than fight a war he most of all viewed as a distraction from him getting the chance to driving domestic changes.

6. Excessive secrecy played a role both in the case of the Bay of Pigs invasion as well as in the case of escalating the Vietnam War. President Johnson was secretive by nature, leaving out people rather than including them in his most important decision-making processing.

7. In the cases of the Korean War, Pearl Harbor and the Vietnam War, wishful thinking became dominant. In the Korean War setting, General McArthur's far too positive assessment on his ability to reach the Yalu River (i.e. entirely liberating both Koreas) was believed too eagerly.

   The context on the ground, however, differed from that at the desks of the State Department, the Pentagon and McArthur's headquarter. The Red Chinese government had only just demobilized their winning armies from the long civil war against the Kuomintang forces. North Korea had been China's ally for most of the past ten centuries. On top, North Korea shared the communist political worldview opposing the capitalist-led UN coalition. Still, the US policy in-group expected the new Chinese warrior leaders that had just won a brutal war to accept a US-led UN coalition to conquer and occupy a next-door neighbor ally (North Korea).

   The US, fighting thousands of miles from home to defend their distant South Korean ally thus anticipated the Chinese as not assisting in defending an ally's territory adjacent to their own border. The wishful thinking was that the US policy makers believed the Red Chinese government not to dare oppose the clear winners of the Pacific Theatre of the Second World War. Dean Rusk, US Secretary of State in the Kennedy and Johnson administrations, in 1951 was assistant Secretary of State tasked with Far Eastern affairs. When a CIA analyst briefed Rusk that the Red Chinese had surreptitiously introduced their forces into North Korea, Rusk is reported to have listened politely to the briefing if only to arrogantly conclude it with a beautiful example of wishful thinking (Clark, 2007e):

   *"Young man, they wouldn't dare."*

   In the case of Pearl Harbor, multiple early warning signals were ignored, as an attack on Pearl Harbor was simply unthinkable, so any signal pointing even at the possibility of such an attack was treated with arrogant contempt. In the case of the Vietnam War, the dominant belief was that the North Vietnamese government would give in – they were just a bit stubborn still, but they would after all. They didn't.

8. Ethnocentric biases fed erroneous US decisions in several cases. In the Vietnam War, the resilience and hardship tolerance of the North Vietnamese forces were underestimated. US soldiers and the US homefront at large may not have been prepared to endure the losses the North Vietnamese took. The North Vietnamese and their allies within the South, however, in their struggle for self-determination did. The ethnocentric idea was that the North Vietnamese would be bombed into submitting to Western superiority. After colonialism and war that concept was not on North Vietnamese' leaders minds.

   In the case of Pearl Harbor, multiple stereotypes blinded US military decision-makers, including:

   - Japanese can't fly a plane (they could).
   - Japanese can't develop torpedoes that can be used in shallow waters (such as Pearl Harbor). (they had devastatingly effective torpedoes in Pearl Harbor at that time).
   - The Japanese leaders will not risk their aircraft carriers by attacking us as US Navy as far out as Pearl Harbor (they did).
   - The Japanese leaders will not attack so powerful an adversary as the US (they did).

   Partly ethnocentric bias, partly wishful thinking, these assumptions all proved flawed.

9. The 2002 Iraqi WMD intelligence case has been documented well (Corera, 2012b). The available narrative suggests features of groupthink and yesmanship, as the following quote illustrates, even when CIA sources believe there was no groupthink (see footnote 4):

> *"[Sir Richard Dearlove, head of MI6] believed that the crowd round the vice-president [Cheney] was playing fast and loose with the evidence. In his view, it was never about 'fixing' the intelligence itself but rather about the undisciplined manner in which the intelligence was being used."*

Gordon and Trainor postulate that the 1990–1 Persian Gulf War (the Iraqi invasion and subsequent allied liberation of Kuwait) could have been prevented, if only when the US government wouldn't have been the victim of groupthink (Gordon, 1995a):

> *"Instead of seeing Iraq's war preparations for what they were, it had embraced the most benign explanations of the Iraqi moves. Only those outside the policy consensus [...] could see the Iraqi moves for what they were."*

10. Janis proposes the following criteria for sound decision-making by groups (Janis, 1982n):
    - Thoroughly canvassed a wide range of alternative courses of action.
    - Surveyed the objectives and the values implicated.
    - Carefully weighed the costs, drawbacks, and subtle risks of negative consequences, as well as the positive consequences that could flow from what initially seemed the most advantageous course of action.
    - Continuously searched for relevant information for evaluating the policy alternatives.
    - Conscientiously took account of the information and the expert judgments to which they were exposed, even when the information or judgments did not support the course of action they initially preferred.
    - Re-examined the positive and negative consequences of all the main alternatives, including those originally considered unacceptable, before making a final choice.
    - Made detailed provisions for executing the chosen course-of-action, with special attention to contingency plans that might be required if various known risks were to materialize.
11. Statements in *Tables 17.2-17.4* are empirically based on my personal observations in almost three decades of work experience. Neither scientific method nor pretense relates to these statements.

# CHAPTER 18

1. Believe me or not but I am not a specialist in law and thus cannot accept any liability related to the readers use of opinions on economic law provided for in this book.
2. As so often the EEA came into being in response to an event (Rothke, 2002). The creation of the EEA was triggered by the highly publicized trade secret – related conflict between General Motors and Volkswagen AG. This conflict emerged when a top executive of General Motors, Mr Jose Lopez, was persuaded to join Volkswagen AG. VAG's courting Mr Lopez partly originated from the fact that his coming would offer VAG a large number of GM's trade secrets. Rothke remarks:

    > *"GM sought to take action against VAG in the US but found its remedies limited. Criminal action was basically foreclosed by the absence of trade secrets legislation."*
3. Dumpster diving is a traditional yet unethical intelligence tool. During the Second World War British intelligence regularly applied dumpster diving to foreign embassies' wastebins as part of their efforts to break encrypted communication of others nations (Aldrich, 2011d).
4. Credits to D.C. Martin (Martin, 2003) who so elegantly framed a situation where nobody knows who is working for whom at what time as a 'wilderness of mirrors'.
5. SCIP stands for Society of Competitive Intelligence Professionals. This society has compiled the following code of ethics for practicing market intelligence (McGonagle, 2008):
    - To continually strive to increase the recognition and respect of the profession.
    - To comply with all applicable laws, domestic and international.
    - To accurately disclose all relevant information, including one's identity and organization prior to all interviews.
    - To avoid conflicts of interest in fulfilling one's duties.

- To provide honest and realistic recommendations and conclusions in the execution of one's duties.
- To promote this code of ethics within one's company, with third-party contractors and within the entire profession.
- To faithfully adhere to and abide by one's company policies, objectives and guidelines.

The SCIP code of ethics is broadly used by market intelligence-collection contractors as a sign of professionalism in ethical execution.

## CHAPTER 19

1. The frailty of human memory has long been acknowledged. According to Dr Marsel Mesulam, in 1994 head of the neurology department at Beth Israel Hospital at Harvard Medical School (Goleman, 1994):

   *"The lay expectation is that whatever we remember should be true, but memory does not work like a video camera. From the point of view of neuroscience, every memory is a fragile reconstruction of what the nervous system actually witnessed."*

   Work by Dr Charles Brainerd, also quoted by Goleman, reports:

   *"the context – the time and place – in which you acquire a memory is the quickest part of the memory to decay and the easiest to interfere with."*

   Given the scientific evidence for the frailty of memory,

   *"The miracle is that anything we remember is true," according to Dr. Mesulam, "not that there is distortion."*

   This is a sobering thought and a warning to anyone involved in strategic analysis, where true facts are the basis for any analysis deliverable that ultimately is to underpin a corporate decision. Structured filing of data as they appear when they appear is probably the best mitigation to the risk of distortion *post* the acquisition of those data. It, however, in collection from human sources doesn't solve any distortion of the truth, either intentionally as deception or inadvertently due to memory frailty.

   The most savvy collectors of data from humans that apply elicitation, regardless of the ethical dimension involved, are trained to intentionally distort the memory of their sources. Sources are not to remember that they shared (sensitive) data by intentionally loading their memory with experiences that were so gratifying that neither the relevant data given nor the de facto theft thereof is stored in the memory, let alone that these facts are accessible for remembering later by the source. This serves to protect the collector (and his principal) from being unmasked. It is taking the intelligence paradigm of 'not leaving traces' as far as is possible. It is outside the scope of this text to discuss further details, mainly for ethical reasons. This is not a book on how to succeed in data theft from humans.

2. Multiple providers offer financial data for companies in pre-defined formats. These providers do not tend to emphasize the little issues mentioned regarding differences in definitions. The quality of such providers varies widely. In the reports of such providers it is often not transparent how differently defined original data have been 'structured'. Some providers offer all companies' financial statements in US$ regardless of the original reporting currency, but all too often for the sake of convenience the exchange rate corresponding with the last day of the book year has been used in the conversion, rather than for instance a year-average exchange rate. Thus, critical information may get lost or distorted 'in translation'.

3. There is catch here. Filing copies in a data management system that is only accessible by a single person is generally legally possible. Do check the terms and conditions that may apply to filing data in the country or countries of operation that are applicable to your situation (especially the copyright on news texts and/or photographs).

   However, filing news items on a data management system that offers access to that news to multiple users, like a corporate intranet or equivalent, is generally not allowed by most countries' copyright or other applicable law. This means that with the publisher of the data or with the data collector to whom news collection has been outsourced, copyright-related agreements need to be concluded, so as to ensure copyright law compliance.

Doing so may increase the cost of filing or may limit the time that a file can be retained on file. As a rule, it is critical to be compliant and the filing of most qualitative data is worth paying for.

4. Digitalization should consist of two steps. First the hard copy is scanned. This results usually in a PDF-format file, with the data/text being stored as an image. This file should be processed with OCR or optical character recognition. The latter allows all the text in the scan to be recognized as text, turning a hard copy via an image into a text file (i.e. a Microsoft Word file or a PDF). Assuming the OCR process to be sufficiently accurate, the overall process turns a hard copy via an image into a text file that may be analyzed automatically with natural language processing.
5. The information technology term for adding metadata is "to tag" metadata to a data point
6. Preferably users can select the number of emails they would like to receive from the system, e.g. choosing to have one email a day containing all their relevant hits or e.g. a real-time, single data point alert for a particular query
7. At the very beginning of the design of the qualitative knowledge management system it is recommended to decide that any data related to the own company would only and exclusively be featured in the system as long as that information was already available in the public domain. The system thus under no circumstance distributes data, information, knowledge or intelligence on the own company that in any way is company confidential. This approach takes away any barriers to open up the system to any employee worldwide: even when some employee may join a competitor as their next employer, the employee can, through the system, never access confidential data on the own company, unforeseen distribution of which could be detrimental to the own company's interests

# CHAPTER 20

1. Competitive intelligence specialist Ellen Naylor describes vividly how she set up a competitive intelligence department at Verizon (Naylor, 2007). In Motorola, former strategic intelligence methodologies and practices have been embraced from day one as in Motorola a former CIA team had been hired to build the in-house capability.
2. In preparation for and during the Second World War, both the German and the British intelligence services needed to be expanded. When in Germany the Nazis took power in 1933, part of the military establishment (and not only they) frowned upon the new ruling party. They viewed them as uncivilized lower-class rascals. A bulwark of German upper-class society was the Abwehr, the military intelligence service, led by the shrewd Admiral Wilhelm Canaris. As the Nazi-party realized cooperation with the Abwehr would not come naturally, the State Security office (ReichsSicherheitsHauptAmt, RSHA) set up its own parallel foreign intelligence service. This was a correct assessment as the Abwehr would form a nodal point in the military coup against Hitler, executed July 20, 1944.

   The state security-based foreign intelligence service was to be led by a young lawyer named Walter Schellenberg. Given his inevitable allegiance with the SS, he carried co-responsibility for war crimes. After the war, he was sentenced a short prison term at Neurenberg. In prison he wrote his memoirs in which he reflected on setting up his intelligence service, including the setup of a foreign network of human sources. Even when the differences between a wartime government intelligence service serving one of the most brutal and despicable regimes that ever existed on earth and strategic analysis in business in terms of aims and methods are vastly different and shall neither methodologically nor ethically be stepped over too lightly, Schellenberg provides a lesson which has relevance to strategic analysis in business (Schellenberg, 2000):

   > *"I decided that the worst thing was to try to prepare and carry out intelligence work under [time] pressure. An intelligence network has to be built up step-by-step. On foreign soil it must*

*be nurtured like a plant and allowed to take root. Only then will there be healthy growth and a plentiful harvest."*

To the west of the North Sea, MI6 the UK foreign intelligence service at the start of the Second World War faced similar problems (Jeffery, 2011f):

*"[it took] years to develop reliable and dependable sources."*

*"First class sources in foreign countries cannot be created at short notice [but required] careful and prolonged cultivation."*

If there is one single reason why success in strategic analysis doesn't come quickly and tenure has a disproportional value, it is the building and maintaining of a network also when sources as in business practice only operate ethically and compliant with all applicable law.

3. For the record: the Dutch government intelligence service, AIVD, reportedly has an annual budget for 2014 of about €250 million, which is between 0.03 and 0.04% of the Dutch GDP – a remarkably comparable percentage to what companies spend on their strategic analysis function.

4. Both in the case of the Pearl Harbor Attack in 1941, as well as in the case of 9/11, poor sharing contributed to flawed analysis (Bruce, 2008c). He writes:

   *"Poor sharing of limited collection greatly impeded warning analysis."*

5. The role of corporate strategy as a department often mirrors the role of the Chief Strategy Officer or CSO. The choice for the role of the department is often determined by the CEO of the firm, who subsequently selects a CSO that matches the profile of the role the CEO wants the department to take. Powell and Angwin identify four different characteristic roles of CSOs (Powell, 2012):

| Role: | Mainly in scope: | Less or not in scope: |
|---|---|---|
| • The internal consultant | Top-down strategy formulation | Implementation |
| • Specialist | Functional specialism e.g. M&A | New strategy formulation |
| • Coach | Bottom-up strategy formulation facilitating business units | P&L responsibility |
| • Change agent | Execution-oriented facilitators | New strategy formulation |

The above roles do not need to be mutually exclusive, but usually one role is by far dominant. Strategic analysis as function fits best in a corporate strategy department when the CSO's focus is that of the internal consultant or that of the coach. The change agent will tend to be more focused on strategy execution and less on strategy design, in doing so requiring management monitoring information rather than strategic analysis of the business environment.

The specialist may create a good home for strategic analysis when for example his specialism is to build the organization's innovation capabilities. Designing an innovation strategy requires a sharp view where to compete, prior to deciding how to compete through innovation. This is where strategic environment analysis fits in nicely.

6. Research carried out with teams of US intelligence analysts showed that (Grant, 2013):

   *"The single strongest predictor of group effectiveness was the amount of help that analysts gave to each other. In the highest-performing teams, analysts invested extensive time and energy in coaching, teaching, and consulting with their colleagues. These contributions helped analysts question their own assumptions, fill gaps in their knowledge, gain access to novel perspectives, and recognize patterns in seemingly disconnected threads of information."*

7. GIA itself describes its world class MI roadmap as follows (GIA, 2011):

   *"The World Class Market Intelligence Roadmap by GIA is a pragmatic approach to setting up an intelligence program from the ground up. It involves several steps including conducting*

*a needs analysis and setting the scope of the intelligence activity, planning the intelligence process, defining deliverables, implementing tools and techniques, activating the organization, and marketing the intelligence program to its internal users. The Roadmap framework serves as a yardstick for measuring progress in taking the intelligence program to a world class level."*

8. Regardless of the level of sophistication, firefighting will always inevitably be part of the assignment portfolio of a strategic analysis function. To experienced and a bit frustrated-turned-cynical staff firefighting may also be known by its government intelligence nickname: "the tyranny of current intelligence"

# LITERATURE


AchieveGlobal [2010], Winning Account Strategies training program; see www.achieveglobal.com visited Feb. 2012.

AIVD [2016], Annual report (in Dutch), www.aivd.nl, visited April 22, 2016.

Albright, D. [2003], Iraq's Aluminum Tubes: Separating Fact from Fiction; http://www.isis-online.org/publications/iraq/IraqAluminumTubes12-5-03.pdf, visited Feb. 1, 2014.

Aldrich, R.J. [2011a], *GCHQ The Uncensored Story of Britain's Most Secret Intelligence Agency*, Harper Press, London, pp. 520-521.

Aldrich, R.J. [2011b], ibid, pp. 245-246.

Aldrich, R.J. [2011c], ibid, p. 388.

Aldrich, R.J. [2011d], ibid, p. 56.

Aldrich, R.J. [2011e], ibid.

Aldrich, R.J. [2011f], ibid, p. 362.

Alford, S. [2013a], *The Watchers – a secret history of the Reign of Elizabeth I*, Penguin, London, UK, p. 54.

Alford, S. [2013b], p. 263.

Andrew, C., Mitrokhin, V. [2001a] *The Sword and the Shield*, Basic Books (paperback), New York, p. 51.

Andrew, C. [2001b], ibid, p. 95.

Andrew, C. [2001c], ibid, foreword and introduction to the paperback edition.

Andrew, C. [2001d], ibid, p. 480.

Andrew, C.,[2001e], ibid, p. 107.

Andrew, C. [2001f], ibid, p. 480.

Andrew, C. [2001g], ibid, p. 475.

Axelrod, A. [1999], *Patton on Leadership: Strategic Lessons for Corporate Warfare*, Prentice Hall press, Paramus NJ, p. 205-206.

Baeza-Yates, R. (2014), 'Data vs. Right Data', paper presented at the GIA conference "Intelligence 3.0", 3–4 June, Helsinki, Finland.

Baker, E.H. (2014), 'Looking Outward with Big Data: A Q & A with Tom Davenport', *Strategy & Business* online edition, 31 March.

Bassett, R. (2005), *Hitler's Spy Chief: The Wilhelm Canaris Mystery*, Cassell, London, pp. 101–2, 104.

Benedict, R. (1954), *The Chrysanthemum and the Sword; Patterns of Japanese Culture*, Tuttle Publishing, Tokyo / Periplus Edition reprint, p. 216.

Berle, A.A. (1969a), *Power*, Harcourt, Brace & World, Inc., New York, p. 553.

Berle, A.A. (1969b), ibid, p. 59.

Berlinski, C. (2010), 'Smile and Smile: Turkey's Feel-Good Foreign Policy', *World Affairs*, July/August.

Bird, A. (2009), 'McKinsey Conversations with Global Leaders: Paul Polman of Unilever', *McKinsey Quarterly*, October 2009.

Bird, K. (2014), *The Good Spy: The Life and Death of Robert Ames*, Broadway Books, New York, p. 194.

Borum, R. (2006), 'Approaching Truth: Behavioral Science Lessons on Educing Information from Human Sources', in: *Educing Information – Interrogation: Science and Art?*, NDIC Press, Washington DC, pp. 17-43.

Bower, J.L, Doz, Y., (1979), 'Strategy Formulation: A Social and Political Process', in: D. Schendel and C. Hofer (eds.) *Strategic Management: A New View of Business Policy and Planning,* Little Brown and Co., Boston, MA.

Box, G.E.P., Hunter, J.S., Hunter, W.G. (2005), *Statistics for Experimenters: Design, Innovation and Discovery*, 2nd Ed., J. Wiley & Sons, Hoboken, NY p. 440.

Bradley, C., Dawson, A, Montard, A. (2013), 'Mastering the Building Blocks of Strategy', *McKinsey Quarterly*, October 2013.

Brown, B., Gottlieb, J. (2016), 'The Need to Lead in Data Analytics', *McKinsey Quarterly*, 22 April.

Bruce, J.B., George, R.Z. (2008a), 'Intelligence Analysis – The Emergence of a Discipline', in: R.Z. George, J.B. Bruce (eds), *Analyzing Intelligence: Origins, Obstacles, and Innovations,* Georgetown University Press, Washington DC, pp. 6-10.

Bruce, J.B. (2008b), 'Making Analysis More Reliable: Why Epistemology Matters in Intelligence', in: R.Z. George, J.B. Bruce (eds), *Analyzing Intelligence: Origins, Obstacles, and Innovations*, Georgetown University Press, Washington DC, pp. 171–190.

Bruce, J.B. (2008c), 'The Missing Link: The Analyst-collector Relationship', in: R.Z. George, J.B. Bruce (Editors), *Analyzing Intelligence: Origins, Obstacles, and Innovations*, Georgetown University Press, Washington DC, pp. 191–210.

Bruce, J.B., Bennett, M. (2008d), 'Foreign Denial and Deception: Analytical Imperatives', in: R.Z. George, J.B. Bruce (eds), *Analyzing Intelligence: Origins, Obstacles, and Innovations*, Georgetown University Press, Washington DC, p. 123.

Bruce, J.B., Bennett, M. (2008e), ibid, pp. 126-135.

Bryan, L. (2009), 'Dynamic Management: Better Decision in Uncertain Times', *McKinsey Quarterly,* December 2009.

Bughin, J. et al. (2011), 'The Impact of Internet Technologies: Search', McKinsey & Company Report.

Burrough, B., Helyar, J. (1991), *Barbarians at the Gate: The Fall of RJR Nabisco*, HarperPerennial, New York.

Canadian Land Forces (2001), Land Force Information Operations, Field Manual Intelligence, http://armyapp.forces.gc.ca/ael/pubs/B-GL-357-001-FP-001.pdf, website visited 12 February 2011, pp. 12–13.

Canadian Land Forces (2001b) ibid, p. 145.

Canadian Land Forces (2001c) ibid, pp. 130–131.

Canadian Land Forces (2001d), ibid, p. 52.

Capozzi, M.M., Dye, R., Howe, A. (2011), 'Sparking Creativity in Teams: An Executive's Guide', *McKinsey Quarterly*, April.

Carpe, D. (2005), 'The Ups and Downs of Elicitation', *SCIP Magazine*, Vol. 8, no. 5, September-October.

CEB, Corporate Executive Board (2007), Informal Intelligence Network: Capturing the Organization's Tacit Knowledge, Featuring General Motors Corporation, Market Research Executive Board MRC177M069.

Chandler Jr., A.D. (1962), *Strategy and Structure: Chapters in the History of the American Industrial Enterprise*, MIT Press, Boston, MA.

Cheevers, J. (2014), *Act of War: Lyndon Johnson, North Korea, and the Capture of the Spy Ship Pueblo*, Penguin, New York, p. 344.

Cherkashin, V. (2005) with Feifer, G., *Spy Handler: Memoir of a KGB Officer. The True Story of the Man who Recruited Robert Hanssen and Aldrich Ames*, Basic Books, New York, p. 114.

Christensen, C.M. (2000), *The Innovator's Dilemma*, HarperCollins, New York

Chui, M., Manyika, J., Van Kuiken, S, (2014), 'What Executives Should Know About Open Data', *McKinsey Quarterly*, January.

Clark, C. (2013a), *The Sleepwalkers: How Europe Went to War in 1914*, Penguin, London, pp. 41, 61.

Clark, C. (2013b), ibid, p. 345.

Clark, R.M. (2007a), *Intelligence Analysis: A Target-centric Approach*, CQ Press, Washington DC p. 151.

Clark, R.M. (2007b), ibid.

Clark, R.M. (2007c), ibid, p. 56.

Clark, R.M. (2007d), ibid, pp. 123–31.

Clark, R.M. (2007e), ibid, p. 283.

Clark, R.M. (2007f), ibid, p. 111.

Clark, R.M. (2007g), ibid, p. 163.

von Clausewitz, C. (1980) (based on edition of 1832-1834), *Vom Kriege*, Philip Reclam, Stuttgart.

Collins, J.C. (2005), 'Level 5 Leadership: The Triumph of Humility and Fierce Resolve', *Harvard Business Review*, July-August, pp. 136–46.

Collins, J.C. (2009), *How the Mighty Fall and Why Some Companies Never Give In*, Random House Business Books, London p. 78.

Cooper, J.R. (2005a), 'Curing Analytic Pathologies: Pathways to Improved Intelligence Analysis', Center for the Study of Intelligence, December (www.cia.gov) p.26.

Cooper, J.R. (2005b), ibid, pp. 33-34.

Cooper, J.R. (2005c), ibid, pp. 35-37.

Corera, G. (2012a), *MI6: Life and Death in the British Secret Service*, Phoenix – Orionbooks, London, p. 267.

Corera, G. (2012b), ibid, p. 359.

Coutu, D.L., (2005), 'Strategic Intensity: A Conversation with World Chess Champion Garry Kasparov', *Harvard Business Research*, April pp. 49-53.

Cramm, S. (2013), 'Are You Disabling Your Organization with Advice?', *Strategy & Business*, 14 November.

Cusack, J., McKnight, M, McPherson, R. (2010), 'The Intelligence Challenge: Lessons from the Private Sector', *Harvard Business Review Spotlight on Leadership Lessons from the Military*, 18 November.

Davenport, T.H. (2014a), *Big Data @ Work: Dispelling the Myths, Uncovering the Opportunities*, Harvard Business Review Press, Boston MA, p. 141.

Davenport, T.H. (2014b), ibid, p. 96.

Davenport, T.H. (2014c), ibid, p. 102.

Davenport, T.H. (2014d), ibid, p. 3.

Davenport, T.H. (2014e), ibid, p. 187.

Davenport, T.H. (2014f), ibid, p. 192.

Davis, J. (1997), 'A Compendium of Analytic Tradecraft Notes', Directorate of Intelligence, CIA, Vol. I, Note 10 *Tradecraft and Counterintelligence*, p. 42.

Davis, J. (2008), Why bad things happen to good analysts, In: R.Z. George, J.B. Bruce (Editors), Analyzing Intelligence – origins, obstacles, and innovations, Georgetown University Press, Washington DC, pp. 157-170.

Deacon, R., (1982a), *A History of the Japanese Secret Service*, Frederick Muller Ltd., Wimbledon, p. 59.

Deacon, R. (1982b), ibid, p. 52.

Deacon, R., (1982c), ibid, p. 142.

Deacon, R., (1982d), ibid, p. 263.

Deacon, R., (1982e), ibid, p. 4.

Deacon, R., (1982f), ibid, pp. 248-249.

Dean, D., Webb, C. (2011), 'Recovering From Information Overload', *McKinsey Quarterly*, January.

De Bondt, W.F.M., Thaler, R. (1985), 'Does the Stock Market Overreact?', *Journal of Finance*, Vol. 40, No. 3, Papers and Proceedings of the Forty-Third Annual Meeting American Finance Association, Dallas, TX, 28–30 December 1984. (July 1985), pp. 793–805.

Delattre, L, (2006), *Betraying Hitler*, Atlantic Books, London, p. 238.

Denrell, J. (2005), 'Selection Bias and the Perils of Benchmarking', *Harvard Business Review*, April, pp. 114-19.

Dobbs, M. (2009a), *One Minute to Midnight*, Knopf, Random House, New York, p. 175.

Dobbs, M. (2009b), ibid, p. 4.

Dobbs, M. (2009c), ibid, p. 15.

Dobbs, M. (2009d), ibid, p. 168.

Dobbs, M. (2009e), ibid, p. 3 and photo catern opposite p. 62.

Dobbs, M. (2009f), ibid, p. 184.

Donovan, J.B. (1964), *Strangers on a bridge: The Case of Colonel Abel*, Atheneum, New York, p. 332.

Dörner, D., (1996a), *The Logic of Failure: Recognizing and Avoiding Error in Complex Situations*, Basic Books, New York, p. 24.

Dörner, D., (1996b), ibid, p. 101.

Dörner, D., (1996c), ibid, p. 16.

Dörner, D., (1996d), ibid, p. 181.

Doty, E. (2014), 'Integrity is Free', *Strategy + Business* online edition, 16 December.

Drucker, P. (c. 1990), quote attributed to him but without formal source at http://en.wikiquote.org/wiki/Talk:Peter_Drucker, visited 17 March 2012.

*Economist* (2014), 'Intelligent Intelligence', 19 July, p. 69.

Edward, S., Tokcan, S. (2014), 'The Power of Human Intelligence', paper presented at the GIA conference "Intelligence 3.0", Helsinki, Finland, June.

EEA (1997), 'The Economic Espionage Act of 1996', *Competitive Intelligence Review*, 8 (3) pp. 4-6.

Ehrlich, C. (2006), 'Phantom Interview and the False Flag Job Seeker', *Competitive Intelligence Magazine*, 9 (3), May-June.

Engelen, D. (2007), *Frontdienst, de BVD in de koude oorlog*, Boom, Amsterdam, 179.

Favaro, K., Yacteen, N. (2013), 'The Right Ideas in all the Wrong Places', *Strategy + Business* online edition, 11 March 2013.

FBI (2014), Elicitation Brochure, www.fbi.gov, visited 1 March 2014.

Fedewa, D, Kothari, A., Narayanan, A.S. (2009), 'Squeezing More Ideas from Product Teardowns', *McKinsey Quarterly*, July.

Fehringer, D., Hohhof, B. (2006), 'Competitive Intelligence Ethics: Navigating the Gray Zone', *Topics in Competitive Intelligence*, Vol. I, Competitive Intelligence Foundation, www.scip.org.

Fenton-O'Creevy, M., Soane, E. (2000), 'The Subjective Perception of Risk', *Financial Times*, 25 April Appendix on Mastering Risk.

Figes, O. (2011), *Crimea: The Last Crusade*, Penguin, London, p. 309.

Fillié, J.P. (2010), 'Half a Century of BI: From Inception to BI 2.0', *Cutter IT Journal*, June edition, pp. 22-26.

Fine, N.R. (1997), 'The Economic Espionage Act: Turning Fear into Compliance', *Competitive Intelligence Review*, 8 (3), pp. 20–4.

Fisher, R., Johnston, R. (2008), 'Is Intelligence Analysis a Aiscipline?', in: R.Z. George, J.B. Bruce (Eds), *Analyzing Intelligence: Origins, Obstacles, and Innovations*, Georgetown University Press, Washington DC, pp. 55-68.

Fisher, J. (2014), 'Competitive Intelligence: A Case Study of Motorola's Corporate Competitive Intelligence Group, 1983-2009', Intelligencer: Journal of US Intelligence Studies, Spring/Summer 2014, pp. 55-8.

Frank, C.J., Magnone, P. (2011a), *Drinking from the Fire Hose: Making Smarter Decisions without Drowning in Information*, Portfolio Penguin, London UK, pp. 41–2.

Frank, C.J., Magnone, P. (2011b), ibid, pp. 187–201.

Frank, C.J., Magnone, P. (2011c), ibid, p. 130.

Frank, C.J., Magnone, P. (2011d), ibid, p. 116.

Freedman, Sir L. (2013a), *Strategy: A History*, Oxford University Press, Oxford, p. 324.

Freedman, Sir L. (2013b), ibid, p. 153.

Freedman, Sir L. (2013c), ibid, pp. 599–606.

Freedman, Sir L. (2013d), ibid, p. 483.

Freedman, Sir L. (2013e), ibid, p. 569.

Freedman, Sir L. (2013f), ibid, p. 239.

Friedman, G. (2009), 'Strategic Calculus and the Afghan War', www.stratfor.com, geopolitics column, 13 July 2009.

Friedman, G. (2010a), 'Russian Spies and Strategic Intelligence', www.stratfor.com, geopolitics column, 13 July 2010.

Friedman, G. (2010b), 'Rethinking American Options on Iran', www.stratfor.com, geopolitics column, 31 August 2010.

Friedman, G. (2013), 'Russia after Putin: Inherent Leadership Struggles', www.stratfor.com, analysis column, 24 June 2013.

Friedman, U. (2012), 'The Ten Biggest American Intelligence Failures', *Foreign Policy*, 3 January, online issue.

Gavetti, G., Rivkin, J.W. (2005), 'How Strategists Really Think: Tapping the Power of Analogy', Harvard *Business Review*, April.

George, R. Z. (2008a), 'The Art of Strategy and Intelligence', in: R.Z. George, J.B. Bruce (eds), *Analyzing Intelligence: Origins, Obstacles, and Innovations*, Georgetown University Press, Washington DC, p. 111.

George, R. Z. (2008b), 'The Art of Strategy and Intelligence', in: R.Z. George, J.B. Bruce (eds), *Analyzing Intelligence: Origins, Obstacles, and Innovations*, Georgetown University Press, Washington DC, p. 113.

George, R.Z., Bruce, J.B. (2008b), 'Conclusion: The Age of Analysis', in: R.Z. George, J.B. Bruce (eds), *Analyzing Intelligence: Origins, Obstacles, and Innovations*, Georgetown University Press, Washington DC, p. 305.

Gerstner, L.V. Jr. (2003), *Who Says Elephants Can't Dance? Inside IBM's Historic Turnaround*, Harper-Collins Publishers, London, pp. 229–30.

GIA; Global Intelligence Alliance (2005), 'Competitive Intelligence in Large Companies – Global Study'; GIA White Paper 4/2005.

GIA; Global Intelligence Alliance (2011), 'Market Intelligence in Global Organizations: Survey Findings in 2011'; GIA White Paper 2/2011.

Gilad, B., Gilad, T. (1988), *The Business Intelligence System*, Amacon, New York, pp. 158–186.

Gladwell, M. (2000a), *The Tipping Point*, Back Bay Books, Little, Brown and Company, New York, p. 118.

Gladwell, M. (2000b), ibid, pp. 133–92.

Gladwell, M. (2005), *Blink: The Power of Thinking Without Thinking*, Little, Brown and Company, New York, pp. 21–38.

Gladwell, M. (2009a), 'Cocksure: Banks, Battles and the Psychology of Overconfidence', *The New Yorker*, 27 July.

Gladwell, M. (2009b), *Outliers: The Story of Success*, Penguin, London, p. 89.

Gladwell, M. (2009c), ibid, pp. 206–61.

Godin, S. (2007), *The Dip: The Extraordinary Benefits of Knowing When to Quit (And When to Stick)*, Little Brown Book Group, London, p. 17.

Goleman, D., 'Miscoding is Seen As The Root of False Memories', *New York Times*, 31 May 1994.

Gordon, M.R., Trainor, B.E. (1995a), *The General's War: The Inside Story of the Conflict in the Gulf*, Little Brown Book Group, New York, p. 29.

Gordon, M.R., Trainor, B.E. (1995b), ibid, p. xiv.

Gordon, M.R., Trainor, B.E. (1995c), ibid, pp. 4–6.

Graaff, B. de (2015), 'Is intelligence Information?', Paper presented at the VOGIN-IP conference, Amsterdam, 26 March 2015.

Grant, A. (2013), 'Givers Take All: The Hidden Dimension of Corporate Culture', *McKinsey Quarterly*, April edition

Grey, S. (2016a), *The New Spymasters: Inside Espionage from the Cold War to Global Terror*, Penguin, London p. 137.

Grey, S. (2016b), ibid, pp. 142–3.

Grey, S. (2016c), ibid, p. 40.

Grey, S. (2016d), ibid, p. 239.

Grey, S. (2016e), ibid, p. 242.

Grey, S. (2016f), ibid.

Grey, S. (2016g), ibid, p. 49.

Grey, S. (2016h), ibid, p. 56.

Guderian, H. (1999), *Achtung Panzer!*, English translation based on 1937 German original, Cassell Military Paperbacks, London.

Gudlavelleti, S, Gupta, S., Narayanan, A.S. (2013), 'Developing Winning Products for Emerging Markets', *McKinsey Quarterly*, May 2013.

Guszcza, J., Lucker, J. (2012), 'A Delicate Balance: Organizational Barriers to Evidence-based Management', *Deloitte Review*, 6 April 2012.

Halberstam, D. (1992a), The Best and The Brightest, Random House, New York, p. 171.

Halberstam, D. (1992b), ibid, p. 457.

Halberstam, D. (1992c), ibid, p. 581.

Halberstam, D. (1992d), ibid, pp. 186–7.

Halberstam, D. (1992e), ibid, p. 231.

Halberstam, D. (1992f), ibid, p. 595.

Halberstam, D. (2009), *The Coldest Winter*, Pan MacMillan, London, pp. 15, 378–9.

Halligan, R.M. (1997), 'The Theft of Trade Secrets is Now a Federal Crime', *Competitive Intelligence Review*, 8 (3), pp. 7–12.

Hansen, J.H. (2007), 'Soviet Deception in the Cuban Missile Crisis', viewed at https://www.cia.gov/library/center-for-the-study-of-intelligence/csi-publications/csi-studies/studies/vol46no1/article06.html, site visited 25 January 2014.

Hawker, S. (ed.) (2006), *Little Oxford English Dictionary*, 9th Edition, Oxford University Press, Oxford.

Hedin, H., Hirvensalo, I., Vaarnas, M. (2011), *The Handbook of Market Intelligence: Understand, Compete and Grow in Global Markets*, 1st Edition, J. Wiley & Sons, Chichester, pp. 210–11.

Helgesen, S. (2008), 'The Practical Wisdom of Ikujiro Nonaka', *Strategy+Business*, Vol. 53, Winter issue.

Herring, J.P. (2006), 'Developing Ethical Guidelines: Getting Started', in: Fehringer, D. and Hohhof, B. [eds.], *Competitive Intelligence Ethics: Navigating the Gray Zone, Topics in Competitive Intelligence*, Vol. I, Competitive Intelligence Foundation, pp. 7–8.

van der Heijden, K. (1997a), *Scenarios: The Art of Strategic Conversation*, J. Wiley & Sons, Chichester, p. 3.

Heuer Jr., R.J., (1999a), *The Psychology of Intelligence Analysis*, Center for the Study of Intelligence, CIA,, pp. 4–5, 8–11 and 31.

Heuer Jr., R.J., (1999b), ibid, pp. 23–6.

Heuer Jr., R.J., (1999c), ibid, p. 29.

Heuer Jr., R.J., (1999d), ibid, pp. 129–31.

Heuer Jr., R.J., (1999e), ibid, p. 153.

Heuer Jr., R.J., (1999f), ibid, pp. 70–1.

Heuer Jr., R.J., (1999g), ibid, p. 33.

Heuer Jr., R.J., (1999h), ibid, p. 46.

Heuer Jr., R.J. (1999i), ibid, p. 124.

Heuer Jr., R.J. (1999j), ibid, p. 52.

Heuer Jr., R.J. (1999k), ibid, pp. 18–19.

Heuer Jr., R.J. (1999l), ibid, p. 121.

Heuer Jr., R.J., (1999m), ibid, p. xiv.

Heuer Jr. , R.J. (1999o), ibid, p. 67.

Heuer Jr., R.J. (1999p), ibid, p. 30.

Heuer Jr. R.J., (2005), 'Improving Intelligence Analysis with ACH', November 2005; www.pherson.org visited 22 February 2014.

Heuer Jr., R.J. (2008), 'Computer-aided Analysis of Competing Hypotheses', in: R.Z. George, J.B. Bruce (Editors), *Analyzing Intelligence: Origins, Obstacles, and innovations*, Georgetown University Press, Washington DC, pp. 251-65.

Hoffman, D.E. (2011a) *The Dead Hand*, Icon Books, London, p. 340.

Hoffman, D.E. (2011b), ibid, p. 190.

Hoffman, D.E. (2011c), ibid, pp. 76-9.

Hoffman, D.E. (2011d), ibid, p. 146.

Hoffman, D.E. (2015), *The Billion Dollar Spy: A True Story of Cold War Espionage and Betrayal*, Doubleday, New York, p. 156.

Hopkirk, P. (1994), *The Great Game: The Struggle for Empire in Central Asia*, Kodansha America, New York, p. 456.

Horowitz, R. (1997), 'The Economic Espionage Act: The Rules Have Not Changed', *Competitive Intelligence Review*, 9 (3) pp. 30–8.

Houston, P., Floyd, M., Carnicero, S., Tennant, D. (2012a), *Spy the Lie: Former CIA Officers Teach You How to Detect Deception*, Icon Books, London, pp. 51–72, 93–102.

Houston, P., Floyd, M., Carnicero, S., Tennant, D. (2012b), ibid, p. 149.

Houston, P., Floyd, M., Carnicero, S., Tennant, D. (2012c), ibid, pp. 127–36.

Jacobsen, A., (2014), *Operation Paperclip: The Secret Intelligence Program that Brought Nazi Scientists to America*, Little, Brown & Co., New York, p. 315.

Jähne, P., (2009), Handouts, SAGEBSSB Business Intelligence Training and Personal Communication.

Janis, I.L, (1982a), *Groupthink: Psychological Studies of Policy Decisions and Fiascoes*, 2nd revised and enlarged edition, Wadsworth Centage Learning, Boston, MA, p. 83.

Janis, I.L. (1982b), ibid, p. 129.

Janis, I.L. (1982c), ibid, p. 177.

Janis, I.L, (1982d), ibid, pp. 11–13.

Janis, I.L. (1982e), ibid, p. 9.

Janis, I.L. (1982f), ibid, p. 35.

Janis, I.L. (1982g), ibid, p. 244.

Janis, I.L. (1982h), ibid, pp. 141–2.

Janis, I.L. (1982i), ibid, p. 3.

Janis, I.L. (1982j), ibid, p. 193.

Janis, I.L. (1982k), ibid, p. 243.

Janis, I.L. (1982l), ibid, p. 257.

Janis, I.L. (1982m), ibid, p. 172.

Janis, I.L. (1982n), ibid, p. 136.

Janis, I.L. (1982o), ibid, pp. 155 and 157.

Javers, E. (2011), *Broker, Trader, Lawyer, Spy: The Secret World of Corporate Espionage*, HarperCollins Publishers, New York, p. 276.

Javers, E. (2011b), ibid, pp. 183–4.

Javers, E. (2011c), ibid.

Jeffery, K., (2011a), MI6: *The History of the Secret Intelligence Service 1909–1949*, Bloomsbury, London, p. 747.

Jeffery, K. (2011b), ibid, pp. 334–5.

Jeffery, K. (2011c), ibid, p. 34.

Jeffery, K. (2011d), ibid, p. 576.

Jeffery, K. (2011e), ibid, p. 188.

Jeffery, K. (2011f), ibid, p. 677.

Jeffery, K. (2011g), ibid, p. 248.

Jervis, R. (2010a), *Why Intelligence Fails: Lessons from the Iranian Revolution and the Iraq War*, Cornell University Press, Ithaca and London, p. vi.

Jervis, R. (2010b), ibid, p. 127.

Jervis, R. (2010c), ibid, p. 38.

Jervis, R. (2010d), ibid, p. 140.

Jervis, R. (2010e), ibid, p. 169.

Jervis, R. (2010f), ibid, p. 150.

Jervis, R. (2010g), ibid, p. 159.

Jervis, R. (2010h), ibid, p. 142.

Johnson, W.R. (2009a), *Thwarting Enemies at Home and Abroad: How to be a Counterintelligence Officer*, Georgetown University Press, Washington DC, p. 181.

Johnson, W.R. (2009b), ibid, pp. 9 and.197.

Johnson, W.R. (2009c), ibid, pp. 36–8.

Johnson, W.R. (2009d), ibid, pp. 9-10.

Johnston, R. (2005a), 'Chapter Three: A Taxonomy of intelligence Variables', *Analytic Culture in the US Intelligence Community*, CIA, Washington DC.

Johnston, R. (2005b), 'Chapter Two: Findings', ibid.

Johnston, R. (2005c), 'Chapter Six: The Question of Foreign Cultures, Combating Ethnocentrism in Intelligence Analysis', ibid.

Johnston, R. (2005d), 'Chapter One: Definitions', ibid.

Jones, C. (2007), 'Intelligence Reform: The Logic of information Sharing', *Intelligence and National Security*, Vol. 22, no. 3 pp. 384–401.

Jones, R.V. (1978a), *Most Secret War: British Scientific intelligence 1939-1945*; edition used: Penguin, London 2009. p. 161.

Jones, R.V. (1978b), ibid, p. 446-450.

Jones, R.V. (1978c), ibid, p. 323.

Jones, R.V. (1978d), ibid, p. 523.

Jones, R.V. (1978e), ibid, p. 76.

Joyner, M. (2007), *Simpleology: The Simple Science of Getting What You Want*, J. Wiley & Sons, Hoboken, NJ, pp. 63–5.

Just-Food, 'Switzerland: Court Convicts Nestlé of "Spying" on Protest Group', 30 January 2013.

Kahneman, D. (2010), 'Strategic Decisions: When Can You Trust Your Gut?', *McKinsey Quarterly*, March 2010.

Kahneman, D. (2011a), *Thinking Fast and Slow*, Penguin, London, p. 10.

Kahneman, D. (2011b), ibid, p. 117–18.

Kahneman, D. (2011c), ibid, p. 100.

Kahneman, D. (2011d), ibid, p. 170.

Kahneman, D. (2011e), ibid, p. 417.

Kahneman, D. (2011f), ibid, pp. 62–4 and 87.

Kahneman, D. (2011g), ibid, p. 249.

Kahneman, D. (2011h), ibid, pp. 126–7.

Kahneman, D. (2011i), ibid, p. 201.

Kahneman, D. (2011j), ibid, p. 87.

Kahneman, D. (2011k), ibid, p.79.

Kahneman, D. (2011l), ibid, pp. 19–24.

Kahneman, D. (2011m), ibid, pp. 256–9, 263–5.

Kahneman, D. (2011n), ibid, pp. 238–41.

Kalitka, P.F. (1997), 'Counterintelligence and Law Enforcement: The Economic Espionage Act of 1996 Versus Competitive Intelligence', *Competitive Intelligence Review*, 8 (3) pp. 25–8.

Keegan, J. (2003a), *Intelligence in War: Knowledge of the Enemy from Napolean to Al-Qaeda*, A.A. Knopf – Random House, New York, p. 196.

Keegan, J. (2003b), ibid, p. 174.

Keegan, J. (2003c), ibid, p. 183.

Keough, D.R. (2008a), *The Ten Commandments for Business Failure*, Penguin London, Chapter 7; pp. 8–9.

Keough, D.R. (2008b), ibid, pp. 97–114.

Kerr, R.J. (2008a), 'The Track Record: CIA Analysis from 1950 to 2000', in: R.Z. George, J.B. Bruce (eds), *Analyzing Intelligence: Origins, Obstacles, and Innovations*, Georgetown University Press, Washington DC, p. 51.

Kerr, R.J. (2008b), ibid p. 39.

Kindler, T.J. (2006), 'Putting an Ethics Policy in Place', in: Fehringer, D. and Hohhof, B. (eds), 'Competitive Intelligence Ethics: Navigating the Gray Zone', *Topics in Competitive Intelligence*, Vol. I, Competitive Intelligence Foundation, pp. 9-11.

Kipling, R. (1980), *Just So Stories*, Watermill Press, Mahwah, NJ, p. 42.

Kirkland, R. (2010), 'Anne Mulcahy, Timeliness Trumps Perfection', *McKinsey Quarterly*, March 2010.

Klein, G. (1999a), *Sources of Power: How People Make Decisions*, MIT Press, Cambridge, MA, p. 189.

Klein, G. (1999b), ibid, pp. 271–84.

Klein, G. (1999c), ibid, pp. 17, 20, 25–30, 34, 92, 93, 95, 96, 100–3.

Klein, G. (1999d), ibid.

Klein, G. (1999e), ibid, pp. 156–7.

Kübler-Ross, E. (1973), *On Death and Dying*, Routledge, Abingdon-on-Thames.

Lacey, R. (1986), *Ford: The Man and the Machine*, Little, Brown and Company, Boston, MA.

Larkin, E. (2005), *Secret Histories: Finding George Orwell in a Burmese Teashop*, John Murray Publishers, London.

Lauder, M. (2009), 'Red Dawn: The Emergence of a Red Teaming Capability in the Canadian Forces', *Canadian Forces' Canadian Army Journal*, Vol. 12, issue 2 (Summer), pp. 25–36.

Lawrence, T.E. (2011), *Revolt in the Desert*, Tauris Parke, London, p. 73.

Lencioni, P. [2002], The five dysfunctions of a team – a leadership fable, Jossey-Bass, San Francisco, CA.

Lermontov, M.J. (1916), *A Hero of Our Time*, translated from the 1840 original by J.H. Wisdom Marr Murray, Alfred A. Knopf, New York, p. 188.

Liddell Hart, B.H. (1991a), *Strategy*, 2nd revised edition, Meridian, London, p. 230.

Liddell Hart, B.H. (1991b), ibid, pp. 319–25.

Lovallo, D., Sibony, O. (2010a), 'The Case for Behavioral Strategy', *McKinsey Quarterly*, March edition.

Lovallo, D., Sibony, O. (2010b), 'Taking the Bias Out of Meetings', *McKinsey Quarterly*, April edition.

Lowenthal, M.M. (2008), 'Intelligence in Transition: Analysis after September 11 and Iraq', in: R.Z. George, J.B. Bruce (eds), *Analyzing Intelligence: Origins, Obstacles, and Innovations*, Georgetown University Press, Washington DC, pp. 226–37.

Luhn, H.P. (1958), 'A Business Intelligence System', *IBM Journal*, October issue, pp. 314–19.

Macintyre, B. (2007), *Agent Zigzag*, Bloomsbury, London, p. 69.

Macintyre, B. (2010a), *Operation Mincemeat*, Bloomsbury, London, p. 129–30.

Macintyre, B. (2010b), ibid, p. 61.

Macintyre, B. (2010c), ibid.

Macintyre, B. (2010d), ibid, pp. 80–1.

Macintyre, B. (2010e), ibid, p. 38.

Macintyre, B. (2010f), ibid, p. 251.

Macintyre, B. (2010g), ibid, p. 26.

Macintyre, B. (2010h), ibid, p. 151.

Macintyre, B. (2010i), ibid, p. 192.

Macintyre, B. (2012), *Double Cross*, Bloomsbury, London.

Macintyre, B. (2014), A spy among friends – Kim Philby and the great betrayal, Crown Publishers, New York, p. 163.

Makridakis, S.G. (1990), *Forecasting, Planning and Strategy for the 21st Century*, The Free Press, New York,, pp. 22–48.

Malandro, L., 'Discover Your Leadership Blind Spots', *Business Week*, 6 September 2009.

Mandel, D.R., Barnes, A. (2014), 'Accuracy of Forecasts in Strategic Intelligence', *Proceedings of the National Academy of Science*, Vol. 111, no. 30, pp. 10984–9.

Mark, K. (2002), *Procter & Gamble: Managing Competitive Intelligence*, Richard Ivey School of Business, The University of Western Ontario, Business Case 9B02C002.

Martin, D.C. (2003), *The Wilderness of Mirrors*, The Lyons Press, Guilford, CO (reprint from original edition of 1980).

May, E.R. (1973a), *Lessons of the Past: The Use and Misuse of History in American Foreign Policy*, Oxford University Press, New York, p. xi.

May, E.R. (1973b), ibid, p. 16.

May, E.R. (1973c), ibid, p. 18.

May, E.R. (1973d), ibid, pp. 50–1.

May, E.R. (1973e), ibid, p. 83.

May, E.R. (1973f), ibid, p. 116.

May, E.R. (1973g), ibid, pp. 137 and 162.

McBeth, M.S. (2002), 'Approaches to Enhancing Sensemaking for Intelligence Analysis', Report to Dean of Academics, Naval War College, Newport, RI, issued May, 17.

McDonald, L. (2009), *A Colossal Failure of Common Sense: The Incredible Inside Story of the Collapse of Lehman Brothers*, Ebury Press, New York, p. 81.

McGonagle, J.J. (2008), 'Ethical Codes: Do it Yourself', *Competitive Intelligence Magazine*, 11 (2), pp. 43–4.

McLaughlin, J. (2008a), 'Serving the National Policymaker', in: R.Z. George, J.B. Bruce (eds), *Analyzing Intelligence: Origins, Obstacles, and Innovations*, Georgetown University Press, Washington DC, p. 71.

McLaughlin, J. (2008b), ibid, p. 79.

McLaughlin, J. (2008c), ibid, pp. 73–4.

McNulty, E.J., 'In Praise of Long-tenure' Cultures, *Strategy & Business* (online), 25 November 2013..

McTaggart, J.M., Kontes, P.W., Mankins, M.C. (1994), *The Value Imperative: Managing for Superior Shareholder Returns*, The Free Press, New York, pp. 221–37.

Medina, C.A., (2008), 'The New Analysis', in: R.Z. George, J.B. Bruce (eds), *Analyzing Intelligence: Origins, Obstacles, and Innovations*, Georgetown University Press, Washington DC, p. 238.

Meister Johnston, J., Johnston, R. (2005), 'Testing the Intelligence Cycle Through Systems Modeling and Simulation', in Johnston (2005a).

Mellers, B. et al. (2015), 'The Psychology of Intelligence Analysis: Drivers of Prediction Accuracy in World Politics', *Journal of Experimental Psychology: Applied*, Vol. 21, No. 1 pp. 1-14.

Mercado, S.C. (2009a), 'Reexamining the Distinction Between Open Information and Secrets', Centre for the Study of Intelligence publications, www.cia.gov/library, visited 18 June 2009 (and sources quoted therein).

Mercado, S.C. (2009b), 'Sailing the Sea of OSINT in the Information Age: A Venerable Source in a New Era', Centre for the Study of Intelligence publications, www.cia.gov/library, visited 18 June 2009 (and sources quoted therein).

Merriam-Webster (2013), http://www.merriam-webster.com/dictionary/analysis, visited 24 November 2013.

Milton, G. (2014), *Russian Roulette: How British Spies Defeated Lenin*, Hodder & Stoughton, London, p. 199.

Minto, B. (2008), *The Pyramid Principle: Logic in Thinking and Writing*, 3rd Ed. FT/Prentice Hall, London.

Mintzberg, H., Ahlstrand, B., Lampel, J. (1998), *Strategy Safari: A Guided Tour Through the Wilds of Strategic Management*, Free Press, New York, pp. 69-71.

Montgomery, C.A. (2012a) *The Strategist: Be the Leader Your Business Needs*, HarperCollins Publishers, London, p. 67.

Montgomery, C.A. (2012b), ibid p. 153.

Moore, D.T. (2007a), 'Critical Thinking and Intelligence Analysis', National Defense Intelligence College, Occasional paper no. 14, Washington DC, p. 24.

Moore, D.T. (2007b), ibid, pp. 14–16.

Moore, D.T. (2007c), ibid, p. 82.

Moravec, F. (1975), *Master of Spies: The Memoirs of General Frantisek Moravec*, The Bodley Head Ltd., London, UK, p. 118.

Naylor, E. (2007), 'Setting up Early Warning Cooperatively', *Competitive Intelligence Magazine*, Vol. 10, no. 3, May-June issue.

Noble, D.F. (2004), 'Assessing the Reliability of Open Source Information', Proc. 7th Int. Conference on Information Fusion, Stockholm, Vol. II, pp. 1172–78.

Nonaka, I., Takeuchi, H. (1995), *The Knowledge-Creating Company*, Oxford University Press, Oxford p. 59.

NSA (2007), 'Untangling the Web: A Guide to Internet Research', http://www.nsa.gov/public_info/_files/untangling_the_web.pdf, visited 2 November 2013, p.1 (and sources quoted therein).

ODNI (2007), 'Intelligence Community Directive no. 203 on Analytic Standards', Office Director of National Intelligence, 21 June 2007.

Oleszkiewicz, S., Granhag, P.A., Cancino Montecinos, S., 'The Scharff-Technique: Eliciting Intelligence from Human Sources', *Law and Human Behaviour* (online edition), 7 April 2014.

Pais, A. (1982), *Subtle is the Lord...: The Science and The Life of Albert Einstein*, Oxford University Press, pp. 46–8.

Palmquist, M., '(Tacit) Knowledge is Power', *Strategy & Business* blog, 9 April 2014.

Palmquist, M., 'The Dangers of Too Much Workplace Cohesion', *Strategy & Business* blog, 12 February 2015.

Perla, P.P. (2011), *Peter Perla's The Art of Wargaming: A Guide for Professionals and Hobbyists*, John Curry (ed.), US Naval Institute, p. 58.

Peterson, J.J. (2008), 'Appropriate Factors to Consider When Assessing Analytic Confidence in Intelligence Analysis', M.Sc. thesis, Department of Intelligence Studies, Mercyhurst College, Erie, PA.

Philips, E., Vriens, D. (1999), *Business Intelligence*, Kluwer Bedrijfsinformatie, Deventer, pp. 30–2 resp. pp. 117–21.

Pillar, P.R., 'Think Again: Intelligence' www.foreignpolicy.com, Jan/Feb 2012, visited 24 February 2012.

Pollack, K.M. (2004), 'Spies, Lies, and Weapons: What Went Wrong?', *The Atlantic*, Jan/Feb issue.

Pooley, J. (1997), 'Criminal Consequences of Trade Secret Theft: The EEA and Compliance Plans', *Competitive Intelligence Review*, 8 (3) pp. 13–19.

Porter, M.E., 'How Competitive Forces Shape Strategy', *Harvard Business Review*, March-April 1979, pp. 137–45.

Porter, M.E. (2004), *Competitive Strategy: Techniques for Analyzing Industries and Competitors*, The Free Press, New York, p. 74 (reprint from 1980 edition).

Powell, J. (2011a), *The New Machiavelli: How to Wield Power and Influence in the Modern World*, Vintage, London, p. 104.

Powell, J. (2011b), Ibid., pp. 285–6.

Powell, T.H., Angwin, D.N. (2012), 'The Role of the Chief Strategy Officer', *MIT Sloan Management Review*, Fall 2012, Vol. 54, No. 1, pp. 15–16.

Reger, R.K. et al. (1994), 'Reframing the Organization: Why Implementing Total Quality Management is Easier Said Than Done', *Academy of Management Review*, Vol. 19 pp. 565–84.

Reuser, A. (2012), Personal Communication: see www.reuser.biz for A. Reuser's advanced OSINT training references

Rivkin, J.W., Cullen, A. (2010), 'Finding Information for Industry Analysis', Harvard Business School note 9-708-481.

Robarge, D.S. (2007), *Richard Helms: The Intelligence Professional Personified*, CSI-studies, Vol. 46, no. 4, article no. 6.

Rohrbeck, R., Heuer, J., Arnold, H. (2006), The Technology RADAR: An Instrument of Technology Intelligence and Innovation Strategy', The 3rd IEEE international Conference on Management of Innovation and Technology, 2006, Singapore, pp. 978–83.

Rosenzweig, P., (2014), 'The Benefits – and Limits – of Decision Models', *McKinsey Quarterly*, Feb. Edition.

Rothke, B., 'Corporate Espionage and What Can Be Done to Prevent It', *Information Systems Security*, November/December 2002, pp. 10-15.

Roussel, P.A., Saad, K.M. and Erickson, T.J. (1991), *Third Generation R&D*, Harvard Business School Press, Boston MA.

Roxburgh, C. (2003), 'Hidden Flaws in Strategy', *McKinsey Quarterly*, May issue.

Rumelt, R.P. (2012a), *Good Strategy, Bad Strategy*, Profile Books Ltd., London, p. 298.

Rumelt, R.P. (2012b), ibid, pp. 266, 267, 271.

Schellenberg, W. (2000), *The Labyrinth: Memoirs of Walter Schellenberg, Hitler's Chief of Counterintelligence*, Da Capo Press, Cambridge, MA, p. 41.

Schoemaker, P.J.H. (2009), 'Eyes Wide Open: Embracing Uncertainty Through Scenario Planning', HBR-blog, http://knowledge.wharton.upenn.edu/article/eyes-wide-open-embracing-uncertainty-through-scenario-planning/ visited 8 November 2014.

Shalev, A. (2014a), *Israel's Intelligence Assessment Before the Yom Kippur War*, Sussex Academic Press, Eastbourne, p. 78.

Shulsky, A., Schmitt, G.J. (2002), *Silent Warfare: Understanding the World of Intelligence*, 3rd Ed., Potomac Books, Dulles, VA, p. 67.

Silver, N. (2013a), *The Signal and The Noise*, Penguin, London, p. 44.

Silver, N. (2013b), ibid, p. 198.

Silver, N. (2013c), ibid, p. 191.

Silver, N. (2013d), ibid, p. 272.

Silver, N. (2013e), ibid, pp. 52–4.

Silver, N. (2013f), ibid, p. 367.

Silver, N. (2013g), ibid, p. 389.

Silver, N. (2013h), ibid, p. 57.

Silver, N. (2013i), ibid, pp. 72–3.

Silver, N. (2013j), ibid., pp. 5-6.

Sinclair, R.S. (2010), *Thinking and Writing: Cognitive Science and Intelligence Analysis*, Revised Ed., Centre for the Study of Intelligence, Washington DC.

Smith, T.J. (2008), 'Predictive Warning: Teams, Networks and Scientific Method', in: R.Z. George, J.B. Bruce (eds), *Analyzing Intelligence: Origins, Obstacles, and Innovations*, Georgetown University Press, Washington DC, p. 271.

Sontag, S., Drew, C. (1998a), *Blind Man's Bluff: The Untold Story of American Submarine Espionage*, Public Affairs, New York, pp. 75–80.

Sontag, S., Drew, C. (1998b), ibid, p. 26 and 81.

Sontag, S., Drew, C. (1998c), ibid, p. 274.

Snowden, D. (2002), 'Complex Acts of Knowing: Paradox and Descriptive Self-awareness', *Journal of Knowledge Management*, 6, no. 2 (May) pp. 1-14.

Steinberg, J.B. (2008), 'The Policymaker's Perspective: Transparency and Partnership', in: R.Z. George, J.B. Bruce (eds), *Analyzing Intelligence: Origins, Obstacles, and Innovations*, Georgetown University Press, Washington DC, pp. 82–90.

Stewart, S., 'Analyzing Breaking Events', www.stratfor.com, 31 October 2013.

Sunstein, C.R., Hastie, R. (2015a), *Wiser: Getting Beyond Groupthink to Make Groups Smarter*, Harvard Business Review Press, Boston, MA, p. 124.

Sunstein, C.R., Hastie, R. (2015b), ibid, pp. 57–75.

Sunstein, C.R., Hastie, R. (2015c), ibid, pp. 6-7.

Sunstein, C.R., Hastie, R. (2015d), ibid, p. 56.

Surowiecki, J. (2005a), *The Wisdom of Crowds*, Anchor Books, Random House, New York, p. xv.

Surowiecki, J. (2005b), ibid, pp. 207–8.

Surowiecki, J. (2005c), ibid, pp. xix and 180.

Surowiecki, J. (2005d), ibid, p. 220.

Surowiecki, J. (2005e), ibid, p. 72.

Surowiecki, J. (2005f), Ibid., p. 10.

Suvorov, V. (1984), *Inside Soviet Military Intelligence*, MacMillan Publishing Co. New York.

Talbot, D. (2015), *The Devil's Chessboard: Allen Dulles, the CIA, and the Rise of America's Secret Government*, WilliamCollins, London p. 404.

Taleb, N.N. (2007a), The Black Swan: The Impact of the Highly Improbable, Penguin, London, p. 36.

Taleb, N.N. (2007b), ibid, pp. 156–7.

Taleb, N.N. (2007c), ibid.

Taleb, N.N. (2007d), ibid, pp. 79–80.

Taleb, N.N. (2007e), ibid, p. 19.

Taleb, N.N. (2007f), ibid, pp. 146–50.

Taleb, N.N. (2007g), ibid, p. 8.

Taleb, N.N. (2007h), ibid, pp. 119–20.

TheFreeDictionary (2013), www.thefreedictionary.com, visited 24 November 2013

Tradoc (2010), 'Red Teaming', Tradoc Information Pamphlet, US Army, Fort Monroe, VA, www.tradoc.army.mil/pao/index.htm

Treverton, G.F. (2008), 'Intelligence Analysis: Between "Politicization" and Irrelevance', in: R.Z. George, J.B. Bruce (eds), *Analyzing Intelligence: Origins, Obstacles, and Innovations*, Georgetown University Press, Washington DC, pp. 91–106.

Trompenaars, F. (2007), Personal Communication During a FrieslandFoods Company Seminar on the Value of Values.

Tversky, A., Kahneman, D. (1973), 'Availability: A Heuristic for Judging Frequency and Probability', *Cognitive Psychology*, Vol. 5 pp. 207–32.

Tyson, K., Swanson, K. (1992), 'Executive Information Systems Approach for Business Intelligence', *Competitive Intelligence Review*, Spring issue, pp. 16–20.

Tyson, K. (1995), 'Competitive Knowledge Development: Reengineering Competitive Intelligence for Maximum Success', *Competitive Intelligence Review*, Vol. 6(4), pp. 14–21.

Tyson, K. (2006), 'Implementing an Effective Ethics Policy', in: Fehringer, D. and Hohhof, B. (eds), 'Competitive Intelligence Ethics: Navigating the Gray Zone', *Topics in Competitive Intelligence*, Vol. I, Competitive Intelligence Foundation, pp. 13–14.

University of Minnesota (2013), 'Falsification of History', http://www.tc.umn.edu/~hick0088/classes/csci_2101/false.html, visited 29 October 2013.

US Army (2006a), *Human Intelligence Debriefing Handbook* (S//NF) TC 2-22.305, pp. 9–15.

US Army (2006b), ibid, pp. 9–10.

Von Baeyer, H.C. (1993), *The Fermi Solution: Essays on Science,*, Random House, Portland, OR p. 212.

Weiner, T. (2008a), *Legacy of Ashes: The History of the CIA*, Penguin, London, p. 225.

Weiner, T. (2008b), ibid, pp. 284–6.

Weiner, T. (2008c), ibid, p. 425.

Weiner, T. (2008d), ibid, p. 309.

Weiner, T. (2008e), ibid, p. 343.

Weiner, T. (2008f), ibid, p. 553.

West, N. (1999), *Venona: The Greatest Secret of The Cold War*, HarperCollins Publishers, London, p. 61.

Whymant, R. (2006), *Stalin's Spy: Richard Sorge and the Tokyo Espionage Ring*, I.B. Tauris, London, p. 91.

Wikipedia (2013), https://en.wikipedia.org/wiki/Alexander_Suvorov, site visited 17 July 2013.

Wiroreno, W. (2008), Personal Communication to the Author.

Wolf, M., McElvoy, A. (1998), Memoirs of a Spymaster: The Man Who Waged a Secret War Against the West, Pimlico, London

Wohlstetter, R. (1965a), 'Cuba and Pearl Harbor: Hindsight and Foresight', Memorandum RM-4328-ISA, April, Rand Corporation, Santa Monica, CA p. 20.

Wohlstetter, R. (1965b), ibid, pp. 2 and 36.

Wohlstetter, R. (1965c), ibid, p. 13.

Woodward, B. (2001), *Maestro: Greenspan's FED and the American Boom*, Touchstone, Simon & Schuster, New York.

Wright, P., Greengrass, P. (1987), *Spy-catcher*, Heinemann, Richmond, Victoria,.

Yarhi-Milo, K. (2014a), *Knowing the Adversary: Leaders, Intelligence and Assessment of Intentions in International Relations*, Princeton University Press, Princeton NJ, p. 193.

Yarhi-Milo, K. (2014b), ibid, p. 42.

Yarhi-Milo, K. (2014c), ibid, pp. 176 and 200.

Zeldes, N., Sward, D., Louchheim, S. (2007), 'Infomania: Why We Can't Afford to Ignore It Any Longer', *First Monday*, Vol. 12, no. 8.

Zook, C., Allen, J. (2012a), *Repeatability: Build Enduring Businesses for a World of Constant Change*, Harvard Business Review Press, Boston MA.

Zook, C., Allen, J. (2012b), ibid, p. 189.